Heisenberg and the Nazi Atomic Bomb Project

Werner Heisenberg in the late 1930s.

HEISENBERG

and the Nazi Atomic Bomb Project

A STUDY IN GERMAN CULTURE

PAUL LAWRENCE ROSE

UNIVERSITY OF CALIFORNIA PRESS
Berkeley   Los Angeles   London

BY THE SAME AUTHOR:

The Italian Renaissance of Mathematics: Humanists and Mathematicians from Petrarch to Galileo. Geneva: Librairie Droz, 1976.

Bodin and the Great God of Nature: The Moral and Religious Universe of a Judaiser. Geneva: Librairie Droz, 1980.

German Question/Jewish Question: Revolutionary Antisemitism in Germany from Kant to Wagner. Princeton University Press, 1990; 2d ed., 1992.

Wagner: Race and Revolution. Yale University Press, 1992; reissued, 1996.

University of California Press
Berkeley and Los Angeles, California

University of California Press, Ltd.
London, England

© 1998 by
The Regents of the University of California

Library of Congress Cataloging-in-Publication Data

Rose, Paul Lawrence.
Heisenberg and the Nazi atomic bomb project: A study in German culture /
Paul Lawrence Rose.
p.   cm.
Includes bibliographical references and index.
ISBN 0-520-21077-8 (alk. paper)
1. Heisenberg, Werner, 1901–1976—Views on atomic bomb.   2. Physicists—
Political activity.   3. Atomic bomb—Germany—History.   4. Germany—Politics and
government—1933–1945.   I. Title.
QC16.H35R67   1998

355.8'25119'092—dc21

97-18143
CIP

Printed in the United States of America
9 8 7 6 5 4 3 2 1

In affectionate memory of Brian Dalton (1924—1996),
Scholar, gentleman, leader, friend

And in honor of my father's 80th birthday
לאבי מורי

Science without conscience is the ruin of the soul.

RABELAIS, *Gargantua*

And, after all, what is a lie? 'Tis but
The truth in masquerade.

BYRON, *Don Juan*

Contents

Acknowledgments

For hospitality during various phases of work on this book I am grateful to Aryeh Dvoretzky, Director of the Institute of Advanced Studies of the Hebrew University of Jerusalem, whose invitation there allowed me to begin work on the book while on sabbatical leave from James Cook University of North Queensland, Australia, in 1983; and to those colleagues whose good offices made it possible for me to resume research on the subject while a visiting professor at York University and the University of Toronto, Canada, in 1990–92. Grants from the College of the Liberal Arts and the Institute for the Arts and Humanistic Studies of The Pennsylvania State University enabled me to complete the research and writing of the book.

I am indebted to a great many scientists and other colleagues who kindly supplied information at various points, including R. Peierls, H. Bethe, R. Serber, I. Unna, Y. Wagschall, R. V. Jones, G. Born, F. H. Hinsley, M. Gowing, W. Williams, C. Fraser, G. Holton, D. C. Cassidy, M. Beller, K. Macrakis, R. L. Sime, H. Henisch, R. Anshen, A. Pais, R. H. March, C. Dilworth-Occhialini, N. Dawidoff, J. Dippel, T. H. von Laue, S. Rozental, T. Powers, D. Irving, C.-F. von Weizsäcker, M. von Ardenne, E. Bagge, K. Wirtz, K.-H. Höcker, and D. Hoffmann. Several fellow historians also supplied encouragement, particularly B. Z. Kedar, Roy Porter, John Maguire, Conor Cruise O'Brien, and the late Sir Geoffrey Elton. To P. O. Kristeller, my teacher in another field, I am also deeply indebted.

Among those archivists who helpfully answered inquiries and procured copies of documentation are E. Meese, W. Mahoney, B. Crystal, K. Molholm, M. Blakeslee, S. Weart, Z. Rosenkranz, F. Aaserud, F. Pors, H. Rechenberg, M. Rasch, C. Tietz, A. Kerkmann, R. Heinrich, E. Henning, M. Kazemi, and H. Bachmann. My son Alexander—a historian in his own right—also obtained various materials for me.

I owe a special debt of thanks to three scientists who have given critical readings to portions or all of the manuscript and have been generous with advice and information. They are Arnold Kramish, Jonothan Logan, and Sir Charles Frank. My wife, Susan, also read the manuscript and suggested numerous improvements (as ever).

In writing of the experiences of German professors during the 1930s I have drawn on my observation of how former colleagues of the University of Newcastle, Australia—David Frost, Tony Guttmann, and Don Parkes—reacted honorably to injustice in their midst. The late Brian Dalton, to whom the book is dedicated, was an inspiration in every way, personally and professionally, to all those who were fortunate enough to work with him in building a genuinely first-rate research and teaching department at James Cook University. His response to bullying assertion of managerial authority, of a kind slightly reminiscent of that which reigned unchecked in German universities in the 1930s, is illustrated by an anecdote whose veracity I can attest. Late for a meeting one day, Brian was obliged to park for a few minutes in a space designated for an overbearing senior administrator who was rarely present. That day, the official did come in and he telephoned Brian, shouting with rage and menace down the line. Brian hung up, and then called him back, saying urbanely, "My dear ———, I think you ought to know that someone has just been impersonating you on the telephone. He appeared to be drunk." This story has a certain relevance to some aspects of the subject of this book.

Paul Lawrence Rose
6 February 1997

Abbreviations

AIP	Niels Bohr Library, American Institute of Physics, College Park, Md.
BA	Bundesarchiv, Koblenz
BAS	*Bulletin of the Atomic Scientists*
BSC	Bohr Scientific Correspondence, microfilms in Archive for History of Quantum Physics, Berkeley; AIP; and elsewhere
Cassidy	D. C. Cassidy, *Uncertainty: The Life and Science of Werner Heisenberg* (New York, 1992)
FHT	Farm Hall transcripts (Public Record Office, London, WO208/5019; also in U.S. National Archives, College Park, Md., RG 77, entry 22, box 163)
G-*x*	German Atomic Research Reports, U.S. National Archives, College Park, Md., RG 242, Captured German Records, microfiche (also in AIP); *x* = document number
GWH *x y*	W. Heisenberg, *Gesammelte Werke / Collected Works*, ed. W. Blum, H.-P. Duerr, and H. Rechenberg (Berlin, Munich, and New York, 1984–); *x* = series, *y* = part
HPNS	K. Hentschel and A. Hentschel, eds., *Physics and National Socialism: An Anthology of Primary Sources* (Basel, Boston, and Berlin, 1996)
HWA	Heereswaffenamt (Army Weapons Department)
HWA WaF	Heereswaffenamt, Waffenforschung (HWA Weapons Research Office)
HWA WaF/1a	Heereswaffenamt, Waffenforschung: Kernphysik (HWA Weapons Research Office/1a: Nuclear Physics)
IMF	D. Irving, comp. *Records and Documents Relating to the Third Reich*, group 11, *German Atomic Research* (Wakefield, Yorks., 1973), microfilms 29–32
KWG	Kaiser-Wilhelm-Society/Kaiser-Wilhelm Gesellschaft
KWIP	Kaiser-Wilhelm-Institut for Physics, Berlin
LC	Library of Congress, Washington, D.C.
MPG	Max-Planck-Gesellschaft, Berlin
NA	National Archives, Archives II, College Park, Md.

OE	*Operation Epsilon: The Farm Hall Transcripts,* ed. Sir Charles Frank (Berkeley, 1993)
OHI	Oral History Interviews, Neils Bohr Library, American Institute of Physics, College Park, Md.
PRO	Public Record Office, Kew, London
PRO, AB	Public Record Office, Atomic Energy Series
PRO, CAB	Public Record Office, Cabinet Office Series
PRO, FO	Public Record Office, Foreign Office Series

A Note on Three New Sources

Three important books were published after the completion of the present work. Several of the German documents, particularly those bearing on the politics of Heisenberg and other German physicists during the Nazi period, are now available in English translation in K. Hentschel and A. Hentschel, *Physics and National Socialism: An Anthology of Primary Sources* (Basel, Boston, and Berlin, 1996). Further material on the compromises of Otto Hahn and others is to be found in R. L. Sime, *Lise Meitner: A Life in Physics* (Berkeley, 1996). And a running critical commentary on the Farm Hall transcripts has been provided by J. Bernstein, *Hitler's Uranium Club* (Woodbury, N.Y., 1996). Attention should also be drawn to the reissue of S. Goudsmit's *ALSOS*, with a new introduction by D. C. Cassidy (Woodbury, N.Y., 1996). Though unable to have made full use of these new sources, I have added a few references to them in the footnotes, which may prove useful to readers wishing to have access to certain documents in translation.

Preface: Why Heisenberg?

Why Heisenberg? Werner Heisenberg (1901 – 76) is at once an emblem of twentieth-century physics and of the crisis of German culture and society during the Hitler period. Heisenberg's invention and development of matrix mechanics in 1925 in rivalry with Erwin Schrödinger's wave mechanics rescued traditional quantum theory from its various impasses and opened the way to the quantum mechanics that has dominated physical thinking in the last three-quarters of a century. This breakthrough, along with his formulation of the Uncertainty Principle in 1927, has assured Heisenberg a permanent place among the great physicists—an achievement recognized by the award of the Nobel Prize in 1933.

But in that same year Hitler came to power, and though Heisenberg might well have preferred not to think about him, Hitler opened the door to a *crise de conscience* for German physicists, as well as for the rest of the German cultural elite: Should we stay on (some asked themselves) and keep quiet, waiting for the storm to pass? Or was open protest, accompanied or not by actual political resistance, a viable alternative? Or again, was the only proper course of action to pack up and leave Germany and resist from outside? Heisenberg made a firm decision, reaffirmed during the six years before the outbreak of the Second World War in 1939, to stay on. The extent to which he agreed or disagreed politically with the Nazi regime has been a matter of bitter controversy for the last sixty years. But the point on which recrimination—and apology too—have focused has been Heisenberg's participation in the Nazi atomic bomb project. And here there is indeed massive uncertainty and disputation. On the purely scientific and technical side, did Heisenberg understand accurately how an atomic bomb would work and how to make it? And from the political and ethical point of view, did Heisenberg recognize the moral problem of becoming involved in the bomb project at all, let alone actually producing one for Hitler's use?

Since the war an apologetic campaign has been mounted by Heisenberg and other German physicists and historians to demonstrate that he understood fully both the moral and scientific issues involved in his work as chief physicist for the Nazi atomic bomb project from 1939 to 1945. Unsurprisingly, this has been countered on many fronts by less sympathetic American and British critics. The present book attempts to penetrate Heisenberg's mask to reconstruct his thinking and sensibility, and his conceptions of politics, morality, and duty. It will try to explain how his purely scientific work on the project must be set firmly in the German cultural climate and social context in which he always saw himself firmly situated. As Heisenberg himself avowed, he was above all a German. If we are to understand Heisenberg as he really was, we must enter into the German frame of mind, or mentality, or mind-set and sensibility, that had evolved out of the German culture of the nineteenth and twentieth centuries, strange though that mentality appears now to non-Germans, and even to those Germans who have been shaped by the changed and Westernized German culture that has been developing since 1945.

I cannot say that my British background has made me entirely sympathetic to German culture. Although I would be the first to admit its outstanding achievements in science, music, and intellectual life in general, its insistent abstraction as well as the more sinister traditions that accompanied it induce in me a certain skepticism and even aversion. As the American liberal philosopher John Dewey once observed, even Kant's categorical imperative has a whiff of the Prussian drill sergeant about it; the grand moral principle depended, despite its apparent universal reasonableness, on an all too German demand for conforming obedience. Some readers may be put off by what seems, following this spirit of distrust of Kant, the *Tendenz* of the present book, its lack of sympathy with German culture, and its seeming moral and scientific denigration of a great physicist who found himself born into an evil time. Some may also find distasteful the recurrent moral judgments passed on Heisenberg, and ask what I—or anyone else—would have done if placed in Heisenberg's position in Nazi Germany. Who made me a judge over Heisenberg? But this is to mistake the proper role of the historian, which is to reconstruct the historical truth, and then, in cases where moral judgment is clearly required, to judge as fairly as one may, either by implicit suggestion and shaping of the material, or by more open statement where the conceptual and analytical elements are often obscured or misunderstood. This role does not require the historian personally to be a moral paragon or blameless. Consequently, the truth of any historical or moral portrait of Heisenberg cannot be discredited merely by stating that the historian needs to have been in Heisenberg's shoes before being able to judge. Certainly, any historian should be able to think himself or herself by an effort of historical imagination into Heisenberg's predicament, but that sort of empathetic understanding is something quite different from sympathetic abstention from moral judgments. The only real test of the historical truth of the present reconstruction is whether it makes better sense of the central problems of the Heisenberg affair and conforms more exactly to the facts as far as we may know them about Heisenberg, the German atomic bomb project, and German culture and society before, during, and after the Third Reich than do other versions.

This book began as a chapter in an intended book of essays that would explore the mentality and sensibility of a selection of German cultural figures who found themselves facing what one might have thought to be moral dilemmas during the Hitler years. These figures included Furtwängler, Heidegger, Heisenberg, Riefenstahl, and Jünger, among others. I had originally expected the Heisenberg chapter to be straightforward. It turned out otherwise, and the resolution of the difficulties of the case—stemming from both its scientific and its moral obscurities—have taken me nearly fourteen years to resolve. During this period, which was spent in Australia, Israel, Canada, and the United States, I was able to become more familiar with German patterns of thought and behavior through detailed work on such major cultural emblems as Kant, Fichte, Wagner, and Thomas Mann, as well as a range of lesser-known antisemitic thinkers. This increasing familiarity has convinced me of the difference and alienness—in a word, uniqueness—of German life and thought in recent centuries, and of the enduring nature of what one might call the "deep culture" of Germany. Readers are free to accept or reject my characterizations, but I hope that in neither case will they accuse me of unthinkingly preaching a crude view of German "national character," whatever that term may mean. I also hope they will not dismiss out of hand the central thrust of the book: It is only by understanding Heisenberg in his specifically *German* context that we are likely to come to a true knowledge of his political and moral behavior and attitudes, as well as his scientific activity, during the Nazi era. In insisting on this German context, I believe I am being historically true to Heisenberg's own perception and priorities, for he saw himself in the end as a German more than even as a physicist.

· · ·

In this book I have tried to penetrate into how Germans think—or rather, perhaps, used to think—and to show how radically different are German and what I have termed "Western" mentalities and sensibilities. My regret is that in order to expose the nature and fallacies of much of this German thinking and feeling, I have, I fear, often been forced to be tediously analytical. This is not, in consequence, a graceful book, I am sorry to confess, but perhaps Heisenberg and company have benefited too long from grace of various sorts.

A Note on Historical Terminology
of the First Nuclear Age,
1939 – 45

ATOMIC URANIUM BOMB

This is an explosive chain reaction taking place in pure or almost pure U235. It is produced by fast neutrons fissioning in a very short time the separated rare isotope U235, which is usually fissioned by slow neutrons of low energy. Heisenberg grasped this notion of a fast-neutron U235 bomb, but failed to understand that the critical mass required for such a bomb would be comparatively small.

REACTOR

During the first nuclear age (1939 – 45) the reactor (or pile) was envisaged as a device to produce a chain reaction in a suitably arranged mass of unseparated uranium or uranium with an enriched U235 content. The reaction was comparatively slow and nonexplosive, and understood to be generated by slow neutrons fissioning the U235 that was present. In order to prevent the fast neutrons produced by fission from losing the amount of energy that would result in their being captured uselessly in the predominant mass of U238 before reaching the lower energy where they would fission the U235, a moderator such as heavy water or graphite would be employed to absorb enough of the neutrons' energy to carry them below the U238 "resonance bands." This also improved the efficiency of the reaction.

REACTOR-BOMB

Before the scientific principle of the atomic uranium bomb was clearly understood (i.e., that fast neutrons produced in a small critical mass of U235 an explosive chain reaction), suggestions were made as to how an explosion could be created in U235 by slow neutrons in a reactor stocked with either unseparated uranium or enriched uranium. In Germany research was pursued on the hypothesis that such a reactor-bomb would essentially be an unstable reactor using a moderator and highly enriched U235. This was seen in Germany as a solution to the insurmountable problem of obtaining the tons of U235 thought to be required for a U235 bomb.

The Heisenberg Problem

Deception and Self-Deception

We do not know where Heisenberg stands on the question, whether the German scientists could not, or could and would not, work on the making of atom bombs.

RUDOLF PEIERLS, 1971

Investigation of the technical sides of the atomic bomb problem—for example, of the so-called critical size—was, however, not undertaken.

WERNER HEISENBERG, 1946-47

In the upshot the German scientists were spared the decision as to whether or not they should aim at producing atomic bombs.

HEISENBERG, 1946

Dr. Hahn, Dr. von Laue and I falsified the mathematics in order to avoid the development of the atom bomb by German scientists.

HEISENBERG, 1970

The whole story of "a kind of confrontation" [with Bohr in 1947] . . . is a typical Heisenberg fabrication—maybe a bit brighter than a thousand others, but like them all a product of his Blut und Boden *guilt complex, which he rationalizes that quickly that the stories become for him the truth. . . . Pitiful, in a man of his mental stature.*

RONALD FRASER (BRITISH SCIENTIFIC INTELLIGENCE OFFICER WHO AIDED HEISENBERG'S REINTEGRATION INTO THE EUROPEAN SCIENTIFIC COMMUNITY AFTER THE WAR)

Dear Professor Einstein,
As a representative Nobel Prizewinner, would you make the generalization that Nobel Prizewinners "do not lie"? Mr. Waldemar Kaempffert makes precisely this statement [in defending Heisenberg against the accusations of S. Goudsmit's book ALSOS*].*

HENRY SCHUMAN (PUBLISHER OF *ALSOS*), 11 NOVEMBER 1947

Dear Mr. Schuman,
Concerning Nobel Prizewinners, Mr. Kaempffert could only rightly say: One does not get the Nobel Prize for lying, but this does not exclude that some of the fortunates may lie under the pressure of certain situations.

ALBERT EINSTEIN, 17 NOVEMBER 1947

Werner Heisenberg's involvement in the Nazi atomic energy project from 1939 to 1945 is shrouded in mystery and confusion, some of it created perhaps intentionally, some of it the result of Western incomprehension of German mentality and patterns of mental and social behavior.[1] Why did Heisenberg, as the chief physicist of the project, not produce a design for an atomic bomb? How could Heisenberg, by his own admission, not have calculated the critical mass of U235 required for a bomb? Why did a civilized man like Heisenberg, so esteemed by his fellow Western scientists such as Niels Bohr, consent to work for Hitler on a project of such frightening consequences? Why did Heisenberg, again by his own admission, never make a "moral decision" on whether or not to build a bomb for Hitler? What indeed was a "moral decision" in Heisenberg's view? These questions involve issues bearing not merely on technical scientific matters, but also on less tangible problems of morality and politics.

Along with these mixed scientific/moral puzzles there also stands an array of purely moral and political riddles: Why did Heisenberg, who refused to join the Nazi Party, nevertheless choose to remain in Germany and so lend his prestige to the Nazi regime? Why did he, despite his aversion to Nazi antisemitism and his defense of "Jewish physics," justify Nazi war victories to his colleagues in occupied Denmark and Holland? Why, after the war, was he so oblivious to the offense he gave Western friends by his rationalizations of the Nazi regime?

To date these questions have received largely contradictory and unsatisfactory answers, rooted in a failure, for the most part, to understand Heisenberg's actions, thoughts, and personality in the relevant cultural and scientific contexts. What appears to a reader of Western sensibility and outlook to be almost nonsensical in Heisenberg's political statements becomes clear and comprehensible when put into a "German" context—for example, Heisenberg's claim never to have made a "moral decision" about the bomb when, in Western terms, participation itself in Hitler's war effort was a moral decision. At the same time, Heisenberg's omission of a calculation of the critical mass of a bomb—and any physicist in charge of a bomb project surely would have had to make such a fundamental calculation at the outset—becomes understandable only when viewed in the scientific context of German nuclear theorizing in 1939–40.

We must, however, beware of separating the cultural and scientific contexts in this way. Although such a separation may be essential for an initial analysis, it obscures a crucial aspect of the Heisenberg problem: the peculiar interaction of German moral and cultural contexts with purely technical, scientific issues. In

1. The sources of the introductory quotations are as follows: The quotation from R. Peierls is from "Atomic Germans," *New York Review of Books*, 1 July 1971, pp. 23–24, reviewing Heisenberg's *Physics and Beyond*. The Heisenberg quotations of 1946–47 are from GWH, C V, 30 and 32, and GWH, B, 416 f., discussed below in chap. 1. The 1970 quotation is from a letter to Ruth Anshen (see chap. 2). R. Fraser made his comment in a letter to D. Irving, 27 August 1966 (in IMF 32; see below, chap. 21). The Einstein-Schuman correspondence is in the Einstein Archives, Jewish National and University Library, Hebrew University of Jerusalem; I am grateful to the curator, Ze'ev Rosenkranz, for providing copies.

other words, understanding why Heisenberg did not produce a bomb for Hitler requires a knowledge not only of his atomic theories, but also of his general mentality, particularly his conception of duty to the state and his visions of science and the role of the scientist.

It could be said that many of these questions might just as validly be put to the Allied scientists who were engaged on the Los Alamos bomb project, that there is nothing specifically "German" about the Heisenberg case. Though it is true that for many of the Allied scientists the atomic bomb represented an entanglement of scientific and moral issues, most were willing to work on the bomb because they believed in the rightfulness of the Allied cause. To claim a symmetry here with the German scientists, therefore, raises serious problems; symmetry would require that Heisenberg also believed in the rightfulness of his own country's aggressive war. As it happens, it seems that he did, but then how is that to be squared with his non-Nazi attitudes? If, on the other hand, he did not think that Germany's cause was just, why should he have served the state as a scientist? One might say that patriotism motivated the Allied and German scientists alike. But then the problem arises as to whether the horrors of the Nazi regime should have precluded patriotic loyalty of the kind claimed by any normal state. A simple comparison of the German project to the Allied one, therefore, soon raises very complicated issues requiring explanations grounded in the peculiarities of German mentality.

Sometimes these peculiarities verge on the bizarre, the absurd, and even the comical, as readers of the Farm Hall transcripts will know. One of the most curious of these peculiarities is the German capacity for self-delusion (oft remarked by German authors), a trait exemplified to an astonishing degree in Heisenberg himself. Indeed, if we are to unravel the Heisenberg case fully, it is essential to appreciate the degree to which this culturally conditioned mental trait has informed German life since at least the nineteenth century, rising to a climax in the Nazi and post-Nazi eras. Many skeptical non-Germans have long been suspicious of German efforts at deception through half-truths and falsifications, and it is certainly tempting for a Western analyst to dismiss several of Heisenberg's statements as simple lies.[2] But that is to miss the essence of the matter. Heisenberg was so apt and quick to rationalize not only his own behavior, but the situation around him, that it is not immediately clear just how much he was deluding himself as opposed to trying only to mislead others.

This sort of ambivalence is indeed a general problem for historians of the Nazi period; one comes across so many seemingly absurd cases where obvious Nazis or fellow travelers deny their complicity, even to the point of claiming to be resisters, that it is difficult to know how far they were consciously lying and how far resort-

---

2. For a recent investigation of the "lies" of another German figure, see G. Sereny, *Albert Speer: His Battle with Truth* (New York, 1995), though the author seems to underrate the opportunism in Speer's deception and self-deception, as well as accepting too readily that Speer ever really wanted to know the "truth." See now D. van der Vat, *The Good Nazi* (Boston, 1997).

ing to ingrained behavioral traits developed to evade moral and civic responsibility. This resourcefulness in self-exculpation and rationalization is too complex to be written off simply as "lying" (though in the end, one is usually forced to conclude, it was just that).

In the Heisenberg case, the instinct for self-delusion produced in the space of two nights in August 1945 a fully elaborated myth of the German project, embodying both scientific and political elements. This myth became immediately the actual "truth" for all concerned. For those who believe a myth, it is, after all, the truth, and we might be able to understand the Heisenberg case better if we look at it in terms of self-delusion rather than outright lying. Still, the case is more complicated than that, for combined with self-delusion, there was also present an intention (even if sometimes barely conscious) to mislead outsiders. This capacity for self-contradiction—an ability to hold incompatible views and attitudes in separate compartments of the mind and not allow them to emerge into an open clash of contradictions—is deeply characteristic of German culture and is one of the most potent sources of confusion for non-Germans approaching German culture.

Much of what follows will seem extraordinary, both for its reconstruction of Heisenberg's fundamental misunderstandings of the scientific principles of an atomic bomb, and for its depiction of the selective amnesia that has gripped German scientists for the last fifty years. Nevertheless it is, I believe, a truer picture of Heisenberg's understanding of the atomic bomb than has so far been available, in that it applies conceptual approaches developed in the course of analyzing German cultural and thought patterns, especially those that structured the German antisemitic mentality and sensibility of the modern period since Kant. At the same time, since the problem of Heisenberg's perception of the atomic bomb is ultimately a scientific one, the bulk of the book seeks to re-create in terms accessible to the general reader those technical arguments and concepts through which the German physicists of the war years understood the atomic bomb problem. After the war, the correct scientific theory of the bomb seemed so obvious to Heisenberg that he was unable to conceive how he could ever have been so mistaken during the war (just as after the Allied victory it was nearly impossible for many Germans to understand how they could ever have believed in the desirability of a Nazi victory). When the mechanics and dynamics of this mental illusion, or self-deception, are exposed, then much of what seems incomprehensible—both scientifically and morally—about Heisenberg's participation in the atomic bomb project no longer seems quite so bewildering.

.   .   .

Part I of this book (chapters 1–3) presents a critical survey of Heisenberg's own version of the history of the German atomic bomb project, combined with an account of how the version was elaborated by German scientists and various historians, and subjected to fierce criticism by mainly Allied scientists. The confused state of the primary and secondary literature, as well as the intrinsic difficulty of the subject, requires an analysis of some intricacy and complexity, which may seem tediously detailed but which, it is hoped, may help to strip away the various layers of deception and confusion that have accreted around the subject since 1945, and are now feeding what has become an endless and often sterile controversy.

Part II (chapters 4–14) is devoted to a largely technical investigation of German thinking about the nature of an atomic bomb during the period of the war. It is argued that Heisenberg failed to understand the practical scientific principle of an atomic bomb until 14 August 1945. His various conceptions of a bomb from December 1939 until 14 August 1945 were all flawed, impossible, and chimerical. Evidence is drawn from numerous unpublished and previously uncited German official and private documents.

Having established Heisenberg's essential ignorance of the scientific principle of an atomic bomb, this book turns in part III (chapters 15–21) to questions that can be answered only in the context of Heisenberg's "German" mentality. Why did Heisenberg—and, one might say, the other German scientists too—work on this dangerous and amoral Nazi atomic project when it seemed in 1939–40 that it might have a serious chance of success? Would Heisenberg have built a bomb had he indeed known how to do so between 1939 and 1945? Why did Heisenberg remain in Germany, despite the urgings of his American friends to leave in 1938–39? Which elements in Nazi Germany did he find congenial, which unacceptable? Why, finally, did he feel the necessity of constructing a version of events that was historically false and morally corrupt?

PART I

History:
The Heisenberg Version
and Its Critics

Quantum theory always enables us to give full reasons for the occurrence of an event after it has actually taken place.[1]

HEISENBERG, 1936

"I have done that," says my memory. "I could not have done that," says my pride, and remains inexorable. Finally, my memory yields.

NIETZSCHE, *Beyond Good and Evil*

1. Heisenberg, "Questions of Principle in Modern Physics" (1936), in his *Philosophical Problems of Nuclear Science* (London, 1952) (GWH, C I, 118).

CHAPTER 1

The Heisenberg Version and Its First Critic, 1945–49

The claim of Heisenberg and others that he had understood completely the principle of an atomic bomb from early on in the war is rooted in the rather fortunate ambiguity and vagueness of the wartime papers he prepared for the German uranium project.[1] But just why were these papers so strangely ambiguous and imprecise? As this book will argue, it was not merely a matter of good luck that these war papers were so cryptic about the atomic bomb that they could later be used as evidence of Heisenberg's scientific prescience; the enigmatic statements to be found in these papers stemmed from the fact that Heisenberg had reached false conclusions in his first paper (G-39) and in further work done in 1940 which suggested that an atomic bomb was a virtual impossibility on account of the huge quantities of U235 that would be required. Thereafter, Heisenberg failed to give any serious attention to the matter of the bomb, and so gave no further thought—whether conceptually or in terms of quantities—to the basic problem of critical mass. There is, astoundingly, no mention in these wartime papers of three of the essential elements of a correct conceptualization of an atomic bomb—namely,

1. a calculation of the critical mass of a U235 bomb;
2. a statement that a U235 bomb would depend on a fast-neutron reaction;
3. an equation for the internal multiplication of neutrons with respect to time in the case of a fast-neutron reaction.[2]

Admittedly Heisenberg's remarks during his internment at Farm Hall, near

---

1. For a short incisive history of what I call "the Heisenberg version," see D. C. Cassidy, *Uncertainty: The Life and Science of Werner Heisenberg* (New York, 1992), chap. 26, pp. 501 ff.

2. These claims will be demonstrated in the course of chaps. 4–14. Most of the German physicists seem to have worked under the impression that the bomb would be a slow-neutron device, as will be seen.

Cambridge, England, in 1945 indicate that he understood that the U235 bomb would have to be a fast-neutron reaction, but it is suggestive of his somewhat relaxed attitude to the whole bomb problem that he had not felt obliged to incorporate such an explicit statement into any of his wartime papers.[3] As we shall see, the reason for this silence was that Heisenberg's initial erroneous assumptions ruled out the need for any precise thinking on this and related subjects. Hence the general air of imprecision that governed the whole project and became manifest in the dismayed and ignorant reactions of the German scientists at Farm Hall to the news of Hiroshima.

Still shocked by the news of the Allies' success in building a bomb where they had failed, the interned German scientists drew up a memorandum at Farm Hall on 7–8 August 1945 in which the main lines of all later apologies were set out.[4] It must be emphasized that when they prepared this first apology, Heisenberg and his colleagues had no idea of how the bomb had been made; its material and its physical principles were mysteries to them. They were thus forced to compose a statement that would imply they understood the bomb and indicate its nature without actually showing too much of their own hand. This extremely cautious statement, therefore, did not give any details of German scientific thinking on the character of an atomic bomb. The nuclear material was not specified, nor was its critical mass. Instead, a few well-known ideas about a reactor were alluded to, including its use of heavy water as a moderator and the possible obviation of the need for heavy water by resort to enriched U235. The uranium project was described largely in terms of its concentration on the design of a reactor rather than of a bomb:

3. *OE*, p. 83. In a recent paper, a noted German historian observes that "the prime reason for the comparative failure of the German Uranium Project seems to have been the sheer arrogance with which the Germans looked down on scientists elsewhere. . . . This arrogance comes out quite clearly in the Farm Hall transcripts. . . . There is also strong evidence that the myth deliberately spread by von Weizsäcker, Heisenberg and others . . . was created in a collective act of the group and this was done for the purpose of protecting each other's career prospects. . . . What might be called von Weizsäcker's myth . . . contributed to their moral arrogance. . . . The existence of nuclear weapons was viewed by them as blatant evidence of American imperialism or aggressiveness. Here, too, lies one of the roots of anti-Americanism in Germany" (W. Krieger, *The Germans and the Nuclear Question*, Fifth Alois Mertes Memorial Lecture 1995, German Historical Institute, Washington, D.C., Occasional Paper no. 14, p. 13).

4. Memorandum of 7 August 1945, printed in German in GWH, C V, 26–27 (reprinted in IMF, pp. 140–142). The GWH version comes from the Heisenberg papers and seems to be a variant first draft. A page of the draft in Heisenberg's hand with Gerlach's corrections is reproduced—presumably from the Heisenberg-Archiv, Munich—at p. 41 of Dieter Hoffmann's German edition of the Farm Hall transcripts, *Operation Epsilon: Die Farm-Hall-Protokolle oder die Angst der Alliierten vor der deutschen Atombombe* (Berlin, 1993). Several pages of the memorandum manuscript with Gerlach's and Wirtz's emendations are reproduced in H. Rechenberg, *Farm-Hall-Berichte: Die abgehörten Gespräche der 1945–46 in England internierten deutschen Atomwissenschaftler: Ein Kommentar* (Stuttgart, 1994), pp. 49–54 (and more legibly in his earlier draft, *Die langerwarteten Farm-Hall-Berichte—Sensation oder "Alter Schnee"?* [Munich, 1993]). A second German version of the memorandum with English translation is printed in the Farm Hall transcripts (*OE*, pp. 102–104; English at pp. 105–106).

The discussion in the transcripts (*OE*, pp. 93–94) shows that the memorandum was drafted on 7 August, whereas the final version (p. 102) is dated 8 August.

1. The nuclear fission of uranium was discovered in December 1938 by Hahn and Strassmann at the Kaiser-Wilhelm-Institute for Chemistry in Berlin as the fruit of pure scientific research which had nothing to do with practical purposes.
2. Not until the beginning of the war was a group of researchers convened in Germany, whose task it was to investigate the question of the practical exploitation of nuclear energy in connection with Hahn's discovery. Preparatory scientific work had towards the end of 1941 led to the result that it would be possible to apply nuclear energy to the running of machines. On the other hand, it was the view of the researchers that the resources for the production of a bomb were not available in the context of the technical possibilities prevailing in Germany. Further work concentrated therefore on the problem of machines, for which heavy water was needed in addition to uranium.[5]

Already one sees the crystallization of a version of the German project that would merge scientific omniscience with moral superiority. The emphasis on the reactor focus of the project enabled the German scientists to represent themselves as working largely on a comparatively benign project, one that might give rise to certain military applications such as submarine engines, but more fundamentally, as had been envisaged since 1939, to civilian usage as a power generator. That a reactor might actually produce nuclear material (plutonium) for a bomb was well known to the German team from 1940, but not thought worthy of mention here. A further aspect of the German scientists' discretion was the vague statement that sufficient technical resources were not available in Germany for the production of a bomb. Such a statement would suggest to Allied and other readers that Heisenberg and company were perfectly aware of the resources needed for a bomb, while avoiding the need to state exactly what these were. It was assumed that Allied scientists would read Heisenberg's shrewdly vague remark in terms of their own awareness of what it had taken, both materially and conceptually, to manufacture an atomic bomb and so credit Heisenberg with the same insight and understanding. True, Heisenberg had himself stated during the war to Speer that Germany possessed inadequate resources for the building of a bomb, and, equally true, Heisenberg found his own assessment confirmed by reading in the newspaper on 7 August 1945 that the Allies had deployed 150,000 personnel in their bomb project, in contrast to the few hundred active in the German enterprise.[6] But this does not mean that Heisenberg and the Allied scientists had the same understanding of just why so many personnel were required, of what they were doing, and of the actual design principle of the bomb. Heisenberg at this stage was, as the Farm Hall transcripts show quite graphically, still very much in the dark about the basic nature of the Hiroshima bomb and convinced that its critical mass would be in the realm of tons—not kilograms—of $U235$.[7]

5. GWH, C V, 26.
6. *OE*, pp. 75, 103.
7. See below, chap. 14, for an analysis of Heisenberg's thinking at Farm Hall.

In order to understand the forms of half-truth and evasion favored by Heisenberg and his colleagues, it is worth looking at apparently minor discrepancies in the two variant versions of the Farm Hall memorandum. The first is from Heisenberg's *Collected Works;* the second, a revision of the first, is from the Farm Hall transcripts:

> On the question of the atomic bomb it must be stressed that the undersigned knew of no investigations by other groups in Germany that might have had the immediate aim of the production of the bomb. If such efforts should nevertheless have been undertaken, they were, however, pursued by dilettantes and were not to be taken seriously.

> On the question of the atomic bomb it must be stressed that the undersigned knew of no investigations by other groups in Germany on the uranium problem that were to be taken seriously.[8]

The nuancing here is noticeable. First, there is the rather blunt allusion in the initial GWH version to German work on "the bomb." In the subsequent *OE* variant, however, "the bomb" is softened to "the uranium problem." Second, the GWH version denies knowledge of other German groups possibly working on "the bomb," but then implicitly contradicts itself by stating with great assurance that any work by such groups was pursued by dilettantes and not to be taken seriously. (How could Heisenberg have been so sure unless he already knew the personnel and work of those groups?) This contradiction—with its rather too emphatic condemnation of other groups being assuredly "dilettante"—is ironed away in the *OE* version by the less problematic statement that the Heisenberg team merely "knew of no other groups to be taken seriously."

Taken together, and with due attention being paid to their tone and phrasing, these variants actually set the model for later German pronouncements on the history of the atomic bomb project. For, although seeming forthright and unambiguous on the surface, they actually are deeply evasive and largely half-truths. Thus, Heisenberg knew perfectly well in 1945 that there were at least three other official projects aimed at the building of an atomic bomb: the Ardenne laboratory's work under the joint aegis of the Post Office and the Reichsforschungsrat; the Dällenbach project under Reichsforschungsrat, AEG, and Kaiser-Wilhelm-Society auspices, for which he himself had acted as consultant; and the SS bomb proposal of 1944.[9] Thus, the first draft's unrestrained contempt toward Heisenberg's rivals as

---

8. GWH, C V, 27: "Zur Frage der Atombombe sei noch festgestellt, dass den Unterzeichneten keine Untersuchungen etwa anderer Gruppen in Deutschland bekannt worden sind, die unmittelbar die Herstellung der Bombe zum Ziel gehabt hätten. Wenn solche Versuche doch unternommen sein sollten, so waren sie jedenfalls von Dilettanten durchgeführt und nicht ernst zu nehmen."

OE, p. 103: "Zur Frage der Atombombe sei noch festgestellt, dass den Unterzeichneten keine ernst zu nehmenden Untersuchungen etwa anderer Gruppen in Deutschland über das Uranproblem bekannt geworden sind."

9. These projects are described in the chapters that follow.

"dilettantes" betrayed the fact that Heisenberg actually did know of other bomb projects, but by the time of the final version, Heisenberg and his colleagues had controlled their feelings enough to substitute a rather more effective half-truth ("not taken seriously") that would tacitly admit the existence of the other projects without admitting their official status. The object of this carefulness was to mis-lead the Allied reader without actually telling an outright lie; through such equiv-ocation, Heisenberg was able to maintain—in his own mind—his integrity. Whether the reader is obliged to accept Heisenberg's self-evaluation is, of course, open to question.

Following the German scientists' return to Germany, Heisenberg wrote up for publication an account of the wartime uranium project and in late 1946 circulated a draft of this for comment to several colleagues, including Walther Bothe.[10] In a basic historical sense, this article is useless for establishing just what Heisenberg had understood about the atomic bomb problem during the war years, since it was written with knowledge of the Smyth Report, the official technical history of the Allied bomb project published in late 1945.[11] The present interest of Heisenberg's article lies rather in how this 1946 paper represents the first detailed German quasi-official history of the uranium project.

Heisenberg records that in September 1939 many nuclear physicists were "en-listed"—or, as the published version has it, "ordered"—to work on the atomic project. It was understood early on that $U235$ could be used in both a reactor and a bomb, but "separation of $U235$ was a problem that could be solved only with the greatest technical application."[12] Here Heisenberg presents a typical half-truth: While his scientific writings of the period show that he did appreciate that a bomb could be made with $U235$, he had grievously overestimated the amount of $U235$ that was required. He could not now mention this calculation, since it would have exposed a fatal error that lay at the heart of his work for the German

10. The original draft (cited hereafter as MS Draft) is in the Archiv zur Geschichte der Max-Planck-Gesellschaft, Berlin, III Abt., Rep. 6, Bothe Nachlass, along with the Bothe-Heisenberg corre-spondence of 29 November and 7 December 1946 on the matter. M. Walker, *German National Socialism and the Quest for Nuclear Power, 1939–1949* (Cambridge, 1989), pp. 205–210, discusses well the interesting mentality behind the different versions of the article, but rather strangely concludes, notwithstanding, that it is "an honest, sincere account" (p. 209)! (Walker [p. 209] also wrongly asserts that Heisenberg claimed in the paper to have "willfully hindered" the bomb project.)

The article was printed as W. Heisenberg, "Über die Arbeiten zur technischen Ausnutzung der Atomkernenergie in Deutschland," *Die Naturwissenschaften* 33 (1946): 325–329. Reprinted in GWH, C V, 28–32; and in IMF, pp. 143–157. Received 14 January 1947.

The "slightly abridged" English version, "Research in Germany on the Technical Application of Atomic Energy," *Nature*, no. 4059 (16 August 1947): 211–215, is reprinted in GWH, series B, 414–418. (The article was translated by Ronald Fraser; see below, chap. 21).

11. H. DeW. Smyth, *Atomic Energy for Military Purposes: The Official Report on the Development of the Atomic Bomb* (Princeton, 1945).

12. MS Draft, p. 2: "Aber natürlich war die Abtrennung des $U235$ ein Problem, das schliesslich nur mit grösstem technischen Aufwand zu lösen war."

project. The best course of action now was simply to state his awareness of the possibility of a U235 bomb and leave his readers to assume that, of course, Heisenberg would also have been as aware of its true critical mass as his Western colleagues had been. Later in the paper Heisenberg continues to mislead his readers by attributing the virtual abandonment of the bomb project to the tremendous difficulty of separating U235: "The production of an atomic explosive [could not be achieved] without a wholly colossal—and thus not to be considered—technical effort."[13] Heisenberg does not say that at the time he believed that tons of U235 would be required, but prefers to allow his readers to assume that he saw the technical effort in the same light as the Allies, who built their separation plants in the expectation that only kilograms would be required for each bomb. It was true that a huge industrial effort would be needed even for this small amount, but that had not deterred the British from entering upon it in 1940. Again Heisenberg is letting his readers assume that the same scientific knowledge governed both the Allied and the German decisions as to whether or not to proceed with the bomb.

Heisenberg next gives credit to his intimate friend Carl-Friedrich von Weizsäcker for perceiving an alternative route to an atomic bomb. Weizsäcker in 1940 had argued that an operating reactor would produce a new fissionable element suitable for use as an explosive. "An energy-producing uranium reactor [says Heisenberg] can thus be used for the manufacture of an atomic explosive," as indeed the Americans found with plutonium.[14] Here Heisenberg is a little too glib, since Weizsäcker had wrongly identified element 93 (neptunium) rather than element 94 (plutonium) as the explosive, though other German colleagues did eventually arrive at the correct interpretation. The usefulness of a reactor for the eventual production of a bomb is emphasized by Heisenberg later in the paper when he cites the famous Harnack-Haus meeting of 1942.

For Heisenberg the pivotal point of the uranium project was the major meeting held at this Berlin facility of the Kaiser-Wilhelm-Institute for Physics in June 1942, where Armaments Minister Albert Speer and a large group of military leaders were briefed by the scientists. The conclusion of the meeting was that the bomb would be deferred as a long-term possibility and work concentrated on the building of a reactor that would serve not only as a possible power source for military vessels, but also as the source of plutonium as a nuclear explosive.

> It was definitely established that the technical application of atomic energy was possible in a uranium reactor. Furthermore, it was to be expected that an explosive for atomic bombs could be produced in a uranium pile. However, more significance was placed on the determination that the energy developed in a uranium reactor could be used for the driving of engines. No procedure was known for the separation of

13. Ibid., p. 4; quoted more fully below.
14. Ibid., p. 3. "Ein energieerzeugender Uranbrenner kann also zur Herstellung eines Atomsprengstoffes benutzt werden."

isotopes that would achieve the production of an atomic explosive without a wholly colossal—and thus not to be considered—technical effort.[15]

Heisenberg's main historical point is that the German project focused on the development of a reactor rather than a bomb program, and that this priority was finally imposed by Speer in 1942. This leaves Heisenberg with the awkward task of explaining how it was that Fermi had succeeded in constructing a critical reactor in December 1942 while the Germans had not yet succeeded in having a reactor go critical by the end of the war in 1945 despite much effort and theorizing over the preceding six years.

One reasonable explanation for this failure was the Allied bombing and the shortage of raw materials such as heavy water that delayed German work, and indeed it is hard to imagine the German project having any real chance of success under these conditions. But here again there is a great deal of concealed equivocation. In December 1939 Heisenberg had suggested that either pure graphite or heavy water might serve as a moderator that would enable a reactor to achieve criticality, but subsequently he had opted for heavy water. This left the Germans vulnerable to Allied raids as well as shortages, since the only good source of the material was the Norwegian Norsk-Hydro plant. But the plant was crippled through Allied action in 1943, and eventually Heisenberg switched to graphite instead. Three crucial years, however, had been lost by this misjudgment. Characteristically, Heisenberg refused to accept the responsibility even though he was the chief scientist on the project. He attempted rather disingenuously to shift the blame to his colleague Walther Bothe, claiming in this draft paper that the Heidelberg scientist in 1941 had used slightly impure graphite for his measurements of neutron absorption and so wrongly concluded that graphite would not serve as a moderator. "Clearly [says Heisenberg] the graphite used was not pure enough. Yet it was falsely concluded from this that even absolutely pure graphite would not be suitable for the construction of a reactor."[16] It was only later that Bothe in conjunction with Heisenberg's own Berlin team found that graphite would indeed be suitable. The final, properly accurate experiments were carried out by Heisenberg's close associate Wirtz in late 1944 (an implicit reflection on Bothe's competence).[17] Bothe, however, was having none of this; in his

15. Ibid., p. 4: "Es war der sichere Nachweis vorhanden, dass die technische Ausnützung der Atomenergie in einem Uranpile möglich ist. Ferner war zu erwarten, dass man in einem Uranpile Sprengstoff für Atombomben herstellen kann. Jedoch wurde mehr Wert auf die Feststellung gelegt, dass man die im Uranbrenner entwickelte Energie zum Betrieb von Maschinen benützen kann. In der Isotopentrennung war kein Verfahren bekannt, das die Herstellung eines Atomsprengstoffes ohne einen ganz ungeheuerlichen und deshalb nicht in Betracht kommenden technischen Aufwand geleistet hätte."

16. MS Draft, p. 3: "Offenbar war der benützte Elektrographit nicht rein genug. Allerdings wurde damals fälschlicherweise geschlossen, dass auch absolut reine Kohle nicht zum Bau von Uranbrenner geeignet sei." On this subject, see below, chap. 9.

17. MS Draft, pp. 3, 5.

comments to Heisenberg in 1946 he crossed out the offending sentences, rewording them thus: "The graphite was pure . . . but on the basis of current theory the conclusion was that even with the purest material, graphite would not be suitable for a reactor."[18] In his letter to Heisenberg, Bothe coolly remarked: "I am not so convinced that our absorption cross-section for pure graphite is so very wrong, if we had also given greater attention to the occluding nitrogen. If you should know something about more exact American results, I would be very grateful to you for a short note." In other words, Bothe held that the graphite had been pure, that the experimental results were correct, and that theory confirmed experiment and led to the elimination of graphite—and, of course, as Heisenberg was made to understand, theory had been his domain. Though Bothe was successful on this occasion in forcing Heisenberg to retract his evasion, in later years Heisenberg could not refrain from trying again to put forward this particular line of self-exculpation.[19]

The last section of Heisenberg's 1946 draft conflates technical arguments with moral ones, developing a tendency already set down in the Farm Hall memorandum. Heisenberg starts out by implausibly claiming that until 1942 the Allied and German projects had progressed equally.

> Both sides had reached roughly the same results at roughly the same time except in the area of isotope separation, where the Americans had made essentially greater progress. It had now to be decided what the technical consequences of these results should be, and the decision on both sides turned out to be different. In America it was decided to attempt the production of atomic bombs with an effort that would constitute a large part of the collective American war effort. In Germany an effort one thousandth the scale of the American was applied to the problem of producing atomic energy that would drive engines.[20]

This claim to equality with the Allied project as late as 1942 is quite self-deluding, to say the least. The Allies had by 1942 acquired a large body of relevant experimental data relating to the cross-sections for fission and other fast-neutron pro-

---

18. Ibid., p. 7, in Bothe's hand: " . . . und daraus auf das Verhalten des reinen Kohlenstoffs geschlossen; das Ergebnis war, dass nach dem damaligen Stande der Theorie auch reinste Kohle eben nicht mehr für die Herstellung eines Uranbrenners geeignet sein sollte."

19. As in his discussions with David Irving; see below.

20. MS Draft, p. 6: "[1942] Auf beiden Seiten kam man ungefähr gleichzeitig zu ungefähr denselben Resultaten, mit Ausnahme des Gebiets der Isotopentrennung, auf dem die Amerikaner wesentlich grössere Fortschritte erzielt hatten. Nun musste entschieden werden, welche technischen Konsequenzen aus diesen Ergebnissen zu Ziehen seien, und diese Entscheidung ist auf beiden Seiten verschieden ausgefallen. In Amerika entschloss man sich, mit einem Aufwand, der einen nicht unbeträchtlichen Teil des gesamten amerikanischen Kriegsaufwandes ausgemacht haben dürfte, die Herstellung von Atombomben zu versuchen. In Deutschland wandte man sich, mit einem Aufwand, der etwa den tausendsten Teil der amerikanischen betrug, dem Problem der mit Atomenergie betriebenen Maschine zu."

cesses in U235 that were directly relevant to bomb design; they also had a correct concept of explosive critical mass and detailed calculations thereof, and were about to launch a large-scale project at Los Alamos. The British MAUD Report of 1941 is conceptually and experimentally in a different universe from the comparable German Heereswaffenamt (HWA; Army Weapons Office) Report of February 1942. To reduce this qualitative and quantitative advantage, as Heisenberg does, to a mere technical lead in isotope separation is disingenuous.

The moral content of the passage quoted is equally fallacious. It carries an implied moral judgment on the Allied scientists for their having opted for atomic bombs without regard to the central moral issue. For Heisenberg and later German writers, the moral issue was that atomic bombs were bad per se and should not have been developed. The fallacy here is that it is not atomic bombs that are the primary moral problem, but rather the evilness of Nazi Germany. By suppressing the Nazi and the Allied contexts, Heisenberg creates a false symmetry between the moral predicaments of the Allied and German scientists. It is as though the scientists are acting in a political vacuum simply as scientists, rather than as fighters for their respective causes. Given this political neutralism, the action of the Allied physicists in choosing to manufacture an atomic bomb thus becomes morally reprehensible. Heisenberg never says anything in his accounts about the fact that the Allied scientists were behaving morally by virtue of the fact that they were developing weapons for the defense of a moral cause against an evil one. Never in any of his writings or interviews or letters did Heisenberg bring himself to concede the morality of the Allied cause, nor the morality of its atomic scientists. His only concession—symptomatic of the moral vacuum of the German scientists—was to state that he had "the greatest admiration for the *efficiency* [emphasis added] of the American physicists"; their *morality* did not come into it.[21]

This unpleasant imputation is worsened by Heisenberg's explanation of the German inability to construct a bomb. There are two elements to this argument, one moral, the other scientific:

> It is often asked us by the English and Americans why no attempt was made in Germany to produce atomic bombs. The simplest answer that can be given is this: be-

21. Heisenberg to the *New York Times*, 30 January 1949, reprinted in GWH, C V, 42 (see below). Perhaps I should clarify this by noting that Heisenberg and his colleagues were motivated by a German morality of their own, but this morality was quite different from the Western code of morality, as will be seen below in part III.

This blindness to what in the West would be seen as the fundamental moral issue of Nazism, a blindness manifested in attempts to equate Nazi atrocities with purported Allied atrocities such as the use of atomic bombs, is characteristic of a great deal of German thinking. Heidegger's obtuse likening of Auschwitz to the deportations of eastern Germans from Poland in 1945 is only more rashly expressed than Heisenberg's and Weizsäcker's attitudes. See the revealing correspondence in R. Wolin, ed., *The Heidegger Controversy: A Critical Reader* (New York, 1991), pp. 160–164.

cause this enterprise could not have succeeded during the war. It could not have succeeded on technical grounds, for even in America with its much greater resources . . .
free of enemy action, the bomb was not ready before the end of the war with Germany.[22]

One might also mention that Heisenberg is here implying that he was always presciently aware of just how long the war would last, though in 1939 – 41 Heisenberg
was actually expecting a rather short war. So the pressures of the Russian war, especially on men and materials, and of the Allied bombing of Germany, together
with the regime's concentration on short-term weapons development, blocked any
possible successful outcome of a bomb project. Thus, we have added to Heisenberg's original scientific explanation that U235 isotope separation was too great an
undertaking the political one that the war itself precluded any successful bomb
project's being pursued. This is all plausible enough, but Heisenberg rashly adds a
moral explanation claiming that the German scientists did indeed from the start
have a moral awareness of the dangers of their work, but were thankful to have
been relieved in 1942 by "external circumstances" of the responsibility of making
a moral decision as to whether they should actually work on a bomb.

> For the scientists who worked on the uranium project this decision had still another,
> human, side. These physicists were aware of the great responsibility that a person
> who could unleash such powers of nature had to bear. Conscious of this, they had
> worked with much effort to retain control of the project in their hands. They had
> obliged themselves from the beginning to face the difficult question of whether the
> cause was good for which they should bring into action the greatest powers of na-
> ture. External circumstances had removed from their hands the difficult moral deci-
> sion whether they should produce atomic bombs.[23]

"From the beginning," claims Heisenberg, the German scientists had been
aware of the moral dilemma of making a bomb for a cause that may not have
been "good" (he cannot bring himself to say the word "evil"). But if this is so, why
did Heisenberg and his friends work at all on the project for almost three years
(September 1939 to June 1942) when it was considered feasible that some sort of

22. MS Draft, p. 6: "Es ist uns oft, auch von englischer und amerikanischer Seite, die Frage gestellt
worden, warum man damals nicht auch in Deutschland den Versuch unternommen habe, Atombomben zu erzeugen. Die einfachste Antwort, die man auf diese Frage geben kann, lautet: weil dieses
Unternehmen während des Kriegs nicht mehr gelingen konnte. Es konnte schon aus technischen Gru-
enden nicht gelingen; denn selbst in Amerika, mit seinen viel grösseren Reserven . . . ohne Feindein-
wirkung . . . ist die Bombe, ja erst nach dem Ende des Kriegs mit Deutschland fertiggeworden."

23. MS Draft, p. 6: "Für die Forscher, die am Uranvorhaben mitarbeiteten, hatte diese Entscheidung noch eine andere, menschliche Seite. Diese Physiker wussten von den grossen Verantwortung, die
ein Mensch zu tragen hat, der solche Naturkräfte entfesseln kann, und sie haben von vornherein be-
wusst und mit viel Mühe darauf hingearbeitet, die Kontrolle über das Vorhaben in der Hand zu be-
halten. Sie haben sich auch von Anfang an die schwere Frage vorlegen müssen, ob die Sache gut sei,
für die hier die grössten Naturkräfte eingesetzt werden sollen. Die äusseren Umstände haben ihnen die
schwere moralische Entscheidung, ob sie Atombomben herstellen sollten, aus der Hand genommen."

bomb could be made and indeed when it was possible that the government might order the project to proceed as a priority? To have worked on the project in this state of uncertainty as to whether the project might actually produce a bomb or not—but potentially could—belies any claim to moral principle. The morality of Heisenberg and his colleagues consisted simply in their agonizing a little, as would any physicist, over whether it was a good idea to build a bomb. There was no real moral consideration here of the fundamental evil of Nazism, but simply otiose and self-indulgent moralizing.

Underlying all this tortuous argument is the strong implication that, if the scientists had ever been forced to make a moral decision, their preexisting moral consciousness of the issue would have led them to refuse to make a bomb. Far from displaying Heisenberg's moral courage, however, the intricate reasoning only illustrates vividly the anxiety of the German physicists to evade acceptance of any true responsibility. This characteristic, which has often been argued to be deeply rooted in German culture and behavioral patterns,[24] would in all likelihood have led them to work diligently, no doubt with conscientious misgivings, on a bomb had they been so ordered; they would then have shifted the blame for their work onto "the regime." Negative "external circumstances"—Speer, the government, shortages, Allied bombing, the cost—had been used by Heisenberg to justify his not working on the bomb after 1942. But had "external circumstances" turned out to be favorable instead, then they would have been used to justify working on the bomb. This is the hidden mentality that animates Heisenberg's mixing of contradictory scientific, political, and moral explanations. The emotional, characteristically German, motivation for it all emerges quite tellingly in Heisenberg's explanation of why the Germans worked on the uranium project, especially after 1942. It was because they were driven by the conviction that

> the possibility [of nuclear energy] had first been created through the discovery of the German scientists Hahn and Strassmann; so it seemed to us right and fair that the great technical development of this discovery that must result with peace should have one of its beginnings in Germany and bear fruits for Germany.[25]

Naturally, a reader of this passage in 1946 was expected to agree that Heisenberg's work had been done during the war with an eye to the peace that would follow; but some of his most enthusiastic research on the problem—including its bomb aspect—had been done during the high tide of German military success, when he was visiting colleagues in occupied countries and telling them what a benefit German victory would be for the whole of Europe.[26]

---

24. See below, chap. 15.

25. MS Draft, p. 6: " . . . die Möglichkeit dazu war erst durch die Entdeckung der deutschen Forscher Hahn und Strassmann geschaffen worden; so schien es uns recht und billig, dass die grosse technische Entwicklung, die sich auch im Frieden an diese Entwicklung anschliessen musste, in Deutschland einen ihrer Anfänge haben und für Deutschland Früchte tragen sollte."

26. For these views see below, and also chap. 19.

In sum, this first detailed account in Heisenberg's manuscript is extraordinarily revealing, but should be handled with the greatest caution. Its web of half-truths, equivocations, evasions, and inaccuracies is intended to disarm non-German readers by luring them into thinking that the German scientists shared the same assumptions—both physical and moral—as their Allied counterparts.

Heisenberg's reworked German version of his historical paper was published in December 1946. There are several interesting changes:

1. Where the manuscript draft simply said that the German official project was set up in September 1939 in the light of information received concerning "atomic energy work in America," the new version rather more bare-facedly attributes the German project to the fear aroused by news of "American military offices making funds available for investigation of the atomic problem. In the light of the possibility that atomic weapons would be developed by the Anglo-Saxon side, the Heereswaffenamt [Army Weapons Office] set up its research body."[27]

2. Heisenberg yielded to Bothe's criticism of his earlier version of the mistaken measurements of the graphite cross-section. He had little choice in this if he was to preserve a united front by the German physicists, since Bothe would not have been inclined to let stand an official version that laid the blame for the failure of the reactor program at his door.[28]

3. Weizsäcker's plutonium suggestion of 1940 is shaded in two ways. Its imprecision about whether the explosive is element 93 or 94 is excused by the claim that without a suitable cyclotron in Germany, the resolving experiments could not be carried out. As to the insight that the reactor might thus be used to produce an atomic explosive, the word "probably" (*wahrscheinlich*) is used to soften the draft's certainty that this was so, and a proviso is quietly inserted that "to this end, however, no practical development was yet discussed at that time," thus removing any moral stain from the proposal.[29]

   Heisenberg has more to say about plutonium when he summarizes the results of the meetings of February and June 1942, which he says, unblushingly, were attended by leading figures in military-weapons research. As if to show how little practical interest there was in obtaining plutonium for a bomb, Heisenberg mentions that "protoactinium was also drawn attention to as an atomic explosive . . . since it might be amenable to a chain reaction with fast neutrons; the obtaining of such large amounts of protoactinium

---

27. *Naturwissenschaften* (1946), "Über die Arbeiten," p. 326. Reprinted in GWH, C. The campaign was launched with a rather vague newspaper report: "Das deutsche Atombomben-Geheimnis: Interview mit Professor Werner Heisenberg," *Die Welt*, no. 39 (12 August 1946): 3. The piece is not printed in GWH, though it is mentioned there at C V, 7, 9, where it is dated 13 August. Heisenberg's words are not given verbatim.

28. "Über die Arbeiten," p. 327. GWH, C V, 30.

29. Ibid.

was, however, concluded to be hopeless."[30] Plutonium was bracketed with protoactinium in this way as an obviously far-fetched possibility for a bomb, thus making it respectable and safe for Heisenberg and his colleagues to work on the reactor program without fear of having to face a decision about actually building a bomb within the foreseeable future. In this context, Heisenberg's lack of scientific success again allowed him to remain "moral" within his own mind while working on the uranium project. (But what if he were to have achieved an unexpected success with the reactor that suddenly made a plutonium bomb a practical proposition . . . ?)

4. In the published version there is the astonishing new claim that Heisenberg made no investigations as to the critical mass of an atomic bomb:

> Furthermore, it was to be expected that an explosive for atomic bombs could be produced in a uranium pile. *No investigations, however, were initiated on the technical side of the atomic bomb problem, for example, on the smallest size of a bomb.* [Emphasis added.] However, more significance was placed on the determination that the energy developed in a uranium reactor could be used for the driving of engines.[31]

The second sentence (the one that I have italicized) is new, placed between two sentences that were already there in the manuscript draft. It is a typical Heisenberg half-truth, designed to mislead in two respects. First, since it figures in the context of the discussion of a reactor producing plutonium, the sentence means that Heisenberg can equivocate and in good conscience keep silent about his 1940 calculation of the critical mass of a U235 bomb. Second, the phrasing is literally accurate: no investigations of the "technical side" of the problem were initiated (such as those that were done at Los Alamos) that applied to a practical bomb. Heisenberg's earlier notion—not, in his mind, a "technical investigation"—of the huge critical mass of uranium and his current difficulty in conceiving a project for the extraction of plutonium together effectively ruled out the development of an atomic bomb for the rest of the war. There was, therefore, no need in June 1942 for him to "investigate" on a technically detailed level the critical mass of a bomb; he did not have to say he had indeed already (as we shall see) carried out a very rough calculation that would not be deemed a precise "technical investigation." If his readers did not know this, it was not his responsibility to tell them about it.[32]

5. Heisenberg holds to his eccentric belief that until "the turning point" in 1942, the Allied and German projects were roughly equal (aside from U235 separation). But since he seems to have been advised that as it stood, this

---

30. Ibid. The prospects of protoactinium as an explosive had already been discussed at Farm Hall in August 1945. See below, chap. 14.

31. "Über die Arbeiten," p. 327. GWH, C V, 30.

32. For this rough calculation of 1940, see below, chap. 7.

would not wash with an Allied readership, Heisenberg now refers specifically to Fermi's successful Chicago reactor of December 1942, and—trying to skate over the fact that he is contradicting himself—attributes the American success to "the much more significant preparatory work for the large-scale technical effort of the uranium project that had already been made in America, so that as a consequence the practical execution of the major experimentation could go much faster; the first energy-producing reactor was therefore already completed by December 1942."[33] Heisenberg smoothly attempts to mislead his readers into forgetting that this "much more significant preparatory work" meant that the two sides were not, as he asserts in these same paragraphs, "roughly" equal until 1942, when the Allies decided to make atomic bombs while the Germans determined to shelve that bellicose program in favor of developing a reactor.

6. The printed version rings an interesting change on the question of the physicist's recommendation (or rather non-recommendation) to Speer that the bomb project be shelved. The manuscript draft had this: "To achieve the necessary support, the experts would have had to make a promise concerning its expected success that they could not have kept." The printed version adds to this the gloss that "the experts did not attempt, in view of the known situation of the highest leadership, to procure a great industrial effort for the production of atomic bombs." This is a rather strangely negative way of putting the matter, suggesting that there was no moral decision involved in this non-recommendation and that it was motivated by purely practical considerations. However, at Farm Hall, Heisenberg had made an interesting remark that reveals what lay behind this cryptic expression; he had observed then that "we wouldn't have had the moral courage to recommend to the Government in the spring of 1942 that they should employ 120,000 men just for building the thing up."[34] There had indeed been a moral decision implicit in the failure to advise Speer to undertake a massive development for the bomb, but it had not been the one that might have been expected. For Heisenberg, the moral issue had been simply whether the unpromising technical prognosis for the project justified the large-scale commitment of resources. This was Heisenberg's idea of a dilemma requiring "moral courage"; almost verging on the absurd in Western eyes, such thinking is rather typical of a great deal of German moral reflection during the Third Reich—and after. In a section added to a republished version in 1956, Heisenberg explained how for him the moral problem was not whether to work on a preparatory investigation, nor whether to tell Hitler that a bomb was indeed feasible, but rather whether to obey a Hitler order to make the bomb: "The physicists were

33. "Über die Arbeiten," pp. 328 f. GWH, C V, 31–32.
34. OE, p. 76.

spared the hard moral decision with which they would be faced by an order to produce atomic bombs."[35]

Heisenberg had his German account translated for publication in the British journal *Nature* in 1947, and this became his standard version of his work on the German atomic project: The Germans had fully understood that atomic bombs could be made with U235 and plutonium; the German project had maintained parity with the Allied one until the "turning point" of 1942, when the "external circumstances" of the war had led to Speer's ordering that the bomb project be abandoned in favor of the reactor program; the German scientists had made no moral decision as to whether or not nuclear weapons should be developed. This was the version he maintained—with one amazing exception—in subsequent interviews, papers, and memoirs.

Heisenberg's efforts to establish his own German historiography through his December 1946 *Naturwissenschaften* article and its British version in *Nature* (August 1947), along with its American reprint (September 1947),[36] provoked a sharp American response from Samuel Goudsmit, the Dutch-American physicist who had been the scientific leader of the Allied ALSOS wartime mission charged with obtaining scientific intelligence of the German uranium project. An old friend of Heisenberg's, Goudsmit had been sadly disillusioned by the conduct of Heisenberg and other German scientists under the Nazi regime. He now attempted to counter the Heisenberg version of events in the American scientific media, beginning with a talk at the American Physical Society's meeting of May 1947. Goudsmit's campaign induced Heisenberg to write to him privately in September 1947 to correct his allegedly false impressions, particularly his view that the German scientists had been engaged in a race against the Americans to develop the bomb. Heisenberg, however, glides over the fact that the Germans were indeed racing for a bomb in 1939−41, nor does he admit that the Germans abandoned the race after 1942 because of his mistaken view that a U235 bomb would require tons of the isotope, rather than solely on account of the difficulties of building a reactor-bomb and obtaining enough plutonium.

Even more questionable than these scientific half-truths are the moral ones. Heisenberg alleges in his first letter to Goudsmit that the German scientists adopted a passive attitude toward the bomb project because "it was clear to us that on the one hand a European victory of National Socialism would have terrible consequences; on the other hand, however, in view of the hatred sown by National Socialism, one could not have a hopeful view of a complete defeat of Germany." The first part of this statement is proven false by well-substantiated reports of Heisenberg's optimistic comments about the prospects of a German victory made

35. Postscript to Heisenberg, "Über die Arbeiten," in *Helle Zeit—Dunkle Zeit*, ed. C. Seelig (Zurich, 1956), p. 144.

36. Reprinted in *Chemical and Engineering News* (U.S.), 15 September 1947.

in the course of his visits to occupied countries in 1940–42.[37] The phrasing of the second part of the statement reveals the extent to which Heisenberg's thinking was skewed by his intense German patriotism, which forced him, like most Germans, to conclude that a Nazi victory was preferable to defeat at the hands of the Allies, as had happened in 1918. Taken as a whole, the sentence represents a false dilemma: The moral issue was not a choice between Nazi victory and Allied vengeance, as Heisenberg would have it, but rather a choice between Nazi victory and the preservation of European civilization and values. Compare Heisenberg's pusillanimity to Thomas Mann's courageous recognition that any disaster that might befall his own beloved Germany was preferable to a German victory.[38]

Heisenberg's hand was forced no doubt by rumors that Goudsmit was about to publish a book that would document his charges of German scientific ignorance and German moral ignominy alike. In two popular articles in the autumn of 1947, Goudsmit roundly attacked Heisenberg's *Nature* article, which he called "Heisenberg's Smyth Report . . . his answer to the German people." Hiroshima had put the German scientists on the defensive. They had been arrogant in their belief that if they had not developed a bomb, then no one else could. Now

> they had to explain why the supposedly superior German science had failed. . . . Heisenberg's report is a tale of success. . . . But they were on the wrong path as far as the bomb was concerned. It is not right to blame this on a ruling by Armament Minister Speer or the war conditions in Germany.[39]

What particularly irked Goudsmit was Heisenberg's apparent inability to admit that what had really wrecked the German project—as it had German science in general—was the dictatorial and racist policy of the Nazi regime. Blame instead was laid by Heisenberg on the fact that "public interest in atomic physics was negligibly small in Germany between the years 1933 and 1939."

Goudsmit's book, *ALSOS*, a memoir of the Allied atomic-intelligence team's investigation of Nazi science, itself appeared in October 1947, just under a year after Heisenberg's apologetic article. Despite some flaws, *ALSOS* was a remarkable piece of work, rich in its critical insights into the fallacies of the German conception of the atomic bomb as well as providing a shrewd grasp of the extent to which German science and scientists had been corrupted by the Nazi era. Drawing on his own store of captured documentation, Goudsmit scathingly dismissed the

37. M. Walker, "Physics and Propaganda: Werner Heisenberg's Foreign Lectures under National Socialism," *Historical Studies in the Physical Sciences* 22 (1992): 339–389. See below, chap. 16, for details.

38. Heisenberg to Goudsmit, 23 September 1947. This and ensuing correspondence between Heisenberg and Goudsmit quoted below are in Goudsmit Papers, AIP, box 10, folders 93–97. See also below, chaps. 19–21.

39. S. Goudsmit, "Heisenberg on the German Uranium Project," *BAS* 3 (1947): 343. See also S. Goudsmit, "Nazis' Atomic Secrets," *Life*, 20 October 1947, 124–134. In a letter of 27 October 1947 to Rosbaud, Goudsmit stated that he was "furious about Heisenberg's article"; Goudsmit Papers, box 28, folder 43.

moral pretensions of the German physicists, printing documents that exposed Heisenberg's dealings with Himmler as well as Weizsäcker's involvement with the SS in determining official policy toward "Jewish physics." As to the Germans' understanding of the atomic bomb, Goudsmit forthrightly exposed their fundamental ignorance. From his study of the captured German documents and American intelligence reports (including a perhaps too rapid inspection of the Farm Hall transcripts) Goudsmit concluded—mistakenly—that Heisenberg had never understood the U235 bomb to be a fast-neutron reaction. Properly aware of the actual German interest in unwieldy and unrealistic reactor-bombs, Goudsmit deduced wrongly that these notions of a reactor-bomb constituted Heisenberg's slow-neutron U235 bomb. This was not so; in fact, since the slow-neutron reactor-bomb was actually a separate concept from the pure-U235 bomb. Goudsmit had thus conflated two quite different German bomb concepts into a single one—though, given the fragmentary and often cryptic state of evidence then available, this error was understandable. Finally, Goudsmit erred in arguing that the Germans had not realized that plutonium could also be used as an atomic explosive.[40]

Though Goudsmit was generally correct and fair-minded in his estimation that the German scientists had achieved no clear or true idea of an atomic bomb and were indeed woefully ignorant of its scientific principles, the particular errors in *ALSOS* opened up an easy avenue for Heisenberg and his friends to counterattack. First and foremost, Goudsmit's charge that the Germans did not conceive clearly of plutonium as an explosive could be persuasively refuted by reference to Weizsäcker's 1940 paper on the subject (G-50), imprecise though it was about whether element 93 (neptunium) or 94 (plutonium) would be the explosive.[41] Heisenberg found an ally in Waldemar Kaempffert, the scientific correspondent of the *New York Times*, who, in a review of Goudsmit's book and Heisenberg's reprinted *Nature* article, openly preferred the Heisenberg version for its objectivity, which he found reminiscent (not surprisingly, according to Goudsmit!) of the Smyth Report.[42] Goudsmit reacted in a published letter, to which Kaempffert made the rather lame rejoinder that Heisenberg must be telling the truth since

40. S. Goudsmit, *ALSOS* (New York, 1947; reprint, Los Angeles, 1983), pp. 176 f., 179, 183. M. Walker, "Heisenberg, Goudsmit, and the German Atomic Bomb," *Physics Today*, January 1990, 52–60, and the ensuing letters critical of Walker's distorted portrayal of Goudsmit, ibid., May 1991, 13–15, 90–96; February 1992, 126. Characteristic of Walker's article is its suppression of Goudsmit's readiness to correct his account in print when Heisenberg provided proper evidence. Walker's account is fatally flawed by its assumption that Heisenberg was telling the truth about his wartime knowledge of the atomic bomb and that Goudsmit was therefore unreasonable, biased, and wrong throughout the correspondence. For example, Walker (p. 55) describes as erroneous Goudsmit's claim that the Germans conceived of an atomic bomb as a reactor gone out of control. As we shall see in chap. 8, this was indeed one of Heisenberg's conceptions of the atomic bomb, though Goudsmit was somewhat misled by the ambiguous documentation into thinking that this was the only German conception of a bomb.

41. See below, chap. 9.

42. W. Kaempffert, "Why the Germans Failed to Develop an Atomic Bomb Is Now Revealed in Two Reports," *New York Times*, 26 October 1947.

"liars do not win the Nobel Prize." This was followed by the somewhat perverse statement that "it was no more discreditable for German than for American physicists to engage in research that might lead to an atomic bomb"—as though there were no moral difference between working for Hitler and for the Allies.[43]

Among those who found Kaempffert's arguments distasteful, if not risible, was Goudsmit's friend Paul Rosbaud, who wrote:

> I was distressed when I read his apologia for Heisenberg (Nobel-prize winners don't tell lies! How cheap an argument, besides I could tell him of several who have told lies. It is just as ridiculous as if one would say that ministers and diplomats never tell lies).[44]

Rosbaud was certainly in a position to know. Because of his hatred for the Nazi regime, Rosbaud had remained on as an Allied agent in wartime Germany. His position as a scientific editor and his wide circle of scientific acquaintances kept him knowledgeable about technical developments in numerous fields, including atomic research. In 1939 Rosbaud had influenced Hahn to publish the news of uranium fission in his journal *Die Naturwissenschaften* so as to prevent the knowledge from becoming a German monopoly, and later that same year had informed the British through R. S. Hutton and John Cockcroft of the formation of the German "Uranium Club."[45] Throughout the war Rosbaud had kept British intelligence abreast of the latest German work on atomic energy, exploiting his close personal relationship with Walter Gerlach, the head of the uranium project from 1944. After the war Rosbaud moved to England and kept up a steady correspondence with Goudsmit, ensuring that his *ALSOS* book was reviewed (by himself!) in the *Times Literary Supplement*.[46] As Rosbaud observed to Goudsmit, "I am sure that Heisenberg and his club will not like it very much," but although it was desirable that someone write a letter to the periodical supporting the review, he was not sanguine about finding someone in England to do so since "you know it is difficult to find an English scientist who understands how it is possible to fight his own country." Niels Bohr seemed a possibility, but he was in the United States, "and besides I don't know whether he would do it; he likes Heisenberg too much."[47]

Meanwhile, privately replying to Heisenberg's earlier letter in December 1947,

---

43. Letters of Goudsmit and Kaempffert in the *New York Times,* 9 November 1947.

44. Rosbaud to Goudsmit, 11 June 1948, Goudsmit Papers, box 28, folder 43.

45. On 5 August 1945 Rosbaud wrote up an anecdotal eleven-page account of the history of the German uranium project, which reached Goudsmit (now in Goudsmit Papers, box 28, folder 42).

46. *Times Literary Supplement,* 5 June 1948; see below, chap. 3. For the authorship of the anonymous review, see Rosbaud to Goudsmit, 11 June 1948, Goudsmit Papers, box 28, folder 43. For Rosbaud, see A. Kramish, *The Griffin* (Boston, 1986); also see below, chaps. 2 and 3, as well as subsequent chaps., esp. chap. 21.

47. Rosbaud to Goudsmit, 25 April 1948, Goudsmit Papers, box 28, folder 43. For Bohr's sometimes difficult relationship with Heisenberg, see below, chaps. 10, 19, and 21.

Goudsmit promised to send him a copy of *ALSOS* and reiterated his belief, based on documentary evidence, that the

> German scientists had incorrect ideas about an atomic bomb. By not stressing certain points [in your article] you give the casual reader the impression that you knew all the time how one should solve the problem. You put all the blame on a decision by Speer and the lack of resources.

However, Goudsmit's main concern was with the dubious moral smoke screen that Heisenberg had thrown up. Goudsmit was "shocked and surprised" by the omissions and understatements in the Heisenberg article, which "to me seemed merely meant as a defense of German physics under Hitler." The impossibility of a "compromise" with Nazism should have been as obvious to Heisenberg as it had been to Max von Laue. Even now, accused Goudsmit, Heisenberg and other Germans were proving themselves unable to make a frank admission of their mistaken approach to Hitler. Hoping to jolt Heisenberg into recognizing the folly of his compromising approach, Goudsmit enclosed a statement by Himmler concerning the recruiting of his correspondent to Nazi purposes. In words that probably cut closer to the bone than he realized, Goudsmit concluded: "Too many German scientists are still convinced that they deserved to win the war. . . . too many are merely concerned with the 'prestige' of German science."[48]

Heisenberg responded to Goudsmit with a long refutation in a letter of 5 January 1948.[49] He refers Goudsmit to Weizsäcker's paper of 1940 for evidence that the Germans were aware of the explosive possibility of plutonium. As to the basic principle of a bomb, Heisenberg insists that he understood it to be self-evident that a chain reaction with fast neutrons was possible in $U235$, and he refers to a slide diagram he had presented to meetings in 1942–43 that purportedly proved this. Unfortunately, the diagram is rather more ambiguous than Heisenberg lets on; in neither the slide nor its published accompanying text is it stated explicitly that the reaction uses fast neutrons.[50] Heisenberg himself may well have appreciated that fast neutrons were involved in the bomb, but there is no indication that his audiences were made aware of the fact. More important, Heisenberg as usual maintains a half-truth: He confines his answer to Goudsmit on this matter to the fact that he (Heisenberg) understood the bomb to use fast neutrons; but he keeps silent about what the critical mass of such a pure-$U235$ bomb would have been. Heisenberg thus avoids—here as elsewhere—the need to tell an actual lie. As far as I know, Heisenberg never claimed directly to have understood during the war

---

48. Goudsmit to Heisenberg, 1 December 1947, Goudsmit Papers.

49. Heisenberg to Goudsmit, 5 January 1948, Goudsmit Papers, box 10, folders 95–96 (IMF 29-1185/1189).

50. See the published lecture of 1943, "Die Energiegewinnung aus der Atomkernspaltung" (G-217), reprinted in GWH, A II, 570, which includes the diagram. But cf. the critical comment on the paper below, chap. 10.

period that the critical mass of a U235 bomb was relatively small. Where he intimated that this was so, he preferred to cite other persons' memories, such as that of Ernst Telschow of the Kaiser-Wilhelm-Society, as will be seen.

As an example of how adept Heisenberg was at spinning a plausible tale from scientific ambiguity, it is instructive to examine his letter's use of protoactinium as an analogy for U235 in order to prove his full understanding of a U235 bomb. In trying to prove to Goudsmit that he had, in fact, understood the bomb to be a fast-neutron reaction, Heisenberg falls into a trap of his own making:

> As proof of this assertion about the German physicists, I wish firstly to point out a passage in a secret report (article by Bothe about fast neutrons) . . . in which it is surmised that pure protoactinium in sufficient quantities would explode through a chain reaction of fast neutrons. It was known that protoactinium does not fission at all with slow neutrons. In your opinion, how would one explain this sentence about protoactinium if not in this way: that we were thoroughly aware of the chain reaction of all fast neutrons?"[51]

But what did Bothe actually say? The paper in question, *Machines Exploiting Fission by Fast Neutrons* (1941), investigates the use of fast neutrons to fission not U235— but U238 in piles. At the end of section 3, Bothe concludes that U238 on its own will not work, but in a footnote he indicates the possibility of mixing in some protoactinium, which has a seven times larger fission cross-section than U238 and a neutron multiplication factor of slightly more than one neutron per fission: "If the question arose at any time of obtaining a very large quantity of protoactinium, then one would have to reckon with the possibility of an explosion."[52]

Apart from the ambiguity as to whether Bothe is adumbrating the potential of protoactinium as a nuclear explosive or is merely observing that a reactor containing the element may explode, it should be noticed that there is no attempt in the Bothe paper to compare protoactinium fission with that of U235. The comparison is, in fact, with that of U238 in a reactor. When Heisenberg rehashed the

51. The question was repeated in a subsequent letter of 3 October 1948 (IMF 29-1192/1194).

This line is rehearsed in a FIAT (= Field Information Agency, Technical) paper of the same year prepared for the Allied authorities by O. Haxel: "[Protoactinium] with its seven times greater cross-section [than U238] would produce a neutron multiplication factor of slightly over one [per fission]. Thus, if larger masses of protoactinium could be obtained, one would have an explosion. This goes naturally in greater measure for the isolated U235 isotope." (O. Haxel, "Der Beitrag der schnellen Neutronen zur Neutronenvermehrung im Uran," in *FIAT [Field Information Agency, Technical] Review of German Science, 1939–1946: Nuclear Physics and Cosmic Rays*, ed. W. Bothe and S. Flügge [Wiesbaden, 1948], pt. II, p. 173.) Haxel seems to be referring to a paper by Bothe et al. on the 1945 Haigerloch reactor, rather than a bomb.

52. W. Bothe, "Maschinen mit Ausnutzung der Spaltung durch schnelle Neutronen" (G-128), December 2, 1941, p. 48 (IMF 30-028): "Käme also jemals die Gewinnung sehr grösser Pa-Mengen in Frage, so müsste mit der Möglichkeit einer Explosion gerechnet werden." This appears as a footnote to the statement: "Mit einer Energiegewinnung aus reines 38-Metall allein kann also nach unserem Versuch kaum noch gerechnet werden."

story for David Irving in 1965–66, he took it a stage further. Heisenberg now claimed that at the June 1942 Speer conference he had argued that a supercritical mass of protoactinium would detonate spontaneously in the same way as plutonium or U235, though a sufficient quantity could never be obtained.[53] But the main point here in reality is that the Bothe report seems to contradict the idea that the critical mass of a U235 bomb would be small, for Bothe speaks of "a very large quantity of protoactinium." If there were indeed an analogy between protoactinium and U235 fission, as Heisenberg claims, then the analogy would have been that both required large quantities for an explosion to take place.

Heisenberg also sidestepped the moral charges raised by Goudsmit. Stung by Goudsmit's exasperation that he had ever thought he could deal with the Nazi regime, Heisenberg repeated that he had done so to prevent worse catastrophes and that though improbable, the prospect was not hopeless. (This was not a line of argument likely to convince Goudsmit, whose opinion was based on the essential evil of Nazism; one made compromises with normal governments, not with the powers of evil.) In this context Heisenberg makes the extraordinary remark that he had discussed his Himmler dealings with Niels Bohr himself, who had approved his effort. Although Heisenberg may have himself believed this to be true, it is impossible to credit that Bohr's character would have inclined him to confer any such approval on a line of conduct that would have seemed to him at best folly and at worst immoral.

Heisenberg attempted again to drag Bohr into the moral debate later that year in a letter to the Dutch scientist B. L. van der Waerden.

When at the end of 1941 I realized that the reactor would work and that atomic bombs could probably be made (with plutonium; U235 separation still appeared to me a fantasy—in both cases I estimated the effort to be greater than it actually was)—then I was deeply frightened of the possibility that such weapons might be placed in the hands of whatever holders of power, not only Hitler. . . . When I spoke to Niels Bohr in Copenhagen in the autumn of 1941 I asked him whether physicists had the moral right to work on atomic problems in wartime . . . I certainly thought it a crime to make atomic bombs for Hitler; but I find it also not good to give them to other holders of power.[54]

This was typical of Heisenberg's repeated attempts—rejected by Bohr—to annex the Danish physicist to his own apology. Bohr, of course, thought atomic weapons evil, and even during the war was seeking to organize political action to

53. D. Irving, *The German Atomic Bomb* (New York, 1967; published in the United Kingdom as *The Virus House*), p. 120, seemingly quoting Ernst Telschow. The text of Heisenberg's talk is conveniently lost. One might conjecture that in it U235 was also written off as being needed in impossibly large amounts.

54. Heisenberg to B. L. van der Waerden, 28 April 1948, in IMF 29-1130/1131. For the moral aspect of the Copenhagen visit to Bohr, see below, chap. 19; the scientific aspect of the visit is discussed in chap. 10.

control and perhaps abolish them. But Bohr also recognized that in the face of Nazi evil, the moral imperative was that the Allies should produce atomic bombs, and indeed he worked on them himself at Los Alamos in 1944. Heisenberg and his colleagues never understood Bohr's ethical perception. Indeed, at Farm Hall, even the tolerant Otto Hahn sanctimoniously commented that "if Niels Bohr helped [with the bomb], then I must say that he has gone down in my estimation."[55] The peculiarity of Heisenberg's moral thinking, even in 1948, is revealed by his casual remark about his fear of giving politicians in general—"not only Hitler"—the atomic bomb. The specifically German nature of the moral problem of working for Hitler is here universalized into suspicion of all politicians and a condemnation of nuclear weapons in general, while the particular evils of Hitler and the German cause are forgotten.

Goudsmit waited a long time before answering Heisenberg's letter of January 1948. "I am in a rather sad and violent correspondence with Heisenberg," he told Paul Rosbaud.

> He still does not see the bigger issues and is mad because I probably underestimated his knowledge about plutonium. He fights me like he did Himmler. . . . Ramsauer's articles are much nearer to what is needed than the boastful article by Heisenberg in *Nature*. . . . All he knows about is that "his honor is being attacked" or that "German" physics is being frustrated.

Here Goudsmit had grasped the essential motivation behind all of Heisenberg's twists and turns, his evasions and subterfuges, and his compromises and collusions with the Nazi regime—namely, the preservation of his own "honor" as supreme value.[56]

In the meantime Goudsmit had had long talks with van der Waerden, and he also made special trips to Washington to study again the secret German reports, including Weizsäcker's. As Goudsmit notes in his letter to Heisenberg of 20 September 1948, this last paper, however, dealt with element 93 rather than plutonium, though he concedes that by 1942 Heisenberg himself certainly knew that element 94 was the explosive. But Goudsmit stresses that Weizsäcker's and other German reports (including, one might add, P. O. Müller's 1940 paper on a reactor-bomb) never specify fast-neutron reactions for a bomb, and indeed are clearly referring to slow neutrons. "The authors may have thought about fast neutrons, but if the picture had been clear in their minds they certainly would have stressed this important point repeatedly." On the moral side, Goudsmit complained yet again that Heisenberg seemed interested in describing the triumphs of German science rather than its corruption under the Nazis.[57]

55. *OE*, p. 91. For Carl Ramsauer, see Cassidy, p. 480.
56. See below, pt. III, esp. chap. 18.
57. Goudsmit to Heisenberg, 20 September 1948, Goudsmit Papers.

In his long reply to Goudsmit on 3 October 1948, Heisenberg criticized the characterizations in *ALSOS* and told Goudsmit that the correct description of the German position should have been:

> The German physicists knew at least so much about the manufacture and construction of atomic bombs that it was clear to them that the manufacture of bombs in Germany could not succeed during the war. For this reason, they were spared the moral decision whether they should make an atomic bomb and they had only worked on the uranium engine.[58]

One may imagine how Goudsmit received Heisenberg's suggestion that he publish a "rectification" of his book along these lines in the *Bulletin of the Atomic Scientists*.

Heisenberg was gratified by Goudsmit's concession that the Germans knew of plutonium, but wanted him further to admit they had also appreciated the bomb to be a fast-neutron reaction. In order to force the issue, Heisenberg disingenuously referred Goudsmit to a paper by F. H. Houtermans that had discussed fast-neutron reactions. The trouble is that the paper in question treats fast neutrons in U238, not U235, and is concerned with a reactor.[59] Heisenberg tries to enhance this sophistry by referring to German knowledge that a fast-neutron explosion could also take place in protoactinium and saying that this proves that "we are completely acquainted with the chain reaction by fast neutrons." This "complete acquaintance" does not quite jibe with what Heisenberg had confessed in a less guarded moment at Farm Hall in 1945:

> We have done little research in the field of completed fast-neutron reactions because we could not see how we could do it because we did not have this element [94], and we saw no prospect of being able to obtain it.[60]

Given Heisenberg's selective memory, we should not place much store in his next reminiscence, especially as he carefully says that the former Director-General at the Kaiser-Wilhelm-Society and a secretary had to remind him about it.[61] Heisenberg claims that at the famous military-scientific meeting attended by Speer in June 1942, Field Marshal Milch had asked him how large an atomic bomb would have to be to destroy a city.

58. Heisenberg to Goudsmit, 3 October 1948, Goudsmit Papers. Walker, "German Atomic Bomb," p. 57, is wrong to say that there is no record that Heisenberg ever read *ALSOS;* this letter gives quotations and page references to the book.
59. The paper by Houtermans, "The Problem of Releasing a Nuclear Chain Reaction" (G-94 and G-267), 1941, discusses fast-neutron reactions in sec. 3 and fig. 1. For this paper see below, chap. 9.
Since slow neutrons do not fission in U238, fast neutrons are needed to fission it, whether for a chain reaction in a "reactor" or in a putative explosion. But, though the neutrons used in the reactor U238 are fast, the actual chain reaction goes slowly.
60. *OE*, p. 117. See below, chap. 14.
61. Heisenberg to Irving, 10 June 1966 (IMF 32). See below, chap. 12.

> I answered at that time that the bomb, that is the essentially active part, would have to be about the size of a pineapple. This statement, of course, caused a surprise, especially with the known physicists, and it has therefore remained in the memory of several participants.[62]

What stands out here is that the small critical mass of a bomb came as news to the *physicists* present, who evidently still believed that a large mass was needed. But other aspects of the episode are quite incredible. If the statement had caused such a sensation at the time, it would assuredly have led to a massive drive being launched to obtain such a small amount of U235, as had been the case in Britain. The truth is that by 1942 Heisenberg had virtually given up on the possibility of separating U235 on the scale of the tons—rather than kilograms—that he believed would be needed for a bomb.[63] If indeed he did make a statement about a pineapple, then it related to one of two things: First, it might refer to the actual amount of U235 that had to be "burned" efficiently in an explosion. This was many orders of magnitude smaller than the amount of U235 that Heisenberg believed was needed to ensure this "burning." Or, second, the amount might have referred speculatively to plutonium, which was assumed to be more fissionable than U235, and which the Germans had guessed in January 1942 might have a critical mass of only 10 to 100 kg.[64] The latter possibility seems more likely, for it would explain how Heisenberg was able to hold off the enthusiasm of the assembled military and political leaders. Heisenberg would have been careful to explain that work on the plutonium-producing reactor was proceeding with all dispatch, but that it was a long-term project whose success he would report to them as soon as it was achieved.

Regardless of the exact meaning of Heisenberg's pineapple remark, it stands out in the history of the Heisenberg version because it seems to be the sole occasion when he claimed more or less explicitly to have understood that the critical mass of a bomb would be relatively small. In all his other references Heisenberg always leaves things vague enough for the reader to assume that, since he knew the principle of the bomb, ipso facto he also knew the critical mass to be small. Yet even in the present case Heisenberg's claim tends to be implicit, rather than the explicit statement it seems to be: The explosive material is not specified, and Heisenberg is careful not to make the claim himself (thus avoiding telling a lie), but rather to let others remind him that he had made the pineapple statement.

By now Heisenberg was ready to raise the whole dispute with Goudsmit onto a more public stage. As a counterattack to Goudsmit's *ALSOS*, Heisenberg tried in 1948 to have his *Naturwissenschaften* essay along with two more technical pieces on the German reactor program reprinted by a German publisher. Nothing came of the enterprise, but Heisenberg's manuscript foreword to the intended book has re-

62. Ibid. Cf. Irving, *German Atomic Bomb*, p. 120.
63. See below, chaps. 6, 7, and 14.
64. See below, chap. 11, for the 1942 HWA report.

cently been printed. For Heisenberg, the American advantage was merely a matter of "technology," since the Germans had a full understanding of nuclear matters. Not only did the Germans completely grasp the principles of the uranium reactor, but among them "the chain reaction with fast neutrons that leads to the atomic bomb was thoroughly known" as well. This seems a rather egregious claim, since among all the German wartime technical papers, there is not one that discusses the technicalities of a fast-neutron chain reaction in U235. Moreover, as the Farm Hall transcripts show, the fact that an atomic bomb would depend on a fast-neutron chain reaction was news to the assembled German scientists. With the advantage of hindsight, Heisenberg angrily declares that all this German scientific knowledge "expressly contradicts the current portrayals in the foreign press; it was not the ignorance of the basic physical principles that was the prime reason that no atomic bombs were produced in Germany." It was, of course, the Allied air attacks, inadequate German industrial capacity, the government priority given to short-term projects—assuredly not lack of scientific knowledge—that frustrated a German atomic bomb. And, of course, all these external factors spared the physicists from having to make a decision.[65]

A further boost to the Heisenberg version was given by Waldemar Kaempffert's decision to publish an interview with the physicist in the *New York Times* (28 December 1948).[66] The main moral defense advanced was—in Heisenberg's own words—that though the "leading scientists disliked the totalitarian system, yet as patriots who loved their country they could not refuse to work for the Government when called upon." This is an enormous admission. It does not blame the Nazi terror for forcing the scientists to work on the project out of fear; rather, it makes their atomic bomb project a patriotic duty. As Kaempffert rather too sympathetically put it, "these German research physicists were torn between their dislike of the Nazi regime and their duty as patriots. Should they as patriots develop an atomic bomb?" In this curious conception of "patriotism," Heisenberg conformed to the fundamental German moral code of duty of obedience to political authority, regardless of its evil. In a Western context, the idea of moral and patriotic duty would have been quite the opposite: It would have been the patriotic duty of a Western scientist to refuse to work for an evil government, whereas in Germany the patriot's duty was not to refuse. In Western thinking, the thought that "patriotism" could be defined in terms of willingness to make an atomic bomb for Hitler was a paradox that rendered such a "patriotism" meaningless as well as repugnant.

Heisenberg then moves to his second moral defense. In order to deflect the anticipated American revulsion toward the German scientists for having worked on

65. *Unveröffentliches Vorwort zu einer Aufsatzsammlung* (1948), GWH, C V, 35–36 (cf. p. 7).

66. "Nazis Spurned Idea of an Atomic Bomb: Dr. Heisenberg Says German's Research Was Far Advanced but Lacked Hitler Support," *New York Times*, 28 December 1948. Reprinted in GWH, C V, 37–40.

an atomic bomb for Hitler, Heisenberg invokes his earlier theme that the scientists were fortunate in that an atomic bomb was, because of "external circumstances," never a possibility in Germany, and hence they never really worked on the bomb. Then Heisenberg declares: "Fortunately they never had to make a moral decision, and this for the reason that they and the Army agreed on the utter impossibility of producing a bomb during the war." The problem with this argument from a Western point of view is that the German scientists had made a moral decision to work on the bomb project in September 1939; that it turned out to be a failure—as much because of Heisenberg's own mistakes as because of "external circumstances"—does not change the fact that a moral decision had been taken at the outset. The "moral decision" that Heisenberg imagined would have had to be faced at a later stage was a fiction; it had been preempted by his decision in late 1939 to agree to investigate the possibility of atomic weapons.

As to Goudsmit's charges of scientific ignorance, Heisenberg pointed out that his discussions at Farm Hall in the wake of Hiroshima could scarcely have been followed by "scientifically untrained guards." Far from their being ignorant of the difference between a reactor and a bomb, or of the possibilities of plutonium, "the truth is that the general principles which must of necessity underlie the design and construction of an atomic bomb were well known to German physicists." Heisenberg thus neatly skated with a half-truth over the awkward fact that he had set his own assistant in 1940 to exploring the possibility of using an exploding reactor as a bomb.[67]

Three times in this interview Heisenberg insists on the "obviousness" of atomic bomb principles to German and other scientists from 1939 on. "That theoretically a bomb could be made of U235 was obvious to every physicist before the war, Dr. Heisenberg emphasized." But when these seductively plausible arguments are looked at critically, it emerges, as so often with Heisenberg, that they are nothing more than half-truths. Of course, in 1939 many scientists imagined that some sort of bomb might theoretically be made with U235. The problem, as we shall see in chapter 4, is that virtually every scientist assumed that the reaction would be a slow-neutron affair that would require a bomb mass of many tons. It was never so obvious a matter as Heisenberg so glibly pretended with the full advantage of hindsight and the desperate need for self-justification. The extent of this self-delusion is evident in his concluding remark:

> The [captured German] reports in Washington show that our reasoning was just like that of your physicists. With all this information available, at least to privileged persons, I cannot understand why it is generally held in the United States that we completely missed the basic principle of the bomb until after Hiroshima.

It cannot be stressed enough that in the nearly four hundred captured German reports, there is no clear declaration that the bomb is a fast-neutron reaction, there

67. See below, chap. 8.

is no calculation of the critical mass of a U235 bomb, and there are no accurate measurements of the crucial cross-sections for a fast-neutron bomb except for two almost incidental and seemingly neglected indirect measurements in 1941 and 1943–44 of the fast-neutron fission cross-section of U235.[68] Indeed, an official scientific review of German progress in nuclear physics published by one of Heisenberg's close colleagues in 1948 admitted that "necessary experimental values for [calculating the critical mass of a fast-neutron reaction in U235], including the essential neutron multiplication factor and inelastic cross-section, are known inexactly, and experiments in this direction were not carried out." Just how vital these obscure cross-sections were for the calculation of the critical mass of a bomb is blithely admitted by the same writer in a preceding sentence: "From the considerations of Bothe and Heisenberg it may be deduced without difficulties [*sic*] how great a sphere of pure U235 or enriched mixture must be if a chain reaction with fast neutrons is to take place. Such an estimate had, however, to be declined [*abgesehen*]"[69] in view of the crucial missing experimental data. Had Heisenberg thought he needed these data for a feasible bomb, it can scarcely be doubted that

68. There are two German figures for the fast-neutron fission cross-section in U235, neither very precise, and neither given much prominence. The first is by G. von Droste, which was reported by Droste to a meeting at the Kaiser-Wilhelm-Institute for Physics on March 13–14, 1941. (See G-84 and G-346, p. 25.) W. Bothe, "Einige Eigenschaften der U und der Bremsstoffe" (G-66), March 8, 1941, p. 7 (IMF 31-117), cites Droste's value for the U235 fission cross-section as 3.6 barns, but it is unclear whether the neutron energy here is 200 eV or in the MeV range. Droste's original paper does not appear to be listed in his own postwar survey of the literature ("Wirkungsquerschnitte von Uran," in Bothe and Flügge, *FIAT Review*, pt. II, pp. 197–208). Here (p. 207) Droste cites only the second figure, calculated by W. Jentschke and K. Lintner in 1943–44 ("Schnelle Neutronen in Uran. V" [G-227], February 1944, p. 95 [IMF 30-461]), giving the fast-neutron fission cross-section for U235 as 3.7 plus or minus 0.5. (In connection with *thermal* neutrons, however, Droste does give references to two of his own earlier papers of 1940–41, which I have not been able to see: "Der Spaltquerschnitt von Uran fur thermische Neutronen" [1941] and "Die Vermehrung der Neutronen an 2 t Uran" [1940]. Cf. G-24, G-77, G-78, G-84.)

Heisenberg seems to have assumed a cross-section in U235 of 0.5×10^{-24} cm^2, to judge from Haxel's reference ("Beitrag der schnellen Neutronen," p. 172). In the Farm Hall transcripts, however, Heisenberg comes up with two different figures: on 9 August 1945 (*OE*, p. 122), the figure used is 0.5: but on 14 August (*OE*, p. 127) he adopts a more optimistic range of 0.5 to 2.5 (see below, chap. 14).

A curious example of Heisenberg's false reconstruction of facts hangs thereby: Heisenberg, writing to Irving on 10 June 1966, recalls in a marginal note to Irving's typescript that "the figures quoted in my report of Aug. 8th 1945 in Farm Hall were probably improved versions of Houtermans' figures, improved by later measurements of Jentschke and Lintner" (IMF-32). However, the paper by Jentschke and Lintner had calculated the fast-neutron fission cross-section in U235 as 3.7 plus or minus 0.5. This figure obviously aroused little interest, since Heisenberg by the time of Farm Hall had forgotten it, adopting quite different figures instead. His reconstruction in 1966 was therefore false.

Measurements by Jentschke, Stetter, Lintner, and Droste generally pertain to fast neutrons in unseparated uranium and U238. See the references in Droste ("Wirkungsquerschnitte von Uran") and Haxel ("Beitrag der schnellen Neutronen," pp. 166, 172 f), and the Stetter and Lintner measurements in G-192 and G-193 (IMF 30-371).

69. Haxel, "Beitrag der schnellen Neutronen," p. 173.

the experiments would have been carried out somehow. How Heisenberg in the light of these glaring omissions could have claimed that his reasoning was "just like that of your physicists" is as much a cause for amazement as for amusement.

Goudsmit could not let this go unanswered, and in a letter published in the *New York Times* on 9 January 1949 he asserted that on his reading of them, "the German secret reports show clearly that their scientists had only a very vague notion of the working of the atomic bomb." Admitting that he had oversimplified the situation in his book, Goudsmit shrewdly pointed out that although Heisenberg may have understood the nature of plutonium, conversations with one of his inner circle in 1945 (probably Weizsäcker) showed that the impression prevailed that element 93 and not plutonium (94) was the nuclear explosive. Goudsmit repeated his earlier charge that the Germans had not understood the U235 bomb to be based on fast neutrons; as it happens, though, while Heisenberg may have appreciated the bomb to be a fast-neutron reaction, it is apparent from the Farm Hall transcripts that hardly anyone else present with him in the room knew this.[70]

Replying in the *New York Times* on 30 January 1949, Heisenberg noted with satisfaction that Goudsmit had withdrawn some of his statements, and he smugly quoted in his defense the American physicist Eugene Wigner's view that as far as reactor design was concerned, "the whole [Fermi] work was duplicated, apparently without any major deviation, also, by the German nuclear physicists."[71] Even if this were to be true of the reactor program—which it is not—Wigner's judgment does not apply to the bomb programs.

Meanwhile, the private exchanges between Goudsmit and Heisenberg had resumed with a letter from Goudsmit written on 11 February 1949. Suggesting that they put an end to the public debate, Goudsmit tartly remarked that the Kaempffert interview and Heisenberg's letter to the *New York Times* had "not made a good impression."

> Your desire to save the prestige of German science is totally superfluous. . . . What you claim about the physics achievements during the Hitler regime is really not so. It may be true that you and Fräulein Bellmann and administrator Dr. Telschow knew that the bomb was probably the size of a "pineapple," but Houtermans, "with whom you discussed the uranium problem regularly," or Flügge, whose writings deal with this point, or even Gerlach, the "Reichsmarschall für Kernphysik," were not aware of it.[72]

Goudsmit informed Heisenberg that he was arranging to have an unbiased selection of the more important German reports copied and distributed, and out of fairness even asked his correspondent to list the most significant. As to Heisen-

70. *OE*, p. 83. See below, chap. 14.
71. Reprinted in GWH, C V, 41–42.
72. Goudsmit to Heisenberg, 11 February 1949, Goudsmit Papers.

berg's bringing up the "moral problem" in his letter, Goudsmit observed that "this is resented by some of the colleagues here to whom I have shown your letter."

Heisenberg's cold reply to Goudsmit in April 1949 accused him of publishing false information in the American press; therefore, it was only right for Heisenberg to use the same forum to publish a correct version of the matter.[73] This hurt protestation would have been more convincing had Heisenberg's version been more truthful than it was, and it provoked a last exasperated response from Goudsmit on 3 June 1949.

> This is the last letter on our controversial subject. I am afraid that we might lose our tempers and the suggestion I made to stop this discussion seems to be a good one. However, I hope that we shall continue to correspond about other matters.[74]

As with all his other writings on the subject, this final letter of Goudsmit's stressed that his main concern was the apparent inability of Heisenberg to admit fully to the disastrous influence of the Nazi years for German science. On a superficial level, Heisenberg agreed with him, often blaming the Nazi government for placing obstacles in the way of the physicists, for being scientifically ignorant, and for disrupting the profession. But Goudsmit's real concern was a deeper one: that the German scientists admit the profound evil of the regime they had served and see that the Allied democratic cause had always been morally superior. This Heisenberg was very reluctant to do in an open way; even when condemning Hitler, he would always obscure the moral issue with a universalizing or relativizing posture, as when in his letter to van der Waerden he had transformed the problem of supplying an evil dictator with an atomic bomb into the vaguer universal problem of supplying any political leader with such a weapon. Heisenberg seems to have believed that all power was amoral—a common prejudice in German culture. But this politically immature attitude was dangerous in that it promoted moral and political cowardice. For if all power was amoral, then no political cause was good, and hence the Allied cause was hardly superior to that of Hitler. In the end, the only thing that mattered politically for Heisenberg was the German nation. It was this patriotic, nationalist core of Heisenberg's sensibility that Goudsmit kept irritating like a hidden sore spot throughout their correspondence: Goudsmit was desperate to have Heisenberg disown the belief that was— along with science itself—the central pillar of his existence.

Given the fact that the book was an attack on the German mentality that had made the Nazi disaster possible and not merely a critique of some technical errors, it was not surprising that *ALSOS* itself became a taboo in Germany. Rosbaud noted that

73. Heisenberg to Goudsmit, 20 April 1949, Goudsmit Papers.
74. Goudsmit to Heisenberg, 3 June 1949, Goudsmit Papers.

Heisenberg is, of course, very powerful and has a very great influence and I know that several bigshots of the COG or Military Government like very much to discuss things with him and ask for his advice. *ALSOS* is regarded by almost every German scientist as an outrageous atrocity.[75]

Goudsmit himself neatly observed that "I'm proud of the fact that the Germans consider *ALSOS* the most infamous book ever written. What I write must be true, otherwise they wouldn't be so angry about it."[76]

75. Rosbaud to Goudsmit, 27 January 1947, Goudsmit Papers, box 28, folder 43. See also below, chap. 21.

76. Goudsmit to Rosbaud, 21 November 1949, Goudsmit Papers, box 28, folder 45.

CHAPTER 2

Elaborating the Heisenberg Version, 1945–76

No way was found to expedite the [uranium] development quickly so that it could be utilized. As I learned from various talks with Professor Heisenberg, it was not the fault of our leaders but that [sic] the reason was more that science itself did not feel that it was possible to obtain immediate results.[1]

DR. LIEB, TECHNICAL ADVISER TO ALBERT SPEER, AUGUST 1945

I do hope Heisenberg is not now claiming that they tried, for reasons of principle, to sabotage the project by asking for such minimal support![2]

ALBERT SPEER, 1953

The origins of the Heisenberg version are to be found in the Farm Hall Memorandum of 7–8 August 1945, which the ten interned German physicists had signed and certified as true. At that time, however, the scientists were still mystified by the Allied success in building a bomb that Heisenberg believed would require tons of U235. The Farm Hall transcripts have shown how Heisenberg's fallacious concept of an explosive critical mass of tons of U235 prevailed in the explanations he outlined to his colleagues between 6 and 9 August. By 14 August, however, this picture changed with Hciscnbcrg's rethinking of the whole problem and his radically new conclusion that the critical mass had to be in the region of kilograms rather than tons.

This placed the scientists in a predicament: How could they support their now official version? Their best plan lay in following Heisenberg's lead and convincing themselves that they had essentially taken the correct scientific path, that the bomb could never have been made—regardless of its critical mass—in the difficult conditions of wartime Germany, and that, when all was said and done, the question of whether or not its critical mass was large or small was a mere techni-

---

1. Dr. Lieb, *The Handling of the Problem of Nuclear Physics by the Ministry of Armament and War Production* (USAF Historical Research Agency, Maxwell AFB, Alabama, U.S. 9th Air Force, P/W Interrogation Detachment, Military Intelligence Service, in folder "Interrogations" 533.619, B-5 1945, no. 4, *Atomic Bomb—German, Investigations, Research, Developments and Practical Use*, 19 August 1945 = Microfilm B. 5737). See below, chap. 12.

2. Unpublished version of memoirs, 1953, quoted in G. Sereny, *Albert Speer: His Battle with Truth* (New York, 1995), p. 319.

cal detail. They might well say in good conscience, therefore, that they had indeed understood the bomb. This was a plausible rationalization of Heisenberg's error, though if they had known in the early years that the Allies had recorded their discussions, the German physicists might have been willing to make a clean breast of the matter. The public revelation in 1962 by the American military head of the Manhattan Project, General Leslie Groves, of the existence of the Farm Hall transcripts was followed, however, by David Irving's complimentary account of the German project, which heartened Heisenberg to launch a fresh wave of self-justifications. A major feature of this was the neat circumvention of the more embarrassing contents of his transcribed conversations of 1945.

This background explains why the German scientists' support of the Heisenberg version was surprisingly weak and reticent in the postwar years. Heisenberg's defense of the German position was as strong as it could feasibly be, and any elaboration at this time risked exposing its many inherent weak points. Their main approach was to quote fragmentary phrases out of context, suppress awkward material, and leave the reader to draw a mistaken but favorable impression of German abilities.

Otto Hahn's diary of the events at Farm Hall following the news of Hiroshima is a case in point. In the various published texts of the entry for 6 August 1945, a puzzling elision occurs. After the news of the bomb has broken, Hahn remarks "We discuss . . . " and then the text skips to "I go soon to my room to sleep."[3] Just what the scientists "discussed" during those first three elision dots is omitted. As to the technical conversations of subsequent days, there too the diary's published version is largely silent. Fortunately for the Heisenberg version, the original manuscript is not open to public inspection, but one may conjecture that the omitted passages would not show Heisenberg in a favorable light. By 1946 Hahn had come to accept the official Heisenberg version, writing a historical essay of his own (which was not published at the time). Hahn argued that "for the production of a bomb the effort needed had to be enormous. . . . The Germans did not have this option," because German industry had been interdicted by Allied bombing.[4] What is alarming about this endorsement of the Heisenberg version is that Hahn was well aware of Heisenberg's mistaken notion of the critical mass of a U235 bomb being in the region of tons; Heisenberg had carefully explained it to him in

3. Hahn diary, 6 August 1945. Passage printed, with omission marks, in E. Berninger, *Otto Hahn in Selbstzeugnissen und Bilddokumenten* (Reinbek, 1974), pp. 89 f. The MS text in Archiv zur Geschichte der Max-Planck-Gesellschaft, Berlin, is closed until 1998. "Wir diskutieren . . . [*sic!*] Ich gehe bald auf mein Zimmer, um mich bald schlafen zu legen." There is a suggestion in L. Badash, "Otto Hahn, Science, and Social Responsibility" (in *Otto Hahn and the Rise of Nuclear Physics*, ed. W. R. Shea [Dordrecht, 1983], pp. 167–180), that he had been shown the complete text; no elided material is given.

The printed portion does show that Hahn himself was relieved that the Germans had thought the bomb not a feasible proposition during the war, a view corroborated by the Farm Hall transcripts.

4. Hahn, *Die deutschen Arbeiten über Atomenergie*, 2 February 1946, MS in Archiv zur Geschichte der Max-Planck-Gesellschaft. Text closed until 1998. Abridged version in Berninger, *Otto Hahn*, pp. 74–76.

the Farm Hall transcripts. This raises serious problems about the integrity of even the most decent German scientists.[5]

Another diary relating to Farm Hall was kept by Erich Bagge. Bagge's diary mentions the discussions that went on during the night of 6 August and also describes Heisenberg's colloquium of August 14, in which he finally presented the right solution to the atomic bomb problem. Bagge's juxtaposition of these two episodes is intended to suggest that Heisenberg knew as much about the bomb's design on 6 August (and before) as he did on the 14 August. But the Farm Hall transcripts now show that this is not the case, and that his thinking underwent a radical transformation between 6 and 14 August.[6] In 1957 Bagge and Kurt Diebner, who had headed the uranium project for a time, prepared a historical narrative that included long excerpts from a most important source, the official Army Weapons Office (HWA) Report of 1942. The HWA Report proved that the Germans were guessing that the critical mass of a plutonium bomb might be as low as 10 to 100 kg. Unfortunately, the portions of the report that were not printed reveal that Heisenberg's team was not quite as prescient about other aspects of the atomic bomb

5. It was not only in the matter of scientific truth that Hahn showed himself to be less than ingenuous; even his behavior toward Lise Meitner in 1938 is open to reevaluation. Hahn had originally caved in to Nazi pressure to abandon Meitner, and it was only because he was shamed by Paul Rosbaud into changing his stance that he helped his old colleague and friend to escape from Germany. What some would regard as his almost indecent acceptance of the Nobel Prize in 1946 while Meitner was denied her due share of recognition shows how easy it was for him to succumb to the conviction that German scientific honor had to be restored at all costs. That he knew his action to be unjust personally to Meitner (who had given a mystified Hahn the physical explanation of what exactly had occurred in his crucial experiment) is demonstrated by his donating a portion of the prize money to his former colleague. Hahn might not have been so unshaken in his patriotism had he received the intercepted letter of June 1945 in which Meitner had finally exploded in exasperation at his and the other German scientists' complacent and morally blind conduct under the Nazis, dismissing with contempt their efforts at moral apologizing. See R. L. Sime, "Lise Meitner's Escape from Germany," *American Journal of Physics* 58 (March 1990): 262–267; idem, "A Split Decision?" *Chemistry in Britain,* June 1994, 482–484; idem, *Lise Meitner: A Life in Physics* (Berkeley, 1996), pp. 185, 341–346. For Meitner's letter of 27 June 1945 (copy in the Meitner Papers, Churchill College Archives, Cambridge), see below, chap. 20. Another copy is printed in F. Krafft, *Im Schatten der Sensation: Leben und Wirken von Fritz Strassmann* (Weinheim, 1981), pp. 181–182. There is also some implicit disagreement in Krafft with the usual hagiographical portrait of Hahn. (See below, chaps. 20 and 21.)

6. Some of the diary entries for 1945 are printed in E. Bagge, K. Diebner, and K. Jay, *Von der Uranspaltung bis Calder Hall* (Hamburg, 1957), pp. 43–71. Copies and transcripts of the diaries are in IMF 29-106/159. It should be noted (as Irving points out in his index to IMF 29–145) that the diary excerpts for the war period have been edited and rewritten. It is clear from the microfilm that considerable cutting and pasting has gone on.

In a letter to me of 30 March 1984 Professor Bagge declares firmly that the portion of his diary written at Farm Hall "has been published without any changes at all. . . . Nothing has been 'improved.'" As for the longer period of the war, 1940–45, Bagge tells me in a later letter of 7 October 1991 that "nothing of real historical significance has been dropped" apart from the names of some German scientists responsible for the lack of progress in nuclear physics in the 1930s. (The gaps in the diary covering the meetings of February and June 1942 are to be regretted.)

problem; no critical mass for a U235 bomb was proposed, while a great deal of attention was paid to the possibility of developing an explosive reactor-bomb.[7]

A few unenlightening passages from another diary of the Farm Hall period have been published by Karl Wirtz, who with Carl-Friedrich von Weizsäcker formed Heisenberg's closest circle of physicists. There is nothing in the published version bearing on the technical discussions at Farm Hall, but Wirtz's historical accounts of the German project have faithfully followed the Heisenberg version.[8] In a lecture at the meeting of the German Physical Society on 5 September 1947, Wirtz gave a précis of his more technical FIAT report on the reactor experiments, prepared for the Allies in the postwar period. He stated that in 1939 it was known that a chain reaction was "very probable with pure U235, which is fissionable by fast and slow neutrons. It would probably take place explosively. But this road was immediately [zunächst] blocked, since it appeared impossible without a great expenditure." (Wirtz jumps the gun here, since the official version has it that the prospect of enormous expenditure finished off the bomb only in 1942, rather than in 1939–40.) Any discussion of a U235 bomb was evaded in this lecture, leaving the audience to take it for granted that the bomb was fully understood at the outset.[9]

Wirtz's memoirs afforded a more detailed history, again based on the prescience of the German scientists. "The scientists had many chances, both at the beginning and during the war, to remark that the building of atomic bombs was possible if sufficient amounts of U235 or plutonium (in both cases about a few kilograms) were available."[10] With this evasive phrasing, Wirtz tried to suggest that the Germans during the war understood "sufficient amounts" to be around a few kilograms. As to reactor-bombs, in 1945 Gerlach, the head of the project, visited Wirtz's experimental reactor at Haigerloch and seemed to think it could be used as a bomb. Wirtz tries to write this off as an incomprehensible mistake and says that he explained to Gerlach that this was not a bomb. But this is hardly convincing; Gerlach was an excellent physicist and had been head of the project for some time. It simply is not credible that he would have thought the Wirtz-Heisenberg reactor potentially a bomb if he had been unaware of earlier proposals for a reactor-bomb.[11]

7. E. Bagge and K. Diebner, "Zur Entwicklung der Kernenergieverwertung in Deutschland," in Bagge, Diebner, and Jay, Von der Uranspaltung, pp. 9–80. (For plutonium, see p. 39.) For the HWA Report, see below, chap. 9.

Cf. W. Tautorus [K. Diebner], "Die deutschen Geheimarbeiten zur Kernenergieverwertung während des zweiten Weltkrieges, 1939–1945," Atomkernenergie 1 (1956): 368–370, 423–425; W. Hanle and E. R. Bagge, "Peaceful Use of Nuclear Energy during 40 Years," Atomkernenergie-Kerntechnik 40 (1982): 1–10.

8. Excerpts from Wirtz's diary are printed in K. Wirtz, Im Umkreis der Physik (Karlsruhe, 1988), pp. 161–165.

9. K. Wirtz, "Historisches zu den Uranarbeiten in Deutschland in den Jahren 1940–1945," Physikalische Blätter 3 (1947): 371–379.

10. Wirtz, Im Umkreis der Physik, pp. 29–69, at pp. 38 f., 56.

11. Ibid., p. 61.

Like Heisenberg in his postwar writings, Wirtz blamed Bothe's error for the failure of the German reactor program. However, time allowed Wirtz to be more generous to Kurt Diebner (the Nazi chief administrator of the uranium project), who had previously been shunned by the Heisenberg camp and seen, with Bothe, as the author of the German failure. Diebner was now viewed as a cooperative scientist, welcoming Heisenberg's takeover of the Kaiser-Wilhelm-Institute for Physics.[12]

Wirtz's warders at Farm Hall had a very poor view of his veracity, and his memory also seems to have been open to question. When an old friend, Charles Frank—then involved with British scientific intelligence—visited him at Farm Hall, Wirtz admitted in a private talk that the Heisenberg group had indeed concluded early on that the critical mass of a U235 bomb would be enormous. Recently, however, Wirtz has denied ever saying this and maintained that the Germans were all along aware of the small critical mass for U235.[13]

As one of the originators of the Heisenberg version during the Farm Hall discussions and the preparation of the original memorandum, Carl-Friedrich von Weizsäcker was an early if cautious defender of the version against Goudsmit's *ALSOS*.[14] In 1948 Weizsäcker compiled some comments on the book, but did not publish them at the time. In 1956, however, Weizsäcker printed some judiciously short excerpts, his main point being that during the war the German physicists had justified atomic research on the negative ground that "through research they had to make sure that America developed no atomic bombs." The physicists dared not hold out any hope of atomic bombs to their own authorities in case they were immediately ordered to produce them within six months. This characteristically specious line of argument was really somewhat silly, and never adopted by those with more common sense, including Heisenberg himself. Weizsäcker also tested credulity when he confessed that they were surprised that in the last year of the war, the SS, "which had its hand in everything, did not concern itself with the uranium project." The fact is, as Heisenberg and others were

12. Ibid., p. 45. Earlier K. Winnacker and K. Wirtz, *Nuclear Energy in Germany,* trans. (La Grange Park, Ill., 1979), pp. 21, 27, saw the failure as the fault of Bothe (for his mistake about graphite) and Diebner for hogging the uranium stocks that would have allowed the Heisenberg reactor to go critical in 1945.

13. See below, chap. 14. In a letter to me of 29 November 1984, Professor Wirtz declared that he knew of no meeting in 1940 that received Heisenberg's view that several tons of U235 would be required for a bomb. Wirtz's memory on other matters in this is less than firm: He says that Heisenberg's "pineapple" conjecture about the size of the critical mass was presented to the German Academy for Air Research in 1943, whereas it was actually mentioned at the Speer meeting of June 1942; and he asserts that on 6 August 1945 "Heisenberg repeated [*sic*] a short calculation of the critical mass of U235 that proved to be more or less correct." The Farm Hall transcripts, however, show that this calculation produced a figure of tons of U235. See *OE*, pp. 73, 84, 91, 117, analyzed below in chap. 14.

14. For Weizsäcker's Nazi connections and flexible moral attitudes, see below, chaps. 19–21.

well aware of at the time, the SS became actively interested in atomic bomb research in 1944.[15]

A published letter of 14 October 1955 was more adventurous in its defense of Heisenberg.

> Everything significant [about the German atomic project] you will find in Heisenberg's essay. . . . We never undertook or proposed anything concrete for the building of a bomb. Heisenberg discusses the general background in the last two pages of his essay. I would above all underline the point that we German atomic physicists were not confronted with the decision of whether we wanted to make bombs or not. Should we have faced this decision, it is certain that each of us would have reacted in different ways. Some certainly would have wanted to make bombs, others certainly not so. . . . We knew the difficulty of the problem and perhaps somewhat overestimated it, and we had underestimated the resources available in America.

If only, lamented Weizsäcker, the Americans had realized that the Germans had no intention of producing an atomic bomb, perhaps then they would have desisted and the Hiroshima catastrophe would never have occurred. And if only Einstein had been aware of the elder Weizsäcker's "resistance" to the Nazis! Instead, Einstein's famous letter of 1939 to Roosevelt had warned of the possible role of Weizsäcker's father in transmitting to Hitler the younger Weizsäcker's scientific knowledge about atomic energy.[16]

The facile reasoning here needs to be seen in the light of a comment made by Goudsmit about Weizsäcker's glibness. Goudsmit recalled how Weizsäcker after receiving the Erasmus Prize in Holland in 1969 had "used the occasion to criticize me very strongly in a Dutch magazine. . . . [After] my Dutch fight with Weizsäcker, I gave him a copy [of my reply], but he never sent me any of the articles in which he criticizes me." Goudsmit discerned Weizsäcker's voice in the weak letter

---

15. Weizsäcker's remarks of 1948 are printed in C. Seelig, ed., *Helle Zeit—Dunkle Zeit* (Zurich, 1956), pp. 132–133. Replying in a letter of 20 January 1966 (copy supplied by Irving) to David Irving's request to see these "alten Aufzeichnungen," Weizsäcker says that he has not been able to find them, but will search. He then pointedly says that he recalls showing them to the author Robert Jungk, who consulted at length carefully with him in the writing of his book so as to bring out the "true motives" of the German scientists; Weizsäcker then remarks that he is not yet sure whether Irving is likely to be as diligently reliable! In a letter to me of 22 March 1984 Professor von Weizsäcker stated that he believed he had his MS critique of the Goudsmit book in a chest in his cellar, but lacked the time to unearth it; he suggested that a copy might be available in the Max-Planck-Institut für Physik in Munich. After Jungk in 1990 recanted his pro-Heisenberg line, Weizsäcker transferred his allegiance to Thomas Powers's work (see below) and condemned Jungk's laxness in interviewing him in the 1950s! (Interview by Dieter Hoffmann et al. with Weizsäcker in 1993, cited in note 34 to chap. 3 below.)

For the SS role in the uranium project, see below, chap. 13.

16. C. F. von Weizsäcker, "Die Illusion deutscher Atombomben: Aus einem Brief an den Herausgeber, Göttingen, 14 October 1955," in Seelig, *Helle Zeit*, pp. 130–132. For Ernst von Weizsäcker's so-called resistance, see below, chaps. 19 and 20.

with which Heisenberg had intervened on behalf of Goudsmit's deported parents in 1943: it "must have been dictated by Weizsäcker . . . the same non-committal style," he dryly commented.[17]

One important theme did emerge in Weizsäcker's thought which was only implicit in the Heisenberg version, but that may well contain an essential truth about the German uranium project. This was the admission that Weizsäcker decided to pursue investigation of the bomb problem in 1939–40 in order to see whether a bomb could indeed be made. In this sense, as Heisenberg asserted, no "moral decision" was made; the scientists would face that decision if and when they concluded that a bomb was feasible. But they were saved from that crisis of decision because their technical research forced them to conclude that though bombs were theoretically possible, they certainly could not be constructed within the time span of the war. As in the Heisenberg version, Weizsäcker explained this was so because of the "external circumstances" of disruptive war conditions and the sheer scale of the effort required to separate $U235$; as for plutonium, that seemed a very long-term possibility in view of Bothe's "error," which had ruled out graphite as a moderator, thus forcing the Germans into reliance on the rare heavy water. However, if we read into this scheme what we know from other evidence, then it becomes quite plausible that the German research project by 1940 had become essentially a "negative" research effort, exploring various bomb possibilities and giving up on each of them as impractical. This is what Heisenberg and Weizsäcker were trying to conceal under a camouflage of diversionary argument.

This becomes apparent if we consider the three directions of research that were being pursued in 1939–41 by Heisenberg himself, his assistant Paul Müller, and Weizsäcker. First, by 1940, Heisenberg had concluded that a $U235$ bomb was theoretically possible, but would require several tons of pure $U235$. Either the whole of this mass would be fissioned (as his later paper of February 1942 suggests) or the large mass would be needed instead to explode properly the "few kilos" of $U235$ that had to be fissioned.[18] Second, a reactor-bomb of considerably less explosive power than a true atomic bomb was also possible in theory, but again it seemed practically remote. Heisenberg in early 1940 had assigned Müller to work out the "critical mass" (for want of a better term) of such an unlikely bomb.[19]

17. Goudsmit to A. Hermann, letters of 18 October 1976 and 5 January 1977, in Goudsmit Papers, AIP. For the 1977 letter see below, chap. 19. Walker and others have rather callously used this letter to denigrate Goudsmit for launching a campaign against Heisenberg; Goudsmit is alleged to have lost his scientific judgment because of Heisenberg's failure to rescue his parents. It seems to me that such an opinion shows a basic misunderstanding of Goudsmit's character, which, if anything, was rather too forgiving.

18. For the 1942 paper, see below, chap. 10. For the problematic suggestion to Ardenne and Hahn that only "a few kilos" would explode, see chaps. 9 and 12.

19. See below, chap. 8.

Third, a plutonium bomb was theoretically in order (as Weizsäcker realized by July 1940), but to obtain enough of the new element was a long-term project that would require the operation of numerous reactors over a substantial period of time.[20] By this threefold analysis of the problem, the German scientists could in 1940 reassure themselves that no bomb was practically possible in the foreseeable future, and so they never had to make what they thought of as their "moral decision." Unfortunately, neither Heisenberg nor Weizsäcker was ever able to admit that they had reached this conclusion through their own scientific mistakes and technical misjudgments; it was always Bothe's error or "external circumstances" that were at fault.[21]

As to the man who did make the "decision" (if it were one) not to proceed with a bomb, Albert Speer had plenty of time to read during his twenty-odd-year imprisonment for war crimes and subsequent leisure to look into the archives. Speer concluded that Heisenberg had been correct in saying the whole project could never have been realized in wartime Germany. Indeed, even if Hitler himself had favored the project with full resources, it would not have been enough. The bomb project was bound to fail because it needed massive industrial resources that were beyond Germany's capability. Speer's misconception, however, arose from hindsight; he looked at the German project in terms of what he later learned about the scale of the Allied effort. This legitimated his decision of 1942 to "scuttle the project." Looked at historically, however, the true reason for giving up was not that the American scale showed the venture to be impossible for Germany. It was rather that Heisenberg's crucial mistake in vastly overestimating the amount of U235 needed, combined with his failure to design a successful reactor for producing plutonium as effectively and quickly as the Americans, misled Speer into thinking that there was no hope of a successful outcome within a reasonable time. Despite the specious justifications, the project had, in fact, been scuttled for the wrong reasons. Had Heisenberg been more clearheaded and more dynamic, Speer would most likely have been very willing to allocate much greater resources to the enterprise and—who knows?—with German technical ingenuity, some breakthrough might well have been achieved with isotope separation or plutonium production.[22]

The implication that Heisenberg never showed the right spirit is implicit in the memoirs of Helmut Fischer, who otherwise generally accepts the Heisenberg version. Fischer was an SS officer and scientific expert in charge of one of the SS offices concerned with cultural and scientific affairs and actually had specific dealings with the uranium project in 1943–44. Much of Fischer's technical informa-

---

20. See below, chap. 9.

21. See especially Weizsäcker's interview "Wir waren heilfroh . . . ," in *Stern*, August 1984, pp. 55–56, reprinted in his *Bewusstseinswandel* (Munich, 1988), p. 367. Weizsäcker was here willing to admit that the Americans could make the bomb with good conscience since they were on the right side. See below, chaps. 20 and 21.

22. A. Speer, *Inside the Third Reich* (New York, 1970), pp. 225–229. See below, chap. 12.

tion appears to have derived from later accounts rather than his own direct experience, but there are some indications in his text that suggest he may have had more information than he cared to divulge.[23]

Not everyone was enchanted with Heisenberg's role in the project, especially his Farm Hall companion Paul Harteck, one of the most able people in the venture. Though he remained loyal at the time, Harteck in an interview many years later expressed his opinion that Heisenberg and the other physicists

> may have been very clever, but their work did not help other people very much. . . .
> I believe that if Gustav Hertz had a leading position in this group, the first working reactor in the world would have been built in Germany [Hertz was partly Jewish and so officially under a cloud]. . . . How could [Heisenberg and Weizsäcker] think they could lead the development of a new technology? That was poor judgment; it is almost unbelievable . . . [in 1939] we, including myself, backed [Heisenberg] . . . but after a year he disappointed us.[24]

Another disgruntled scientist was Manfred von Ardenne, who had evaded Farm Hall, having been otherwise detained by the Russians for work on their atomic bomb. During the war Ardenne had entertained the leading German atomic scientists on visits to his private laboratory in Berlin, where his own nuclear research was financed by the German Post Office. In his later memoirs Ardenne recalled various seemingly contradictory remarks about atomic bombs from his guests. On the one hand, on being asked in 1940 how much U235 would be needed for a bomb, Hahn and Heisenberg reportedly told their host it would be only "a few kilograms." But on the other hand, Weizsäcker, who was very much in Heisenberg's confidence, blankly told Ardenne that a bomb was impractical because of the reduction of the cross-sections as the temperature rises, thus breaking off the reaction.[25] These strange remarks can be understood only when placed in the correct contexts: first, of the general position of the bomb project in 1940; and second, of Heisenberg's detailed thinking (as shared with Weizsäcker) on the bomb project.

The general context was that Heisenberg and Weizsäcker had concluded by late 1940 that no matter what the theoretical possibility of a bomb might be, it lay beyond the reach of practicality. The specific thinking that led to this conclusion was that three types of bombs—U235, reactor-bombs, and plutonium—had been considered and ruled out of consideration for differing reasons. Thus, Weizsäcker would have been referring either to a bomb using ordinary uranium or too small

---

23. Helmut J. Fischer, *Hitler und die Atombombe: Bericht eines Zeitzeugen* (Asendorf, 1987). Idem, *Erinnerungen* (Ingolstadt, 1984–85). See below, chap. 13.

24. Interview with Paul Harteck in J. J. Ermenc, *Atomic Bomb Scientists: Memoirs, 1939–1945* (Westport, Conn., 1989), pp. 102, 113, 115, 123.

25. Ardenne's original typescript memoirs of the 1960s are reproduced in IMF 32; the relevant passage occurs at pp. 116–117. See below, chap. 9.

a quantity of U235 that would expand before an explosion could occur, or alternatively to a reactor-bomb, in which the reaction would be too slow to achieve a true nuclear explosion. Heisenberg's remark about a "few kilograms," however, refers to the amount of U235 needed to be exploded in a proper atomic explosion. But, in Heisenberg's thinking in 1940, to explode this amount efficiently required, as we shall see, a far larger quantity of U235. Of course, Heisenberg appreciated this confirmation in the 1960s by Ardenne of the fact that he had truly understood the crucial principle of the small critical mass of U235 during the war; but this raised dangers for the Heisenberg version that had to be explained away. Why was an enthusiastic and resourceful technician like Ardenne being told information about a "few kilograms" that might start him off on a possibly successful crash program to extract that small amount of U235 for a bomb? Heisenberg explained it away thus, somewhat unconvincingly, in a letter of 1966:

> We were always skeptical toward Ardenne . . . with his influence in government circles. Since we knew that Ardenne was interested in the atomic bomb question, we feared that he would get something big going on the matter. . . . Naturally we wanted to block this at any price. Weizsäcker's talk of 10 October 1940 with him . . . served with great probability to deflect him from such plans. In my first talk of 1940 with Ardenne I had probably answered somewhat rashly what I knew, namely that an atomic bomb could be made with a few kilograms of U235. . . . I assumed that Weizsäcker's words served in the first place to deflect Ardenne from his operation. Whether Weizsäcker did express these views, which miss the mark, or whether Ardenne just misunderstood these words, I naturally cannot judge. In any case I still feel very fortunate that these words prevented Ardenne from starting a big campaign for the production of atomic bombs.[26]

Weizsäcker agreed that he and Heisenberg had feared that the influential Ardenne might initiate a major drive for an atomic bomb. But Weizsäcker declared that, though he remembered the conversation with Ardenne, he could not recall any of its details. Nonetheless, "I definitely never held the view that an atomic bomb was impossible. . . . Should I have expressed myself exactly as Ardenne reports, it could only have been because I wished to deter him." Nevertheless, Ardenne's inconvenient recollections of this matter in an East German lecture of 1955 destroyed a friendship based on family ties.[27] Ardenne, moreover, continues to affirm the accuracy of his report of Weizsäcker's error.[28]

The most instructive case in these German reconstructions is that of Max von Laue, whose moral integrity was unimpeachable; he had rejected Nazi honors and openly defied the regime. Yet even he wilted initially under the collective pressure of his colleagues at Farm Hall and after. Standing outside the uranium project

26. Heisenberg to Irving, 17 May 1966, in IMF 32.
27. Weizsäcker to Irving, 14 June 1966, in IMF 32.
28. Ardenne to author, 9 August 1984. See the later editions of his memoirs, cited below, chap. 9.

during the war and also absent during some of the key Heisenberg technical conversations at Farm Hall, Laue was ready to swallow the official version. Laue's letter of 7 August 1945 describing the German reaction to Hiroshima for his son, whom he had sent to America before the war, innocently rehearses the Heisenberg version: None of the Germans could foresee the possibility of making a bomb in Germany, and in any case no one wanted to give such a weapon to Hitler. The project had been dedicated to building a reactor. No one had any idea of how the Allied bomb had been made.[29]

Laue's deep-seated loyalty to Germany took sharper expression in an indignant article he wrote in 1947 in defense of his colleagues. An English version appeared the following year.[30] Laue angrily retorted to Philip Morrison's accusation that many German scientists—Laue and Gentner were notable exceptions—had been the "armourers of Himmler and Auschwitz." Laue perhaps too loyally sprang to Heisenberg's defense, arguing that those who lost relatives to the Nazis were incapable of unbiased judgment in this matter. Moreover, the position of leading scientists like Heisenberg was very complicated; they had little choice in placing their institutes at the disposal of the Hitler regime, but even then they were able to do a little good, helping to save Jews and others in danger. The scientists, insisted Laue, had not aided an evil government, and articles like Morrison's only kept hatred alive. This was an honest plea, but unfortunately Laue was perhaps too decent himself to understand that the motives of others were less pure than his own. As Morrison stated in his reply, "many of the most able and distinguished men of German science, moved doubtless by sentiments of national loyalty, by traditional response to the authority over them, and by simple fear, worked for the advantage of the Nazi state. . . . Are we to forget the tragic failure of those German men of learning?" And in a clear reference to Heisenberg, Morrison concluded that it is not Goudsmit who was biased and who should be pained by the mention of Auschwitz, but rather "many a famous German physicist in Göttingen today, many a man of insight and responsibility, who could live for a decade in the Third Reich, and never once risk his position of comfort and authority in real opposition to the men who could build that infamous place of death."[31] The journal editor reinforced this charge by observing that Morrison's "criticism applies to some men of great prominence in science, whose apparently unreserved collaboration with the criminals in power helped to subdue the qualms of many a rank-and-file German scientist." Needless to say, Goudsmit himself was "upset" by Laue's article, while Paul Rosbaud feared the worst even before seeing it, since he was "some-

29. Max von Laue to Theodor von Laue (at Princeton, N.J.), 7 August 1945, Deutsches Museum, Munich; copy in Goudsmit Papers, box 14, folder 142. (Copy supplied to author by T. H. von Laue.)

30. "Die Kriegsaktivitätkeit der deutschen Physiker," *Physikalische Blätter* 4 (1948): 424–425; reprint, from the manuscript, in E. Henning, "Der Nachlass Max von Laues," *Physikalische Blätter* 48 (1992): 938–940. Translated under the title "The Wartime Activities of German Scientists," *BAS* 4 (1948): 103.

31. P. Morrison, "Reply to Dr. Von Laue," *BAS* 4 (1948): 104.

times afraid of Laue's impulsive way."[32] Lise Meitner, one of Laue's firmest friends, wrote that "I am afraid that with his inclination to defend everything that has happened—out of an understandable attachment to Germany—Laue is not helping Germany but risks achieving the opposite. Since I know that he's going to America very soon, I think it important to make him aware of this danger."[33]

Laue's loyalty to his German colleagues seems even more misplaced when one reads in one of his later letters to Paul Rosbaud of the petty persecutions at Farm Hall he had suffered at their hands—"particularly from Weizsäcker. . . . I attribute it to his influence, which he knows how to use with everybody who happens to be in power."[34] By 1959 the scales had fallen from Laue's eyes completely, and he wrote again to Rosbaud in confidence. Provoked by the misrepresentations in a new book by Robert Jungk, Laue now characterized the German project as a "somewhat comical secret affair. . . . It seemed to be a rather muddled business." Recalling Farm Hall, Laue said nothing about Heisenberg's early conversations suggesting a critical mass of tons (he had probably been out of the room during much of the discussion), but he did recollect Heisenberg's giving a lecture on the subject. Laue, however, was more concerned now with disowning the moral excuses that emerged at Farm Hall.

> During our table conversation the version [*Lesart*] was developed that the German atomic physicists really had not wanted the atomic bomb, either because it was impossible to achieve it during the expected duration of the war, or because they simply did not want to have it at all. The leader in these discussions was Weizsäcker. I did not hear the mention of any ethical point of view. Heisenberg was mostly silent.[35]

By now the Heisenberg version had reached a high point with the publication of Robert Jungk's already mentioned best-seller *Brighter Than a Thousand Suns* in

32. Goudsmit to Rosbaud, 7 April 1948; Rosbaud to Goudsmit, 25 April 1948; Goudsmit Papers, box 28, folder 43.

33. Meitner to Hahn, 6 June 1948, Meitner Papers, Churchill College, Cambridge; printed in Krafft, *Im Schatten der Sensation*, p. 186; translated in *HPNS*, p. 402. At this time Laue was so overcome by the need to apologize for Germany that he even blamed Einstein's expulsion from the Prussian Academy on the victim's own political involvement—a far cry from what Laue had believed at the time, when he had actively resisted it. Meitner dismissed this "so naive" view. See Sime, *Lise Meitner*, p. 356.

34. Laue to Rosbaud, n.d., printed in A. Kramish, *The Griffin* (Boston, 1986), pp. 244 f. Kramish cites the letter as being in the R. S. Hutton Papers at Cambridge, but has informed me in a letter of 1 June 1995 that the Rosbaud correspondence is now held by one of Rosbaud's relatives and is inaccessible for the time being. Hutton's papers are now mostly in the John Rylands University Library, Manchester, but the head of Special Collections there informs me that no material relevant to Laue or Rosbaud is included. Cf. R. S. Hutton, *Recollections of a Technologist* (London, 1964), pp. 180 f., for Rosbaud's warning of 1939 about German work on atomic energy.

35. Laue to Rosbaud, 4 May 1959, printed in Kramish, *The Griffin*, pp. 245–247. See below for Rosbaud's view of the Jungk book.

1956, which scandalously portrayed the German physicists as the moral conscience of the world in contrast to the reckless, if not immoral, Americans.[36] The book draws heavily on Heisenberg's and Weizsäcker's accounts and advances interpretations that they had not dared to put forward in their own writings. Particularly appalling is the depiction of Heisenberg's notorious visit in 1941 to Niels Bohr, which is seen as the pinnacle of conscientious behavior. Bohr was taken aback by the evident untruth of Jungk's account; some years later at a reception attended by Heisenberg and Weizsäcker, Mrs. Bohr burst out from across the room, "I don't care what they say—their visit in 1941 was a hostile act."[37] Needless to say, in Jungk's view the German scientists had a complete understanding of the scientific aspects of the atomic bomb, especially of the utility of plutonium as allegedly explained by F. H. Houtermans, a rather eccentric, partly Jewish former communist character whom Heisenberg had helped place in Ardenne's laboratory.[38] Jungk's work served to inspire a new major theme in German histories of the atomic bomb—namely, the pure morality as well as the omniscience of Heisenberg.[39]

The next landmark in the Heisenberg version was David Irving's *The German Atomic Bomb* (1967), which was the first work to make extensive use of the captured German documents.[40] Irving's microfilmed source materials for the work are still of the greatest value for anyone interested in the subject.[41] Nevertheless, the book must be handled with care, since Irving's tendency to sensationalize and his general perversity of judgment figured prominently even in this most sober of his books. Already Irving was entangled in the ugly revisionist historical scandals, including that of the bombing of Dresden, which became his trademark; he was later to descend into a mire of apologetic writing for Hitler and join neo-Nazi circles.

For his book Irving industriously interviewed and corresponded with most of the German scientists, particularly Heisenberg, who also commented on draft typescript pages.[42] His relationship with Weizsäcker, however, was less congenial,

36. R. Jungk, *Brighter Than a Thousand Suns: A Personal History of the Atomic Scientists*, trans. (Harmondsworth, 1960; reprint, 1982). In the light of recent revelations, Jungk has recanted some of his whitewash. See R. Jungk, *Trotzdem: Mein Leben für die Zukunft* (Munich, 1993). See also M. Walker, *Nazi Science: Myth, Truth, and the German Atomic Bomb* (New York, 1995), p. 256.

37. See below, chap. 10, for the scientific aspects of the visit, and chap. 19 for its moral and political significance.

38. For Houtermans, whose role remains enigmatic, see below, chap. 9.

39. See, for example, A. Hermann, *Die Jahrhundertwissenschaft: Werner Heisenberg und die Physik seiner Zeit* (Stuttgart, 1977); idem, *Wie die Wissenschaft ihre Unschuld verlor: Macht und Missbrauch der Forscher* (Stuttgart, 1982). Other examples are listed in M. Walker, *German National Socialism and the Quest for Nuclear Power, 1939–1949* (Cambridge, 1989), p. 264.

40. *The German Atomic Bomb: The History of Nuclear Research in Germany* (New York, 1967); published in the United Kingdom under the title *The Virus House* (London, 1967).

41. *Records and Documents Relating to the Third Reich*, group 2, *German Atomic Research* (Wakefield, Yorks., 1973), microfilms 29, 30, 31, 32.

42. As in the matter of the Paul Müller episode; see below, chap. 8.

and this showed in the eventual shape of the book's arguments, which were not entirely to the liking of the German scientists. This was largely due to Irving's cynicism about German claims to moral virtue, which emerged in snide remarks about Weizsäcker in particular, and a rather sneering account of the German conduct at Farm Hall in the light of leaked information then available from General Groves's memoirs. As Irving recalled to Goudsmit concerning his 1966 talk with Heisenberg and Weizsäcker, "it was a long interview, in which they wasted a lot of time talking about the moral issues."[43] However, these lapses were in large measure pardoned because of Irving's sterling service in vindicating in more detail than ever before the Heisenberg version's insistence that the Germans had fully understood the scientific principles of the atomic bomb, and indeed had only through bad luck—namely, Bothe's mistake and Allied bombing—failed to achieve a critical reactor by the end of the war. Indeed, so persuaded by Heisenberg's coaching was Irving that he decided to remove completely from his text any mention of Goudsmit's technical criticisms of German ignorance of the scientific principles of the atomic bomb—and this despite the fact that Irving had interviewed and corresponded with Goudsmit, who had supplied him with a great many key German documents from his own files.[44] It is not clear whose idea it was that the best treatment for Goudsmit was silence. Nor was it to be the last time that a supposedly serious historian sought to deal with the Goudsmit problem simply by purging mention of the *ALSOS* allegations from his own book.[45] Curiously, Irving seems to have misled Goudsmit into thinking that they were in agreement. Goudsmit told a former member of British scientific intelligence, "Irving writes me that he has incorporated my views into his book and has sent me a few revised pages. His recent interview with Heisenberg and von Weizsäcker seems to have convinced him that I was right."[46]

43. Irving to Goudsmit, 31 July 1966 (copy supplied to author by D. Irving). See the mutually recriminatory correspondence between Irving and Weizsäcker of 1966: "[Our] interview gave me the impression that you fundamentally distrust the people you are interviewing," Weizsäcker to Irving, 20 January 1966. Cf. similar letter of 16 February 1966, and Irving's reply of 25 January (copies supplied to author by D. Irving). This animus of Irving's against Weizsäcker was not much to Heisenberg's taste.

44. Interview notes with Goudsmit are in IMF 31-1353/1356C. Correspondence of January–July (copies supplied to author by D. Irving) shows that Irving was diffident about bringing up Goudsmit's specific charges of German ignorance of the bomb principle (except very diplomatically in his first letter to Goudsmit of 12 January 1966).

45. Irving (*German Atomic Bomb*, p. 92) refers abstractly to "various historians" who charge that the Germans did not understand the nature of the atomic bomb, but he does not cite Goudsmit as being among them. The only one named is Margaret Gowing, the author of the official British nuclear history (see below).

Walker's *German National Socialism* is another case in point where Goudsmit's scientific arguments against Heisenberg are magically "disappeared."

46. Goudsmit to Michael Perrin, 4 August 1966, Goudsmit Papers, box 17, folder 180. Perrin replied to Goudsmit, 11 August 1966, that "I think you know that I have always been in general agreement with you about both Heisenberg and von Weizsäcker," ibid.

Irving's credulous acceptance of Heisenberg's scientific claims led him into making several erroneous statements in his book:

1. Irving claims that a Houtermans paper of August 1941 "for the first time made explicit calculations on fast-neutron reactions and the critical mass of U235. . . . Houtermans certainly did both." In fact, Houtermans made no such calculation of the critical mass, and although he did carry out some fast-neutron calculations, these pertained not to U235 but to fast neutrons in unseparated uranium in a reactor "without isotope separation," as he clearly says. The critical size of a reactor using both fast and slow neutrons in unseparated uranium is given, but it applies neither to a bomb nor to pure U235. When Houtermans does mention a bomb, it is only to stress the difficulty of separating U235 and to compare it unfavorably with plutonium as a possible nuclear fuel and explosive.[47]

2. According to Irving, Heisenberg in a lecture of 1943 "improved on Houtermans's criticality theory on the basis of 1943 fast-neutron fission measurements of U235 made by the Viennese physicists Jentschke and Lintner." However, nothing is to be found in the lecture in question about these measurements. Irving also gives the Jentschke cross-section for U235 as $7.0 \pm 0.5 \times 10^{-24}$ cm^2, rather than 3.7 ± 0.5 as in the actual paper, which was circulated in February 1944. In any case, the Jentschke-Lintner paper bears on reactor theory, and there is no indication that the measurement was performed in order to obtain data for the theory of a bomb. The measurement was never used by Heisenberg in any of his extant wartime papers, although he claims to have availed himself of it for his 1945 calculation of the critical mass of the Hiroshima bomb. As noted above, there is no evidence of the Jentschke-Lintner value, nor of a similar figure of 3.6 reported by Droste to a Kaiser-Wilhelm-Institute for Physics meeting in 1941, being welcomed during the war by Heisenberg as a breakthrough for the theory of a U235 bomb. Heisenberg had forgotten both figures by the time of Farm Hall.[48]

3. Much is made by Irving of Heisenberg's famous remark of June 1942 that the explosive part of a bomb would be about the size of a "pineapple." As

47. Irving, *German Atomic Bomb*, p. 92, citing Houtermans (G-94, pp. 119–124, for fast neutrons in uranium; pp. 136–137 for the critical size of a reactor; p. 139 for U235 and plutonium as explosives; reproduced along with its variant version G-267 in IMF 30-545 and 30-704). See below, chap. 9.

48. Irving, *German Atomic Bomb*, pp. 93, 309, citing the Jentschke and Lintner calculation of 3.7 in their "Schnelle Neutronen in Uran. V" (G-227) (IMF 30-461). See above for Heisenberg's claim to have used this at Farm Hall in 1945, and also for Droste's figure of 3.6.

The Heisenberg lecture in question is "Die Energiegewinnung aus der Atomkernspaltung," 6 May 1943 (G-217) (IMF 31-197).

For Heisenberg's claim to have used the Jentschke-Lintner value at Farm Hall, see his letter to Irving of 10 June 1966, cited above (IMF 32). See also below, chap. 14.

has been argued above, however, this comment is problematic, and nothing secure can be erected upon it.[49]

Heisenberg naturally welcomed Irving's book, and in a review of this "historically correct description" happily commented that "it is satisfying that Irving's investigation confirms the German report [viz., the FIAT report and Heisenberg's own 1946 *Naturwissenschaften* version] in all important points."[50] This approbation was scarcely surprising since Heisenberg had exchanged a great deal of correspondence with Irving in 1966, meticulously correcting his typescripts and encouraging Irving to provide a "new picture" that would refute the "prejudiced" and "false version"—a formula repeatedly used—of Groves and Goudsmit.[51] The usual facts are rehearsed, though with some peculiar twists of phrasing. For instance, Heisenberg curiously says that in June 1942 "no serious attempt to construct an atom bomb was ordered by the German authorities after the [June 1942] Conference," leaving open an escape clause that (as was indeed the case) less than "serious" attempts were ordered in the summer of 1944, as Heisenberg well knew.[52] Again, Heisenberg states that a supposed government order prohibiting long-term projects "spared the German physicists the decision whether to plead [*sic*] for an attempt to produce atom bombs."[53] Does this mean that Heisenberg and company were open to the eventuality that they might have to pressure the government to produce atomic bombs rather than vice versa? As ever, "external circumstances" are blamed for the German failure to progress both with the reactor and with the bomb after 1942. The account is so glib that one may come away from it without noticing an astounding omission: There is no mention of the critical mass of a U_{235} bomb, nor of any explanation as to why it was not calculated—seriously or otherwise. Heisenberg had clearly come to realize that it was better to keep quiet on this point, rather than to flag it as he had done in his 1946 version.

49. Irving, *German Atomic Bomb*, p. 92, also suggests that a paper by S. Flügge ("Kann man eine Uranmaschine mit schnellen Neutronen betreiben?" [G-142], September 1942 [IMF 30-720]) is advocating a U_{235} bomb using fast neutrons. However, the whole point of Flügge's paper is that a U_{238} reactor using fast neutrons would be impractical and that a "Uran-bombe" would have to consist of U_{235} and employ the slow-neutron reaction. It is unclear here whether Flügge had in mind a reactor-bomb or was simply using the term "Uran-bombe" to mean an engine of some sort.

50. W. Heisenberg, "The Third Reich and the Atomic Bomb," *BAS* 24 (1968): 34–35. The German text, "Das Dritte Reich versuchte nicht, die Atombombe zu bauen," was published in the *Frankfurter Allgemeine Zeitung*, 9 December 1967, and reprinted in GWH, C V, 50–52.

51. See Heisenberg's letters to Irving of 23 and 24 May, 10 June, 6 July, 1 August, and 19 December 1966, in IMF 32. Not all of Heisenberg's suggestions were adopted; Irving's Farm Hall account, for example, continued to show Heisenberg in a poor light.

52. "Kein ernsthafter Versuch," in the German. For the SS efforts of 1944 to make a bomb, see below, chap. 13.

53. In the German text: " . . . ob sie für einen Versuch zur Herstellung von Atombomben plädieren sollten."

Where Heisenberg expresses reservations with Irving's book is in the psychological area of "motivation" and "atmosphere." Of the difficulty of living in a terror state that fractured the trust between scientists, Irving "obviously knows but little." This criticism was a veiled defense of Weizsäcker from Irving's implicit contempt; Weizsäcker, after all, was seen to be the great diplomatic maneuverer on behalf of Heisenberg and true theoretical physics in the Third Reich, who had been obliged—like his father—to make what seemed cowardly and ignoble compromises with Nazism on behalf of a higher cause. The dangers of such a psychological "misinterpretation" as Irving's, pronounces Heisenberg, is to be seen in an English review "in which the essence of the book was not correctly understood." The reference seems to be to Paul Rosbaud's review (discussed below in chapter 3). Since Rosbaud had been present in Germany and involved with many of the participants in the uranium project including Heisenberg (whom he greatly disliked), Heisenberg doubtless felt obliged to attempt to discredit his all too informed skepticism about both the decency and the scientific acumen of the German team.[54] The disreputable character of Heisenberg's own review emerges in the final paragraph, where he denounces the hostile Allied view of the German official version as a species of victor's justice. "After a great war, history is written by the victors and legends develop which glorify them." For Heisenberg, the Goudsmit version was the scientific parallel to the "victor's justice" meted out at Nuremberg and by the denazification tribunals: Both were equally false. Like so many German intellectuals after the war who sought to rationalize their current misfortunes as simply the fortunes of war, Heisenberg was oblivious of his moral blindness. He turned out to be as adept at misleading the denazification investigators and pleading on behalf of former Nazis and SS members as he was at refuting such Allied scientists as Goudsmit.[55]

A group of three extended interviews given by Heisenberg in the 1960s and after are interesting for the manner in which they illustrate a certain tension present in his recounting his versions. Heisenberg does go over smoothly his now canonical version, but there are curious silences and gaps, and occasional slips, that suggest that he was not as happy with his account as he presented himself to be. The chief irritant seems to have been General Groves's publication of passages from the Farm Hall transcripts concerning Heisenberg's calculations of a critical mass of tons of $U235$; even the balm of Irving's considerate exclusion of Groves's figure from his book and his favorable portrayal of German scientific prescience had not been enough. Indeed, the outstanding characteristic of all three of these interviews is the absence of any discussion of the alleged tons of $U235$ that Heisenberg had, according to Groves, believed to be the critical mass of a bomb.

54. Rosbaud's suspicion and dislike of Heisenberg's character and stance during the Nazi period and after are discussed in chaps. 3 and 21 below.
55. For the dishonest denazification "Persil-certificates" written by Heisenberg, see below, chap. 21.

In the interview with Irving of 1965, Heisenberg tries to reassure his interlocutor (and perhaps himself) that he had understood the critical mass correctly from the beginning as a small quantity. He recalls the "pineapple" size he had suggested at the Speer meeting of June 1942 (here said to be a "football or a coconut"). Then Heisenberg telescopes what happened at Farm Hall; he claims that it was the "next day" (7 August) that he worked out the mass of the Hiroshima-type bomb to be 14 kg. The truth is, however, that he originally adhered to calculations running into tons, repeating these figures from 6 through 9 August, and only on 14 August did he finally arrive—after jettisoning his earlier approach—at the correct answer of a kilogram-size critical mass. In the interview Heisenberg says nothing about the Groves charge, nor about his earlier calculations of critical mass (apart from the famous "pineapple"). He is very evasive, and Irving was too naive to press him on the subject.[56]

The other recurring feature of these interviews is Heisenberg's concern with setting the record straight on his famous visit of 1941 to Niels Bohr. This will be examined later, but it is of relevance here for the manner in which Heisenberg's anxiety to justify himself leads him into stronger statements than usual about the nature of the German uranium project.[57] The visit was made necessary, Heisenberg unhesitatingly states, because "we saw truly from September 1941 an open road to the atomic bomb before us" and so wanted to consult Bohr for moral advice.[58] Heisenberg does not appear to notice that this is an admission that he worked hard enough on the bomb project to bring it to a point where a decision was required as to its future course (though, of course, unpolitical as he was, he left that decision to politicians). There is no indication here or anywhere else in Heisenberg's writings, it should be emphasized, that he had decided that he would refuse to make an atomic bomb for Hitler; the most he will say is that it troubled him, and that he was thankful the decision was taken out of his hands. It is all too easy for a Western reader to glide over this crucial distinction and simply assume that since Heisenberg had some moral qualms about making a bomb for Hitler, he would not have done so. However, all the weight of German behavior and mentality, and Heisenberg's own nationalist attitude with its tradition of duty and obedience, would have ensured that he would have worked on a bomb, had he been ordered to do so.

56. Interview by D. Irving, 23 October 1965, 42 pp., in IMF 31-526/567; see p. 39 (IMF 31-564).

Irving's manuscript notes on a joint interview of 19 July 1966 with both Heisenberg and Weizsäcker recount an amusing exchange where Heisenberg tries to prod Weizsäcker into recalling that he had calculated the mass at 14 kilograms. Weizsäcker says coyly: "My memory is a blank. . . . I hesitate to [suggest a figure]. If you said a figure, I could say a straight yes or no." Heisenberg, "a bit put out," asks if it was 14 kilograms, and Weizsäcker replies: "Well, now you say that, I can say that I was going to say you said 15 kg, but I hesitated" (IMF 31-616/620).

57. See below, chaps. 10 and 15.

58. Interview with Irving, p. 16 (IMF 31-541). See below, chap. 19.

The interviewer for the magazine *Der Spiegel* in 1967 simply assumed that the German calculations for critical mass had always been on track when he asked Heisenberg: "The German physicists knew from their calculations how many kilograms were needed to build an atomic bomb—and these figures agreed well, as was shown after the war, with the American ones?" Heisenberg answered, "Most figures of this sort, not only those for the size of the atomic bomb, agreed almost exactly. . . ." Heisenberg's reply here has a certain fuzziness to it, evident in the use of the word *most*; no mention is made of Groves's allegation of a critical-mass figure of tons, nor is Heisenberg's own second Farm Hall figure of 14 kg cited.[59]

The third and last interview, of 29 August 1967, is somewhat more explicit, especially in its attacks on the Allied critics of the Heisenberg version. The interviewer, J. J. Ermenc, reads out some conclusions from Margaret Gowing's official British atomic history about the errors of the German project, asserting that the Germans had failed to ask basic questions about cross-sections for U235 at various energies, as well as the character of the U235 reaction. Heisenberg, who asserts he had not read Gowing's book, reacts angrily. "That's all wrong. Every sentence is wrong. It's all nonsense. It simply does not correspond with the facts. . . . [At Farm Hall I] gave the figure of 14 kilos or so of U235. . . . Her statements are just nonsense."[60] The sentences from Gowing were indeed read out of context and made it sound as though no work was done at all on the cross-sections of U235, so Heisenberg could quite reasonably repudiate these charges of ignorance.[61] Moreover, since Gowing did not cite the "tons" of U235 calculation that Groves had attributed to Heisenberg, there was no difficulty in his responding with genuine indignation to her reported charges. *That* calculation, though, would not have been so easy to fob off. But, alas, the interviewer fails to confront Heisenberg with Groves's Farm Hall quotations.

Later in the interview Ermenc does ask Heisenberg if he had read Groves's book, and Heisenberg again—as he had with Gowing—says that he has not read it and immediately refers to the Farm Hall tape recordings: "I understand Groves has used some of these conversations in his book."[62] This admission is surprising; one would have thought that curiosity would have led Heisenberg to look over the Groves memoirs, which had been published in 1963, as well as the Gowing history, which appeared in 1964. However, the opportunity of a fruitful discussion of Groves's quotations from Farm Hall is lost as Ermenc hastens to assure his subject that he had not intended to refer to the Farm Hall evidence, but to a more

59. " 'Gott sei Dank, wir konnten sie nicht bauen'—Spiegel-Gespräch mit . . . Werner Heisenberg," *Der Spiegel* 28 (3 July 1967): 79–83, esp. 80. Reprinted in GWH, C V, 45–49. In German, Heisenberg's answer ran: "Die meisten Zahlen dieser Art, nicht nur die über die Grösse der Atombombe, haben sich fast genau gedeckt, bis auf die erwähnte Kohlenstoffmessung."

60. Interview in Ermenc, *Atomic Bomb Scientists*, pp. 43–45.

61. See M. Gowing, *Britain and Atomic Energy, 1939–1945* (London, 1964), p. 42, discussed below.

62. Ermenc, *Atomic Bomb Scientists*, p. 67.

general point about the government and military funding of science. Having failed to press Heisenberg on the crucial matter of the critical-mass calculation, Ermenc cannot be expected to do much better with the third Allied critique, Goudsmit's *ALSOS*, which Heisenberg dismisses thus: "I did not like the book of Goudsmit. It was not a good book. I felt that he wrote it for political propaganda . . . I can only say that Irving really has studied the documents much better than Goudsmit has. In Irving you get the facts practically correct. He has done very careful work."[63]

Heisenberg was rather incautious in this interview in explaining why he worked on the atomic project at all. Indeed, he concedes that the bomb was an active aim of the project until 1942:

> In the later stages, after 1942, the idea was to work on the reactors but certainly not on the atomic bomb. We considered the bomb project as much too dangerous and besides that it could not be ready by the end of the war.

This admission that he was working on the project during the phase when the possibility of an atomic bomb was still being investigated before June 1942 effectively robs Heisenberg of his moral justification, as indeed he seems to sense.[64] But at various stages in the interview Heisenberg's attempt to smooth over this awkward fact leads him into unwittingly giving away rather more of his own character—and German character in general—than he intended. The fact that he is so lacking in awareness of what he is saying and how it might affect non-German readers is very suggestive of a blind spot in German self-perception. Thus, Heisenberg stresses repeatedly that he was in the project only for the benefit of physics and doing interesting experiments. The bomb, he asserts, was never a practical possibility. This is meant to show that Heisenberg was innocent of wanting to make an atomic bomb; unfortunately, it also suggests a certain cynicism and opportunism in his character.[65] Again, a certain selfishness is evident in the remark that the German physicists did not urge their project's merits on the regime because if it had been given high priority and failed, "this could have had extremely disagreeable consequences for us"—hardly a remark of moral or patriotic earnestness.[66] Finally, Heisenberg recalls approvingly that Speer had himself recollected that the scientists at the June 1942 meeting had said that a bomb could be made but would take at least five years. Speer had played down his report to Hitler in order to dampen enthusiasm, so that all ended up for the best. The difficulty here, however, is that Heisenberg had described to Speer a possible, though very difficult, project and then left him and Hitler with the decision. This was a seemingly satisfactory state of affairs as far as Heisenberg was concerned. But in real-

63. Ibid., pp. 56, 59.
64. Ibid., p. 64.
65. Ibid., pp. 23, 33.
66. Ibid., p. 34.

ity it represented an abdication of all responsibility by Heisenberg, who shows himself totally unaware of its implications. What would have happened had Hitler decided on an all-out campaign?

There is a certain ostrichlike quality in these interviews and writings with their apparent ignorance of how non-German readers perceived the implicit scientific and moral problems that makes one suspect that Heisenberg had really convinced himself that he had correctly calculated the critical mass all along, and now just wanted to forget everything that indicated otherwise. He never deals with the Groves figure of tons, and he skates over the difficult issues of his own wartime behavior in cooperating with the Nazi regime. It would be too crude to call such strategies of deception "lies"; they were meant more, perhaps, to deceive and reassure himself about his—and Germany's—moral and scientific integrity than to deceive others.

This urge to justify himself led Heisenberg to explore the inner meaning of his involvement in the Nazi uranium project in an unusual memoir published in 1969. Heisenberg's *Physics and Beyond* is an intellectual autobiography cast in the form of a philosophical novella—a highly selective and stylized memoir consisting of dialogues between almost symbolic characters representative of various ideas and situations. It is scarcely a factual history, but rather a literary account that takes great liberties with the purely factual record, openly interpreting Heisenberg's experiences as part of a life's journey whose meaning becomes manifest only with time. Much of the work is occupied by reconstructed conversations that can no more be taken as accurate verbatim accounts than the speeches that punctuate Thucydides. This caveat should apply particularly to the reported conversations he had with Weizsäcker in Berlin in 1939–41. Here Heisenberg justifies both his scientific and moral awareness at the time, but again there are telling omissions and slips. Thus, Heisenberg now implies in his conversation that only "several kilograms" are required for a bomb and that even that amount would be too difficult to obtain technically, but he says nothing about his calculations of critical mass, nor of Groves's allegations. On the moral side, Weizsäcker opines that they should "say little or nothing about the possibility of building atomic bombs to the authorities. Naturally, we shall have to keep this possibility constantly in mind, if only to be prepared for what the other side may have up their sleeves."[67] In other words, if the Allies produce an atomic bomb, Weizsäcker is willing to produce one for Hitler in German self-defense! Heisenberg recounts this opinion as though he were quite oblivious of its implication. The entire text is as remarkable for its blithe and glib moralizing as for its attempt to impose moral meaning on situations where moral understanding was absent at the time. For most non-German readers, the analysis of the morality involved is always slightly out of focus, just missing what seems in

---

67. W. Heisenberg, *Physics and Beyond: Encounters and Conversations*, trans. (New York, 1972), p. 174; originally published as *Der Teil und das Ganze* (Munich, 1969; reprinted in GWH, C III).

commonsense terms to be the essential moral point in favor of some seemingly more profound moral insight.[68]

One statement that catches the eye is that by the end of 1941 or early 1942, "we were happily able to give the authorities an absolutely honest account of the latest development, and yet feel certain that no serious attempt to construct atom bombs would be made in Germany."[69] The words *absolutely honest* ring ironic in view of a letter which Heisenberg wrote in 1970 to Ruth Nanda Anshen, the American editor of his memoir. That year Anshen had also edited a collection of essays by I. I. Rabi that reprinted Rabi's approving review of Goudsmit's *ALSOS*.[70] A bizarre letter now arrived on Anshen's desk from Heisenberg.

Dear Dr. Anshen:

I have finished reading in your Perspectives in Humanism series the volume written by Professor I. I. Rabi entitled *Science: The Center of Culture*. I should like to review this important volume. However, I must say to you that I shall have to take exception to Dr. Rabi's statement that "such a tremendous undertaking as Oak Ridge, with huge, combined efforts of science, engineering, industry and the Army, would have been impossible in bomb-ridden Germany.["]

Dr. Hahn, Dr. von Laue and I falsified the mathematics in order to avoid the development of the atom bomb by German scientists.

Sincerely yours,
Werner Heisenberg[71]

Anshen was puzzled by this missive and consulted Rabi. After holding Heisenberg's letter for a week, Rabi returned it, asking Anshen to write to Heisenberg and tell him that he (Rabi) was honored by his wish to review the book, but "I should not wish to enter a public controversy with so eminent a scientist as he." Anshen was astounded at this reluctance to discuss openly such a historically im-

---

68. This matter is developed below in part III.

69. Heisenberg, *Physics and Beyond*, p. 180.

70. I. I. Rabi, *Science: The Center of Culture* (New York, 1970), pp. 94–100.

71. Printed (without date, but apparently written in May or June 1970) in Ruth Nanda Anshen, *Biography of an Idea* (Mt. Kisco, N.Y., 1986), p. 171. Mrs. Anshen was an admirer of Heisenberg's, but has some incisive observations about his character: "extraordinarily intelligent, but also compassionate despite a lurking ambiguity" (p. 39); "Though he welcomed agreement within the limits of the possible, he was determined not to compromise where he would not follow. . . . A patriotic German, his life was lived in difficult times" (p. 40); "Heisenberg, as ever, had a ready and convincing argument to offer" (p. 169). As to whether Rabi or Heisenberg was right about the German failure to make the bomb, Dr. Anshen—who is in general extremely sympathetic to Heisenberg—states that "my own inclination is to believe Rabi's statement" (p. 172).

portant matter, but Rabi gave her only "a direct glance, nothing more." A few days later, on 16 June 1970, she wrote to Heisenberg as Rabi had requested.[72]

The mystery is deepened by the fact that the original Heisenberg letter seems to have disappeared. Mrs. Anshen gave her papers and correspondence en bloc to Columbia University Library in the 1980s, but the letter has not been found among them. Nor has Mrs. Anshen been able to discover it among the records retained in her possession.[73] Nevertheless, it seems beyond doubt that the letter was genuine; its quotation in the Anshen memoirs is direct, and the letter itself is so startling that it could scarcely have been invented.

If we assume the letter to be accurately quoted in Anshen's book, it suggests that Heisenberg had been provoked to an outburst by a fellow Nobel laureate's rehearsal of the old Goudsmit libels as he saw them, and just when it seemed in the aftermath of Irving's work that the Heisenberg version had finally been vindicated beyond any doubt. The republication of Rabi's review at precisely this juncture by his own American editor—itself an act of betrayal, it must have seemed—would naturally have appeared to such a formalist as Heisenberg to have been an open declaration that the American scientific establishment regarded him as a liar. Hence, Heisenberg might well have felt desperate enough to reply in such a combative way, and to make the sensational claim that he had actually derailed the German bomb project by "falsifying the mathematics."

What did he mean by this? The answer that comes to mind is, of course, Heisenberg's wartime calculations—rehearsed at Farm Hall—that the critical mass of a $U235$ bomb would be in the region of tons of $U235$. This niggling memory of his error could now erupt again under great provocation and be twisted to form the basis of a new, self-justifying version: The wartime calculation had been an intentional attempt to mislead the Nazi regime into thinking a bomb was impossible, Heisenberg having been aware all along that it was a false calculation; thus he was able to preserve his claim to a true scientific understanding of the real critical mass from the outset. At any rate, Heisenberg's cleverness did not desert him even at this moment of great emotional turmoil; he still had enough presence of mind to insist that Hahn and Laue had been his accomplices in the deception. Conveniently, Laue had died in 1960 and Hahn in 1968, so Heisenberg's claim could be neither contradicted nor confirmed. But in none of Hahn's or Laue's writings, nor in the Farm Hall transcripts, are there any indications that they had aided Heisenberg in "falsifying the mathematics." Rather, they seem to have been quite ignorant of any of the "mathematics" involved, as is all too apparent in the published transcripts.

72. Information from Bernard Crystal, Curator of Manuscripts, Special Collections, Columbia University Library.

73. In telephone conversations with me in 1993, Mrs. Anshen was insistent that the letter had been given to Columbia with her other papers. Consultations on the matter have since taken place between Mrs. Anshen and the Columbia staff.

CHAPTER 3

Criticizing the Version, 1948–94

Skepticism about the Heisenberg version was always deep-rooted among Allied scientists; knowledge of the damaging contents of the Farm Hall transcripts ensured that from the beginning. But Heisenberg's own conduct hardened that skepticism. His unrepentant and insensitive remarks in personal conversation after the war, even in the diluted form in which they appeared in his printed writings, greatly antagonized American and other physicists. As Luis Alvarez observed about his meeting Heisenberg in 1948, "those of us who had worked on the Manhattan Project held Heisenberg in low esteem because of some demonstrably untrue and self-serving statements he made at the end of the war."[1]

The intelligence received from Germany during the war had given British officials a clear idea of German scientific deficiencies and shaped a hostile opinion of Heisenberg's opportunistic character. Heisenberg's visit to Bohr in 1941 was well known in Britain, of course, having aroused the disgust of Lise Meitner (then in Sweden), which she had communicated to Max von Laue and no doubt to British agents.[2] Similar distrust of Heisenberg was shared by Paul Rosbaud, who was the main source of scientific intelligence for Britain.[3] Rosbaud's role as an Allied agent has only recently emerged, and even now there are many gaps in the record of his activity. Austrian by birth and trained in physics at Berlin, Rosbaud in the 1930s was a scientific editor for the Springer-Verlag's leading journal, *Die Naturwissenschaften*. He had excellent relationships with many leading German scientists, and indeed it was he who ensured that Hahn's discovery of fission was given as

---

1. L. Alvarez, *Alvarez* (New York, 1987), p. 162. For Heisenberg's distasteful remarks to Allied scientists—including former German-Jewish colleagues—after the war, see below, chap. 21.

2. See below, chaps. 19 and 21, for the Meitner letter in question.

3. A. Kramish, *The Griffin* (Boston, 1986). For Rosbaud's supply of information to Britain, see below, chap. 10.

wide publicity as possible in that publication in January 1939. Though his wife and daughter spent the war in Britain, Rosbaud remained in Germany, gathering much material on visits abroad to Scandinavia as well as throughout Germany. Both during and after the war Rosbaud was held in the highest regard by anti-Nazi scientists, particularly by Max von Laue, who communicated to Rosbaud (as we have seen) his own misgivings about the behavior of his German colleagues even long after the war had ended.

Rosbaud was well informed of the progress of the uranium project.[4] A few days after the Speer meeting of June 1942, Rosbaud learned of its outcome at a gathering of the German Physical Society. That evening at a café near the Kurfürstendamm, the physicists professed their relief at not being ordered to develop a bomb. Rosbaud remained quiet during this display of cant until he was finally provoked to exclaim: "Nonsense! If you knew how to build it, you'd present it to your Führer on a silver platter!" The stunned scientists, fearful of Rosbaud's being an agent provocateur who might be trying to get them into trouble with the Gestapo, dispersed quietly.[5]

Rosbaud had been so shocked by a conversation with Heisenberg in 1940 in which the physicist had looked forward to Germany's winning the war that he refused to have any further discussion with him during the next few years except to exchange greetings. Even after the war, Rosbaud found that nothing much had changed in Heisenberg's attitudes. As he told Goudsmit in 1950, "I am shocked and depressed about the childish and, I almost would say immoral, views of such a great scientist. He has not changed a bit and has not learned anything."[6]

In 1948 Rosbaud's warm review of Goudsmit's *ALSOS* in the *Times Literary Supplement* confirmed British distrust of Heisenberg, coming as it did from someone who had been on the inside, even though Rosbaud accepted the Goudsmit charge that the Germans had not thought of using plutonium for a bomb. The Germans, recounted Rosbaud, had been deterred by the difficulty of obtaining adequate U235 and so caught at the idea of using a uranium pile with heavy water as a bomb. The review insisted that true German patriotism during the war should have aimed at the defeat of Germany, and in this respect Rosbaud generously praised the integrity of Hahn and Laue, which had been manifested in either passive or active resistance to Nazism. Heisenberg's name is notably absent from this

4. See Rosbaud's long report of 5 August 1945 on the German uranium project, reproduced in IMF 29-1174/1184; he had been on particularly good terms with Gerlach, who became head of the project in 1944, and was a rich source of information.

5. Kramish, *The Griffin*, p. 129. See Rosbaud's own recollection in Goudsmit Papers, box 28, folder 44, quoted below, chap. 21.

6. Rosbaud to Goudsmit, 25 October 1950, communicated by Arnold Kramish from original in Goudsmit Papers, AIP, box 28, folder 45 (see below, chap. 21). The conversation of 1940 is also described in the report on Heisenberg that Rosbaud wrote on 12 August 1945 (ibid.). For more on this matter, see below, chap. 21.

roll of honor, and Rosbaud implies that it should appear on a different list—of those "who would have been only too glad to [produce an atomic bomb] if they had known how."[7]

Naturally, Rosbaud damned Jungk's whitewashing book when it appeared in English in 1959. The Heisenberg version was dismissed as follows:

> Heisenberg's statement in 1946 that "external circumstances" had relieved the German atomic experts from the need "to take the difficult decision whether or not to produce atom bombs" may be regarded as correct—if ignorance of how to do so is taken to be synonymous with "external circumstances."

Rosbaud found that Jungk had omitted the most important reason for the German failure to construct a bomb:

> The Germans knew that in principle a bomb *could* be made; they had no idea *how*. A detailed theory of the A-bomb had never been developed in Germany. . . . As far as the reviewer is aware, no member of the German team has admitted this ignorance of how to prepare a bomb.[8]

Rosbaud, of course, had no access to the Farm Hall transcripts and could not refer to the fallacious argument used by Heisenberg, which would have justified his skepticism. The evidence Rosbaud does cite is mainly Bagge's partly published diary, which even in its edited form betrays the long-standing German mystification as to how a bomb could be built. In private, however, Rosbaud worried about the impact of Jungk's book.

> I do not doubt the sincerity of the author but I have every doubt in the sincerity of some of the people he has interviewed. His main sources in Germany were apparently Houtermans and von Weizsäcker. H. in his *Geltungsbedürfnis* claims the H-bomb and W. the diplomat knew how to produce the A-bomb, and so did everyone else of the Verein. And, I am afraid, this will now be the official German version.[9]

A major blow was dealt to the Heisenberg version, however, by the publication of unauthorized excerpts from the Farm Hall transcripts in General Groves's memoirs in 1962. Probably the most damaging passage for Heisenberg's self-respect was that in which Otto Hahn called Heisenberg a "second-rater," not once, but twice: "If the Americans have a uranium bomb then you're all second-raters. Poor old Heisenberg. . . . At any rate Heisenberg, you're just second-raters, and you

---

7. P. Rosbaud, "Secret Mission," *Times Literary Supplement*, 5 June 1948, 320. See above, chap. 1.

8. P. Rosbaud, review of Jungk's *Brighter Than a Thousand Suns*, *Discovery* 20 (March 1959): 96–97. See also Rosbaud's condemnation of the disastrous effect of the Jungk book on German self-delusion: Rosbaud to Goudsmit, 30 April 1958, Goudsmit Papers, box 28, folder 44. Goudsmit wrote to Rosbaud (5 January 1959, Goudsmit Papers, box 28, folder 45) that "Jungk's misrepresentation of the facts in this and many other cases borders on the criminal."

9. Rosbaud to Goudsmit, 30 June 1958, Goudsmit Papers, box 28, folder 45.

may as well pack up." Heisenberg's own frustration was almost comically vented: "Well, how have they actually done it? I find it is a disgrace if we, the professors who have worked on it, cannot at least work out how they did it." But though these passages cannot have been amusing for Heisenberg to have read—his insistence in his interview with Ermenc that he had not read Groves's book seems a little too self-protective—at least he was spared the verbatim quotation of his fallacious calculation of a critical mass of tons of U235. Curiously, Groves contented himself on this crucial point with a one-sentence paraphrase: "But the most surprising statement came from Heisenberg. He wondered how we were able to separate the two tons of U235 needed for a bomb." Groves then interpreted this "two tons" as confirming Goudsmit's view that the Germans had arrived at this grotesque figure by failing to understand that the bomb was a fast-neutron device. Today we know that Heisenberg had indeed grasped that the reaction must depend on fast neutrons; his mistake was to misunderstand the efficiency of the reaction and use a misconceived calculation to ensure an efficiency that resulted in a greatly exaggerated magnitude of tons, rather than kilograms. But Groves's failure to give Heisenberg's explanation of his wrong calculation and the actual figure in direct quotation allowed Heisenberg to wriggle off the hook. And when Irving provided the new official German history with his 1967 book, it carefully omitted any mention of the embarrassing "two tons" that Groves had cited.[10]

Groves's mistake in laying stress upon the alleged German incomprehension of the fast-neutron principle of the atomic bomb was repeated in the official British nuclear history by Margaret Gowing in 1964. An introductory chapter by the British physicist Kenneth Jay affirmed that "mercifully, the difference [in effectiveness of slow and fast neutrons in producing a nuclear explosion] was never appreciated by German scientists, at least during the war." Gowing then implied that this failure to understand the role of fast neutrons in pure U235 had resulted in Heisenberg's failure to ask the right questions about the explosive fission process in pure U235. Of course, Heisenberg believed that he had indeed asked the crucial questions; he had understood the bomb to be a fast-neutron reaction, he had had a rough idea of the fission cross-section, and he had calculated the critical mass of pure U235. All this is evident from the Farm Hall transcripts of the period 6–9 August 1945. The only trouble was that he had not understood the nature of a U235 bomb well enough and had calculated a critical mass in a totally misconceived way. Unfortunately, Gowing never took up Groves's reference to the "two tons" of U235 that would be required, and so Heisenberg felt it easy not to take

10. L. R. Groves, *Now It Can Be Told: The Story of the Manhattan Project* (London, 1963), pp. 333, 335 f., 338. Cf. the Groves interview in J. J. Ermenc, *Atomic Bomb Scientists: Memoirs, 1939–1945* (Westport, Conn., 1989), p. 253, where the two tons is misstated to be "20 tons." Groves comments that after his book was published, the Germans "realized that we knew what they had said. After that they were just scared to talk." Irving's book, however, proved a wonderful escape from their enforced silence.

the charges seriously, appalled as he seemed to be when Ermenc read them out to him in his interview.[11]

A publication that Heisenberg would have had more difficulty in writing off was the detailed memoir of British scientific intelligence by R. V. Jones, but this appeared only in 1978, two years after Heisenberg's death. Since Jones, and more especially his colleague Sir Charles Frank, were well acquainted with German atomic bomb thinking through their knowledge of the then still classified Farm Hall transcripts, great importance should have been attached to whatever they had to say. The kernel of Jones's recollection about the Farm Hall discussion was his explanation of just why Heisenberg had arrived at the figure of tons of pure U235 as the critical mass that had already been reported so tantalizingly by Groves. Heisenberg, argued Jones, had set himself a fictitious problem of how one might be completely sure of exploding a given amount of U235 before the mass disintegrated and broke off the reaction. This amount was a "mole," which comprised 10^{24} atoms—a number roughly equivalent to 2^{80}. Assuming two neutrons were released per fission, this meant that exploding 10^{24} atoms would require a chain of 80 fissions before the reaction stopped. By means of a basic statistical analysis known as the drunkard's (or random) walk, Heisenberg worked out that the radius of the critical mass would have to be 80 cm—a mass of many tons—if the explosion of a chain of 80 fissions were to be completed in time. (The fallacy lay in the fact that this calculation represented the upper limit, rather than the lower limit, for an explosive chain reaction).[12] Jones, therefore, concluded that "if our memories [Frank's and his own memories of Heisenberg's argument] are correct, then one explanation of why the Germans did not go for a bomb is that they thought that far too much uranium would be required." Somewhat uncomfortable with the idea that a physicist as brilliant as Heisenberg should have made such an error of judgment, Jones cautiously added the proviso: "But it is conceivable that we both misunderstood what Heisenberg said; and in fairness to a great physicist it is regrettable that the transcript has never been published." Alas for Heisenberg, when the transcript eventually became available in 1992 it showed all too clearly that Jones had not misunderstood him at all.[13]

Rather surprisingly, Jones's accurate analysis was not taken up in the Heisenberg literature. It was not for lack of public awareness; Jones had already explained it to David Irving in an interview of January 1966, but Irving chose to suppress it from his final text, though a transcript of the interview was made available to scholars in the microfilm edition of Irving sources.[14] Moreover, in 1983 Jones

11. M. Gowing, *Britain and Atomic Energy, 1939–1945* (London, 1964), pp. 30, 42. See above for the Ermenc interview. It will be recalled that Heisenberg claimed at that time that he had not read Gowing's book.

12. See below, chap. 14, for a detailed analysis.

13. R. V. Jones, *Most Secret War: British Scientific Intelligence, 1939–1945* (London, 1979; published in the United States as *The Wizard War* [New York, 1978]), pp. 606–607.

14. IMF 31-344.

repeated his analysis and added to it Charles Frank's testimony in an introduction to the reprint of Goudsmit's *ALSOS*.[15]

There was no excuse, then, for ignorance of this critical contribution to the Heisenberg problem, yet Mark Walker in the most detailed and best-known scholarly book on the German atomic project, *German National Socialism and the Quest for Nuclear Power, 1939–1949*, chose to remain silent about the issue and even omitted any mention of Jones's introduction from his bibliographical listing of the *ALSOS* reprint.[16] Nor was Jones's own memoir of 1978 cited. This is all the more remarkable since Walker had been extensively briefed about Heisenberg's crucial error in the course of a long interview in 1985 with Jones's colleague Sir Charles Frank. The transcript of this interview shows Frank explaining twice to Walker just where Heisenberg had made his crucial error in calculating the critical mass of a $U235$ bomb as being tons. But even though Walker recalls here that he had read about it in R. V. Jones's book, it was evidently something that he felt had no merit in an account of Heisenberg's involvement in the atomic project.[17] Inexplicably for a work of scholarship, no direct reference is to be found in Walker's book to the key point about a critical mass of tons of $U235$ that had been made by Groves, Jones, and Frank.

There is, however, an oblique reference in Walker to the matter, where it is linked to an unrelated point and used to draw a quite false conclusion. Walker took Frank's point that Heisenberg was mistakenly trying to find an "upper limit" for the critical mass of the bomb, whereas Frisch and Peierls had been looking for a "lower limit." But then this idea of upper and lower limits—which leads respec-

15. Published by Tomash, Los Angeles, 1983, pp. xv–xvi.

16. M. Walker, *German National Socialism and the Quest for Nuclear Power, 1939–1949* (Cambridge, 1989), p. 275. Jones's name does not appear in the index. In his recent book, *Nazi Science: Myth, Truth, and the German Atomic Bomb* (New York, 1995), p. 226 f., Walker does mention Jones and Frank on Heisenberg's mistaken conception of an atomic bomb, but he seems to think that this citation invalidates the Goudsmit and Groves accounts of how the Farm Hall transcripts expose Heisenberg's erroneous thinking. And he concludes that Heisenberg did calculate a small critical mass during the war: "During the war Heisenberg *most probably* [emphasis added] made a rough estimate which was comparable to contemporary Allied estimates" (p. 227). Walker seems to be unable to believe what Frank had told him in an interview and what is apparent in the Farm Hall transcripts—namely, that until 14 August 1945 Heisenberg believed the critical mass to be very large. In his essay "Legends Surrounding the German Atomic Bomb," in *Science, Medicine, and Cultural Imperialism*, ed. T. Meade and M. Walker (London, 1991), p. 187, Walker asserts that "the German achievement, although admittedly modest when compared to the completed Manhattan Project, included no gross scientific errors," though it was clear from Jones's memoirs that it included at least one pretty fundamental error. Walker (pp. 199–201) accuses Arnold Kramish of "a lack of objectivity and scholarly rigor. . . . As an author, Kramish is apparently intent only on attacking Heisenberg. Historical accuracy is of secondary importance." One might say something about glass houses here, considering Walker's own handling of evidence.

17. C. Frank, interview, 12 April 1985, OHI, pp. 9–11, 14–16. Walker (*German National Socialism*, p. 14) remarks that he has read about the random-walk calculation in R. V. Jones's book. See below, chap. 14.

tively to masses of tons and kilograms—is misapplied by Walker to the uncertainty surrounding the precise figure for a bomb. Taking an estimate in a German source of 1942 of 10 to 100 kg for plutonium, Walker leads the reader to believe, first, that this applies to U235, and second, that these figures represented the "lower" and "upper" limits sought respectively by the Allied scientists and the Germans. The conclusion is that the differences in the Allied and German estimates were merely details:

> The estimate of explosive critical mass mentioned by the Germans in January of 1942, 10 to 100 kilograms, is comparable to the American estimate reported in December of 1941, 2 to 100 kilograms. Arguably the Americans and British were more confident that the lower limit was correct, while the Germans—who apparently never made more exact calculations of critical mass—inclined more to the upper limit, but the Germans were nevertheless close to their Allied rivals.[18]

This is a gross distortion of the issue. The alleged similar "upper limit" of 100 kg shared by the Germans and the Allies is not the "upper limit" calculated by Heisenberg. The Allied figure is merely the upper limit of a band of values for what is properly called by Frank the "lower limit" of a bomb; this band depends on the precise data used and ranges from 2 to 100 kg. Heisenberg's "upper limit" is a quite different approach. It is a maximum band of values that would ensure an explosion without wasting a neutron, and it leads to a figure of from one to many tons of U235, as opposed to the kilograms calculated by Frisch and Peierls in Britain in 1940. It is not a difference of *detail*, but one of *conception*, that is at stake.[19]

Even worse than the treatment of critical mass found in his book of 1989 is Walker's handling of the Farm Hall transcripts after they had become available in 1992 and so made plain for all to see the erroneous reasoning behind Heisenberg's calculation. In his account of the transcripts in *Nature*, Walker suppressed the argument that Heisenberg had given twice at Farm Hall for concluding that tons of U235 would be required for a bomb. Walker (who for some reason inflates the figure given in the transcripts to "hundreds of tons of U235") makes it seem as though Heisenberg at that stage still believed that the critical mass was about 50 kg, though it is clear from what follows in the transcripts that this was not so. This allows Walker to conclude falsely that "the transcripts corroborate Heisenberg's understanding and have cleared up the last remaining matter, that of critical mass."[20] The transcripts have indeed cleared up the matter of critical mass, but

18. Walker, *German National Socialism*, p. 172.

19. For the reasoning behind Heisenberg's calculation, see below, chaps. 7 and 14.

20. M. Walker, "Myths of the German Atomic Bomb," *Nature* 359 (8 October 1992): 473 f. A highly critical reply by J. L. Logan and R. Serber to this note was published as "Heisenberg and the Bomb," *Nature* 362 (11 March 1993): 117, accusing Walker of misunderstanding essential issues involved in the transcripts. Serber, who was one of the designers of the Los Alamos bomb, finds even Heisenberg's more or less "correct" analysis of the bomb in his lecture of 14 August 1945 " primitive" and "unso-

they do so by showing that Heisenberg understood the critical mass of a U235 bomb to be on the order of tons.[21]

This conformity to the basic assertion of the Heisenberg version—that the Germans had understood correctly the science of the bomb—is all the more peculiar since Walker has been perhaps the most incisive critic of the moral aspects of the official version. His book was marked by the most acute dissection of the various layers of deception and self-deception that Heisenberg had constructed to protect his moral integrity. Walker quite brilliantly showed that Heisenberg's wartime visits to occupied countries were a conscious endorsement of German strategy, and he demonstrated that Heisenberg felt free during those visits to inform his hapless colleagues there of the rightness and inevitability of a Nazi victory.[22] Indeed, Walker's analysis was convincing enough to persuade Robert Jungk to recant his former adulation of German moral supremacy and contribute a foreword to the German translation of *German National Socialism*.[23] Had Walker been as critical-minded in dealing with Heisenberg's scientific claims as he was with the moral ones, his book would not have been disfigured as it is by serious mistakes of historical judgment and the suppression of relevant evidence.

Significantly, Walker seems to have realized at one point that his endorsement of the scientific Heisenberg version could not hold. In a published exchange of correspondence with the author in 1990, Walker was obliged to admit that Heisenberg had after all misunderstood the bomb in his paper of December 1939, but he now insisted that by 1942 Heisenberg had "changed his mind" and arrived at a correct conception.[24] However, Walker gave no evidence for why Heisenberg should have

---

phisticated." See also I. Klotz, "Germans at Farm Hall Knew Little of Atomic Bombs," *Physics Today*, October 1993, 11 – 15, 135. (Cf. M. Walker, "Selbstreflexionen deutscher Atomphysiker: Die Farm-Hall-Protokolle und die 'deutsche Atombombe,'" *Vierteljahrshefte für Zeitgeschichte* 41 [1993]: 519 – 542.)

21. Heisenberg was never precise about practical physical calculations; at Farm Hall, he gave varying masses, ranging from 1 ton (*OE*, p. 84) to 10 tons (p. 72). This variation seems largely due to assuming varying values for the main cross-sections. Others have tried to correct Heisenberg's mathematics, taking various values. Jones (*Most Secret War*, p. 607), taking a large radius, estimates the mass at 40 tons, whereas Frank in his introduction to *OE*, p. 5, works out Heisenberg's mass to be 6 tons. Logan and Serber ("Heisenberg and the Bomb") conclude that it was 13 tons.

22. Walker, *German National Socialism*, pp. 105 – 118. See also M. Walker, "Physics and Propaganda: Werner Heisenberg's Foreign Lectures," *Historical Studies in the Physical Sciences* 22 (1992): 339 – 389.

23. M. Walker, *Die Uranmaschine: Mythos und Wirklichkeit der deutschen Atombombe*, with "Vorwort" by Jungk (Berlin, 1990).

24. P. L. Rose, "Did Heisenberg Misconceive the Atomic Bomb?" *Physics Today*, February 1992, 126; M. Walker, reply to P. L. Rose, ibid. Walker concedes that Heisenberg's paper of December 1939 (G-39) "is a good source for his understanding of the problem at that time, but people can change their minds." I had argued that G-39 indicated that Heisenberg's conception of the bomb was confused. Although at that time I believed that this confusion issued from Heisenberg's conception of the bomb as a slow-neutron reaction, it may well be that he had already conceived of it as a fast-neutron device, as the Farm Hall transcripts have finally made plain. Nevertheless, it is far from clear that Heisenberg's fast-neutron view had been formed in 1939 at the time he wrote G-39, and it may represent a later in-

changed his mind in 1942, and he continued to rely on an erroneous interpretation of a document of that year for evidence of Heisenberg's change of mind. According to Walker, the Army Weapons Office (HWA) Report of 1942 showed that the Germans believed the critical mass of U235 to be 10 to 100 kg. But this false assertion cannot survive a reading of the relevant passage in the report, which shows that the 10 to 100 kg figure refers to plutonium, not U235. Moreover, the report also proposes such chimerical conceptions as U235 reactor-bombs, an inconvenient detail about which Walker's book also remains silent, as it does too about the research done on the same subject by Heisenberg's assistant Paul Müller in 1940.[25]

In sum, therefore, Walker successfully discredited most of the myths about German moral integrity, but at the cost of preserving the equally untrue scientific foundations of the Heisenberg version. This he did by concentrating on Goudsmit's errors and cutting out any reference to the crucial argument of Heisenberg's that resulted in a critical mass of tons of U235, as well as by omitting the material on German conceptions of reactor-bombs that was to be found in the HWA Report as well as in Paul Müller's papers and elsewhere in the documentary record. Finally, the 10 to 100 kg critical-mass figure was misleadingly applied to U235 instead of to plutonium, its proper reference.

Thanks to the influence of Walker's book, a new set of myths has grown up in the last few years concerning Heisenberg's scientific omniscience, even in the face of the damning evidence of the declassified Farm Hall transcripts, which have been consistently misrepresented by Walker and others. Foremost among these is Thomas Powers, who has now propagated the greatest of all Heisenberg myths, one that goes far beyond the orthodox Heisenberg version.[26] Heisenberg indeed assumes the role of an icon of moral and scientific resistance to Nazism. Endowed with a complete scientific understanding of the bomb, Heisenberg in this new version intentionally sabotages the bomb project out of moral scruples. Like Jungk's earlier book, Powers's *Heisenberg's War* is journalistic, highly readable, and entirely bogus, imposing wrongheaded interpretations on the historical and scientific ma-

---

sight, formed perhaps in 1940 in connection with his random-walk analysis. In any event, G-39 is highly obscure in its thinking about an atomic bomb. (See below, chap. 6.)

I regret that when I wrote my letter I had not yet reached a final analysis of the Heisenberg problem and so placed too much emphasis on the Goudsmit-Groves charge that Heisenberg at Farm Hall still believed the bomb to depend on slow neutrons. It would have been wiser to have given a fuller account of R. V. Jones's report of the random-walk reasoning behind Heisenberg's calculation of a critical mass of tons instead of mistakenly affirming as I did that Heisenberg had not glimpsed the fast-neutron principle. (At the time of writing I had not seen the text of the crucial interview between Walker and Charles Frank; nor had the Farm Hall transcripts been declassified.)

The correspondence resulted from M. Walker, "Heisenberg, Goudsmit, and the German Atomic Bomb," *Physics Today,* January 1990, 52–60.

25. Walker (*German National Socialism,* p. 172) also cites the figure of 10–100 kg carelessly, as though it were for U235. For Müller's paper, listed but not discussed in Walker, see below, chap. 8.

26. T. Powers, *Heisenberg's War: The Secret History of the German Bomb* (New York, 1993).

terial alike. One fundamental methodological problem that invalidates this historical travesty from the outset is that Heisenberg always denied making a moral decision about the bomb. Again, Heisenberg's outburst in his 1970 letter to Anshen that he "falsified" the mathematics is taken as confirming Powers's general thesis of a sabotaging Heisenberg; the problem, however, is that if Heisenberg was telling the truth here, it meant he had been lying for the previous thirty years in all his repetitions of the Heisenberg version. What credence therefore can be placed in anything he ever said?[27]

To sustain this fantasy, Powers has assembled a vast compilation of fragmented factual and pseudofactual material, without being able to distinguish the relative value and meaning of the various species of evidence—hearsay, conjecture, document, reconstruction—that he adduces. The lack of any critical understanding of the nature of the evidence and how it needs to be handled renders Powers's material suspect and unusable by other scholars unless it is corroborated by other sources and set in historical context. This critical deficiency applies to both the moral and the scientific aspects of the problem. Powers's incomprehension of German mentality, culture, and behavior leads him to impute concepts of resistance to Heisenberg that might make sense in a non-German context, but are wholly improbable when projected onto Heisenberg. A similar ignorance permeates Powers's handling of the scientific aspects of the bomb; there is very little discussion of the technical contents of the secret German wartime reports, and the revelatory paper by Müller dealing with the reactor-bomb is not even mentioned in this verbose book of nearly six hundred pages.[28]

The flavor of Powers's approach can be gathered from his curious handling of the Farm Hall transcripts. Unlike Walker, Powers at least provides the Jones/Frank analysis of Heisenberg's fundamental error in calculating the critical mass of a bomb as being of the order of tons of $U235$. But then he asks why Heisenberg also seemed to agree with Hahn that the figure might have been in the realm of kilograms even before working it out precisely in his lecture of 14 August 1945. Powers concludes that the contradictory masses given by Heisenberg in the transcripts show, first, that he did know the critical mass to be small, and second, that he had kept quiet about this during the war and misled the authorities with his calculation of a huge mass. The "mistake" was intentional:

> The Farm Hall transcripts offer strong evidence . . . that Heisenberg cooked up a plausible method of estimating critical mass which gave an answer in tons, and that he well knew how to make a bomb with far less, but kept the knowledge to himself.[29]

27. Powers, *Heisenberg's War*, p. 507. Powers says that Dr. Anshen "declined" to show him the original of the letter, but she has affirmed to me that she told him she no longer had it in her possession and had donated it to Columbia University Library (see above).

28. Müller is mentioned solely in passing at p. 98 as an assistant of Weizsäcker's. (Actually, he was Heisenberg's assistant.)

29. Powers, *Heisenberg's War*, pp. 447, 452, 576 f. At p. 449, Powers strangely attributes an earlier figure of a one-ton critical mass to a Heisenberg paper of February 1942 (*Die theoretischen Grundlagen für die*

This schizophrenic Heisenberg is hardly convincing. According to Powers's portrait, Heisenberg at Farm Hall hardly knew what he was thinking at any one time: Was the mass kilograms or tons? The mistake Powers makes here is to take interjections by Hahn about Heisenberg's having mentioned a small mass of kilograms during the war, and then to assume that these represented Heisenberg's current thinking on 6–9 August 1945. Looked at in the historical context of Heisenberg's wartime papers and other evidence, and also in the context of the Farm Hall conversations themselves, Hahn's general ignorance of bomb design is obvious and it is clear that he had misunderstood what Heisenberg had told him during the war. In the transcripts, one can almost hear Heisenberg's impatience with Hahn's questions and his offhanded replies as he intensely pursues the matter preoccupying him at the time—the random-walk calculation that produces a large critical mass. One simply cannot take all the stray figures mentioned in Farm Hall as equally representative of Heisenberg's thinking at the time, yet this cardinal methodological point is lost on Powers, who, as always, fails both to discriminate between species of evidence and to interpret his evidence within a secure historical context.

This combination of scientific and cultural ignorance renders the whole book a scholarly disaster, a book that because of its elephantine proportions and wide publicity is likely to distort the general reader's image of Heisenberg for a long time to come. Heisenberg specialists have been less impressed than lay reviewers by the book. The leading biographer of Heisenberg, David Cassidy, for instance, has condemned it as "so superficial and . . . so prejudiced as to render his account, though plausible, quite unacceptable. . . . [It rests upon] faulty interpretations, misrepresentations and shallow scholarship. . . . [It] stretch[es] credulity, and the historical record, beyond the breaking point."[30]

Energiegewinnung aus der Uranspaltung, in GWH, A II, 517–521; IMF 29-1005); but in context Heisenberg is clearly referring here to the explosive energy in one ton of unseparated uranium rather than to the critical mass of a $U235$ bomb. (See below, chap. 12, for this paper.)

Similarly fanciful playing with the Farm Hall "critical masses" occurs in S. Goldberg and T. Powers, "Declassified Files Reopen 'Nazi Bomb' Debate," *BAS* 48 (September 1992): 32–40.

30. D. C. Cassidy, "Atomic Conspiracies," review of *Heisenberg's War,* by T. Powers, *Nature* 363 (27 May 1993): 311–312. (The phrase beginning "faulty interpretations" appears in a circulated typed version, but is omitted from the printed copy.) Another critical review, by Jeremy Bernstein (*Science* 259 [26 March 1993]: 1923–1926), recommends that the book be "handled with extreme caution," while Paul Forman, in the *American Historical Review* 99 (1994): 1715–1717, characterizes the book as a "tendentious, as well as a journalistic, construction. . . . An immersion experience more appropriate to a novel than to a work of scholarship. . . . Disingenuous." Forman condemns especially Powers's distorting selectivity and draws attention to the fact that his documentation is "completely absent at many points, and everywhere severely restricted by Powers's reliance on translators for all materials in German." Mark Walker, in the *Times Higher Education Supplement,* 4 March 1994, 22, rejects the book's thesis of moral resistance and states that "Powers systematically distorts or shades evidence," and also dismisses his analysis of Farm Hall as "unconvincing and lack[ing] understanding." Among Powers's defenders is Brian Pippard (*Times Literary Supplement,* 28 May 1993, 3): "Heisenberg's reputation as a great physicist

Cassidy had himself just before the release of the Farm Hall transcripts produced the definitive biography of Heisenberg, a work rich in analytical insight and psychological and political perception. Exploring Heisenberg's German mentality with great sophistication, Cassidy's *Uncertainty* (1992) depicted the moral equivocation of Heisenberg and the near-mindless German nationalist instincts, which, together with his quasi-religious worship of science and his personal ambition, had impelled him to acquiesce in and ingratiate himself with the Nazi regime. Cassidy gave a penetrating critique of the moral aspects of the Heisenberg version: He was scathing about the German scientists' Farm Hall Memorandum, dismissed Heisenberg's *Nature* article of 1947 as a "preposterous account," and declared that if Heisenberg had been able to get his reactor working, he "would surely have advanced to the next step: extracting weapons-grade plutonium from the machine." Nevertheless, Cassidy was less willing to commit himself (in the absence, no doubt, of the Farm Hall transcripts) to an equally incisive critique of the scientific aspects of the Heisenberg version, and was content to state simply that the Groves excerpts showed that "apparently, [Heisenberg] had never determined in detail the actual size of an explosive."[31] The availability of the transcripts has enabled Cassidy subsequently to be more categorical in this matter.[32]

Given the entrenchment of the Heisenberg version in Germany, it is not surprising that the transcripts have failed to shake the established view of Heisenberg's involvement in the uranium project and his omniscience about the scientific principles of the atomic bomb from the beginning. Recent writings are indeed marked by the same refusal to consider Heisenberg's random-walk calculation of a critical mass of tons of U_{235}—a calculation given three times in the transcripts between 6 and 9 August. Emphasis instead has gone to the quite different approach used in his lecture of 14 August.[33]

---

is unchallenged, and his name has been cleared of . . . imputations." For an account of some of the controversy aroused by Powers's book, see W. J. Broad, "Saboteur or Savant of Nazi Drive for A-Bomb," *New York Times: Science Times,* 1 September 1992, C1 and C5.

One might also cite a less-noticed book of similar import to that of Powers and equally a work of fantasy: G. Brooks, *Hitler's Nuclear Weapons* (Barnsley, England, 1992).

31. D. C. Cassidy, *Uncertainty: The Life and Science of Werner Heisenberg* (New York, 1992), chap. 26, pp. 505 ff., 510; a general account of Heisenberg's involvement in the uranium project is given in the course of chaps. 22–26. Cassidy's article on Heisenberg in the *Dictionary of Scientific Biography* (New York, 1990), supp., 17:394–403, also declines to judge the matter. The useful history of the Kaiser-Wilhelm-Society by K. Macrakis, *Surviving the Swastika: Scientific Research in Nazi Germany* (New York, 1993), pp. 162–186, 247, is similarly reticent about giving a final judgment on whether Heisenberg did understand properly the physics of the bomb.

32. As in the review of Powers's book for *Nature,* cited above, where strong skepticism is shown toward the claim that Heisenberg understood the idea of a small critical mass all along.

33. The lecture has been edited by H. Rechenberg: "Über die Uranbombe (1945)," *Physikalische Blätter* 48 (1992): 994–1001. Rechenberg's *Farm-Hall-Berichte . . .* (Stuttgart, 1994), pp. 42 ff., 96, quotes Heisenberg's figure of tons but dismisses it as either a lapse of memory or as the result of simple variations of values for the mean free path; no mention is made of the random-walk argument on which

Weizsäcker himself continues to be as evasive as ever on the problems of the Heisenberg version. When asked about Laue's complaint of 1959 to Rosbaud that a "version" (*Lesart*) had been concocted at Farm Hall, Weizsäcker smoothly observes that Laue's letter to his son of August 1945 agreed "exactly with what he afterward portrays as my version."[34] Challenged about Gerlach's confused 1944 idea of a reactor-bomb, Weizsäcker says he cannot contradict what was in Gerlach's mind, but that he himself certainly was not confused about such things. As to why the Farm Hall transcripts depict the German scientists listening to Heisenberg's bomb lecture of 14 August as though they were students hearing the explanation for the first time, Weizsäcker explains this by saying that it was done on a pedagogical level for the benefit of Laue—and now Gerlach is opportunely added—who did not really know much about the subject. This does not explain the naïveté of Weizsäcker's own questions during the lecture, as recorded in the transcripts.

Weizsäcker's handling of the moral issues is somewhat more distasteful and reveals the gulf in mentality and sensibility that exists between German and non-German perceptions of the atomic bomb issue and indeed of Nazism. Without any sense of shame Weizsäcker depicts his visit with Heisenberg to Niels Bohr in Copenhagen in September 1941 as an act of resistance on their part, designed to preserve Bohr's institute. He sees Bohr's refusal to meet them as almost stupidly obstinate. What Weizsäcker cannot understand is just why the Heisenberg-Weizsäcker visit under the aegis of the German occupation authorities was regarded with such disgust. For instance, he remarks that one Danish physicist, B. Stromgren, was better disposed toward them than most Danes, and adds that after the war Stromgren was regarded with hostility by his international colleagues. Weizsäcker says this with some mystification, as though unable to comprehend that Stromgren had acted as a "collaborator" and this was why he was condemned.[35] Again, Weizsäcker is silent about some of his own behavior in Copenhagen. Thus, he states that he went to see Bohr, but what he does not say is that he had to push his way into Bohr's office, since Bohr had declined to see him. Clearly,

---

Heisenberg's figure of tons actually depends. (See below, chap. 14.) Rechenberg denounces the "erroneous and hairsplitting arguments of Walker" (*Farm-Hall-Berichte*, p. 56) as well as Jeremy Bernstein's "petty and prejudiced critique of Heisenberg which repeats Goudsmit's mistakes 45 years later" (p. 92).

For interesting quasi-legal reasons the text of the lecture is omitted from Dieter Hoffmann's German edition of the transcripts, *Operation Epsilon: Die Farm-Hall-Protokolle oder die Angst der Alliierten vor der deutschen Atombombe* (Berlin, 1993), which simply mentions the "tons" figure (p. 37) but omits any analysis or explanation of the actual reasoning used by Heisenberg.

34. C.-F. von Weizsäcker, interview of 3 June 1993 by D. Hoffmann, H. Rechenberg, and T. Spengler, in Hoffmann, *Operation Epsilon,* p. 349. The questions are asked anonymously, and one wonders who posed the more difficult questions.

35. Ibid., pp. 352–353. At p. 353 Weizsäcker voices his approval of Powers's "very good description and analysis" of the visit to Bohr. One has the impression that somehow Weizsäcker has aided the publication of the Powers book.

Weizsäcker's arrogance blinded him to how his conduct and attitude were perceived by non-Germans. Even if he went to Copenhagen for the best of reasons in his own mind, his conduct there only reinforced natural Danish suspicions and resentment of German arrogance. But even this may be conceding too much to Weizsäcker's purity of intention; any benevolence was mixed with the insensitivity of feelings of German superiority nourished by the Nazi victories of 1940–41. Heisenberg and Weizsäcker alike were incapable of comprehending how patronizing and offensive their favors must have seemed to the Danes. This German solipsism and the resentment it provoked are a recurrent theme in accounts by non-German scientists of Heisenberg's wartime visitations—and the theme continues into the postwar encounters between Heisenberg and Allied scientists, including German refugee physicists such as Max Born, Francis Simon, Goudsmit, and many others.[36] Indeed, in his 1993 interview Weizsäcker seems still not to have fully understood the criminality of Nazi Germany and the justice of the Allied cause; he sees the Nuremberg trials as the judgment of "the guilty by the guilty," and regards Hiroshima as virtually a crime of the same order as the Holocaust.[37] Perhaps, after all, as Lise Meitner observed, the German physicists just could not understand why their attitudes and conduct were so offensive to their Allied colleagues.[38] The conditioning of German culture and behavioral patterns made the mentality and feeling of Heisenberg and his colleagues an alien intellectual and moral universe that their Allied counterparts could regard only with disgust and bemusement—and sometimes amusement.

Other revealing admissions were made in unpublished lectures and ensuing discussion by Weizsäcker at the European Nuclear Research Center in January 1988. On the moral level, Weizsäcker concedes that on the evening in February 1939 when he heard of the secondary emission of neutrons that would make a bomb possible, he "discussed the problem all night, and our conclusion was that from then on, the only political task for mankind was to abolish the institution of war and that we had to struggle for that. . . . No other solution would work . . . I will skip what we did during the war."[39] Weizsäcker was interested not in the rather more immediate problem of abolishing Hitler, but simply in the grand problem of "war" in the universal. Without any awareness of contradicting himself, Weizsäcker then confesses he did actually want to work on the bomb, consoling himself with the knowledge that it would not be constructed before the end of the war; even so, he concedes that it might have been completed on time. For a year it had seemed indeed that a bomb was feasible.

36. See below, chap. 21.
37. Weizsäcker, interview in Hoffmann, pp. 356 f.
38. See her outburst to Hahn in the letter of 27 June 1945, quoted below, chap. 21.
39. C.-F. von Weizsäcker, *Ideas on the Philosophy of Science; The Meaning of Quantum Mechanics; The Political and Moral Consequences of Science* (lectures given at CERN, Geneva, January 1988), pp. 14, 30. (Dr. Jonothan Logan kindly supplied me with the transcription.)

In fact, I wanted to participate in the work. I did not expect that the bomb would be made during the war which Hitler had started. Still, this was not certain, and it might well have been possible, and if it had Heisenberg and I and others would have been in a horrible situation, because we did not actually want to give Hitler such a weapon . . . though great damage might have been done if we had been able to make a bomb. Then, after a year or so, we realized that so much was needed to make a bomb that we had no chance of making it. From that moment on, the moral problem more or less disappeared for us.[40]

And of course Heisenberg knew perfectly well how to make a bomb:

It was quite clear that Hahn was not the man to make a bomb . . . Heisenberg was fully able to imagine a bomb, and to make the plans for it. . . . In September or October 1939 Heisenberg told me the following: "Well, we must do it. Hitler will lose his war. . . . Much of Germany will be destroyed. . . . and it is necessary that science should live through the war, and we must do something for that. And therefore we must enter into that enterprise."[41]

How, one wonders, could working on an atomic bomb preserve German science, unless one reduces the atomic bomb project to a form of indoor relief for the scientific classes?

In these passages Weizsäcker fully admits that he and Heisenberg worked seriously on an atomic bomb in 1939–40 for a whole year though realizing there would be a serious problem if they actually succeeded in producing one. He does not say anywhere that he and his mentor would have withheld the weapon from Hitler. The only safety lock was that the bomb might turn out to be too difficult to make. Such admissions patently belie the original version devised at Farm Hall in 1945.

In America and Britain, the opening of the Farm Hall material has solidified the long-standing criticism of the Heisenberg version in both its scientific and moral aspects.[42] Above all, Sir Charles Frank's edition contains an invaluable preface that should finally have laid to rest the scientific claims of the Heisenberg version. Frank points out the three rehearsals of the random-walk calculation yielding tons during the days following Hiroshima before Heisenberg finally arrived at a correct conception and calculation in his lecture of 14 August. And Frank also states that Wirtz, an old friend of Frank's from before the war, had admitted to him in the garden of Farm Hall that a wrong calculation of this type had actually

40. Weizsäcker, CERN lectures, p. 42.
41. Ibid.
42. See, for instance, Logan and Serber, "Heisenberg and the Bomb"; J. Logan, "The Critical Mass," *American Scientist* 84 (May–June 1996): 263–277; Cassidy, "Atomic Conspiracies"; J. Bernstein, "The Farm Hall Transcripts: The German Scientists and the Bomb," *New York Review of Books* 13, no. 14 (13 August 1992): 47–53. See also the new critical work by J. Bernstein, *Hitler's Uranium Club* (Woodbury, N.Y., 1996), published after the completion of my manuscript.

been confided to his circle by Heisenberg at a meeting held in 1940.[43] This would mean that the reason why the atomic bomb was never intensively pursued in Germany was not because of moral scruples on the part of the scientists, nor because of shortages of heavy water or wrong graphite measurements, nor because of Allied bombing, nor because of the government's insistence that only short-term projects were to be pressed. It was because of none of these "external circumstances" that Heisenberg gave up on the bomb project by 1942; it was because he believed from 1940 on that an impossibly huge amount of $U235$ would be required for a $U235$ bomb, an amount that would not be obtainable within several decades, let alone before the end of the war. During 1940–42 and even afterward Heisenberg and other German scientists continued to play with alternative versions of a bomb: It might be designed as an unstable reactor-bomb, or it might ultimately be built with plutonium. A plutonium bomb, though, would also be a long-term enterprise, requiring the development of a reactor program, which now became the principal avenue of research. References in the German documentation to these alternative types of bomb have often been confused by later historians with the pure-$U235$ bomb, giving rise to a complicated and contradictory picture of German thinking about atomic bombs of various sorts that the present book attempts to unravel. Nevertheless, the fact remains that it was Heisenberg's fundamental scientific error in 1940 that precluded him from recommending an all-out attack on the atomic bomb problem. This was the true reason why Nazi Germany failed to achieve the bomb, and it was a truth that the Heisenberg version was designed to conceal—and continues to conceal.

43. C. H. Frank, ed., *Operation Epsilon: The Farm Hall Transcripts* (Berkeley, 1993), p. 3; and private correspondence with Sir Charles Frank. See below, chap. 14.

PART II

Science:
Conceptions and Misconceptions of Physics

CHAPTER 4

The Atomic Bomb Problem, 1939

In Berlin in mid-December 1938 the prominent German chemist Otto Hahn discovered to his amazement that when bombarded by neutrons, the nucleus of the heaviest natural element, uranium, yielded nuclei of barium, an element roughly halfway down the periodic table. Hahn gave word of this extraordinary phenomenon to his friend Paul Rosbaud, who as an editor of the Springer press's prestigious scientific weekly journal, *Die Naturwissenschaften*, saw to its rapid publication on 6 January 1939.[1]

The first person to have been informed, however, was not Rosbaud, but rather Lise Meitner, Hahn's long-term collaborator on the research program that had led to the discovery.[2] An Austrian-Jewish physicist, Meitner had worked with Hahn at the Kaiser-Wilhelm-Institute for Chemistry until the intensifying persecution of the Jews and her vulnerability as an Austrian citizen after the annexation of Austria forced her to flee Germany with the help of Hahn and Rosbaud in July 1938. Now, on 19 December Hahn sent his old colleague a letter with the news of his discovery that reached her in Sweden two days later.[3] Like Hahn, she found the phe-

---

1. A. Kramish, *The Griffin* (Boston, 1986), pp. 50 ff. (The book reconstructs Rosbaud's astounding career as a British agent.) Texts in H. G. Graetzer and D. L. Anderson, *The Discovery of Nuclear Fission* (New York, 1971).

2. For Hahn's somewhat disingenuous suppression of crucial aspects of Meitner's contribution to the discovery of fission, see the important article by R. L. Sime, "A Split Decision?" *Chemistry in Britain,* June 1994, 482–484. On Hahn's temptation to dismiss Meitner in 1938, see idem, "Lise Meitner's Escape from Germany," *American Journal of Physics* 58, no. 3 (March 1990): 262–267; idem, *Lise Meitner: A Life in Physics* (Berkeley, 1996), p. 185.

3. Printed in O. Hahn, *My Life: The Autobiography of a Scientist* (New York, 1970), pp. 150 f. (The original is in the Meitner Papers, Churchill College Archives, Cambridge.) Hahn believed that the "radium isotopes behave not like radium, but like barium." A second letter sent two days later strengthened this chemical conclusion, but again without coming to any physical deduction: The isotopes "are not ra-

nomenon puzzling and very difficult to explain. But when Meitner's physicist nephew, Otto Frisch, visited her at Christmas, the pair came up with an explanation for the appearance of barium: the nucleus had been fissioned into two large parts by the incoming neutron, releasing kinetic energies of 200 million electron volts (200 MeV), thanks to the loss of a small amount of mass that was converted to energy. Frisch managed to acquaint his mentor Niels Bohr with this revolutionary finding in Copenhagen on 3 January, just before Bohr left for America, where his news of it was to create a sensation among physicists. Frisch and Meitner's formal report in a letter dated 16 January to *Nature* (published on 11 February) ensured the rapid circulation of the idea among the international scientific community.[4]

But Frisch and Meitner had missed what the former himself called the "most important" thing of all, though it was quickly brought to his attention by a Copenhagen colleague, Christian Møller.[5] Elementary theory indicated that the two lighter elements formed from uranium would not require as much "neutron glue" to hold together their individual nuclei as did the massive uranium atom. A number of surplus neutrons would, therefore, be ejected in the fission process, and these could go on in turn to disintegrate further uranium atoms, which would in their turn yield more neutrons to multiply the process exponentially. Through this phenomenon of the "chain reaction," it was conceivable that the miniature energies released on the atomic level might be scaled up to produce prodigious energies in the everyday world, whether in a reactor generating controlled energy, or in an unrestrained explosion of immense power. By March 1939 teams including Szilard and Fermi in the United States and the Halban and Joliot group in Paris had reported results of experiments on the rate of neutron reproduction in fission. They established that the rate—ranging from 2.3 to 3.5 neutrons released per fission—was high enough to maintain a chain reaction.[6]

---

dium at all but, from the chemist's point of view, barium" (ibid., p. 152). Hahn's other memoir, *A Scientific Autobiography*, trans. (New York, 1966), acknowledges (p. 158) that he was inclined to interpret the results mistakenly in terms of the then prevailing theory of transuranics, whereas "the correct explanation" was published by Meitner and Frisch. But in a little-known third letter of 28 December, Hahn himself asked Meitner what she thought about his "barium fantasy"—meaning "the possibility that the U239 could split into one Barium and one Masurium." (Letter translated in P. Rife, "Lise Meitner: The Life and Times of a Jewish Woman Physicist" [Ph.D. diss., Union for Experimenting Colleges and Universities, 1983], p. 285, from Dietrich Hahn, *Otto Hahn: Erlebnisse und Erkenntnisse* [Düsseldorf, 1975], p. 82.)

4. O. R. Frisch, *What Little I Remember* (Cambridge, 1979), pp. 115–119.

5. Ibid., p. 118. The Frisch-Meitner paper of 16 January 1939 mentions neither neutron reproduction nor chain reaction (reprinted in Graetzer and Anderson, *Discovery of Nuclear Fission*, pp. 51 ff.).

6. The article by H. von Halban, F. Joliot, and L. Kowarski, "Liberation of Neutrons in the Nuclear Explosion of Uranium," *Nature* 143 (1939): 470 (dated 18 March), is reprinted in Graetzer and Anderson, *Discovery of Nuclear Fission*, pp. 74 ff. (see p. 72 for the other papers). *Explosion* here is a synonym for "fission."

That the energies involved in a chain reaction might have military application in the form of a uranium bomb was quickly grasped. Speculation about the nature and feasibility of such a bomb was rife throughout 1939 and was conducted not only through scientific media but also in the general press, which reported on the excitement animating physicists' meetings. In April 1939, for example, the *New York Times* announced the physicists' "vision [of] earth rocked by isotope blast."[7]

Bohr's American trip of January–May 1939 fueled much of the scientific speculation about a uranium bomb. After first electrifying the Americans with his news of Frisch's hypothesis, Bohr had come up with a theory of his own about the nature of uranium fission. At a breakfast conversation in Princeton on 5 February 1939 it suddenly occurred to Bohr that nearly all the observed fission in uranium was due to a rare isotope, U235, present in natural uranium only in a proportion of roughly 1 to 140, virtually the whole of the remainder being composed of U238. In two brilliant papers of February and August 1939, Bohr argued that the plentiful isotope U238 would indeed fission, but only with fast neutrons of a high energy, most neutrons either being simply captured by the U238 nucleus or rebounding "inelastically" after a collision, as a result of which they frequently lost energy and so became unable to cause fission in subsequent collisions. The factors of simple capture and collision without fission were dominant enough to render dependence on U238 fission alone an unfeasible source of power. But this did not hold for U235. The latter's nuclei were easily fissioned by slow neutrons (as well as by the even slower thermal neutrons). This insight had the effect of channeling the interest of physicists into the phenomenon of slow-neutron fission in U235, somewhat eclipsing the study of fast neutrons. Bohr himself, however, had been careful to suggest that U235 might also be fissionable by fast neutrons, though the effect was masked by the fast-neutron fission process occurring in the omnipresent U238.[8]

Shortly after his remarkable insight, Bohr discussed with his Princeton friends the possibility of an atomic bomb, which he clearly understood would have to depend on U235 fission. But, given the extreme difficulty of extracting U235 from natural uranium, Bohr concluded that it was preposterous to think of ever being able to separate sufficient U235: "It would take the entire efforts of a country to

---

7. *New York Times*, 30 April 1939, quoted at p. 214 of L. Badash, E. Hodes, and A. Tiddens, "Nuclear Fission: Reaction to the Discovery in 1939," *Proceedings of the American Philosophical Society* 130, no. 2 (1986): 196–231: R. Rhodes, *The Making of the Atomic Bomb* (New York, 1986), is the most complete account available of the development of the bomb.

8. N. Bohr, "Resonance in Uranium and Thorium Disintegrations and the Phenomenon of Nuclear Fission," *Physical Review* 55 (1939): 418–419; N. Bohr and J. A. Wheeler, "The Mechanism of Nuclear Fission," *Physical Review* 56 (1939): 426–450; L. Rosenfeld, *Selected Papers* (Boston, 1979), pp. 343 f.; J. A. Wheeler, "Niels Bohr and Nuclear Physics," *Physics Today*, October 1963, 36–45, esp. p. 42; Rhodes, *Atomic Bomb*, pp. 284–288; A. Pais, *Niels Bohr's Times in Physics, Philosophy, and Polity* (Oxford, 1991), pp. 454–458. See the clear account in Rhodes, *Atomic Bomb*, pp. 282–288.

make a bomb," he told a colleague.[9] The whole idea of a uranium bomb seemed so chimerical to Bohr that he freely referred to it at the American Physical Society meeting held in Washington at the end of April 1939; his "theoretical possibility" that a chain reaction in pure U235 could destroy everything within a radius of many miles was picked up by the *New York Times* and other papers.[10] According to press reports, Bohr "declared that bombardment of a small amount of the pure Isotope 235 of uranium with slow [*sic*] neutron particles of atoms would start a chain reaction or atomic explosion sufficiently great to blow up a laboratory and the surrounding country for many miles."[11] If this wording is accurate, then Bohr was still not clear in April 1939 that a uranium bomb would have to depend on fast neutrons.

But how big was a "small amount" of U235? One scientist at the meeting believed it might be a sphere of about a yard in diameter.[12] This would mean an incredible mass amounting to tons of pure U235, a quantity that seemed beyond the wildest bounds of possibility, considering that not even a microgram had yet been extracted. When officially consulted by Admiral Stanford Hooper of the U.S. Navy on 17 March 1939 as to how much U235 would be required for a bomb, Enrico Fermi (who had recently discussed fission with Bohr) guessed that it would be "probably less than 500 kilograms [half a ton] of uranium 235." Asked whether the critical mass of a uranium explosive mass (it is not clear whether natural uranium or pure U235 was meant) might be "of practical size," Fermi evasively smiled that it might well be the size of a "small star." At any rate, the critical mass for a bomb was so large as to be hardly worth working out its precise amount; the calculation of a critical mass for a bomb would yield "results [only] of academic interest," and to develop such a bomb would take at least twenty-five to fifty years. Not surprisingly, the navy let the matter drop.

As with so many other pronouncements of 1939 on the bomb, one should be wary of assuming the prescience of Fermi's comments. They seem rather to indicate that Fermi had not thought seriously about the scientific principle of a U235

9. J. A. Wheeler, "The Discovery of Fission," *Physics Today* 20 (November 1967): 49–52, quoted on p. 52 (and misdated to 16 April, rather than 16 March, as in Wheeler's later recollection "Some Men and Moments in Nuclear Physics," in *Nuclear Physics in Retrospect*, ed. R. Stuewer [Minneapolis, 1979], p. 282. The discussion may have been even earlier—in February).

10. Quoted in Badash, Hodes, and Tiddens, "Nuclear Fission," p. 214.

11. Bohr's remark about *slow* neutrons being used in an atomic explosion is taken from the *New York Times* report of 30 April 1939, p. 35.

For the general awareness of the discovery's implications for a bomb, see P. Morrison, *Nothing Is Too Wonderful to Be True* (Woodbury, N.Y., 1995), p. 374: "Even though I was then a naive graduate student, I was able with my friends to draw a funny chalk diagram of a bomb with heavy water and this and that. Even we knew that this was a very likely cause of fearful explosions."

12. Report of 29 April 1939 in the *Washington Post*, quoted in Badash, Hodes, and Tiddens, "Nuclear Fission," p. 214. See also the useful analysis of the problem in J. Logan, "The Critical Mass," *American Scientist* 84 (May–June 1996): 263–277.

bomb; the record of his remarks at the meeting reveals that he was referring to the critical mass of a bomb composed of natural uranium (perhaps enriched with U235), and that U235 concerned him only because it appeared to be the "working" type of uranium fission.[13] At any rate, by November 1940, Fermi had become convinced that no explosion was possible in unseparated uranium.[14]

What is the explanation of these large bomb masses? Part of the answer lies in the fact that experimental data about many of the crucial factors were not available and that the physicists were basing their estimates on the roughest guesses at what the various probabilities of fission, collision, and scattering of neutrons—the "nuclear cross-sections"—might be. More significantly, there was the tendency at this point to think of a bomb as an exploding reactor; as one of the inventors of the bomb later put it, a critical mass of tons was "intuitively expected after thinking about reactors."[15] This intuition arose out of the unspoken assumption that the U235 in the mass would be fissioned almost entirely by slow neutrons and that the probability of fast neutrons fissioning the U235 would be extremely small.[16] Discussions of large critical masses in reactors using ordinary uranium conditioned physicists to conceive of critical masses in a U235 bomb that, though small in relation to unseparated uranium, would still be very great.

There is no evidence that Bohr demurred from the prevailing assumption that a U235 bomb would require an impossibly large quantity of the isotope. It was undoubtedly a great relief to Bohr and others that a bomb made of pure U235, although a theoretical possibility, seemed utterly unachievable in practical terms. As a British physicist later recollected, "in 1939 there was a discussion of the whole [bomb] thing in Copenhagen; it was extraordinarily complete."[17] Such discussions would have provided Bohr with the skeptical arguments against the feasibility of a bomb with which he reassured himself and various audiences in 1939–40.

13. The 500 kg mass is quoted in M. C. MacPherson, *Time Bomb: Fermi, Heisenberg, and the Race for the Atomic Bomb* (New York, 1986), pp. 75 f. L. Strauss, *Men and Decisions* (New York, 1962), pp. 236–238, prints substantial sections of the memorandum of the session taken by Captain G. L. Schuyler (without giving an archival reference). The excerpt does not include any discussion of a bomb made of pure U235, nor is any figure for a critical mass suggested. Cf. Rhodes, *Atomic Bomb*, p. 295. (For Fermi's remark of 1939–40, quoted in Pais, *Niels Bohr's Times*, p. 461, about "one small fission bomb"—which cannot be taken as indicating his awareness of a small critical mass—see below, chap. 12.)

Strauss had corresponded with Szilard about fission in February 1939 and soon after met Bohr; see R. Pfau, *No Sacrifice Too Great: The Life of Lewis L. Strauss* (Charlottesville, Va., 1984), pp. 54 f.

14. Conversation with John Cockcroft, 16 November 1940, reported in PRO, AB 1/495.

15. R. Peierls, "Reflections on the Discovery of Fission," *Nature* 342 (21–28 December 1989): 852–854. See below, chap. 5.

16. Cf. L. Turner, "Nuclear Fission," *Reviews of Modern Physics* 12 (1940): 1–29, at pp. 20 f., which demonstrates the preoccupation with slow-neutron research in 1939–40. Rhodes (*Atomic Bomb*, p. 287) cites a typical simplification of Bohr's argument by physicists in 1940, ascribing fast-neutron fission solely to U238.

17. Blackett speaking to Heisenberg, September 1945, in PRO, WO 208/5019 (Farm Hall Transcripts), no. 7, p. 3 (*OE*, p. 176).

In a lecture delivered at the University of Birmingham just before the beginning of the war and repeated in Denmark in December 1939 and in Norway the following spring, Bohr ruled out the use of unseparated uranium using fast or slow neutrons as the basis of a bomb: "Even if reaction chains can occur [in U238], these will remain too short and too rare for there to be any question of an explosion."[18] As to U235, Bohr allowed that in a "sufficiently large quantity, every neutron would have a very considerable probability of causing further fission . . . and an explosion would be the unavoidable consequence"; but he emphasized that it would be impossible "with present technical means to purify the rare uranium isotope in sufficient quantities to realize the chain reaction discussed above." It is incredible that such a responsible individual as Niels Bohr would have made this public reference to the theory of atomic bombs had he thought that only a reasonable amount of U235—such as might be obtained in the near future by the relatively feasible invention of new technical means—was required. The true reason for Bohr's optimism was that, despite having himself suggested that U235 was fissionable by fast neutrons, he had not thought deeply about the rapidity of the fast-neutron reaction and its significance for the critical mass of a U235 bomb.

This inhibition is evident in a manuscript by Bohr titled "Chain Reactions in Nuclear Fission," dated 5 August 1939. Here Bohr recognizes that a fast-neutron reaction would be possible with

> pure or highly concentrated U(235) [where] the whole situation would be different [than in ordinary uranium] and chain reactions would probably be realisable without any admixture of a lighter substance [to slow neutrons to fissionable thermal velocities] since for all velocities the cross-section for fission would presumably be much larger than the cross-section for radiative capture.[19]

As we shall see in chapter 5, this insight about the efficacy of fast neutrons in U235 was the basis of Frisch and Peierls's scientific conception of an atomic bomb and led to their calculations of a feasible critical mass of U235. But here in 1939 Bohr stopped short of working out the consequences of his own theory; clearly, the assumption that the critical mass of U235 would be huge prevented Bohr from proceeding to ascertain the mass required for a fast-neutron bomb. This may seem

18. "Recent Investigations of the Transmutations of Atomic Nuclei" (1939; published in 1941), printed in N. Bohr, *Collected Works*, ed. E. Rudinger, R. Peierls, et al. (Amsterdam, 1986), 9:443–466, esp. 465 f. See Pais, *Niels Bohr's Times*, pp. 462 f. M. Gowing, *Britain and Atomic Energy, 1939–1945* (London, 1964), p. 248, mentions the lecture being given at Birmingham. Cf. Otto Frisch's recollection of Bohr's argument that (in ordinary uranium) "no effective nuclear explosion [was] possible because the only way to get a chain reaction would be through the use of slow neutrons" and this was too slow a reaction to achieve an explosion; O. R. Frisch, "Recollections," in *All in Our Time*, ed. J. Taylor (Chicago, 1975), p. 54.

19. The manuscript is printed in Bohr, *Collected Works*, 9:395–398. For Bohr's subsequent opinions of 1941–43, formed under the impact of Heisenberg's notorious visit to Copenhagen in October 1941, see chap. 10.

incomprehensible in the light of later knowledge, but the obvious is sometimes invisible; as Bohr had remarked when Frisch originally explained to him his insight that the process Hahn had observed was in fact fission, "What fools we all have been!"[20] Moreover, Bohr would have felt that the sole experimental measurement of the probability of fast neutrons fissioning U235 (the fission cross-section) confirmed his intuition about the impracticably large size of a critical mass of U235; in his fundamental analysis of fission published on 1 September 1939, he had cited a measurement reported by Merle Tuve to a Princeton meeting on 23 June that would have produced a very low figure for the fission cross-section of separated U235.[21]

But if a pure U235 bomb seemed to Bohr to be impractical and a U238 one impossible, several physicists in 1939 thought it might perhaps be feasible to devise an alternative arrangement for a uranium bomb. Some of these proposals depended on the use of uranium in which the percentage of U235 isotope had been enriched and the addition of a moderating substance such as paraffin or water so as to slow down the neutrons to energies where they could more efficiently fission the enriched U235. Other plans suggested the utilization of large masses of uranium, in which fast neutrons stood a better chance of fissioning appreciable numbers of U238 nuclei.[22] Calculations relating to a slow-neutron bomb were carried out by J. B. Fisk and W. Shockley at Bell Telephone Laboratories in mid-1940. In the report, the two scientists first investigated the case of a reactor: "We note that with pure U235 . . . the minimum radius of sphere is still greater than $R_o = 33$ cm." Then, in part II, they reported that

> in addition to increasing the likelihood of a chain reaction, the layer structure may decrease the influence of thermal control upon the reaction and for this reason increase the potentialities of uranium as a high explosive. . . .

Rather Vague Reflections Concerning
the Explosive Aspect of the Chain Reaction

> . . . The energies involved in this state of affairs—uranium layers at several million degrees—would appear to be of highly explosive character.[23]

20. Quoted in Rhodes, *Atomic Bomb*, p. 261.

21. Bohr and Wheeler, "Mechanism of Nuclear Fission," 444. For Chadwick's skepticism about the Tuve measurement and the manner in which Frisch and Peierls arrived at a far larger cross-section by theoretical reasoning, see below, and also chap. 5.

22. Cf. Edward Teller's September 1940 estimate of more than 30 tons of natural uranium being required for a fast-neutron explosion, cited in R. G. Hewlett and O. E. Anderson, Jr., *A History of the United States Atomic Energy Commission*, vol. 1, *The New World, 1939–1946* (University Park, Pa., 1962), p. 32.

23. J. B. Fisk and W. Shockley, "A Study of Uranium as a Source of Power" (July–September 1940), I, p. 15; II, abstract and pp. 10, 12–13; in NA, RG 227, OSRD/S-1 (Bush-Conant Files), Microfilm Publication M-1392, roll 11, folder 170. Cf. S. Weart, "Secrecy, Simultaneous Discovery, and the Theory of Nuclear Reactors," *American Journal of Physics* 45 (1977): 1049–1060, at p. 1056.

These uranium bombs were in effect "reactor-bombs," bizarre schemes that are difficult to comprehend in the light of our current knowledge of the problem, but which sprang naturally to mind in the context of the incomplete and sometimes opaque understanding of atomic energy that prevailed in the United States and Europe in the years immediately following Hahn's discovery.[24] In reading these papers, the questions of whether an author is referring to natural uranium, $U238$ or $U235$, or a mixture, and whether fast or slow neutrons are under consideration must constantly be kept in mind. Many promising remarks that seem to propose a fast-neutron reaction in $U235$ actually do not do so at all, when they are read closely and in historical context. This will become obvious if we cast a rapid glance at the suggestions made about atomic bombs in various countries in 1939.

THE UNITED STATES

When the sensational news of fission reached America, the Hungarian-Jewish émigré Leo Szilard believed that his visionary conjectures dating back to 1933 about chain reactions and atomic power were at last on the verge of realization. By early March 1939 Szilard had applied for a patent on a reactor device using slow-neutron fission in ordinary uranium that could also be adapted to produce "explosions," though of a far lesser order of magnitude than a true nuclear bomb.[25] But later that month he began to consider how fast neutrons might be used to achieve far more destructive explosions. On 31 March 1939 he wrote to Victor Weisskopf that "it appears very likely that a fast neutron bomb will be too heavy to be carried by aeroplane," though it might be transported by boat. Szilard here seems to have in mind a bomb that would depend on the fast-neutron fission of uranium, particularly $U238$.[26] In a memorandum attached to Einstein's famous letter to President Roosevelt of 15 August 1939 advocating research on the atomic bomb, Szilard pursued this conjecture about a fast-neutron bomb:

> At present it is an open question whether such a chain reaction can also be made to work with fast neutrons which are not slowed down.

24. S. Weart, *Nuclear Fear* (Cambridge, Mass., 1988), pp. 78–81. Stanley Weintraub has brought to my attention an anonymous editorial (by C. P. Snow), "A New Means of Destruction," in the British scientific magazine *Discovery*, n.s., 2 (September 1939): 443–444, which bluntly states that "it is no secret: laboratories in the United States, Germany, France and England have been working on it feverishly since the spring. . . . In America, as soon as the possibility came to light, it seemed so urgent that a representative of American physicists telephoned the White House and arranged an interview with the President. That was about three months ago. . . . The principle is simple . . . a slow neutron knocks a uranium nucleus into approximately two pieces, and two or more *faster* neutrons are discharged. . . . These faster neutrons go on to disintegrate other uranium nuclei. . . . If it is not made in America this year, it may be next year in Germany. There is no ethical problem. . . . "

25. L. Szilard, *The Collected Works of Leo Szilard*, ed. B. T. Feld and G. W. Szilard (Cambridge, Mass., 1972), 1:464 ff., 656, 671 ff., 680. For Szilard's idea of a reactor-bomb, see below, chap. 10.

26. Quoted in Badash, Hodes, and Tiddens, "Nuclear Fission," p. 214.

There is reason to believe that, if fast neutrons could be used, it would be easy to construct extremely dangerous bombs. The destructive power of these bombs can only roughly be estimated, but there is no doubt that it would go far beyond all military conceptions. It appears likely that such bombs would be too heavy to be transported be airplane, but still they could be transported by boat and exploded in port with disastrous results.[27]

A subsequent memorandum of April 1940 to Alexander Sachs, his contact with Roosevelt, makes it clear that Szilard was thinking of a fast-neutron bomb using predominantly U238, not pure U235:

A chain reaction of this second type [i.e., one "in which neutrons are not slowed down and in which the bulk of the ordinary uranium could be utilized"] would make it possible to bring about explosions of extraordinary intensity.[28]

In his "Recollections" Szilard recalled how this notion of a fast-neutron bomb using ordinary uranium took him into a dead end:

During this early period I was also haunted by the fear that it might be possible to detonate uranium metal by fast neutrons, if a sufficiently large quantity of this material were assembled. . . . Whether or not a chain reaction can be maintained depends on how fast the neutrons emitted from fission are slowed down so that they might lose their effectiveness [in splitting] further uranium [U238]. Dr. [?] and I therefore pursued a side-line investigation to determine how fast uranium metal slows down fast neutrons. We did not stop this investigation until we were satisfied that uranium metal could not be used to make a bomb.[29]

As to using fast neutrons in pure U235, Szilard was convinced, like everyone else, that this would also require a huge critical mass (though with hindsight he blamed his blindness on the scientific blockages caused by excessive security).

It so happens that I actually measured the cross-section of U235 for medium-velocity neutrons in the first half of 1939. From this I could have computed how much U235 it takes to make a bomb. The amount seemed fairly large and I did not know that it was possible to separate such quantities of U235. Urey's contract specified that he was not supposed to discuss his results with Fermi and me, who were not cleared. Therefore we were not able to put two and two together and come up with a simple statement that bombs could be made out of reasonable quantities of U235. . . .

After November 1940 Urey was not free to continue these discussions [on centrifuge]. I felt so discouraged by this that I failed even to work up and write down some earlier nuclear measurements which Zinn and I made in 1939. These measurements gave information on the fission cross-section of U235. Had our values

27. Szilard, *Collected Works*, 1:202 f.
28. L. Szilard, *Leo Szilard: His Version of the Facts*, ed. S. R. Weart and G. W. Szilard (Cambridge, Mass., 1978), p. 125.
29. Ibid., p. 177.

been known to Urey and had we been aware that separation of the uranium isotopes would receive adequate support, we certainly would have gone through the simple calculations.[30]

The reigning confusion among physicists of the time about the basic principle of the atomic bomb is well attested by Szilard's hindsighted claim here that in 1939 he had measured the fission cross-section for medium-velocity neutrons in U235, but had not gone on to make the "simple calculations" of the critical mass of a U235 bomb![31] Those scientists who did, like Fisk and Shockley at Bell, came up with wrong answers: "We note that with pure U235 ... the minimum radius of sphere is still greater than $R_o = 33$ cm"—a critical radius approximating to tons of U235![32]

FRANCE

In France research into a uranium bomb pursued a parallel course. One of its first fruits was the development of a technique for calculating the critical mass of uranium required for initiating and sustaining a chain reaction. In March 1939 Francis Perrin was recruited by the Halban/Joliot team to give advice on the theory of chain reactions. In a paper of 1 May, Perrin introduced the concept of a critical size—the minimum amount of uranium needed for a self-sustaining chain reaction, in which the rate of neutron multiplication by fission would exceed the loss of neutrons by capture, scattering, and escape. Perrin's work, however, seems to have been carried out in ignorance of Bohr's theory about U235 as the main fissionable material; his formula for the critical size for an explosive chain reaction was based solely on fissioning by fast neutrons in uranium oxide, and he saw no need in a bomb to slow down the neutrons to enhance their fissioning of U235. Assuming (wrongly) that all fast neutrons would fission on collision with uranium nuclei, Perrin calculated that a uranium bomb would have a critical radius of 130 cm, approximating to 40 tons of uranium oxide. (It is reported that the idea of carrying out a secret experiment in the Sahara was discussed at the time.)

Despite its apparent impracticability, the French scientists devised a design for a uranium bomb for which they submitted a patent application on 4 May 1939. The critical mass for a fast-neutron reaction in uranium powder is given as "several tens of tons," that for denser uranium metal as "some tons"—both figures being reducible if a tamper is employed or if hydrogenous material can be utilized. The bomb is clearly a very active reactor, since its explosion is prevented by the presence of cadmium and other neutron absorbers. The rapid assembly of the critical mass would be achieved by means of the compression effected by conven-

30. Ibid., pp. 144, 177.
31. Ibid., p. 177.
32. Fisk and Shockley, "Study of Uranium," pt. I, p. 15.

tional explosives. The "design" is very vague and makes no mention of Bohr's recently announced theory that U235 is the prime fissionable isotope. This omission was rectified by a secret paper of 30 October 1939 (sealed until 1948) that recommended the use of enriched uranium and deuterium in a reactor. But then the prospect of a bomb receded as Perrin became aware that any explosion in such a large mass would be premature and inefficient: "We saw clearly that when the chain reaction began to develop, before any extremely violent explosion could occur, the rise in temperature would blow up the system [and] disperse it." Joliot's team therefore switched their efforts to the development of a slower but controlled reaction, exploiting the fission of unseparated uranium by thermal neutrons.[33]

BRITAIN

The French work, notably the Halban-Joliot estimate of neutron reproduction, had an impact on British physicists, prompting G. P. Thomson in April 1939 to approach the government for uranium for experimental purposes. In May 1939 A. M. Tyndall reported to the Committee of Imperial Defence that a uranium bomb might well be decisive in the next war; Tyndall's report worried about the vagueness of vital data, but suggested that a large mass would be needed, as well as conjecturing that U235 was the active isotope.[34] With war imminent, in August 1939 Thomson wrote a false report (to be planted with the Germans) on the successful explosion of "half-ton uranium bombs" using a hydrogen mixture and cadmium "trigger," which it was hoped would deter Germany from war. Nevertheless, in a covering letter Thomson informed Sir Henry Tizard that "the serious side of the work goes well, and I see no reason to change my view that it will work."[35] By the time war broke out, however, Thomson had concluded that no amount of uranium oxide in water would produce a nuclear explosion, though a suggestion was made that perhaps a 15 to 20% enrichment of U235 might work.[36]

Meanwhile, at Birmingham, Rudolf Peierls had refined Perrin's formula for

33. F. Perrin, "Calcul relatif aux conditions éventuelles de transmutation en chaîne de l'uranium," *Comptes Rendus de l'Académie des Sciences* 208 (1 May 1939): 1394–1396. A second paper of the same title (ibid. 208 [15 May 1939]: 1573–1575) turns to the theory of reactors and moderators. For the bomb proposal of May 1939 by Halban, Joliot, Kowarski, and Perrin ("Perfectionnement aux charges explosives"), see F. Joliot-Curie and I. Joliot-Curie, *Oeuvres scientifiques complètes* (Paris, 1961), pp. 687–691; the file of 30 October 1939 is printed ibid., pp. 673–677. Perrin's later remark comes from an interview of 1973, cited in S. Weart, *Scientists in Power* (Cambridge, Mass., 1979), pp. 94, 305. Cf. Weart, "Secrecy," pp. 1052 f. For the Sahara test see B. Goldschmidt, *Atomic Rivals* (New Brunswick, N.J., 1990), pp. 49 ff.

34. A. M. Tyndall, *The Possibility of Producing an Atomic Bomb*, 3 May 1939, in PRO, AB 1/9 (summarized in AB 1/37). Cited also in R. W. Clark, *The Greatest Power on Earth* (New York, 1980), p. 59.

35. R. W. Clark, *Tizard* (Cambridge, Mass., 1965), pp. 184–186.

36. G. P. Thomson, "Anglo-U.S. Cooperation on Atomic Energy," *BAS* 9, no. 2 (1953): 46–48. Weart, "Secrecy," p. 1052. Gowing, *Britain and Atomic Energy*, pp. 34 ff., 39 f. R. W. Clark, *The Birth of the Bomb* (London, 1961), pp. 36 f.

critical size by a more sophisticated theory of neutron multiplication and diffusion. Peierls stressed that for simplicity's sake he had considered only the case of fast neutrons, but conceded (with acknowledgment to Bohr) that the bulk of the fission effect was probably due to slow neutrons in U235. This understanding seems to have convinced Peierls that his formula could have no significance for the development of an atomic bomb, and so he submitted a paper with his "rather academic" calculation to a Cambridge journal in June 1939.[37] Peierls's new colleague at Birmingham, Otto Frisch, "saw no reason against having my paper published, since Bohr had shown that an atomic bomb was not a realistic proposition."[38] According to the formula, the critical mass of natural uranium would be "of the order of tons. It therefore appeared to me that the paper had no relevance to a nuclear weapon. The whole mass . . . would have been the size of the present Windscale reactor."[39] (In the summer of 1940 Frisch and Peierls actually calculated that a critical mass for fast neutrons in unseparated uranium would be "at least 28 tons").[40] As it happened, Peierls's Cambridge paper was not published until October, after war had broken out, and it does not seem to have been known in Germany during the war, nor, to judge from the lack of citations, elsewhere in 1939–40 except to the British nuclear physicist James Chadwick and local readers.[41] But, as we shall see, the paper was in the spring of 1940 to play a crucial role in the invention of nuclear weapons.

Meanwhile, Frisch himself during the winter of 1939 considered further the impossibility of creating an atomic bomb in a review of the year's developments in nuclear fission that he was asked to prepare for the British Chemical Society. Here he pointed out that Perrin's critical-size formula was flawed by its assumption that fast neutrons would maintain their energy even after collisions until they could fission a U238 nucleus. But this was mistaken; such collisions greatly reduced the energy of the neutrons (inelastic scattering), leaving them incapable of fissioning U238. Nor could the neutrons survive to the low thermal energies associated with the fission of U235 nuclei, for they were intercepted on the way down and simply captured by the U238 without fissioning. Enriching the U235 even tenfold would probably achieve a chain reaction, but not an explosive one. Consider-

37. R. Peierls, "Critical Conditions in Neutron Multiplication," *Proceedings of the Cambridge Philosophical Society* 35 (1939): 610–615. A major motive for writing the paper was to clarify the concept of "critical size." See the interview with Peierls, 11–13 August 1969, pp. 79–81 (OHI).

38. R. Peierls, *Bird of Passage* (Princeton, 1985), p. 153. Peierls (OHI interview, p. 80) mentions that Frisch had reassured him that the Bohr-Wheeler attribution of fission to U235 meant that a chain reaction was impossible in unseparated uranium.

39. From a letter quoted in Clark, *Birth of the Bomb*, p. 43. See also Clark, *Greatest Power on Earth*, p. 85.

40. Gowing, *Britain and Atomic Energy*, p. 55.

41. Peierls was surprised when Philip Moon, who was on the government uranium committee, asked him for a copy of the paper; Peierls, OHI interview, p. 90.

ing a slow-neutron bomb, Frisch concluded (on the basis of Bohr's arguments) that enriching U235

> would not, however, form an effective basis for the construction of a super-bomb, at any rate according to present knowledge, because the reaction is not fast enough. The time required for a neutron to become thermal is about 10^{-5} sec.; a further 10^{-4} sec. is lost, on an average, before the neutron hits a uranium [U235] nucleus. So the "reproduction cycle" takes about 10^{-4} sec., and the time required to double the "population" of neutrons is probably several times longer. As soon as the temperature has reached several thousand degrees the container will be broken, and in a time of 10^{-4} sec. the parts of the bomb will be well separated. The neutrons will then be able to escape and the reaction will stop. Consequently, the energy liberated will be only about sufficient to break the container or, in other words, of the same order as with ordinary explosives.[42]

The opinions of the most distinguished British nuclear physicist of the time, James Chadwick, exemplify the foggy conception of atomic bomb principles that was pervasive in the international community of physicists in 1939. Approached for advice by the government in October 1939, Chadwick replied that perhaps "several tons" of pure uranium were required and that he understood a bomb to be a thermal-neutron fission process. He believed an explosive chain reaction to be possible with natural uranium and promised to pursue the matter.[43] A second letter of 5 December was more developed: By now, Chadwick had seen a further paper of the Halban and Joliot team and also read Peierls's refinement of the critical-size formula. He now believed that two types of explosion were feasible. The first depended on fission by thermal neutrons in a uranium and hydrogen (water) mixture—namely, a reactor-bomb. The hydrogen material was needed as a moderator to prevent the neutrons from being captured by the U238 nuclei without fis-

42. O. R. Frisch, "Nuclear Fission," in *Annual Reports on the Progress of Chemistry for 1939* (London: The Chemical Society, 1940), 7–24, at pp. 16 f. In his article "Early Steps towards the Chain Reaction," in *Rudolf Peierls and Theoretical Physics* (Oxford, 1977), pp. 18–27, Frisch relates (p. 22) that "Bohr had advanced very good arguments—which I quoted—that such a reaction could not lead to an explosion of any significance. . . . Bohr had pointed out that U238 would probably not support such a reaction. . . . The only chance he could see of creating the chain reaction would be to add some kind of moderator . . . [to] bring the neutrons down to the very low energy where they were likely to cause fission in U235" (but that would be too slow for a bomb). See also the Frisch interview of 3 May 1967, p. 39 (OHI), for his citation of Bohr for having shown that the only way to make a chain reaction was by the use of slowed-down neutrons, which ruled out an explosion.

43. Chadwick to E. V. Appleton, Secretary of the Department of Scientific and Industrial Research, 31 October 1939, PRO, CAB 104/186.

M. Gowing, "James Chadwick and the Atomic Bomb," *Notes and Records of the Royal Society of London* 47 (1993): 79–92, has much of interest on Chadwick's involvement in the atomic bomb project after 1940, but is disappointingly imprecise on the subject of his thinking and activities in 1939–40. Chadwick's change of mind seems to be attributed somewhat improbably to a belated reading of Bohr and Wheeler, and his correspondence with Appleton, and later in 1943 with Niels Bohr, is not accurately analyzed.

sion. A chain reaction was probable in the right arrangement, though "perhaps more than a ton of uranium [would be] required." However, the second proposal was for a fast-neutron explosive chain reaction in uranium. Chadwick felt that this would be inhibited only by the effect of inelastic scattering—that is, by collisions in which neutrons lost energy and became subject to simple capture by U238. This meant that Chadwick was thinking of the fast-neutron fission of U235, but within a mass of unseparated uranium. "I think the explosion is almost certain to occur if one had enough uranium . . . from about 1 ton to 30 or 40, according to the data adopted."[44] Curiously, in a later interview Chadwick recollected that he had been thinking not of unseparated uranium, but of U235 itself.[45] Though this is not evident in the text of the letter, it is quite possible that indeed he had had in mind the case of separated U235 as well as that of the U235 in unseparated uranium. In any event, relying on an erroneous measurement of the fast-neutron cross-section in unseparated uranium reported by Bohr,[46] Chadwick derived the cross-section for U235 and then, with his colleague Maurice Pryce, calculated, on the basis of the Peierls formula, that "getting on for a ton of U235" would be needed. Chadwick later recalled: "Well, it certainly would have made a hell of an explosion, but it was not feasible to think that one could separate a ton of U235. So when I wrote to Appleton, I said something to the effect that there didn't seem to be much in either possibility."[47]

In this letter Chadwick had made no specific mention of U235 in the context of fast-neutron fission, though it seems from his later recollection that this was what was actually in his mind, as we have seen. This lack of clarity extended to other aspects of his conception of a bomb, which is characteristic of early nuclear-weapons thinking in general: First, Chadwick is primarily considering the use of natural uranium for a bomb, with or without a moderator; and second, the critical masses for a bomb proposed—even for one made of pure U235—are grotesquely huge and apparently preclude the construction of a practicable bomb that might be carried in an aircraft. Not surprisingly, the government found Chadwick's comments very reassuring.[48] But, uneasy about this reassurance, Chadwick was to reflect further on the matter and, as we shall see in the next chapter, to have a dramatic change of mind.

The conventional wisdom, therefore, in Britain and in many other countries by

44. Chadwick to Appleton, 5 December 1939, PRO, CAB 21/1262. Cf. Gowing, *Britain and Atomic Energy*, pp. 38 f.; Clark, *Birth of the Bomb*, p. 46. (A. Brown, *The Neutron and the Bomb: A Biography of Sir James Chadwick* [Oxford, 1997], p. 180 ff., cites discussions on the fast-neutron bomb between Chadwick and his colleague Joseph Rotblat.)

45. In an extended interview of 1967 Chadwick recalled that the critical mass of 1 ton for a fast-neutron bomb pertains to U235, not unseparated uranium (interview of 3 May 1967, p. 103 [OHI]). The letter itself, however, does not specify U235.

46. For the measurement by Merle Tuve, see below, chap. 5.

47. Chadwick, OHI interview, pp. 102 f.

48. See the Appleton/Hankey/Chatfield correspondence in PRO, CAB 21/1262.

late 1939 when the initial flush of enthusiasm generated by the Perrin paper and other publications had worn off, was that an atomic bomb was theoretically only a slight possibility; the practical design of one was something that would have to wait for the remote future. Thus Churchill, after a briefing from his scientific adviser Lindemann, had written on 5 August 1939 to the Secretary for Air to caution Cabinet against fearing a new super weapon: "The chain process can take place only if the uranium is concentrated in a large mass. . . . As soon as the energy develops, it will explode with a mild detonation before any really violent effects can be produced."[49] As Lord Hankey remarked after receiving news of the Chadwick correspondence of December 1939, "I gather that we may sleep fairly comfortably in our beds."[50]

GERMANY

In Germany scientists had responded very enthusiastically to the suggestions about critical mass and neutron reproduction put forward in the Perrin and Joliot papers. After Halban and Joliot's optimistic findings about neutron reproduction had appeared in *Nature* on 22 April 1939, initiatives were taken by two separate groups of German scientists to obtain serious government support of research into nuclear power. A speech to the Göttingen physics colloquium in late April by Wilhelm Hanle on a "uranium burner" had moved his superior Georg Joos to write to the Reich Minister of Education on the subject. This resulted in a conference being held on 29 April under the chairmanship of Abraham Esau, the head of the German National Bureau of Standards. The meeting decided to set up a "Uranium Club" (*Uranverein*) and recommended that uranium stocks be secured and their export banned. At the same time and independently, Paul Harteck of Hamburg University urged the War Office to pursue research into the explosive potential of uranium. By the summer an office for nuclear research had been set up under Kurt Diebner in the Weapons Research Office of the Army Weapons Department.[51] German nuclear research thus had the backing of two government offices within the Education and War Ministries before the outbreak of war in September 1939.

The most complete exposition of German nuclear knowledge in this initial period is to be found in an article published in June 1939 by Siegfried Flügge (a col-

49. Winston Churchill, *The Gathering Storm* (New York, 1948), pp. 386 ff.

50. Hankey to Lord Chatfield, 12 December 1939, PRO, CAB 21/1262.

A memorandum of 16 May 1940 from Professor A. V. Hill, then in Washington, concludes that the U235 reaction in natural uranium is too slow for a bomb, and reports that the Americans think the idea of a bomb is "a waste of time" at present (PRO, AB 1/9).

51. D. Irving, *The German Atomic Bomb: The History of Nuclear Research in Nazi Germany*, 2d ed. (New York, 1983; published in the United Kingdom as *The Virus House* [London, 1967]), pp. 34–44; M. Walker, *German National Socialism and the Quest for Nuclear Power, 1939–1945* (Cambridge, 1989), pp. 17 f.

league of Heisenberg's at Hahn's institute in Berlin), entitled "Can the Energy Content of the Atomic Nucleus Be Exploited Technically?" Flügge tantalizingly estimated that one cubic meter of uranium oxide contained enough energy to lift a cubic kilometer of water 27 km high. The essential condition for the conversion of this mass into energy was whether it could "in a space of time of less that 1/100 [*sic*] second be set free." Flügge envisaged two different species of explosions in reactor-bombs, based on different times and different materials and neutrons.

1. The first type takes place within one ten-thousandth of a second, occurs in natural uranium metal, and is effected mainly by fast neutrons. "In less than 10^{-4} seconds the whole of the uranium is converted. The liberation of the energy thus happens in such a short time that it produces an extraordinarily violent explosion."
2. The second type is achieved within one-tenth of a second, but it happens in uranium oxide mixed with a moderator, and the agents are slow neutrons. "The conversion of the uranium takes place in about 1/10th of a second. The liberation of the energy proceeds certainly more slowly than with fast neutrons, but it is still nevertheless explosive."[52]

Flügge's fastest time of 10^{-4} (one ten-thousandth of a second) for the explosive chain reaction in his "reactor-bomb" was, as Frisch and Bohr realized, far too slow. By then, the bomb would have expanded and the reaction come to a halt. As we shall see, a time of the order of 10^{-8} seconds (one one-hundred-millionth of a second) was more realistic. Moreover, Flügge shared the widespread opinion of physicists (Bohr apart) in 1939 that an explosion in natural uranium might be conceivable. His notion of a slower explosion in a reactor-bomb using slow neutrons in a mixture of uranium oxide and moderator is also typical of the context of uranium-bomb thinking in 1939. There is no evidence that anyone in Germany disagreed with the article's premises when it appeared in the summer of 1939. (The major proposals offered in 1939 for a uranium bomb are summarized in table 1.)

That goes for Heisenberg too. Soon after the appearance of Flügge's paper, Heisenberg visited the United States and discussed the idea of a uranium bomb with Fermi and other physicists. They agreed it to be a rather remote and long-term proposition.[53] But things were to change after his return to Germany and the

52. S. Flügge, "Kann der Energieinhalt der Atomkerne technisch nutzbar gemacht werden?" *Die Naturwissenschaften* 27 (9 June 1939): 402–410. Quotations are taken from pp. 403, 406, 407. A popular newspaper version, entitled "Die Ausnutzung der Atomenergie," was published by Flügge in the *Deutsche Allgemeine Zeitung*, no. 385–386, "Beiblatt," 15 August 1939. Here Flügge indicates that the chain reaction would be explosive in a mass of "a few meters" diameter, evidently of unseparated uranium, for he does not show any awareness of Bohr's finding that U235 is the primary fissionable isotope (translated in *HPNS*, p. 197).

53. For Heisenberg's American visit, see below, chap. 18. One must use with caution Heisenberg's recollection of the meeting in his *Physics and Beyond: Encounters and Conversations*, trans. (New York, 1972), pp. 169 ff., written after the war. His intention there is to justify his participation in the Nazi wartime

Table of Uranium Bomb Proposals in 1939

	Uranium/ U238	Moderator	Enriched U235	U235	Fast	Slow	Critical Mass
Bohr			*	*			large
Fermi			*	*	?	?	500 kg U235
Szilard	*	*				*	tons
Teller (1940)	*				*		30 tons
Perrin							
1st Proposal	*				*		40 tons
2d Proposal	*				*		tons
Thomson			*				large
Peierls	*					*	tons
Chadwick							
1st Proposal	*					*	tons
2d Proposal	*	*				*	1 ton+
3d Proposal			?	?	*		1–40 tons
Flügge							
1st Proposal	*				*		tons
2d Proposal	*	*				*	tons

Column headings: unseparated uranium/U238; moderator; enriched U235; pure U235; fast neutrons; slow neutrons; critical mass.

outbreak of war. September 1939 saw the hurried formation of a unified uranium-bomb research team under the control of the Army Weapons Department, which immediately co-opted Heisenberg as its scientific leader.[54] Like Bohr, Fermi,

---

uranium project by arguing that he did not believe a bomb could be achieved within the duration of the coming war and therefore he might work on it with a clear conscience. (See D. C. Cassidy, *Uncertainty: The Life and Science of Werner Heisenberg* [New York, 1992], pp. 414, 420 f.) Whether or not this was his true thinking at the time may be debated, but he certainly threw himself into the project with enthusiasm, and it seemed for a time in 1939–40 that a bomb might indeed be feasible, as shall be seen.

54. For a detailed angry account of how the Education Ministry's Reich Research Council's uranium project was hijacked by the Army Weapons Department, see Abraham Esau's letter of complaint to General Karl Becker of 13 November 1939, Goudsmit Papers, AIP, box 25, folder 15 (IMF 29-098/101).

Frisch, and many others, Heisenberg was well aware of the theoretical objections to the idea of an atomic bomb, but he aggressively set himself to overcome them. By the end of 1939, he had worked out the theoretical basis of a nuclear reactor and thought up the germ of a twofold approach to the design of an atomic bomb. But his theorizing only convinced him of the impracticality of the enterprise. Moreover, one of his approaches to the bomb was a misconceived reactor-bomb, while the other failed to consider properly the nature of a U235 bomb. It was these scientific flaws that deterred him from launching a major effort to develop a German atomic bomb. For the duration of the war, Heisenberg never felt impelled to amend in a serious way his initial analysis of the bomb, even though he did add a third approach based on plutonium. It was only in August 1945 that the fact of Hiroshima forced him at last to recognize that the Allies must have come up with a different, realistic solution to the problem of devising an atomic bomb.

CHAPTER 5

The Frisch-Peierls Solution, 1940

Wrapped up in an overcoat in his freezing room at Birmingham in the winter of 1939, Otto Frisch had written his reassuring Chemical Society report concluding that a slow-neutron uranium bomb was an impossibility. But he could not let go of the problem, and finally in February 1940 the inspiration came to him.

> However, by writing this article, I had been made to think about the problem much more thoroughly than before. I had become aware of Peierls's calculation and I asked him for the formula, and just sort of playfully I put in an estimated cross-section for U235 . . . the result was a critical mass of the order of a pound or so.[1]

> After writing that report I wondered . . . if one could . . . produce enough U235 to make a truly explosive chain reaction possible, not dependent on slow neutrons. How much of the isotope would be needed? I used a formula derived by . . . Perrin and refined by Peierls. . . . To my amazement it was very much smaller than I had expected; it was not a matter of tons, but something like a pound or two.
> Of course, I discussed that result with Peierls at once. . . . We stared at each other and realized that an atomic bomb might after all be possible.[2]

> I had always thought in terms of tons, without really thinking much, because one doesn't need a Peierls formula; one needs a bit of common sense to get a critical size, an approximate one.[3]

Frisch had found a way of conceiving a practicable fast-neutron chain reaction that had eluded his international colleagues in 1939–40, who had failed in their

1. O. R. Frisch, "Early Steps towards the Chain Reaction," in *Rudolf Peierls and Theoretical Physics*, Progress in Nuclear Physics, vol. 13 (Oxford, 1977), pp. 18–27, esp. p. 22.
2. O. R. Frisch, *What Little I Remember* (Cambridge, 1979), p. 126.
3. O. R. Frisch, interview, 3 May 1967, p. 39 (OHI).

attempts to harness the rapidity of fast neutrons (which may travel ten thousand times faster than slow ones) to the design of a nuclear explosion. The conceptual breakthrough here is camouflaged by Frisch's light reduction of the problem to one of inserting the likely cross-section in Peierls's formula. Frisch would never have thought in the first place of asking Peierls for a formula into which he could insert data for fast-neutron fission of U235 had he not already perceived that fast neutrons would play an important role in the fissioning of pure U235. In other words, Frisch had already asked himself the fundamental conceptual questions: Would the chain reaction proceed differently in a mass of pure U235 than in a mixture of U235 and U238? Would U235 be fissioned effectively by fast neutrons in its pure state in a way that it was not in a mixture?

Peierls recalls how they elaborated the solution together, using his 1939 formula to calculate, first, the critical mass of U235, and second, the rate at which the reaction would proceed (and hence its effectiveness as an explosion):

> Then one day, in February or March 1940, Frisch said, "Suppose someone gave you a quantity of pure 235 isotope of uranium—what would happen?" We started working out the consequences. The work of Bohr and Wheeler seemed to suggest that every neutron that hits a 235 nucleus should produce fission. Since the number of secondary neutrons per fission had been measured approximately, we had all the data to insert in my formula for the critical size, and we were amazed how small this turned out to be. We estimated the critical size to be about a pound, whereas speculations concerned with natural uranium had tended to come out with tons. . . . That still left the question how far the chain reaction would go before the developing pressure would disperse the uranium. A rough estimate—on the back of the proverbial envelope—showed that a substantial fraction of the uranium would be split.[4]

We were staggered to find that the critical size, or mass, was only pounds, instead of the tons one intuitively expected after thinking about reactors.[5]

With pure U235, in fact, an almost qualitative shift took place in the rate of fission and neutron multiplication, which went counter to all prevailing expectations of critical mass:

> Now, one was used to thinking of critical mass in terms of tons of ordinary uranium. And you don't intuitively appreciate how much the fact that a factor of a hundred in the concentration means increasing the effective cross-section by something like a

4. R. Peierls, *Bird of Passage: Recollections of a Physicist* (Princeton, 1985), pp. 154 f. See also R. W. Clark, *The Birth of the Bomb* (London, 1961), pp. 51 ff.; idem, *The Greatest Power on Earth* (London, 1980), pp. 88 f.; R. Peierls, interview, 11–13 August 1969, pp. 90 f. (OHI).

5. R. Peierls, "Reflections on the Discovery of Fission," *Nature* 342 (21–28 December 1989): 852–854. For Bohr's influence on the assumption that the U235 critical mass would be huge, see Clark, *Birth of the Bomb*, p. 39.

hundred, which means almost a hundred in the linear dimension, and therefore a fantastic factor in the mass.[6]

The key here to Frisch and Peierls's solution lay in their understanding of the implications of the Niels Bohr articles of 1939 on fission—above all, the concept of the continuous fissionability of U235 by neutrons of all energies, not just slow ones. This meant that the various factors that militated against fast-neutron fission of U235 in mixtures—such as capture by U238, inelastic scattering—could be discounted. Even if a fast neutron were scattered on hitting a U235 nucleus, the time taken before its next strike would be very short (2.6×10^{-9} seconds).

> We had read the paper of Bohr-Wheeler and had understood it, and it seemed to convince us that in those circumstances for neutrons in U235 the cross-section would be dominated by fission, and that scattering and . . . capture cross-sections and so on would be negligible. . . . Then also you could reasonably assume that the total cross-section for not too low energies would be the geometric cross-section of the nucleus—if a neutron hit the nucleus something was bound to happen.[7]

This fresh conceptualization of the problem gave them a new intuitive and crucially large estimate for the cross-section for U235 fast-neutron fission (10^{-23} cm^2) for insertion in their critical-mass formula. Such a large theoretical estimate went against experimental indications, published in Bohr-Wheeler, that it should be an order of magnitude less. As it happened, the Frisch-Peierls figure was ten times too large and led to a critical mass that was a hundred times too small, though their failure to consider a neutron reflector in the bomb design (Frisch later claimed) compensated somewhat for this. The figure, along with other details, was corrected in the later official British MAUD report to 10^{-24}.[8]

Whether a bomb using the fast-neutron chain reaction would work depended on the rapidity of the process. Would the rate of increase of fissions be fast enough to achieve a large explosion in a very short time? In other words, would a sufficient amount of the U235's energy be released before the expansion of the explosion brought the chain reaction to a halt?[9] Frisch and Peierls estimated that the chain reaction would indeed be fast enough, since each fast neutron would spend only the extremely short time of 2.6×10^{-9} seconds before it was bound to strike a nucleus:

6. Peierls, OHI interview, p. 91.

7. Peierls's discussion in Frisch, "Early Steps," p. 24. Also Peierls, OHI interview, p. 90. Cf. M. Gowing, *Britain and Atomic Energy, 1939–1945* (London, 1964), pp. 41 f., 401.

8. Frisch, "Early Steps," pp. 22, 24 f. For the experimental data of Merle Tuve reported by Bohr, see below, and for Szilard's unpublished measurement of 1939, see above, chap. 4. The 1941 MAUD report is in Gowing, *Britain and Atomic Energy*, pp. 401 ff.

For the underestimate, see below, note 19.

9. See Peierls, OHI interview, p. 91. To analyze the problem, Peierls availed himself of work he had earlier done on hydrodynamics as well as the first steps toward understanding the time scale of neutron multiplication taken in his 1939 Cambridge paper.

In the expression e^t/Tau for the increase of neutron density with time, [the reaction] would be about 4×10^{-9} seconds, very much shorter than in the case of a chain reaction depending on slow neutrons.[10]

Peierls calculated that there would be time enough for, say, 80 generations of neutrons to fission ($1 \times 2 \times 4 \times 8 \times 16 \ldots$) and so produce a big explosion that would use up 2^{80} atoms of U235 within hundred-millionths of a second (10^{-8} seconds).[11] The tremendous rapidity of a fast-neutron explosion overwhelmed quickly the escape of neutrons from the surface of the critical mass before they had time to affect strongly a slow-neutron chain reaction and so prevent an explosion. Some of this had been implicit in Bohr's writings and lectures of 1939, but Bohr evidently had not considered explicitly the kinetics of the chain reaction and the necessity of a fast chain reaction for producing an efficient explosion. It was Frisch and Peierls who drew it all out.

At the suggestion of Mark Oliphant, the Australian head of physics at Birmingham, Frisch and Peierls compiled a memorandum explaining their theoretical considerations and suggesting how the separation of sufficient U235 could be practically achieved within a reasonable time. Oliphant took the memorandum to a fellow member of the Air-Warfare and Defence Committee, George Thomson, and declared himself convinced by his colleagues' proposals.[12] Relying on Thomson's own pessimistic findings that fast neutrons were ineffective in ordinary uranium mixtures, the committee had been about to abandon uranium work, but, impressed by the new proposals, it now set up a special uranium subcommittee (later known as MAUD) that included Oliphant, Thomson, and Chadwick among its membership.[13] To this group on 24 April 1940 the new chairman, Thomson, presented the views of Frisch and Peierls on the possibility of a fast-neutron bomb:

---

10. From their memorandum of 1940, printed in Gowing, *Britain and Atomic Energy*, p. 391. Tau is the time taken to increase neutron density by a factor e (the natural logarithmic base used widely in calculations of exponential growth).

11. R. Rhodes, *The Making of the Atomic Bomb* (New York, 1986), p. 323, says that Peierls was thinking of 80 generations of neutrons, but the source he cites does not specify this number. Nevertheless, 80 was taken as the working figure by both Heisenberg and the Los Alamos team for reasons of scientific convenience. See below, chap. 7.

The Frisch-Peierls memorandum (Gowing, *Britain and Atomic Energy*, p. 391) gives the time for each generation of neutrons as 10^{-9} seconds; the MAUD report gives the time for completion of the final avalanche of fissions as 10^{-8} seconds (Gowing, *Britain and Atomic Energy*, p. 402).

12. The main text of the Frisch-Peierls Memorandum is printed in Gowing, *Britain and Atomic Energy*, pp. 389–393. A nontechnical supplement found among Tizard's papers is printed (along with Oliphant's covering letter) in R. W. Clark, *Tizard* (Cambridge, Mass., 1965), pp. 214–217. Both texts are reprinted in R. Serber, *The Los Alamos Primer* (Berkeley, 1992), pp. 79–88. See M. Oliphant, "The Beginning: Chadwick and the Neutron," *BAS* 38, no. 10 (1982): 14–18, at p. 17, for his statement that he "took" it to Thomson (rather than forwarding it to him through Tizard, as Gowing [*Britain and Atomic Energy*, p. 43] says).

13. Gowing, *Britain and Atomic Energy*, p. 39. Clark, *Birth of the Bomb*, pp. 36 f.

The Committee generally was electrified by the possibility, but Chadwick, who was also a member, was embarrassed, confessing that he had reached similar conclusions, but did not feel justified in reporting them until more was known about the neutron cross-sections from experiments. Peierls and Frisch had used calculated values.[14]

In chapter 4 we left Chadwick in early December 1939 still on the wrong path; he had been thinking either of a slow-neutron reactor-bomb exploiting U235 fission by means of a moderator, or of a fast-neutron explosion of pure or mixed U235 with a critical mass of a ton or more. But at the end of December he glimpsed a new possibility: that the fast-neutron fission of U235 might require a far lesser mass than he had earlier calculated. On 26 December 1939, Chadwick cautiously wrote a personal letter to E. V. Appleton, Secretary of the Department of Scientific and Industrial Research, saying that he thought there might be an interesting military application of uranium fission by fast—not slow—neutrons and asking what work was being done generally on fission. Appleton referred him to Thomson; Chadwick did not tell Thomson about his fast-neutrons idea, and so Thomson merely informed his correspondent that he had done some work of his own on slow neutrons but given up the project.[15]

Chadwick had thus reached the right conclusion about the fast-neutron principle of an atomic bomb, but what he was now pursuing was the critical mass. His own earlier estimate of a ton or more of U235 bothered him, as it had been based on Merle Tuve's very low measurement (as reported by Bohr) of the fission cross-section for fast neutrons of 0.6 MeV in unseparated uranium as being 0.003×10^{-24} cm^2.[16] Deducing that the U235 content alone was being fissioned at this energy, Chadwick had derived the fission cross-section of U235 itself by multiplying Tuve's measurement by 139 (1/139 being taken as the ratio of U235 to other isotopes in unseparated uranium) to arrive at the conclusion that in pure U235 the cross-section would be 0.4×10^{-24} cm^2. This was the value that Chadwick's colleague, Maurice Pryce, had put into the Peierls formula. However, this underestimate of the cross-section by a factor of three, combined with a failure to consider tamping (reflection of escaping neutrons back into the critical mass) and other factors, resulted in a critical mass of a ton or more of U235.[17] (It seems

14. Oliphant, "Chadwick and the Neutron," p. 17.

15. I have not yet been able to locate Chadwick's handwritten letter, which is summarized in Clark, *Birth of the Bomb*, p. 47. (It seems to be alluded to in Gowing, *Britain and Atomic Energy*, p. 42.) Chadwick's papers are to be found at Churchill College, Cambridge, and among the PRO, AB files on atomic energy. In 1969 Chadwick himself was unable to trace the correspondence and presumed it had been destroyed. See Chadwick's interview of 15–21 April 1969, pp. 101, 103 (OHI). It is possible that a copy may have survived in the E. V. Appleton Papers in the University of Edinburgh Library.

16. Reported in N. Bohr and J. A. Wheeler, "The Mechanism of Nuclear Fission," *Physical Review* 56 (1939): 444. See also above, chap. 4.

17. Chadwick, OHI interview, p. 102. S. Weart, *Scientists in Power* (Cambridge, Mass., 1979), pp. 313 f., states that Chadwick's figure for the critical mass was "many kilograms," but Chadwick clearly re-

that Fermi at this point had also been led astray by the same measurement.)[18]

By late December 1939, however, Chadwick began to suspect that the cross-section was "too damn low altogether," on the theoretical ground that it yielded a figure much smaller than what the geometrical cross-section of the nucleus suggested it should be.[19] Chadwick, therefore, began working on his own measurements at Liverpool in the first months of 1940, and it was at this point that he was presented with Frisch and Peierls's proposal.[20] Their proposal must have been quite a shock; it not only presented a new conceptual approach to the problem, but also boldly adopted a value for the fission cross-section of U235 that was enormously greater than that implied by the Tuve measurement (10×10^{-24} cm^2, compared with a mere 0.4×10^{-24} cm^2). Although Chadwick saw no justification for their assumption that in pure U235 neutrons of any energy would be effective, he believed it still a possibility and good reason for urgent investigation of the fissionability of fast neutrons in U235.[21] Thus was the British atomic bomb project proper born.

Frisch and Peierls's breakthrough had stemmed from their ability to ask the right questions about the behavior of fast neutrons and the rapidity of the reaction in pure U235. As the official historian of the British project has written:

> The questions may seem obvious enough today but they were not at the time. In America they were not asked for many months, until after the British work was available. The German physicists, including the brilliant Heisenberg, apparently did not ask them at all. In Britain, by the spring of 1940, practically everyone had more or less ruled out a uranium bomb as a serious proposition for the Second World War.[22]

---

members the figure being of the order of tons, as is borne out by his letter of 5 December, quoted above in chap. 4. See also Gowing, *Britain and Atomic Energy*, pp. 42, 61; the fast-neutron fission discussed at p. 38 refers to Chadwick's earlier suggestion of a fast reaction in ordinary uranium.

18. See Weart, *Scientists in Power*, p. 314.

19. Chadwick suspected that the Tuve cross-section was too small a fraction of the total cross-section of the nucleus to explain the fission phenomenon, given the fact that the total cross-section must have been of the order of the nuclear diameter. (Chadwick, OHI interview, p. 102; for these cross-sections see Serber, *Los Alamos Primer*, pp. 13, 16, 18.) Frisch and Peierls, who seemed to have missed the Tuve reference in Bohr's article, assumed that the fission cross-section would roughly correspond to the geometrical cross-section, which they rounded up to 1×10^{-23} ($= 10 \times 10^{-24}$) and hence arrived at an encouragingly small figure for critical mass of 0.6 kg instead of the true 60 kg or so. (See Peierls, OHI interview, p. 90. Chadwick's memory slips in recollecting [OHI interview, p. 103] that Frisch and Peierls had guessed the fission cross-section to be 2×10^{-24}.) They compensated to some extent for this overestimate, however, by omitting the tamping factor, though not as completely as Frisch and Peierls individually have recalled. Tamping would reduce the mass perhaps by a factor of two or three, to 30 or 20 kg.

20. Chadwick, OHI interview, p. 103.

21. The MAUD Committee learned during the summer of 1940 of new data on the fission cross-section of fast neutrons obtained by the Tuve team at the Carnegie Institution's Department of Terrestrial Magnetism, Washington (report of 27 July 1940, in PRO, AB 1/9).

22. Gowing, *Britain and Atomic Energy*, p. 42. In fact, the feasibility of a fast-neutron uranium bomb with a small critical mass was not understood in the United States until the summer of 1941! See below, chap. 9.

As George Thomson himself put it later: "[An atomic bomb] seemed nearly impossible, and if this conclusion now seems disgraceful blindness, I can only plead that to the end of the war the most distinguished physicists in Germany thought the same."[23]

Only when set in the complicated historical context of the confused state of atomic bomb theorizing that prevailed in 1939–40 may the astonishingly wrong path taken by Heisenberg be comprehended.

23. G. P. Thomson, "Anglo-U.S. Cooperation on Atomic Energy," *BAS* 9, no. 2 (1953): 46–48. Clark, *Birth of the Bomb*, p. 37.

CHAPTER 6

Heisenberg's False Foundations, 1939

The outbreak of war in September 1939 quickly crystallized existing German initiatives for the invention of a uranium fission bomb. On 16 September the Army Weapons Research Office (HWA WaF) held a meeting in Berlin presided over by Kurt Diebner and attended by Heisenberg's former assistant Erich Bagge at which it was decided that Heisenberg himself should be "invited" by military order to the next meeting on 26 September. Here the scientists were conscripted into a serious research project, pursuing theoretical and experimental avenues as well as technological applications. The Uranium Club (*Uranverein*), as it was informally known, came to number about sixty scientists ranging from loyal Nazis like Diebner and Bagge, to those who later described themselves as "apolitical" types such as Heisenberg and Weizsäcker, to genuinely nonpolitical scientists like Hahn and even anti-Nazis like Laue and Gentner. Among the research centers where the project established teams were the Kaiser-Wilhelm-Institutes for Chemistry and Physics in Berlin and several universities including those in Hamburg, Heidelberg, Vienna, and Heisenberg's own Leipzig base.[1] In the course of the war, the project circulated nearly four hundred secret reports (known as "G" reports from their later American numeration), ranging from highly theoretical pa-

---

1. See D. C. Cassidy, *Uncertainty: The Life and Science of Werner Heisenberg* (New York, 1992), pp. 418, 420, 622. General accounts of the German project are M. Walker, *German National Socialism and the Quest for Nuclear Power, 1939–1949* (Cambridge, 1989); D. Irving, *The German Atomic Bomb: The History of Nuclear Research in Nazi Germany*, 2d ed. (New York, 1983); E. Bagge, K. Diebner, and K. Jay, *Von der Uranspaltung bis Calder Hall* (Hamburg, 1957), pp. 22–26. Bagge was one of the main movers of the September meetings, which were chaired by Diebner. For the conflict between the Education Ministry's Reich Research Council (Reichsforschungsrat) and the Army Weapons Department (HWA) over control of the uranium project, see Esau's letter to General Becker of 13 November 1939 (IMF 29-098/101) and K. Zierold, *Forschungsförderung in drei Epochen: Deutsche Forschungsgemeinschaft* (Wiesbaden, 1968), pp. 259 ff.

pers to experimental reports and nontechnical presentations for political and military personnel.[2]

In the two months following his enlistment in the uranium project Heisenberg submerged himself in the scientific literature concerning nuclear fission, and in early December he circulated a long synoptic paper that laid down the theoretical foundation for the wartime German uranium project. This was entitled "The Possibility of Technical Energy Production from Uranium Fission" (G-39), and dated 6 December 1939.[3] It set out for the first time a detailed theory of a nuclear reactor that could produce a controlled fission reaction in uranium; and, more cryptically, it made reference to the other possibility opened up by nuclear power: a uranium bomb. But Heisenberg's reactor theory contained a flaw that was to prove almost physically fatal to him, while the bomb theory did not go beyond the public scientific understanding of the atomic bomb that prevailed in 1939.

This first report of Heisenberg's shows a wide reading of French and American reports, and is particularly indebted for its understanding of fission to his old teacher Bohr, and for its treatment of the complex problem of neutron diffusion to Fermi and others. Though there is no indication here (or elsewhere) that Heisenberg had read Peierls's article on fast-neutron fission, he was well informed of foreign work on slow neutrons and the critical sizes of reactors.[4] In attempting to provide a comprehensive theory of a nuclear reactor, G-39 gives an extended treatment of the diffusion equation that describes the movement, collision, and escape of neutrons through uranium. This permits the calculation of a critical size for a chain reaction that is initiated when the number of neutrons generated internally exceeds the number escaping from the surface and lost to other nonfission processes. One strange feature of this discussion is Heisenberg's conviction that a reactor would be self-stabilizing, since (he believed) it would automatically seek a state of temperature equilibrium owing to the widening of the capturing $U238$ resonance bands through the nuclear Doppler effect, the reduction of den-

2. Listed with synopses in *German Reports on Atomic Energy: A Bibliography of Unclassified Literature*, USAEC-TID-3030, ed. L. R. David and I. A. Warheit (Oak Ridge, Tenn., 1952); a shorter list, but containing several entries not in the American list, is printed in W. Tautorus (i.e., K. Diebner), "Die deutschen Geheimarbeiten zur Kernenergieverwertung während des zweiten Weltkrieges, 1939–1945," *Atomkernenergie* 1 (1956): 368–370; 423–425. Many of the titles are also given in Walker, *German National Socialism*, pp. 268–274. The original reports were at one time to be found at the Oak Ridge Laboratory. Microfiche copies are obtainable from the U.S. National Archives, Washington, D.C., RG 242, Captured German Documents: TID-3030, and may also be found in the Niels Bohr Library of the American Institute of Physics, College Park, Md. Numerous reports are reproduced in IMF. Texts of the twenty-odd papers on uranium authored by Heisenberg are printed in GWH, A II.

3. "Die Möglichkeit der technischen Energiegewinnung aus der Uranspaltung" (= G-39), printed in GWH, A II, pp. 378–396.

4. Heisenberg cites Bohr and Wheeler's fundamental article as well as experimental data reported by Anderson, Fermi, and Szilard. On Fermi, see below. For the uncited Peierls paper of 1939, see above, chap. 4.

sities through heat expansion, and the energy increase of protons. This means that at a temperature of 800 degrees, the diffusion length (letter l) of neutrons has increased so greatly that unbounded neutron multiplication ceases: The mean free paths (Greek letter lambda) lengthen, the fission cross-sections diminish, and so fission events become rarer, and the reaction is no longer sustainable. At this point, the reactor would then stabilize itself without the need for cadmium or other control rods to restrain the chain reaction. Heisenberg was so confident about this finding (which actually applies to only one species of reactor) that he never bothered to work out a quantitative theory of the cadmium regulators that might be needed; he was content in his 1942 experiments with having a "lump" of cadmium on hand to drop into the reactor in case it came to criticality, and his final experiment in 1945 was scarcely better protected.[5] Moreover, Heisenberg was ignorant—and remained so throughout the war—of the crucial factor in running a controlled reactor—namely, the role of delayed neutrons.[6] In

5. G-39, pp. 15–17 (GWH, A II, 389 ff.). In G-161 ("Bemerkungen zu dem geplanten halbtechnischen Versuch . . . ," 31 July 1942; GWH, A II, 551), Heisenberg refers to the use of cadmium as suggested by Joliot in case the reactor becomes unstable, but does not anticipate any difficulty in restoring its stability. The difficulty is much underrated here. (Cf. Irving, *German Atomic Bomb*, pp. 270, 302; Walker, *German National Socialism*, p. 85.) For other 1939 recommendations of cadmium by Adler and Halban as well as Flügge, see below, chap. 8.

See below, chap. 8, for Heisenberg's conception of a nonstabilizing reactor as a "reactor-bomb."

Szilard was independently aware of the kind of thermal equilibrium reactor envisaged by Heisenberg: "If a chain reaction could be maintained in a homogeneous mixture of water and uranium or carbon and uranium it would have a certain natural stability in the sense that with rising temperature there would be a decrease in the neutron production. The reason for this is the fact that the absorption of both uranium and hydrogen obey the $1/v$ law in the thermal region and thus at higher temperatures the range of thermal neutrons in the mixture is larger. Correspondingly, at higher temperatures a larger fraction of the thermal neutrons will escape across the boundary of the mixture without having reacted with the uranium in the mixture. This natural stability could even be enhanced by having bodies of strong thermal neutron absorbers inserted in the mixture." But Szilard then goes beyond Heisenberg to argue that most reactors will actually be unstable: "A system, on the other hand, in which uranium bodies which are almost 'black' for thermal neutrons are embedded in carbon . . . has no such stability. This is due to the fact that with rising temperature the capture cross-section of the carbon decreases whereas the absorption by the uranium spheres remains almost unchanged. Accordingly, at higher temperatures, a larger fraction of the thermal neutrons is absorbed by carbon and this leads to an increase in q_e [?] and thermal instability.

"It is, however, quite easy artificially to stabilize the chain reaction by slowly shifting the position of absorbing bodies within the system." (L. Szilard, *The Collected Works of Leo Szilard*, ed. B. T. Feld and G. W. Szilard, vol. 1, *Scientific Papers* (Cambridge Mass., 1972), p. 252, cf. p. 217.) Szilard withheld from publication his paper of February 1940, "Divergent Chain Reactions in Systems Composed of Uranium and Carbon." (For Szilard's conception of a reactor-bomb, see below, chap. 10.)

On the American side, see also the Fisk-Shockley report, discussed above, chap. 4. Cf. E. Fermi, "The Temperature Effect on a Chain Reacting Unit" (1942), in *Collected Papers* (Chicago, 1962–65), 2:149–151.

6. See the letter of Alvin Weinberg published in *Physics Today*, December 1994, p. 84. Weinberg had examined the captured German reports in 1945, but confesses he wrongly assumed that the Germans were aware of delayed neutrons.

any event, the belief in a self-stabilizing reactor became a central tenet of German reactor theory, as may be seen in the papers of Houtermans, Müller, and Weizsäcker, as well as in the anonymous Army Weapons Research Office (HWA WaF) Report of 1942.[7]

What is particularly interesting about the reactor-temperature discussion in G-39, however, is that it impels Heisenberg to insert a parenthetical paragraph about a possible uranium bomb immediately after giving a formula (number 38) linking the temperature of a reactor to its radius and the diffusion lengths of the neutrons:

> Equation 38 ceases to apply if the temperature rises so high that the coefficients v [Greek letter nu, for neutron production coefficient] are no longer temperature-independent. For the natural mixture of U238 and U235 this happens with neutron energies of a few eV since from this energy up the U238 capture outweighs the U235 fission considerably. In mixtures of natural uranium therefore the temperature will not rise above the temperature of known good explosives. But enrichment of the U235 would permit the temperature to rise further. If the U235 were to be so much enriched that temperatures could be attained corresponding to a neutron energy of 300 eV—which according to equation 38 pertains to a radius R of the order of 10 π l, then without any further increase of the radius the temperature would rise at a stroke to about 10^{12} degrees; that is, the whole radiation energy of all the available uranium atoms would be liberated at once. For at 300 eV the fission cross-section of U235 has sunk to around 5×10^{-24} cm^2 and cannot sink further for geometrical reasons. Above neutron energies of 300 eV, l [diffusion length] no longer increases with temperature. But this explosive transformation of uranium atoms can occur only in almost pure [*fast reinem*] U235, since already in small admixtures of U238 the neutrons are captured into the U238 resonance band.[8]

Heisenberg's point here about a bomb is that if a neutron energy of 300 eV (corresponding to a temperature of 3.5 million degrees) could be reached, then there is nothing to stop a massive explosion occurring since the fission cross-section for all neutrons, including fast ones above 300 eV, cannot diminish further.

There are many perplexing aspects to this crucial passage, of which five in particular stand out. First, the minimum fission cross-section given for U235 of 5×10^{-24} cm^2 is, in the context of nuclear data available in 1939, much too large a number to be referring to fast neutrons in U235; 0.4 or 0.5×10^{-24} cm^2 would be closer to contemporary estimates, as suggested by Tuve, Bohr, Chadwick—and Ladenburg, who is actually cited earlier in the paper by Heisenberg. It is possible that the figure of 5.0 may therefore be simply a misprint for the much lower "0.5." On the other hand, it may be read in context as being actually a minimum cross-section for slow neutrons in U235 in unseparated uranium; Heisenberg would then be inappropriately applying reactor concepts and data to the bomb prob-

7. See below, chaps. 8–11.
8. G-39, pp. 15 f. (GWH, A II, 389).

lem.[9] Either way, this apparently trivial slip reveals a great deal of loose and erroneous thinking about the nature of a U235 bomb.

Second, there is the temperature argument. Heisenberg's bomb temperature of 10^{12} (= a thousand billion) degrees is wild, and seems to indicate some enormous radius. Most important, the simple application of the reactor's temperature/radius formula (number 38) to the rather different case of a bomb is misleading and likely to result in a distorted idea of a bomb as well as an exaggerated critical size. Heisenberg actually specifies that applying this formula yields a critical radius approximating to $10\,\pi\,l$; depending on the enrichment of U235, the diffusion length l would vary. Though Heisenberg does not give the values to be inserted here, his tabulated measurements for slow-neutron diffusion are quite high; if we concede that he may (improbably, as some critics may carp) have had in mind for fast neutrons a low value of, say, 2 cm for l, then inserting it in his formula yields a critical radius of no less than 63 cm—equivalent to tens of tons of "almost pure" U235! Heisenberg does not even bother to calculate the mass, since any contemporary reader must have understood at once that he believed a uranium bomb based on his reactor theory in G-39 to be so chimerical as to be hardly worth discussing at this point.

Third, Heisenberg does not formulate any expression for the exponential increase of neutrons such as e^t/Tau, which is the key to the Frisch-Peierls bomb concept; instead he stops at an equation (number 30)—useful for reactors—that gives a simple instantaneous balance of internal neutron multiplication and neutron escape. When this approach is applied to conceiving a bomb, it is again, like the temperature-stabilization idea, misleading. It mistakes the crucial condition of a bomb, which is not, as Heisenberg had it, that "the escape of neutrons from its surface *be small* [emphasis added] compared with the internal neutron multiplication," but rather that there be an excess of internal neutron multiplication over neutrons lost to escape and other nonfission processes. This is equivalent to saying that the rate of internal neutron multiplication be such that, of the number of free neutrons released in each nuclear fission, slightly more than one neutron on aver-

9. In G-39 (p. 12) Heisenberg cites a measurement of 0.5×10^{-25} cm^2 by R. Ladenburg ("Study of Uranium and Thorium Fission Produced by Fast Neutrons of Nearly Homogeneous Energy," *Physical Review* 56 [July 1939]: 168–170) for fast neutrons in unseparated uranium (GWH, A II, 387). A paper (G-7) of December 1939 by one of Heisenberg's assistants, Paul Müller, gives the fast-neutron fission cross-section of unseparated uranium as 0.5×10^{-24} cm^2 and assumes, from Bohr-Wheeler, that this value holds for both main isotopes, U238 and U235. Though a later report of February 1944 by W. Jentschke and K. Lintner, "Schnelle Neutronen in Uran. V" (G-227), calculates the cross-section for fast-neutron fission in U235 as 3.7×10^{-24} cm^2, that far larger figure does not appear to have been absorbed by Heisenberg, to judge from the Farm Hall transcripts, which show him adhering still to 0.5×10^{-24} cm^2 as the minimum value for U235 (FHT, no. 5, p. 15; *OE*, p. 122). See below, chap. 14.

Chadwick used the geometrical cross-section to reason for a large fission cross-section for fast neutrons in U235, but Heisenberg's argument is quite different and cannot be related to fast neutrons in the same way. See above, chaps. 4 and 5.

age should fission another nucleus. Heisenberg's condition does define the critical mass for a chain reaction, but if applied to a bomb without realistic consideration of the rate of neutron multiplication and exponential increase, it produces a larger "critical mass" than is really needed.[10] This is because it requires an unnecessarily high degree of efficiency in the fissioning of nuclei, whereas as long as the chain reaction is sustained by positive neutron multiplication—however small—even a large majority of neutrons may be allowed to escape, in contradiction to Heisenberg's condition. The rapidity of the fast-neutron reaction is what makes all this possible.[11] However, in Heisenberg's mind, the essential condition is that the efficiency of this reaction depends on the escape of neutrons being "small" compared to the internal multiplication. If the excess of multiplying over escaping neutrons is very small, then (as Frisch and Peierls had recognized) the chain reaction will grow too slowly to permit an efficient explosion, and calculations are necessary to determine how much additional material is required to guarantee a desired yield. Because Heisenberg had not sufficiently grasped the principle of the fast-neutron reaction in pure U235, he telescoped the efficiency question into the critical-mass criterion and for working purposes assumed the "critical mass" for a bomb to be the mass required for an *efficient* bomb.

Fourth, Heisenberg does not seem to be interested in analyzing Frisch and Peierls's crucial case of a bomb made of pure U235. Heisenberg's phrasing is telling here: He speaks of "almost pure U235." Despite his disclaimer about "small admixtures of U238," he effectively leaves the door open to consideration of bombs that might employ uranium mixtures or a moderator designed to pre-

10. I have placed *critical mass* in quotation marks here and elsewhere because it represents the practical or effective amount of material needed, according to Heisenberg's theory, to produce an explosion. Heisenberg, of course, understood perfectly well what a critical mass for a chain reaction (fast or slow) would be, but believed that an enormously greater mass of U235 would have to be used to obtain an explosion. He was led to this peculiar view of the *practical* "critical mass" needed for an efficient explosion by his failure to understand the full implications of a fast-neutron reaction as Frisch and Peierls had grasped them.

11. For this vital "loose detail of thinking," see R. V. Jones, *Most Secret War* (London, 1978), p. 594 n. Heisenberg's extension of the simple critical-mass concept to a bomb was a common assumption at the time; see, for example, L. Turner, "Nuclear Fission," *Reviews of Modern Physics* 12 (1940): 1–29, at p. 21: "For a sample of reasonable size, many neutrons will escape without producing further ones so that the quantity $A_f v / A_{tot}$ will have to be even greater if *explosive* [emphasis added] release of nuclear energy is to occur."

On Heisenberg's misapplication of the correct theory of critical mass to a bomb, see below, chaps. 7, 12, and 14.

A paper by C. F. von Weizsäcker, Paul Müller, and K.-H. Höcker, "Berechnung der Energiegewinnung in der Uranmaschine" (G-60), 26 February 1940, p. 1, gives a formula for neutron multiplication as proportional to neutron number that is derived from G-39, but it does not include a time factor.

In a private communication to me of 27 December 1984, Professor Sir Rudolf Peierls distinguishes between "critical size . . . [and] the extent to which the chain reaction proceeds, a question apparently ignored by Heisenberg."

vent the neutrons from being captured by the U238 present in such a mixed bomb.[12] As he states ambiguously at the end of the paper, "the enrichment of U235 is the only method with which to make the volume of the machine small as compared to 1 cubic meter. It is furthermore the only method to produce an explosive that exceeds the strongest existing explosives by several powers of ten."[13] For the bomb, Heisenberg does not propose the extraction of pure U235, but merely its enrichment to an "almost pure" state.

Fifth and finally, the last sentence in the passage quoted above suggests that Heisenberg has not fully understood the role played by fast neutrons in a uranium bomb: It is irrelevant in a bomb whether neutrons of lower energies are "captured into the U238 resonance band," since the bomb reaction depends entirely on the fast neutrons alone. Heisenberg here seems to be thinking vaguely of using, in his "almost pure" U235 bomb, neutrons other than those too fast to be absorbed by U238; in other words, he has not understood in any precise way that the bomb is a fast-neutron explosion.

This sequence of seemingly trivial errors and loose scientific details may appear unimportant when broken down into discrete slips, but, taken together as a sequence, these slips fall into a pattern that has a cumulative power to illustrate just how nebulous, primitive, and misconceived Heisenberg's thinking about the bomb was in December 1939. The impression gained from G-39 of Heisenberg's idea of a U235 bomb is that it is essentially an extrapolation of his thinking about reactors; like Bohr, he has assumed from his study of fission reactors that a bomb of U235 must have a large critical mass. It must be remembered, in any case, that after the Bohr-Wheeler paper of August 1939 the treatment of neutron diffusion usually focused on cases of slow neutrons, and physicists were accustomed to working with data characteristic of slow-neutron reactors. It was easy, therefore, to assume that with fast neutrons, the vital data would be even less favorable, or alternatively that the dominant process even in a bomb would be the same slow-neutron reaction—somehow speeded up to overcome the temperature stabilization—that was the basis of the reactor.[14] In G-39 Heisenberg conceived a bomb as a device operating with uranium that was enriched in U235 sufficiently to raise the temperature to a level corresponding to 300 eV, at which point a full nuclear explosion would suddenly take place.

---

12. The Hiroshima bomb itself did, of course, include a mixture with 10% U238, but that design was arrived at only after the crucial theoretical first step had been taken of considering a reaction in pure U235. However, Heisenberg had not understood the first step, and so any discussion of U238 admixtures was necessarily misconceived.

13. G-39, p. 24 (GWH, A II, p. 396).

14. Note that the basis for Heisenberg's diffusion theory was the paper by E. Amaldi and E. Fermi, "On the Absorption and the Diffusion of Slow Neutrons," *Physical Review* 50 (1936): 899–928 (reprinted in E. Fermi, *Collected Papers* [Chicago, 1962], esp. p. 941). In an interview of 1967 (J. J. Ermenc, *Atomic Bomb Scientists: Memoirs, 1939–1945* [Westport, Conn., 1989], p. 46), Heisenberg recalls that he improved on Fermi's existing theory of neutron diffusion. See below, chap. 7, for quotation.

We may allow that Heisenberg, like Niels Bohr, believed that the bomb had, in principle, to be a fast-neutron reaction (though this recognition would seem to have been formed only in 1940);[15] nevertheless, it is clear from G-39 that in December 1939 Heisenberg regarded the uranium bomb as essentially an exploding reactor. An incremental enrichment of the U235 content of the uranium in the "reactor" would overcome the temperature-stabilization barrier and gradually bring the device closer to the point of an explosion; the actual point of ignition, however, would have to be reached very rapidly by some technical trick in order to avoid a meltdown. From all this it is obvious that in G-39 Heisenberg had not yet thought out rigorously any proposal for a bomb. Indeed, he seems to have conflated what later became two separate proposals, one for a reactor-bomb, the other for a "nearly pure U235" bomb. This is apparent from the otherwise puzzling fact that he makes no attempt to calculate the critical mass of a bomb as opposed to a reactor. In the context of his misconceived approach, there was indeed no reason for him to do so at this early juncture: Given the implicit requirement (as a consequence of his reactor theory) of a very large mass of highly enriched uranium for a bomb, it would hardly have been worth working out the precise mass at this stage. When Heisenberg did get to working out the critical mass in 1940, however, he was to introduce yet another error into his already fallacious way of thinking about the bomb, as will be seen.

.   .   .

Let us try to get inside Heisenberg's mind in 1939 and to summarize the peculiar assumptions and perspectives that shaped and constrained his understanding of the problem of a uranium bomb as revealed rather tortuously in his fundamental paper G-39.

The strange obscurities and omissions in G-39 derive from Heisenberg's two basic ways of thinking about an atomic bomb at this early crucial stage of the German uranium project. The first of these considers a uranium bomb as being at the end of a sliding scale that runs from reactors to bombs. This explains why he feels no need to discuss at this stage whether fast or slow neutrons drive the bomb reaction; after all, if a bomb reaction is conceived as being on a sliding scale from bomb to reactor, if there is no sharp qualitative distinction between a bomb and reactor, then it would have been in his mind premature to judge whether different kinds of reactions were involved in bombs and reactors. That verdict must belong to a later stage of development of bomb theory.

Second, G-39 takes a reactor-bomb as the implicit model for consideration of a uranium bomb. Again, a sliding scale seems to be dominating Heisenberg's thinking. A reactor-bomb could be made of slightly enriched uranium, highly enriched, or—for the sake of argument—"almost pure U235," or even 100% pure

15. *OE*, pp. 83 f. See below, chap. 14.

U235. Because of this continuum, the whole analysis is blurred: There is no need to distinguish strictly between slow- and fast-neutron reactions, nor to consider seriously the role of fast neutrons in a reactor-bomb. Heisenberg thus removes the need to analyze in precise terms the phenomenon of a fast reaction, in particular the crucial question as to whether a fast-neutron reaction would proceed differently in pure U235 than it would in a mixture. Since he does not ask himself this question, Heisenberg consequently does not go on to answer it in the manner of Frisch and Peierls, and so conclude that the critical mass of a pure-U235 bomb would in fact be very small. Thus, although Heisenberg gives no calculation in G-39 for the mass of his bomb, his imprecision about fast and slow reactions, together with his basic notion of the bomb as a reactor using up to 100% pure U235, must have led him to assume that it would obviously be a very large critical mass.

In summary, then, Heisenberg is concerned here with a chimera and its own distorted reflection. First there is the chimera itself—an "almost pure" U235 bomb that is not really a bomb at all but rather a kind of reactor. And then there is its reflection—a reactor-bomb that may use "almost pure" U235. The inchoate nature of Heisenberg's thinking about atomic bombs at this stage, compared with the understanding of Frisch and Peierls, is evident from the astonishing facts that in this foundation paper he does not give a critical mass for a U235 bomb, does not spell out the unique characteristics of pure U235 as opposed to mixtures, and finally does not raise the question of whether the reaction is to be based on fast or slow neutrons.

CHAPTER 7

The Bomb as Reactor

The U235 Bomb Misconceived, 1940

Heisenberg's basic conceptual error in his G-39 paper of December 1939 was to think of the bomb in terms of reactor theory. On this false foundation he constructed in the months that followed an equally fallacious solution to the problem of the critical mass of a U235 bomb. Misapplying a basic feature of diffusion theory, Heisenberg arrived at an impossibly high figure for a critical mass of pure U235. This was done by means of a seductively simple "back of an envelope" calculation in 1940, as is recollected by Sir Charles Frank—one of the two British intelligence scientists most involved with the investigation of the German project:

> According to my information (which derives chiefly from the Farm Hall seminar and conversations with [Karl] Wirtz) Heisenberg first gave the back-of-the-envelope calculation to a private meeting of German physicists early in 1940, at which they decided what their strategy for the war period was going to be.[1]

A likely occasion for Heisenberg's confiding the calculation to his colleagues may have been a meeting held in Berlin at the beginning of January 1940 with Kurt Diebner, the head of the Army Weapons Research Office's uranium project,

---

1. This comment is taken from a private letter of 5 June 1984 from Professor Sir Charles Frank to me.
The Wirtz conversation is also recounted in Frank's interview by Mark Walker of 12 April 1985, pp. 9 f., 14 ff.(OHI). Frank and Wirtz had been good friends before the war, and at Farm Hall on 2 November 1945 (*OE*, p. 237) they walked after lunch in the garden, where Wirtz related the 1940 meeting and back-of-an-envelope calculation. Frank, however, mentions in the interview that in recent letters to him Wirtz has denied saying this; in his recent account of the Wirtz conversation (*OE*, pp. 2–3), Sir Charles has omitted any mention of Wirtz's admission of the back-of-an-envelope calculation. (For another convenient memory lapse by Wirtz, see below, chap. 10.) Strangely, no trace of this crucial information is to be found in M. Walker, *German National Socialism and the Quest for Nuclear Power, 1939–1949* (Cambridge, 1989), and one wonders why; it is perhaps the most extraordinary of Walker's suppressions and renders the whole technical argumentation of the book suspect and invalid. (It must be ad-

and attended by Heisenberg and Wirtz; or the calculation may have been unveiled at a larger conference that seems to have taken place on 24 April 1940. (The calculation may have been carried out in the context of more formal investigations of the critical size for a reactor that were reported in late February 1940.)[2]

Since Heisenberg (falsely) claimed in 1946–47 that "investigation of the technical sides of the atomic bomb problem—for example, of the so-called critical size—was, however, not undertaken" during the war, we cannot be absolutely sure of what that back-of-an-envelope calculation consisted.[3] Still, Heisenberg's suave production of a critical-mass calculation for pure U235—like a magician's pulling a rabbit out of a hat—the day after Hiroshima for the benefit of his fellow internees at Farm Hall in 1945 suggests that the trick had been prepared long before, and that he was actually just repeating an old familiar argument rather than thinking up something quite new to him. It seems plausible that Heisenberg's Farm Hall calculation was indeed the one that he had performed previously for some of his German colleagues in 1940.[4]

---

mitted that Sir Charles Frank's OHI interview telescopes some of Heisenberg's thinking, but his recall of the general picture seems accurate. See below, chap. 14.)

After receiving the Frank information, I wrote to Karl Wirtz for his comment on the matter, but his reply of 29 November 1985 evaded the issue.

R.V. Jones, in his introduction to the reprint of S. Goudsmit's *ALSOS* (Los Angeles, 1988), p. xvi, quotes a letter of Sir Charles of 1967 that also refers to a "crude and faulty calculation" presented to a conference in 1940.

2. For the meeting of "Anfang Januar" 1940 (called to discuss heavy-water production), see Heisenberg to Harteck, 18 January 1940, in IMF 29-626; also D. Irving, *The German Atomic Bomb* (New York, 1967), p. 59. Rudolf Fleischmann's notebook (G-346), p. 26, seems to refer to a meeting on 24 April 1940. There were probably other such meetings in the first months of the year. Unfortunately, Erich Bagge's diary entries for the first half of 1940 are missing, as he informs me by private communication. (Earlier and later passages of his diary are in IMF 29-106/159.)

Heisenberg's sequel to G-39, "Bericht über die Möglichkeit technischer Energiegewinnung aus der Uranspaltung (II)" (G-40), 29 February 1940, in GWH, A II, 397, contains phrasing (including the use of *Bericht* in the title) suggesting that it was to be discussed along with other papers at a meeting of the *Uranverein;* the last page (GWH, A II, 418) concludes with the comment that "von Weizsäcker ausführliche Berechnungen über diesen Gegenstand durchgeführt hat und wohl demnächst mitteilen wird"; this may indicate an imminent meeting where Weizsäcker would present his calculations (or it may simply be referring to the imminent circulation of a report by Weizsäcker). Another paper dating from the same month of February by Heisenberg's associates Weizsäcker, Paul Müller, and Karl-Heinz Höcker deals with the critical size of a reactor (G-60, 26 February 1940, cited below, chap. 8).

3. For the various critical masses of U235, plutonium, and reactor-bombs that were in fact calculated by Heisenberg and other German physicists during the war, see below, chaps. 11–13, 15. For the disingenuous claim that investigation of the critical mass for a bomb was not pursued, see W. Heisenberg, "Über die Arbeiten zur technischen Ausnutzung der Atomkernenergie in Deutschland," *Die Naturwissenschaften* 33 (1946): 325–329 (reprinted with a postscript in the Einstein commemorative volume *Helle Zeit—Dunkle Zeit,* ed. C. Seelig [Zurich, 1956], pp. 133–144). Translated in part as "Research in Germany on the Technical Application of Atomic Energy," *Nature,* no. 4059 (August 16, 1947): 211–215, at p. 213 (reprinted in GWH, ser. B, 416).

4. What follows is reconstructed from significant—if cryptic—remarks in Heisenberg's papers of 26 February 1942 (printed in GWH, A II, 517 ff.; IMF, 29-1005; misfiled in G-323) and 6 May 1943

Heisenberg's argument solved (he thought) neatly what seemed to be a major theoretical objection to the bomb: Once the critical size of a uranium bomb has been reached and the chain reaction launched, the expansion of the bomb means that the chances of neutrons fissioning nuclei within the critical mass fall as the neutrons escape at an increasing rate from the enlarging mass, and so the chain reaction is cut off before (thought Heisenberg) enough nuclei have been fissioned to create a true atomic explosion. Heisenberg was actually setting himself a false problem: What was, he asked himself, the minimum amount of U235 required to ensure that a sufficient quantity of the bomb fuel—anything, say, from a few hundred grams of U235 to a few kilograms—would be "burned" so as to produce a large explosion? This approach must have represented to Heisenberg a solution to the difficulties of applying the idea of "critical mass" to a bomb as opposed to a reactor. By 1940, Heisenberg evidently had realized that simple reactor theory could not be applied to the theory of a bomb without major modifications. But this new sophisticated understanding of the U235 bomb resulted in an unconventional conception of "critical mass." In effect, Heisenberg was not interested in ascertaining what we would call the critical mass of U235 in the sense of it defining the minimum mass at which an explosive chain reaction would be initiated. Heisenberg's concern was rather the much larger mass that would not only initiate the fast-neutron chain reaction, but also statistically assure the efficient explosion of a given minimum amount of U235 before the point was reached at which more neutrons were escaping than being internally generated. For example, if through the first generation of 100 fissions, 300 neutrons were released from split nuclei, 160 might escape through the surface, leaving a minority of 140 behind to carry on the next generation of fissions. As the reaction continues, the proportion of escaping neutrons rises exponentially, soon cutting off the reaction. In effect, Heisenberg was trying to find an upper limit for the practical or effective "critical mass" of a U235 bomb that could be exploded while all the original neutrons were still within the sphere—a most unrealistic approach, for reasons that will soon be explained.

For this purpose of finding a minimum certain "critical mass" for an efficient explosion (rather than the critical mass in its proper sense), Heisenberg thought up a temptingly simple argument and calculation: To be sure that 10^{24} U235 nuclei (roughly Avogadro's number of U235 nuclei—6×10^{23} of them [a *mole*, a standard unit in atomic calculations]—or 235 grams of U235, but rounded up to 10^{24} so as to equal 370 grams) were fissioned before the chain reaction was broken off by the escape of neutrons and the expansion of the bomb, Heisenberg plausibly rea-

_____

(G-217; printed in GWH, A II, 570 ff.; misdated 5 May), and from his exposition of 7 August 1945, in the Farm Hall transcripts, no. 4, pp. 24–25 (*OE*, p. 91). For analysis of the two papers, see below, chap. 12. For the details of the random walk, see below, chap. 14.

Sir Charles Frank's OHI interview, pp. 10, 14, strongly suggests that the Farm Hall random-walk calculation was indeed the same back-of-an-envelope calculation that Heisenberg devised in 1940.

soned that all that was necessary was that there should be enough uranium present to be assured that 80 generations of fissions would be completed within a sphere of U235 before it expanded. The idea was to burn a mole of U235 not as a continuous, consolidated mass, but rather as a thread of sequential nuclei, spread throughout the larger mass (10^{24} = approximately 2^{80}, so that if two neutrons are produced per fission, then after 80 generations of fission, 10^{24} nuclei will have been burned).[5] In order to work out the size of the sphere needed to satisfy this condition, Heisenberg availed himself of a basic statistical technique known to him from Einstein's work on the random movement of particles in Brownian motion, which had been developed by Fermi into a theory of neutron diffusion.[6] The technique was known as the "random walk" (or, more colloquially, the "drunkard's walk"), and it illustrated how the reaction spreads through a sphere by the diffusion of neutrons.[7] What distance will a neutron (or its descendants) be from the center of a sphere after taking 80 steps between fissions of a standard length, but in random zigzagging directions? The answer is calculated by taking the length of each

5. The use of 80 as the figure for the number of neutron generations required to fission Avogadro's number of atoms was instinctive at the time. Cf. R. Serber, *The Los Alamos Primer* (Berkeley, 1992), p. 10; S. Glasstone, *Sourcebook on Nuclear Energy*, 2d ed. (Princeton, 1958), pp. 417 f. (though in the 3d ed. [Princeton, 1967], p. 511, the figure is refined to an actual 56 generations).

Fascinating computer simulations of chain reactions are described in A. K. Dewdney, *The Magic Machine: A Handbook of Computer Sorcery* (New York, 1990), chap. 23.

6. In a 1967 interview, Heisenberg noted that "there was a theory of neutron diffusion already worked out by Fermi before the war. But then we had to improve on it. We had to take into account the different velocities of the neutrons—the fast and slow neutrons. This was finally a rather elaborate and I think quite good theory which we used for the reactor experiments" (J. J. Ermenc, *Atomic Bomb Scientists: Memoirs, 1939–1945* [Westport, Conn., 1989], p. 46). Heisenberg's knowledge of Fermi's papers is evident, for example, in GWH, A II, 388, 408 (G-39 and G-40).

For Fermi's influential diffusion theory and neutron-diffusion equations see E. Amaldi and E. Fermi, "On the Absorption and the Diffusion of Slow Neutrons," *Physical Review* 50 (1936): 899–928 (reprinted in Fermi, *Collected Papers* [Chicago, 1962–65], 1:892–942); and E. Fermi, "On the Motion of Neutrons in Hydrogenous Substances" (1936), in his *Collected Papers*, 1:980–1016. Cf. E. Fermi, *Nuclear Physics*, rev. ed. (Chicago, 1950), pp. 187–194, where he uses the "root mean square path" to calculate the diffusion of thermal neutrons in a pile ("nascent neutrons of the Gaussian distribution"). See also the lucid account in *Encyclopaedia Britannica*, 1971 ed., 7:422 ff., s.v. "Diffusion Theory."

On the earlier application of statistical analysis to Brownian movement, see A. Einstein, *Investigations on the Theory of the Brownian Movement* (London, 1926), pp. 11–17; M. Smoluchowski, *Abhandlungen über die Brownsche Bewegung und verwandte Erscheinungen* (Leipzig, 1923); J. Perrin, *Les atomes*, 2d ed. (Paris, 1936), chap. 4.

7. On diffusion theory and random walks see R. Feynman, *The Feynman Lectures on Physics* (Reading, Mass., 1963), vol. 1, secs. 41.4 and 43; and the popular presentation by G. Gamow, *One, Two, Three . . . Infinity*, 2d ed. (New York, 1961), pp. 199–203, which explains that the random-walk aspect of diffusion theory allows one to calculate how many neutrons remain within a sphere of given radius after a given number of collisions, and may be linked to the number of generations of neutrons within a set time that would liberate a given threshold of energy. For analogous biological applications, see H. C. Berg, *Random Walks in Biology* (Princeton, 1983). Cf. A. Joffé, *Promenades aléatoires et mouvement Brownien* (Montreal, 1969).

step (the mean free path)—say, in Heisenberg's thinking, 6 cm—and multiplying it by the square root of the number of steps: Thus, 6 cm × √80 = 54 cm. This means that the critical radius needed to ensure an explosion is 54 cm, which is equivalent to 13 tons of pure U235, a quantity that it would have seemed pure fantasy in 1940 even to think of extracting. Heisenberg was thus able to convince himself that a pure-U235 bomb based on fast neutrons was a practical impossibility because of its gigantic "critical mass."

In the Farm Hall transcripts Heisenberg states the explanation for his calculation twice to Otto Hahn on two successive days:

> In order to make 10^{24} neutrons I need 80 reactions one after the other. . . . In order to make 80 collisions, I must have a lump of a radius of about 54 centimeters and this would be about a ton [6 August 1945]. . . .
> . . . In order to produce fissions in 10^{25} [*sic*] atoms you need 80 steps in the chain so that the whole reaction is complete in 10^{-8} seconds. . . . I need 10^{25} neutrons and that is 2^{80}. I need 80 steps in the chain and then I have made 2^{80} neutrons [7 August 1945].[8]

That Heisenberg was quite mistaken in his approach to calculating the critical mass of a bomb is clearly proven by the evidence. But perhaps it may be useful to try to reconstruct some of the thinking that led to his error by looking at how his reasoning was fallacious in four respects. The major source of the fallacy lies in Heisenberg's attempt to calculate the critical mass for a case in which the explosion would occur without wasting a neutron. The point is to find the critical size at which the original chain of 80 fission generations would still be within the mass. It ignores the fact that the divergent chains will be sufficient to produce an explosion even after the original ancestral neutron may have escaped, and is thus a quite unnecessary argument. This is demanding an unreasonable and unnecessary certainty. The calculation would admittedly yield an upper limit for the critical mass, but at the cost of neglecting the far smaller practical, true critical limit for a bomb. In other words, Heisenberg's critical mass is technically correct, but is too exigent in its requirement for certainty of explosion. As one physicist has commented:

> There is nothing wrong with the formula itself, as a simple estimate of neutron diffusion. Heisenberg's mistake is in the unnecessarily demanding requirement that each neutron starting from the center of the uranium mass must give rise to N fissions before exiting through the surface of the mass. . . . The big mistake is the conceptual one, of defining the minimum mass by the requirement that a hypothetical neutron at the center must give rise to the fission of a kilogram [*sic*, for *mole*] of uranium before its work is done and it exits.[9]

8. *OE*, pp. 84, 91. See below, chap. 14, for fuller quotation and further analysis.

9. J. Logan, letter to author, 7 June 1995. For a detailed analysis of the misunderstanding concealed in Heisenberg's Farm Hall calculation, see J. Logan, "The Critical Mass," *American Scientist* 84 (May–June 1996): 263–277.

The second fallacy is that the random-walk analysis is applied to cases of infinite mass, where no consideration of boundary conditions is involved. However, boundary conditions are of crucial importance for cases of finite mass, such as a bomb or a reactor. There is, therefore, an essential fallacy in applying the random-walk argument to determining the finite mass of a bomb. Heisenberg, it might be said, was carried away here by his own cleverness and delight in the simplicity of his argument.[10]

The third element of fallacy is reflected in the surprising absence from Heisenberg's wartime writings on the bomb of an expression for the internal multiplication of neutrons with respect to time. The random-walk argument seemingly averted the need to work out such an expression as that of Frisch and Peierls and so foreclosed Heisenberg's mind to the most fruitful method of conceiving the U235 bomb. Heisenberg was forced to present the relevant equation only on 14 August 1945, after he had abandoned the random-walk back-of-an-envelope calculation as misleading though attractive. The lack of this expression until then, however, had been a major deficiency in Heisenberg's thinking about the atomic bomb and had worsened the conceptual imprecision surrounding his whole approach to the bomb problem. (He had, however, used such an expression once in 1942 in connection with a reactor; see below, p. 125.)

Fourth, the preoccupation of Heisenberg that no neutron should have escaped before 80 generations of fission had been completed led him to misunderstand a basic implication of the neutron-escape process for the U235 bomb. Heisenberg failed to appreciate clearly that the reaction is so rapid that as long as an average of slightly more than one neutron released per fission goes on to fission another, the process overwhelms the effect of the escape of the majority of neutrons from the surface.[11] This can be grasped by considering the different perceptions of the problem of the bomb's "expansion" held by Heisenberg and Frisch. In his pessimistic Chemical Society report of 1939–40, Frisch had concluded that the possibility of a bomb was blocked by the explosive expansion of the critical mass; but he had been thinking of the bomb as a slow-neutron reaction, which would be far too slow to be completed—no matter how large the mass—before the expansion took place. As soon as he conceived in February 1940 the reaction rather to be based on fast neutrons, Frisch understood that the rapidity of the reaction removed the major obstacle as he had seen it to achieving an explosion; expansion was no longer a problem. So too the American physicist Robert Serber in his 1943 bomb orientation lecture at Los Alamos explained the bomb in terms of using 80 generations of fissions to fission 2^{80} atoms, but, not sharing Heisenberg's criterion

10. See Frank's comments in his OHI interview, p. 14 (and below, chap. 14): "It's brilliantly simple, and had it given the right answer, you would say how clever, it takes a clever man like Heisenberg to see how to do such a difficult problem so simply."

11. R. V. Jones, *Most Secret War: British Scientific Intelligence, 1939–1945* (London, 1979), p. 594, has pointed out this imprecision as a "loose detail of thinking" that had serious consequences for the calculation of critical mass.

that the difference in the neutron balance between escape and generation must not be "small," he found no need to veer off into Heisenberg's misapplied random-walk argument.[12]

Heisenberg, on the other hand, did not truly comprehend the fast-neutron reaction because of his misconception of a bomb's practical "critical mass" as primarily a matter of the escape of neutrons through the surface being "small" compared with internal neutron multiplication, rather than as depending on the neutron multiplication factor (with allowance made for surface escape) being greater than one. This perception seems to have been rooted in his general approach to the bomb in terms of reactor theory; in G-39 he had presented neutron multiplication in terms of a balance between neutron increase and neutron escape, where it would appear intuitively the case that the difference between neutron escape and neutron multiplication should not be "small" if the chain reaction were to keep going.[13] But the same criterion in the case of a bomb led to too high an estimate of the mass needed for an efficient explosion. In other words, Heisenberg did not truly appreciate the nature of a fast-neutron bomb and the implications of the rapidity of the reaction involved.[14] Hence, his resort to the fallacious argument of the random walk to allow time for 80 generations of fissions to be completed. As we shall see, Heisenberg held to this fallacy in his wartime papers, even expounding it to his German colleagues as late as 7 August 1945, until finally a week later on 14 August he realized at last his total misconception of the problem and abandoned the whole random-walk argument.[15]

It is also possible that Heisenberg held so stubbornly to his random-walk argument because it originated conceptually in the particle-physics research he was pursuing in the late 1930s and after, centering on the problem of cosmic-ray showers. At the time there were two rival theories of the showers—namely, the "cascade" and the "explosion" theories. Oppenheimer and other physicists perceived the cosmic-ray shower as being formed not by an instantaneous explosion, but by a succession of individual "braking radiations" as a high-energy particle bounced between atoms after hitting a thin piece of matter in a series of cascades. But Heisenberg strongly fought for an opposing conception, seeing the shower forma-

12. Serber, *Los Alamos Primer,* pp. 10 f., 25–28; for his later consideration of neutron escape, see pp. 67–75.

13. G-39, pp. 14 f. (GWH, A II, 388 ff.), esp. equations 36, 37. See also G-126, "Vorläufiger Bericht über Ergebnisse an einer Schichtenkugel aus 38-Metall und Paraffin [B III]," coauthored with F. Bopp et al., 6 January 1942 (IMF 30-015), in GWH, A II, 515, discussing the "Neutronenbilanz" in an experimental reactor; and his paper with R. Döpel and K. Döpel, "Die Neutronenvermehrung in 38-Metall durch rasche Neutronen" (G-137), 26–28 February 1942 (IMF 30-125), in GWH, A II, 531.

14. That most of Heisenberg's colleagues, except for the favored few, were poorly informed about the fast-neutron principle of the bomb and the random-walk calculation of its critical mass is apparent from the way in which the matters were explained and received in the Farm Hall transcripts. See chap. 14.

15. See below, chap. 14.

tion as a single event or explosion, rather than a series of "new" events.[16] It would have been easy for such an intuitive physicist as Heisenberg to leap to the analogy between the cosmic-ray model and a nuclear explosive chain reaction. The chain reaction would be envisaged as emanations of a single event—that is, the original neutron beginning the reaction and that neutron's fate—rather than a cascading series in which each fission marked the start of a "new" series of showers, so rendering the movement of the original neutron irrelevant. Thus, Heisenberg's random-walk analysis depends on the condition of a single neutron fissioning the rest as though in a sequential unified explosion along one path. The Frisch-Peierls approach, on the other hand, saw the chain reaction as a cascade series of fissions along various paths. Heisenberg's whole approach to physics in the 1930s, therefore, may have predisposed him to invent his fallacious analysis of the atomic bomb in 1940.

16. See D. C. Cassidy, *Uncertainty: The Life and Science of Werner Heisenberg* (New York, 1992), pp. 361 f., for cosmic-shower theories.

CHAPTER 8

The Reactor as Bomb

Explosive Reactor-Bombs, 1940

In his G-39 paper Heisenberg had seen the U235 bomb as a crude extrapolation of his reactor theory, looking at the atomic bomb as though it were perhaps a "fast" reactor using "almost pure" U235. His back-of-an-envelope calculation in early 1940 had then effectively ruled out the development of such a U235 bomb, since his random-walk analysis entailed a critical mass of tons of U235. But in 1940 Heisenberg began to investigate another avenue that was implied in G-39.

G-39 had postulated that a chain reaction with slow neutrons would be self-regulating, with a reactor temperature stabilizing itself at 800 degrees. But would it be possible to design a reactor with enriched U235 and a moderator that could overcome this temperature barrier and produce an explosion? Such an explosion, Heisenberg well realized, would not be a true nuclear explosion such as might be obtained with his "almost pure U235" bomb using fast neutrons that would efficiently fission an adequate amount of the U235. Nevertheless, it should be feasible somehow to exploit the slow-neutron chain reaction. A paper of 1939 by the French physicists F. Adler and H. von Halban had cautioned that the "danger that a system containing uranium in high concentration might explode, once the chain reaction starts, is considerable"; the authors proposed the use of cadmium absorbers to control the reaction.[1] This notion had been picked up by Siegfried Flügge in his widely circulated article of June 1939, which warned that in the absence of cadmium controls "the reaction would soar straightaway to a stationary

---

1. F. Adler and H. von Halban, "Control of the Chain Reaction Involved in Fission of the Uranium Nucleus," *Nature* 143 (13 May 1939): 793. The fear of an instantaneous explosion is actually fallacious, since it fails to take account of the effect of the delayed neutrons that allow the reaction to be kept under control. For cadmium controls, see above, chap. 6, and GWH, A II, 551.

temperature of 100,000 degrees C."[2] Heisenberg believed that his theory of the reactor as outlined in G-39 obviated this danger, since it showed how the increasing U238 resonance bands captured enough neutrons to prevent an explosive rise in temperature.[3] But would it be possible to circumvent this temperature-stabilization barrier by greatly enriching the U235 and using a specific moderator to reduce the U238 resonance capture? This would render the reactor unstable and result in a substantial blast with messy radiation once the chain reaction had begun. It would not, however, be a true nuclear explosion, since its use of slow neutrons would not fission sufficient U235 for a large-scale explosion. In his theorizing, Heisenberg's ignorance of the role of delayed neutrons in the control of reactors left him committed to reactors that were essentially what would now be called "prompt-critical."[4] Such devices could be controlled (he believed) only by their inherent tendency to self-stabilize at a temperature of 800°C since the neutron multiplication took place in too small a fraction of a second to be otherwise restrained. But in a non-stabilizing reactor of this same putative type, the slow-neutron chain reaction would produce enough heat to break through the 800-degree barrier, the reactor would become unstable ("labile"), and it would subsequently explode. It would not be the 3.5 million degrees (= 300 eV) needed for a true explosion (as concluded in G-39), but it might be large enough to be worthwhile pursuing.[5] The problem, however, as Heisenberg obviously realized from the start, was that, first, any such exploding reactor would have to weigh far too many tons to be carried by plane, and second, as it turned out, the extent of U235 enrichment would be enormous, leading to an actual content of tons of U235 in the explosive fuel mixture. Moreover, it would obviously be a more difficult reactor to construct than the normal "critical" machine envisaged as the culmination of the first stage of the uranium project. These factors made the reactor-bomb nearly as much a monster for Heisenberg as the "almost pure" U235 bomb. Still, since the theory seemed set, and since the development of a critical reactor was after July 1940 the unavoidable and essential first stage in the development of a true fast-neutron bomb, Heisenberg never really abandoned the idea of the reactor-bomb. Though it was in effect an impracticable sideline to the main thrust of a true atomic bomb, the reactor-bomb remained a salient feature of German nuclear thinking for the duration of the war, as will be seen.

2. S. Flügge, "Kann die Energieinhalt der Atomkerne technisch nutzbar gemacht werden?" *Die Naturwissenschaften* 27 (9 June 1939): 408. For Flügge's later proposal of a reactor-bomb, see below, chap. 13.

3. The U238 energy bands increase owing to the nuclear Doppler effect, and the widening of the capture peaks causes the capture of more neutrons. Cf. GWH, A II, 387 ff., 395 f.

4. See Irving to Goudsmit, 31 July 1966 (copy from David Irving), referring to "the Germans' ignorance of delayed neutrons (as confirmed to me by Heisenberg)."

5. The explosion of the Soviet reactor at Chernobyl in 1986 seems to have been due to "prompt-neutrons"; it is estimated to have been equivalent to 10 to 20 tons of TNT. (I owe this information to

The shadow of the reactor-bomb looms over Heisenberg's description in his later reactor papers of the need to be sure that an explosive instability does not occur with the start of the chain reaction. A key paper of July 1942 on a proposed large-scale reactor experiment is fraught with fear of an explosion and meltdown:

> As criticality is approached, the nuclear process (fission) sets in with great intensity so that it is easily seen that almost only the U238 metal will heat up, but scarcely the moderator. . . .
>
> The concept of stability requires clarification: One must immediately fear that the whole fissioning of the uranium nuclei in an explosive manner in a fraction of a second will occur. In this explosion, the water would remain practically cold. The stability of the boiler [reactor] as opposed to this explosion will be decided through the behavior of the resonance lines of the uranium. But even if the machine is in this perception unstable, yet the following process may start: The metal reaches, to start with, a particular temperature, so stabilizing the machine through the broadening of the resonance lines of the uranium. . . . [Even] if the arrangement is not itself stable, one could intervene through dispositions of the sort that Joliot and others have described. . . . On the contrary, the first described process is very dangerous, since if the broadening of the resonance lines is not sufficient for stabilization, clearly no other process can hinder the nearly complete discharge of the chain reaction. This process would in a very large reactor take place in a fraction of a second. . . . For $\bar{\nu}$ [mean time absorption coefficient of the system] $= -400$ sec^{-1} . . . the number of neutrons would multiply to 10^{28} . . . which would be enough in practice for complete destruction . . . in a time of 0.16 seconds. . . . The investigation of the stability of the rise in metal temperature alone is one of the most urgent problems of U238 research. . . .
>
> Before implementing any experiment that has the objective of reaching or exceeding criticality, we must elucidate the stability of the machine by investigation of the temperature coefficient in heated uranium.[6]

Early in 1940 Heisenberg set three of his younger colleagues at the Kaiser-Wilhelm-Institute for Physics to work on the problem of reactor criticality, U238 resonance capture, and moderators, so as to obtain a fuller understanding of the conditions for stabilization.[7] The leader of the team was Heisenberg's most intimate confidant, Carl-Friedrich von Weizsäcker, and the other two members were Karl-Heinz Höcker and Paul O. Müller. The last named continued with further

---

Robert H. March of the Department of Physics, University of Wisconsin at Madison; Professor March also tells me that a self-stabilizing homogeneous "warm neutron" reactor was built at Los Alamos after the war.)

Heisenberg seems to have ignored the crucial role of delayed neutrons in controlling a nuclear reactor.

6. "Bemerkungen zu dem geplanten halbtechnischen Versuch mit 1.5 to D_2O und 3 to 38-Metall" (G-161), 31 July 1942, in GWH, A II, 548, 550 f., 552.

7. See the 26 February 1940 report by C.-F. von Weizsäcker, P. O. Müller, and K.-H. Höcker, "Berechnung der Energieerzeugung in der Uranmaschine" (G-60). Cf. M. Walker, *German National Socialism and the Quest for Nuclear Power, 1939–1949* (Cambridge 1989), p. 37.

investigations of fast neutrons in U238 and of the use of heavy water as moderator, whose results were circulated in April.[8] Müller then proceeded to calculate the U235 enrichment required, presenting his findings in a paper of May 1940 entitled "A Condition for the Application of Uranium as an Explosive" (G-50), which has never been discussed in any of the published literature on the German atomic project.[9] A British intelligence assessment of 1945, however, recognized its importance, stating baldly that "once more in 1940, the question of an atomic bomb was raised. Müller calculated, assuming a uranium-water mixture, that the uranium must be so enriched that there would be 70% more 235 present than 238. This appears to be the last occasion on which an explosive reactor was seriously considered."[10] It is worth quoting Müller's concept of a reactor-bomb at length:

> This work investigates the minimum strength to which the isotope U235 must be enriched to yield an actual explosive. . . . An exponential increase in the number of neutrons occurs, and with that a rise in temperature. The consumption of the U235 and the increase of fission products . . . counteract this rise, while the reduction of U238 nuclei as a consequence of the capture of resonance neutrons involves a decrease in the probability of absorption of the fission neutrons. It may easily be estimated that this rise in temperature must come to a stop relatively soon—not perhaps on account of the impoverishment of active nuclei or the rising absorption by fission products whenever the substance is slightly or halfway pure, but rather because after reaching the first resonance of 25 eV the absorption by U238 sets in extraordinarily strongly.
>
> But if the temperature rise comes to a halt at 25 eV, a minimal portion of the U235 nuclei (about 0.006%) is converted, at a temperature equivalent to about 3×10^5 degrees, roughly only 100 times the temperature of a dynamite explosion. In order to obtain an extraordinarily active explosive and exploit as many as possible of the available U235 nuclei for the production of energy, the isotope U235 has to be strongly enriched so as to be able to overcome the resonances for the absorption by U238. Because of this strong absorption, a very large percentage of slowing moderator is required, which will slow the fission neutrons down as quickly as possible. When the first critical resonance is passed, neutron multiplication will again take place until at the next resonance the same circumstances appear. (p. 1)
>
> We want now to investigate what must be the least proportion of the number of U235 atoms to the number of heavier U238 nuclei and how great must be the ad-

8. P. O. Müller, "Die Energiegewinnung aus dem Uranspaltungsprozess durch schnelle Neutronen" (G-49), 25 April 1940, examines whether fast neutrons can be applied to a uranium machine, but regards it as very unlikely since the scatter cross-section is four times greater than that for fission. Idem, "Berechnung der Energieerzeugung in der Uranmaschine III: Schweres Wasser" (G-53), 29 April 1940 (IMF 29-434).

9. P. O. Müller, "Eine Bedingung für die Verwendbarkeit von Uran als Sprengstoff" (G-50; IMF 29-437).

10. "Notes on Captured German Reports on Nuclear Physics," 1945 (for/by Michael Perrin?), PRO, AB 1/356. There were later proposals for reactor-bombs by Heisenberg and others (see following chapters), but Müller's detailed calculations seem not to have been superseded.

mixture of scattering substance (water) in order to overcome the first resonance at 25 eV. (p.2)

Müller's technical discussion of the problem concludes (p. 6):

Thus, to maintain a temperature rise above 25 eV, that is, above 3×10^5 degrees, there must be present in the solution at least 70% more U235 atoms than U238 atoms. . . . In the most favorable mixture . . . the numbers of atoms will be:

$$U235 = 6.15 \times 10^{20}$$
$$U238 = 3.62 \times 10^{20}$$
$$\text{Hydrogen} = 6.50 \times 10^{22}$$
$$\text{Oxygen} = 3.25 \times 10^{22}.$$

Müller thus conceives of the reactor-bomb as a nonstabilizing reactor, made unstable by the use of a moderator to overcome the stabilization of the 25 eV resonance threshold. An enrichment of the U235 content of uranium by 70% would be needed to do this, a clearly daunting project.

The whole paper is heavily indebted to Heisenberg for its basic theory, and its origin can probably be traced back to a typically unclear remark made in the conclusion of G-39:

The enrichment of U235 is the only method by which the volume of the machine can be made small compared with one cubic meter. It is moreover the only method for producing an explosive material that exceeds by several powers of ten the explosive power of the strongest existing explosives.[11]

Heisenberg is unclear as to whether the explosive would simply be an "enriched" U235, and if so to what degree.

Müller specifically cites (pp. 1, 5) Heisenberg's G-40 of February 1940, the sequel to G-39. In G-40 Heisenberg had observed that "neutron multiplication sets in whenever the isotope U235 is enriched by a factor of 2.5 or more," and this had probably given Müller his cue to start working out the results of higher enrichment factors.[12]

In a subsequent paper, "On the Dependency on Temperature of the Uranium Machine" (G-52, 26 September 1940), Müller spelled out how the unstable reactor's overcoming of the temperature-stabilization barrier would transform it into a bomb:

Since at low temperatures the relationship of scattering to absorption is always unfavorable, ν [nu, for neutron multiplication factor] must with decreasing temperature sink and consequently a uranium machine becomes generally impossible. At a higher temperature the relationship worsens through the constantly stronger escape

---

11. G-39, p. 24 (GWH, A II, 396).

12. Heisenberg, "Bericht über die Möglichkeit technischer Energiegewinnung aus der Uranspaltung (II)" (G-40), 29 February 1940 (IMF 29–398), p. 25 (GWH, A II, 416 f.).

of neutrons from the machine, so that with rising temperature, neutron multiplications approach zero, an effect that at lower temperatures does not possess this overwhelming significance. . . .

From this relationship of ν the following operational aspects of the uranium machine may be stipulated: The machine is generally first active above a certain temperature T_1, so that at the beginning of its operation in general an ignition of the machine is required. At this temperature T_1 an unstable equilibrium predominates, and this takes place through the increasing neutron multiplication as long as the temperature is rising, until the stable equilibrium temperature T_2 is reached. It is now possible through variation of the layer thicknesses to attain a shift of these temperatures T_1 and T_2. . . . The operating temperature is $T_2 = 2T_0$, which is feasible for technical purposes.

It would be possible through variation of the layer thicknesses also to achieve an application of uranium as an explosive. To prevent a premature explosion one must by means of the appropriate choice of layer thicknesses shift the ignition temperature T_1 sufficiently high above the room temperature. The machine is surrounded with a conventional explosive; this ignition enables the machine to be brought to the temperature necessary for neutron multiplication and thus the chain reaction of neutron multiplication is produced.[13]

In 1966 Heisenberg effectively censored a reference to this scheme in David Irving's book. Irving had written in a typed draft sent to Heisenberg:

> In Berlin, K.-H. Höcker reported during April that he thought a reactor could be built . . . and a few weeks later P. O. Müller wrote a paper on *A Requirement for the Utilisation of Uranium as an Explosive* which showed clearly that the Germans' thinking on uranium bombs was still very backward . . . there would have to be at least 70 per cent more uranium 235 atoms in the explosive than uranium 238 . . . water would have to be present as a moderator; in other words that the explosion would be caused by slow neutrons.

Heisenberg favored Irving with a critique of his draft, striking out "the Germans'"(thinking) and substituting "Mr. Müller's" (thinking), and noting in the margin: "Müller's opinions were not taken very seriously in the K.W.I. [Kaiser-Wilhelm-Institute] in Berlin." Irving declared himself convinced by the emendations and stated that he was "cutting out any reference to Müller's work on U-235 als Sprengstoff [as explosive], as I think your objections well-founded."[14] However,

---

13. P. O. Müller, "Über die Temperaturabhängigkeit der Uranmaschine" (G-52), pp. 5, 7 (IMF 29-456).

14. The emended page of typescript with Heisenberg's handwritten annotations is in IMF 32 (frame not numbered), as are Heisenberg's letter of 10 June 1966 and Irving's reply of 16 June 1966. Though Walker (*German National Socialism*, p. 269) lists G-50 and G-52 in his bibliography, he too fails to say what these papers contained.

Sir Charles Frank, however, in a private communication finds Heisenberg's criticism of Müller to be substantiated by the error made in G-50 in assuming the equivalence of energy per particle to temperature (whereas Heisenberg would surely have been aware that at the temperatures concerned en-

this manipulation of Irving by Heisenberg in 1966 does not square with his sponsorship of Müller's work in 1940. Müller worked with Heisenberg for a year, producing at least seven uranium papers for him, the first of which thanked Heisenberg "for his valuable advice and discussion" and Weizsäcker for his inspiration and help.[15] Heisenberg had not deterred Müller from his explorations of the reactor-bomb between April and September 1940—a six-month period, when he would have been well aware of what his assistant was doing, if only through Weizsäcker, who was also based in the same building. Most significantly, Heisenberg had allowed the Müller reports to be circulated officially and not sought to refute their findings, which suggests that they reflected the Heisenberg group's orthodoxy at the time. Weizsäcker not only coauthored a major paper with Müller, but indeed prominently and approvingly cited Müller's work in tandem with Heisenberg's in a paper of his own in September 1941.[16] According to Weizsäcker, Müller had provided the theory for reactor stability at low temperatures, as Heisenberg did for high temperatures.[17] Müller left the Heisenberg team only because, like Höcker, he was conscripted for military service in late 1940 or 1941. By the time Heisenberg was able to have Höcker released back to the Kaiser-Wilhelm-Institute in the spring of 1942, Müller was dead. Höcker states that "I myself have continued his work in 1942–44," which suggests strongly that, far from not having been taken "seriously" at the KWI, Müller was in fact well regarded.[18]

Though practically a dead end, the road to the reactor-bomb was assiduously followed right through the war. The German progress along that road is marked by indicators in the official reports, as well as in the loose comments made by Ger-

---

ergy principally resides in radiation). This "naïveté" of Müller's would have been enough to ensure that his contract was not renewed at the end of the year. Nevertheless, Sir Charles observes, "it was probably useful for Heisenberg to have somebody to do a bit of calculation just to demonstrate that the use of a reactor-bomb would not be cost effective" (Frank to author, 20 March 1994).

15. P. O. Müller, "Die Wirkungsquerschnitt der Uranspaltung," (G-7), Max-Planck-Institut, Berlin-Dahlem, December 1939, p. 10. On the basis of Bohr-Wheeler, Müller investigated the fission cross-section for fast neutrons in ordinary uranium, finding it to sink after a certain threshold.

The other Müller papers are (in chronological order): G-7, G-60, G-49, G-51, G-53 (IMF 29-434), G-50 (IMF 29-437), G-52 (IMF 29-456).

16. Weizsäcker, Müller, and Höcker, "Berechnung der Energieerzeugung."

17. C. F. von Weizsäcker, "Über den Temperatureffekt der Schichtenmaschine" (G-121), 1 September 1941, p. 1 (IMF 30-017).

18. K.-H. Höcker to author, 20 August 1991. In a subsequent reply of 18 August 1993 to a request for his comments on copies of two papers by Müller that were provided to him, Professor Höcker was somewhat cryptic, but significantly did not impugn his former colleague's scientific ability. The entire main text of his reply runs (in translation): "I am glad that you are interested from the standpoint of the historian in those scientific works that might enable the leap from the knowledge of scientific facts to their eventual application through still hypothetical technical applications. Mr. Müller in his work made modeling assumptions in elaborating the consequences of the liberating of energy from the release of elemental processes."

man scientists over the years 1939–45 that we shall come to in due course. Its misconception was rooted deeply in Heisenberg's whole reactor theory, rather than being an illogical aberration. And it was accepted by Heisenberg's own working circle, rather than being the figment of some eccentric physicists' imaginations.

After the war Heisenberg admitted with his customary ambiguity that his group had actually considered reactor-bombs. Though he tried unconvincingly to make this out as a passing, trivial interest, the glib phrasing hints that the interest may have been somewhat more serious:

> At Farm Hall the possibility was discussed that the Americans had dropped a reactor on Japan which through the resulting radioactive contamination had possibly injured or killed many people. In support of this possibility it could be said that we knew that it was much easier to build a reactor than an atomic bomb, and that consequently through the radioactive contamination of a reactor vaporized in a supercritical state massive damage could be produced. But I am sure that this possibility, if it was discussed for a short time, nevertheless was very soon rejected as unrealistic.[19]

Heisenberg here had come perilously close to admitting that he had seriously considered a reactor-bomb, even if it were only "for a short time."[20]

19. Heisenberg to Irving, 10 June 1966, p. 3 (IMF 32).

20. In an early report probably dating from mid-1940, Peierls had also considered a slow-neutron "radiation" bomb that would result if the reactor were "left to explode" (R. Peierls, "Summary of Information on the Uranium Problem," PRO, AB 1/494, "MS 2").

CHAPTER 9

The Reactor and the Bomb

Plutonium, 1940–41

By the middle of 1940 it appeared to Heisenberg that both routes to an atomic bomb were virtually impassable. He and his associates had worked out that an "almost pure" U235 bomb would require a staggeringly huge critical mass of the rare isotope (which in any case was proving more difficult to isolate than imagined, even in very small amounts). As to the other route, the reactor-bomb, Müller's work had made it obvious just how improbable a monstrosity such a device would be. But it was now that a third path suddenly opened up.

Weizsäcker was an assiduous reader of the *Physical Review,* which he would often peruse on the Berlin subway. He would certainly have seen an article in a January 1940 issue by the American L. Turner that cited one of his own papers. Turner had argued that when U238 captured a neutron to become U239, it would decay to the new element "93 Eka Re239," which he conjectured to be the ancestor of U235. This new element, known later as neptunium, would according to Bohr-Wheeler be fissile by fast as well as thermal neutrons.[1] The search for the long-lived isotope of this element had been pursued keenly in 1939–40, since it would obviously be at least as fissile as U235. Moreover, unlike U235, the new isotope would be chemically different from uranium and so much more easily separated from uranium than was U235. However, it seems to have taken until July 1940 for the penny to drop in Weizsäcker's mind that such a highly fissile, relatively easily separable isotope would also be as explosive as U235.

Weizsäcker's paper for the Army Weapons Research Office of July 1940, "A Possibility of Gaining Energy from U238," first lists the disadvantages of using U235/U238 mixtures, including the fact that "because of the resonance absorption of neutrons in the U238, even the energy of the U235 cannot be liberated

---

1. L. Turner, "The Nonexistence of Transuranic Elements," *Physical Review* 57 (15 January 1940): 157.

suddenly at a very high temperature; hence its use as a practical explosive comes to nothing."[2] (This remark, reminiscent of Heisenberg's phrases in G-39, suggests strongly that Weizsäcker had not considered accurately the case of a pure-U235 bomb.) But, continues Weizsäcker, "all these difficulties may be overcome" if one considers that U238 may, by capturing a neutron, produce an unstable 23-minute U239, which would then decay into a stable element 93 "Eka Re239." This element 93 is assumed by Weizsäcker to be long-lived and, as a result of Bohr-Wheeler, fissile like U235. It will also be separable by chemical methods.

> In this way, two-thirds of our U238 may be transformed into Eka Re. This Eka Re can be used in three ways:
>
> 1. To construct very small machines.
> 2. As explosive.
> 3. For the transformation—by mixing—of other elements in large quantities.

Weizsäcker's enthusiasm about the explosive potential of the element produced in the reactor is all too clear. It exposes the dishonesty of his later claims that he had never intended to provide the Nazis with an atomic bomb, was interested only in physics, and, moreover, had from the start held a high moral position on the matter. Given the fact that the actual difficulty of separating the transuranic was not yet properly appreciated and that a reactor to produce it seemed feasible, Weizsäcker's enthusiastic proposal of the explosive potential of the new "reactor element" to the Nazi military weapons development office belies any claim he has made to be an arbiter of moral conscience. He was intentionally dangling the bait of an atomic bomb before his Nazified military sponsors.[3]

Ironically, Weizsäcker's speculation that element 93 was the stable end of the decay series was already outdated by the time he wrote of it. In an article published in the *Physical Review* on 15 June 1940, E. McMillan and P. Abelson had announced their discovery that neptunium was in fact a short-lived 2.3-day element 93, which would decay in turn into a stable isotope of element 94—plutonium. This, obviously, would be the explosive element, and not 93, as Weizsäcker had believed.[4] After reading the McMillan-Abelson article, however, the Germans were quick to realize the correctness of this interpretation and adopted 94 as the stable nuclear explosive. Weizsäcker claims that he had arrived at his idea of a transuranic explosive independently of the June *Physical Review* article—a typical half-truth, since it was the earlier Turner article of January, rather than the McMillan and Abelson paper of June, that inspired his own report and produced its erroneous conclusion about element 93. In any event, it took the published

---

2. C.-F. von Weizsäcker, "Eine Möglichkeit der Energiegewinnung aus U238" (G-59), 17 July 1940 (IMF 29-451).

3. For Weizsäcker's moral pretensions, see below, chaps. 14 and 15.

4. E. McMillan and P. Abelson, "Radioactive Element 93," *Physical Review* 57 (15 June 1940): 1185 f.

American work to identify for the Germans precisely which of the transuranics would be the stable practicable explosive.[5]

The McMillan-Abelson article was the last crucial paper on fission to be published before the embargo campaigned for by Leo Szilard on the publication of such potentially dangerous information came into force. The article greatly alarmed Chadwick, who had the British government complain to the U.S. authorities about its publication.[6] His concern was hardly surprising, since the implication of the paper that plutonium would be highly fissile entailed some startling consequences. If a critical reactor could be built, it would provide a steady source of explosive material for a bomb. The material would be in a purified state, the fission cross-sections larger than in $U235$, and thus the critical mass might be conjectured to be much smaller than for $U235$. Measurements and calculations, though very tentative, seemed to bear out these implications The result of the circulation of the McMillan-Abelson paper in America was that plutonium eclipsed $U235$ as the atomic explosive of choice during 1940 and until the late summer of 1941 in the United States.[7] The same happened in Germany, where Weizsäcker's and Heisenberg's swift assimilation of the significance of element 94 made them understand

5. See D. Irving, *The German Atomic Bomb*, 2d ed. (New York, 1983), p. 73, for Weizsäcker's claim of independent discovery. Actually, Weizsäcker had simply followed up Turner's idea that the daughter of $U239$ might be the origin of the actinide series.

6. For Chadwick's concern, see M. Gowing, *Britain and Atomic Energy, 1939–1945* (London, 1964), p. 60. This led to the withholding from publication until 1946 of Seaborg's important paper on plutonium of March 1941; see G. Seaborg et al., *The Transuranium Elements* (New York, 1949), pp. 5–7.

7. The United States neglected the $U235$ bomb in 1940–41 despite repeated British urging. Lyman Briggs, the head of the American uranium committee, simply kept the startlingly optimistic British reports in his safe, declining to show them to his colleagues. It was only when Oliphant in desperation visited the United States in the summer of 1941 and informed an unhappy Ernest Lawrence of the situation that immediate and dramatic action was taken. (M. Oliphant, "Notes on Conversation with E. O. Lawrence, 23–24 September 1941," PRO, AB 1/495.) The result was the launching of the American bomb effort in August 1941, which led in due course to the Manhattan Project. See M. Oliphant, "The Beginning: Chadwick and the Neutron," *BAS* 38 (1982): 14–18; Gowing, *Britain and Atomic Energy*, pp. 42, 115–117; A. H. Compton, *Atomic Quest: A Personal Narrative* (New York, 1956), pp. 53 f.; R. G. Hewlett and O. E. Anderson, *The New World, 1939–1946: A History of the USAEC* (University Park, Pa., 1962), 1:41–44; J. Conant, *My Several Lives* (New York, 1970), pp. 274–282 (now fleshed out in J. G. Hershberg, *James B. Conant: Harvard to Hiroshima and the Making of the Nuclear Age* [New York, 1993]). The American neglect of $U235$ in 1940–41 is astonishing and requires further investigation. Even Fermi was careless about the matter of a $U235$ bomb; see his "Report A-26" (6 October 1941), in his *Collected Papers* (Chicago, 1962–65), 2:98–103, which guesses at a $U235$ critical mass of 130 kg, but disarmingly admits that it could be anywhere between 20 kg and "one or more tons"!

Even after the British work had been taken to heart by the Americans, the fact of the small critical mass of $U235$ was not fully absorbed. The secret National Academy of Sciences Third Report of 6 November 1941, prepared by Compton, estimated the critical mass to range from 26 kg to 720 kg, or, if tamped, from 3.4 kg to 87 kg (NA, RG 227, OSRD/S-1, microfilm M-1392, roll 1, folder 1, S-1 Historical File, Bush-Conant Files, sec. A, app. A).

For calculations and measurements of the fissionability of plutonium, see Hewlett and Anderson, *The New World*, pp. 41 f.; R. Rhodes, *The Making of the Atomic Bomb* (New York, 1986), pp. 366, 368.

their reactor program to be all the more vital.[8] The military significance attached by Weizsäcker to his theorizing was picked up and broadcast by Heisenberg. In a lecture intended for Nazi dignitaries including Himmler held in Berlin on 26 February 1942, Heisenberg stated:

> As soon as such a machine is in operation, the question of the production of a new explosive takes a new turn, according to an idea of von Weizsäcker. The transformation of uranium in the machine produces, in fact, a new substance (element 94), which is most probably, just like U235, an explosive of the same unimaginable effect. This substance can be obtained much more easily from uranium than is U235 because it may be separated chemically from the uranium.[9]

The unpromising avenues to a U235 bomb and a reactor-bomb were now largely given up and the reactor embraced as the royal road, not only to power generation and the development of an atomic engine, but also to the plutonium atomic bomb.

That Heisenberg was unable, for all his efforts, to achieve criticality with his various reactor experiments during the war was due in large part to his ready acceptance of a wrong measurement of the properties of graphite as a moderator. Walter Bothe's misleading experimental data on graphite had been supported by Heisenberg's theory and ruled out the construction of a graphite reactor, and induced the German team to commit itself to heavy water for its moderator.[10] Difficult to manufacture and coming from a vulnerable plant in Norway, heavy water proved awkward on various counts and undoubtedly slowed down the German project. Yet even when Heisenberg was informed of the true data for graphite, he was

8. J. Schintlmeister and E. Hernegger ("Über ein bisher unbekanntes, alpha-strahlendes chemisches Element" [G-55], June 1940, and its two sequels of May 1941 [G-112 and G-111; IMF 31-001/056]) believed they had found plutonium, though their colleagues were skeptical, according to M. Walker, *German National Socialism and the Quest for Nuclear Power, 1939–1949* (Cambridge, 1989), p. 23, citing Kurt Starke. Schintlmeister concluded that, like U235, element 94 would be fissionable by thermal neutrons (IMF 31-047/048). There was certainly not enough plutonium to measure the cross-sections.

The Germans were relaxed about keeping secret their research on transuranics and permitted reports on element 93 by Hahn and Strassmann (G-151) and Starke (G-113) to be printed in *Die Naturwissenschaften* 30 (1942). One may discern here the hand of Paul Rosbaud, who was probably trying to alert the Allies to German interest in plutonium.

9. "Die theoretischen Grundlagen für die Energiegewinnung aus der Uranspaltung" (no G number), 26 February 1942 (IMF 29-1005), in GWH, A II, 517–521, at p. 520. Himmler was invited to the meeting, but did not attend; see below, chap. 12.

10. W. Bothe and P. Jensen, "Die Absorption thermischer Neutronen in Elektrographit," 20 January 1941 (G-71; printed version in IMF 31-915), amending an earlier paper (G-12) of 7 June 1940. The HWA Report of 1942 (see below, chap. 11), pp. 87 f., also cites the former Bothe-Jensen paper for its rejection of a graphite reactor and observes that "since the more exact investigation of the graphite used yielded later a small boron content, the true capture cross-section is clearly smaller. But since carbon with a higher purity than the type used cannot be practically produced, it may scarcely be considered as a moderator."

incapable of changing direction and continued with heavy water.[11] After the war, Heisenberg tried to blame the failure of the German reactor program on Bothe's "mistake," but some colleagues were more inclined to attribute it to Heisenberg's insistence on knowing best all the time. Bothe defended himself by arguing that Heisenberg's theoretical estimates agreed with his own experimental results and had been welcomed for that reason.[12] In any case, Heisenberg's omniscience should be contrasted with the careful experimental approach of Szilard and Fermi, who had been aware from the start of the difficulty of obtaining the requisite purity of graphite for their work and had taken great care to verify the purity of their material and to screen out other factors.[13]

Among the physicists friendly with Heisenberg who investigated the production of plutonium was the Austrian Fritz Houtermans. He was a curious character, half Jew and whole communist, who had worked in Russia in the 1930s, where he was arrested by the secret police before being returned to Germany in care of the Gestapo after the outbreak of the war. Thanks to somewhat obscure interventions on his behalf, Houtermans had eventually been released and found through Max von Laue a research post in the Berlin laboratory of Baron Manfred von Ardenne, where he worked on an atomic research project funded by the German Post Office. There he produced in 1941 a detailed research report on the construction of a reactor that could be used to produce plutonium for a bomb. Houtermans

11. W. Hanle, "Über den Nachweis von Bor und Cadmium in Kohle" (G-85), 18 April 1941, criticized Bothe's measurement and the impurity of his graphite samples. Cf. G. Joos to HWA WaF/1a, 29 March 1940 (G-46; IMF 31-110). (See Walker, *German National Socialism*, p. 26.) The Army Weapons Research Office decided, however, to continue with heavy water on the grounds that the graphite would be too expensive to produce and that in any case the graphite was required for the rocket program. Moreover, the graphite would be contaminated by radioactivity, whereas the heavy water could be used indefinitely. Heisenberg claimed not to have been informed of these corrected data, though it is difficult to believe that, as the senior physicist of the project, he would not have seen the circulated reports, or at least been told of the results by the HWA.

12. See above, chap. 1, for Bothe's cool comments of 1946. See also Walker, *German National Socialism*, pp. 207, 264 f.; Cassidy, p. 423. But D. Irving, *The German Atomic Bomb* (New York, 1967), pp. 58 f., 84 f., naively accepts Heisenberg's attempt to shift the blame to Bothe; Wirtz depicts Bothe's "error" as "blocking the way" to the reactor (K. Winnacker and K. Wirtz, *Nuclear Energy in Germany*, trans. [La Grange Park, Ill., 1979], p. 21). However, the HWA was well aware of the potential of graphite, but on account of pressure from Heisenberg (G-39, p. 26; G-40, p. 1a) as well as the prohibitive cost of producing the graphite, it opted for heavy water (Walker, *German National Socialism*, pp. 26 f.). Even with Bothe's "error," a reactor could have been built, though it would have required much more uranium as well as a higher enrichment of the U235. The interview with Paul Harteck in J. J. Ermenc, *Atomic Bomb Scientists: Memoirs, 1939–1945* (Westport, Conn., 1989), pp. 112–115, 123, shows a near contempt for Heisenberg's proprietorial attitude.

13. L. Szilard, *Leo Szilard: His Version of the Facts,* ed. S. R. Weart and G. W. Szilard (Cambridge, Mass., 1978), pp. 116 f.; W. Lanouette, *Genius in the Shadows: A Biography of Leo Szilard* (New York, 1993), pp. 216 f. The Szilard-Fermi figure was kept secret; it was later printed in Fermi, "Report A-21," in *Collected Papers*, 2:31–40.

claimed plausibly enough that he had worked for the Nazi regime to save his own life, and indeed in the spring of 1941 he had contrived to send the Americans a warning about the success of the German project.[14] Nevertheless, the dedication of his research raises questions about his actions and his honesty. Indeed, Houtermans admitted to Weizsäcker that to protect himself he had been obliged to provide the Nazi regime with promising military research.[15]

Like Houtermans, Ardenne (1907–97) was highly adaptable politically. A gifted inventor, he worked happily first for the Nazi government, then for Stalin on the production of the Soviet atomic bomb, and then for East Germany, where he was honored for his political as well as scientific contributions, before finally coming through as a self-styled hero of the peaceful revolution that resulted in German re-unification in 1989.[16]

Ardenne had written to the Nazi Post Office minister Wilhelm Ohnesorge in December 1939 with a request to sponsor nuclear-fission research at his laboratory.[17] Subsequently this extraordinary operator had inveigled Heisenberg, Weizsäcker, Hahn, and many other distinguished physicists to visit his baronial mansion-cum-laboratory. On 10 October 1940, Ardenne recalled in the original typescript of his memoirs, he was visited by Weizsäcker, who told him that he and his mentor Heisenberg both had concluded that an atomic (i.e., uranium) bomb was impossible:

> Because of the decline of the effective cross-sections at high temperatures, the chain reaction would be broken off prematurely. On this account the chain reaction could

14. See the end of this chapter for a discussion of the 1941 warning.
15. IMF 31-620 (see below). The heroic portrait of Houtermans in R. Jungk, *Brighter Than a Thousand Suns* (Harmondsworth, 1960), pp. 92–95, is as absurd as his depictions of the other German physicists. Jungk falsely states that Houtermans kept his 1941 report secret until 1944 and that only Harteck among the other German scientists understood the plutonium idea; the truth is that the Houtermans paper was circulated in 1941 and that Heisenberg and Weizsäcker besides others had promoted the plutonium idea from 1940. Not a word in Jungk should be taken as true. For references see below.
16. The title of Ardenne's autobiography changes as often as his politics: *Ein glückliches Leben für Forschung und Technik* (Zurich, 1972); 2d ed., *Sechzig Jahre für Forschung und Fortschritt: Autobiographie* (Berlin, 1984); 3d ed., *Die Erinnerungen* (Munich, 1991). A very hostile portrait of Ardenne was drawn in 1945 by Paul Rosbaud, the Allied agent in Berlin. Describing Ardenne's contingency plans in early 1945 for continuing his enterprises after the war, Rosbaud told Walter Gerlach, then the head of the German atomic project, that Ardenne had forgotten just one thing: The Russians would be in Berlin in a few months and would pack up Ardenne together with his scientific equipment and manorial suits of armor and send them all off east. Gerlach commented presciently: "And there, I am sure, he will rebuild everything, perhaps ten times larger than before, and he will be glad to continue his work." (Rosbaud, *Report* on German atomic science for ALSOS Mission, 5 August 1945, [IMF 29-1183/4].)
In his review of T. Powers, *Heisenbergs Krieg* (Hamburg, 1993), the German edition of *Heisenberg's War*, Ardenne shamelessly claims that all his and Houtermans's wartime work on nuclear physics was intended "for peaceful aims" (*Die Welt*, 8 May 1993, book section).
17. Ardenne, *Sechzig Jahre*, p. 481. An American target list of 1944 refers to Ardenne as a "well-known Nazi inventor. Boasted of U bomb" (NA, RG 77, MED Decimal Files 319.1, "Reports," box 50).

be employed only in a reactor where the temperatures remain relatively low. This conclusion proved to be an error of historical importance. Because I did not keep silent about it in some details I recollected in 1955, Herr von Weizsäcker, with whom I had until then been in friendly relations, has never pardoned me. My description of these conclusions stands in opposition to the official version proclaimed by Herr von Weizsäcker after Hiroshima, which held that atom bombs were not worked on in Germany in order to withhold them from Hitler.[18]

This rather too frank passage was deleted in the published versions of the memoirs, which nevertheless contained some plain speaking:

My theoretical interest in a sudden explosive [*momentan ablaufenden*] chain reaction had been squashed by an evening visit at the beginning of 1942 by Weizsäcker and his wife. . . . [I was informed that] the cross-section for uranium fission at high temperature was strongly reduced, so that no explosive chain reaction could occur. . . . In this error Heisenberg and Weizsäcker remained caught until the day of Hiroshima, as the [Farm Hall] recording reveals. . . . Thankfully, the caution, errors, and chances of early initiatives prevented the development of an atomic bomb.[19]

When David Irving heard about this from Ardenne in 1965–66, he naturally consulted Heisenberg and Weizsäcker for their views, and he got an indignant response to the effect that they'd never been close to "that man"—a mere manager who would produce a bomb for anyone. If the Weizsäcker conversation ever took place, Heisenberg insisted, it must have been a ploy to prevent Ardenne from getting the Nazi politicians all enthused about making a bomb, which, claimed Heisenberg, he and Weizsäcker had "naturally wanted to prevent at any price."[20] Weizsäcker himself sadly denied that a man of Ardenne's "political" bent and he had ever been close, and asserted that he had no recollection of ever telling Ardenne that an atomic bomb was not possible. Ardenne's tales to Irving must have been the last straw for Weizsäcker, who, despite their family friendship during the war period, had already broken off relations with Ardenne over incautious remarks made in lectures in the 1950s.[21] The two were reconciled in 1986 through

18. Reproduced in IMF 32, typescript pp. 116–117. In correspondence of 9 August 1984 Professor von Ardenne told me that in 1940 he and Weizsäcker were on close terms following the deaths of their brothers, who had been in the same regiment. Ardenne is convinced that Weizsäcker was not trying to put him off the scent, but was genuinely conveying Heisenberg's and his own "understanding that the uranium bomb wouldn't work because at high temperatures the fission cross-section decreased critically. [This] bespoke their true thinking at the time."

19. Ardenne, *Sechzig Jahre*, pp. 162 f.

20. Irving, *German Atomic Bomb*, pp. 71 f. Heisenberg to Irving, May 17, 1966 (IMF 32), strongly objects to Ardenne's recollection of the Weizsäcker visit of October 10, 1940. So too does Weizsäcker to Irving, June 14, 1966 (IMF 32). See above, chap. 2.

21. In a letter to me of 9 August 1984, Ardenne emphatically stated that his conversations with Weizsäcker during the war were, on account of their family connection, conducted "in complete openness"; the fact that Weizsäcker visited Ardenne's house with his wife suggests that this is true. Ardenne says that he had lectured on the Weizsäcker and Heisenberg mistake to a "Kongress der Kammer der

the efforts of West German President Richard von Weizsäcker, resulting in the spectacle of Carl-Friedrich being invited by Ardenne to East Germany to speak on the nuclear threat to world peace.[22] Here again is confirmation of the need to take Weizsäcker's words with caution; if he had indeed believed Ardenne to be a liar, he would scarcely have accepted his invitation.

Heisenberg's letter of complaint about Ardenne was also self-incriminating in that it conceded he had informed the entrepreneur during 1940—as Ardenne claimed—that the mass of a uranium bomb would be very small. After explaining how concerned he and Weizsäcker were to throw Ardenne off the scent of the bomb by their temperature argument, Heisenberg casually observes: "Obviously I had incautiously answered Ardenne in my first conversation of 1940 what I believed to be known, namely that an atomic bomb could be made with a few kilograms of U235."[23] One might think this a somewhat inadequate explanation of how Heisenberg had let such a crucial piece of scientific information slip into the hands of a dynamic man known to be politically unsound. The motivation for all this to-ing and fro-ing is given out to be Heisenberg's moral decision to deny Hitler a bomb, yet he maintained after the war that he had never made such a moral decision. Apart from this inconsistency, the actual dates of the Weizsäcker and Heisenberg visits also point to the falseness of these lame excuses. Weizsäcker had visited Ardenne on 10 October 1940 and again in early 1942, and on both of these visits, according to Ardenne, as we have seen, he had explained how a temperature rise frustrated the bomb. Heisenberg also seems to have visited twice—once in 1940 when he dropped the remark about the "few kilos" of U235, and again on 28 November 1941 when he outlined the temperature objection. Why did he wait a year to tell Ardenne that "a few kilos" would not work after all? Such a delay hardly indicates anxiety about letting Ardenne give Hitler a bomb.

There is, furthermore, evidence to suggest that Heisenberg's memory was faulty and that he made only one visit, not two, to Ardenne, and that it was in 1941, not 1940. Ardenne recalls:

In their visits [to my laboratory] in 1940 I had asked Otto Hahn and also Werner Heisenberg the question, how many grams of the pure isotope U235 would be needed for the unleashing of a sudden explosive chain reaction. They answered me: "A few kilograms." In these conversations I advocated the production of several kilograms of U235, it being certainly technically possible with the help of the highly developed magnetic mass separator, which we had at that time planned conceptually, if

Technik" in the 1950s. He also thinks Weizsäcker was angry at his having worked in Russia from 1945 to 1955 in order to achieve world peace through a balance of nuclear weapons. The reader may take his choice between the self-avowed moral stands of the pair.

22. Ardenne, *Sechzig Jahre*, pp. 451 f.; idem, *Ein glückliches Leben*, pp. 257–260; and letters from Ardenne to the author.

23. Heisenberg to Irving, 17 May 1966 (IMF 32).

a large electrical company could be involved in it. Fortunately, no collaborative step could be taken in this direction.[24]

The difficulty here is that Ardenne's guest book (which is the safest documentary evidence for these various visitations) does not indicate a visit from Heisenberg in 1940, but only one for 28 November 1941. Moreover, Hahn's visit is from around the same time, 10 December 1941.[25] This gives us a clue to a characteristic Heisenberg lie. When Irving presented Heisenberg with Ardenne's original misdating of a visit to 1940, he obviously triggered Heisenberg's usual facile rationalizing ability so that he imagined there must have also been a visit in 1940 during which he mentioned the few kilos recalled by Ardenne; Heisenberg then went on glibly to recollect that he would have nullified this dangerous remark at his (now he thought) second meeting of 1941. The problem with this double sequence is Hahn's corroboration of the "few kilos" figure. Hahn, who depended for his knowledge of the critical mass on Heisenberg, visited Ardenne only two weeks after Heisenberg and reiterated that the mass would be only a few kilos (probably 50 kg, to judge from a remark at Farm Hall).[26] It certainly would have surprised Ardenne if Hahn's few kilos had contradicted what he had just heard from Heisenberg; obviously Hahn had, for Ardenne, reinforced Heisenberg's opinion, rather than being at odds with it. So, if Heisenberg did say something about a few kilos of U235 as he and Ardenne claimed, then it would have been at the single meeting he had with Ardenne in November 1941; the message about the temperature problem would have been carried much earlier by Weizsäcker. In any event, it is perilous to accept Heisenberg's recollection of a double visit as it is presented in his letter of 1966.[27]

The contradictions in this episode deepen when Ardenne's behavior is consid-

24. Ardenne, *Ein glückliches Leben*, p. 153.

25. Ardenne, *Sechzig Jahre*, p. 482. In this edition, Ardenne also (p. 162) corrects the date of the "few kilos" conversations to 1941. K. Hoffmann, *Otto Hahn* (Berlin, 1979), pp. 225 f., wrongly conflates the separate visits of Hahn and Heisenberg into a single visit.

26. In the Farm Hall transcripts (FHT, no. 4, p. 4; *OE*, p. 73), Hahn queried Heisenberg as to why he had told him during the war that "50 kg" of U235 were needed to "do anything." Heisenberg shrugged this off and insisted that it was actually 2 tons that were needed! The "few kilos" may refer to the amount of U235 containing enough energy to make a big bang; it might be embedded in a far larger quantity of U235 itself, or perhaps it might simply signify the weight of enriched U235 in a given mass of uranium, or refer to the amount of U235 needed to be contained in either pure or mixed form in a reactor-bomb. Hahn had obviously misunderstood Heisenberg, who had doubtless been too impatient to explain his reasoning. Or it may be simply a case of Heisenberg's famous cavalier attitude to numbers; as he says in the transcripts, the critical mass could be anywhere from 50 to 5,000 kg depending on the values of the mean free path—hardly a precise or serious approach to the problem. (See chap. 14.)

27. To complicate matters even further, in a letter to me dated 19 August 1991 Ardenne states that the critical-mass figure was mentioned to him not by Heisenberg at all, but solely by Hahn. If Ardenne's statement is correct, then the delusory nature of Heisenberg's memory is evident. On the other hand, if Heisenberg did mention "a few kilos," one runs into the problems discussed in the text.

ered. If only a few kilos of U235 were needed, why did not the ambitious Ardenne press ahead urgently with his mass separator? And why did Hahn—who definitely did have moral compunctions about producing a bomb for the Nazi regime—also hang out the tempting bait of a "few kilos"? The answer is to be found in Heisenberg's analyses of the uranium bomb problem: A pure U235 bomb would require an enormous surrounding mass of the isotope in order to assure the efficient explosion of the "few kilos," while a uranium reactor-bomb using an enriched stock of "a few kilos" of pure U235 would also be impractical because of the diminishing cross-sections. In other words, both Heisenberg and Hahn were able to throw off their dangerous remarks to Ardenne because they were able immediately to tell him that even if "a few kilos" were obtained, it still would not work.[28]

Perhaps the simplest explanation for these confusing pieces of evidence is that Heisenberg and Weizsäcker were referring obscurely to different types of bombs and that they were too cryptic and close-lipped for Ardenne (like Hahn) to understand clearly what they had in mind. The "few kilos" that Heisenberg had divulged to Hahn pertained to the amount needed to be burned in a pure U235 bomb, which would, however, require a vastly greater "critical mass" to be sure of exploding. References to mean free paths being too long also probably referred to the U235 bomb, just as Heisenberg used the phrase at Farm Hall in 1945 to introduce his random-walk calculation. On the other hand, references to high temperatures cutting off the reaction most likely relate to the reactor-bomb idea. It is, however, impossible to be sure what really happened between Ardenne and Heisenberg and Weizsäcker, since Ardenne was writing so many years after the event and was still rather confused by the whole matter. Nevertheless, there still seems to be a ring of truth in his recounting of the peculiar reasons given so dissuasively to him by Heisenberg and Weizsäcker.

It was in this environment of murky political and scientific thinking that Houtermans spent 1941 preparing an extensive paper on the production of plutonium (or rather an unspecified transuranic) as a bomb fuel. Houtermans seems to have worked, to judge from his references, without benefit of seeing the various secret German scientific reports, but he was evidently aware of Heisenberg's idea that reactors would be self-stabilizing; and he did, it seems, enjoy the confidence of both Heisenberg and Weizsäcker.[29] At any rate, Heisenberg's preoccupation

---

28. In a letter to me of 9 August 1984 Ardenne repeats that he accepted the Heisenberg-Weizsäcker view that the bomb was impossible. As to why he failed earlier to persuade Heisenberg himself to let him pursue the isotope separation of a few kilos of U235, Ardenne observes that Heisenberg had little influence and that anyway he (Ardenne), on account of *his* dislike of the Nazis, was interested only in the scientific problem of isotopes and so never attempted to persuade his patron, the Nazi Post Office minister Ohnesorge, nor the Siemens company to develop the separation process. (However, see below, chap. 13, for evidence that Ardenne in 1944–45 was keen to show how his mass separator would have been successful.) Ardenne's remarks, like Heisenberg's, should be treated with due skepticism.

29. Heisenberg to Irving, 10 June 1966 (IMF 32), says he often discussed nuclear subjects with Houtermans, and insists that Houtermans's 1941 report was circulated (despite Jungk's assertion

with neutron escape as the temperature rises also figures in the Houtermans paper of August 1941 entitled "On the Release of Nuclear Chain Reactions":

> This even happens with pure $U235$, where the not as yet treated probability of the neutrons escaping from the finite experimental volume without releasing a neutron must rise with the multiplication of neutrons and $T^{-1/2}$ [temperature law] and thus likewise operate as self-regulating.[30]

Houtermans's self-stabilizing reactor, however, was rather different from Heisenberg's since it aimed at the production not of energy, but of radioactive isotopes. For this reason, it would be able to operate at low temperature using liquid methane as a moderator, rather than heavy water or graphite. This meant that it would be an efficient producer of an "element 93 or higher" that could be chemically separated and used as a nuclear explosive. Houtermans here echoes Weizsäcker's opinion that the long-lived 239 descendent of $U238$ is a more viable road to the atomic bomb than $U235$. (His imprecision about whether it would be element 93 or 94 that would be the long-lived 239 isotope also recalls Weizsäcker's paper of 1940.)

> In all conceivable apparatuses permitting a chain reaction in separated [*sic*] $U235$, only 1/139th of the total available uranium mass would be used as *burning fuel* or *explosive* [*als "Brennstoff" oder "Explosivstoff"*].

[*Brighter Than a Thousand Suns*, pp. 92–95] that it was suppressed by its author for reasons of conscience). Houtermans's letter of 9 April 1945 to Patrick Blackett (IMF 31-1148/9) refers to intimate conversations with Heisenberg. (See below, chap. 15.)

According to British reports in PRO, AB 1/356 (Chadwick to Perrin, and Fuchs to Perrin, March–April 1942), it was known that Houtermans was working in Ardenne's laboratory and had published an article on isotope separation in the *Annalen der Physik* 40 (November 1941): 493. Furthermore, Houtermans was thought to be a regular abstractor of papers on fission for the *Physikalische Berichte*. Klaus Fuchs states that he had met Houtermans in 1934 in England, and that his Russian wife and two children were now in the United States. (The isotope-separation paper is also mentioned in a 7 November 1944 report on German scientific literature in the same file.)

30. F. G. Houtermans, *Zur Frage der Auslösung von Kern-Kettenreaktionen*, Mitteilung aus dem Laboratorium Manfred von Ardenne, Berlin-Lichterfelde-Ost, August 1941, p. 24. The paper has been reissued in photocopy by the Forschungsinstitut Manfred von Ardenne, Dresden, 1987, under the title "Nachdruck als Beitrag zur Geschichte der Kernspaltung in Deutschland." The paper was retyped in October 1943 and circulated in November 1943 in the volume *Sonderhefte der Forschungsanstalt der Deutschen Reichspost, Abteilung für Kernphysik* ("Oktober 1943"), pp. 115–145 (G-94; IMF 30-704); see p. 135.

The words "even with pure U235" (*selbst bei reinem U235*) are omitted from the third issue of the paper (G-267, p. 27). G-267 had been retyped and a *Nachwort* added for its appearance in October 1944 in the series of *Forschungsberichte* of the official nuclear program then headed by W. Gerlach; the typescript is dated August 1944, from the "Physik. Techn. Reichsanstalt, Berlin," to which Houtermans had by now moved, before going on to Göttingen.

On Houtermans's reactor theory see S. R. Weart, "Secrecy, Simultaneous Discovery, and the Theory of Nuclear Reactors," *American Journal of Physics* 45 (1977): 1054.

M. Gowing, "Niels Bohr and Nuclear Weapons," in *Niels Bohr: A Centenary Volume*, ed. A. P. French and J. P. Kennedy (Cambridge, Mass., 1985), p. 267, slips in saying that Houtermans's paper "calculated the critical mass of U235."

We can therefore view an apparatus whose energy return on weighable amounts of U235 permits a chain reaction to take place as being at the same time an isotope-transformation apparatus. . . . Its advantage over an isotope separator is that the newly created product, with nuclear charge of 93 or higher, is no longer chemically identical with uranium and hence may be separated by conventional chemical methods. . . . This is of much greater value than isotope separation, which permits only the U235 to be of use.[31]

Though Houtermans's report may not have been officially circulated in 1941, Heisenberg and other scientists—including, of course, Ardenne, who presumably showed it to his master Ohnesorge—saw copies of it that year, and it seems probable that Heisenberg would have discussed it with Houtermans during his visit to the Ardenne laboratory that November.[32] It was, however, reissued in 1943 and 1944 in two variants and thus entered a fairly wide official circulation. Houtermans claimed he had always wanted to restrict it severely, but the language of both the 1943 and 1944 versions is extremely irresponsible in its promotion of the reactor as a realistic means of producing a transuranic nuclear explosive. After the war, Houtermans admitted that he had felt obliged to produce good military research results such as the plutonium findings.[33] The fact that he was willing to provide such potentially dangerous ideas to his Nazi superiors raises a serious question about his scientific and moral judgment. This lack of discrimination may help explain how Houtermans was able in 1945 to see virtually all his German colleagues as "resisters" of one sort or another.[34] In any event, nothing that Houtermans has to say should be accepted as truth, since he lied to Jungk about the crucial point; he claimed that he had known about the transuranic explosive produced in the reactor in July 1941, but that in his August paper he "did not report on this aspect of his work, since he did not wish to draw the attention of the state authorities to the possibility of the construction of atomic bombs."[35] This was a blatant lie; Houtermans's paper had explicitly proposed the use of his reactor to produce a transuranic explosive and even used the term "Explosivstoff."

31. Houtermans, "Zur Frage der Auslösung" (1941 version), pp. 31, 33 (G-94, pp. 139 f.). The word *Explosivstoff* is omitted from G-267, p. 33.

"Separated U235" may mean here that the reaction occurs only in the U235, rather than that the reactor contains only U235. In G-267 Houtermans uses "getrenntem" and in G-94 "isoliertem."

32. Ardenne's editorial note to his reissue of the 1941 Houtermans paper claims it was sent at the time to Bothe, Diebner, Hahn, Flügge, Heisenberg, Weizsäcker, and others. S. Flügge, "Kann man eine Uranmaschine mit schnellen Neutronen betreiben?" (G-142), September 1942, pp. 152, 155 (IMF 30-720), cites a Reichspostforschung secret report of 1942 by Houtermans.

33. Irving has noted, concerning an interview with Weizsäcker, 19 July 1966 (IMF 31-620): "According to Weizsäcker, Houtermans talked with him at great length about the plutonium question. He explained to W. that his position was so delicate as a political suspect that he had to make some *military* [emphasis added; PLR] contribution." (Houtermans also went to Russia during the war to collect scientific intelligence for the Germans on the Soviet nuclear project; see below.)

34. Houtermans to Blackett, 9 April 1945, Goudsmit Papers, AIP, box 10, folder 93 (IMF 31-1149).

35. Jungk, *Brighter Than a Thousand Suns*, p. 94.

Yet this was the same man who reportedly had arranged for an emigrating German physicist (Fritz Reiche) in March 1941 to carry a message to his friends in America that was reported eventually to the head of the U.S. uranium project thus:

A large number of German physicists are working intensively on the uranium bomb under the direction of Heisenberg. . . . Heisenberg tries to delay the work as much as possible, fearing the catastrophic results of a success. But he cannot help fulfilling the orders given to him, and if the problem can be solved, it will be solved probably in the near future. So he [Houtermans] gave the advice to us to hurry up if U.S.A. will not come too late.

Incidentally, Reiche, who had carried the warning, later inclined to skepticism about Heisenberg's white-knight act.[36]

There is no reason to doubt Houtermans's sincerity in giving this warning; he was still well esteemed at this stage by such a man of conscience as the Allied agent Paul Rosbaud, who had known him since 1929.[37] Unhappily, the evidence suggests that Houtermans lost his footing a little later that year after the German invasion of Russia. First there came his rash plutonium proposal in his August 1941 report. Then there was his dubious participation in October–November 1941 in a mission for German intelligence to report on Soviet scientific work at Kiev, Kharkov, and other laboratories. The report submitted by Houtermans on the mission concluded with the distasteful words: "Of course, it will be necessary to check in each case the political idea."[38] After the war, Houtermans put a favorable gloss on this visit, claiming he had agreed to go in order to help his former Russian colleagues.[39]

36. R. Ladenburg to L. Briggs, 14 April 1941, in NA, RG 227, OSRD/S-1, Briggs, box 5, Ladenburg folder, quoted in T. Powers, *Heisenberg's War* (New York, 1993), pp. 107 f. See Fritz Reiche's own recollection in his interview of 9 May 1962, p. 8 (OHI), where he expresses doubt about the truth of Heisenberg's opposition to the bomb project: "I thought really it is so, that Heisenberg was strictly opposed to the whole thing. Obviously not. This was not so, I think." This reconsideration is not reported by Powers.

Wigner's recollections in S. R. Weart, "The Road to Los Alamos," *Journal de Physique* 43, no. 12 (December 1982), Supplément (*International Colloquium on the History of Particle Physics, 21–23 July* [= *Colloque C8*]), p. 317, and in *The Recollections of Eugene P. Wigner* (New York, 1992), p. 241, confuse the Houtermans message with one received a year later by Szilard, via Friedrich Dessauer, as do most existing accounts (e.g., A. Kramish, *The Griffin* [Boston, 1986], p. 162 f.). See Powers, *Heisenberg's War*, pp. 103–109, 162 f., 507, 519, citing Szilard to Arthur Compton, 1 June 1942, NA, RG 227, OSRD/S-1, microfilm M-1392, roll 7, folder 75 (Bush-Conant Files).

37. Kramish, *The Griffin*, pp. 122–124, describes the mission as being run for German Naval Intelligence.

38. F. G. Houtermans, "Evaluation of the Quality, Political Inclination, and Present Situation of Physicists, Engineers, and Technically Trained Helpers in Sowjetrussland" (American OSS translation), 31 December 1941, submitted to Admiral Witzell of German Naval Intelligence. I am grateful to Arnold Kramish for supplying a copy of this translated document from the Goudsmit Papers, which I verified to be in box 27, folder 35. The original may be in the OSS records of the National Archives, since the OSS had prepared the translation.

39. See Powers, *Heisenberg's War*, pp. 413 ff.

On this subject, however, Houtermans seems to have been less than frank during his April 1945 interrogation at Göttingen by Goudsmit, who may have allowed himself to be misled by Houtermans's silence about his proposal for plutonium as an explosive.[40] On the other hand, Goudsmit reports that Houtermans gave him a manuscript copy of his secret published paper on the "chain reaction at low temperature." This was the "Auslösung" paper with the discreet deletions about the explosive potential of plutonium, as per its 1944 revision described above. Indeed at Göttingen in April 1945, Houtermans was not at all informative about Heisenberg and the German uranium project. His main concern, it seems, was to get the German physics institutes running again at full steam as though there had not been a war.[41]

What became known of Houtermans's wartime activities disturbed some of his former friends. Houtermans had reportedly gone east in company with Diebner and Schumann of the Heereswaffenamt, who were accustomed to travel in uniform, and it appears that Paul Rosbaud may have lost faith in his old friend on hearing that he too had been seen at Kharkov wearing a military cap. Certainly Rosbaud found Houtermans's postwar personal behavior "disgusting," thought him "not the type of man Germany and German science needs today," and hoped that he might be prevented from coming to work in the United States.[42] Rumors about Houtermans's activities in Russia (including the allegation that he looted the Soviet laboratories) were known after the war to the Italian physicist Giuseppe Occhialini, who also was friendly with Rosbaud.[43] While based at the Free University of Brussels about 1950, Occhialini severely questioned the visiting Houtermans about these matters and was so "fed up" with the discussion that he left the house to go to a cinema, leaving his wife to get a clear statement from Houtermans.[44] In general, so pervasive was the suspicion of Houtermans that Goudsmit

40. Goudsmit's report of 23 April 1945, titled "Conversation with Houtermans," is in NA, RG 77, MED, Foreign Intelligence Unit, entry 22, box 167, folder 202.3, "London Office" (not RG 65, as Powers [*Heisenberg's War*, p. 567] states). Cf. NA, RG 77, MED, microfilm A-1218, roll 5 (*Manhattan History*, vol. 14, Supplement 1, "Foreign Intelligence"), 4.31, where Houtermans admits that he was "sent to Russia by the Germans to learn of nuclear research there."

41. Houtermans to Blackett, 9 April 1945, loc. cit.

42. Rosbaud to Goudsmit, 17 February 1947, Goudsmit Papers, box 28, folder 43.

43. C. F. Powell and G. P. S. Occhialini, in their *Nuclear Physics in Photographs* (Oxford, 1947), thank Rosbaud in the preface for having proposed the idea of the book.

44. Using the notes and letters of Mrs. Occhialini (Connie Dilworth), Powers (*Heisenberg's War*, pp. 471, 505) reports this incident. The details of Diebner's and Schumann's accompanying of Houtermans, as well as Rosbaud's hearing about the military garb of Houtermans (Powers, *Heisenberg's War*, pp. 413–415, 471), also appear to come from Occhialini. In a letter to me of 5 November 1993 Professor Connie Dilworth tells me she has discussed the subject with her husband, Professor Occhialini, and corrects several aspects of the Powers account. Occhialini says that the source of the statement about the Nazi uniform was not Rosbaud, but Houtermans himself, who stated that "they will tell you also that I went there [to Kharkov] wearing a Nazi cap. It is not true." Neither Occhialini nor Dilworth have any information as to the source of Powers's remark that Houtermans went to Kharkov in the

had to tell Houtermans's ex-wife that he thought the chances of his ever being allowed to come to America were slim.[45]

The impression left by all of this is that until the summer of 1941 Houtermans was firmly anti-Nazi, but that the German successes in Russia led to both his active participation in the German atomic project and his involvement in distasteful Nazi missions to occupied countries. The result was that by 1945 he was so morally compromised that he became willingly enmeshed in the net of lies and deception that Heisenberg, Weizsäcker, and his other friends had spun.

Yet even were we to accept that Houtermans remained anti-Nazi throughout, the question remains: If a political, radically inclined anti-Nazi such as Houtermans was able to lie about his recommendation of plutonium as an explosive in this fashion, what credence may be attached to the recollections of those "apolitical" German scientists who had rather more to hide after the war?

---

company of Schumann and Diebner. Interestingly, Occhialini had had a first talk for several hours in London with Houtermans (in which, it may be surmised, British Intelligence had had an interest), and had expected it would turn out badly. But he was impressed enough to invite Houtermans to Brussels to meet the geophysicists there for the main discussion. In a further letter to me of 15 March 1995, Professor Dilworth modifies some of Powers's description of the unpleasant nature of the Brussels meeting, characterizing it as "heated" rather than "difficult" and noting that her husband had not been "distressed" but simply had got "fed up." Professor Dilworth would also read the final phrase of Houtermans's Kharkov report as being "a necessary protection against possible mishaps."

Houtermans is an enigmatic character. An apparently favorably inclined Italian estimation may be found in Edoardo Amaldi's unpublished manuscript, "The Adventurous Life of Friedrich-Georg Houtermans, Physicist (1903–1966)" (see Powers, *Heisenberg's War,* p. 502). F. Herneck, "Ein alarmierende Botschaft," in his *Wissenschaftsgeschichte* (Berlin, 1984), pp. 190–200, cites Gustav Hertz's description of Houtermans as "a coffee-house physicist" (p. 197). H. Casimir, *Haphazard Reality* (New York, 1983), pp. 220–223, has some amusing recollections, but seems disturbed by Houtermans's services to the Germans in Russia.

Diebner's and Schumann's plundering trips to occupied countries are noted by Goudsmit in his letter to Vannevar Bush, 15 August 1945 (Goudsmit Papers), cited in Walker, *German National Socialism,* p. 149. Heisenberg in 1967 recalled that "Houtermans did speak frequently with Weizsäcker, Wirtz, and probably Diebner" (J. J. Ermenc, *Atomic Bomb Scientists: Memoirs 1939–1945* [Westport, Conn., 1989], p. 69).

45. Goudsmit to Charlotte Houtermans, 7 November 1947, Goudsmit Papers, box 28, folder 52.

CHAPTER 10

The Reactor-Bomb Patent
and the Heisenberg/Bohr Drawing, 1941

THE PATENT

When the German physicists were trying at Farm Hall in 1945 to draw up a memorandum recapitulating (or rather, justifying) the story of their wartime work on the uranium bomb,

> Wirtz remarked that they should remember that there was a patent for the production of such a bomb at the Kaiser-Wilhelm-Institute for Physics. This patent was taken out in 1941.[1]

The memory of this patent has been conveniently suppressed for the last fifty years. Nevertheless, traces of it exist in the German sources. A comprehensive survey of the uranium project prepared by the Army Weapons Research Office (HWA WaF) in February 1942—which includes a detailed discussion of reactor-bombs—contains in its bibliography the following reference:

> P1. Patentanmeldung Technische Energiegewinnung, Neutronenerzeugung und Herstellung neuer Elemente durch Spaltung von Uran oder verwandten schwerem Elementen 28.8.1941. 14 S.[2]

Though the title of this patent seems to relate only to the description of a reactor, let us speculate that it also included suggestions for a bomb, as Wirtz recollected. And let us further speculate that the bomb in question was actually a reactor-bomb. We have already seen that Heisenberg's assistant Müller had worked out calculations for a reactor-bomb, and we know that other patents of these early

---

1. FHT, no. 4, p. 27, 7 August 1945; *OE*, p. 94. Patents are also referred to in *OE*, pp. 61, 65 f., 73.
2. *Deutsche Geheimberichte zur Nutzbarmachung der Kernenergie aus den Jahren 1939–1942*, p. 141. (Copy supplied by Professor Erich Bagge; see below, chap. 11.) The version of the extracted bibliography in IMF 29-695 ff. does not seem to include this patent title.

years such as Joliot's and Szilard's treated reactor-bombs as part of a general reactor patent application.[3] So it is not unreasonable to proceed, with due caution, on the assumption that the harmless-sounding PI patent included a section describing a reactor-bomb that could be drawn on by the authors of the HWA Report for their own section detailing such a type of bomb.

Who had prepared the PI patent application? Since it would undoubtedly have been a secret patent, it would most likely have been registered in the name of the organization and possibly the officials, rather than the true inventors. Although much of the work of Heisenberg's team was carried out at the Kaiser-Wilhelm-Institute for Physics, the organization in charge of the project in 1941 was still the Nuclear Physics Section of the Weapons Research Office (HWA WaF/1a), whose administrative head was H. Basche and whose scientific leader was Diebner. Now, we find in a list of German reports published by Diebner in 1956 (under the pseudonym "W. Tautorus") the following item:

T-45. K. Diebner, H. Basche u.a.
Geheimpatent über Uranmaschine mit verschiedenen geometrischen Anordnungen von Uran und Bremssubstanz.[4]

The Diebner/Tautorus list was drawn up from a collection of documents in the possession of Diebner that has never been made available to scholars working on the subject and that apparently disappeared after Diebner's death in 1964. (Basche was killed in the last days of the war.) Efforts to trace the Diebner collection have failed to date, so we cannot know the exact title and contents of his T-45 secret patent, but one may reasonably speculate that T-45 was, in fact, identifiable with the PI patent listed in the HWA bibliography.[5]

The patent has left some traces in the official correspondence of the Weapons Research Office, which suggest that it may have been prepared and circulated in 1941–42, but not actually submitted to the Reichspatentamt until after August 1942. On 4 February 1942 Basche, the HWA WaF/1a administrator, sent the following request to Paul Harteck (and presumably the other institute heads of the project):

Ref: Patent Application.

The Patent Application "Uranium Pile" [*Uranmaschine*] is sent to you attached for your information as to important results of common efforts. By means of this appli-

3. For Joliot, see above, chap. 4; for Szilard, below, chap. 10.

4. W. Tautorus [K. Diebner], "Die deutschen Geheimarbeiten zur Kernenergieverwertung während des zweiten Weltkrieges, 1939–1945," *Atomkernenergie* 1 (1956): 368–370; 423–425, at p. 369, numbered T-45.

5. Although the HWA Report's bibliography of February 1942 does not cite any patent with the title or authorship of Diebner's T-45, the title given by Tautorus is vaguely generic and so should not automatically be taken to exclude T-45's identification with PI. Moreover, a KWIP secret military patent in 1941 would undoubtedly have been submitted under the auspices of the head office of the whole project, the HWA WaF/1a, headed by Basche and Diebner.

cation it may be determined what other patentable ideas your Institute may have over and beyond those already set down in the [application] "Uranium Pile."

Further, information is requested as to what persons of your Institute collaborated on the "Uranium Pile" and who accordingly are to be listed with the Patent Office as inventors. Prof. Bothe suggests that the patent be looked upon as [the result of] common effort by all institutes."[6]

In August 1942 Basche tried to finalize the patent by giving institute directors two weeks to submit their comments. On 20 August 1942 Basche wrote to Otto Hahn, enclosing the *Patentanmeldung "Uranmaschine,"* which he described as an important product of teamwork. Basche wished to know which gentlemen of Hahn's institute had contributed and should be recognized as co-inventors. Again, Bothe's proposal that all the institutes be credited for collective work is mentioned approvingly. Basche asked for comments and the "return of the enclosed *Patentanmeldung* within 14 days." This Hahn did on 28 August, adding on 4 September a list of sixteen "co-inventors" from his institute, including H. Bomke, who was, according to the Farm Hall Transcripts, regarded as a Nazi plant.[7]

It is possible that the *Uranmaschine* secret patent was submitted by the Weapons Research Office to a central agency, the OKW Zentralstelle Patentstelle, set up by the Armed Forces High Command's Scientific Division (OKW AWA/W Wiss [III]), the Army's OKH Heereswaffenamt (representing the Weapons Research Office), the Reichsforschungsrat, and the Reichspatentamt. This central agency was functioning by late 1944, since correspondence is extant concerning Walther Gerlach's attempt to introduce a separate unit for nuclear patents at the Patent Office under his control, only to be informed that an agency already existed to coordinate secret patents of military value.[8] Whether this agency was operative as early as 1942 and would have received the patent is unclear.

Efforts by American intelligence in 1945 to find this general *Uranmaschine* patent proved fruitless, though several related patents concerning heavy-water production and isotope-separation centrifuges were retrieved.[9] (Some of these had in-

6. Basche to Harteck, 4 February 1942, NA, RG 77, MED Foreign Intelligence Unit, entry 22, box 166, folder 32.23—I, "Patents."

7. Basche (OKH WaF /1a) to Hahn, 20 August 1942; Hahn to Basche, 28 August and 4 September 1942. NA, RG 77, MED Foreign Intelligence Unit, entry 22, box 166, folder 32.23—I, "Patents." For Bomke, see FHT, no. 4, p. 7; *OE*, p. 75.

8. Gerlach was by then in charge of the nuclear program as the Reichsmarschall's Plenipotentiary for Nuclear Physics and was based at the Reichsforschungsrat. (See below, chap. 13.) For the correspondence, see Gerlach's letters to the Chief Engineer of the Weapons Research Office (HWA WaF) and other officials of 17 October 1944 and the subsequent chastening replies of December 1944 in NA, RG 77, MED Foreign Intelligence Unit, entry 22, box 166, folder 32.23—I, "Patents," item IX; ibid., box 169, folder 32.21, "Germany—Research—General," papers marked "Betr. OKW—Zentrale Patentstelle."

9. NA, RG 77, MED Foreign Intelligence Unit, entry 22, box 166, folder 32.23—I, "Patents," items I–VIII, include much patent material.

See below for the Allied search for the secret patents in 1945.

volved a dispute with I. G. Farben.) These were later included among the nearly four hundred German reports captured by the ALSOS team (the "G" reports).[10] Unfortunately, there is no trace in the "G"-papers collection of the HWA PI patent, Tautorus's T-45, or the *Uranmaschine* patent.

It is possible, however, that the secret patent or patents may have been preserved in two other collections of captured German papers now in Washington. In 1945–48 the Allied scientific and technical intelligence authorities in Germany seized as reparations large amounts of German technical materials (a practice complained of by Otto Hahn at the time).[11] Among these were 144,000 German patents and applications then held in the Reichspatentamt in Berlin. These were microfilmed and the titles individually listed—out of sequence but by subject—in installments. As they became available, the titles of the patents were announced for purchase in the Office of Technical Service's *Bibliography of Scientific and Industrial Research Reports*. The microfilms were kept in the scientific reference section of the Library of Congress.[12] Though there are a few nuclear-physics titles, a de-

---

10. The originals of the "G" reports are reported to be in the USAEC Technical Information Service, Oak Ridge, Tennessee. Microfiche sets are in NA, RG 242, Captured German Records, TID 3030; AIP; and the Library of the Kernforschungszentrum, Karlsruhe.

Among the patents in the "G" reports are:

G-137: K. Clusius and Linde Company, "Patentanmeldung über Verfahren zur Gewinnung von schwerem Wasserstoff" (see M. Walker, *German National Socialism and the Quest for Nuclear Energy, 1939–1949* [Cambridge, 1989], p. 144).

G-209: W. Dällenbach, "Patent Application and General Correspondence with the German Patent Office on a Particle Accelerator," 1943 (see below, chap. 13; J. V. H. Dippel, *Two Against Hitler* [New York, 1992], p.183; also FHT, no. 3, pp. 3 f.; *OE*, pp. 66 f.).

G-341, vol. 1, fiche 2, refers to an I. G. Farben secret patent for heavy water of July 1944, under the patent application number R.112.465 IV b/12 i geh, which may be a clue to the *Uranmaschine* patent's number.

G-378: G. Stetter, "Technische Energiegewinnung mit Hilfe von Kernreaktionen" (7 *Patent-Ansprüche* [patent titles] for a reactor; at p. 2 discusses a deuterium explosion).

The Tautorus list includes:

T-45: K. Diebner, H. Basche, et al., "Geheimpatent über Uranmaschine mit verschiedenen geometrischen Anordnungen von Uran und Bremssubstanz" (n.d.).

T-100: P. Harteck, "Patentanmeldung: Die Niederdruckkolonne."

T-101: P. Harteck and H. Suess, "Patentanmeldung: Schwerwasseranreicherung durch Austauschreaktionen." (Harteck claimed in his interview in J. J. Ermenc, *Atomic Bomb Scientists: Memoirs* [Westport, Conn., 1989], pp. 100 f., to have been uninterested in taking out patents.)

For the uranium project's dispute with I. G. Farben over a heavy-water production process in 1943, see G-268 (IMF 29-759; cf. IMF 29-716).

11. O. Hahn and F. H. Rein, "Einladung nach USA," *Physikalische Blätter* 3 (1947): 33–35.

12. J. Gimbel, *Science, Technology, and Reparations: Exploitation and Plunder in Postwar Germany* (Stanford, Calif., 1990), p. 63, states that over a million pages were microfilmed, amounting to 17 miles of microfilm. Curiously, Gimbel never examined these, nor did he give their location as the Library of Congress—though at p. 62 he mentions that all the materials microfilmed in Germany were to be sent back

tailed search of these "PB" (Publication Board) listings has not produced any of the secret patents that emanated from the German government's uranium project. (A few private ones have been found.)[13]

A second Library of Congress source is a collection of over seven hundred files confiscated by the ALSOS mission, which include several Reichsforschungsrat (RFR; Reich Research Council) administrative files. The originals of these have recently been restored to the German Federal Archives, but microfilms have been retained in Washington. Since the RFR in early 1942 took over control from the HWA of the uranium project (including supervision of the Heisenberg unit at the Kaiser-Wilhelm-Institute for Physics [KWIP]), it is possible that the RFR may thus also have acquired any secret patents formerly held by the HWA. So far, a sample search has not produced any positive results, but a more detailed investigation is now under way.[14]

Could the patents still be held by German repositories? It is conceivable that the patent applications were lodged with the Munich or Nuremberg offices, rather than the Berlin Reichspatentamt, but the fact that the HWA was based in Berlin renders this unlikely. Moreover, it seems that nearly all German secret patents and applications were destroyed by the Nazi regime toward the war's end. A British scientific intelligence report of 1946 noted that of the twelve thousand secret

---

via FIAT (Field Information Agency, Technical) to the Office of Technical Services (OTS) of the Department of Commerce and refers (pp. 68, 94 f.) to the distribution of FIAT material in the OTS's periodical *Bibliography of Scientific and Industrial Research Reports (BSIR)*.

Guides to the these patents are: *FIAT—Berlin Patent Office Activities*, FIAT Technical Bulletin T-50 (Office of Military Government for Germany—U.S., 29 May 1947); Association for the Use and Diffusion of Documentation (UDD), *Subject Outline of the Unpublished Applications for Patents Filed at the German Patent Office during 1940 to 1945* (Paris, 1950); *An Informal Introduction to German Patent Applications (1940–1945) in the Library of Congress* (typed guide, Library of Congress, n.d.); Dept. of Commerce, Office of Technical Services, *FIAT Microfilm Reel Index* (= microfilm PB-92000), available from LC, Photoduplication Service; idem, *Auszüge deutscher Patent-Anmeldungen* (index to microfilmed German patents), in LC, Photoduplication Service Room; idem, *Bibliography of Scientific and Industrial Reports, Prepared by the Office of Technical Services* (Washington, D.C.), vol. 6, no. 1 (4 July 1947), and subsequent issues to 1948 (includes listings of microfilmed German patents). These reports are indexed in idem, *Numerical Index to the Bibliography of Scientific and Industrial Reports, Volumes 1–10, 1946–1948* (Washington, D.C., 1948), and G. Runge, ed., *Correlation Index: Document Series and PB Reports,* (New York, 1953). On the imminent expiry of the project, see A. Leggin, "Potomac Postscripts," *Chemical and Engineering News* 26, no. 11 (15 March 1948): 733.

The FIAT teams were instructed particularly to look for "secret patent applications" (Gimbel, *Science, Technology, and Reparations*, p. 62), but I have been unable yet to discover whether they found any.

13. PB nos. 70080 (BSIR/OTS, vol. 6, p. 261), 70081 (vol. 5, p. 724), 70082 (vol. 7, pp. 74, 78), 70083 (vol. 7, p. 70), 70084 (vol. 6, pp. 931 ff., 934 f.), 70093 (vol. 6, p. 929), 83283 (vol. 8, p. 917).

14. A fifty-page finding list for these ALSOS documents is available in the Library of Congress, which gives reels 141 and 143 for relevant RFR and KWG documents. For the file numbers see the *Correlation Index*, cited above.

For the history of the RFR, see L. E. Simon, *German Research in World War II* (New York, 1947), pp. 104–107; K. Zierold, *Forschungsförderung in drei Epochen* (Wiesbaden, 1968).

patents and further twenty-five thousand–plus secret patent applications in the Berlin office, nearly all had been destroyed by the Germans as the war ended. It not very hopefully suggested that some of these secret patents and applications might be reconstructed through copies in companies' archives. However, the British team also reported that a summary register of these remained in the Berlin Patent Office.[15] This register has, it seems, since vanished.[16]

It seems, however, that a "registry book" of the secret patents was extant in 1945 and indeed microfilmed by the Americans for General Groves's office. On 6 July 1945 the U.S. Legal Group reported that "a small part of the records including fragments of the secret files, which the Germans had endeavored to destroy in the [Heringen] mine, were removed under the supervision of Mr. Childs, Archivist, to Frankfurt where they are stored in the Reichsbank."[17] A report in the *Washington Evening Star* on 23 July 1945 that American authorities led by Colonel Ernest McLendon seized the seven-hundred-room German Patent Office and found "almost all" the patent records intact in a deep sub-basement led to Groves's staff contacting McLendon in Berlin on 15 August. They were informed that about 150 tons of unclassified patents and related papers in the Berlin Patent Office had been saved. "In regard to secret German patents, the only evidence recovered to date is the German secret patent registry book which merely gives the name of the patent and title of the patent. This document is being microfilmed and will be ready for examination shortly. While McLendon has learned that the original secret patent files were destroyed it is still hoped that a duplicate set will be found and an extensive search is going ahead with that in mind. . . . It is requested that this office be advised as to what information about patents was obtained from the captured TA documents."[18]

15. R. Jones et al., *German Patent Records,* 16 pp. (March 1946), p. 2 (BIOS Final Report no. 538, item no. 28; Defense Technical Information Center [DTIC], Cameron Station Army Base, Virginia, accession no. ATI 70297 / JIOA [vol. 1 of BIOS Reports, 1949]). Supplied by Kurt Molholm, Administrator of DTIC, January 1993. BIOS Final Reports are also held in the Library of Congress, as well as in the British Library Documentary Supply Centre, Wetherby, West Yorkshire, and the Imperial War Museum, London.

16. Although Dr. Manfred Rasch (Archiv, Thyssen Aktiengesellschaft) has mentioned to me a "Namenskartei der Anmelder Geheim-Patenten 1939–1943/44" held in the Patent-Recherche-Abteilung of the Bundespatentamt, Berlin, the index relates to normal—not secret—patents, according to Dr. Christa Tietz of the staff. During researches that Dr. Tietz kindly undertook for me, no trace of any relevant nuclear patent was found.

17. Col. John B. Marsh, U.S. Legal Group CC, to Col. Dix, OSS, 6 July 1945, NA, RG 77, MED Foreign Intelligence Unit, entry 22, box 166, folder 32.23—I, "Patents."

18. Calvert (London) to Smith (Washington), 22 August 1945, NA, RG 77, MED Foreign Intelligence Unit, entry 22, box 169, folder 32.21, "Germany—Research—General." Calvert was informed on 1 September 1945 that "no further information is available or has been obtained from the captured TA documents regarding the German patents."

I have not traced the microfilm of the registry book in NA RG 77; it is perhaps to be found in the Military Government (OMGUS) records.

Further discussions on 25 October with American and British officers in Berlin concluded

> that all secret classified German patents were destroyed by the Germans in a city called Herringen near Kassel, Germany. Lt. Col. Kessenick inspected the charred remains of these documents and stated that they were incapable of being restored to legibility. Over 180,000 unclassified patent applications are now being processed and catalogued. Of those thus far catalogued no indication has been found that patents of interest to General Groves' office are among them. . . . Lt. Warner was advised that the American and British authorities have definite information that 40 truckloads of "patent material" were removed by the Russians prior to British and American entry into Berlin. The Russians are stated as having denied this, however.[19]

Another possible source for the 1941 patent itself is the archives of the Kaiser-Wilhelm-Gesellschaft (KWG; Kaiser-Wilhelm-Society) in Berlin. The KWG, which controlled the various Kaiser-Wilhelm-Institutes, was actively interested in pursuing patents during the war and indeed set up an agency for this purpose in 1941 under the direction of its legal adviser (*Syndikus*), Herbert Rainer Müller. It is possible that this bureau may have handled secret as well as open patents.[20] Here one comes to an interesting connection, for Müller (who died in 1972) was anti-Nazi and tried to place bureaucratic obstacles in the way of the nuclear research being pursued in the KWIP.[21] Moreover, he is now known to have supplied the major Allied agent Erwin Respondek (died 1971) with information on this research.[22] Respondek also had other informants at the KWG, knew Max Planck

19. NA, RG 77, MED Foreign Intelligence Unit, entry 22, box 169, folder 32.21, Calvert to Britt (Washington), 30 October 1945, loc. cit.; information repeated in Shuler's memorandum to Groves, 15 November 1945, loc. cit.

20. Dippel, *Two Against Hitler,* p. 178. See the 1956 report "Entstehung der 'Forschungsschutz GmbH—Gesellschaft zum Schutz der Urheber- und Erfinderrechte der Kaiser-Wilhelm-Gesellschaft zur Förderung der Wissenschaften,'" Generalverwaltung, I Abt., Rep. 1A, no. 1935, Archiv zur Geschichte der Max-Planck-Gesellschaft, Berlin. See also E. Henning and M. Kazemi, *Chronik der Kaiser-Wilhelm-Gesellschaft zur Förderung der Wissenschaften,* Veröffentlichungen aus dem Archiv der Max-Planck-Gesellschaft, vol. 1 (Berlin, 1988), pp. 106, 109. K. Macrakis's history of the KWG during the war, *Surviving the Swastika* (New York, 1993), does not contain references to patents, nor does the chapter by H. Albrecht and A. Hermann, "Die Kaiser-Wilhelm-Gesellschaft im Dritten Reich (1933–1945)," in *Forschung im Spannungsfeld von Politik und Gesellschaft: Geschichte und Struktur der Kaiser-Wilhelm-/Max-Planck-Gesellschaft,* ed. R. Vierhaus and B. vom Brocke (Stuttgart, 1990), pp. 356–406. The pre-1918 patents policy of the KWG is mentioned in J. A. Johnson, *The Kaiser's Chemists: Science and Modernization in Imperial Germany* (Chapel Hill, N.C., 1990), pp. 154 f.

21. Dippel, *Two Against Hitler,* pp. 81 f., 92 ff.

22. See Woods's memorandum of 1945 to Hull, in the Cordell Hull Papers, Library of Congress, MS Division, folder 184 (first located by Dippel). Respondek's "Report on the History of the KWG," 12 November 1970, Generalverwaltung, II Abt., Rep. 1A Gründung, no. 1/1–4, Archiv zur Geschichte der Max-Planck-Gesellschaft, Berlin, has little on this aspect of his activities.

Dippel's book (*Two Against Hitler*) is an extraordinary piece of scholarly detective work that uncovers for the first time the crucial contributions of both Sam Woods and Respondek to Allied intelligence.

well, and was acquainted through him with Hahn and Heisenberg, though relations with the latter were not warm.[23]

Respondek duly passed the information obtained from Müller and other sources to his handler in Berlin, the legendary American diplomat and spy Sam Woods, in the form of a report dated 6 March 1941 entitled "Status and Recent Activity of German Scientific Developments in Recent Months." Forwarded by Woods to the U.S. War Department, the report contained passing references to work on nuclear physics and fission at the Kaiser-Wilhelm-Institutes for Physics and Chemistry in Berlin, but no details on uranium.[24]

It is entirely possible that the patent will eventually surface, even if not from the sources discussed, since copies of it are known to have been held in two archives, copies that at present remain untraced but may well materialize at some later stage. One of these archives is the Diebner collection; the other is the archive of the HWA WaF itself. Only a few files of the latter (copied from British sources) are now in the Military Division of the German Federal Archives at Freiburg; but though the major part of the archive was probably destroyed during the war, there is a chance that it may have fallen, like many other German records in Berlin, into the hands of the Russians.[25] (There is also a chance that a copy may have been held by Speer's own departmental patent office within the Ministry of Armaments.)[26]

Is there any way of discovering the contents of the 1941 patent or patents for a bomb that were taken out by the HWA Weapons Research Office and/or the

23. Dippel, *Two Against Hitler,* pp. 80 f., 86, 177, 180.

24. NA, RG 165, G-2, Military Intelligence Division, Correspondence, 1917–1941, box 1573, 2655-B-392/3 (= MID Report no. 18,214). See Dippel, *Two Against Hitler,* pp. 61, 82, 178. (For Respondek's later reports of 1943 in RG 59 and RG 84, see below, note 50.)

25. For the HWA's Weapons Research Office (WaF; Waffenforschung), see Simon, *German Research,* pp. 54 f., 67, 71, 78–89, 98–101; and the analysis by its chief from 1940–45, General Emil Leeb, *Aus der Rüstung des Dritten Reiches (Das Heereswaffenamt, 1938–1945): Ein authentischer Bericht des letzten Chefs des Heereswaffenamtes (= Wehrtechnische Monatshefte,* Beiheft 4) (Berlin and Frankfurt, 1958), pp. 12, 22.

The Bundesarchiv's Militärarchiv in Freiburg has in its HWA series (RH8) the following three volumes of WaF records: RH8/1362, 1714, and 1771. These are actually copied from holdings formerly in British Intelligence's Halstead Exploitation Centre, which were later transferred to the National Lending Library, Boston Spa, Yorkshire, and then to the Imperial War Museum, London. The War Museum materials are now reportedly kept at its Duxford depot, and inquiries indicate that they contain no relevant material on the WaF's atomic program. (Some additional holdings from captured German records in American hands have recently been transferred to the Militärarchiv, under the series marks RH8 I, II, and III.)

The British television program *The Red Bomb* (Rapide Productions, 1994) recently displayed papers relating to the German atomic project found by Russians on the body of a German officer; the research staff of the production have, however, informed me that these are merely reconstructions, the originals being inaccessible. Inquiries to Russian archives have not succeeded in tracing any HWA WaF records.

26. The head of this patent office was Dr. Lieb, who discussed atomic bomb matters often with Heisenberg after 1942. For Lieb's 1945 interrogation see above, chap. 2, and below, chap. 12.

Kaiser-Wilhelm-Gesellschaft? Notwithstanding German awareness of plutonium and U235 as nuclear explosives, the most likely subject of a patent would have been a reactor-bomb, since speculation on the possibility of such a device continued throughout the war. A notorious episode of 1941 may also support this conclusion.

BOHR AND THE HEISENBERG DRAWING

In chapter 4, we left Niels Bohr in 1939 at the stage where he had ruled out the possibility of a fast-neutron bomb using pure U235 on the ground that no way could be seen of extracting sufficiently large quantities of U235—quantities that he, like other physicists of the time, assumed would be very substantial indeed. In the same lecture in which he had rejected this possibility, Bohr had also argued— he thought, conclusively—that neither was there a chance of making a reactor-bomb that would utilize slow neutrons in a uranium mixture with a moderator:

> The decisive question is therefore how far the natural mixture of uranium isotopes can be used to release energy on a large scale. The obvious approach would be to mix uranium with materials containing hydrogen so as to ensure that the neutrons produced in the fission will subsequently be slowed down, by collision with the protons, sufficiently to react with the rare isotope with sufficient probability. . . . But it is clear beforehand that with this approach there can never be a question of explosions which would suddenly release a substantial part of the atomic energy.
>
> For such explosions to occur, the temperature would have to rise to milliards [i.e., billions] of degrees, but as soon as the temperature reaches just a few thousand degrees the process will stop because the protons in the mixture will have too high a kinetic energy to slow down the fission neutrons sufficiently. Indeed, the probability of a neutron reacting with the rare uranium isotope decreases rapidly with rising neutron energy, and already at energies of a few electron volt [*sic*] it is less than the probability of neutron capture in the abundant isotope.[27]

This lecture was particularly memorable to those who heard it, such as Bohr's colleagues Christian Møller and Stefan Rozental, and it seemed to lay to rest all fears of an atomic bomb being feasible.[28] But Bohr had omitted one important area of consideration in his treatment; he had dealt with the cases of pure U235 and unseparated uranium. But what about the case of the *enrichment*, as opposed to the extraction, of U235? This was the case that P. O. Müller worked out for Heisenberg in 1940 and that in all probability was developed in the patent argued above to have been submitted by the KWIP through the Weapons Research Office

27. N. Bohr, "Recent Investigations of the Transmutations of Atomic Nuclei" (1939; published in 1941), printed in Bohr, *Collected Works,* ed. E. Rudinger, R. Peierls, et al. (Amsterdam, 1986), 9:443–466, esp. pp. 465 f.

28. R. H. Stuewer, "Niels Bohr and Nuclear Physics," in *Niels Bohr: A Centenary Volume,* ed. A. P. French and P. J. Kennedy (Cambridge, Mass., 1985), p. 219.

in August 1941. It may well also have been the case that was brought to Bohr's alarmed attention when Heisenberg made his notorious unwelcome visit to Copenhagen in September 1941.

This "unforgivable"—and unforgiven—visit was arranged in the framework of German attempts to inveigle Bohr and his institute into collaboration with the German army of occupation.[29] It originated in a proposal of 22 July 1941 by Weizsäcker that Heisenberg and he (together with three other scientists) be invited to attend a German Cultural Institute conference in Copenhagen on physics and astronomy—a transparent propaganda exercise.[30] Bohr tried with all his powers to resist the efforts of Heisenberg and Weizsäcker to involve him publicly in this scarcely disguised collaborationist venture. The result was that Weizsäcker was so frustrated that he resorted to thrusting the director of the so-called Cultural Institute past Bohr's secretary into the physicist's office.[31] Both Heisenberg and Weizsäcker showed an utter disregard for the sensibilities of the Danes, with Heisenberg blithely justifying the German attack on Russia and domination of Europe and smoothly rationalizing the Nazi regime. The abysmal climax to the visit came when, in a private conversation with Bohr, Heisenberg raised the possibility of constructing nuclear weapons. Bohr was deeply shocked by the fact that Heisenberg seemed to be participating in a serious Nazi atomic project and, worse still, it appeared, was seeking to recruit Bohr to the project, or at least to winkle useful scientific advice out of him, perhaps also trying to discover from Bohr whether the Allies too were working on uranium. After the meeting Bohr communicated his distress to colleagues at his Institute, though the episode was so upsetting to him that he declined to give details of it. What is certain is that Bohr never forgave Heisenberg for the visit and that their formerly close relations cooled into a formal politeness that continued even long after the war had ended.[32]

There seems to be little doubt that Heisenberg used the conversation as a fishing expedition to discover how far (if at all) the Allies had progressed with the development of an atomic bomb. Before coming to Copenhagen, Weizsäcker had written two urgent letters, one to the Army Weapons Research Office, the other to Reichsminister Rust, head of the Education Ministry, which had controlled the

29. On 27 June 1945 Lise Meitner wrote to the interned Otto Hahn of Heisenberg's "unforgivable visit to Denmark" (Meitner Papers, Churchill College Archives, Cambridge). (See below, chap. 21.) The unsavory political and moral context of this visit is described in detail in M. Walker, *German National Socialism and the Quest for Nuclear Power, 1939–1949* (Cambridge, 1989), pp. 223–227, and amplified in his article "Physics and Propaganda: Werner Heisenberg's Foreign Lectures under National Socialism," *Historical Studies in the Physical Sciences* 22 (1992): 339–389, esp. pp. 361 ff.

30. G-343B calendars the proposal of Weizsäcker to the German Academic Exchange Service: "I suggest that Prof. Kienle . . . Unsold . . . Biermann . . . Heisenberg and myself be invited to attend the Copenhagen conference." See below for the probable motive for this letter.

31. J. G. Crowther, *Science in Liberated Europe* (London, 1949), p. 107.

32. For Danish and other reactions to this visit and what the whole affair reveals of Heisenberg's character and capacity for self-deluding apology, see below, chaps. 19 and 21.

earlier Reich Research Council uranium project of 1939. Weizsäcker wrote to alert officials to a report in a Stockholm newspaper that experiments were being made in the United States in connection with a new kind of bomb:

> The material used in the bomb is uranium, and if the energy contained in this element were released, explosions of heretofore-undreamt-of power could be achieved. Thus, a five-kilogram bomb could create a crater 1 kilometer deep and 40 kilometers in radius. All buildings within a range of 150 kilometers would be demolished.[33]

Weizsäcker had learned in July of the Swedish report through the press office of the Foreign Ministry, in which his father was the senior permanent official. He had then sought an interview with Rust to warn him of the reported American advantage and as a result written up a report that he now submitted with his letter of 5 September. It seems plausible that Weizsäcker had asked his father in July to see to it that the German Academic Exchange Service immediately arrange a conference in Copenhagen as a pretext to cover the Heisenberg visit.[34] But even if Weizsäcker had not proposed the Copenhagen visit in July as an immediate consequence of hearing about the Stockholm report, by the time he and Heisenberg reached Denmark in September, the possibility of an American bomb must have been very much on their minds. It was doubtless this anxiety that drove the two German physicists into their disastrous approaches to Bohr.

In later years Heisenberg tried to depict the whole encounter as a misunderstanding by Bohr. Nevertheless, Heisenberg did admit that the subject of the discussion was the possibility of making a bomb.[35] It may be conjectured that Heisenberg explained to an increasingly nervous, though skeptical, Bohr how they both understood that the difficulty of extracting large amounts of pure $U235$ precluded a $U235$ bomb, while slow neutrons would be unable to bring about an explosion in unseparated uranium. Perhaps plutonium was also mooted.[36] The discussion must have become quite technically specific on these matters, for it occasioned Heisenberg's production of a drawing of a possible design for an atomic

---

33. Weizsäcker's letters of 4 and 5 September 1941, respectively to OKW HWA WaF/1a and Rust, are in *Manhattan History*, vol. 14, *Foreign Intelligence*, supp. 1, app. A, in NA, RG 77, MED, microfilm A-1218, roll 5.

34. Weizsäcker's report is not included in the *Manhattan History* appendix, cited above. For Weizsäcker's proposal of the mission, see his letter of 22 July quoted above.

35. W. Heisenberg, *Physics and Beyond* (New York, 1971), p. 182, recollects that he hinted that "it was now possible in principle to build atomic bombs." A. Pais, *Niels Bohr's Times in Physics, Philosophy, and Polity* (Oxford, 1991), pp. 481–485, says that Aage Bohr confirmed to him in conversation that "it was his father's clear impression that Heis [i.e., Heisenberg] was engaged in atomic war work."

36. N. Blaedel, *Harmony and Unity: The Life of Niels Bohr* (Madison, Wisc., 1988), p. 235, states that even before the Heisenberg visit, "earlier the same autumn, he [Bohr] had learned about a paper written by the German physicist F. G. Houtermans that clearly showed that the German physicists understood how to achieve nuclear fission." No source is given for this claim.

bomb—undoubtedly a reactor-bomb—whose meaning and subsequent fate will be discussed below.[37]

It must be assumed that Heisenberg did not cause Bohr to think that an atomic bomb was an imminent possibility, or even that it would be achieved within the foreseeable future. Otherwise Bohr would certainly have taken some action to alert his Allied contacts of the danger. In fact, it was not until Bohr was approached clandestinely at Chadwick's instance in January 1943 that he began to think seriously again about the feasibility of an atomic bomb based upon slow neutrons.[38] Bohr was obviously struck by Chadwick's invitation to him to come to work in England on the project, but, though he declined for the time being out of consideration for the need to protect his friends and colleagues in Denmark, he still replied that he would have come all the same had he thought any danger was presented by nuclear science in the near future.

> Above all, I have to the best of my judgement convinced myself that, in spite of all future prospects, any immediate use of the latest marvellous discoveries of atomic physics is impracticable.[39]

But rumors of German large-scale preparations for the production of metallic uranium and heavy water caused Bohr to reflect seriously on what Heisenberg had let slip, and in a second letter to Chadwick written two months later he recounted how he had been obliged to think over the whole question of a slow-neutron reactor-bomb, and he now proposed a possible method of designing a bomb using unseparated uranium and a heavy-water moderator. The idea was to achieve an explosive rise in the temperature of the uranium before the reaction was cut off by the reduction in moderator efficiency caused by the heavy water's own rise in temperature.

> In view of the rumours going round the world, that large scale preparations are being made for the production of metallic Uranium and heavy water to be used in atom bombs, I wish to modify my statement as regards the impracticability of an immediate

37. Aage Bohr, "The War Years and the Prospects Raised by the Atomic Weapons," in *Niels Bohr: His Life and Work As Seen by His Friends and Colleagues*, ed. S. Rozental (Amsterdam and New York, 1967), pp. 191–214: "In a private conversation with my father Heisenberg brought up the question of the military applications of atomic energy. My father was very reticent and expressed his scepticism because of the great technical difficulties that had to be overcome, but he had the impression that Heisenberg thought that the new possibilities could decide the outcome of the war if the war dragged on.... The very scanty contact with the German physicists during the occupation contributed—as already mentioned—to strengthen the impression that the German authorities attributed great military importance to atomic energy" (pp. 193 f.).

38. Chadwick to Bohr, 25 January 1943; original in the Niels Bohr Archive, Copenhagen; printed in Pais, *Neils Bohr's Times*, p. 486.

39. Bohr to Chadwick, undated, but February 1943. Dr. Finn Aaserud has kindly forwarded me a text of the copy in the Niels Bohr Archive, Copenhagen. It is also quoted in Aage Bohr, "The War Years," pp. 193 f.; and M. Gowing, *Britain and Atomic Energy, 1939–1945* (London, 1964), pp. 246 f.

use of the discoveries in nuclear physics. Taking for granted that it is impossible to separate the U-isotopes in sufficient amount, any use of the natural isotopic mixture
would as well-known depend on the possibility to retard the fission neutrons to such a
degree that their effect on the rare $U235$ isotope exceeds neutron capture in the isotope
$U238$. Although it might not be excluded to obtain this result in a mixture of Uranium
and Deuterium, there will surely be a limit to the degree to which atomic energy could
be released in such a mixture, due to the decrease of the retarding effect with rising
temperature. This limit would seem to be set by a temperature of the D corresponding
to about 1 Volt pro atom, and this would, therefore, be the limit of the explosion power
of a thorough mixture. If, however, as often suggested, solid pieces of U are placed in
a large tank of heavy water, it might be possible to obtain a far higher temperature
within the U before the critical D-temperature is reached. Since, however, at least 1 pct.
of the average energy set free will independently of the amount of the U used obviously never be greater than about 100 times that required to heat the water to the critical temperature [*sic*].[40] Even if this is very great compared with that obtainable with
ordinary chemical explosives, it would in view of the large scale bombing already
achieved hardly be responsible to rely on the effect of a single bomb of this type
procurable only with an enormous effort. The situation, however, is of course quite
different, if it is true that enough heavy water can be made to manufacture a large
number of eventual atom-bombs, and although I am convinced that the arguments
here outlined are familiar to experts, I hasten therefore to modify my statement.[41]

40. "Critical temperature" may be understood here as the temperature of the liquid-vapor critical
point—that is, the temperature above which the water has no liquid-vapor transition. But as J. Logan
has suggested to me, it is more likely to be the temperature at which deuterium ceases to be an effective moderator for the reaction. (The sentence lacks a main clause in the original.)

41. Dr. Aaserud has supplied a copy of the undated transcript of Bohr's second letter to Chadwick
(written about April 1943), now in the Niels Bohr Archive, Copenhagen. There seems to be an omitted
main clause in the sentence marked *sic* in my quotation, but it may be due to Bohr's English style. The
letter is quoted briefly in F. H. Hinsley, *British Intelligence in the Second World War* (Cambridge, 1988), vol.
3, pt. 2, pp. 584 f. (where it is dated to June 1943), but no source reference is given. Professor Hinsley
has kindly informed me that he believes the letter now to be in the still classified PRO, CAB 126/39.
This file has been retained by the Cabinet Office, which has, however, informed me that Bohr's letter
has not been found there. The Records Office of the UKAEA has also been unable to trace it in their
classified files, nor have I been able to find it in the PRO, AB series, nor in the Chadwick Papers at
Churchill College Archives, Cambridge.

See Aage Bohr's account, "The War Years," p. 194, which states that the second letter to Chadwick
was written two months after the first, whereas Pais (*Niels Bohr's Times*, p. 487) asserts that it was written
only two weeks later. (Cf. Gowing, *Britain and Atomic Energy*, p. 246.) The explanation of this discrepancy
may be found in information in A. Kramish, *The Griffin* (Boston, 1986), p. 193, where, using documents
shown to him by Michael Perrin, Kramish cites two letters of 4 and 19 June 1943 in which Bohr discusses the atomic bomb problem. The former of these may well be the February letter quoted above,
if one stretches the period between February and June into "two months," for on 4 June, "two months
later," Bohr wrote a second time. And finally, "two weeks later," on 19 June, Bohr may have written his
third letter. (Dr. Kramish is currently searching his files for further information.)

The letter of 19 June reportedly explains at length why an atomic bomb was not possible. This referred presumably to a true nuclear explosion, as opposed to a reactor-bomb. (The parallels between
Heisenberg's thinking in G-39 and Bohr's 1943 letters are, not surprisingly, marked.)

As the opening of the letter suggests, it would seem that part of the reason for Bohr's active interest in the design of a bomb in 1943 was the information he was receiving on the German atomic project from the British intelligence officer Eric Welsh, whose source was Paul Rosbaud in Berlin.[42]

In October 1943 the dangerous situation of the Jews in Denmark finally persuaded Bohr (who was himself half-Jewish) to escape to England, where he arrived in London on 6 October, to be greeted by Chadwick and a secret-service officer. Bohr dined at the Savoy on 8 October with a group of British scientists including the Chancellor Sir John Anderson (then in charge of the British atomic project), Lord Cherwell, R. V. Jones and Charles Frank of scientific intelligence, Michael Perrin of the British atomic project, and others. There Bohr was acquainted with Allied progress on the atomic bomb, including the secret of the small critical mass resulting from the work of Frisch and Peierls. Apparently, Bohr was astounded by the briefing, both by the fact that the bomb was indeed possible after all and by the rate of its development. His son Aage, who arrived a week later, reported "how profoundly surprised Niels was by what he was told that day about the status of the Anglo-American atomic weapons effort."[43] A few days later Bohr had a long discussion with Cherwell as to the correctness of the theory of the bomb, the results of which were reported to Churchill.[44] Cherwell also suggested to Bohr that

42. Kramish, *The Griffin*, pp. 195 f. Dr. Kramish tells me that he believes that the postwar correspondence between Bohr and Welsh reported to be in the Niels Bohr Archive, Copenhagen, may throw further light on a number of problems.

A memorandum of 3 July 1944 by Bohr recalls that in the first years of the war he believed that Germany had not made a large-scale effort to extract U235, but that in 1943 there seemed to be a surge of "feverish German activity" that worried him. (National Archives, microfilm M-1108, Harrison-Bundy Files, roll 2, folder 19.)

43. See Kramish, *The Griffin*, pp. 193-196, for the fullest account (based on information and documents supplied by the late Michael Perrin, who was effectively in charge of atomic bomb intelligence). See also R. V. Jones, *Most Secret War* (London, 1979), pp. 596 f.; idem, "Meetings in Wartime and After," in *Niels Bohr Centenary Volume*, ed. French and Kennedy, pp. 278-287.

Even though Bohr was accommodated in conditions of great secrecy, there was an astonishing lapse of security when the *New York Times* carried in its issue of 9 October an Associated Press report of Bohr's arrival in which he is described as bearing "plans for a new invention involving atomic explosions. The plans were described as of the greatest importance to the Allied war effort." The AP dispatch is reprinted in Pais, *Niels Bohr's Times*, p. 491. The reaction of General Groves may be imagined. (Further lapses are to be found among the clippings in PRO, AB 1/40: The *Evening Standard* of 11 November reported Bohr's meeting at the Savoy; the *Daily Sketch* of 15 December noted that "Bohr has gone to the US on a special mission after consultations with Lord Cherwell. Prof. Bohr . . . is an expert on explosives. We understand that this subject is connected with his trip, and that he is taking to the US some new ideas"; and the *New York Daily Mirror* of 20 December observed that "the Germans believe he has a vast knowledge of atomic warfare—the miracle that might save Germany.") Could these security leaks have been deliberate?

44. T. Powers, *Heisenberg's War: The Secret History of the German Bomb* (New York, 1993), p. 238, conflates the Savoy dinner with the Cherwell conversation, citing Irving's interview with Michael Perrin (IMF 31-1333). The interview, however, does not date the Cherwell exchange to the evening at the Savoy. Kramish, *The Griffin*, p. 196, gives the correct chronology.

he might wish to visit the American side of the project, and so Bohr duly arrived in New York on 6 December.[45]

During five or six conversations with General Groves's security assistant Robert Furman in Washington later in the month, Bohr was questioned about the German project and Heisenberg's visit to Copenhagen. On 16 December, Groves himself met with Bohr in his office, and when Bohr traveled by train to Los Alamos, he was joined en route in Chicago by the general. Over a two-day period, Groves and Bohr were in each other's company for many hours, and by the time they arrived Bohr seems to have convinced his companion that there was a serious possibility that Heisenberg's reactor-bomb idea might work.[46] The result was that a meeting was convened in Oppenheimer's office to discuss Bohr's fears on 31 December, attended by Bohr and his son, Hans Bethe, Edward Teller, Victor Weisskopf, Robert Serber, and others.

At this meeting Bohr went over with his colleagues the drawing of a reactor-bomb that Heisenberg had sketched for him in 1941, resembling a crude box shape with rods sticking out of the top. The physicists found it difficult to take the sketch seriously. Weisskopf thought that Bohr's anti-German prejudice had deceived his better judgment, while Bethe was bewildered by the whole thing:

> A little drawing . . . [was] sent [brought?] to the United States after he [Bohr] had escaped from Denmark to Sweden in 1943. The drawing, attributed to Heisenberg, had been made when Heisenberg had visited Bohr in Copenhagen. Bohr sent [took?] it to Los Alamos, where several of us, including Oppenheimer, Teller, and myself, puzzled over its meaning. As far as we could see, the drawing represented a nuclear power reactor with control rods. But we had the preconceived notion that it was supposed to represent an atom bomb. So we wondered: Are the Germans crazy? Do they want to drop a nuclear reactor on London?[47]

45. R. W. Clark, *The Birth of the Bomb* (New York, 1961), p. 179. Kramish, *The Griffin*, p. 196. For British concern to keep Bohr out of "the American orbit," see the telegrams of 25 November and 28 December 1943 in PRO, AB 1/40.

46. Powers, *Heisenberg's War*, pp. 242 f., 246–248.

47. H. Bethe, "Niels Bohr and His Institute," in *Niels Bohr Centenary Volume*, pp. 232–234, at p. 233; idem, "Bethe on the German Bomb Program," *BAS*, January–February 1993, pp. 53–54. For interview quotations see J. Bernstein, *Hans Bethe, Prophet of Energy* (New York, 1980), pp. 77 f. Despite Bohr's insistence that Heisenberg was thinking of a bomb, Bethe concluded in retrospect that the proposal was so eccentric that the drawing must refer to a simple reactor, and that Heisenberg may have been trying to assure Bohr, who was "ignorant of these matters," that the Germans were not working on a bomb! This is underrating Bohr's knowledge. He may—like Heisenberg—have been ignorant of the small critical mass of U235, and he may also have taken too seriously Heisenberg's notion of an exploding reactor-bomb, but Bohr was certainly as well aware as Heisenberg of the difference between a reactor-bomb and a true atomic bomb. In any case, the context of reactor-bomb thinking renders the Heisenberg proposal less strange, as well as less innocuous.

Powers, *Heisenberg's War*, pp. 246–248, 252–254, 536, is confusing about the whole matter. He accepts that there was a drawing and that Bohr believed it was the design for a reactor-bomb; but he con-

Perhaps the crucial point here, indicating that Heisenberg's drawing did indeed refer to a bomb—and not a reactor—is the mention of control rods. We know that in 1941 (and for long afterward as well) Heisenberg did not consider control rods to be necessary in a "normal" $U238$ reactor, which would be self-stabilizing. At this stage of Heisenberg's thinking, the only conceivable reason for control rods was not to quench the reaction, but rather to use them somehow to engineer an explosion in a specific kind of reactor using enriched $U235$.

There is no written record of what exactly was said at the Los Alamos meeting, and all the participants' memories—even Bethe's, which is the best of them—are extremely hazy.[48] Nor has the drawing itself been found.[49] It is, however, certain that the reactor-bomb concept was discussed in detail and that Bohr's fears were laid to rest, since the outcome of the meeting was that Bethe and Teller were asked by Oppenheimer to prepare a report on the possibility of such a weapon. (Bethe and Teller were well chosen to write the report, since only a few months before they had written to Oppenheimer of their concern about press notices suggesting that a German bomb might be ready very soon.)[50]

---

cludes that the drawing was actually of a reactor. The result is that Bohr is made to seem rather foolish for believing that it was meant to be a bomb.

R. Rhodes, *The Making of the Atomic Bomb* (New York, 1986), pp. 384, 513, also wrongly concludes that the drawing was of an "experimental heavy-water reactor," rather than a reactor-bomb.

48. I have not traced the two later accounts of the meeting by Groves—his letter to Oppenheimer of 18 December 1964, and his notes of 13 December 1962—cited by Powers (*Heisenberg's War*, p. 535) as being in NA, RG 200, Groves Papers. Nor have I been able to find any comment or discussion among Chadwick's reports from Los Alamos to England (though these appear to be incomplete) in PRO, AB 1/485/566/581/615. An evaluation of 22 December 1943 by Furman and Groves of the British belief that the German bomb project was no longer serious cites Bohr as now agreeing with the British view (NA, RG 77, MED, Foreign Intelligence Unit, entry 22, box 170, folder 32.60-1, "German Summary Reports, June '43–June '44").

In private correspondence of 11 May 1996 Jeremy Bernstein tells me that Aage Bohr now "insists that Bohr made it up. But at Los Alamos he presented it as a German design. Serber, who was at the meeting, recalls that when Oppenheimer called it Heisenberg's, Bohr did not contradict him." Conceivably, Bohr was imputing his own design to Heisenberg and trying to guess what device Heisenberg had in mind. See below.

49. Searches in the Los Alamos Scientific Laboratory Archives, the U.S. National Archives, the Oppenheimer Papers in both the Library of Congress and the Niels Bohr Archive in Copenhagen, and the U.K. Atomic Energy files retained by the Cabinet Office and the Ministry of Defence, as well as the PRO Atomic Energy Files (AB 1), have so far failed to trace the drawing.

50. Bethe and Teller to Oppenheimer, 21 August 1943, Oppenheimer Papers, Library of Congress, box 20, quoted in Rhodes, *Making of the Atomic Bomb*, pp. 511 f., who dates it variously to July and August. The reports seem to have been triggered by information on the Dällenbach nuclear project (see below, chap. 13) and other German bomb projects that may have been connected with the Respondek-Woods espionage link (see above). For the 1943 intelligence reports of Woods in NA, RG 59, 740.0011, EW/29326, Telegram no. 109, parts 6/7 (13–15 May 1943) (= microfilm M-982, roll 158) and NA, RG 84, Decimal Files 863.4, Bern Confidential File, box 14, "Uranium" folder, see Dippel, *Two Against Hitler*, pp. 92–98. In the RG 84 correspondence the following statement suggests that some sort of cyclotron bomb was envisaged: "Experiments being conducted by AEG with uranium atom smashing for

Bethe and Teller proposed in their report to

show that the explosion of an inhomogeneous pile will liberate energies which are probably smaller . . . than those obtainable by the explosion of an equal mass of TNT.

The proposed pile consists of uranium sheets immersed into heavy water. In the course of the explosion the major part of the energy is liberated in the uranium plates in the form of heat. This will cause vaporization of the uranium. . . .

After the uranium is vaporized it will expand and transfer its energy to the surrounding heavy water; this in turn may transfer part of its energy to the case which contains the pile. . . . The major part of the energy will be in the form of kinetic energy of the heavy water and the casing, and perhaps of the uranium itself.

The velocities of these materials may be estimated by dividing the distance through which matter has to move in order to stop multiplication by the time in which the neutron density in the pile is multiplied by a factor e. . . .

The multiplication is expected to stop when the pile has expanded to roughly twice its initial linear dimensions. Even if the pile is very highly supercritical so that multiplication does not actually stop upon such an expansion, the time between fissions is so much increased that the energy production comes practically to an end. . . .

Not counting the escape of neutrons from the surface of the pile the neutrons will need not less than about 1.3×10^{-3} sec. to be multiplied by a factor e. . . .

[This] means an energy liberation of about one quarter of that due to the same mass of TNT.

The above figure is actually an over-estimate because it neglects the neutron escape from the surface. This escape will increase the effective time scale and decrease the needed expansion distance. If these effects are taken into account, a forty ton pile will actually liberate only an energy corresponding to about one ton of TNT.[51]

---

high explosive purposes. . . . The invention stems from a Swiss. . . . Indications are that the idea is to release a neutron or two in, say, a cubic meter of uranium oxide powder" (Harrison to State Dept., no. 2958, 14 May 1943, RG 84, loc. cit.); "Our informant believes that experiments have not yet resulted in elimination of extremely heavy zyklotron in which bombing of atoms takes place. If so, would preclude use as practical explosive. Nevertheless, research in Germany is continuing" (Harrison to Legge, 29 May 1943, RG 84, loc. cit.). Urgent requests on 2 June and 15 August for elucidation of these reports seem to have produced no further details in the file. However, the reply from Harrison to Long of 18 August 1943 (Bern telegram no. 5062) states that "every endeavor will be made by the contact to request Ralph for the information desired by you" and also promises that "as soon as it is received, the report promised with regard to 'secret weapons' will be telegraphed" (though it is not clear whether the "secret weapons" remark pertains to atomic weapons). Detailed information from Ralph [Respondek] via Woods on the general impact of Allied bombing on German industry is contained in Bern telegram no. 5078, Harrison to Berle and Long, 19 August 1943 (RG 59, Decimal Files 740.0011 EW 30782; also on microfilm M-982, roll 168). The latter promises that "concerning announcement of destructive reprisal measures of militarily decisive nature by 'secret weapons' factual report will be made." I have not yet been able to locate the follow-up report on "secret weapons"—whether they were of an atomic or other nature.

See below, chap. 13, for the Swiss Dällenbach's connection with this intelligence.

51. H. Bethe and E. Teller, "Explosion of an Inhomogenous Uranium-Heavy Water Pile," in NA, RG 77, MED Decimal Files 337, box 63, "Conferences."

The Bethe-Teller report deals with the case of a reactor using unseparated uranium; might it therefore really be considering Bohr's own conception of a reactor-bomb (such as that described above in his letter of June 1943) rather than a German reactor-bomb of the Müller type using highly enriched uranium? If we go back to Heisenberg's visit of 1941 to Bohr, it seems plausible to assume that Heisenberg would not have divulged to Bohr the highly secret key to the Müller proposal (and, presumably, also the secret patent application)—namely, that the reactor would be using enriched uranium to achieve much higher temperatures before the reaction terminated. Bohr himself, moreover, does not seem to have been interested in such a case, for no indication has been found that he worked out the figures for an enriched-$U235$ reactor-bomb. This suggests the conclusion that Heisenberg's true proposal for a reactor-bomb was not known to Bohr and so never discussed at all in Oppenheimer's office. On the other hand, it seems certain that Bohr himself truly believed it was Heisenberg's scheme that he had presented to the meeting. This is reinforced by the concluding sentence of Oppenheimer's covering letter to Groves, which offers a "formal assurance" that the Bohr "arrangement" would not work. For if Bohr and Groves did not believe that the "arrangement" was indeed Heisenberg's own idea, then they would not have been so worried about the whole affair out of concern that the Germans—and not just Bohr—had thought up a new kind of atomic bomb. In his letter Oppenheimer wrote:

> I am enclosing a memorandum written by Bethe and Teller after the conference yesterday. . . . The calculations referred to and described in the accompanying memorandum were carried out by Bethe and Teller, but the fundamental physics was quite fully discussed and the results and methods have been understood and agreed to by Baker [= Bohr].
>
> No complete assurance can be given that with a new idea or a new arrangement, something along these lines might not work. It is, however, true that many of us have given thought to the matter in the past, and that neither then nor now has any possibility suggested itself which had the least promise. The purpose of the enclosed memorandum is to give you a formal assurance, together with the reasons therefore, that the arrangement suggested to you by Baker [Bohr] would be a quite useless military weapon.[52]

Slow-neutron reactor-bombs had, as Oppenheimer's letter testifies, been the subject of research and continued to be so. In 1939 Szilard had described an explosive arrangement in an American patent application:

> The invention teaches that it is possible to produce a nuclear chain reaction and to maintain the stationary conditions in such chain reactions. It also teaches that it is possible to have explosive bodies in which an explosion is brought about at will by a sudden change in the distribution of matter. . . .

52. Oppenheimer to Groves, 1 January 1944, in NA, RG 77, MED Decimal Files 337, box 63.

Variation of Critical Thickness

If slow neutrons are used, the critical thickness can be increased by having a slow neutron absorber within the hollow sphere in the center. . . . By removing such absorbing matter from the inside of the chain reaction layer, the critical thickness may be reduced below the actual thickness, and thus an explosion may be brought about. The explosion will be all the more violent the more quickly the absorbing substance is removed. . . .

Mild explosions can be brought about by slowly changing the space distribution of matter and also by arranging layers. . . . On the contrary, if a strong destructive explosion is wanted, it can be brought about by providing for such an outflow [of water/boron salt]. . . .

. . . [And] by changing the distribution of matter within or without the chain reaction layer and the increase carried to the point where the critical thickness of the arrangement is exceeded so that a chain reaction leading to an EXPLOSION takes place.[53]

In 1940 the Fisk-Shockley report pursued the possibility of an exploding reactor, stating in words similar to Heisenberg's that "all of these factors tend to reduce fission with increasing temperature and hold the reaction in check."[54] And in December 1942 Groves compiled a questionnaire that included this query about a reactor-bomb:

When [*sic*] is the "critical mass" of "25" and "49" [= U235 and plutonium] required to produce an explosion in conjunction with heavy water? How much heavy water is required?[55]

And six months after Bethe and Teller had refuted the Bohr-Heisenberg design, Oppenheimer pointed out to Groves in a memorandum on the explosive character of a fast-neutron reaction that:

Systems involving slow neutrons can be explosive only if: (1) they do need the delayed neutrons to sustain the delayed chain reaction; (2) they can be made appreciably over-critical (multiplication rates some tenths of the value for infinite masses); and (3) they are not thermally self-quenching. Many such systems have been proposed, and it is probable that some will be developed in the future. To be effective, they should be so designed that the initial effects of the high pressures generated by the chain reaction increase the activity of the configuration.[56]

53. Patent application of 9 March 1939, in L. Szilard, *The Collected Works of Leo Szilard*, ed. B. T. Feld and G. W. Szilard, vol. 1, *Scientific Papers* (Cambridge, Mass., 1972), pp. 656, 671 ff., 680. See also above, chap. 4.

54. Nevertheless, it was believed possible to reach a temperature of 2 million degrees Kelvin. See J. B. Fisk and W. Shockley, "A Study of Uranium as a Source of Power" (July–September 1940), pt. II, p. 10, in NA, RG 227, OSRD/S-1, Bush-Conant Files, microfilm M-1392, roll 11, folder 170. See also the quotations from the report given above, chap. 4.

55. Groves to Conant (at OSRD), 9 December 1942, NA, RG 77, MED Decimal Files 334, box 60.

56. Memorandum from Oppenheimer to Groves, "Explosion from Fast Neutron Reactions," 27 May 1944, NA, RG 77, MED Decimal Files 319.1, box 50. (A revised version of 29 May with a covering letter is in box 53.)

One other possibility of the exact meaning of the Heisenberg drawing remains to be considered. According to a memoir by Robert Wilson, Bohr during a scientific conversation with him at Los Alamos in early 1944 pulled out of his pocket a drawing that seemed to relate to an experiment for an "autocatalytic bomb."[57]

Wilson believed that Bohr was suggesting a method of enhancing a nuclear explosion by having wedges of boron forced out during the reaction—an idea that had already occurred to Wilson and about which he was skeptical. It is very likely, however, that Bohr was thinking of a way of initiating, rather than merely enhancing, an atomic explosion, and so reverting to the Heisenberg design for a reactor-bomb that would be started by withdrawing boron control rods. That Wilson and Bohr were indeed at cross-purposes in this conversation is strongly suggested by Bohr's own brief description of an "autocatalytic bomb" that survives in a draft report on the bomb project that he prepared on 3 March 1944. This bomb would use neutron absorbers in a highly reactive, supercritical material. An explosive reaction would occur through the sudden removal or compression of these absorbers.

> Devices are conceivable by which to a certain extent the nuclear explosion will cause an increase rather than a decrease of the reactivity of the system and thus may be exploited to create by itself the conditions necessary for the attainment of high efficiencies.
>
> Such effects, usually referred to as autocatalysis, may be obtained by introducing into active material, otherwise in a highly supercritical state, neutron absorbers in sufficient amount to prevent a chain from developing. In fact, if a system of this type is rendered just slightly supercritical as is easily done f. inst. by removing a small absorber, the resulting expansion of the active material may, provided the absorbers are arranged in an appropriate manner, be able to expel them or compress them, thereby reducing their surface and consequently their effectivity. Of course, this removal of brakes on the process will be accompanied by a general expansion of the whole system tending to decrease its reactivity, but especially if the enclosure material is heavier than the absorber material, the former effect may dominate by proceeding the faster and the active material thus work itself into a more and more supercritical state.
>
> Clearly such autocatalytic schemes present great advantages for avoiding many of the most intricate problems of assembly.

The drawback was that large amounts of enriched material would be required to overcome the intrinsically poor efficiency of such an arrangement. Nevertheless, Bohr believed this direction to "afford the richest possibilities" for future work.[58]

57. R. R. Wilson, "Niels Bohr and the Young Scientists," *BAS* 41 (August 1985): 23–26.

58. The typed report with handwritten revisions is in PRO, AB 1/646, sec. III, 13. I have quoted here the original typed phrasing.

Seen in this context, both Heisenberg's secret patent application of 1941 for a reactor-bomb (if our speculation is true) and his sketch of a reactor-bomb for Bohr in September of that year do not seem quite so bizarre and improbable, but on the contrary arise naturally out of the contemporary ways of thinking about nuclear physics. Impractical though it might have been, the reactor-bomb using slow neutrons and a heavy-water moderator was conceptually respectable.

CHAPTER 11

The Weapons Research
Office Report of 1942

Plutonium and the Reactor-Bomb

By late 1941 the Army Weapons Department (HWA) was beset with urgent war requirements and undertook a reassessment of its research priorities. As no immediate result—whether in the form of a reactor-bomb, a pure-U235 bomb, or a plutonium bomb—seemed likely to materialize from the uranium project, the Weapons Research Office (HWA WaF) became interested in transferring its control to the Education Ministry and its agency, the Reich Research Council (Reichsforschungsrat), which had closer relations with the university and Kaiser-Wilhelm-Society institutes and laboratories, where most of the research was being done. On 5 December 1941 Erich Schumann, the head of the Weapons Research Office, summoned the project's leading scientists to a discussion at his office to assess progress, informing them (in the most excruciatingly bureaucratic German) that

> after the drawing up of a collective report on the state of the experiments and after further planning with the setting of target dates for conclusion of components of the problem, I shall inform the chief of the Army Weapons Department of the result of the discussion and bring about in a higher place the decision on the matter of the further handling of the subject.[1]

At the discussion held on 16 December and attended by Heisenberg, Hahn, and others, it was decided that a comprehensive survey of the state of the project should be prepared by the Nuclear Physics Section of the Weapons Research Office (HWA WaF/1a), which was headed by Kurt Diebner.[2] Compiled over the

---

1. E. Schumann to P. Harteck and other project directors, 5 December 1941 (IMF 29-687); printed in E. Bagge, K. Diebner, and K. Jay, *Von der Uranspaltung bis Calder Hall* (Hamburg, 1957), p. 28.

2. Aktennotiz aus Personalakten Peter Debye, 22 January 1942, Archiv zur Geschichte der Max-Planck-Gesellschaft, Berlin-Dahlem, I. Abt., Rep. 1A, no. 1652, lists those present and recounts Schumann's attempt to name Bothe as the new director of the KWIP.

next two months, the HWA Report ran to 144 pages, and included a nine-page bibliography of German atomic reports from 1939 to February 1942 (pp. 136–144). There is only one known original typed copy of this survey, and it is currently in private hands.[3] Though its initial four pages are lacking, a preface on the first extant page (p. 5) is dated February 1942, and a later manuscript annotation in Erich Bagge's hand reads: "*Deutsche Geheimberichte zur Nutzbarmachung der Kernenergie aus dem Jahren 1939–1942*" (German secret reports on the exploitation of nuclear energy from the years 1939–1942).[4] Despite the possibility of later emendations, the report seems to be entirely authentic as far as can be seen. What speaks in favor of its authenticity is that it contains a great deal of what might be called incriminating material, in the sense that it exposes with startling clarity the mistaken ideas about the atomic bomb that dominated German thinking during the war and shows how those ideas were shaped by Heisenberg. Essentially a large-scale elaboration of Heisenberg's fundamental paper G-39, the HWA Report links the reactor-bomb approach of Paul Müller with Heisenberg's research strategy, and explicitly states that the reactor-bomb will use a heavy-water moderator. It was never repudiated by Heisenberg, either during the war or after.

The first chapter cursorily describes the dual application of atomic energy as a reactor and as a bomb. "If the chain reaction proceeds slowly, the uranium represents a heat-producing machine; if it goes rapidly, it is an explosive of the highest effectiveness. . . . A temperature of 1000 to 2000 degrees is a heat machine; 10^{10} degrees is an explosion." Following Heisenberg, it asserts that with rising temperature, neutron escape increases, eventually bringing neutron multiplication to a stop; the reactor is thus in thermal equilibrium (pp. 9–11). Turning to explosives, the HWA Report points out that since U238 quenches fission as the temperature rises, "an explosive must therefore include the very smallest amount of U238." Because separation of U235 is difficult, it is proposed that element 94 be adopted as a preferable explosive. Even though its qualities are as yet unknown, 94 must be even more fissionable than U235, and so has the advantage of a small critical mass:

> Since in every substance a few free neutrons are to be found, it would suffice for the ignition of the explosive to bring together in space an adequate mass (perhaps about 10–100 kg).[5]

3. Professor Erich Bagge kindly supplied a copy of the report from his private papers. I have not been able to trace a copy in any other archive or collection. Excerpts from it were printed in Bagge, Diebner, and Jay, *Von der Uranspaltung*, pp. 30–32. The account of it given in M. Walker, *German National Socialism and the Quest for Nuclear Power, 1939–1949* (Cambridge, 1989), pp. 47–49, is quite wrong in crucial respects.

4. D. Irving, who had not seen a copy, states (*The German Atomic Bomb* [New York, 1967], p. 111) that the report was circulated after the 26 February meeting; but it seems more likely to have been prepared before then.

5. HWA Report, p. 13: "Da sich in jeder Substanz einige freie Neutronen befinden, würde es zur Entzündung des Sprengstoffs genügen, eine hinreichende Menge (vermutlich etwa 10—100 kg) räumlich zu vereinigen."

This critical mass of "10–100 kg" has often falsely been cited as proof that Heisenberg and the German project scientists were aware that the critical mass of a *U235* bomb would be small, or at least practicable. However, it is quite clear from the context of the sentence in the HWA Report that the figure refers to the critical mass of *plutonium*, not of U235, and that the figure is a purely speculative one, without any justified calculation being offered.[6]

This opening chapter concludes discouragingly with the observation that the production of an explosive requires either "a very large isotope separation plant or the successful extraction of element 94 in large quantity from a reactor" (p. 17). In other words, both the U235 and plutonium bombs were seen as very long-term projects indeed and hardly practicable within the duration of the war. This was very much Heisenberg's attitude, but then in the following chapter the authors pursue Heisenberg's third idea of an atomic bomb that was neither pure U235 nor plutonium, but rather an enriched-U235 reactor-bomb.

Chapter 2, section 5, is divided into three subsections, each dealing with an aspect of reactor temperatures. The first of these, "Operating Temperature" (pp. 37–38), draws on G-39 to conclude that at higher temperatures the critical radius must be larger because diffusion lengths are greater. But in the second section, "Running Process" (pp. 38–42), the authors argue, relying on findings by Weizsäcker and Müller, that a layered pile would alter the situation, since it would reduce neutron escape and keep slowed neutrons inside the pile, where they would continue the fission process. By this means, the temperature level at which the reactor remains stable may be raised and the chain reaction can continue to a point where a high enough rise in temperature again renders the reactor unstable and an explosion may take place.

> With the building up of the reactor to a temperature T_1 below T_k, an unstable equilibrium will for the time being be reached, which in an explosive manner will pass over in the following conditions into the much hotter stable temperature T_2.[7]

This leads naturally to the third section, "Possibility of the Explosive" (pp. 42–43), which explicitly cites the work of Heisenberg and Müller as the theoretical basis for its proposal of a reactor-bomb with moderator.

> We must speak still of a third temperature effect, which becomes apparent only in conditions of a quite different sort and whose discussion will be important for judg-

6. There is no excuse for the misleading phrasing by Walker (*German National Socialism*, p. 48) that the figure applies to both U235 and plutonium, since it is clear from the excerpts quoted by both Irving (*German Atomic Bomb*, p. 111) and Bagge, Diebner, and Jay (*Von der Uranspaltung*, p.39) that the critical mass here refers exclusively to plutonium and not U235. (Like Walker, Irving [*German Atomic Bomb*, p. 111] also misrepresents the "10–100 kg" as referring to U235.)

7. HWA Report, p. 41: "Beim Aufbau der Maschine bei einer Temperatur T_1 unterhalb T_k wird zunächst eine labile Gleichgewichtslage erreicht, die explosionsartig in die unter Umständen viel heissere stabile Temperatur T_2 übergehen wird."

ing the question of whether the nuclear fission of uranium is adaptable for the production of highly explosive material (see Heisenberg H1, Müller M3) [= G-39 and G-50]. If the whole fission energy can be liberated at a stroke, this means (with 2×10^8 eV of energy being liberated per fission) a sudden jump in temperature of about 10^{12} degrees (1 eV being equivalent to 10^4 degrees). According to our current considerations, this should be possible if sufficiently large masses of the material are present. (In this connection the critical volume diminishes with increasing concentration of the active isotope U235.) This rise in temperature, however, soon is limited by the resonance onset at 7.5 eV (thus at around 180,000 degrees). For if the thermal energy becomes equal to the resonance energy, the latter absorption prevails in general over fission in order of magnitude.

To overcome this critical point, the U235 must be so strongly enriched that the resonance absorption subsides quantitatively, and at the same time very large amounts of moderator must be selected. The latter point may be understood in the following manner. If a neutron has already almost reached thermal energy, it may happen that the particle after colliding with a nucleus of the moderator has more energy than it did before. This means that the slowing process at the last energy level occurs more slowly than at the start. If the thermal level lies closely below that of the resonance band, then the retardation of the slowing process occurs precisely in the resonance band and also causes a rise in absorption. This can be avoided only through the further enrichment of U235 or through increasing the number of collisions with the moderator by increasing its concentration. According to Müller, loc. cit. [= G-50], the temperature rises over the resonance value in a uranium-water mixture in which the concentration of hydrogen is about 100 times greater than that of the uranium, for which the proportion of U235 atoms to U238 atoms is 1 to 7. This estimate is based on obsolete data, so that the figures have only a qualitative significance. It shows that with natural or weakly enriched isotope mixtures heat-producing reactors may certainly be built, but that no explosive can be made that would exceed conventional explosives by two orders of magnitude. In mixtures with very much U235, however, an extreme explosive effect is possible.[8]

8. Ibid., pp. 42 f.: "Wir müssen noch von einem dritten Temperatureffekt sprechen, der aber erst unter gänzlich andersartigen Bedingungen in Erscheinung tritt und dessen Diskussion wichtig wird bei der Beurteilung der Frage, ob sich die Kernspaltung von U zur Herstellung hochbrisanter Sprengstoffe eignet (vgl. *Heisenberg* H1, *Müller* M3). Wenn sämtliche Spaltungsenergie mit einem Schlage frei wird, bedeutet dies (bei etw 2. 10^8eV frei werdender Energie pro Spaltung) eine plötzliche Temperaturerhöhung von etwa 10^{12} Grad (1 eV äquivalent 10^4 Grad). Nach unsern bisherigen Überlegungen sollte dies möglich sein, wenn nur hinreichend grosse Substanzmengen vorhanden sind. (Dabei sinkt das kritische Volumen mit wachsender Konzentration des wirksamen Isotops 235). Dieser Temperaturanstieg findet aber bald eine Begrenzung durch [p. 43] den Resonanzeinfang bei 7.5 eV (also bei etwa 180,000 Grad). Denn wenn die thermische Energie gleich der Resonanzenergie wird, überwiegt die letzte Absorption im allgemeinen die der Spaltung grössenordnungsmässig.

"Um diesen kritischen Punkt zu überwinden, muss man das Isotop 235 so stark anreichern, dass die Resonanzabsorption quantitativ zurücktritt, und zugleich sehr grosse Mengen Bremssubstanz wählen. Den letzten Punkt kann man folgendermassen verstehen. Wenn ein Neutron bereits annähernd thermische Energie erreicht hat, dann kann es vorkommen, dass das Teilchen nach dem Stoss mit einem Kern des Bremsmittels mehr Energie hat als zuvor. Das bedeutet, dass die Abbremsung im letzten En-

The point is driven home in the summary of the chapter:

> Uranium in its natural isotope mixture is not usable as an explosive; with a strong enrichment of the isotope [235] and at the same time an increase in the moderator, an explosive liberation of the whole fission energy is possible.[9]

Here is the smoking gun of the German reactor-bomb. Its concept is fully described here and related to Heisenberg's theory and Müller's approach. There is no evidence that Heisenberg ever disagreed with this description in the official HWA Report any more than he did with Müller's G-50 paper. On the contrary, a paper (G-161) written by Heisenberg in July 1942 describing a proposed large-scale experiment with a reactor contains the following passage, which is clearly related to the reactor-bomb described in the HWA Report. After pointing out that the reactor will through rising temperature reach a state of stability, Heisenberg observes:

> The concept *stability* still needs the clarification: It is immediately to be feared that the whole fission disintegration of the uranium nuclei in an explosive fashion will proceed in a fraction of a second. In this explosion the water will remain practically cold. The stability of the burner against this explosion will be decided by the characteristic of the resonance lines of the uranium. But even if the machine in this respect is unstable, the following process might occur: The metal might immediately reach a specific temperature at which the machine stabilizes itself through the broadening of the resonance lines.[10]

---

ergiebereich langsamer erfolgt als angangs. Liegt nun der thermische Bereich knapp unter den der Resonanzstelle, so tritt die Verzögerung der Abbremsung gerade im Resonanzgebiet ein und bewirkt ebenfalls eine erhöhte Absorption. Dem kann man nur entgehen durch abermalige Anreicherung des Isotops 235 oder durch Erhöhung des Stosszahl mit der Bremssubstanz, also durch Vergrösserung der Bremsstoffkonzentration. Nach *Müller* (l.c.) steigt die Temperatur über den Resonanzwert in einer U-Wassermischung, in der die Wasserstoffkonzentration etwa hundertmal grösser ist als die des Urans und für die sich als Isotopenverhältnis $N_{235} : N_{238} = 1.7$ ergibt. Diese Abschätzung beruht auf überholten Daten, so dass den Zahlen nur qualitative Bedeutung zukommt. Sie zeigt, dass mit gewöhnlichen oder nur schwach angereicherten Isotopengemischen zwar Wärmemaschinen, aber keine Sprengstoffe gemacht werden können, die den gebräuchlichen um mehr als zwei Grössenordnungen überlagen wären. Bei Gemischen mit sehr viel U235 ist jedoch eine extreme Sprengstoffwirkung möglich."

9. Ibid., p. 49: "Uran in gewöhnlicher Isotopenmischung ist nicht als Sprengstoff brauchbar; bei starker Anreicherung des Isotops und gleichzeitiger Vermehrung der Bremssubstanz ist eine explosionsartige Freisetzung der gesamten Spaltungsenergie möglich."

Walker, *German National Socialism*, pp. 48 f., deliberately suppresses the HWA Report's extensive discussion of the reactor-bomb proposal, so misrepresenting not only the content of the document but also the whole history of the German atomic project.

10. W. Heisenberg, "Bemerkungen zu dem geplanten halbtechnischen Versuch mit 1.5 to D_2O und 3 to 38-Metall" (G-161), 31 July 1942, in GWH, A II, 550–551: "Der Begriff *Stabilität* bedarf hierbei noch der Klärung: Man wird zunächst fürchten müssen, dass der ganze Spaltungszerfall der Urankerne explosionsartig in einem Bruchteil einer Sekunde vor sich geht. Bei dieser Explosion würde das Wasser praktisch kalt bleiben. Die Stabilität des Brenners gegenüber dieser Explosion wird durch

It may be reasonably conjectured that the reactor-bomb of the HWA Report and Heisenberg's G-161 was the same as that for which (as Wirtz recollected) a patent had been submitted in 1941. Indeed, the bibliography attached to the Report lists as "P1" the patent application for the production of nuclear energy that we sought to trace in the preceding chapter. But even if P1 did not contain the proposal for a reactor-bomb, it still seems highly probable that the design was included in the T-45 secret patent that Diebner's own HWA Nuclear Physics Section had prepared, which must have been available to Diebner's team while preparing the HWA Report (assuming, of course, that T-45 had been formulated by February 1942).[11]

---

das Verhalten der Resonanzlinien des Urans entschieden. Aber selbst wenn die Maschine in dieser Hinsicht labil ist, so könnte noch folgender Prozess eintreten: Das Metall würde sich zunächst bis zu einer bestimmten Temperatur erhitzen, bei der sich die Maschine durch Verbreiterung der Resonanzlinien stabilisiert."

11. I am conceding here for the sake of argument that P1 and T-45 are not identical, though it has been speculated above in chap. 10 that they were indeed so.

CHAPTER 12

The Two Conferences of 1942

Loose Details, Non-decisions, and Pineapples

Even before the HWA Report had been completed, a meeting took place in February 1942—attended by the head of the Army Weapons Department (HWA), General Emil Leeb; the chief of the HWA's Weapons Research Office (HWA WaF), Erich Schumann; and the president of the Kaiser-Wilhelm-Society, Albert Vögler—at which it was decided to release the uranium project from the HWA and assign it to the Education Ministry. From January to April 1942, Bernhard Rust, the minister of education, allowed the project to be run by the Kaiser-Wilhelm-Society, to the delight of the scientists at the Kaiser-Wilhelm-Institute for Physics (KWIP), who were happy to be free of military control. However, by April, Abraham Esau, the head of the Physics Section of the ministry's research agency, the Reichsforschungsrat (RFR; Reich Research Council), had persuaded Rust to restore to him the control of the uranium project, of which he had been deprived in 1939 at the behest of the HWA. Esau was under the supervision of Rudolf Mentzel, an SS brigadier who ran the RFR's funding arm, the Deutsche Forschungsgemeinschaft (German Research Society), as well as being a vice president of the Kaiser-Wilhelm-Society. This was rather like a game of musical chairs, since there was considerable interaction between the HWA and the RFR; General Karl Becker had been head of the HWA as well as president of the RFR in 1939–40 until succeeded by Rust in the latter post, while Erich Schumann, the chief of the HWA's Weapons Research Office, was also on the board of the RFR and had been head of the Education Ministry's Scientific Research Section.[1] Even after the transfer of the project to the RFR, Diebner's HWA Nuclear Physics Section

---

1. It was said of Schumann that he had five different offices in Berlin, in none of which he was to be found. Serious searchers looked for him rather at the Telschow café (Friedrich Glum, *Zwischen Wissenschaft, Wirtschaft, und Politik* [Bonn, 1964], pp. 451 f.). Schumann had been a political activist in the Nazi party since September 1932, and in 1934 was appointed both head of the HWA WaF and of the

(HWA WaF/1a) was permitted to continue its work in a semi-independent way. The rationale for this reorganization was that, since it was now clear that the uranium project was unlikely to yield practical military applications for some years to come, it would be better managed for the time being by a research administration rather than a military one.[2]

The changing of the guard was acknowledged by two large conferences that took place on 26–28 February 1942. The context in which these meetings took place was provided by the recommendations of the HWA Report. Although it encouraged the continued investigation of possible methods of isotope separation and enrichment that might provide the explosive for a pure-$U235$ bomb in the very long run, the main thrust of the Report was the construction of a reactor. Apart from being a feasible objective within the short term, reactor research would also be the path to the two most promising species of atomic bombs, a reactor-bomb and a plutonium bomb.[3]

The first of the two conferences was announced in January by Erich Schumann while the uranium project was still an HWA affair. Over twenty-five technical papers were to be presented at a three-day meeting at the Harnack-Haus of the Kaiser-Wilhelm-Society between 26 and 28 February.[4] But by February when the meeting's program was circulated, the RFR was bidding for control and decided to mount a more popular event that would take place at its House of German Research (Haus der deutschen Forschung) in Berlin-Steglitz on the morning preceding the Harnack-Haus meeting, scheduled to begin later in the day. Numerous Nazi and military leaders, including Himmler, were invited to the RFR's meeting (which was announced as being under the joint sponsorship of the RFR and the HWA), but it seems that a secretarial mix-up resulted in these luminaries' being sent the program of the rather less inviting technical conference and so finding themselves otherwise engaged.[5] The RFR event consisted of eight short lec-

Education Ministry's Scientific Research Section. See K.-H. Ludwig, *Technik und Ingenieure im Dritten Reich* (Düsseldorf, 1974), pp. 215 f., 230, 268.

2. M. Walker, *German National Socialism and the Quest for Nuclear Power, 1939–1949* (Cambridge, 1989), pp. 49, 59. D. Irving, *The German Atomic Bomb* (New York, 1967), pp. 104 ff. For the structure and history of the RFR, see K. Zierold, *Forschungsförderung in drei Epochen: Deutsche Forschungsgemeinschaft* (Wiesbaden, 1968), pp. 236–266, esp. pp. 260 f.; and Ludwig, *Technik*, chap. 6. On the various posts held by Schumann, Mentzel, et al., see K. Macrakis, *Surviving the Swastika: Scientific Research in Nazi Germany* (New York, 1993), pp. 90–96, 135–137, 165 f.

For the negotiations, see Archiv zur Geschichte der Max-Planck-Gesellschaft, Berlin-Dahlem, I Abt., Rep. 1A, nos. 1652, 1653.

3. See HWA Report, pp. 47 f., 134: "Über die Möglichkeiten der Herstellung von 'Kernsprengstoffen' kann erst nach Anlaufen der ersten Uranmaschine bezw. nach erfolgter Isotopentrennung in technischen Ausmasse entschieden werden."

4. Irving, *German Atomic Bomb*, pp. 105–107. Walker, *German National Socialism*, p. 53, slips in dating the conference to January. The program is in IMF 29-998, and many of the papers are in IMF 30-117/224.

5. Irving, *German Atomic Bomb*, pp. 106–112. Walker, *German National Socialism*, pp. 55 ff. (where the Haus der deutschen Forschung is wrongly located at Berlin-Dahlem, which was the home of the

tures, followed by a rather unappetizing "experimental lunch" of foods enhanced with soya, synthetic fat, and the like.[6] Schumann opened with a lecture titled "Nuclear Physics as a Weapon" and was followed by Hahn, Heisenberg, and others.[7]

Heisenberg's lecture, "The Theoretical Foundations for the Production of Energy from Uranium Fission," pointed out that natural uranium cannot sustain neutron multiplication in a chain reaction. Heisenberg, therefore, turned to the possibility of U235 enrichment or isolation:

> An increase in the number of fissions can be achieved if the rare—but fissionable at low energies—isotope U235 is enriched. If one succeeded even in producing pure U235, the situation shown on the right side of figure 1 would occur. Every neutron would, after one or more collisions, cause a further fission, unless it escaped first through the surface. The probability of the loss of the neutron through capture as opposed to that of its reproduction is here vanishingly small. If one can therefore only accumulate so great a mass of U235 that the neutron loss through the surface remains small compared to the multiplication of neutrons within, the number of neutrons in the shortest time would multiply enormously and the whole fission energy of 15 billion calories per ton would be liberated in a fraction of a second. Pure U235 would therefore represent undoubtedly an explosive of quite unimaginable power. However, this explosive is very difficult to produce.[8]

This passage has misled later historians into thinking that it is a clear exposition of a pure-U235 bomb that would have a small critical mass. In fact, the description is anything but clear in its grasp of the physics of an atomic bomb. It mistakes the basic scientific principle of the bomb when it states that the critical mass of the bomb depends on the condition "that the neutron loss through the surface remains small compared to the multiplication of neutrons within." This is not necessarily so; the essential condition is that, of the number of free neutrons released in each fission, slightly more than one neutron on average should collide with a U235 nucleus and cause it to fission.[9] (Given the speed of the fast-neutron reac-

---

KWG's Harnack-Haus). Himmler to Rust, 23 February 1942, Goudsmit Papers, AIP, box 27, folder 38, declined the invitation.

6. For the lunch menu see S. Goudsmit, *ALSOS* (New York, 1947), p. 170.

7. The program is reproduced in Irving, *German Atomic Bomb*, p. 109 (from IMF 29-705).

8. W. Heisenberg, "Die theoretischen Grundlagen für die Energiegewinnung aus der Uranspaltung" (no G number), 26 February 1942, p. 4 (IMF 29-1005; GWH, A II, 518 f.). This paper has no "G" number. A translation by D. C. Cassidy and W. Sweet appears in Heisenberg, "A Lecture on Bomb Physics: February 1942," *Physics Today*, August 1995, 27–30. The editors rather charitably remark that the talk "is accurate about bomb physics in all essentials, as far as it goes"—which is not very far, as one of the essentials missing is the critical mass of U235. (Also translated in *HPNS*, p. 294.)

9. As R. V. Jones shrewdly pointed out in *Most Secret War* (London, 1979), p. 594 n. I ought to mention Sir Charles Frank's criticism of this conclusion in a private communication to me dated 20 March 1994. Pointing out that if the effective neutron multiplication factor is only slightly above unity, then only a very inefficient explosion will occur, Sir Charles finds that Heisenberg "did indeed grossly overestimate the required amount of nuclear explosive, but *not* . . . by overestimating the role of neutron-escape—[but] rather by not giving it sufficiently detailed attention"—as is evident in Heisenberg's

tion, this condition assures that the explosive chain reaction will occur.) Heisenberg's false condition—his "loose detail" of scientific thinking, as R.V. Jones has called it—led him to an overestimation of the role of neutron escape, to his failure to comprehend the significance of the fast-neutron bomb, and to an erroneous conception of the idea of critical mass as applied to a bomb. (The "loose detail" was repeated in another lecture given by Heisenberg to the Academy of Aeronautical Research in May 1943.)[10]

It should be noted also that Heisenberg's phrasing here is consistent with his random-walk argument in favor of a huge critical mass for U235. He states that "if one can therefore only accumulate so great a mass of U235 that the neutron loss through the surface remains small compared to the multiplication of neutrons within," then a vast explosion would occur. That this mass would be very large is implied by a phrase of Heisenberg's that appears unexceptional, but is in fact rather curious for being stated so baldly: "Every neutron would, after one or more collisions, cause a further fission, unless it escaped first through the surface." *Unless it escaped first through the surface*—this singular condition strongly suggests that Heisenberg would be calculating the critical mass of a bomb on the supposition that the explosion must be sure to take place before the original fissioning neutron in the chain had escaped from the surface—that is, the case for which his random-walk argument had originally been devised.[11]

In this lecture, Heisenberg declined to specify a figure for the critical mass of a U235 bomb, but another phrase hints that he had not changed his mind since his 1940 back-of-an-envelope calculation that it would be in the range of tons. Giving a figure for the energy release of a U235 bomb, Heisenberg works the figure out in terms of "per ton": "The whole fission energy of 15 billion calories per ton would be liberated in a fraction of a second."[12]

It has to be assumed that it was made clear to the conference that the amount of U235 required for a bomb was so massive as to rule out any possibility of its being acquired even through a crash program in the remote future. Otherwise the pressures applied to the physicists by the military and political establishments to isolate a small amount of U235 would have been overwhelming. Throughout the war, the German physicists were able to conduct the uranium project as a very long-term research project, without the urgency that drove both the British project

---

phrase *small compared to.* Sir Charles observes that Heisenberg had no precise definition of the term "critical mass" before 1945.

10. W. Heisenberg, "Die Energiegewinnung aus der Uranspaltung" (G-217), 6 May 1943, in GWH, A II, 571 (which misdates it to 5 May). A curiosity of the diagram attached to the paper is that the depiction of fission in pure U235 shows too large a number of nonfissioning collisions. This suggests again Heisenberg's incomplete understanding of the nature of a fast-neutron explosion in U235.

11. See above, chap. 6, for the random-walk argument.

12. Neither Walker (*German National Socialism,* pp. 56–58) nor Irving (*German Atomic Bomb,* pp. 108–11) actually state that the critical mass would be small, but their general arguments are that Heisenberg understood the critical mass of a U235 bomb to be small.

from the moment that the Frisch-Peierls memorandum was submitted and the American once it was understood in the summer of 1941 that the critical mass of U235 was in fact quite small. Despite an initial flurry of anxiety in Germany as everywhere in September 1939, once Heisenberg had completed his reassuring G-39 paper in December 1939, we find wholly lacking there the alarmed response characteristic of Allied scientists. Thus, the February 1942 meeting concluded on a happy and calming note. Bagge reported that

> toward the end of the session Professors Heisenberg and Bothe were asked whether with the aid of uranium energy it might be possible in the course of three-quarters of a year to produce a weapon that would decide the war. Both had realistically and in consideration of the handicapped situation arising out of the war to agree to answer no.[13]

Even if the given time period had been three or four years, the answer would still have been the same (as indeed it was on subsequent occasions). Contrast the alarm evinced in Britain and America as soon as it was understood that the critical mass of a U235 bomb would be only a few kilograms. Clearly, Heisenberg and the German scientists never understood during the war the fundamental point about critical bomb mass that would have made an emergency bomb project inevitable.

Though Heisenberg's lecture of February 1942 does not deal with the possibility of a reactor-bomb, there is nothing in it to contradict the received German idea of such a device. Heisenberg advances his usual theory of a reactor using natural uranium and a moderator as being essentially self-stabilizing, but he does not discuss the case of an enriched-U235 reactor that would be the sort in which an arrangement could be made so as to render it unstable and explosive. Indeed, he says very little about how enriched U235 would affect the operation of a reactor of any kind, even though he points out twice that the atomic project must aim at both the *enrichment* and the *extraction* of U235. The reactor-bomb concept, therefore, remains only implicit in Heisenberg's text.[14]

A remarkable aspect of this 1942 lecture is its enthusiastic endorsement of plutonium as a nuclear explosive. After describing the chances of building a natural-uranium reactor with moderator, Heisenberg remarks:

---

13. W. Hanle and E. Bagge, "40 Jahre Nutzung der Kernenergie," *Atomkernenergie* 40 (1982): 3–7, at p. 5. (The English version, "Peaceful Use of Nuclear Energy during 40 Years," ibid., 1–3, is not as explicit as the German.)

14. GWH, A II, 519, 521 ("Problem der Anreicherung bzw. der Reindarstellung des Isotops U235"; "Die Energiegewinnung aus der Uranspaltung ist zweifellos möglich, wenn die Anreicherung des Isotops U235 gelingt. Die *Reindarstellung* von U235 würde zu einem Sprengstoff von unvorstellbarer Wirkung führen"). Heisenberg already has argued that with the right moderator, a chain reaction would probably occur in a reactor fueled by natural uranium. He now suggests—without explanation—that enriched U235 would guarantee the chain reaction; but, of course, the use of enriched U235 would also mean that the reactor might be rendered unstable. (Cf. Heisenberg's paper of 31 July 1942, G-161, discussed above, chap. 11.)

As soon as such a machine is in operation, the question of producing an explosive takes on, according to an idea of von Weizsäcker's, a new twist. With the transformation of uranium in the machine, a new substance (element number 94) is created that has the highest probability of being an explosive of equally unimaginable power as pure U235.[15]

This is a crucial statement for the understanding of the mentality behind the whole German atomic project. With uranium seeming a very long and uncertain path to the bomb, plutonium had the merit of being in all likelihood a shorter and safer bet. Certainly, Heisenberg believed that even plutonium might take many years to be developed as a practical explosive and so was able to reassure himself he was not actually producing a bomb for Hitler. But the crucial point is that he fully understood the reactor to be the path to the bomb and was willing to announce it as such to what was intended to be a political-military-scientific gathering in February 1942.[16] Nor was this a momentary indiscretion; it was to be repeated at a full-scale armaments meeting held in the presence of the munitions minister, Albert Speer, and several generals a few months later in June 1942.

Speer had been brought into the organization of atomic research in April 1942 by Vögler, the head of the KWG, who was anxious to gain independence for the KWIP's project from what was already becoming the oppressive hand of Esau and Rust's Education Ministry. The result was that Speer by the time of the June conference had already arranged with Hitler himself for the transfer of the entire Reichsforschungsrat, including the uranium project, from Rust to Goering. In effect, this meant that Esau's old RFR controller Rudolf Mentzel would be more likely to be restrained, since Mentzel himself would be answerable to Goering. These bureaucratic maneuvers were very necessary for Heisenberg to enjoy a certain scientific independence in his research, and in the process he himself was in late April appointed to be director of the KWIP, effective from October. In this official capacity, Heisenberg was well positioned to exploit the sympathetic interest of Speer through personal contact.[17]

15. GWH, A II, 520.

16. When word of it reached Goebbels, he became quite enthused about the potential of an atomic bomb (J. Goebbels, *Tagebücher, 1942–1943,* ed. L. P. Lochner [Zurich, 1948], p. 136, 21 March 1942; idem, *The Goebbels Diaries,* ed. and trans. L. P. Lochner [London, 1948], p. 90).

17. Albert Speer, *Inside the Third Reich* (New York, 1970), pp. 225 ff.; Ludwig, *Technik,* pp. 234 ff.; Walker, *German National Socialism,* pp. 77–79; Macrakis, *Surviving the Swastika,* p. 174. For the KWIP appointment, see Elisabeth Heisenberg, *Inner Exile* (Boston, 1984), pp. 83, 91; Walker, *German National Socialism,* p. 86. Macrakis, *Surviving the Swastika,* p. 170, establishes October as the starting date. For the efforts of Schumann to have Bothe nominated as director, and for the countermeasures at the KWIP in favor of Heisenberg, see Archiv zur Geschichte der Max-Planck-Gesellschaft, Berlin-Dahlem, I Abt., Rep. 1A, nos. 1652, 1653. (Harteck had complained to the KWG regarding Schumann's "impulsive" nomination of Bothe.)

It was to recruit Speer's full support that the Kaiser-Wilhelm-Society held a high-level meeting in the Helmholtz lecture room of its Harnack-Haus on 4 June 1942, attended by several senior scientists including Heisenberg and Hahn, and on the military side by Speer; his technical chief, Karl-Otto Saur; General Fromm of the Army High Command, and the heads of the Army Weapons Department and its Air Force and Navy counterparts (General Leeb, Field Marshal Milch, and Admiral Witzell, respectively).[18] It was an imposing gathering of about fifty military men and scientists, as a photograph of the occasion shows.[19] No record of Heisenberg's lecture on this occasion survives, but it is reported to have been unabashed in its talk of nuclear weapons.[20] According to Irving (drawing on accounts by Heisenberg and others present), Heisenberg opened with a discussion of the military applications of nuclear energy and explained how an atomic bomb could be made.[21] The frankness of the discussion of a bomb is said to have staggered some of the audience.[22] Heisenberg identified U235 and plutonium as possible explosives, and also reported that Bothe's work had shown that protoactinium was also

18. Irving, *German Atomic Bomb*, pp. 118–122, gives the most detailed account of the meeting, based on interviews with the participants, but it should be treated with caution. So far no detailed documentary evidence has been found. As Macrakis, *Surviving the Swastika*, p. 170, points out, the event has become the object of some mythology, and the reliability of Heisenberg's and other recollections is called into question by various contradictions. (Walker, *German National Socialism*, p. 78, seriously understates the significance of this meeting.)

Harnack-Haus was the KWG's guest house, not far from the KWIP in Berlin-Dahlem.

19. See the plate in Irving, *German Atomic Bomb*. The U.S. Air Force report of the interrogation of a Dr. Lieb—Speer's technical adviser—is vague in its technical details of a uranium bomb, and it also has Lieb dating the meeting to early 1943, but he evidently remembered the event well. In his statement "The Handling of the Problem of Nuclear Physics by the Ministry of Armament and War Production" (USAF Historical Research Agency, Maxwell AFB, Alabama, US 9th Air Force, P/W Interrogation Detachment, Military Intelligence Service, folder "Interrogations" 533.619, B-5 1945. no. 4, *Atomic Bomb—German, Investigations, Research, Developments, and Practical Use*, 19 August 1945 = microfilm B-5737), Lieb—a physical chemist and head of the patent office in the Speer ministry—recalls the meeting having been attended by about fifty people including Schumann, Milch, and Rhein and their staffs (representing the Army, Luftwaffe, and Navy) as well as a group of scientists including Heisenberg, Hahn, Strassmann, Harteck, Jensen, Groth, Bothe, Clusius, Sommerfeld (!), Joos, Ardenne, and many others. It was felt by the participants that the results of this research could not affect the war, but some people pointed out that having such a weapon would "assure the country having it undisputed superiority for a long time." Lieb says he had many subsequent talks with Heisenberg, who felt that the problem would not admit of swift progress.

20. Heisenberg to Irving, 24 May 1966, p. 2 (IMF 32), seems to refer to his having circulated his *Bericht* for the meeting to Hahn and other scientists.

21. Irving, *German Atomic Bomb*, p. 120.

22. Such as (allegedly) E. Telschow, the director general of the KWG, a time server whose word about anything should be treated with caution. The scientists and the military men could not have been so surprised; after the war Lieutenant-General Erich Schneider of the Heereswaffenamt in an interview recalled that the scientists were absolutely clear that the military authorities expected from them a destructive weapon (Ludwig, *Technik*, p. 240).

fissionable by fast neutrons and so likely to form supercritical masses that would detonate spontaneously. But, Heisenberg was emphatic, protoactinium could never be produced in sufficient quantities.[23]

Such is the Heisenberg version, but it must be treated with caution. Where it can be checked, for instance, in its account of Bothe's work on protoactinium, it seems to misrepresent the significance of the Bothe paper, which more likely envisaged protoactinium as a possible additive to a $U238$ reactor-bomb rather than as a pure explosive capable of spontaneous detonation in supercritical mass, as Heisenberg asserts.[24]

The same caveat applies to the famous estimate of a critical mass suggested to the meeting by Heisenberg. When asked by Milch how much nuclear explosive was needed to destroy a city, Heisenberg replied that it would be (the image varies) "as large as a pineapple" or "as big as a football."[25] Heisenberg and others have tried to claim that this remark proves that the Germans understood (like Frisch and Peierls) the critical mass of a $U235$ bomb to be very small.[26] But the pineapple analogy has no precedent in Heisenberg's thinking about a pure-$U235$ bomb; it is, how-

23. Reported in Irving, *German Atomic Bomb*, p. 120, drawing on Heisenberg's recollection. See his interview with Heisenberg, 23 October 1965, pp. 21 ff. (IMF 31-546 ff.).

24. W. Bothe, "Maschinen mit Ausnutzung der Spaltung durch schnelle Neutronen" ("Machines Exploiting Fission by Fast Neutrons") (G-128), 2 December 1941, p. 48 (IMF 30-028), investigates the use of fast neutrons to fission $U238$ in piles. At the end of section 3, Bothe concludes that $U238$ itself will not work, but in a footnote he indicates the possibility of mixing in some protoactinium, which has a seven-times-larger fission cross-section than $U238$ and a neutron multiplication factor of slightly more than one neutron per fission: "If the question arose at any time of obtaining a very large quantity of protoactinium, then one would have to reckon with the possibility of an explosion." Apart from the ambiguity as to whether Bothe is adumbrating the potential of protoactinium as a nuclear explosive or is merely worried that a reactor containing the element may explode, it should be noticed that he does not attempt to compare protoactinium fission to that of $U235$. The comparison is, in fact, to that of $U238$ fission in a reactor. The question remains of whether Bothe—and Heisenberg—conceived protoactinium to be primarily a possibility for a reactor-bomb. (Protoactinium is also discussed in FHT, no. 5, pp. 11, 13 f., 17 f.; *OE*, pp. 118 ff., 123 f.)

Heisenberg's letters to Goudsmit of 5 January and 3 October 1948 (IMF 29-1185) use Bothe's findings somewhat unwarrantedly to justify his claim to have understood fully the fast-neutron reaction in $U235$. (Originals in Goudsmit Papers, box 10, folders 95, 96.) But see above, chap. 1. So too O. Haxel, "Der Beitrag der schnellen Neutronen zur Neutronenvermehrung im Uran," in *FIAT [= Field Information Agency, Technical] Review of German Science, 1939–1946: Nuclear Physics and Cosmic Rays*, ed. W. Bothe and S. Flügge (Wiesbaden, 1948), pt. II, pp. 165–173, at p. 173, though the reference is erroneous, being to an unrelated paper by Bothe on the Haigerloch reactor. As Irving points out in speaking of Heisenberg's own *FIAT Review* paper, "some of the claims should be treated with caution and compared with original documents" (IMF inventory). Goudsmit also believed that the *FIAT Review* reports were not to be trusted, written as they were with the advantage of hindsight (Goudsmit to Irving, 11 February 1966, IMF 32).

25. Irving, *German Atomic Bomb*, p. 120. See Heisenberg's letter to Irving of 10 June 1966 (IMF 32) for his hazy recall of this episode.

26. For instance, Heisenberg to Irving, 10 June 1966, p. 2, which refers to his image of a "football of $U235$"; and the interview of 1965, p. 22 (IMF 31-547).

ever, anticipated by the figure of 10 to 100 kg given in the HWA Report a few months earlier as the critical mass of a plutonium bomb.[27] After the war, Heisenberg conveniently forgot about his "pineapple," when he declared as early as 1947 that "investigation of the technical sides of the atomic bomb problem—for example, of the so-called critical size—was, however, not undertaken."[28] Except in the very limited sense that a formal and detailed calculation was not undertaken similar to that in the Frisch-Peierls memorandum, this statement is false.[29] Only a year after making this remark of 1947, Heisenberg would contradict himself by making his first reference to his June 1942 response that the "essentially active part of a bomb would be the size of a pineapple."[30]

Heisenberg's strategy at the conference succeeded beyond expectations. It comprised several elements. First, it would be demonstrated that no practical out-

27. T. Powers, *Heisenberg's War: The Secret History of the German Bomb* (New York, 1993), p. 147, accepts Heisenberg's postwar claim (interview with Irving, 23 October 1965, pp. 21 f. [IMF 31-546/547]) that he intentionally did not mention plutonium in his June 1942 lecture. But the contemporary evidence is largely from silence (Speer did not specify plutonium) or ambiguous (Lieb was confused over the discussion of transuranics). On the contrary, Heisenberg had already spoken forcefully about plutonium in his February talk. Even if Heisenberg did not discuss plutonium in his formal Harnack-Haus lecture, he undoubtedly had plutonium in mind when he answered the question with his remark about the pineapple. (Irving, *German Atomic Bomb*, p. 120, asserts that plutonium was referred to along with U235 as an explosive.)

I should note here that some observers are of the opinion that no significance should be attached either to the unelaborated HWA reference to "10–100 kg" or to the "pineapple" remark. This use of Occam's razor would certainly remove the need for a good deal of speculative argument. Still, the former occurs in an official and I believe authentic document that was assuredly circulated to Heisenberg, and there seems to be a link between the two statements. It certainly would be interesting to learn the means by which the "10–100 kg" figure was reached and by whom.

28. W. Heisenberg, "Research in Germany on the Technical Application of Atomic Energy," *Nature*, no. 4059 (16 August 1947): 211–215, at p. 213 (GWH, ser. B, 416).

29. Whether or not Heisenberg accurately understood the concept of critical mass as applied to a U235 bomb is, in any case, open to doubt, as argued above in chap. 7. There is, furthermore, a possibility that when he made his pineapple remark, he was alluding not to the actual size of the plutonium critical mass, but rather to the amount of U235 or plutonium containing the energy needed to destroy a city. This was widely known at the time. For example, Abraham Pais, in *Niels Bohr's Times in Physics: Philosophy and Polity* (Oxford, 1991), p. 461, recalls that in February 1939 Fermi's office mate Uhlenbeck told him "how one day Fermi had stood at the window of their office in Pupin Laboratory, looking out over the city, then had turned around, and said: 'You realize, George, that one small fission bomb could destroy most of what we see outside?'" Yet at the time Fermi believed (see above, chap. 4) that the critical mass of a U235 bomb would be enormous. He was referring merely to the amount of U235 that could theoretically cause that destruction; the quantity, or critical mass, of U235 needed to ensure that that smaller amount was exploded was a different problem. (Pais, *Neils Bohr's Times*, p.462, quotes one of the many popular articles that described the quantity of energy available in small amounts of U235: "Physicists here debate whether experiments will blow up 2 miles of the landscape" [*Washington Post*, 29 April 1939]). For the general knowledge from 1939 on that 1 kg of U235 could destroy a city—and for the general ignorance of how it could be exploded—see the *New York Times* article of 5 May 1940, quoted in W. L. Laurence, *Men and Atoms* (New York, 1959), pp. xii, 43, 46–49.

30. Heisenberg to Goudsmit, 3 October 1948, in Goudsmit Papers. See above, chap. 1.

come could be expected from the uranium project within the foreseeable future. Second, Heisenberg would show that German research was going ahead with all possible urgency on the reactor, which would lead to the bomb.

Third, given these facts, Speer would be reassured that the Allies could not possibly be ahead of the German project. Fourth, it would be stressed how important the project was in the long run to Germany. And fifth, Heisenberg would secure Speer's approval of the continuation of the project, despite its lack of immediate practical results, by dangling the long-run bait of a "pineapple" atomic bomb that would emerge from the reactor. It appears it was never the intention of Heisenberg to develop a reactor merely as an engine or a heat machine; the ultimate significance of the reactor always remained its capacity to produce plutonium.[31] Believing that he needed only sufficient funds to achieve the building of a critical reactor and that he would then take whatever step was needed after that stage had been reached, Heisenberg felt no compunction in speaking so temptingly of pineapple-sized critical masses of plutonium. At any rate, he was prepared to throw the whole weight of his scientific authority behind the claim that his research program was the right and indeed the only way to attain a bomb, that no more could be done than was being done, and that there was no point in launching an all-out industrial drive. Everything had to be done in a scientifically orderly way, as determined by Heisenberg.

After the meeting, Heisenberg sought to enlist Speer's personal attention while showing the minister over the Kaiser-Wilhelm-Institute for Physics. Heisenberg claims to have hinted to Speer his pessimism about the end of the war, a hint responded to by a long silence. The upshot of the whole affair was that Speer asked Heisenberg how much he needed for the project, felt amused by the small sum— an increase of 75,000 marks to reach a budget of 350,000 marks—that was requested, but assured Heisenberg of his continued support and interest.[32] This would enable the building of a new reactor bunker for the KWIP in which the reactor experiments B-VI and B-VII would be conducted through 1944. (After the war, Heisenberg claimed that he had lacked the "moral courage" to recommend to Speer that such a speculative project requisition the "120,000" staff needed to pursue it on a large scale.)[33] For his part, Speer ordered the reorganization of the RFR on 9 June, and on 23 June dutifully notified Hitler of the meeting of 4 June

31. After talking to Diebner, Harteck wrote on 26 June 1942 to the War Office asking for continued support for uranium enrichment. Though the project was now aiming for a reactor using natural uranium, Harteck urged that enriched $U235$ be used as fuel: "The latter method is, furthermore, more akin to the manufacture of explosives" (IMF 29-719, quoted in Irving, *German Atomic Bomb*, p. 128).

32. Speer, *Inside the Third Reich*, p. 226. Heisenberg's letter of 11 June 1942 to Telschow (KWG), outlining his budget (Heisenberg Archiv, Munich) cited in Powers *Heisenberg's War*, p. 149.

33. FHT, no. 4, p. 9; *OE*, p. 76.

and of his support for the uranium project.[34] (Hitler's acquaintance with the project became known to some of the scientists.)[35]

Had Heisenberg really believed that only a few kilograms or "pineapple" of U235 were needed for a bomb and so informed Speer, there seems little doubt that the minister would have seized the chance to begin a massive crash program to isolate those few kilograms, just as happened in England (but not in the United States, where, as in Germany, the small critical mass of U235 was not appreciated, despite British information, until the summer of 1941). The production of plutonium, however, could not be hurried and would have to wait until Heisenberg's methodical experiments with his uranium and heavy-water reactor had come to their orderly conclusion.

Speer had thus accepted Heisenberg's opinion in its rather paradoxical central aspect— namely, that the uranium project would have no practical outcome in the near future, but was worth supporting since its "research" program was going ahead with all possible speed. This great success, as it seemed, of Heisenberg's relieved the German physicists of having to make what after the war he himself termed "a moral decision."[36] Word soon filtered down to the other physicists involved in the project. A few nights later, after a meeting of the Physical Society, some of the participants repaired to a café by the Kurfürstendamm and professed their relief at not having to develop a bomb. The Allied agent Paul Rosbaud, who was present, listened with mounting indignation to this cant, until he was at last provoked to exclaim: "Nonsense! If you knew how to build it, you'd present it to your Führer on a silver platter." The physicists were stunned, alarmed that Rosbaud might be an agent provocateur, but also fearful of reporting him, consider-

---

34. W. A. Boelcke, ed., *Deutschlands Rüstung im Zweiten Weltkrieg: Hitlers Konferenzen mit Albert Speer, 1942–1945* (Frankfurt, 1969), p. 137. Ludwig, *Technik*, p. 242. (The report is in BA, R 3/1504). Cf. Walker, *German National Socialism*, p. 78. The matter was raised with Hitler as item 15, not item 16 as Irving, *German Atomic Bomb*, p.121, declares.

35. An ALSOS report compiled by Goudsmit after examining captured documents of Weizsäcker at Strasbourg and interrogating German physicists there, including Rudolf Fleischmann (see below, chap. 13) in December 1944, observes: "There are also indications that energy production rather than an explosive is the principal German goal, though the latter has not been overlooked. Hitler has been informed of the T.A. [Allied code for atomic bomb project] possibilities as far back as 1942; his reaction is unknown." (Goudsmit to War Department, Military Intelligence Section G-2, 31 January 1945, in *Manhattan History* [NA Mflm. A- 1218, roll 5, vol. 14, supp. 1, "Foreign Intelligence," appendix].) The information must have come from either the Weizsäcker or Fleischmann papers; according to F. H. Hinsley, *British Intelligence in the Second World War* (Cambridge, 1988), vol. 3, pt. 2, p. 591, the source was the Weizsäcker papers. (A letter from Telschow to the President of the KWG, A. Vögler, dated 24 July 1942, states that Schumann's proposals should be conveyed along with Speer's by Keitel to Hitler in the coming weeks; Archiv zur Geschichte der Max-Planck-Geschichte, Berlin-Dahlem, I Abt. Rep. 1A, no. 1653.)

36. See above, chap. 1.

ing their own less than patriotic remarks. The gathering dissolved in an uncomfortable silence.[37]

For the rest of the war Heisenberg's plan was to construct a natural-uranium reactor that would be the door to the development of both atomic engines and atomic plutonium bombs. Uranium enrichment, which seemed too replete with technical difficulties, was investigated, but not as the central thrust of the project. On the other hand, once the funds and the continuation of the uranium project had been assured by Speer, neither Heisenberg nor his organizational superiors in the Reichsforschungsrat were interested in emphasizing any longer the attractive ease of obtaining plutonium as opposed to U235, since that might invite unpleasant pressure from both Speer and Hitler to achieve some practical results.[38] This tactfulness comes through in another of Heisenberg's "popular" presentations, the lecture delivered to the Academy of Aeronautical Research in May 1943, where Heisenberg suppresses any mention of plutonium, while referring to ongoing research into the enrichment of U235 and his theory of a pure-U235 bomb where "the escape of neutrons from the surface will be outweighed . . . by the internal neutron multiplication."[39] By 1942, therefore, Heisenberg was convinced that no atomic bomb could be developed during the course of the war: A U235 bomb, like a reactor-bomb, seemed chimerical, while the plutonium bomb depended first on the slow stages to a successful reactor, followed by the running of such reactors over a lengthy period of time. No wonder Heisenberg felt he had not yet reached the stage of having to make a moral decision. His erroneous scientific decisions had protected him from that.

37. A. Kramish, *The Griffin* (Boston, 1986), p. 129. For slightly different wording, see below, chap. 21. For Respondek's learning of the June conference's results through his contacts in the Speer ministry, see J. V. H. Dippel, *Two against Hitler* (New York, 1992), p. 87.

38. See Walker, *German National Socialism,* p. 94.

39. "Energiegewinnung aus der Atomkernspaltung" (G-217), in GWH, A II, 571.

CHAPTER 13

Reactor-Bombs, Plutonium Bombs, and the SS

The Report of Activities of 1944

Though the Harnack-Haus conference of June 1942 firmly established that the main thrust of the uranium project must now be the building of a reactor (after which would come plutonium), the idea of a reactor-bomb that might be invented along the way never really left the minds of the German physicists and their administrative masters. In July 1942 Heisenberg set the example for this kind of wishful thinking when in his paper on a proposed large-scale reactor experiment (G-161) he stated that

> the whole fission disintegration of the uranium nuclei in an explosive fashion will proceed in a fraction of a second. . . . The stability of the burner as opposed to this explosion will be decided by the characteristic of the resonance lines of the uranium.[1]

Since Heisenberg himself had laid down this principle of an explosive unstable reactor, it was only natural that his colleagues should have kept it in mind as the model of a reactor-bomb. There is some evidence, moreover, that he fostered these hopes.

In May 1942 a pro-Nazi Swiss inventor named Walter Dällenbach, who was much disliked by both the Allied agents Rosbaud and Respondek, approached Heisenberg with a proposal for a new powerful type of cyclotron. Heisenberg recommended Dällenbach to Speer, who in December 1942 helped arrange the backing of the head of the giant AEG electrical company, Hermann Bücher—then a member of the Armaments Ministry's board on new weapons projects—for the inventor's efforts to develop new devices for "atomic-energy purposes." By July 1943 Dällenbach had set himself up in a well-funded special research facility at

---

1. W. Heisenberg, "Bemerkungen zu dem geplanten halbtechnischen Versuch mit 1.5 to D_2O und 3 to 38-Metall" (G-161), 31 July 1942, in GWH, A II, 550–551 (quoted more fully above in chap. 11).

Bisingen (*Forschungstelle D*). After the war, of course, Dällenbach claimed that his interest in a cyclotron was purely scientific, but he seems to have solicited funding for it on the basis of its military potential. Thus, in 1943 Dällenbach's patron Bücher boasted to Respondek that he had—or would have—a new weapon capable of destroying the Allies. Respondek reported through Switzerland to Washington on the funding of the Dällenbach project, stating that "the inventor of the bomb" was said to be a Swiss under contract to AEG and that the idea seemed to be to "release one or two neutrons in . . . one cubic meter of uranium oxide powder."[2] This points clearly to a reactor-bomb, and it seems likely that the idea—approved in principle by Heisenberg—was not so much to obtain the large quantities needed for a pure-U235 bomb, but rather to use the cyclotron to produce moderate amounts of U235 that might be used to "seed" the reactor and render it explosively unstable. Nevertheless, Heisenberg resented Dällenbach enough to want to keep him out of the KWIP, and after the war in 1949 he recommended severing contacts between the Max-Planck-Society (the successor to the KWG) and the Swiss scientist.[3]

Other echoes of Heisenberg's thinking about a reactor-bomb may be found in the records relating to the physicist Rudolf Fleischmann (born 1903), who was active in the official uranium project as Bothe's assistant at Heidelberg before being appointed head of the Department of Physics in the Medical Research Institute of the Faculty of Medicine at the Nazified University of Strasbourg in November 1941.[4] Colleagues in the medical faculty included scientists who were involved in human experimentation on Jewish and other prisoners;[5] not surprisingly, when

2. Harrison to State Dept., no. 2958, 14 May 1943, NA, RG 84, Decimal Files 863.4, Bern Confidential File, box 14, quoted above, chap. 10.

3. For Dällenbach and the alarmed reception of Respondek's reports in Washington, see J. V. H. Dippel, *Two against Hitler* (New York, 1992), pp. 87–93.

Dippel (pp. 90 f., 182 f.) draws on materials in the Heisenberg-Archiv in Munich and the Archiv der Max-Planck-Gesellschaft in Berlin for relations between Heisenberg and Dällenbach. (At p. 183, the break with Dällenbach seems to be dated to 1946; but see pp. 90 f.) For Heisenberg's exclusion of Dällenbach from the KWIP, see FHT, no. 3, pp. 3 f.; *OE*, pp. 66 f.. Heisenberg seems to have regarded Dällenbach both as a "foreign spy" and as a Nazi protégé of Bormann's.

Rosbaud's dislike of Dällenbach's Nazi sentiments is expressed in his letter of 5 September 1945 to Goudsmit (Goudsmit Papers, AIP, folder 42, ser. IV), cited in Dippel (p. 91).

Dällenbach's patent application for certain features of his cyclotron is in G-209, dated 1943. See above, chap. 10, for Dällenbach's other patents.

Evaluations by Oppenheimer and others of the OSS's report of November 1944 on Dällenbach are in NA, RG 77, MED Foreign Intelligence Unit, entry 22, box 166, folder 32.24—1, "German Research Institutes." The folder contains a report that Laue and Heisenberg were on a committee that met with Dällenbach every week.

4. See B. Ring, *Origines du Centre de Recherches Nucléaires*, vol. 1, *Implantation d'un générateur de neutrons aux Hospices Civils de Strasbourg, 1941–1944* (Strasbourg, [1988?]). R. Fleischmann, "Warum Forschungsinstitut der Medizinischen Fakultät der Reichsuniversität Strassburg?" (lecture, 1988).

5. See S. Goudsmit, *ALSOS* (New York, 1947), pp. 73 f., 207, concerning A. Hirt and E. Haagen. Files on Haagen are to be found in the Library of Congress ALSOS records, e.g., LC MS 18,806.2,

Goudsmit interrogated Fleischmann on 4 December 1944, he found his subject to be "an extreme Nazi" and not at all "cooperative."[6] At Strasbourg, Fleischmann's main fellow physicist was Carl-Friedrich von Weizsäcker, who, as Heisenberg's closest friend, would have been able to keep Fleischmann informed of progress at the Berlin KWIP.[7]

Active in soliciting research funds from the German government for a neutron generator and cyclotron, Fleischmann on 19 May 1942 visited Dr. Schieber, a Munitions Ministry official and head of the Reich Technicians Group for Chemistry of the National Socialist Union of German Researchers, to appeal for equipment funds. In a memorandum to Schieber dated 22 May, Fleischmann justified his case by stating that the uranium machine would make an excellent engine and then continued:

Use of the Cyclotron

For research work, especially for such work as has to do with the construction of the uranium machine. . . .
    . . . If the uranium machine succeeds, its chief value will be the small use of combustibles. For example, it appears possible to build a ship with great speed. . . . It might also be possible by means of a rapid ignition to give the uranium machine the character of a buzz bomb. Because of the great weight of the apparatus and the presumed difficulty of a voluntary and instantaneous ignition, it is probable that the uranium machine is more important as a source of industrial energy.[8]

A later report, "The Physics of the Atomic Nucleus and the Prospects of Its Practical Application," contains a similar reference:

The question of whether the uranium machine will work is being considered (details

---

container 230, reel 134: ALSOS 104 (microfilm PB 20503). Cf. R. J. Lifton, *The Nazi Doctors* (New York, 1986), pp. 285 f.; M. Kater, *Doctors under Hitler* (Chapel Hill, N.C., 1989), p. 237; and idem, *Das "Ahnenerbe" der SS, 1935–1945* (Stuttgart, 1974), pp. 245–255, 261 f.

6. Goudsmit's ALSOS reports, cited below, footnote 10.

7. In a letter to me of 11 July 1993, Fleischmann claims that after November 1941 he "was no longer entitled to read the official reports on the uranium problem. Nor had I the time and connection to do so." Nevertheless, Fleischmann attended meetings after November 1941 and also worked with Weizsäcker (see IMF 31-1057, 1060).

8. G-343B, an abstract of correspondence by Fleischmann and Weizsäcker found at Strasbourg. A follow-up on this subject appears in Fleischmann's notes of 1 June 1942 (also in G-343B):

Question: Is the main use for energy or destruction?
Answer: Energy
Q: Also on destruction. Difficulties arise.
. . . The question of defense is important. Can a bomb be detected in the distance by means of rays?
A: No.

The German original is not given, but is to be found in RG 77, MED Foreign Intelligence Unit, entry 22, box 164, folder "Germany."

remain secret). Previous investigations make it probable that the uranium machine will work. . . . For the time being it may be allowed as less probable that the uranium machine can be used as a gigantic bomb.[9]

Fleischmann was captured by the ALSOS team at Strasbourg in late November 1944 and interrogated in a friendly way by Goudsmit and F. Wardenburg, who were careful about giving away their interest in the German nuclear program. When asked about "secret" papers found in Weizsäcker's office, Fleischmann suggested that they had to do with a ship's engine proposal.[10] Fleischmann's nuclear expertise, as well as his strongly Nazi attitude, induced Goudsmit to have him transferred after a brief hospital stay to America for further questioning in February 1945.[11] Fleischmann now denies having ever known or said anything about a reactor-bomb, though this is contradicted by the written evidence quoted above.[12] (In June 1946 Fleischmann asked to see Goudsmit, who recommended his immediate release and return to Germany, where he managed to survive Denazification and become a professor at Hamburg in 1947. This may serve as a corrective to recent efforts to depict Goudsmit as crazed by anti-German prejudice after the war.)

Another reference to reactor-bombs appears in a 1942 research paper by Sieg-

9. R. Fleischmann, "Die Physik der Atomkern und die Aussichten ihrer praktischen Anwendung" (G-384), p. 3: "Die Frage, ob die Uranmaschine geht, steht etwa so (Einzelheiten sind geheim). Die bisherigen Untersuchungen machen es sehr wahrscheinlich dass die Uranmaschine gehen wird. . . . Im Augenblick darf es als weniger wahrscheinlich gelten, dass die Uranmaschine als riesige Bombe benützt werden kann." The report is not dated but appears to have been written in late 1942 or 1943.

10. See Goudsmit, *ALSOS,* pp. 67–73. Fleischmann's letter to me of 11 July 1993 refers to two interrogations, of 29 November and 20 December 1944, during the latter of which Goudsmit brought up the question of the secret papers.

These questionings may have been in addition to the other interrogations of 4 and 6 December 1944, which, along with Goudsmit's reports of 6 and 8 December to Military Intelligence G-2 in Washington, are cited in the *Manhattan Project History,* vol. 14, Supplement 1, app. A., NA, RG 77, MED, microfilm A-1218, roll 5, "Foreign Intelligence." Most of the originals are in NA, RG 77, Decimal Files 371.2, box 64, exhibit A, "Goudsmit Mission" folder; RG 227, Bush-Conant Files; OSRD/S-1 Intelligence, folder 5 (= microfilm M-1392, roll 1); and elsewhere.

There may be some unresolved confusion over the dates here.

11. Goudsmit's report of 29 January 1945 to Frank Smith, War Dept., Military Intelligence G-2, Washington, in *Manhattan Project History,* vol. 14, supp. 1, app. A. He suggested confronting Fleischmann with a former ALSOS officer, the nuclear physicist James Fisk of Bell Laboratories, who had worked with him at Heidelberg. (Fisk had been questioning Italian atomic scientists with Boris Pash earlier in 1944 in Italy.)

12. His letter of 11 July 1993 asserts he never spoke of atomic bombs with anyone during the war and that he has no idea what a "reactor-bomb" could be.

Fleischmann was first held in an interrogation camp in Alexandria, Virginia, and then at the Fort Meade prisoner-of-war camp. The reports of Fleischmann's several interrogations between 9 March and 4 April 1945 are to be found in recently declassified ALSOS records in NA, RG 77, MED Foreign Intelligence Unit, entry 22, box 166, folder 32,22-1, "Germany—Research—TA"; and box 167, folder 32.12-2. (*Manhattan Project History,* vol. 14, supp. 1, app. B, lists Fleischmann's interrogation of 9 March 1945 under the reference "CIA NEG 32.12–2." It seems that this reference is unfamiliar to Central Intelligence Agency archivists, who have been unable to trace the item.)

fried Flügge, whose influential *Naturwissenschaften* article of June 1939 had raised the possibility of atomic explosives. There Flügge had cited two different kinds of explosion, one occurring in a ten-thousandth of a second, the other taking place in a slower and less powerful kind of reactor-bomb and taking a tenth of a second.[13] Now in his more sophisticated 1942 paper entitled "Can a Uranium Machine Be Worked with Fast Neutrons?" Flügge speculated that although it would be more convenient to have a reactor that would run on U238, which is fissionable by fast neutrons only, an efficient reactor using ordinary instead of heavy water as a moderator would have to employ uranium enriched in U235, which is fissionable by slow neutrons. Flügge then commented:

> Certainly the separation of the rare fissionable isotope [U235] has the great advantage of producing a considerable reduction in the size of the plant and this greatly extends the scope of application (*Automotor,* "*Uranbombe*").[14]

The "Uranbombe" is a variant of the slow-neutron reactor. It can be made small enough for practical use only because it employs slow neutrons. Any fast-neutron machine would have to be of far greater volume because the mean free paths of neutrons before hitting a nucleus are longer for fast neutrons than for slow ones. Flügge's concept of a "Uranbombe" obviously reflects the thinking about reactor-bombs prevalent in the German uranium project.[15]

This conception of the "Uranbombe" as a reactor-bomb was shared by the masters of the uranium project. Wilhelm Osenberg assumed a major overseeing role in the program when he became head of the Planning Office of the Reichsforschungsrat in 1943. In a summary of the status of atomic physics dated 8 May 1943, Osenberg observed of uranium fission:

1. The *uranium machine* is practicable as a motor if one succeeds in controlling the fission of atomic nuclei within certain limits for a certain time. This will be possible

13. S. Flügge, "Kann der Energieinhalt der Atomkerne technisch nutzbar gemacht werden?" *Die Naturwissenschaften* 27 (9 June 1939): 402–410. See above, chap. 4.

14. S. Flügge, "Kann man eine Uranmaschine mit schnellen Neutronen betreiben?" (G-142), September 1942, p. 149 (IMF 30-721): "Allerdings hat die Abtrennung des seltenen wirksamen Uranisotops den grossen Vorteil, dass eine erhebliche Verkleinerung der Anlage auftritt, die ihren Anwendungsbereich beträchtlich erweitert (Automotor, "Uran-bombe")." This paper is not discussed in M. Walker, *German National Socialism and the Quest for Nuclear Power, 1939–1949* (Cambridge, 1989), while D. Irving, *The German Atomic Bomb* (New York, 1967), p. 92, misleadingly says that Flügge's paper links the discussion of fast-neutron reactions to a pure-U235 bomb using fast neutrons. This is not so. Flügge is considering whether a bomb or reactor using the plentiful U238 fissioned by fast neutrons would work (he believes not). He suggests enriching the U235 as a means of making the volume of the reactor or bomb smaller since the fissionability of U235 by slow neutrons would lead to shorter mean free paths. Flügge does not explicitly (or implicitly) consider the case of a U235 device using fast neutrons. (Throughout the paper Flügge rigidly treats U235 as a slow-neutron case of fission, and U238 as a fast-neutron one.)

15. Despite attempts to interpret the "Uranbombe" here and elsewhere as merely a reactor or reactor engine, Flügge's discussion and language explicitly refer to an explosive bomb of some type. See also Osenberg's 1943 usage of "Uran-Maschine" and "Uran-Bombe" described below.

through the careful provision of a continual small number of neutrons of the right energy to the uranium nuclei. The neutrons released by the fission of the uranium nuclei must be dissipated very rapidly.

2. The *uranium bomb* is then possible if one succeeds in releasing suddenly on the uranium nuclei a certain number of neutrons of the right energy. The neutrons liberated in the fission of the nuclei should not be allowed any possibilities of escape for the time being, but must be so slowed down in their energy—which on account of the fission of the nucleus is quite great—that they can give rise to further nuclear fission. The process propagates itself in an avalanche-like fashion.

Purely computational investigations based on foreign data have shown that processes 1 and 2 are certainly technically possible. Experimental investigation requires the separation of U235 from uranium. So far this purification has not been possible. Foreign admixtures interrupt the desired process.[16]

Three points should be noted here. First, the text distinguishes explicitly between the "uranium machine" and the "uranium bomb," the latter of which is clearly explosive (the usage employed in Flügge's paper of September 1942). Second, both the "machine" and the "bomb" refer to "neutrons of the right energy," which suggests strongly that both are variations of a reactor. Third, the "bomb" requires a moderator to "slow down" the fast neutrons produced by fission to "the right energy."

Osenberg (a member of the SS since 1933) had been brought in as part of the

16. W. Osenberg, "Allgemein verständliche Grundlagen zur Kernphysik," 8 May 1943 (IMF 29-1062/1063): "Der Uran-Zerfall . . . Daneben ergeben sich 2 technische Anwendungsmöglichkeiten: 1. Die *Uran-Maschine* ist als Antriebsmotor brauchbar, wenn es gelingt, den Zerfall von Atomkernen zeitlich in mässigen Grenzen zu steuern. Das wird möglich sein durch vorsichtige Zuführung einer laufend geringen Anzahl von Neutronen richtiger Geschwindigkeit zu den Uran-Atomkernen. Die durch die Spaltung der Urankerne frei werdenden Neutronen müssen schnellstens abgeführt werden.

"2. Die *Uran-Bombe* ist dann möglich, wenn es gelingt, schlagartig eine gewisse Anzahl Neutronen richtiger Geschwindigkeit auf Uran-Kerne loszulassen. Die bei der Kernspaltung frei werdenden Neutronen dürfen zunächst keine Abführungsmöglichkeiten haben, sondern müssen in ihrer—durch den Kernzerfall zu grossen—Geschwindigkeit so abgebremst werden, dass sie weitere Kernspaltung auslösen können. Der Vorgang pflanzt sich dann lawinenartig fort.

"Rein rechnerische Nachprüfungen der ausländischen Unterlagen haben ergeben, dass die Vorgänge 1 und 2 technisch durchaus möglich sind. Zur experimentellen Nachprüfung ist es erforderlich, das Isotop 235 des Uran rein herzustellen. Bisher war diese Reindarstellung nicht möglich. Fremde Beimischungen stören den erwünschten Vorgang."

The text is partially translated in S. Goudsmit, *ALSOS* (New York, 1947), p. 178, without any mention of its authorship by Osenberg. Goudsmit states that the analysis was prepared for the Gestapo (SS/SD); this ties in with the fact that Osenberg was also a senior official in the Gestapo's Cultural Section, III c, in charge of science. Osenberg's files, which contained many reports on the political reliability of German scientists, were tracked down by Goudsmit (ibid., pp. 189 f., 200 f.), many now being dispersed in NA, RG 165, box 139; NA, RG 319, box 12; and PRO, FO 1031/241. The original of this particular report is probably now in the Goudsmit Papers, though I have not been able to find it.

See in general Leo J. Mahoney, "A History of the War Department Scientific Intelligence Mission (ALSOS), 1943–1945" (Ph.D. diss., Kent State University, 1981), pp. 307 f.

new regime that took over administrative control of the uranium project after the Harnack-Haus conference of June 1942. Goering was now nominally in charge, and under him was the uninspiring Abraham Esau (president of the Physikalisch-Technische Reichsanstalt), who was officially known as "Plenipotentiary of the Reich Marshal for Nuclear Physics." The chief administrator was Rudolf Mentzel of the Education Ministry and the Reichsforschungsrat, who reorganized the project, appointing Osenberg to a position of great bureaucratic power as head of the Planning Office of the RFR in June 1943. Though Osenberg was able to secure materials and army exemptions for a great many scientists, his planning mania intimidated the German scientists. (He maintained a card index of fifteen thousand scientists, with which he tried to impress the Allies as to his indispensability in 1945.)[17] These arrangements were scarcely congenial to Heisenberg, who as early as the summer of 1942 was trying to escape the intrusiveness of the RFR and angling for a return to the now seen as happier days of HWA military control.[18] By the end of 1943, however, things were rendered livable by Speer's ouster of Esau and the appointment of the well-known Munich physicist Walther Gerlach as "Plenipotentiary" thanks to Speer's interventions.[19]

While in office Gerlach had to deal with various proposals from inventors and the SS engineering staff about how an atomic bomb might be made. In 1944, indeed, Gerlach sought to establish a special liaison section in the Reich Patent Office to deal with nuclear-physics patents.[20] In handling such proposals, Gerlach naturally resorted to consultations with Heisenberg, and though written communications between the two were sparse, the influence of Heisenberg's advice may be seen at work in a couple of documented episodes.[21] The first of these arose out of a proposal made to Goering as head of the RFR in December 1943 by Werner Mialki, a Dresden engineer, to construct a bomb made from 4.2 tons of uranium oxide. In a report to Mentzel, Gerlach dismissed the proposal as "naive," and, rather curiously, took Mialki's remark that each fission would release two to three neutrons as evidence that he was a stranger to the field of nuclear physics. Gerlach seems mainly, however, to have been irritated by Mialki's accusations that the scientists were not properly cooperating with the Armaments Ministry and not de-

---

17. T. Bower, *The Paperclip Conspiracy* (Boston, 1987), pp. 114 f., 167. Goudsmit, *ALSOS*, pp. 188–201. For Osenberg's bureaucratic maneuvers, see K.-H. Ludwig, *Technik und Ingenieure im Dritten Reich* (Düsseldorf, 1974), pp. 234–271.

18. Walker, *German National Socialism*, p. 86.

19. K. Macrakis, *Surviving the Swastika: Scientific Research in Nazi Germany* (New York, 1993), pp. 174–177. Irving, *German Atomic Bomb*, pp. 198–200. Goudsmit, *ALSOS*, pp. 175 f..

20. See above, chap. 10, for references.

21. For these time-consuming impositions on Heisenberg, see Walker, *German National Socialism*, pp. 91 f.. Inquiries to the Heisenberg-Archiv in Munich and the Gerlach-Nachlass (Deutsches Museum, Munich) have turned up nothing of interest. The respective archivists, Dr. H. Rechenberg and Dr. H. Bachmann, believe that the frequent personal contact between Heisenberg and Gerlach in Berlin obviated the need for written exchanges.

voting themselves as they should to weapons research. To this Gerlach retorted that it was false to say that Heisenberg was not in touch with the ministry officials; in fact, Heisenberg was continually in touch with a Dr. Sommer there. The naming of Heisenberg in this context suggests that Gerlach would have consulted Heisenberg for his opinion on the Mialki proposal, which one may imagine was as peremptory as Gerlach's own dismissal of it.[22]

The second case occurred in November 1944 when an officer of the SS Gas War Office approached the RFR's administrative chief, Mentzel (who was also a brigadier general in the SS and a protégé of Himmler's), with suggestions from an SS Engineer Matzka as to how to expedite the production of a bomb.[23] Matzka seems to have had prior contacts with nuclear physicists in Vienna and so had a general idea of the problem. But Gerlach poured cold water on the idea, informing Mentzel as follows on 18 November 1944:

> As to Mr. Matzka's proposals for an invention I would answer the following: The ideas developed correspond closely on many points with our uranium project. Correct and incorrect ideas are included there.
>
> Unfortunately the fundamental *technical* idea is not right. According to all available experimental and theoretical investigations—which are in full agreement on this precise point—it is not possible to obtain the violent multiplication of nuclear fission with small amounts of material. I can assure you that we have attacked this precise problem repeatedly and from more than one direction. Not even fundamental laboratory measurements on this effect can be done with small amounts; one needs rather at the minimum quantities of material of 2 tons or more, which is one of the reasons for the difficulty of the pursuit of the uranium problem. In this respect, Mr. Matzka's ideas fail to approach hitting the nub of the matter with much sureness.
>
> I should advise you that soon a report on one of the latest uranium-burner experiments will be available, in which again the necessity of an enormously large quantity of material is shown.[24]

22. Gerlach to Mentzel, 30 May 1944, and Mentzel to Goernnert, 13 June 1944, NA, RG 319, ALSOS/RFR Files, box 16, RFR 103H. The file also contains Mialki's proposal.

23. For Mentzel, see Ludwig, *Technik,* pp. 231, 236, and the works by Zierold and Glum cited above in chaps. 11 and 12.

24. The letter is reproduced and partly translated in Goudsmit, *ALSOS,* pp. 179–181: "Zu den Erfindungsvorschlägen von Herrn Matzka erlaube ich mir folgendes zu antworten: Die entwickelten Ideen berühren in vielen Punkten sehr eng unser U-Vorhaben. Es sind richtige und unrichtige Vorstellungen darin enthalten.

"Leider ist der *technische* Grundgedanke nicht richtig. Nach allen bisher vorliegenden Untersuchungen experimenteller und theoretischer Art, die gerade in diesem Punkte in völliger Übereinstimmung sind, ist es nicht möglich, die stürmische Vermehrung der Kernspaltung mit kleinen Substanzmengen zu erhalten. Ich kann Ihnen versichern, dass wir gerade dieses Problem aus mehr als einem Grunde immer wieder angegangen sind. Nicht einmal grundsätzliche Laboratoriumsmessungen über den Effekt sind mit kleinen Mengen durchführbar, vielmehr benutzt man mindestens Sub-

Gerlach's reply echoes an earlier opinion of Heisenberg's of 1942 on the practicality of achieving a chain reaction with a mixture of uranium and moderator. After observing that in "smaller amounts" the neutron escape from the surface remains large compared to internal neutron multiplication, Heisenberg noted that "experiments with very small amounts of substance are for this reason not useful for determining the suitability of mixtures for the chain reaction."[25]

The basic notion that a reactor-bomb would require many tons of uranium percolated through various levels of the scientific-industrial establishment, as is suggested by the interrogation of an anti-Nazi German engineer, Ernest Nagelstein, in late 1944. Nagelstein had lived in Switzerland from 1936 to 1942, and on returning to Germany had from 1942 to 1944 lodged in Berlin with a Frau Friedman, secretary to U. W. Doering, who had a private laboratory in Berlin-Charlottenburg. Doering, an inventor of missiles and a long-distance torpedo, "had knowledge of TA [atomic bomb] work in Germany," and had learned from a member of Hahn's institute that Hahn [*sic*] was working on a bomb, made either of thorium

---

stanzmengen von 2 und mehr Tonnen, einer der Grunde für die Erschwerung der Bearbeitung des U-Problems. Hiermit fallen auch die Vorstellungen des Herrn Matzka über Erreichung grösserer Kerntreffsicherheit.

"Ich darf Sie darauf hinweisen, dass in Kürze ein Bericht über die letzten U-Brenner-Versuche vorliegen wird, in welchen sich wieder die Erforderlichkeit enorm grosser Materialmengen ergibt."

I have not be able to trace the original file, but a letter dated 4 November 1944 from SS Sturmbannführer Waldemar Neitzel to Mentzel, minuted to Gerlach, referring to a discussion about Matzka's proposals appears in one of the captured Reichsforschungsrat files in the Library of Congress, LC MS 18,806.2, container 230, reel 134: ALSOS RFR 104 (microfilm PB 20489). The originals are likely to be either in the Goudsmit Papers or the more than seven hundred ALSOS RFR files formerly in the Library of Congress, where microfilm copies are still held. However, a BIOS index of ALSOS documents taken from the Osenberg RFR files (PRO, FO 1031/241; FO 935/55) gives only the ALSOS RFR 104 reference for this particular subject. (ALSOS RFR 229 is also listed as containing nuclear reports, but this appears to be missing from the *Correlation Index: Document Series and PB Reports*, ed. G. Runge [New York, 1953].)

According to his file obtained from the Berlin Document Center, Neitzel (born 1902) was a longtime Nazi and SS member, specializing in gas warfare. He had purged Jews from the Auergesellschaft in 1935 and became head of the SS's Department of Gas Protection (so one might conjecture that he was somehow connected with the arrangements for the Final Solution). In 1944–45 Neitzel was attached to the SS as a staff officer, concerned with gas, chemical, and rocket subjects, which explains his interest in the uranium project.

It may be noted that M. Walker, "Heisenberg, Goudsmit, and the German Atomic Bomb," *Physics Today*, January 1990, p. 58, alleges that Goudsmit misread this letter, but if there is any misreading it seems to be Walker's.

25. Heisenberg, "Die theoretischen Grundlagen für die Energiegewinnung aus der Uranspaltung" (no G number), 26 February 1942, p. 4 (IMF 29-1005; GWH, A II, 520): "Versuche mit sehr kleinen Substanzmengen sind daher von vornherein unzureichend für die Entscheidung über die Eignung von Mischungen zur Kettenreaktionen."

The passage follows immediately upon a section on the possibility of producing plutonium as an explosive. (See above, chap. 12.) Even if it does not refer to a reactor-bomb as such, but merely to a reactor, the underlying theory is common to both.

or uranium with 2% cadmium to "slow" the reaction: "It has been concluded that the minimum weight for a single bomb is 8 tons."[26] (Gerlach himself at this time was concerned with setting up an arrangement at the Reichspatentamt for the registration of atomic patents.)[27]

Since Gerlach was a talkative friend of Paul Rosbaud's, the Allies were kept abreast of developments and were well aware of how backward German work on atomic bombs and reactors was compared with that in the United States and Britain. Rosbaud's and other British information was pooled with American ALSOS intelligence to produce a report in November 1944 that concluded that there was no likelihood of the German uranium project producing a bomb, since even their experimental reactor had not yet been brought to criticality.[28]

Heisenberg made a last unsuccessful effort in March 1945 to achieve criticality with a pile (B-VIII) at Haigerloch, where the project had relocated. During a visit by the Plenipotentiary (recalls Heisenberg's assistant Karl Wirtz), Gerlach remarked that if the reactor went critical it would yield a suitable bomb with great destructive power. Gerlach obviously had in mind a reactor-bomb, though Wirtz now claims that the remark puzzled him and that he could not make Gerlach understand the difference between a bomb and a reactor. However, Wirtz has had other memory lapses, and as Heisenberg's close colleague he would have been

26. Report of 2 November 1944, in G-343B. (The original interrogation report is in NA, RG 77, MED Foreign Intelligence Unit, entry 22, box 169, folder 32.7002-1.) Anxious as ever to discredit Goudsmit (this time, Goudsmit's allegation that the Germans were thinking of exploding reactors), Walker, *German National Socialism*, p. 155, conjectures that the report had obviously "confused" the reactor with a weapon or reactor-bomb.

27. On patents, see above, chap. 10.

28. F. H. Hinsley, *British Intelligence in the Second World War* (Cambridge, 1979–90), vol. 2, pt. 2, pp. 589–591, and app. 29, pp. 931–944. Goudsmit, *ALSOS*, pp. 68–71. Previously, on 31 July 1944, however, a document titled "Appraisal of Enemy Bomb Production" had been rather more concerned about German nuclear activity (NA, RG 77, MED Foreign Intelligence Unit, entry 22, box 168, folder 202.3-1). (The earlier British report analyzed in an American evaluation by Furman and Groves of December 1943 had been dismissive of the German bomb project; see above, chap. 10, note 48. The evaluation is in NA, RG 77, MED Foreign Intelligence Unit, entry 22, box 170, folder 32.60-1.)

Three main summaries of Goudsmit's conclusions based on evidence captured at Strasbourg are now available in NA, RG 77, MED Foreign Intelligence Unit, entry 22:

1. Box 164, folder "Germany"—"Strassburg Intelligence on German Nuclear Physics and TA", 17 December 1944 (a systematic analysis).
2. Box 164, "TA Strassburg," 16 December 1944 (a compilation of source evidence and analysis). "The enclosed report was put together in very great haste so that Lt. Col. Pash could carry it with him (to Washington)."
3. Box 170, folder 32.60—A, "The Strassburg Summary," 12 February 1945 (a bound volume of more than two hundred pages, probably to be identified with the long sought-after "Strasbourg Report"). chap. 5, sec. 1, head "Technical: Devices: Bomb," is rather skeptical about German progress on the bomb, and relies on Nagelstein's and Fleischmann's testimonies as evidence of German backwardness in thinking about reactor-bombs.

perfectly aware at the time of the idea of an unstable explosive reactor-bomb, just as Gerlach was.[29]

Now complicating the furtherance of atomic research for Gerlach was the rivalry that had developed between Himmler and Speer as patrons of the field. The approach to Osenberg and Gerlach from SS Engineer Matzka had originated in a sudden interest in an atomic bomb taken by the Security Service Department (SD; Sicherheitsdienst) of Himmler's SS in mid-1944. Himmler himself had on 22 June 1944 declared that "with the progress of technology, explosives are suddenly emerging whose speed and effect overshadow the newest explosives of our retaliatory weapons."[30] An SD letter of 26 July 1944 alleged that attempts in the field of nuclear energy by the RFR had failed to yield the required results. The SD now proposed to establish a plan to remove all obstacles to obtaining maximum productive war results from available workers and their research institutes.[31] The result was the creation in August of a War Research Pool run by Osenberg, and nominally headed, like the RFR itself, by Goering.[32] Himmler's own position as an armaments warlord had been strengthened in the aftermath of the July bomb plot. The SS had for some time been trying to develop its own Weapons Office, known from 1944 as the Technical Office of the SS, and in August Himmler became chief of Army Armaments, a position that brought him into rivalry with Speer's Armaments Ministry.[33] Himmler also decided to use his own seat on the board of the RFR to try to wrest control of nuclear physics from Speer, whom he rebuked for neglecting the subject.[34] Speer replied on 23 September 1944 that the research base for atomic physics was too small and could not be increased since it was of no direct use for the war effort.[35]

29. K. Wirtz, *Im Umkreis der Physik* (Karlsruhe, 1987), pp. 61 f.. It will be remembered that Wirtz referred at Farm Hall to a 1941 bomb patent (see chap. 10) and also told Charles Frank of Heisenberg's 1940 back-of-an-envelope calculation of the critical mass of a pure U235 bomb (see chap. 7, and below, chap. 14).

Gerlach was not very informative about the atomic project during his questioning of 13 May and 9 June 1945 (IMF 31-1245/1247).

For photographs of the Haigerloch installation and relevant interrogations and documents, see now NA, RG 77, MED Foreign Intelligence Unit, entry 22, box 166.

30. Report by Supreme SS/Police Commander of South West to Gauleiters of Stuttgart and Strasbourg regarding a meeting with Himmler in Alsace on 22 June 1944 (BA, NS 19/new 371), quoted in A. Speer, *Infiltration* (New York, 1981), pp. 150–152.

31. *Manhattan Project History*, NA mflm. A-1218, roll 5, 4.32.

32. For the setting up of the Wehrforschungs-Gemeinschaft of the RFR, see Goering's letter to Mentzel of 24 August 1944 (IMF 29-1141; also 31-1062/1085). S. Goudsmit and W. F. Colby, "Reports on German Research Organization (RFR) and Reorganization of German War Research," 12 and 23 April 1945, in *Manhattan Project History*, vol. 14., apps. B-29 and B-30. See also Mahoney, "A History," p. 308.

33. See Ludwig, *Technik*, pp. 257, 479.

34. Himmler was appointed to the RFR council in October 1944; see K. Zierold, *Forschungsförderung in drei Epochen: Deutsche Forschungsgemeinschaft* (Wiesbaden, 1968), p. 242.

35. BA, R 3/1583, quoted in Speer, *Infiltration*, pp. 150 f.

The rather credulous head of the SS and his subordinates were not averse to wasting Osenberg's time with technical proposals, and indeed many suggestions originating from the SS, like Matzka's, required at least the pretense of serious investigation before being rejected.[36] Consequently, undue attention was paid to the Matzka proposal, and its rejection helped reinforce the SS's growing sense of failure on the part of the Speer project. In January 1945 the head of the SD, Ohlendorf, accused Speer of neglecting the "Jewish science" of atomic physics and urged the immediate completion of a new research plant, it seems, for heavy water (Construction Project "SH220").[37] Replying to Ohlendorf on 29 January 1945, Speer refused to authorize this despite his own interest in physics: "You know that I was personally interested in nuclear research and that I have granted it all possible support. For this reason, may I ask you to have Professor Gerlach of the nuclear physics section of the RFR apply to me again in about three months."[38] This was simply a runaround, since Gerlach was also Speer's own deputy for nuclear physics. Speer had already squared Gerlach on 19 December by telling him that he could always be assured of small resources for his work: "I place extraordinary value on research in the field of nuclear physics."[39] Speer, of course, had already decided in June 1942 on the basis of Heisenberg's briefing that a uranium or plutonium bomb was something that belonged to the far distant future, and so found no reason now to acquiesce in Himmler's hope that it might be an imminent prospect.[40] (The SS's interest in nuclear physics persisted to the very end of the war; on 2 April 1945 SS General Schwab wrote to Paul Harteck at Hamburg, asking him to take into his institute an SS officer who had been ordered to accelerate research into the production of heavy water.)[41]

. . .

Since the SS, HWA, and RFR records are all incomplete, many intriguing gaps remain in our knowledge of exactly how these various agencies interacted in the matter of atomic research. But recently one hidden key figure has emerged into the light—namely, SS Hauptsturmführer Helmut Joachim Fischer, who from 1938 specialized in scientific policy and from 1943 to 1945 was in charge of scientific affairs in the Reich Main Security Office (RSHA) of the SS, liaising with both the HWA and the RFR. Fischer's posthumous memoirs have left a picture of German work on the atomic bomb that is also tantalizingly incomplete since it is clear that,

36. Speer, *Infiltration*, pp. 146 f.

37. SH200 ("SH220" may be a slip) was the code word for heavy water. Cf. P. Harteck, "Bericht über den Stand der SH200 Gewinnung" (G-262), 15 April 1944 (IMF 29-762).

38. BA, R 3/1593, quoted in Speer, *Infiltration*, p. 151. Cf. Ludwig, *Technik*, pp. 242 f.

39. BA, R 3/1579, folder 1 (cf. Speer, *Infiltration*, pp. 151 f.).

40. See above, chap. 12.

41. Goudsmit to R. R. Furman, 21 May 1945 (IMF 31-1164). The SS officer was H. Clasen, and the letter originated from the Technical Bureau VIII FEP (Research Development—Patents?), SS Führungshauptamt. Cf. Goudsmit, *ALSOS*, p. 201.

though he knew all the principals and understood the technical aspects, he decided not to divulge all that he knew in his book.[42]

After taking a mathematics doctorate at Heidelberg, Fischer had joined the SS's Security Service Department (SD), becoming head of the scientific section, in which capacity he had much to do with Osenberg, Schumann, and Mentzel. Fischer was well aware of the German bomb project, recalling that Schumann had impressed Hitler with its significance in a personal interview. Fischer himself visited Heisenberg at the Kaiser-Wilhelm-Institute for Physics, which he was shown around, promising his host "expressly our help if he should, as the main representative of theoretical physics, ever have any difficulties with party sources." After moving to assume operational control of scientific and technological questions at the SS's Reich Main Security Office (RSHA III C I) in March 1944, Fischer's first task was to prepare a report on Bohr's Copenhagen institute, which Heisenberg had just visited on behalf of the RFR, recommending that German scientists exploit its cyclotron. Fischer continued his own contacts with leading German scientists and scientific administrators, visiting Hahn's laboratory and cooperating with Gerlach, the new scientific chief of atomic research.

Even though written forty years later with the contamination of hindsight, Fischer's remarks on the status of the atomic bomb problem as he found it in the summer of 1944 are revealing. Progress on the enrichment of $U235$ had been discouraging, Esau having shown him a lump of only minimally enriched uranium. Ardenne by the end of 1944 came to have much more success, but Fischer's account suggests that German thinking was still mired in the idea of an enriched-$U235$ reactor-bomb. Esau, he says, was aiming at a "Uranmaschine."

> Once this had produced a chain reaction, the second step would be attempted of raising its energy output to the theoretically possible highest value. This could happen either in a gradual increase of energy production as a sort of uranium burner, or in the shortest space of time, so becoming the uranium bomb.[43]

This description, of course, approximates to Heisenberg's notion of an explosively unstable reactor using enriched $U235$.

Even though he understood that Schumann and the other officials were not treating the bomb project as a priority for fear of provoking political pressure on themselves to produce something tangible, Fischer himself used the scientific intelligence duties of his new position to impress the merits of the atomic project on his superiors, to whom he reported that so far the United States did not appear to

---

42. H. J. Fischer, *Erinnerungen*, 2 vols., Quellenstudien der Zeitgeschichtlichen Forschungsstelle Ingolstadt, vols. 3 and 6 (Ingolstadt, 1984–85). His later book *Hitler und die Atombombe* (Ingolstadt, 1987) is of less value, being based largely on printed sources. Fischer's racial article, "Völkische Bedingtheit von Mathematik und Physik," appeared in *Zeits fur die gesamte Nahrwissenschaft* 3 (1937–38): 422–426.

The following information is taken from Fischer, *Erinnerungen*, 1:125–138, 148 f., 183; 2:1–5, 7 f., 22 f., 31 f., 37 f., 46–52, 56 f., 86 f., 98 f., 101 f., 107, 131, 140–145, 147 f., 172 f., 249, 254, 270.

43. Ibid., 2:50.

have progressed with a bomb. These activities may well have been responsible for triggering the sudden interest in the possibility of a bomb on the part of Himmler in mid-1944, as well as Speer's renewed interest in atomic research that same year. Fischer's overall head at RSHA III C was actually that same Ohlendorf who as we have already seen was involved with both Himmler and Speer concerning atomic matters in 1944–45. Through Ohlendorf, Fischer was able to obtain from Speer experimental materials for Harteck, and he himself entered into discussions with the munitions minister on scientific affairs that secured permission for Osenberg to concentrate scientific manpower. Soon Fischer came to play a more powerful role in scientific policy, drafting letters from Himmler to Speer and entertaining Gerlach and Osenberg in his official guest house, while ensuring that Schumann and Mentzel were gradually excluded from the highest circles. Once Himmler had taken over his own army command, Fischer found himself very much involved with the HWA too.

Fischer's enhanced position in late 1944 enabled him to draw up a proposal for a Scientific-Technical Council that would advise Hitler himself, coordinate military and civil science, and work closely with the Speer ministry. Its members were to include Education Ministry and RFR officials such as Rust, Mentzel, and Schumann, as well as Ardenne's patron Ohnesorge, SS officers, and Speer. The RSHA III C head, Ernst Kaltenbrunner, personally took this SS plan to Hitler, who was delighted, and it seemed that an "unheard-of success for us" was imminent by the end of November. The plan, however, fell through in the aftermath of the failure of the Ardennes offensive.

Amid the German gloom of the spring of 1945 Fischer received an excited telephone call from Gerlach to tell him that Heisenberg's uranium reactor was working. Fischer implies that this news was welcome to the SS because it gave them a bargaining asset to offer to the Western Allies in the course of the clandestine peace negotiations then under way through Schellenberg. This would also make sense of much of the SS's interest in atomic research during 1944, since Himmler's own peace feelers had begun then. It may always have been the SS's intention to use the bomb or other nuclear data as the bait for a separate peace offer.

Fischer himself was lightly punished with probation by a denazification tribunal after the war, thanks to "Persil-certificates" (whitewashes, referring to a European laundry detergent) provided by Gerlach and others who depicted him as an idealist who had protected German science from the likes of Schumann and Mentzel. (Schumann was at the same time portraying himself as the leader of a "scientific resistance group.") This benign picture does not square with some unpleasantly antisemitic remarks in the Fischer memoirs, which depict the physical condition of concentration-camp prisoners at Oranienburg and Dachau as equal or even superior to that of the citizens of Berlin. A typically benevolent Nazi, Fischer diligently explained to his American interrogators that his SS department was not what they thought it was, having little to do with anti-Jewish excesses.

There can be no doubt that Fischer, because of his official position, his under-

THE REPORT OF ACTIVITIES OF 1944

standing of physics, his contacts with Heisenberg, Gerlach, Schumann, and other scientists, and his liaising between Himmler and Speer, is a crucial figure for the understanding of the way in which the German atomic project developed in 1944–45.

. . .

Fischer's activity in the context of renewed interest by both Himmler and Speer in an atomic bomb in the latter part of 1944 may help us to understand a curious and so far unnoticed document of October 1944 that purported to implement an order from Hitler's headquarters authorizing the immediate development of an atomic bomb.[44] The source of this *Rechenschaftsbericht* (*Report of Activities*) is unknown, but from internal evidence there are strong indications that it originated in the German Post Office's atomic research project, headed by Manfred von Ardenne from 1940 to 1945, for which Houtermans had prepared his report on plutonium in 1941.[45] At p. 2 the author refers to a technical report on heavy water available "in our department [*Abteilung*]";[46] and at p. 26, the author adduces "the view of our Research Institution [*Forschungsanstalt*]."[47] Obviously the report emanated from the *Abteilung* of a *Forschungsanstalt*. As it happens, this is precisely the nomenclature used by Ardenne's Reichspost atomic research project in Berlin in late 1944: *Forschungsanstalt der Deutschen Reichspost, Abteilung für Kernphysik* (Research Institution of the German Post Office, Section for Nuclear Physics).[48] There are also references in the text to the work of Gustav Hertz, a major scientist outside the official Reichsforchungsrat uranium project, but one with whom Ardenne is known to have collaborated in 1944–45 (as well as in Russia after the war).[49] The document's emphasis (pp. 16, 18 f.) on the efficacy of the mass spectrograph as a means of isotope separation reinforces its connection with Ardenne, who was deeply committed to the construction of such a device in 1944.[50] For the time being, then,

44. The document's possibly later cover describes it as "Tagung der deutschen Wissenschaftler, Oktober 1944," but I have chosen here to use the title *Rechenschaftsbericht*, as it calls itself at p. 31. It is now in the Wiesenthal Archive in the Yad Vashem Archives, Jerusalem, shelf mark M-0/339. Mr. Wiesenthal obtained the report about 1951, and sent it to Yad Vashem in 1954. Dr. Mara Beller of the Hebrew University of Jerusalem kindly brought this item to my attention. I am grateful to Professor Issachar Unna of the Hebrew University's physics department for useful discussion of the paper.

45. See above, chap. 9, for Houtermans.

46. "Der genaue chemisch-physikalische Herstellungsbericht nebst Konstruktionsplaenen der hiezu [*sic*] nötigen Agr. liegt unter Az. 12/345 1940 in unserer Abteilung auf" (*Rechenschaftsbericht*, p. 2). I have not been able to locate the report alluded to here (*Herstellungsbericht*).

47. "Hierin liegt nach Ansicht unserer Forschungsanstalt der Grund hierfür" (ibid., p. 26).

48. From the title of the collection of the Post Office's research reports published in November 1944 (G-318; IMF 30-646). The papers included a reissue (G-94) of Houtermans's G-267, as well as several reports by S. Flügge (G-141, G-142, G-254, G-255).

49. *Rechenschaftsbericht*, pp. 16, 33. Cf. M. von Ardenne, *Ein glückliches Leben* (Zurich, 1972), pp. 180, 185, 193. For Ardenne, see above, chap. 9.

50. See the paper "Mass Spectography Construction Planned by the German Post Office Department Research Institution" (G-256). Other projects include G-196 (Kiel, 1942) and R. Herzog, "Report

the *Rechenschaftsbericht* may be accepted as authentic, and probably as having some connection to Ardenne's Post Office atomic project.[51]

The meeting for which the *Rechenschaftsbericht* was prepared was, according to its cover, held in October 1944, and it is tempting to see this event as having been called hurriedly to consider the whole project as the result of the order from Hitler to expedite the construction of an atomic bomb that is cited in the text itself. This occurs in the context of a rapid analysis of the possibility of building a plutonium bomb, which seems to be offered reluctantly and in great haste, and with an air of desperate self-justification:

> Since, according to Ord. FHQU 219/44 of 30 September 1944, the construction of the uranium bomb must be forced ahead, we forgo experimenting with small models of the order of a few milligrams, and instead will rely for the building and construction of the uranium bomb essentially on the research findings and theoretical speculations, which nevertheless, as we are now today aware, were correct. . . . The fundamental path is through physical facts that are known to all specialists, though we lack certain details to which we have devoted ourselves in years of research with

---

on Status of Construction of a Large New Mass Spectrograph," (G-375), 1943. Cf. Irving, *German Atomic Bomb,* pp. 235, 298, for the demonstration of an instrument to Gerlach.

I asked Professor Ardenne for his comments on the document, but did not receive them.

51. Arnold Kramish and David Cassidy have suggested to me that the document is in fact of postwar origin, possibly intended to recommend the work of captured German scientists to the Russians. But I do not find their particular arguments convincing for the following reasons:

1. The conjecture of an element no. 98 named "Paulinum" (p. 33)—now known as Californium, and discovered only years after the war—is not necessarily based on postwar American discussions of Paulinum, which were not in any case in the public domain as far as I have been able to discover. The German guess at the existence of an element 98 was reasonable, and the name may well have derived from the German atomic scientist Wolfgang Paul (1913–93; worked at Göttingen 1942–44; Nobel laureate in 1989), rather than from the Jewish Wolfgang Pauli. Element 98 was, in fact, hypothesized as "Eka-Hg" in 1941 in J. Schintlmeister, "Die Stellung des Elementes mit Alphastrahlen von 1.8 cm Reichweite im periodischen System. III. Bericht," 21 May 1941 (G-111; IMF 31-032). (The present reference occurs in the middle of a bizarre passage discussing possible radiation defense weapons, which has an air of desperate invention.)

2. The use of the nomenclature Neptunium and Plutonium for elements 93 and 94 (pp. 10 f., 24) does not necessarily indicate awareness of the Manhattan Project; the planetary-sequence analogy would have been fairly obvious to the Germans at any point.

3. The references to the partly Jewish Gustav Hertz (pp. 16, 33) and Einstein (p.2) are not inconceivable in a document of the Nazi period. The SS was quite willing to allow the positive naming of Jewish—and, more so, half-Jewish—scientists, especially when their work was deemed useful for the success of the German war effort. Indeed, in a speech to RFR and KWG leaders concerned with the uranium project on 6 July 1942, Goering stated that "the Führer rejects a regimentation of science as such. . . . A man who happens to be married to a Jew or because he is half-Jewish . . . this [banning] must be avoided. . . . I have just discussed this with the Führer. . . . The Führer has made exceptions for artists in cases like this. He will make exceptions even more gladly if it is a question of an important research project or researcher" (quoted in Macrakis, *Surviving the Swastika,* p. 92).

great sacrifices. It is these details that in this *Rechenschaftsbericht* we have compiled and are still compiling. All these experiments have cost an enormous amount of effort of every kind, both financially and personally, and we must therefore state that we have prepared this compact *Rechenschaftsbericht* at the command of the FHQU only reluctantly to forward it to a political office, since there is a danger of the total or partial loss of our progress if the content of this report reaches the knowledge of a third person, possibly our enemy.[52]

The Hitler-order reference "Ord. FHQU 219/44 of 30 September 1944" signifies an order (*Befehl*) from Hitler's headquarters (*Führer-Haupt-Quartier*). No single consolidated or complete calendar of Hitler's orders exists, but from partially reconstructed lists we can ascertain that the order took the form of a *Rundschreiben* or circulated order, numbered 219 of the year 1944, sent out by Martin Bormann, Hitler's chief of staff, on 30 September 1944. Although *Rundschreiben* with numbers on either side of 219 have been found, number 219 itself has not yet been traced.[53] It may be presumed that the issuing of *Rundschreiben* 219 was connected somehow with the lively interest in atomic research being taken by Himmler and the SS in the late summer of 1944.

There are clues in the document that its author took advantage of the coincidence that it was also in September that Heisenberg had reported on his group's

52. *Rechenschaftsbericht*, pp. 30 f.: "Da lt. Bef. FHQU 219/44 v. 30 Sept. 1944 der Bau der Uranbombe forciert werden musste, verzichteten wir auf die Arbeiten mit kleinen Modellen in der Grössenordnung von wenigen Milligramm, sonder stützen uns bei dem Bau und der Konstruktion der Uranbombe im Wesentlichen auf die vorhandenen Forschungsergebnisse und theoretische Spekulationen, die sich aber, wie wir heute schon den Beweis haben, richtig waren. . . . Der grundsätzliche Weg ist durch die physikalischen Tatsachen zu machen, die allen Fachleuten bekannt, gegeben, jedoch fehlen diesen die Einzelheiten, die wir in jahrelanger Forschungsarbeit mit grössten Opfern uns angeeignet haben. Es sind dies diese Details, die wir in diesem Rechenschaftsbericht angeführt haben und noch anführen werden. Es kostete alle diese Versuche eine Riesensumme an Einsatz jeglicher Art, sowie finanziell als auch persönlich und machen wir deshalb darauf aufmerksam, dass wir diesen geschlossenen Rechenschaftsbericht, den wir über Befehl FHQU anzufertigen haben nur ungern an eine politische Stelle weiterleiten, da die Gefahr des Totalen, oder teilweisen Verlustes unseres Vorsprunges besteht, wenn der Inhalt dieses Berichtes zur Kenntnis einer dritten Person, womöglich gar unserer Gegner, gelangt." ("30" may be a misprint for "3" September. See next note.)

53. That *Rundschreiben* 219 existed is proven by a reference in a letter of 29 September 1944 from Diebner to Harteck, which refers to the "Rundschreiben des Reichsleiters Bormann an allen Gauleitern vom 3.9.44," in Harteck's papers (G-341, vol. 1). For references to *Rundschreiben* numbered 216 (4 September 1944?) and 302 (6 October 1944), see the Institut für Zeitgeschichte's publication *Akten der Partei-Kanzlei der NSDAP: Rekonstruktion* . . . (Munich, 1983), "Regesten," 2:1051; 3: *199. *Rundschreiben* 217 (from Martin Bormann, Reichsleiter der NS Partei-Kanzlei, under the heading "Führer-Haupt-Quartier," 3–7 September 1944, regarding the War Research Pool and especially concerning Osenberg) is reproduced in IMF 31-1074/1076 in both its typed and telegraphed formats, and is referred to in Gerlach's letter of 16 December 1944 to Bormann in IMF 29-1156 (original in NA, RG 77, MED Foreign Intelligence Unit, entry 22, box 166, folder 32.22-1). These and related materials including *Rundschreiben* 294 and 338 of 1 October 1944 are also to be found in NA, microfilm T-580, roll 872. Inquiries to the Bundesarchiv Koblenz, the Munich Institut für Zeitgeschichte, the Berlin Document Center, and other sources have so far proved fruitless in tracing no. 219.

experiments with their new reactor design known as B-VI. The *Rechenschaftsbericht* states at p. 28 that "in January 1944 the new significantly improved uranium battery was assembled," apparently referring to the beginning of the series of B-VI experiments at the Kaiser-Wilhelm-Institute for Physics that ran from January to the late summer of 1944.[54] In September, Heisenberg compiled an evaluation (G-220) of the various B-VI experiments conducted between January and August 1944.[55] Heisenberg himself later described this report as having discussed "research reports of September 1944 by Bopp, Borrmann, Bothe, Fischer, Fünfer, Jensen, Heisenberg, Ritter, Wirtz."[56] It seems feasible that these reports together with Heisenberg's G-220 formed the basis for discussion at the "Meeting of German Scientists" in October that had resulted from the sudden issue of the Hitler-Bormann *Rundschreiben* 219 a few weeks before. And the *Rechenschaftsbericht* itself may well be a hasty effort undertaken by Ardenne at summing up the implications of all this research for bomb making. Certainly the document bears many marks of incompletion; it lacks many equations and data for which spaces have been left, as well as a bibliography to which references are made, and—lastly—diagrams for the construction of an atomic bomb. The omission of the quantities of uranium, heavy paraffin, and graphite required for a 100,000-kW reactor, for example, suggests that the author had neither the time—nor the knowledge—to calculate them.[57]

The *Rechenschaftsbericht*'s whole thrust is toward the construction of a bomb, rather than being a general discussion of reactors and bombs on the lines of the HWA Report of 1942.

> But these epochal discoveries, faced with the demand to forge most urgently weapons that would give our people a notable superiority in all war operations, were yet only of trivial importance, since they could be exploited only in the long run and not immediately. The problem was this: How does one get from the uranium battery to the uranium bomb? [*Es trat die Frage auf: Wie kommt man von der Uranbatterie zur Uranbombe?*] (pp. 23 f.)

54. "Im Jänner 1944 die neue, bedeutend verbesserte Uranbatterie Aufstellung fand," p. 28. See Irving, *German Atomic Bomb*, pp. 233 f., and p. 265 for the demonstration in January 1944 by F. Bopp and E. Fischer ("Einfluss des Rueckstreumantels auf die Neutronenausbeute des U-Brenners" [Effect of the reflector on the neutron yield of the uranium pile] [G-249], 10 January 1944 [IMF 30-418]) that a graphite reflector (not moderator) yielded with heavy water a higher neutron multiplication. Heisenberg insisted on using the less effective uranium plates rather than cubes; had he been less arrogant in rejecting Diebner's cube approach, he might well have achieved criticality by the end of the war.

55. W. Heisenberg, "Theoretische Auswertung der Dahlemer Grossversuche" (G-220), n.d. [September 1944], in GWH, A II, 588.

56. Heisenberg's B-VII report of 3 January 1945 (GWH, A II, 595).

57. See, for instance, pp. 27–30, for blank dotted spaces left for equations and data. At pp. 31–32, the critical masses of uranium and plutonium are not inserted into the spaces left for them. A drawing of the bomb cited at pp. 32 and 35 is not included. "Tabelle" referred to at pp. 27 f. and 36 are missing. "Cited investigations" (p. 27) are lacking, as are the equations for the production of a kilogram of plutonium (p. 27).

Reactors are not described in detail as forms of engine, but rather as the means for obtaining the plutonium needed for a bomb (pp. 10 ff., 22). Moreover, although two types of "Uranbombe" are identified ("UB I" using U235, and "UB II" using plutonium), the author's clear preference is for the plutonium bomb, which is described in detail. ("Plutonium plays an extraordinarily important role in the production of the uranium bomb" [p. 10].) In contrast, the passages dealing with the U235 bomb are very cursory and ambiguous. It is not completely clear, for instance, whether the author has in mind a pure-U235 bomb or a reactor-bomb using enriched U235—or both. Thus, at p. 15, "actino-uranium" (i.e., U235) is proposed as an alternative to using a moderator! And, speaking of how to move from the "Uranbatterie" to the "Uranbombe," the author suggests that a reactor-bomb is blocked for the Heisenbergian reason that the chain reaction will self-stabilize as neutron production and consumption balance (p. 26).

The section headed "The Fission Avalanche and Its Retardation" also shows the impress of Heisenberg's thinking about an explosive reactor, though the author goes beyond Heisenberg in appearing to suggest the use of delayed neutrons to control the chain reaction. "Actually in February 1941 the avalanche became a factor [*kam ins Rollen*], but one still had time to stop it before the explosion occurred" (p. 19).

There follows a reference at p. 22 to an experiment where neutron multiplication had been controlled. Though only half a watt was produced in the reactor, it vindicated the predictions of the feasibility of a chain reaction, and "in fact, 10 days after this experiment, an output of 200 watts was reached." The source of this information seems to be two Heisenberg papers of April 1941 describing his reactor experiments, but the construction placed on them, as already observed, appears to go beyond Heisenberg's own remarks.[58]

On the other hand, the report hints (p. 10) that both the U235 bomb and the plutonium bomb would depend on the fast-neutron reaction ("It must, however, be emphasized that thermal neutrons are better suited for fission than fast neutrons, which will be treated in the later part of this paper in the description of the uranium bomb"). And in the later section on the actual construction of the bomb it is stressed that in either the case of U235 or that of plutonium it must be assembled quickly, since otherwise a slow chain reaction will ensue and 99.9% of the active material will be lost. This seems not to be a case of premature detonation, but rather of the explosion being a slow one and so inefficient. Very fast assembly is needed to

58. See W. Heisenberg, "Bericht über die Versuche mit Schichtenanordnungen von Präparat 38 und Paraffin am Kaiser-Wilhelm-Institut für Physik in Berlin-Dahlem" (G-93), 18 April 1941 (IMF 29-471), in GHW, A II, p. 432. The report itself is dated March 1941 (p. 454), but officially listed as 18 April (p. 374). The second paper, "Versuche mit einer Schichtenanordnung von Wasser und Präparat 38" (G-74), 28 April 1941 (IMF 29-458), written with R. Döpel and K. Döpel, is in GWH, A II, 463.

prevent . . . the avalanche from being completed too early through the slow bringing together of the parts of the bomb and thus the chain reaction beginning. Thereby a small fraction of 0.1% of the total energy of the explosion results and 99.9% of the explosive is wasted without effect, since in the dispersal of the explosive the neutrons liberated by fission can find no more atoms to fission in their turn. From this condition results the following requirement. 1.   2.   [*The two-part requirement is left blank.*] (p. 30)[59]

The section on actual bomb construction (pp. 30–35), which pompously invokes *Rundschreiben* 219 (as already quoted), is notable for its aggressive self-confidence about how to build a bomb, though that cockiness is somewhat undermined by the omission of crucial facts and figures about critical mass and assembly times, as well as the requirements needed to assure the fast-neutron bomb reaction. Nevertheless, the author plunges ahead:

Construction and Execution Report

The most difficult question was how high the critical mass of U235 and plutonium is. This was known only theoretically, not experimentally, since the danger of an unprotected explosion threatened. . . .

   The critical moment of weight of chemically pure ____ [*sic; no substance stated, but U235?*]. The projectile charge lies in a mantle, cross-section ____ of wolfram/lead mixture . . . and is shot through a tube of ____ caliber of ____ mm, with a velocity of ____ m/sec into the target charge. The target charge of plutonium amounts to a mass of ____ g in the form of a sphere. (pp. 31 f.)[60]

Obviously the author had no idea that a gun-assembly method would be too slow for a plutonium bomb, and he continues to discuss his missing sketch (*Planskizze*) of the UB I bomb casing, mentioning such technicalities as the timer for the bomb and the detonating height (again with blanks left for figures). The same specious attention to technical details is evident in the ensuing discussion under the heading "Mechanical Construction of Uranium Bomb Type UB II" (pp. 35 ff.). Though no nuclear information is given, this is presumably the same kind of

---

59. "Verhindern . . . , dass die Lawinenbildung durch langsames Aneinanderbringen schon zu früh erfüllt ist, und somit die Kettenreaktion eintritt. Wobei mit einen kleinen Bruchteil con 0.1% der gesamten Energie der Explosion erfolgt und der Sprengstoff mit 99.9% wirkungslos auseinandergeschleudert wird, weil nach Zerstieben des Sprengstoffes die bei der Spaltung gebildeten Neutronen, keine Atome mehr finden, die sie ihrerseits weiterspalten könnten. Aus dieser Überlegung ergibt sich folgende Forderung: 1.)   2.)   ."

60. "Die schwierigste Frage, nach Klärung des zu verwendeten Materials, war die, wie hoch die kritische Menge bei Actinuran und Plutonium ist. Es war dies wie schon erwähnt nur rechnerisch und nicht experimentell vorauszusagen, da die Gefahr einer unabschirmbaren Explosion drohte . . .

"Das kritische Gewichtsmoment bei chemisch reinem ____. Die Geschossladung liegt in einem Mantel von durchschnittlich ____ Wolfram-Bleigemisch . . . und wird bei einer Rohrlänge von ____ Kaliber von ____ mm mit einer v$_o$ m/sec in die Zielladung geschossen. Die Trefferladung (Zielladung) bei Pu beträgt die Gewichtsmenge von ____ g in Kugelform."

mixed uranium/plutonium bomb as UB I. The difference seems to be that this type is specially designed to be dropped by an AS 12/44 parachute (the drawing—*Zeichnung*—is naturally missing). The author concludes that it would be better to use a V1 or V2 rocket, though there is the danger of it exploding over the homeland. The argument, however, peters out, and the document is left unfinished.

Despite his apparent readiness to build an atomic bomb, the author of the *Rechenschaftsbericht* was daunted by the scale of the enterprise necessary. This is clearly so in the passages discussing four possible methods for the extraction of U235—the centrifuge, the Clusius-Dickl separation tube, Hertz's membranous diffusion, and, most enthusiastically, the mass spectrograph, which is urged as the best technique. Nevertheless, the author admits somewhat despondently that to produce a kilogram of U235 in 24 hours would require 100,000 apparatuses (pp. 18 f.). As for plutonium, the scope of the problem is such that "for the 200-watt reactor to produce a kilogram would take about 11,400 years."[61] One comes away, then, with the impression that for all the author's keen discussion of the practicalities of bomb construction and bomb delivery, he was quite defeated by the practical problem of how to produce enough fissile material for either a U235 or a plutonium bomb. It is little wonder that the piece ends, gaps and all, so inconclusively.

The main interest of this report is the light it sheds on the common knowledge and state of assumptions about the atomic bomb that prevailed among German physicists in 1944. The author draws heavily on Heisenberg's own recent experiments, and it seems a fair assumption that he would have picked up the general principles of an atomic bomb from the October meeting of the physicists seemingly called as a result of the Hitler-Bormann *Rundschreiben* 219. Some of the information acquired was probably vague and almost off-the-cuff, to judge from the generalities in the report. No doubt the scientists present at the meeting had no clear ideas, let alone data, about the bomb, and were simply airing their longstanding assumptions, which, of course, were scarcely encouraging that a bomb could be made. But since the Führer had commanded it, an attempt had to be made to shape the inadequate data and inchoate ideas about a bomb into a concrete proposal for its construction. The result was the *Rechenschaftsbericht*.

61. "Die 200-watt-Batterie würde also rund 11.400 Jahre benötigen, um 1000 g plutonium zu erzeugen" (p. 27).

CHAPTER 14

The Truth

Farm Hall, August 1945

A most unusual source—the Farm Hall transcripts—has recently become available for our understanding of Heisenberg's conceptions of atomic bombs. These transcripts in English translation of the secretly recorded conversations of the group of German nuclear scientists interned at Farm Hall near Cambridge, England, from July to December 1945 afford an almost theatrical insight into the scientific, moral, and political thinking of some of the main members of the German project, including Heisenberg himself, Weizsäcker, Wirtz, Gerlach, Harteck, Hahn, Diebner, Bagge, and Korsching, as well as Max von Laue, who seems to have ended up there largely by chance.[1]

These transcripts are often quite vivid in their portrayal of the various scientists' personalities and the interactions and discussions among them; most important, the transcripts are very specific and detailed—if sometimes cryptic—in their scientific reasoning. Nevertheless, they have already since their declassification in 1992

---

1. The recording and transcription of the German physicists' conversations were done under the code name "Operation Epsilon." The English translations (the German originals have not yet been traced) are available in slightly variant typed copies in the Public Record Office, London, WO 208/5019, and the National Archives, College Park, Md., RG 77, MED Foreign Intelligence Unit, entry 22, box 163. The text has been published with a valuable introduction by Sir Charles Frank under the title *Operation Epsilon: The Farm Hall Transcripts* (Bristol, England, and Berkeley, Calif., 1993). The critical running commentary by J. Bernstein, *Hitler's Uranium Club* (Woodbury, N.Y., 1996), appeared after the completion of this book. There is also a German version edited by D. Hoffmann, *Operation Epsilon: Die Farm-Hall-Protokolle* (Berlin, 1993), but it is retranslated from English and lacks Heisenberg's seminar talk on the atomic bomb of 14 August 1945. For a lucid analysis of the significance of the Farm Hall material, see J. L. Logan, "The Critical Mass," *American Scientist* 84 (May–June 1996): 263–277.

Throughout this chapter I shall be using the term *critical mass* in a very loose sense (sometimes in quotation marks, sometimes combined with *efficient* and/or *practical* in order to reconstruct Heisenberg's notion of what the amount of material needed for a bomb would be); this differs from the proper physical meaning of the term, for which see Logan's article. See below, note 20.

generated conflicting interpretations, some readers believing that they vindicate Heisenberg's later claim to have understood the atomic bomb principle all along, while others come away from the texts with their skepticism about German omniscience reinforced. Some of this is due to the fact that the German originals seem to have been lost, but the main source of debate arises from the fact that the transcripts have been read without any satisfactory historical context having been provided in which their internal contradictions and puzzling references and allusions might be resolved and made sense of. Outside its historical and scientific context, indeed, no document, however transparent it may seem, can really be understood. In large part, the present book's reconstruction of German thinking on atomic bombs of various types in the period 1939–45 is an attempt to provide a context for a properly historical reading of the Farm Hall transcripts. In fact, the materials and analysis contained in the preceding chapters, and the Farm Hall transcripts themselves, should act as mutual controls; if the reconstruction of the various types of bombs of the preceding chapters is correct, then it should be confirmed by the Farm Hall statements, and conversely, if the Farm Hall evidence is to make sense in its entirety, then it should be consistent with the earlier German evidence. The present chapter is written with this fundamental critical principle in mind.

Let us first recall the salient points of German bomb-thinking as reconstructed in the foregoing chapters. First, there is Heisenberg's belief that a U235 bomb would require a huge critical mass, reckoned at the least in hundreds of kilograms and most likely in tons. This assumption was rooted in a widespread misapprehension in the international community of nuclear physicists in 1939 that such huge masses would be entailed; it was then given a quantitative and logical expression by Heisenberg through a misapplied back-of-an-envelope calculation that showed that tons of U235 would be needed for a bomb. Second, attempts were made to design a reactor-bomb using enriched U235; this bomb was conceived as a highly unstable reactor. It was, however, regarded as a somewhat chimerical undertaking. Although a secret patent seems to have been submitted in 1941, German opinion obviously considered that a normal reactor would have to be constructed first and that the enrichment process represented a further obstacle that would have still to be overcome. Third, plutonium was glimpsed as an alternative explosive to U235. Plutonium would be produced through the operation of a U238 reactor and was assumed on general principles to be at least as fissionable as U235. But, like the other bomb versions, a plutonium bomb was envisaged as a very remote practical possibility because of the difficulty of producing sufficient material from the operation of reactors in a given time. In the light of all these assumptions—some of them quite cloudy in their reasoning and devoid of specific calculations—it was not surprising that Heisenberg and his colleagues thought of an atomic bomb as something that could not realistically be achieved during the current war and probably for many decades thereafter. It was natural, therefore, that Heisenberg—convinced as he was by his general scientific conceptualization of the problem, which lacked a proper concept of the critical mass of a bomb, as well as by his simplistic back-of-an-envelope calculation of a critical mass in 1940—should never have attempted any thorough analysis of the bomb problem, and that he should have been overtaken completely by astonishment and disbelief in August 1945 when he heard over the BBC radio news that an atomic bomb had been detonated over Hiroshima.

The Farm Hall transcripts, on a close contextual reading, reveal a fundamental fissure in Heisenberg's thinking about the atomic bomb. From 6 to 9 August 1945, Heisenberg retraces the tracks of his old approaches to the bomb problem, most of which were laid down in 1939—40. Then there is a gap of five days in Heisenberg's technical conversations about the matter with his colleagues. Finally, on 14 August Heisenberg unveils in an impressive lecture to the German scientists a—for him—radically new analysis of the problem, which clearly strikes them as something quite breathtakingly novel. Thus, the first days of utter mystification are followed by the confident revelation of scientific truth.

.   .   .

The two Farm Hall reports containing most of the relevant transcribed conversations are numbers 4 (covering 6–7 August 1945) and 5 (8–22 August); the latter (FHT 5) includes the lecture by Heisenberg given on 14 August in which he describes his reconsidered conception of an atomic bomb, an exposition unprecedented both in its technical detail and also, it will be argued here, in its conceptualization of the whole problem. It is a radically new departure in Heisenberg's whole approach to the atomic bomb, and came about only because he was provoked by the news that the Allies had indeed managed to make a nuclear explosive device. The theory was worked out, it may be deduced from an analysis of the transcripts, between 9 and 14 August. (The original German text of this lecture and discussion appears as an appendix to FHT 5.)

Let us now analyze Heisenberg's various technical remarks on the bomb problem as they appear in sequence in various conversations recorded in the transcripts.

(A) 6 August

Hahn is informed by Major T. H. Rittner, the commanding officer, that the BBC has announced (on the BBC 6:00 P.M. news) that an atomic bomb has been exploded by the Allies. Hahn and Rittner then announce the fact at dinner to the other incredulous German scientists. A conversation on the subject occurs at dinner before the "guests" listen to the 9:00 P.M. news.

Hahn mocks Heisenberg, saying that "if the Americans have a uranium bomb, then you're all second-raters. Poor old Heisenberg. . . . You're just second-raters and you may as well pack up," a sentiment with which Heisenberg expresses agreement, though he expresses doubt whether the Allied bomb was in fact a true nuclear explosion and guesses that some dilettante has tricked the Americans. The scientists, however, conclude that either the Allies have separated U235 or have been running a reactor long enough to produce "element 93" (actually, element 94—viz., plutonium). Heisenberg then alludes to the critical mass required for a U235 bomb: "I still don't believe a word about the bomb but I may be wrong. I consider it perfectly possible that they have about ten tons of enriched uranium, but not that they can have ten tons of pure U235." Clearly, Heisenberg is still here entrenched in his thinking of 1939–40 about the very large mass required for a U235 bomb.

Hahn is surprised by this statement, observing that "I thought that one needed only very little 235," but obviously Heisenberg had never explained to his chemist colleague the different kinds of bombs and masses he as a physicist had been thinking about. Heisenberg replies that "if they only enrich it slightly, they can build an engine which will go but with that they can't make an explosive which will—." This statement is broken off by another query from Hahn and so we do not know which infinitive Heisenberg intended to use. Moreover, we do not have the German original. But even as it stands in English, the exclusion of a slightly enriched U235 explosive may not be as definite as it may seem when read out of historical context. Had Heisenberg meant to say that a reactor using slightly enriched U235 could never produce an explosive, there would have been no need for him to continue into another clause with the words *which will*. Rather, that clause seems to be about to qualify the word *explosive*, most probably by saying that a reactor-bomb using a small amount of U235 in slightly enriched form might explode, but not produce an explosion of the 20,000 tons of TNT equivalent attributed to the Hiroshima bomb. In other words, there is a strong suggestion here that Heisenberg is trying to set Hahn straight on the matter, having told him earlier in the war that very little U235 was required for some sort of atomic explosion—namely, a reactor-bomb. Hahn's confusion about the different types of pure-U235 and reactor-bombs is evident from the question with which he interrupts Heisenberg: "But if they have, let us say, 30 kilogrammes of pure U235, couldn't they make a bomb with it?" Again Heisenberg tries vainly to correct this misapprehension by responding: "But it still wouldn't go off, as the mean free path is still too big." Hahn, now thoroughly puzzled, insists: "But tell me why you used to tell me that one needed 50 kilogrammes of 235 in order to do anything. Now you say one needs two tons."[2] Not willing to explain much to the benighted Hahn, Heisenberg simply says, "I wouldn't like to commit

2. M. von Ardenne, in *Sechzig Jahre für Forschung und Fortschritt* (Berlin, 1988), pp. 162, 482, recalls being told by Otto Hahn (seemingly during a visit on 10 December 1941) that only " a few kilos" of U235 were needed for an explosive chain reaction. See above, chap. 9.

Whatever the figures used during the war, Heisenberg's explanations had evidently deterred Hahn from believing that a bomb was feasible. During a lecture given to the Royal Academy of Sciences at Stockholm in 1943, Hahn referred to the notion of an explosive chain reaction, but concluded that the technical difficulties were insurmountable: "Providence has not wanted the trees to reach to the sky" (quoted in P. Rife, "Lise Meitner: The Life and Times of a Jewish Woman Physicist" [Ph.D. diss., Union for Experimenting Colleges and Universities, 1983], p. 320).

myself for the moment, but it is certainly a fact that the mean free paths are pretty big." Hahn then opines, "I think it's absolutely impossible to produce one ton of U235 by separating isotopes." Heisenberg sees no reason, however, to retreat from his belief that the amount of U235 required would be large:

> If it has been done with U235 then we should be able to work it out properly. It just depends upon whether it is done with 50, 500 or 5,000 kilogrammes and we don't know the order of magnitude. We can assume that they have some method of separating isotopes of which we have no idea.

This explanation of Heisenberg's attempts a twofold reduction of the bomb problem. First, he reduces it to a technical problem of isotope separation, and second, he reduces it to a matter of variation of the values of the mean free paths that can produce critical masses of varying orders of magnitude from 50 to 5,000 kg. Heisenberg cannot bring himself to believe that his original analysis of the bomb problem is invalid and that the Allies may have found an alternative conception of the bomb. This is clear from his following rationalization that "with discoveries one can always be sceptical and many surprises can take place. In the case of inventions, surprises can really occur for people who have not had anything to do with it. It's a bit odd after we have been working on it for five years." Heisenberg is reluctant though willing to credit the Allies with "inventing" a new method of isotope separation, but he cannot even conceive of their having happened upon a new "discovery" of the principle of an atomic bomb that would lead to a far smaller critical mass than he had himself "discovered."[3]

(B) 6 August, after the 9:00 P.M. News

Some time after hearing the BBC 9:00 P.M. news, Hahn and Heisenberg resume a private conversation concerning the question of critical mass, and this time round Heisenberg explains the matter more carefully.

When Heisenberg speculates that with mass spectrographs, the Allies might separate 30 kg of U235 a year, Hahn asks if he thinks they would "need as much as that." This prompts Heisenberg to confess:

> "I think so, certainly, but, quite honestly, I have never worked it out as I never believed one could get pure U235. I always knew it could be done with U235 with fast neu-

---

3. FHT 4, 6 August 1945; *OE*, pp. 71–75. H. Rechenberg, *Farm-Hall-Berichte . . . Ein Kommentar* (Stuttgart, 1994), pp. 44–44, 96, cites this exchange between Hahn and Heisenberg, but seems to ascribe the "10 tons" figure merely to Heisenberg's assuming different mean free paths—or even to Heisenberg's having forgotten his previous figure ("Hahn had to remind him . . . of his earlier estimate")—rather than using a radically different conceptual approach. Rechenberg does not mention the random-walk calculation in his commentary.

It is possible also that the "50 kilogrammes" figure may be derived from a small critical mass of radius 8 cm for a reactor—not a bomb—that Heisenberg had calculated in relation to a 30% enrichment of U235 in his fundamental G-39 paper of December 1939 (GWH, A II, 391).

trons. That's why U235 only can be used as an explosive. One can never make an explosive with slow neutrons, not even with the heavy water machine, as then the neutrons only go with thermal speed, with the result that the reaction is so slow that the thing explodes sooner, before the reaction is complete. It vaporizes at 5,000 degrees and then the reaction is already—" Hahn interrupts: "How does the bomb explode?"

This passage demonstrates that Heisenberg had correctly understood that a true nuclear explosion must be achieved with fast neutrons in order to complete the reaction to a sufficient degree before the device flies apart, breaking off the reaction. This fast-neutron bomb is contrasted with an exploding reactor using slow neutrons whose vaporization at 5,000 degrees would bring the reaction to an end before a true explosion has occurred. The wording shows that Heisenberg obviously did not think a reactor-bomb using slow neutrons was worth pursuing, since its explosive yield would be small. In response to Hahn's interruption "How does the bomb explode?" Heisenberg describes how fast neutrons will produce an explosion in pure U235:

In the case of the bomb it can only be done with the very fast neutrons. The fast neutrons in U235 immediately produce other neutrons so that the very fast neutrons which have a speed of—say—1/30th of that of light make the whole reaction. . . . In ordinary uranium a fast neutron nearly always hits 238 and then gives no fission. . . . Below 600,000 volts I can't do any more fission on the 238, but I can always split the 235. . . . If I have pure U235 each neutron will immediately beget two children and then there must be a chain reaction which goes very quickly.

But then Heisenberg departs from his correct analysis to offer a calculation, which, though accurate, is offering a solution to a false problem.

Then you can reckon as follows. One neutron always makes two others in pure U235. That is to say that in order to make 10^{24} neutrons I need 80 reactions one after the other. Therefore I need 80 collisions and the mean free path is about 6 centimetres. In order to make 80 collisions, I must have a lump of a radius of about 54 centimetres and that would be about a ton.

This was, of course, the brilliantly simple but fallacious back-of-an-envelope calculation based on the random-walk analysis that (as Wirtz informed Sir Charles Frank) Heisenberg had arrived at in 1940. In a later interview Frank commented on the calculation in these terms:

It's brilliantly simple, and had it given the right answer, you would say how clever, it takes a clever man like Heisenberg to see how to do such a difficult problem so simply. . . . Had it not been that it gives you, in the end, a significantly wrong answer for practical conclusions, everyone would have said, it's the brilliance of Heisenberg to see a simple way of calculating it. He did not know that the right way to calculate it had been published by Peierls in . . . 1939.[4]

4. C. Frank, interview by Mark Walker, 12 April 1985, pp. 9 f., 14–16 (OHI). (Astonishingly, no mention of this subject appears in Walker's book.) In this interview, conducted without an opportunity to review the transcripts, Sir Charles conflates Heisenberg's earlier random-walk arguments of 6–9

Thus, what one has here is a correct statement of the fast-neutron-in-U235 principle, combined with a fallacious calculation of the critical mass of U235. Heisenberg was trying to be too sure of exploding a mole of U235; he had set himself the false problem of how one might be 100% sure of exploding a mass of U235 without wasting a neutron. This misconceived anxiety was reinforced by his failure to analyze adequately the phenomenon of neutron escape, which, correctly done, would have exposed the fallacy of his approach. In other words, Heisenberg had set a huge upper limit to the size of the critical mass, which he then took mistakenly as the practical critical mass—which could, as Frisch and Peierls had realized, in fact be much smaller.[5]

(C) 6 August, Later That Night

In a conversation held in Heisenberg's absence, Bagge remarks, "It must be possible to work out at what temperature the thing explodes." This moves Harteck to recall Heisenberg's random-walk argument in a garbled form:

> The multiplication factor with U235 is 2.8, and when one collides with the other how long is the path until it happens? 4 centimetres. Rx is the radius. Then you have to multiply that by the mean free path and divide it by the square root of the multiplication factor. That should be 3.2. R is about 14 centimetres, the weight is 200 kilogrammes, then it explodes.

Harteck has here remembered that Heisenberg had used a square root to work out the critical mass, but he now takes the square root of the wrong quantity. Where Heisenberg had used the square root of the number of fission steps (viz., the square root of 80) and then multiplied that by the mean free path (6 cm), Harteck mistakenly opts for the square root of the multiplication factor, thus rendering the whole argument nonsensical and the critical mass calculation of 200 kg quite bogus.[6] The significance of the passage, however, is its testimony to the fact

---

August 1945 with the solution given in his paper of 14 August, suggesting that the lecture actually began with the random-walk calculation. Nevertheless, Frank's memory is quite clear about Wirtz's admission during their talk of 2 November 1945 (*OE*, p. 237) that Heisenberg had disclosed his back-of-an-envelope calculation to a private meeting of physicists in 1940 or so. (See also above, chap. 7.)

I have found no reference to the Peierls paper of 1939 (see above, chap. 5) anywhere in the extant German literature. The outbreak of war obviously led to its slipping through the usual scientific trawling nets in Germany.

5. FHT 4, 6 August. *OE*, pp. 83 f. See above, chap. 7, and Sir Charles Franks's introduction to *OE*, pp. 5 f., where it is pointed out that the mass of a 54 cm sphere of U235 would actually be 6 tons, not 1 ton. (Logan and Serber, however, correct this figure to 13 tons, assuming a different density; see above, chap. 3.) In a letter to me dated 20 March 1994, Sir Charles wrote that "Heisenberg did indeed grossly overestimate the required amount of nuclear explosive, but *not* . . . by overestimating the role of neutron-escape—rather by not giving it sufficiently detailed attention."

6. This formula for critical radius may not be related in fact to Heisenberg's random-walk, and—with the right data—might actually have yielded a small critical mass. See Bernstein, *Hitler's Uranium Club*, p. 146.

that the German physicists had a vague recollection of a Heisenberg back-of-an-envelope calculation involving a square-root calculation, and that obviously this calculation had been done some time before, since there is no evidence in the Farm Hall transcripts up to this conversation that Heisenberg had expounded his calculation except privately to Hahn earlier that night. This all suggests that early on in the war Heisenberg had announced to his closest colleagues in the uranium project, probably in an offhand way, that according to his reasoning and calculation the critical mass of a bomb would be in the region of tons of U235—and that ever since this obiter dictum the matter had been regarded as closed—closed, that is, until the Hiroshima news reopened the whole issue.[7]

(D) 7 August

After reading the morning newspapers,[8] Heisenberg explains his random-walk view of the bomb to Hahn and Harteck. Hahn asks about the efficiency of the explosion of the uranium: "Is the fission of uranium 0.1%, 1%, 10% or 100%?" Heisenberg replies:

> If it is U235, then for all practical purposes it is the whole lot, as then the reaction goes much quicker than the vaporisation. . . . In order to produce fission in 10^{25} atoms you need 80 steps in the chain so that the whole reaction is complete in 10^{-8} seconds. Then each neutron that flies out of one atom makes two more neutrons when it hits another U235. Now I need 10^{25} neutrons and that is 2^{80}. I need 80 steps in the chain and then I have made 2^{80} neutrons. One step in the chain takes the same time as one neutron to go 5 centimetres, that is 10^{-9} seconds, so that the whole reaction is complete in 10^{-8} seconds. The whole thing probably explodes in that time.

Here again the notion of 100% efficiency in the explosion of the mole of U235 (2^{80} atoms) reflects Heisenberg's unrealistic desire to be absolutely sure of exploding that number of atoms in a given time without wasting a neutron. Setting this upper boundary for the "critical mass" and taking it as the practical mass of a bomb meant that Heisenberg had shut off a priori the possibility of a practical bomb using a far smaller "critical mass."[9]

---

7. *OE*, p. 86. See Frank's introductory comment at p. 6. The paucity of references to plutonium in the Farm Hall ruminations is striking. The explanation seems to be that in the minds of the German scientists the Allies could not possibly have been ahead of them in reactor construction and so could not have obtained any plutonium. Still, it also indicates a lack of serious understanding of the plutonium option.

8. The amount of hard information given in the articles on the atomic bomb in both the London *Times* and the *Manchester Guardian* issues from 7 to 14 August is astonishingly meager. The nuclear explosive is not specified; no critical mass is given (except for an unofficial speculation in the *Times* of 8 August [see below] that it is a mere 1 lb.); and there is no indication that the Hiroshima and Nagasaki bombs used different explosives.

9. *OE*, p. 91. Cf. Frank's introduction, p. 6, for the fallacy in using the upper limit as the actual "critical mass." As Jonothan Logan has pointed out to me, strictly speaking the efficiency problem has

(E) 7 August, Later in the Day

At the suggestion of Major Rittner, the German guests prepare a memorandum on their work on the uranium project. During the considerable discussion that preceded the drawing up of this memorandum, "Wirtz remarked that they should remember that there was a patent for the production of such a bomb at the Kaiser Wilhelm Institute for Physics. The patent was taken out in 1941." The problem of the German patent has already been discussed in detail in chapter 10 above; it appears to have been for some sort of reactor-bomb, using enriched U235. Significantly, no mention of the bomb patent cited by Wirtz appears in the final version of the German scientists' apologetic memorandum, which is framed so as to demonstrate that the German project had never really been organized as an effort to construct an atomic bomb. Reference to a bomb patent, no matter how chimerical, would have been somewhat embarrassing in this context.[10]

(F) 8 August

After reading the newspapers, Heisenberg discusses with Wirtz and Bagge the possibility of a plutonium bomb. Heisenberg finds it difficult to accept that the Allies have obtained plutonium, since according to the newspapers they do not have a running stabilized reactor to produce it. In any case, Heisenberg doubts whether the critical mass of plutonium could be as low as 8 lbs., a figure he seems to have picked up from that morning's newspapers, though the figure given in the *Times* of 8 August is 1 lb., and that is itself a speculation by the paper's science correspondent.[11] (It is possible that Heisenberg's *ein* or *eine* has been misheard by the transcribers as *acht*.)

> I do not see how the reaction can take place in 8 lbs of something, since the mean free paths are fairly long. They have always got mean free paths of 4 cms. In 8 lbs they will surely get no chain reaction whatsoever.

But, still bothered, Heisenberg then conjectures that plutonium might be more fissionable than suspected.

> It could be that this 94 has quite a short mean free path. We have done little research in the field of completed fast neutron reactions because we could not see how we could do it because we did not have this element, and we saw no prospect of being able to obtain it.

---

to do with the kinetics of the evolving chain reaction, not with the question of whether a critical mass is present. By my reconstruction, however, Heisenberg seems to be running the two things together.

10. *OE*, pp. 93 f. See above, chap. 10. The Farm Hall transcripts include several other references to other patents associated with uranium (e.g., *OE*, pp. 61, 65, 73), but not to this one. The memorandum is printed in *OE*, pp. 102–106.

11. "Atomic Bomb Explained," *Times* (London), 8 August 1945, p. 5. The article suggests that U235 separation was the key to the bomb and conjectures that the U.S. industrial effort was devoted to this. The writer remarks that "rough calculation makes it seem likely that the weight of uranium in the bomb just dropped was in the region of a pound."

When Wirtz opines that the Allies do indeed have plutonium and that the bomb is not big, Heisenberg is tempted to agree: "That is to say it might be of the order of 400 kilos." Although Heisenberg is here discussing plutonium, the passage is interesting for the indirect light it throws on his understanding of the large critical mass of a U235 bomb. That is to say, Heisenberg is still convinced that the mean free paths entail a huge critical mass because he is working on the conceptual basis of the upper limit for a critical mass being the practical one for a bomb, whether a plutonium or a uranium one.[12]

(G) 9 August

After the newspapers report that the atomic bomb weighed 200 kg,[13] Heisenberg and Harteck play with the data to make them fit the new weight (or possibly critical mass?). Heisenberg says that reading of the 200 kg figure for the bomb

has worried me considerably, and therefore this evening I have done a few calculations and have seen that it is more probable than we had thought on account of the substantial multiplication factors which one can have with fast neutrons. We have always calculated with a multiplication factor of 1.1. . . . If they have a multiplication factor of 3 or 5 then naturally it is a different matter. We said we need about 80 links in the chain reaction; now the mean free path is 4 cms, therefore we must have 80 long divisions (so was the rough estimate) and this would then come to about a ton. This calculation was right if the multiplication factor is 1.1 because even then we use really every neutron which "escapes" for multiplication. If on the other hand the multiplication factor is 3, things are quite different. Then I can say, if the whole thing is only as big as the mean free path, then one neutron which walks around therein meets another and makes three neutrons. . . . In practice therefore I need only the mean free path for the thing to work.

Harteck then asks what the rest of the 100 to 200 kg around this core are, and Heisenberg rightly replies that it must be a reflector. Nevertheless, Heisenberg finds it difficult to believe his own argument, which depends on an unlikely high neutron multiplication factor, and after a pause he confesses: "Well, how have they actually done it? I find it is a disgrace if we, the Professors who have worked on it, cannot at least work out how they did it." And this leads the two scientists to conjecture as to which other elements might have been used as the nuclear explosive; the most likely candidate is seen to be protoactinium, which Heisenberg believes might actually be what the Allies call "Pluto," with which it shares the same initial letter: "This is almost easier to imagine than all other methods."[14]

12. *OE*, p. 117 (FHT 5).

13. Neither the *Times* nor the *Manchester Guardian* for 9 August report a "200 kg" figure for the bomb. I have not been able to check that day's issues of the *Daily Telegraph*, *Daily Mail*, or *News Chronicle*, one of which may have contained such a speculation.

14. See above, chap. 1, for other references to protoactinium.

In this passage we see Heisenberg once again hung on the spike of his own random-walk argument, which provides only an upper limit for the critical mass. Admittedly, that argument can produce a small figure for the critical mass (1 to 2 kg in the case of protoactinium), but to do so requires unwarranted assumptions about the neutron multiplication factors of plutonium and protoactinium, speculative optimistic numbers that even Heisenberg in the midst of his need is reluctant to try to apply to a uranium bomb.[15]

(H) 9 August, Later in the Day

Heisenberg and others discuss the new bomb again, trying to see if the data for U235 can be made to fit the requirements for a bomb of small critical mass. Heisenberg is convinced throughout this conversation that one of three methods lies behind the Allied bomb: pure protoactinium, isotope separation of U235, or the production of plutonium by means of reactors. Inquiring into the possibility of a small mean free path for U235, Heisenberg asks his colleagues what the fission cross-section of U235 for fast neutrons actually is. (Heisenberg had forgotten the key figure for assessing the feasibility of an atomic bomb!) Diebner then produces a book (perhaps an updated version of his own published compilation of nuclear tables)[16] and states that the figure is 0.5 ($\times 10^{-24}$ cm^2). Heisenberg deduces from this that the mean free path would be 8 cm, which would, of course, end up again in an enormous critical mass. To escape from this dead end, Heisenberg then speculates as he had earlier that the multiplication factor might be higher than suspected; the compensatory figure he selects this time is 5: "I would say that in the most favorable circumstances one would obtain a geometrical cross-section of about 8 cms [obviously a slip; he must intend "mean free path"] and if one then, by some process, obtained out of it 5 neutrons, one need not make the radius

---

15. *OE*, pp. 117–120.

16. K. Diebner and E. Grassmann, *Künstliche Radioaktivität: Experimentelle Ergebnisse* (Leipzig, 1939), with additions published in *Physikalische Zeitschrift* 40 (1939): 297–314; ibid. 41 (1940): 157–194. No figure is given for fast-neutron fission in U235 among the cross-sections at pp. 190 f., though it is possible that Diebner added new data in manuscript to his own copy as they became available. At p. 190, however, Diebner does cite from Ladenburg a general figure for fast-neutron fission in unseparated uranium of 5×10^{-25} (= 0.5×10^{-24}), which could be the figure that he supplies erroneously to Heisenberg in this discussion, as is suggested by a remark in Heisenberg's 14 August lecture, where he says he is unsure of whether the 0.5 figure relates to U235 or to U238 (*OE*, p. 126).

Other German tables published during the war include J. Mattauch and S. Flügge, *Kernphysikalische Tabellen* (Berlin, 1942; trans. as *Nuclear Physics Tables* [New York, 1946]), which gives (p. 67) only a general figure for fast-neutron fission in all uranium isotopes as being of the order of 10^{-25}.

A calculated approximation of 3.7 plus or minus 0.5 appears on p. 95 of a paper by W. Jentschke and K. Lintner circulated in February 1944: "Schnelle Neutronen in Uran. V" (G-227; IMF 30-461). In a letter of 10 June 1966 (IMF 32), Heisenberg claimed to have used this value at Farm Hall in 1945, but this—like so many of Heisenberg's claims—is not borne out by the transcripts in *OE*. See above, chaps. 1 and 2.

any bigger than one mean free path" (assuming the use of a reflector). Here Heisenberg realizes that his estimate of 5 for the neutron multiplication factor of U235 is far too optimistic, for he then goes on, as in his earlier conversation with Harteck, to consider other candidates for the nuclear explosive used in the Allied bomb, again concluding that "they have done it with protoactinium, which to me at the moment appears to be the most likely." (As a postscript, Heisenberg is even willing to agree with Wirtz that the Allies may have "also put a little heavy-water in the bomb in order to raise the factor by 2." This almost trivial aside is a minor indication of how desperate Heisenberg is to find ways of reconciling the awkwardness caused by the small cross-sections of U235 and its large mean free path with the small critical mass of the bomb as speculated in the newspapers.)

Heisenberg is still operating here within the framework of his upper-limit analysis by means of the random-walk calculation. He is allowing for the escape of 4 out of the 5 neutrons produced by each fission, and so looking at what might be called the worst-case scenario of how to be sure of exploding the critical mass while using an excessively optimistic assumption about the multiplication factor. Under these conditions, the critical size would be small, merely the dimensions of one mean free path. He is still hooked on the upper limit for a critical mass being the practical "critical mass" that would ensure a 100% efficiency of the explosion. It is only in the course of the next five days that Heisenberg finally was able to abandon this random-walk analysis and come to a correct understanding of the practical scientific principle of an atomic bomb and of critical mass in its customary sense.[17]

. . .

(I) Heisenberg's Lecture of 14 August 1945

Let us first summarize Heisenberg's conception of the critical mass as it appears in his thinking before the lecture of 14 August 1945.[18] In accordance with established views from 1939 on, Heisenberg regarded critical mass as defined by the balance of escaping and internally produced neutrons; if the internal neutrons exceed those escaping, then the critical mass is realized and a chain reaction is initiated. The problem, however, was to sustain explosively the reaction, since, as Bohr

17. *OE*, pp. 121–125. J. Bernstein and D. Cassidy, in "Bomb Apologetics: Farm Hall, August 1945," *Physics Today*, August 1995, 32–36, seem to depict Heisenberg's random-walk calculation merely as an "arithmetical" error, rather than a fundamental conceptual mistake. The random-walk analysis involves a misconception of "critical mass," rather than being separate from it. Thus, Bernstein and Cassidy rightly point out that Heisenberg "does not seem to know even how to define the critical mass." While this is true if we are thinking of "critical mass" in the correct sense, Heisenberg's random-walk calculation is not simply an arithmetical exercise, but a calculation that is based on a fallacious concept of a "maximum"—and unnecessary—critical mass.

18. The English translation of the lecture and discussion is in *OE*, pp. 125–140, the German at pp. 147–164.

put it, the "chains were too short." To lengthen the chains, in the balance definition of critical mass that appears in Heisenberg's G-39 of December 1939, represented as "n/n'," the excess would have to be large.[19] How large would it have to be for a bomb to explode? To find a solution to the bomb problem, Heisenberg had addressed himself to the problem of ensuring that the reaction continued long enough to fission a large enough number of nuclei—say, 2^{80} nuclei—to produce a large explosion. This led Heisenberg in 1940 to conceive of a practical "critical mass" relevant to a bomb, and he thought of this in terms of an upper limit (as we have seen in chapter 7) arrived at by means of his random-walk back-of-an-envelope calculation. This is the practical "critical mass" for exploding 2^{80} nuclei without "wasting a neutron." It may be a theoretically true construct, but it scarcely represents accurate or serious scientific thought about a bomb. Nevertheless, Heisenberg was content to let his thinking rest on this shaky basis for the remainder of the war. Perhaps the most striking feature of this whole lax approach is that it saved Heisenberg from having to feel any need to apply a general expression for fast-neutron reactions giving internal neutron generation with respect to time (on the lines of Frisch and Peierls's e^t /Tau), which would have led him to perceive that the efficient practical "critical mass" of a bomb could be much smaller than the maximum explosive "critical mass." It is precisely an expression of this kind that Heisenberg finally applied in his lecture of 14 August 1945, which revealed at last the correct practical solution to the critical mass for a bomb.[20]

Heisenberg confidently begins the lecture with a brief recapitulation of the data relevant to U235, but his confidence is belied by two aspects of the talk, one general, the other specific. First, his phrasing and tone and the reactions of his listeners sound very much as though he has only just now understood the solution and that the audience is hearing the correct solution for the first time. Second, Heisenberg is manifestly uncertain as to the crucial data affecting a U235 bomb— above all, the fast-neutron fission cross-section of U235.

Heisenberg is quite certain now that the bomb is a U235 device, and he no longer has to resort to a neutron multiplication factor of 5 to massage the critical mass; 2, 2.5, or 3 neutrons per fission are now sufficient. The principle of the bomb is held to be that the internal multiplication of neutrons must be greater than the

19. GWH, A II, 388 f..

20. In the preceding and other paragraphs in this chapter the term *critical mass* is used, usually in quotation marks, to designate what Heisenberg thought of as the minimum amount of material needed to produce an explosive chain reaction. He arrives at this by his fallacious random-walk calculation, effectively combining two different concepts—that of the critical mass necessary for the chain reaction to begin, and that of the mass of material needed for the efficiency of the reaction. This "efficient" or "practical" critical mass is not to be confused with the true critical mass as the term is generally understood (for which latter see Logan, "The Critical Mass"). See above, note 1.

In his "Bemerkungen" paper of 1942 (G-161), GWH, A II, 551, Heisenberg offers a limited expression in a puzzling negative form for neutron multiplication with respect to the absorption coefficient of a reactor: $e^{-\beta t}$. (See above, chap. 8n6.)

loss of neutrons from the surface of a finite mass. The solution to this matter depends on the mean free paths and nuclear cross-sections. And here Heisenberg produces what he calls a "handy formula"—whose derivation he does not supply— that yields the mean free path for any process in U235: This is 22 cm divided by the cross-section in barns (10^{-24} cm^2) of the particular process.[21] Observing that the "most difficult part is the cross-section for fission," Heisenberg notes that for thermal neutrons in U235 this is very large (and so the mean free path would be very small indeed), but then startlingly admits that he is not sure about the crucial cross-section for fast neutrons and has no real way of calculating it: "There is a figure of 0.5 in Doerrig's [*sic*, for "Diebner's"] Tables, but perhaps it refers to 238 and not 235 . . . I don't quite see how the two fissions can be properly differentiated." In the end, Heisenberg hits upon Frisch and Peierls' theoretical reasoning from Bohr-Wheeler and concludes that the cross-section would be comparable to the geometrical cross-section and that it would be constant over the whole energy range.[22]

Heisenberg now proceeds to assume the following data for U235: 0.5 to 2.5 × 10^{-24} for the fission cross-section for fast neutrons; mean free paths for fission of 9 to 44 cm, and for scattering of 3.7 cm; a neutron multiplication factor of between 2 and 2.5.[23]

Having collected the data, Heisenberg next describes the process of a fast-neutron U235 bomb. For the first time in a discussion of a true atomic bomb, Heisenberg gives a formula for the exponential growth of neutrons within a critical mass: n is proportional to $e^{\nu t}$ (where ν [nu] is the reciprocal time). By thus following in Frisch and Peierls's footsteps, Heisenberg no longer has to be fazed as he had been by the long mean free paths for fission, which had, until now, as a result of his random-walk analysis, produced excessively large critical sizes for a bomb. A mean free path of 6 cm would lead according to the random-walk interpretation to a critical size of a sphere 54 cm in radius, but now Heisenberg is quite happy to take a 9 cm mean free path as the basis of his new calculations. Heisenberg's basic view of the bomb has indeed undergone a revolutionary reconceptualization.[24]

Once Heisenberg has this expression for exponential growth of neutrons in an infinite volume, he moves on to work out how the process develops in a finite volume by applying diffusion theory. He compares the exponential multiplication of neutrons inside the volume to the neutron escape flux, which leads him via a series of well-thought-out steps to resolving the problem for the critical size of a bomb,

---

21. This formula seems to have been obtained very recently by Heisenberg, since if it were used in conjunction with his random-walk analysis and his U235 fast-neutron fission cross-section of 0.5 (accepted on 9 August, but now seen as problematic), it would result in a critical radius of 99 cm (root 80 × 11 cm = 99 cm; each step is 11 cm, since 22 divided by 0.5 [the fission cross-section in barns] = 11).

22. *OE*, pp. 126–127.

23. Ibid., pp. 127–129.

24. Ibid., p. 129. Note that the negative ν (nu) of the 1942 reactor has become positive. See above, chap. 8n6.

which he concludes to be a sphere of radius 6.2 cm, weighing 16 kg.[25] (He is not happy with this greatly reduced critical mass, however, since he has heard that "others"—does he mean the Allies, as reported in the press (see note 11 above)?—have stated that the explosive mass weighed 4 kg; but he conjectures that the 4 kg perhaps refers to the amount of pure $U235$ integrated into a larger uranium mass, or that alternatively the fission cross-section may be much higher, about 6 barns.)[26]

The next problem tackled by Heisenberg in the lecture is the need for rapid assembly of the two hemispheres of the bomb; if they do not come together in a large enough mass quickly enough, then the bomb will be inefficient, since the reaction will not have enough time to be carried through to completion. Heisenberg is able to develop his earlier expression for the exponential growth of neutrons into a new equation that describes how the bomb reaction itself proceeds. Again, this new equation is completely unprecedented in all of Heisenberg's previous writings and utterances on the bomb problem. It is evidence of a wholly new conceptualization of the problem.[27]

The lecture concludes with an estimate of the energy and temperature reached during the explosion.[28]

.　.　.

When read in the full context of Heisenberg's thinking about the various possibilities of atomic bombs during the period 1939–45, the Farm Hall transcripts show clearly that between 6 and 9 August 1945 he did not break out of long-established erroneous conceptions of the bomb. His thinking during the four days after the news of Hiroshima falls nicely into the mold of his preconceived ideas of the previous five years. But, forced by scientific pride as well as intense curiosity to think out the matter far more thoroughly and clearly than he had ever done before, by 14 August Heisenberg had to the evident amazement of his colleagues come up with a detailed analysis of the $U235$ bomb principles that superseded all his previous thinking on the matter.[29] Fortunately, Heisenberg's revelation of 14 August 1945 had already been grasped by Frisch and Peierls in February–March 1940.

25. Ibid., pp. 129–134.

26. Ibid., p. 134. I do not know the source of this 4 kg figure (approximating to the 8 lbs. Heisenberg comes up with earlier from a reading of the newspapers).

27. Ibid., pp. 135–138.

28. Ibid., pp. 138–140.

29. In his OHI interview of 1985 cited above, Sir Charles Frank notes (p. 16): "Overnight or during two or three days that elapsed, after, he did the calculation right and gave them a seminar that showed pretty well what the critical mass should be. And I certainly got the impression that it was brand new, this was the first time he'd done it. That he'd been content with the back-of-an-envelope calculation for about four or five years, and had not looked at it again, and—(*Interviewer interjects:* 'I would believe that—')." Nonetheless, the interviewer (Mark Walker) has since persisted in not believing what he was told here and has consistently argued that Heisenberg had known the true critical-mass calculation for many years before.

On looking over the Farm Hall depictions of the German reaction from 6 to 14 August, two remarkable features of the Farm Hall discussions must impress any reader. The first of these is the evident reigning state of German ignorance of bomb theory. Apart from Heisenberg's own carelessness about calculation and looseness of physical thinking about the concept of critical mass, this ignorance is plainly expressed in Hahn's constant puzzlement and his need to have Heisenberg explain things to him about critical size and so forth. It also emerges in Diebner's plaint: "There is no danger because I don't know anything. For instance I don't know why it is easier to produce fission in element 94. I didn't know all that. It is not in any book."[30] The second striking aspect is the intellectual arrogance of Heisenberg and the other members of his close circle, Wirtz and Weizsäcker. Heisenberg is totally incapable of conceiving that the Allies could have succeeded where he had not. He simply cannot believe that the Americans had been running a reactor since 1942, and so is forced to such bizarre conclusions as the notion that the Allies' plutonium is a derivative of protoactinium, or the desperate idea that protoactinium itself is the explosive.[31] It took Heisenberg until 14 August to dig himself out of the pit created by German ignorance and arrogance.[32]

In the last resort, it was Heisenberg's own genius as well as his arrogance that had thrown him into the pit. As his biographer has noted, the "ability to adopt a serviceable solution regardless of accepted wisdom was a great part of Heisenberg's genius. Born of brilliance, ambition, and youthful ignorance and independence, boldness remained with Heisenberg throughout his career and distinguished his audacious, intuitive style of physics." His motto, indeed, was "success sanctifies the means," and "his legendary intuition permitted him to leap to a bold solution without stumbling over intervening steps. . . . He could even tolerate contradictions in his own final results."[33] But the other side of this intuitive genius was his arrogant insistence on defending with bitter stubbornness even untenable aspects of what he regarded as the general truth of his theories. For five months in 1927 Heisenberg had fought Bohr over his uncertainty paper despite the serious errors that the Danish physicist had criticized. A mere error, thought Heisenberg,

30. *OE*, p. 112. (It is implied by the famous Bohr-Wheeler article on fission published in 1939. See above, chaps. 4 and 5.)

31. *OE*, p. 119.

32. Heisenberg "forgot" about the random-walk error for the rest of his life, and never recalled or discussed it in any of his writings or interviews. When J. J. Ermenc raised the resulting critical mass of "tons" in an interview of 1967 (but without mentioning the random-walk calculation that produced that figure), Heisenberg angrily expostulated that this Farm Hall quotation from Groves's memoirs was obviously ridiculous. The first printed reference to the random-walk analysis seems to be in R. V. Jones, *Most Secret War* (London, 1978). This appeared after Heisenberg's death, though Jones had told David Irving about it in the 1960s and it is conceivable that Irving may have brought up the matter with Heisenberg—and been dissuaded in this, as in several other matters, by a glib Heisenberg response. (See above, chaps. 2 and 3.)

33. Cassidy, pp. 124–126, 291.

should not hold back his great paper.[34] In this case, the general truth of the paper eventually overcame its errors, and so Heisenberg's stubbornness and arrogance were reinforced. It was fortunate for the world that the same traits reemerged in his theory of the atomic bomb. So convinced of the general truth of his atomic bomb theory was Heisenberg from 1939 to 1945 that in the decades following Hiroshima he insisted and believed that the random-walk calculation simply did not matter: It had been a mere technical error compared to the power of his general analysis of the atomic bomb problem.

34. See ibid., p. 242.

PART III

Culture:
German Patriotism, German Morality, and the Truth of Physics

The foregoing chapters have tried to answer the first questions posed in the prologue: Did Heisenberg know how to make a bomb? Did he decide not to? Now we may approach two other questions of a more diffuse and indeed difficult nature: Why did Heisenberg agree to work on the bomb project at all, especially in 1939–40, when it still seemed to hold out a chance of practical success? And, more speculatively, would he have made the bomb, had he known how?

The answers to these questions turn on Heisenberg's way of thinking about moral and political matters, and so we must first examine how his moral character and sensibility were shaped by the specifically German social and cultural environment in which he was raised.

CHAPTER 15

The German Context

Unpolitical Politics

I am not a Nazi, but a German.[1]
HEISENBERG, 1944

We do not have an old democratic tradition, and we Germans are in general grateful when we can turn over the responsibility for public life to our superior authorities.[2]
HEISENBERG, 1951

These extraordinarily gifted people had a childish relationship to the state. State and Fatherland were simply equated. Whatever the state demanded from them, that was demanded by the Fatherland. Hence, their characteristic acquiescence. . . .[3]
WALTER SCHEEL, FEDERAL GERMAN PRESIDENT, 1979

What explains the strange violation of common sense so often encountered in the postwar recollections and excuses offered by major cultural figures of the Nazi period? To any Western European or American viewer, Leni Riefenstahl's *Triumph of the Will* is a blatantly political film, both for its choice of a Nazi Nuremberg Rally as subject matter and for its treatment of the subject in a style glorifying Nazism, Hitler, and the German race. Yet Riefenstahl herself has always claimed that *Triumph of the Will* was an apolitical work of art, not propaganda but merely the artistic documentary filming of an event: "Work and peace are the only messages of *Triumph of the Will*," she recently declared—not the glorification of Hitler.[4] Few Western critics—including modern German critics—have been convinced by these almost pro forma justifications, since the Western mind finds it hard to comprehend how politics and art can be separated in such a self-contradictory and indeed

1. Remark at a dinner in Zurich, December 1944, quoted in N. Dawidoff, *The Catcher Was a Spy: The Mysterious Life of Moe Berg* (New York, 1994), p. 206 (see below, chap. 19).
2. Heisenberg in 1951, quoted in Cassidy, p. 537.
3. Walter Scheel's address to the Einstein-Laue-Hahn-Meitner Centenary Symposium of the Max-Planck-Gesellschaft (*Reden zum 100. Geburtstag von Einstein, Hahn, Meitner, von Laue*, Dokumentationsreihe der Freien Universität Berlin [Berlin, 1979], p. 24). Cf. H. Casimir, *Haphazard Reality* (New York, 1983), p. 193.
4. See the recent comments, for example, on Riefenstahl's *Leni Riefenstahl: A Memoir* (New York, 1993) and on Ray Muller's documentary film *The Wonderful, Horrible Life of Leni Riefenstahl* (1993) in the *New York Times*, 26 September 1993, 14 October 1993, 13 and 16 March 1994.

absurd way. The same may be said of the notorious case of Heidegger. The philosopher claimed to be "apolitical," but to an outside observer he seems to have been mired in practical Nazi politics in 1933–34, seeking to Nazify the German university system, making rectorial speeches at Freiburg in favor of the Nazi revolution, and proclaiming Hitler as the embodiment of German history, past and future. Yet for Heidegger, who thought in German categories, his unshaken faith in the "inner truth and greatness" of Nazism was not a "political" attitude, but rather an unpolitical existential commitment. After the war, of course, even Heidegger recognized that these outspoken remarks needed some glossing if they were to pass the scrutiny of his Western readers, though some of these postwar justifications of his Nazi involvement in themselves must strike a Western reader as bizarre. His depiction of his conduct during the Nazi years as having even been a clear declaration of "spiritual resistance" to the regime—even though he remained a Nazi party member until 1945—seems almost laughable when viewed in the crisp light of Western common sense. Nevertheless, even if Heidegger's various efforts at self-justification are permeated with the sort of half-truths and evasions that are so characteristic of German apologies, they still acquire a certain logic, reasonableness, and consistency when interpreted through the preconceptions of German mentality: Supporting Hitler and wearing a Nazi badge are not really expressions of political belief, but rather of a moral inner closeness to the deepest apolitical ideals of the Nazi regime—work, peace, authenticity, humanity.[5]

The same kind of puzzle is found when we turn to figures who were less tarred with Nazism than Riefenstahl and Heidegger. The conductor Wilhelm Furtwängler had held serious doubts about the Nazi regime, attempting (unsuccessfully) in 1933–34 to defend Jewish musicians and declining to conduct "officially" (though willing to do so in a "freelance" capacity) in occupied France. Yet how is one to close one's eyes to the active and uncritical collusion with Nazism so vividly to be seen in those famous photographs of Furtwängler conducting for a row of Nazi dignitaries with a large swastika in the background, or smilingly chatting with Hitler backstage at Bayreuth?[6]

The solution to these riddles and contradictions is to be sought in the peculiarities of German mentality and sensibility, in the deep mythologies of German culture and its unspoken assumptions and perceptions, in the very un-Western "German" ideas of freedom, truth, and humanity, and in the uniquely German conception of politics and culture.[7] Without these keys to unlock the riddles of

5. Texts in R. Wolin, *The Heidegger Controversy* (New York, 1991). See the complementary treatments in V. Farias, *Heidegger and Nazism*, trans. (Philadelphia, 1989), and H. Ott, *Martin Heidegger: A Political Life*, trans. (New York, 1993).

6. See the penetrating review by R. J. Evans of S. H. Shirakawa's misconceived biography of Furtwängler, *The Devil's Music Master*, in the *Times Literary Supplement*, 13 November 1992.

7. F. Stern, *The Failure of Illiberalism: Essays on the Political Culture of Modern Germany*, rev. ed. (Chicago, 1975), especially the introduction and chap. 1, "The Political Consequences of the Unpolitical Ger-

German history and culture, one cannot comprehend the "otherness" of German life, the peculiarity of German politics and culture, the "German enigma." To understand why the problems of Riefenstahl, Heidegger, Furtwängler—and Heisenberg—have proven so intractable, we must abandon our Western rationality and sensibility and begin to think and feel "German." The false paradoxes and contradictions generated by looking at German history through the distorting lenses of Western liberal and rational thought will then dissolve and allow us to see those great icons in their true image—*as they really were*—and not as they are depicted by their defenders and enemies alike as Western constructs.

The Nazi era intensified certain long-standing German tendencies to an extreme degree, forcing major nonpolitical personalities such as Riefenstahl, Furtwängler, Heidegger, and Heisenberg to become more open and committed than they would have liked, and pushing their logic of acquiescence in Nazism to the limit, while exploiting their ambivalence about a movement that presented itself as the fulfillment of the best aspects of what was "German." In "normal" times, all four might have avoided having to make any concession to the world of politics. Without the Nazi revolution, they would have remained safely isolated in their respective worlds of film, music, philosophy, and physics. But Hitler forced them out of their own domains, and by the time they crossed the border into the realm of the political, they had already internalized the customs of their new Fatherland. The essential dispositions of German national culture had been instilled in them by their own "German formation"—by education, family, religion, and social life—and prepared them for their new life under Nazism. Some of them may have been aware of how Hitler was distorting those traditional German dispositions, but nevertheless they were all too much prisoners of their own culture to escape the attractions of Hitler, no matter how much they had reservations about the new regime. The congruence of the underlying mental reflexes of an older Germany and the Third Reich, for all the distortion and exploitation of the former by the latter, suggests that these celebrated cases of the Nazi era were actually only a special and extreme variation of a more profound and long-standing crux of German mentality in politics and culture.

Of these assumptions, the most fundamental had received its classic formulation by Martin Luther.[8] In his major tracts *On Christian Freedom* (1520) and *On Obedience to Governmental Authority* (1523), Luther had postulated two kinds of freedom,

---

man." See also G. Craig, *The Germans* (New York, 1982). A. Dundes, *Life Is Like a Chicken Coop Ladder: A Portrait of German Culture through Folklore* (New York, 1984), is an interesting, if monothematic, analysis in social-anthropological perspective of what might be called "deep culture," though Dundes uses the misleading term "national character."

8. See the extensive bibliography and discussion (most of it skeptical, however, about Luther's contribution to German authoritarianism) in the essays by J. D. Tracy, T. A. Brady, Jr., and E. W. Gritsch included in *Luther and the Modern State*, Sixteenth Century Essays and Studies, vol. 7, ed. J. D. Tracy (Kirksville, Mo., 1986).

inner and outer. Outer freedom was what a Western political thinker would term true freedom—that is, political and social liberty, the protection of individual rights, the right of resistance to tyranny, and so on. In sixteenth-century France, Protestant rebels against royal Catholic authority had transformed this outer freedom into a practical and theoretical ideology of resistance to unjust power, so laying the foundations of modern liberal democracy. But this was never the case in Germany. There Luther's second freedom, the inner freedom of spiritual salvation, completely eclipsed the first kind. A person was "free" if he was justified by grace and secure in the spiritual certainty of his redemption. It did not matter what happened outside that happy "inner" person; he might be afflicted, oppressed, beaten, killed, but he would still be free. This Lutheran distinction between inner and outer freedom was no abstraction, but a living reality, as the German peasantry and other rival heretics of Luther's found to their cost. In 1525 the German peasants revolted, claiming that Luther's doctrine of spiritual freedom sanctioned their rising up against the godless nobles who oppressed them. Luther at first gave them a *Friendly Admonition* that they were misinterpreting his theology and reading the Gospel "carnally." The two realms of inner Christian freedom and outer carnal political freedom were not to be connected. The peasants' duty as Christians was to obey the worldly power of "the sword," while remaining secure in their inner freedom as true Christians. When the peasants declined to take this advice, Luther was thrown into a panic by his noble patrons' growing suspicion of the soundness of his religious views, and he then uttered one of the most violent incitements in German history, urging the princes to "stab, kill, strangle, and mutilate the rebellious peasants." This political outburst has often been taken by non-German observers as a case of Luther's hypocrisy, inasmuch as he claimed for himself the right to political and religious conscience and resistance against the powers of both church and state while denying the same right to others. Luther himself, however, would never have conceded this, since in his mind the peasants were misreading the Gospel, while he was in possession of the correct religious interpretation, that which justified the political murder of the peasants. It was not he who was letting politics transgress into the realm of religion, but rather the peasants. Nevertheless, though Luther's position may make sense theoretically, it scarcely does so when subjected to the light of reasonable moral scrutiny. Then Luther's conduct seems to be a prime case of bad-faith arguments, instigated by a fit of panic that his mission to save men's souls had been placed in jeopardy by the willful political actions—pretending to religious freedom—of the peasantry.

To appreciate the significance of this (in Western eyes) disreputable reaction by Luther, one must remember that Luther is a crucial figure in the formation of modern German mentality and culture, admired by figures as diverse as Heine, Wagner, and Hitler, and whose impact goes beyond Protestantism in particular, and indeed religion in general. His translation of the Bible, which shaped the German language into its modern form; his invocations of the German nation as a unique people victimized by others; his ferocious attacks on the Jews—all these gave shape to an emerging modern German mentality and sensibility, and so too his conception of inner and outer freedom, entailing the need for obedience to secular power and the illegitimacy of resistance, was internalized to form the structure of modern German political consciousness. The impact of Luther's doctrine of obedience emerges in sharp relief in his translation of a key Pauline text, which in the pre-Lutheran bibles as well as in the English and French versions of the Reformation reads: "Let every soul be subject to higher powers [*höheren Gewalten*], for there is no power but from God" (Paul, Rom. 13:1). Here the phrase "higher powers" has a complex religious rather than a simply political meaning, but Luther chose two singular terms, *Gewalt* (coercive power) and *Obrigkeit* (authority), that would emphasize the political significance of the precept: "Let everyone be subject to the authority that has power [*Gewalt*] . . . for all authority is ordained by God." Even in post-Hitler Germany, this passage continued to exercise its spell in Church and other circles. When Bishop Otto Dibelius, who had during the war urged his Christian friends not to obey the totalitarian state, wrote a pamphlet in 1959 criticizing Luther's authoritarianism, a colleague retorted, "I cannot share Dibelius's views—authority is authority!" Dibelius remembered all too well theologians telling him, "All authority is from God. All, Herr Bishop, all!" causing him to turn away "not entirely without bitterness."[9] For Dietrich Bonhoeffer, Luther's view of the state denied the necessity of resistance to tyranny, while Karl Barth came to regard Luther as a major source of Hitler's tyranny—"the bad dream of the German pagan."[10] This German insistence on obedience to authority should be contrasted to the France of Luther's time, where Calvinist and *politique* emphasis on the individual's private religious conscience produced the nascent doctrine of the political right of resistance. German Calvinism never generated any such liberal democratic sensibility; the Prussian duty of obedience overruled individual conscience.

In the eighteenth century, Luther's religious formula of inner freedom was secularized into the new language of Enlightenment philosophy.[11] Kant redefined inner freedom in terms of his idealist philosophy, which perceived freedom as the free exercise of critical reason. Reason made the individual a moral being and granted him a moral autonomy in his own right. Through his doctrine of the categorical imperative, Kant argued that each man should be regarded as a human being who, as an end in himself, ought never to be treated as though he were merely a means; at the same time, Kant insisted on the universal application of

9. Many interesting observations in A. Elon, *Journey through a Haunted Land: The New Germany* (London, 1967), pp. 169 ff., illustrate vividly how many of the old German traditions that had made Nazism possible survived on in the 1960s, despite the renunciation of Nazism itself.

10. D. Bonhoeffer, *No Rusty Swords: Letters, Lectures, and Notes, 1928–1936*, trans. (New York, 1965), p. 324. K. Barth, *Eine Schweizer Stimme, 1938–1945* (Zurich, 1948), p. 113 (letter of 1939).

11. See Heine's *History of Religion and Philosophy in Germany*, ed. P. L. Rose (North Queensland, 1982), for this process.

moral laws that would prevent privileged exceptions being made that would subvert his first precept. Yet while this might seem like a propounding of liberal individual rights, the categorical imperative was not as liberal as it might appear to a non-German reader. Instead, as John Dewey has observed, it has something of the drill sergeant about it, for its essence lies in the Kantian concept of duty and obedience, which so aptly reflected the Prussian ethos in which the philosopher lived.[12] Even if one's conscience tells one that a particular law is wrong, one may not legitimately resist the state, but rather is bound to obey or submit, should conscience dictate, to punishment. The liberal individualism of Kant's moral writings is weakened further by his political philosophy, which amounts to an endorsement of the rightfulness of the powers that be—no matter how distasteful their actions—provided they have the power to command obedience. The general attitude of Kant, therefore, is very close in practice to Luther's acceptance of the "sword." In sum, Kant's philosophy, which became the major articulation of the rational German tradition of moral and political thinking, accords individual conscience a quite different significance from that of Western liberal thought, where conscience legitimates political resistance. What mattered for Kant was whether the individual could retain his integrity of moral autonomy (that is, inner freedom), rather than whether the individual could practically resist evil in politics. Worse, Kant was quite ruthless in denouncing resistance of any kind. "There is no legitimate resistance by the people. . . . The slightest attempt at this is high treason, and the traitor of this type, as one who seeks to destroy his country, must be punished with no less than death. It is the duty of the people to endure even an intolerable misuse of the supreme power."[13] Kant may have, as sometimes argued, believed that the moral law was superior to the law of the state, but this did not delegitimate the unjust state. Moreover, Germans very rarely went against the prevailing lesson of obedience to authority, or invoked the Antigonian potential of the categorical imperative to justify obedience to the moral law. (A reluctant exception was the philosopher Karl Huber, a member of the anti-Nazi White Rose resistance group in Munich.)[14]

The very ideas of morality and humanity diverged in their Western and German versions. In Kant's philosophy, objective "Reason" had become the arbiter not only of scientific truth, but also of morality, which was thus effectively stripped of its emotional or affective content. One might grasp the impact of this process by noting that whereas for Western liberals "humanity" connoted "humanitarianism" and emotional motivation for the reduction of human suffering, as in the movement for the abolition of slavery, by contrast in the German context *Human-*

12. J. Dewey, *German Philosophy and Politics* (New York, 1915; reissued, New York, 1942 and 1979), p. 57. This remains the most brilliant analysis of the subject, but see now the searching paper by J. R. Silber, "Kant at Auschwitz," in *Proceedings of the Sixth International Kant Congress* (Washington D.C., 1991), I, 177–211. See also L. Dumont, *German Ideology* (Chicago, 1994), for fresh anthropological approaches.

13. Kant, *Metaphysics of Morals,* vol. 1, *Rechtslehre,* trans. (Cambridge, 1991).

14. R. Hanser, *A Noble Treason* (New York, 1979).

ität was essentially a rational concept that could be used, for example, to justify antisemitism. This concept was applied to argue that the Jews lacked "pure humanity" because of their alleged rejection of reason and true "human" freedom. In effect, this argument was a secularization of earlier Christian reproaches of "Jewish stubbornness" in refusing to be redeemed by Christ.[15]

Dewey has admirably described how Kant gave a powerful impulse to the strengthening of the paradoxical (so it seems to outsiders) German tendency to combine an extremely abstract rational idealism with extraordinary efficiency in the realm of practical matters of government and organization, particularly in the fields of bureaucracy, education, and the military. This practical talent was, however, flawed by a notable incapacity to behave with pragmatic common sense in practical politics as understood in liberal democratic societies. Again, the German conception of inner freedom yields the solution to the paradox: Because outer freedom is nugatory, there is no moral impediment as there would be in Western societies to the efficient organizing of the inferior outer world of "phenomena." What mattered was the preservation of the pure inner world, the true and moral universe of rational religion, rational morality and freedom, the universe of scientific and philosophical truth. As long as these remained inviolate, their sullied correlatives in the political world could be disregarded—providing, that is, that efficient order was maintained.

As the modern German nation-state emerged in the nineteenth century, it acquired a philosophical justification and rationalization that were most famously explained by Hegel. Hegel argued that the driving force of world history, the spirit of reason, had animated various nations in sequence, raising each to a peak before deserting it for a fresher culture. Each nation contributed something unique to the progress of universal humanity, but in the modern era the spirit of reason had reached its apogee in the Prussian state, which was the purest exemplar to date of reason and human freedom. The Prussian bureaucracy, the Prussian general staff, the Prussian universities—all were reflections of pure reason. And because (as in Kant) reason and freedom were intertwined, Prussia was not only the most rational but the most free of states—not in a Western liberal sense, of course, since it was an absolute monarchy, but in a transcendentally "human"—and quintessentially "German"—sense. This hymn to Prussian moral supremacy never lacked an appreciative chorus, and it contributed mightily to the atmosphere of arrogant self-righteousness that developed in the later nineteenth century and formed the psychological motor for the later disasters of German history. (Even though Hegel himself may have intended his philosophy to have a covertly subversive meaning and may not perhaps have been the crude Prussian nationalist he seemed, his philosophy was largely taken at its surface level in Germany.)

15. P. L. Rose, *German Question/Jewish Question: Revolutionary Antisemitism in Germany from Kant to Wagner* (Princeton, 1994). For secular transformation in general, see J. L. Talmon, *Political Messianism: The Romantic Phase* (London, 1960).

Although Kant and Hegel may have prepared the way for the authoritarian, obedience-driven German state of the Kaiser, the figure who transformed that ethos into a proto-Nazi mentality was the composer Richard Wagner, whose ferocious antisemitism and prophetic German supremacism powerfully shaped Hitler's own outlook. Wagner followed the German unpolitical tradition of inner freedom, always defining himself as an "artist" and insisting that "art" was separate from "politics." Yet, like so many of his cultural heirs in the Nazi state, Wagner dabbled in some rather heavily political activity, while all the time denying it by invoking his "apolitical" stance. This produced the usual paradoxes: In the 1860s and during the Franco-Prussian War, Wagner would condemn aggressive war and the immorality of the "power state," but found no problem in urging Bismarck on to a war of total destruction of the French and the burning of Paris. Not surprisingly, Wagner's enthusiasm for the new Bismarckian Reich turned to denunciations of its "Jewish" spirit once state support for his own Bayreuth project failed to materialize. The same sort of (to Western minds) contradictory attitudes emerged during the years of Winifred Wagner's alignment of the Bayreuth Festival with Hitler's personal patronage; Winifred was able to keep the festival "artistically" independent while blatantly identifying it with the Nazi spirit of Hitler, who would attend it annually with great pomp. Many years after the war, Winifred uninhibitedly would say that she still regarded Hitler as a human and artistic friend and not at all a politician—this despite the fact that she had earlier taken the very political action of joining the Nazi party in 1923. This confusion of the artistic and the political, of inner and outer freedom, lies at the heart of the experiences of the German intellectual elite under Hitler. The basic mental framework was central to German tradition, even if its full grotesqueness emerged only under the extreme pressures of Nazism.

German thinkers were generally oblivious of how peculiar this muddled complex of ideas and preconceptions was. One of the great exceptions—all the more remarkable because he for a long time subscribed wholeheartedly to it—was the writer Thomas Mann. After the catastrophe of the First World War, however, Mann came gradually to recognize that perhaps Western liberalism gave rise to a less distorted vision of life, and one that was not after all incompatible with the sacred mission of the innerly free "artist." In his *Reflections of an Unpolitical Man* (1918) Mann had extolled at immense length the standard German view of freedom, disparaging the Western view of "outer" individual freedom as shallow and superficial, in contrast to the depth of German spiritual freedom. But by 1920 Mann had changed; now he embraced to a large degree the Western idea of liberal democratic freedom as something that might animate both politics and art. Exiled under Hitler, Mann in his wartime broadcasts and lectures hammered home the disastrous effect of the "unpolitical" ethos on German life. In a 1944 article in the *Atlantic Monthly*, "What Is German," Mann condemned the German unpolitical mentality as not only misguided but dangerous, in that it gave birth to aberrations like Nazism.

The German mentality is essentially indifferent to social and political questions. . . . Translated from political terminology into the psychological, National Socialism means: "I do not want the social at all. I want the folk fairy-tale." But in the political realm, the fairy-tale becomes a murderous lie.[16]

But so profound was the conditioning of the apolitical that even Mann could slip back, in that same essay, into peculiar habits of German thinking (e.g., the idea of the "two Germanies," one artistic and innocent, the other political and evil), which outraged his American readers of the time. Even in his "liberal" period and despite his wife's being of Jewish ancestry, Mann could also evince—like Heisenberg—a peculiarly German antisemitism. After the war, of course, Mann was never forgiven in Germany by those literary colleagues who had stayed on to profit from the patronage of the Nazi regime. Their view, uttered without a tinge of shame, was that by becoming an "outer" political emigrant Mann had betrayed the Germany of art and inner freedom, whereas they, by staying on, had effectively emigrated "innerly," preserving the inner freedom of art and so actually "resisting" Nazi tyranny: Mann had spent his years abroad in comfort, while they had suffered the mental agony of being successful protégés of the Nazi regime! Faced with this incredibly immoral foolishness, Mann refused to live in Germany after the war.

Since 1945 German cultural figures have been adept at exploiting the ambiguities of the unpolitical or apolitical mentality in order to portray their conduct and thinking in terms likely to appeal to Westerners prone to misread these excuses in the context of Western traditions. Such self-serving terms include the difficulties of living under "dictatorship and terror"; the "powerlessness" of the artist in such conditions; the retention of personal integrity nonetheless; that some artists were "apolitical" and so never joined the Nazi party; that those artists who did join the party still disapproved of its policies; that artists could in integrity admire the "good side" of Hitler that resembled Western politics (improved living standards, reduced unemployment); and so forth. These excuses may sound quite persuasive to many a Western reader, but one has to set them in German historical context if their essential fallacies are to be understood. Then it becomes clear that the "good" of Nazism is not really "good" at all in any Western sense, for it is part of an evil whole that distorts and discredits any of the apparent good. Hitler's kindness to children is not really "good," since it occurs in the context of his concept of racial domination, which entails great cruelty toward so many other millions of children. In contrast, normal kindness to children, like Western politics in general, is based on ideals of justice and mercy, which, though often violated, are good in themselves. The evils that occur in normal democratic societies can be tolerated to a degree because of the general morality of the whole system. But the Nazi system was founded on ideals that are intrinsically evil—preeminently the enslavement

16. T. Mann, "What Is German?" *Atlantic Monthly,* May 1944, pp. 78–85.

and murder of other races—and this means that any particular "goods" that the system produces are really not good at all; the only true goods in such a system are those that develop in opposition to the system. Nazism has no "good side"—for the apparently good (which would be truly good in a liberal system) is fused into a whole that is organically bad. Again, in the case of the terror argument, Western liberals are inclined to empathize with the fate of a population subjected to a dictatorship that rules by terror against the will of the people. But to believe that terror alone forced the German people to support Hitler is historically naive. The Gestapo was statistically only a small force; Hitler counted instead on his appeal to profoundly respectable elements of German mentality and tradition to attract the German people and win their consent, if not enthusiasm; the traditional elements that Hitler invoked were military and civic obedience, self-sacrifice, respectability, dignity, and so forth—all virtues in a liberal system, but debased when they served an evil system. As to the excuse that one was not "political," this is persuasive because a Western listener has grown up in a system that actually assumes that everyone is political, in the sense that all have a civic duty that obliges them to act politically whenever moral standards are violated. But in the German context, this is not so. Of *Zivilcourage*, as one German pastor who did resist Hitler put it, "we Germans have no concept, and indeed no authentic German word for it," only a Germanized French term. In German tradition, one's moral sense may be outraged, but that does not entitle one to act politically. Only "politicals" act politically, and they are customarily defined as being people who belong to a political party, rather than the ordinary citizen. Thus, unless one is professionally qualified to make a political protest, one simply keeps quiet. Here a sort of "professionalization" is reinforcing the idea of inner and outer freedom. One may disapprove morally of some aspects of Nazism ("retain one's inner freedom and moral integrity"), but one will not do anything political about it because such action lies in the sphere of outer freedom.[17]

This explains the frequently encountered circular sequence of passing the buck of "conscience" in the Nazi period: The Church passes the duty of resistance on to the politicians, who then pass it on to the military, who return it to the Church, and so on. Moreover, even when certain Germans did, with enormous courage, attempt to assassinate Hitler, one has the impression that the general reason for their individual failures was that their hearts were not really in it. Their German

---

17. See Hedwig Born's analysis of the difference between German and British political culture in H. Born and M. Born, *Der Luxus des Gewissens* (Munich, 1969), pp. 151–170, which points out that whereas British individuals have both a private and a public life in which they are responsible for the good of the family and the nation, Germans have only private lives (though, of course, they are obliged to serve as the state demands). As a typical example of the contrast between British and German sensibility, Mrs. Born recalls a conversation with a German Nazi visitor in 1937 in which he observed condescendingly that the British had no word for *Gemütlichkeit* (a warm coziness). She replied tartly that neither did they have a word for *Schadenfreude* (joy at another's misfortune).

cultural conditioning had been so profound that they could not, at some level of their sensibility, really believe they were doing the right thing in resisting. They had no right to arrogate to themselves the decision of what was politically right.

A final excuse that appeals to Western tastes is that one was simply fighting for one's country, just as the Allied soldiers were: One thus fought out of patriotism, not because of loyalty to the Nazi regime. But again this is a fraudulent argument. In the Western context, one fights for a country that is basically civilized despite one's disapproval of its government or some of its social aspects; but in Germany the "country" was entirely rotted by Nazism and a victory could only produce greater evil. In other words, the excuse of patriotism has validity in a liberal democracy, but not in a Nazi state.

With this German cultural context in mind, let us now turn to the specific case of Heisenberg's moral and political relationship to the Nazi regime.

CHAPTER 16

The Unpolitical Heisenberg

Patriot and Physicist, 1918–33

[Many people in 1933] took a very optimistic view of the situation. They all thought that civilized Germans would not stand for anything really rough happening. The reason I took the opposite position was based on observations of rather small and insignificant things. I noticed that the Germans always took a utilitarian point of view. They asked, "Well, suppose I would oppose this, what good would I do? I wouldn't do very much good, I would just lose my influence. Then, why should I oppose it?" You see, the moral point of view was completely absent, or very weak, and every consideration was simply, what would be the predictable consequence of my action. And on that basis did I reach the conclusion in 1931 that Hitler would get into power, not because the forces of the Nazi revolution were so strong, but rather because I thought that there would be no resistance whatsoever.

LEO SZILARD[1]

Do you not believe that, in the event of a successful revolution along my Party's lines, the brains would not come over to us in droves? Do you believe that the German bourgeoisie [scornfully]— the flower of the intelligentsia—would refuse to follow us and place their brains at our disposal? The German bourgeoisie would, as usual, accept the fait accompli.

ADOLF HITLER, 1931[2]

If Heisenberg had been asked—are you a patriot?—he would have said: "What a pompous word. I think myself a German."

CARL-FRIEDRICH VON WEIZSÄCKER[3]

Heisenberg was not a "Nazi"—at least technically. He was, by his own lights and those of many of his colleagues, a largely decent man, who behaved in what was for him an honorable fashion and who adopted what to him seemed a deeply moral position that preserved at all times his integrity. That non-Germans could judge his actions and words otherwise—judging that his behavior was redolent of shameful compromise, that he acted weakly and confused moral purpose with his own private comfort, that he was a profoundly opportunistic character, that he

---

1. "Reminiscences," in *The Intellectual Migration: Europe and America, 1930–1960,* ed. D. Fleming and B. Bailyn (Cambridge, Mass., 1969), pp. 95 f.
2. E. Calic, *Secret Conversations with Hitler: The Two Newly Discovered 1931 Interviews,* trans. (New York, 1971), p. 36.
3. Interview in *Operation Epsilon: Die Farm-Hall-Protokolle,* ed. D. Hoffmann (Berlin, 1994), p. 336.

failed in his duty as a human being—all these severe judgments seemed to him not only offensive, but utterly incomprehensible. On his deathbed, Heisenberg asked quite sincerely just why it was that "people had so little understood his attempt to act rightly in politics." Yet this very inability of Heisenberg's to comprehend the justice of such accusations is itself in turn incomprehensible to many of his non-German critics. As Heisenberg's more sophisticated friend Carl-Friedrich von Weizsäcker remarked, "what was involved—and unresolvable—was a misunderstanding of a clear [Heisenberg's] moral decision by another clear [Western] moral decision."[4] We encounter here an immense gulf between mentalities, which raises difficult problems of both moral and historical judgment. Though Weizsäcker's relativizing of German and Western morality is rather too facile, we may admit that Heisenberg was acting morally in his own terms, but still conclude that his German morality was mistaken and without true moral insight. The situation is made all the worse by Heisenberg's glib attempts to rationalize the indefensible in an often absurd manner, and the all too ready resort to half-truth, evasion, and self-delusion that has been noted in the opening chapters of this book.

What induced Heisenberg, like so many other decent Germans, to accept the sickening compromises with Nazism—compromises that led him to justify first of all the Nazi regime in the 1930s, and then, worse still, the brutal conquests of Hitler? There is an interesting problem here, because Heisenberg's apologetic tendency was active not only during the war, when it might have been an advantageous or prudential strategy, but even after the war, when Heisenberg had a great deal to lose by putting forth such justifications of German aggression. Obviously Heisenberg's gratuitous apologizing was driven by a very powerful system of belief and values that rendered him oblivious to the moral enormity of what he was saying and the fact that he was giving great offense to his listeners. So deeply conditioned was Heisenberg by the elements of German culture and behavior he had internalized that he was deaf to what he himself was saying. To put it another way, Heisenberg was so persuaded of the essential morality of his German worldview that he could not comprehend how it might appear immoral or indeed evil to anyone else. Even though he gradually learned to curb himself in his expressions, there is no evidence that Heisenberg ever truly confronted his behavior and mentality during the Nazi period in any way meaningful to moral judgment (in the Western sense of the term).

Heisenberg's political attitudes were characteristic of the basic "apolitical" mentality of the German professorial class. That is, he insisted on the separation of his professional duties and moral outlook from "politics." *Politics* here meant what in the West would be called the normal conflict of interested parties and groups, in which individuals participated for either selfish or altruistic reasons. Such political involvement was, however, regarded by German academics as lack-

4. C.-F. von Weizsäcker and B. L. van der Waerden, *Werner Heisenberg* (Munich, 1977), pp. 33–34, 40.

ing respectability; one could fulfill one's civic duty without such political participation as speaking out in support of the Weimar political system when it was under
threat. Worse, from this perspective, the Weimar Republic was an unwelcome
regime of political—that is, democratic—excess whose achievements were to be at
best tolerated by the apolitical scholar, whose political ideal lay either in the conservative Second Empire of the Kaiser, which imposed a constitutional order and
a valid social justice, or in a future Third Reich that would revolutionize human
potential in a metapolitical process. The mundane liberal-democratic ideals of the
Weimar Republic lacked appeal—and legitimacy. It was hardly more than a dis-
pensable interregnum between the German past and the German future, an imposition of victor's justice after the unmerited defeat of 1918, something lacking
truly German roots and reality, and as such destined to pass away. To Westerners,
of course, this inclination for an old authoritarian empire or a new revolutionary
one, and the associated aversion to Weimar democracy, appear as political points
of view. But to Heisenberg and many others, their support of such illiberal states
remained distinctly "apolitical": Their support was spiritual, patriotic, social, national, cultural, moral, natural—indeed, anything but the detested "political" behavior that defense of the Weimar Republic represented. "Politics" was participation in Weimar and illicit, whereas sympathy for anti-Weimar sentiments was
defended as a decently "apolitical" stance. It should be understood, however, that
this basically conservative apolitical stance did not preclude Heisenberg and his
family from supporting a socialist government during the Weimar period; that was
seen as "decent" politics, insofar as it was supporting a government that represented authority. Weimar's socialists could find some legitimation in the public
mind through their covert rearmament and foreign policies, as well as their enforcement of social order by repressing revolutionary left-wing movements while
promoting their own progressive social legislation. Still, even these saving graces
did not really vindicate the Weimar liberal-democratic establishment and inspire
genuine loyalty to it. Weimar remained a mechanical system, rather than something organically German.

Heisenberg was educated—indeed born—into this prevailing mentality.[5] The
outbreak of the Great War in 1914 had produced a swelling of patriotic pride in
the German professoriate that convinced them utterly of the justice of their cause
and blinded them to the fact that by all the civilized international standards of the
time, Germany's violation of Belgian neutrality constituted an act of aggression.
The resulting justifications and rationalizations of the German cause set the
young Heisenberg's mind firmly on the course that led to his own later apologies
for Nazi military victories. Heisenberg's own father volunteered for military service, although the various unpleasantnesses associated with the front led within

5. For a superb analysis of Heisenberg's intellectual and personal formation, see D. C. Cassidy, *Uncertainty: The Life and Science of Werner Heisenberg* (New York, 1991).

some months to his seeking reassignment back home and a diminishing of his military enthusiasm. This family discretion in matters of valor was something that the patriotic Heisenberg never could come fully to terms with, sometimes claiming that a wound had necessitated his father's return.[6] Nevertheless, Heisenberg's own later cautiousness in his dealings with the Third Reich may well have been a family trait. He was certainly patriotic and willing to serve—or alternatively, to resist—at some personal risk, but only to a degree, at which point an almost feline discretion took over.

Heisenberg always saw the 1914 war and 1918 revolution as the crucible in which his mature political and moral sensibility was formed. In his curriculum vitae written for the new Nazi overlords of the universities in 1933, Heisenberg made a deft confession to "political" ideas of the right "unpolitical" kind.

> In 1918 I worked on an Upper Bavarian farm as a Labor Service conscript for half a year, and in 1919 I served for some months as a volunteer on Cavalry Protection Commando 11 in order to take part in the struggle against the Soviet Republic in Munich. These two years had an enormous significance for my human development. My position on political questions was perhaps then decided.[7]

In a subsequent gloss of 1943 Heisenberg made it clear that his unit was part of the political White Terror in specifying that it was attached to the "Freikorps Lützow," one of the right-wing nationalist paramilitary groups that conditioned Germany to the reception of Nazism.[8] Membership in a Freikorps affiliate meant that the young Heisenberg received a strong dose of a reactionary patriotism to reinforce the nationalistic patriotism with which he was already imbued. Given this immersion, it is a testimony to the more decent strands of Heisenberg's character that he did not emerge more deeply affected with antisemitism and militarism than he did.[9] In his post-1945 writings Heisenberg made light of this paramilitary involvement, dismissing it as "nothing serious at all" (though this is about as convincing as Gibbon's famous dismissal of his Catholic conversion at Oxford as a "mere youthful enthusiasm").[10] Since Heisenberg's older brother was a member of Bavarian Colonel Franz Ritter von Epp's bitterly antisemitic Freikorps, it may be assumed that Heisenberg was familiar with the political program of these forma-

6. Cassidy, p. 31.

7. W. Heisenberg, *Selbstbiographie* (1933), written for the Halle Akademie Leopoldina, in GWH, C IV, 12. A letter of 18 January 1938 reminds Sommerfeld of this in connection with his candidacy for the Munich chair (Sommerfeld Nachlass, Deutsches Museum, Munich, 1977–28/A, 136/15). I am grateful to Dr. R. Heinrich of the Deutsches Museum for supplying copies of the Heisenberg-Sommerfeld correspondence.

8. W. Heisenberg, *Lebenslauf*, MS of 1943, in GWH, C IV, 14.

9. For a disturbing analysis of the extreme mental ambience of the Freikorps units, see K. Theweleit, *Male Fantasies*, trans. (Minneapolis, 1987).

10. Cassidy, p. 61. (For the serious problems underlying Gibbon's flippancy see P. Turnbull, "The 'Supposed Infidelity' of Edward Gibbon," *The Historical Journal* 25 [1982]: 23–41.)

tions, even if he did not fully subscribe to it. We may accept as being in character, however, Heisenberg's claim that he managed to save the life of one of the Red prisoners he was guarding prior to execution. Heisenberg did have a sympathetic corner in his nature, but it must also be kept in mind that, even as he tells it, the prisoner was released essentially because he was, on Heisenberg's testimony, a decent chap.[11] There is no indication in Heisenberg's text that he felt compassion for the less decent chaps who were executed. This limitation of sympathy by the needs of the state recurs in Heisenberg's later conduct under Nazism: He would exert himself only for the right kinds of people, and even then only so far. His political sensibility of duty and obedience circumscribed his human compassion in a characteristically German fashion.[12]

After this experience, Heisenberg found an outlet for his need to belong in the nascent German youth movement. This dynamic movement, with its insistence on "rambling as the most German of all innate instincts and the mirror of our national character," was from its inception part of the stream of German nationalism, even though it rejected the beer-hall nationalistic slogans of old official Germany. Many of its adherents saw no problem with excluding Jews from membership while "regarding with contempt all those who call us political."

The gulf between German and Western youth movements is to be seen in the different mentalities of the Anglo-American Boy Scouts and their German counterpart, the Pathfinders (*Pfadfinder*). Already nationalistic, rather than internationalistic on the Baden-Powell model, the German scouts were transformed by the 1914 war and its aftermath into a metapolitical group that aimed at a revolutionary remodeling of society. In August 1919 Heisenberg attended their first postwar gathering at Prunn Castle in Bavaria, where he experienced a quasi-religious epiphany.[13] The "New Pathfinders" and their associated groups, including Heisenberg's own little troop (*Gruppe Heisenberg*), proclaimed a new chivalric ideal, soaked in medieval German and romantic allusion, which they reinterpreted in modern terms; they looked to a new "Empire" (*Reich*) of social justice, duty, obedience, and idealistic purpose, a new spiritual aristocracy of "knighthood" and the "Holy Grail," and they expected the coming of a "Leader" (*Führer*)—a "White Knight" (also the title of their journal) who would guide them out of the morass of materialism, defeat, and national dishonor and destroy the corruption of the masses. In true German fashion, they repudiated Western political culture in favor of a more authentic and profounder German form: "People who preached humanism, the right of everybody to happiness, and the progress of mankind, be-

---

11. Cassidy, pp. 58–61.

12. For the illiberal aspects of the dominant political culture of German "patriotism" in the interwar years, see K. Sontheimer, *Antidemokratisches Denken in der Weimarer Republik: Die politischen Ideen des deutschen Nationalismus zwischen 1918 und 1933*, 2d. ed. (Munich, 1968).

13. W. Heisenberg, *Physics and Beyond: Encounters and Conversations*, trans. (New York, 1971), pp. 10 f. Cf. Cassidy, pp. 66–77.

longed to the camp of civilization, not the camp of culture, and could not be taken seriously."[14] These new knights saw their youth movement as "a freedom movement, which has freed itself from the soulless mechanism and materialism of modern civilization." This was, of course, also the mentality that made Heidegger's philosophy so attractive to so many of the post-1918 generation in search of meaning in place of emptiness, but it was also the mood that led Heidegger himself into his faith in Hitler and Nazism, and prevented any genuine loyalty to the "civilization/materialist" politics of Weimar from forming. As Heisenberg put it, following in the example set by Fichte after the French defeat of Prussia in 1806, "I conclude that it is more correct (as our forefathers [did] a hundred years ago!) to hold the enemy in check by cunning and deceit and fright until a hope exists for weapons. That is precisely what the Reich government appears to be doing." Heisenberg was not a liberal, but a *realpolitiker* supporter of Weimar policy.[15] The Weimar Republic was merely an "unpleasant interlude," which was best passed by engaging in scouting expeditions bringing German culture to other Germanic lands such as Finland, and especially to the German minorities isolated under "foreign occupation," such as the Austrians under Italian domination in the Upper Tyrol. The Heisenberg troop's summer camps were not just mindless fun, but inspired by a serious patriotic purpose and the search for something "new" that would replace the beauty and nobility destroyed by the war, as Heisenberg wrote to his father after visiting the Upper Tyrol in 1922. In this high-minded mission may be seen the model for Heisenberg's later propaganda trips to occupied Europe in 1941–44. Already in 1922 Heisenberg had been so converted to the ideal of German salvation through the spread of German culture that he was simply unable to understand why his patronizing visits as an emissary of victorious Nazi Germany twenty years later should give offense to Dutch or Danish scientists (any more than Martin Heidegger could understand why wearing a Nazi badge during his visit to Rome in 1936 should injure the feelings of an exiled former student he met there).[16]

Heisenberg's involvement with the Pathfinders did not lead him into the plainly Nazi mentality adopted by many of his fellow members (indeed, only one of his troop later joined the Nazi party). For one thing, his respectably social-democratic tastes, as well as an aversion to open political and social antisemitism, militated against that. In a split between the Munich Pathfinder groups over adopting anti-

14. W. Laqueur, *Young Germany: The History of the German Youth Movement* (New York, 1962), pp. 6 f., 33, 75, 105, 133–139. See Cassidy, chaps. 5 and 6, for an immense amount of new material on Heisenberg and the youth movement.

15. Heisenberg to Kurt Pflügel, 31 October 1924, quoted in Cassidy, p. 161. Heisenberg fully embraced the patriotism extolled in J. G. Fichte, *Addresses to the German Nation*, chap. 8, trans. (New York, 1968): "People and Fatherland are a support and guarantee of eternity on earth and far transcend the state. . . . This love of Fatherland is the supreme, final and absolute authority."

16. Cassidy, pp. 132 ff. For Heidegger see K. Löwith, *My Life in Germany before and after 1933*, trans. (Urbana and Chicago, 1994), pp. 59 f.

semitic measures (during which certain leaders even approached Hitler to act as sponsor, sending him a copy of the *White Knight* magazine while he was in jail in 1923), Heisenberg seems to have taken quietly the side of those against such overt antisemitism.[17] Like Heidegger, Heisenberg was willing to have Jews participate in playing chamber music, but both German professors retained a strong implicit antisemitism that had long pervaded, even to a large degree defined, German high culture.[18] Such antisemitism has to be looked for in coded expressions—in Heidegger's strictures against rootlessness, cosmopolitanism, and industrialization, and in Heisenberg's rejection of any interest in politics because "it seemed to me to be a pure money business."[19] Though no overt expression of antisemitism has been found in Heisenberg's correspondence with Jewish physicists, there is, however, one shocking example of Heisenberg's latent antisemitism being forced to the surface; this is his late encounter with Max Born, which will be discussed in the final chapter. In German terms, however, Heisenberg was not sufficiently hostile to Jews or Judaism to be classed as an "antisemite"—but neither was he lacking in prejudice against Jews.

Heisenberg's years with the German youth movement were important for shaping his conduct under Nazism. He developed an existential belief in the ethos of the small group of altruists; loyalty to this group helped to limit the tendency of the Führer leadership ideal to balloon into an all too political loyalty to the Führer principle in politics. Through leading his own small troop of White Knights, Heisenberg set a pattern for his eventual leadership of a small circle of physicists devoted to scientific truth, which would try to preserve a moral ethos in the midst of the political storm of Nazism. Unfortunately, Heisenberg's equally strong devotion to the ethos of German patriotism automatically barred this moral stance from becoming resistance to Hitler. Such a resistance was ruled out by the fact that Hitler was the leader of the German nation, and so to defy him meant being disloyal to the Fatherland. Nevertheless, science, music, and his small groups of Pathfinders and physicists allowed Heisenberg to escape from the peril of a total surrender to Nazi politics, to "withdraw to the woods" when the burden of living in the real political world, whether of Weimar or of the Third Reich, became too much.[20] When Heisenberg met his old friend Goudsmit at Heidelberg in April 1945 and sought to justify his conduct under Nazism by referring to medieval knights and so on, Goudsmit was completely at a loss to understand what the physicist was on about and what it could possibly have to do with the disasters of Hitler.

17. Cassidy, pp. 78–81.

18. See P. L. Rose, *German Question/Jewish Question: Revolutionary Antisemitism from Kant to Wagner,* 2d ed. (Princeton, 1992). My teacher Paul Oskar Kristeller recalls participating (despite his unacceptable background) in chamber-music evenings with the openly Nazi and antisemitic Heidegger in the 1930s.

19. Heisenberg to his brother, 1932, quoted in Cassidy, p. 71; cf. p. 571.

20. For this Heideggerian metaphor of "the woods," see Heisenberg to Pflügel, 24 November [1923], quoted in Cassidy, pp. 162 f.

He irritated me very much. .... He told me about his philosophy, not about his physics, namely some abstract parallel or relationship between Christian ethics, knighthood in the middle ages and the Nazi doctrine. I probably did not understand it.[21]

But Heisenberg was desperate to make Goudsmit understand, because the ethos of knighthood constructed by the Pathfinders was the ethos that directed and justified his entire behavior between 1933 and 1945. It was the key to everything.

The problem, of course, was that these naively idealistic hopes lent themselves to corruption, a potential exploited by Hitler. The Prunn Castle avowal that "we want to submit to our leaders, to whom we give our absolute trust" was German in its extremism of naive sentiment; many of those who evinced this emotionality may have denied that it had any political relevance, but even its apolitical utterance conditioned German youth to the habit of obedience to a strong leader.[22] In Heisenberg's case such a mentality enabled him to find rationalizations for the Nazi regime when it came. Although the Third Reich had an in some ways unacceptable Führer, it was nevertheless found palatable as the precursor to a true German Reich in which the Pathfinders' revolutionary spirit would reign under a good Führer.

Heisenberg's religious elevation of science into a supreme form of truth and even morality also carried within it the same capacity for corruption as did his patriotism and his Pathfinder idealism. Most physicists of the day looked for an inner beauty and truth in science, but in Heisenberg's German context this reverence was distorted. Science became a new kind of redemptive religion, a new form of the inner freedom so sought after in German sensibility. As long as one remained true to one's science, that was pure freedom and even humanity.[23] Here lay the seed of much of Heisenberg's later compromises with the Nazi regime. For as long as his science of theoretical physics was left intact, Heisenberg could tolerate the Third Reich's lack of external political freedom. This mentality led Heisenberg into the most abject compromises with Nazism in the matter of the dismissal and exile of his Jewish colleagues; since science itself was the sacred thing, its priests could themselves be sacrificed to preserve its purity. Heisenberg would try to have Max Born return to Germany in 1936, not as an act of human compassion, but rather to have Born's presence help further the achievements of German science. In this Heisenberg displayed to an astonished Born an insensitivity that recurred in so many of his dealings with German-Jewish and non-German

---

21. Goudsmit to Irving, 4 August 1966 (IMF 32). "Knights" are not mentioned in Goudsmit's "ALSOS Report on Interrogation of Heisenberg," 11 May 1945, NA, RG 77, MED Foreign Intelligence Unit, entry 22, box 167, folder 32.12-2. Cf. S. Goudsmit, *ALSOS* (New York, 1947), pp. 112 f.

22. Cassidy, pp. 71–74.

23. See the opening chapters of *Physics and Beyond*. Though this is a later memoir and suspect in many of its back-readings, its account of Heisenberg's youthful experience and mentality seems largely reliable in a general way.

scientists alike during the 1930s and after. When Born asked if the offer to be allowed to return included his family, Heisenberg, who had kept quiet about this aspect of the deal, sheepishly replied that it did not, and Born was so angered that he broke off the conversation. "We could not understand how Heisenberg, whom we knew as a decent, humane fellow, could have agreed to convey such a message to me."[24] How could any person of average sensitivity—*l'homme moyen sensuel*—have believed that such an offer could be accepted? Heisenberg clearly realized the shamefulness of what he was doing, but nevertheless he felt justified in making the proposal by the knowledge that he was serving the great god of physics—and of Germany.

This religious worship of physics led also to difficulty in Heisenberg's management of his relations with Einstein. Heisenberg revered Einstein's physical theories, and supported him in the 1920s against antisemitic attacks. But, like his revered mentor Arnold Sommerfeld, Heisenberg must have had his veneration and defense of Einstein stretched at times by the Jewish scientist's irritating lack of German patriotism, which it was tempting to ascribe to his race. Though Sommerfeld kept his Munich physics institute free of antisemitic policies, it was certainly not exempt from antisemitic feelings. In March 1919 Sommerfeld confided to a colleague that "because of the Jewish political mischief, I am becoming more and more an anti-Semite" and wondered whether he should publish his new book with the "Jewish" publisher Springer.[25] On the other hand, Sommerfeld was angered at the public antisemitic campaign directed against Einstein, just as Heisenberg was profoundly shocked by his own direct experience of the virulent opposition to Einstein at the first scientific conference he attended in 1922. It was the attack on the new physics by a crudely political antisemitism—"the injection of twisted political passions into scientific life"—that horrified Heisenberg and Sommerfeld, rather than the animosity provoked perhaps understandably by the "unpatriotic" Einstein. The situation could be saved by detaching the physics from the man. When violent opposition erupted over an invitation to Einstein to lecture in Munich, Sommerfeld defended Einstein as a "physicist," not as a "person." This laid the framework for Heisenberg's later compromises with the Nazis over relativity theory. Heisenberg would defend the theory courageously, but consent to the suppression of Einstein's name as its author and, worse, argue glibly that the basis of relativity had been laid by other scientists and that its discovery would have taken place without Einstein. Faced with coercive power, Heisenberg readily surrendered the defense of Einstein's scientific reputation because he had surrendered the defense of Einstein's rights as an individual Jew long before. To paraphrase Goudsmit, Heisenberg was more interested in saving Jewish physics than

24. M. Born, *My Life* (London, 1978), p. 269. For other unpleasant facets of Born's relationship with Heisenberg, see below, chap. 21.

25. M. Eckert et al., eds., *Geheimrat Sommerfeld—Theoretischer Physiker: Eine Dokumentation aus seinem Nachlass (Deutsches Museum)* (Munich, 1984), pp. 132–134.

Jewish physicists.[26] But it was not just Heisenberg's "extreme nationalism," as Goudsmit believed, that produced this behavior. It was rather its combination with a worship of physics—a trait not uncommon in physicists of other nations of the time, but one distorted in Heisenberg and other German scientists by a peculiarly German mentality that demanded quasi-religious absolutes in professional devotion.

26. See S. Goudsmit, letter to *Nuclear News*, October 1970. Cf. Goudsmit to Irving, 22 July 1966, in IMF 32.

CHAPTER 17

Collusion and Compromise under Hitler, 1933–37

One is either born a good German or one is not.[1]
HEISENBERG, 1938–39

With Hitler's legitimized seizure of power in 1933, the apolitical mentality of German academic culture sprang into operation to justify the new regime as one of patriotic order, or, at the least, to proscribe any political resistance to it as being against the ethos of the apolitical scientist. Even those who later distinguished themselves by their refusal to compromise with Nazism were inhibited at first by their cultural formation. In June 1933, after the dismissal of Jewish and other professors had caused outrage in the West, Laue could still reproach Einstein for being "political" and making life difficult. To this highly German point of view, Einstein replied in a Western political manner: "I do not share your view that the scientists should observe silence in political matters. . . . Does not such restraint signify a lack of responsibility? Where would we be had men like Giordano Bruno, Spinoza, Voltaire, and Humboldt thought and behaved in such a fashion?"[2] One unspoken issue here was Einstein's Jewishness, along with that of his other Jewish colleagues. In the eyes of their German Aryan friends, the Jewish scientists were too prone to exaggeration on account of their sensitivity to antisemitism and their personal troubles. In any event, those German scientists who stayed on seemed quite insensitive to the basic political and moral issue of antisemitism that was brought immediately to the fore under the new regime, an issue so great that it demanded an immediate strong reaction. The Germans preferred to see antisemitism as a merely political matter to be avoided, or at best managed, instead of a fundamental moral question for the individual to confront. It was easy, therefore, for them to counsel their Jewish friends to be patient.[3]

Another comforting self-deception that paralyzed any meaningful reaction to

1. From an SS report of 1939, discussed below in chap. 18.
2. Einstein to Laue, 26 May 1933, quoted in Cassidy, p. 302.
3. See Cassidy, pp. 303 ff.

Hitler was the notion of the "good side of Nazism." This "good side" was spring-cleaning the tired and decadent life of Germany and restoring a sense of dignity and honor to it. In October 1933 Heisenberg sagely observed that "much that is good is now also being tried and one should recognize good intentions."[4] Of course, in Western mentality, this is a complete fallacy. There is no "good" side to Hitler any more than there was to Stalin or any other murderous dictator. Any apparent good done by such is rotten, originating as it does in evil motives and having to be seen in a general context of evil. In liberal democracies, governments may have justifiably "good" and "bad" sides, but concerning Nazism such apologies are wrongheaded as well as corrupt, and are symptomatic of a refusal to face up to the moral question of evil. Finding "good" in Nazi evil as he did in 1933 was the beginning of Heisenberg's long slide along the path of well-intentioned compromises.

Closely related to the notion of a "good side" to Nazism was Heisenberg's rationalization that the "bad side" would eventually pass away. In June 1933 he informed Max Born, quite without embarrassment, that "in spite of some nasty things that have been happening here within the workings of science itself [one assumes he means the dismissals of Jewish professors], I know that among those in charge in the new political situation, there are men for whose sake it is worth sticking it out. Certainly in the course of time the splendid things will separate from the hateful."[5] Again there is a wishful self-deluding fallacy involved here; any evil regime can be justified in the present by arguing that historical change erodes its worst aspects. The argument has moral meaning only when applied to democratic societies, where one may put up with badness in expectation that this is only a temporary, rather than an intrinsic, evil—a badness necessary to assure the preservation of the essential good of such societies. But the evil of the Third Reich was intrinsic and essential to it, and the mere fact that it would over time eventually be effaced was a banal historical truism that cannot be used to justify it on a moral level.

Another variation of the fallacious complex of rationalizations that appears in this short excerpt from Heisenberg's letter of 1933 to Max Born is the idea that there are "good" Nazis—friendly to Heisenberg—as opposed to bad ones. Again, the fallacy becomes clear upon a little reflection in Western terms. All Nazis supported the creation of an intrinsically evil system; the fact that some may have differed from some particular policies of the Third Reich (had their own "specialties," as Hitler put it) does not make these particular scrupulous Nazis "good." One can find "scruples" in all kinds of Nazis, ranging up to Himmler and to Hitler himself. But it is morally nonsensical to speak of these scruples as somehow endowing such characters with morality. It is only in a liberal democratic context

4. Heisenberg to his mother, 6 October 1933, quoted in Cassidy, p. 303.

5. Heisenberg to Born, 2 June 1933, in W. Pauli, *Wissenschaftlicher Briefwechsel* (New York and Heidelberg, 1979–93), 2:168. Translated in *HPNS*, p. 62.

that the distinction between "good" and "bad" members (in the eyes of their opponents) makes moral sense. We may see how ingrained this habit of thinking was in Heisenberg's outlook by recalling how after the war he shamelessly—shameless because he remained blissfully unaware of the fallacy involved—supplied deceptive letters of justification and defense for former SS officers to denazification tribunals. No Nazi himself, Heisenberg's German sensibility made him a party to collusion with the Nazi elite. What should seem a cause for guilt in Western eyes appeared natural and decent to Heisenberg after the war.[6]

The pervasiveness of this kind of thinking among German scientists in 1933 is vividly exposed by Otto Hahn's defense of Hitler as a "good Nazi" fighting for a "good cause." While at Cornell University, Hahn was interviewed by the *Toronto Star* for his assessment of the antisemitic boycott of 1 April 1933 and Hitler's anti-Jewish policies. According to the published report, Hahn declared that although he was not a Nazi himself, he believed that Germany's youth respected Hitler as "hero, leader, and saint." Indeed Hahn himself reverentially observed that the Führer "lived like a saint," and he justified any persecution of the Jews as being incidental in the scheme of things to the necessary suppression of communism and disorder.[7]

Even more disturbing an indication of the self-delusion that beset even many German scientists of Jewish ancestry are the comments of Lise Meitner on the occasion of the broadcast of Hitler's reopening of the Reichstag in March 1933:

> It was thoroughly amicable and dignified. . . . Hitler . . . spoke very moderately, tactfully, and personally. Hopefully things will continue in this vein. . . . There is hope for developments turning out well in the end. Periods of transition almost inevitably produce all kinds of blunders, of course. Everything now depends on rational moderation.

And even worse:

> It must surely have been difficult for Haber [the baptized Jewish head of the Kaiser-Wilhelm-Institute for Chemistry] to have to raise the swastika flag. I was glad to hear that . . . he personally gave Kuhn the directions for hoisting the brand-new flag [at the institute]. That is so much more dignified for him than if this requirement had been forced on him.[8]

One wonders how anyone—let alone Lise Meitner—could ever speak of such a wretched act as being "dignified" in any normal sense of the word. In later years she would recall with shame her own attitudes during the Nazi era in Berlin:

---

6. The Farm Hall transcripts show how quickly former members of the Nazi party deceived themselves into thinking they were not really Nazis at all. See below, chap. 20.

7. *Toronto Star,* 8 April 1933, reproduced in D. Hahn, *Otto Hahn: Begründer des Atomzeitalters* (Munich, 1979), pp. 129–130.

8. Meitner to Hahn, 21 March 1933, excerpted in J. Lemmerich, *Die Geschichte der Entdeckung der Kernspaltung* (Berlin, 1988), pp. 112 f. Translated in *HPNS*, p. 17.

It is very clear to me today that I committed a great moral injustice by not leaving in 1933, since, in the end, by staying, I supported Hitlerism after all.[9]

If such a morally aware figure as Lise Meitner could betray herself into these rationalizations, it is not surprising that a more flexible personality such as Heisenberg should, over the course of the twelve years of the Third Reich, elaborate variations on these themes, culminating in his infamous justification of the Nazi conquest of Europe as a "good" thing. Even after the defeat of Germany had exposed the full extent of Nazi murderousness, Heisenberg remained so strongly conditioned by his apolitical acceptance of the good side of Hitler that he failed to comprehend the enormity of his (to him) reasonable apologies for the Third Reich and how they mortally offended Western colleagues, who found it difficult to take in at times what they were hearing from the garrulous and quite unheeding Heisenberg.[10]

These distressing attitudes resulted from the interaction of Heisenberg's own evasive personality with the peculiarities of German mentality. As Heisenberg's biographer has wryly remarked, opposition to Nazism "required a political sensitivity and commitment to democracy that did not exist" by and large in German academic culture, "nor did German academics have much experience with moral action or political commitment."[11] Of the very few great non-Jewish scientists who did leave of their own free will, the most important was Erwin Schrödinger. Schrödinger's standard answer to why he abruptly left his Berlin chair in 1933 was simply "I could not endure being bothered by politics," or as he put it more succinctly to Wolfgang Pauli, "I've had a nosefull—I want to get out"—truly unpolitical statements, as opposed to the false rationalizations of Heisenberg and so many others.[12] It was the very fact that Schrödinger had departed without being forced to do so that made his action especially reprehensible in the eyes of his apolitical colleagues. Heisenberg was very angry, seeing Schrödinger's conduct as traitorous to the cause of German science; why, he had left without fighting to defend German science from political interference.[13] Heisenberg was quite unable to understand that Schrödinger's action was a spontaneous moral reaction to the reality of an evil political system; it would have seemed self-indulgent, quixotic, even immoral to Heisenberg. But the self-righteous condemnation of Schrödinger's own alleged self-righteousness carries also a suggestion of a deeper lingering resentment. Some of Heisenberg's indignation may be traced back to the bitter intellectual hatred he conceived for Schrö-

9. Meitner to Hahn, 6 June 1948, printed in F. Krafft, *Im Schatten der Sensation: Leben und Wirken von Fritz Strassmann* (Weinheim, 1981), pp. 185 f. Translated in *HPNS*, p. 401, and in R. Sime, *Lise Meitner: A Life in Physics* (Berkeley, 1996), p. 356.

10. For Heisenberg's curious remarks during and after the war, see below, chap. 21.

11. Cassidy, p. 305.

12. W. Moore, *Schrödinger: Life and Thought* (Cambridge, 1989), pp. 272 f.

13. Heisenberg to his mother, 17 September 1933, cited in Cassidy, pp. 306 f.

dinger's wave mechanics, which had prevailed over his own matrix mechanics in the 1920s.[14]

In any case, the general opinion was that such conduct as Schrödinger's was as ineffective as it was wrong. When Otto Hahn suggested a mass resignation in support of Jewish colleagues in 1933, he was easily deflected by Max Planck's sagacious advice that such political moves would go unreported and second-rate Nazi scientists would quickly take over the vacated posts.[15] Hahn did, however, resign his University of Berlin professorship, while retaining his Kaiser-Wilhelm-Institute post, partly because he was forced to, and partly under the influence, one suspects, of his more forthright wife, Edith, who had written to James Franck on his resignation: "I could envy you for being Jews . . . and thus for having justice completely on your side and we for ever and ever the humiliation and the inextinguishable shame which can never be made good again."[16] Planck's timid, prudential—and essentially self-interested—argument in the face of the most blatant violation of civilized and academic values was, in Western terms, inadequate, to put it mildly, but it proved all too persuasive and satisfying in Germany in 1933 and after. It was this non-Nazi, apolitical mentality that allowed Hitler to gain power—and to hold on to it. No clear-cut resistance could develop for a long time, because the German elite was not outraged from the very start, preferring to make excuses either for Nazism itself or for their own inaction.

The Western point of view at the time emerges clearly in a letter from Samuel Goudsmit to Charles Galton Darwin of 23 November 1933: "I hope sincerely that Heisenberg has sense and courage enough to make a similar move like Schrödinger in protest to what has been done to his teacher and outstanding colleagues."[17] Writing after the war, Paul Rosbaud, who as we have seen stayed on in Germany to resist, agreed with this analysis in the course of an unrelentingly clear-sighted essay he wrote in 1945 titled "The Attitude of Germans, Especially German Scientists during the Nazi Regime":

> I remember many details, the first Jewish professors who were dismissed—I was waiting for any sign of protest—the expelling of Jewish members of the academies . . . I remember one distinguished member of Göttingen University saying to me: "If they should venture to break our university to pieces by expelling such men as James Franck, Born, Courant, Landau, we shall rise up like one man to protest against it." The next day, the newspapers reported that the same scientists and many others had been dismissed owing to their Jewish race and their disgraceful influence on universities and students. And all the other members of Göttingen University remained sitting and had forgotten their intention to rise and to protest. . . .

14. Cassidy, pp. 213–224. See also below, section on Born, for details.

15. J. L. Heilbron, *The Dilemmas of an Upright Man: Max Planck as Spokesman for German Science* (Berkeley, 1986), p. 150. K. Hoffmann, *Schuld und Verantwortung: Otto Hahn, Konflikte eines Wissenschaftlers* (Berlin, 1993), p. 111.

16. E. Hahn to J. Franck, 22 April 1933, translated in *HPNS*, p. 31.

17. Pauli, *Briefwechsel*, 2:207 n.

The protest of a dozen personalities known not only by everyone in Germany but also of international reputation . . . could have changed the situation. . . .

The general excuse was: "We could not dare to protest, though the expulsion of our Jewish colleagues is completely against all our views and even against our conscience. We could not think of ourselves but of the higher purpose, the university, the academy. We had to avoid the possibility of these institutions having any trouble or their being closed. This was our first duty and so our personal views and interests, as well as those of our Jewish colleagues, had to be kept in the background." Many of them added—and this was probably the first token of the beginning infection and confusion of mind—"Besides, didn't they [the Jews] really go too far with their abstraction in science, and didn't they go too far in accumulating Jewish collaborators? It is their own fault, and they must now pay for it. Perhaps they were really dangerous to our scientific life."

It was my opinion that nobody would have ventured to close all our universities and academies nor to dismiss several hundred university teachers. But even if they had brought some of the learned societies to a preliminary end, their conscience would have remained pure and they could have opened after 12 years triumphantly. I never was in conformity with these views, and I am sorry to say that even today many people don't realize what their duty should have been in those days. The universities did not take advantage of their chance. . . .

The excuses: "I might have had trouble, might lose my job or my pension," all sorts of excuses, and besides, "it makes no difference when I, a single person, am acting against the wishes of the Nazis."[18]

What shows up these pretexts for what they are is the fact that some of Heisenberg's junior colleagues did refuse (unlike Weizsäcker, for instance) to join the Nazi University Lecturers' League (*NS-Dozentenbund*). Though it undoubtedly restricted their careers, the refusal of Fritz Strassmann (Hahn's close associate) and Max Delbrück to collaborate in Nazi academic formations did not lead to their dismissals.[19] At a more senior level, one might point to the case of the chemist Wilhelm Schlenk, who for two years conducted a campaign against the regime, though he eventually gave up and emigrated.[20]

By focusing on their professional as opposed to individual responsibility, Heisenberg and his colleagues spared themselves ethical reflection on the implications of filling positions vacated by unjustly dismissed Jewish scientists. In Western perspective, those implications are fairly obvious; willingness to step into the shoes of Jewish scientists effectively legitimated the dismissals by showing that reasonable men had no ethical problems with doing so, and the happy outcome of the situation proved Hitler right in asserting that science could get on very nicely without the Jews. As David Cassidy has stated, the Nazi regime confronted Germans with

18. Goudsmit Papers, AIP, box 28, folder 42, pp. 1–3.
19. *HPNS*, p. xxxvii.
20. Sime, *Lise Meitner*, p. 146.

most difficult moral and political decisions for which "even the most upright among them were thoroughly unprepared" by their cultural conditioning.[21] Among the behavioral aspects of this conditioning one must cite a certain German predisposition to avoid moral issues and look at things cynically, especially when such an attitude is personally opportune. Anyone who has read the Farm Hall transcripts will recognize the truth of this statement, so blatantly opportunistic and cynical are the comments to be found coming from the mouths of nearly all the internees. Certainly in 1934, Heisenberg showed no awareness of the moral implications of making himself available to replace Max Born at Göttingen; writing to James Franck, he tried cheerily to justify his candidacy by affirming that he would protect Göttingen physics from Nazi intrusions: "I will do everything in my power for our Göttingen, you may be sure." The problem was that for Born and Franck, Göttingen was not "our Göttingen," but Hitler's Göttingen. Heisenberg simply could not see how absurdly monstrous this appropriating of Max Born's shoes appeared to them.[22]

Born was almost amused by the "well-meaning" efforts of such German colleagues as Heisenberg and Max Planck, or at least he was so in 1933, before Heisenberg's insensitivity had developed to its full extent. Ironic amusement was Born's reaction to Heisenberg's excitedly telling him in his "good side of Nazism" letter of 2 June 1933 about Planck's famous visit to Hitler, which seemed to bode well for the physicists.[23] Yet even this visit, which, like Furtwängler's equally celebrated audience, seemed to be a courageous protest to the Führer himself on behalf of Jewish colleagues, turns out on closer examination to be problematic. Indeed, Planck's visit exhibited the same tendency to ambivalence about Nazism and the Jews and the same destructive compromises that characterize Planck's conduct in general.

Planck was a deeply honorable man, but succumbed through the pressure of his own German acculturation to behavior and attitudes that it is difficult to imagine a man of his upright character yielding to who had been brought up in a Western culture. A friend and admirer of Einstein, Planck found his affection for the Jewish physicist strained by the latter's forthright political and moral condemnation of the new Nazi regime in 1933. Planck lectured Einstein that "by your efforts, your racial and religious brethren will not get relief from their situation," positing that the value of an act such as Einstein's public statement against Germany was determined not by its good intentions, but by its likely bad consequences.[24] This moralizing now takes on a certain irony, since what did happen in the face of low-

21. Cassidy, p. 312.
22. Cassidy, pp. 311 f.
23. See Born's remarks in Pauli, *Briefwechsel*, 2:168; and James Franck's similar skepticism, ibid., 2:208.
24. Planck to Einstein, 19 March 1933, in A. Hermann, *Max Planck in Selbstzeugnissen und Bilddokumenten* (Reinbek, 1973), p. 78; see Heilbron, *Dilemmas*, pp. 155 f.

key maneuvers by Planck and Heisenberg most certainly could not have been worse than if Einstein's policy of protest had been followed. But even Planck's good faith itself was tarnished by his subsequent conduct. The Presiding Secretary of the Prussian Academy of Sciences asked Planck to urge Einstein to resign—and astonishingly, Planck complied. He talked himself into this by arguing that Einstein's criticism from abroad barred him from state appointments, as well as by concluding, somewhat self-interestedly, that if Einstein did not resign, his friends would be placed in a difficult situation. This was, of course, precisely the test of conscience that a Western scientist would have thought essential to confront rather than something to be avoided.[25] In a letter that must have seemed honorable to its writer, but would surely have appalled Einstein beyond words, Planck wrote on 31 March 1933:

> If the content of foreign press reports [of your statement] is correct, I am forced to say to you in all honesty that it appears to me that the only way out of your thoughts is that which on the one hand assures you an honorable dissolving of your relations with the Academy, and on the other hand spares your friends an immeasurable amount of sorrow and suffering. I believe I write this to you as an imperative duty.
>
> Above all, it is in my heart to express to you my strong confidence that despite the deep chasm that divides our political points of view, our personal friendly relations should never change.[26]

It is an illustration of the overpowering impress of German cultural mentality that a reasonable man such as Planck could put such insulting, self-interested, and absurd sentiments in writing to his correspondent: Einstein is told to save his friends "sorrow and suffering" by resigning (not a word about Einstein's somewhat greater inconvenience), and then after doing so to continue to behave toward Planck as though nothing had happened.

As it happened, Einstein had already resigned, but the Academy wanted the last word and issued a smug statement stressing its apolitical support of the state ("Our members have always felt themselves bound by the closest ties to the Prussian state, and while abstaining strictly from all political partisanship, have always stressed and remained faithful to the national idea"). This ended with the almost farcically arrogant words that the body "has no reason to regret Einstein's withdrawal."[27] The phrase outraged Laue, who tried in vain to have Planck return for an emergency meeting.[28]

Meanwhile, a further communication of 7 April from the Academy told off Einstein for failing to conform to the culture of German apolitical mentality:

25. Planck to Einstein, 31 March 1933, in Hermann, *Max Planck*, p. 78; see Heilbron, *Dilemmas*, pp. 156 f.
26. Planck to Einstein, 31 March 1933, in Hermann, *Max Planck*, p. 78.
27. A. Einstein, *The World As I See It*, trans. (New York, 1949), pp. 81 f.
28. A. Hermann, *The New Physics* (Bonn, 1979), pp. 75–81.

COLLUSION AND COMPROMISE UNDER HITLER

"Many years of membership in our society must have made [you] familiar with the German character and German habits of thought, [yet you] chose this moment to . . . damage our German people by disseminating erroneous views." Einstein retorted that he "deeply deplored the attitude displayed in your communication."[29] No wonder Einstein wrote a few weeks later to Max Born expressing his disgust at the way in which Planck and others had been corrupted by German mentality. "You know, I think, that I have never had a particularly favorable opinion of the Germans (morally and politically speaking). But I must confess that the degree of their brutality and cowardice came as something of a surprise to me."[30]

Undoubtedly Einstein had Planck in mind in speaking of cowardice. He had urged Planck in early April to speak out publicly against the dismissals and been deeply disappointed at the latter's inaction, but the public betrayal that now ensued was far worse. When Planck finally got back to Berlin in early May, he tried to moderate the earlier insults of the Academy, but his effort only made things worse by laying the blame for Einstein's departure from the Academy on his former colleague's own shoulders. "It is deeply to be regretted that Einstein has by his own political behavior made his continuation in the Academy impossible," stated Planck, and then added as a non sequitur to the minutes an acknowledgment of Einstein's greatness as a physicist.[31] Quite oblivious of the contradiction, Planck used the alleged distinction between politics and physics to justify excluding the great scientist from a scientific academy for purely political reasons. Thenceforth Einstein refused to write to his old friend.[32] Not surprisingly, when Einstein told a colleague at Princeton to convey his greetings to Laue, he pointedly negated an offer to carry them also to Planck. Einstein's instinct in this seems to have been correct, for Planck's failure of principle carried through into his omission of Einstein's name from discussions of relativity theory and physics during the Nazi period, an abject compromise in which he was joined by Heisenberg and others. The omission of the theorist was easily rationalized as a trivial concession compared to the importance of defending the theory itself; but actually agreeing to drop Einstein's name was rather like suppressing Newton's because he was English, and it represents a moral and professional ignominy of immense proportions that no ingenuity of rationalization can explain away. Eventually Planck's basic integrity reasserted itself when in 1943–44 he finally dared to mention and praise Einstein by name in a lecture; he was not given such a chance again.[33]

It was in this treacherously ambivalent frame of mind that Planck went to see

29. Einstein, *World*, pp. 81–87.

30. Einstein to Born, 30 May 1933, in A. Einstein, H. Born, and M. Born, *The Born-Einstein Letters*, ed. and trans. M. Born (New York, 1971), p. 114.

31. Documents in C. Kirsten and H.-J. Treder, *Albert Einstein in Berlin, 1913–1933* (East Berlin, 1979), 1:246–267; see Heilbron, *Dilemmas*, pp. 157–159.

32. Heilbron, *Dilemmas*, p. 200. Einstein wrote to Planck on 6 April 1933 urging him to speak out.

33. See Heilbron, *Dilemmas*, pp. 189–191.

Hitler on 16 May 1933. There is much obscurity about what actually transpired. In 1947 Planck himself published a short paragraph describing the interview. Planck had started (he recalled) by making a plea for the Jewish chemist Fritz Haber, who had resigned from the headship of the Kaiser-Wilhelm-Institute for Physical Chemistry though he could actually have stayed on as a war veteran. (Since Haber had left voluntarily, Planck must have been using this case to make a point about the general damage being done to German science by political interference.) Hitler sophistically disarmed Planck by stating that he had nothing against the Jews as Jews, but rather because they were all communists. When Planck replied by saying that there "were Jews of different types who are worthy and unworthy for humanity" and distinctions must be made, Hitler contradicted himself by insisting that "Jews were Jews," that they do not separate themselves from one another, so why should any distinction be made? Planck then tried again to argue that it would be harmful to German science if "worthy" Jews were forced out. Hitler was in no mood for a rational discussion and started to talk excitedly about other matters, including his own nerves of steel (which made him unflinching from his policy) and eventually flew into such a rage that Planck could only take his leave.[34]

Recent research has shown how this account cannot be taken wholly at its face value. It seems indeed to have been largely written by Planck's wife, with some general direction from the scientist himself. In such a brief document where the wording is crucial, this indirect authorship presents major problems. Moreover, the paragraph needs to be read in the context of postwar German attempts—like the Heisenberg version itself—to read back into scientists' behavior of the Nazi period an anti-Nazi content and motivation. Seen in context, however, that behavior— and especially Planck's visit to Hitler—emerges as part of a campaign of collaboration with, rather than resistance to, Nazism. Planck himself was far more compromised with the Nazi regime than his recollection likes to admit: He had given Hitler-salutes, he had installed busts of Hitler in the Kaiser-Wilhelm-Society offices, he had sent telegrams to Hitler avowing pride in the "national resurrection" that was taking place. In sum, the visit should not be interpreted as an attempt to defend liberal principles (as it might appear to be in a post-1945 context), but rather as an effort to defend German science from the damage caused by political interference.[35]

34. M. Planck, "Mein Besuch bei Adolf Hitler," *Physikalische Blätter* 3 (1947): 143, reprinted with other texts in the German version of Heilbron's biography, *Max Planck: Ein Leben für die Wissenschaft, 1858–1947* (Stuttgart, 1988), p. 253. Cf. Heilbron, *Dilemmas*, p. 153.

35. H. Albrecht, " 'Max Planck: Mein Besuch bei Adolf Hitler'—Anmerkungen zum Wert einer historischen Quelle," in *Naturwissenschaft und Technik in der Geschichte*, ed. H. Albrecht (Stuttgart, 1993), pp. 41–63, provides an elegant analysis. In general see R. Siegmund-Schultze, "The Problem of Anti-Fascist Resistance of 'Apolitical' German Scholars," in *Science, Technology, and National Socialism*, ed. M. Rennenberg and M. Walker (Cambridge, 1994), pp. 312–323.

Most unpleasantly, even the inflected postwar recollection by Planck exposes the latent antisemitism of the educated German academic class that Hitler knew so well how to exploit. The invidious distinction between "Jews . . . who are worthy and unworthy for humanity" invokes the basic premise of German philosophical antisemitism from the time of Kant: Jews are by national character deficient in humanity and morality. Some seemingly "pro-Jewish" (the term is a misnomer) Germans believed that the Jews could educate and moralize themselves so as to become "pure human beings," but an antisemitic prejudice was still at the bottom of such progressive hopes.[36] When Planck came to Hitler hoping to be able through his subtle antisemitism to moderate the more extreme antisemitism of the new government, he was making both a moral and a prudential error, for he had already yielded the essential tactical ground. (The biologist Wolfgang Köhler well understood the ambivalences of the German professoriate about Jews. When he tried to manipulate patriotic and Nazi rhetoric in order to restrain the purges of Jewish scientists, Köhler carefully pointed out that though the professors recognized the need for a solution to the "Jewish Problem" through a purging of "the disproportionately large number of Jews in leadership roles," they had misgivings about the harsh treatment of the genuinely distinguished Jewish scientists such as James Franck and that this alone restrained them from giving their full support to the Nazi government, of which they otherwise approved wholeheartedly. Whatever Köhler's own personal opinions were, he had grasped perfectly the contradictory mixture of "pro-" and "anti-Jewish" feelings that governed such colleagues as Heisenberg and Planck.)[37]

Despite Hitler's temper and his refusal to revoke the Jewish dismissals, Planck's ambivalences about political authority and Jews in science meant that he could carry away from the episode some reassuring hopes for the future. The worst seemed to be over, and it might be assumed that since the only Jews remaining in academic positions were all "worthy" types such as war veterans, they would be secure in their positions. This seems to be the message—though perhaps too optimistically interpreted—that Heisenberg received from Planck soon after the event. In his cheerful letter of 2 June 1933 to Max Born, Heisenberg declared that "Planck has spoken . . . with the head of the regime and received the assurance that the goverment will do nothing beyond the new civil-service law that could hurt our science. . . . The political revolution may take place without any damage to Göttingen physics."[38] In other words, the version of Planck's visit that circulated at the time

36. P. L. Rose, *German Question / Jewish Question: Revolutionary Antisemitism in Germany from Kant to Wagner*, 2d ed. (Princeton, 1992). Planck's original wording seemed to indict "Eastern" Jews as a worthless group. See *HPNS*, p. 360n.

37. W. Köhler, "Gespräche in Deutschland" (Conversations in Germany), in *Deutsche Allgemeine Zeitung*, 28 April 1933 (translated in *HPNS*, pp. 36–38): "[German professors] are of the single opinion that the recent purge could not have been more necessary; they admire the force of the events which for the first time have made Germany into a lasting Reich within a matter of days." In 1935 Köhler gave up trying to change Nazi policy and left Germany for America.

38. Pauli, *Briefwechsel*, 2:168. Cf. Heilbron, *Dilemmas*, p. 154.

was a positive one and certainly not the completely gloomy reading that Planck gave out in 1947, doubtless in good faith even if shaded by self-deception.

The case of Planck, a mature and moral thinker, raises an interesting question about Heisenberg. It would be easy to see the roots of Heisenberg's collaboration with Nazism as growing out of his vulnerable personality: Heisenberg was a conformist, of an adolescent temperament in his lack of moral independence and willingness to accept personal restraints that no seriously moral and mature scientist should have borne. For Heisenberg, attendance at political indoctrination camps and army reserve service, including the notion of participating in a volunteer army sports camp in order "to acquaint myself a little more with this politics," was embraced in a jolly, unthinking way that it is difficult to imagine Planck espousing.[39] In 1936 Heisenberg admitted lightly his attraction to military service in a significant sentence: "It is nice not to have to think for a change, but only to obey. . . . The duty agrees with me in every respect."[40] Yet despite Heisenberg's evident callowness compared with Planck's seriousness, they do have certain reactions to Hitler in common. Both men expected the "storm to pass" and could not face up to the overwhelming moral question posed by the Nazi revolution from the outset. They thought that no really irrevocable moral decision to break with the regime was required by what happened in 1933–34; and afterward they believed that by the time the evil of Nazism had become manifest it was simply too late to resist it. Both physicists showed themselves incapable of understanding that the moral dilemma was not merely one of German science being harmed or a few Jewish colleagues being inconvenienced, and both tended to adopt a prudential, philosophical view of the whole situation; for the sake of German science, they were willing to countenance a "few injustices." Yet to those inside Germany like Laue, or those who had left like Einstein or Born, or those who observed it from afar such as non-Jewish British physicists of the time, the barbarism of these petty injustices was well understood. Moral blindness and noncomprehension were thus characteristic of German mentality, and not just the result of a misjudgment that anyone could have made. A prudential, even tenacious, policy of defending German science from Hitler was no substitute for a forthright moral condemnation of the Nazi regime and resignation. Heisenberg's clever twin policy of, first, trying to fill vacated positions with good physicists and asking Jewish colleagues to hang on while the storm passed, and second, defending theoretical physics itself from Nazi ideological attacks, may have succeeded eventually in safeguarding the teaching of relativity theory—minus the name of its author—in Nazi Germany. But it was politically and morally misconceived. Heisenberg and many others have plausibly argued that in 1933 no one could have expected Nazism to last as long as it did or to become as extreme as it did; waiting for the storm to pass was therefore morally

39. Cassidy, p. 315.
40. Cassidy, p. 364.

and politically reasonable as a course of action. The difficulty with this argument is that in Western sensibility, what had happened or was clearly threatening to happen in 1933–34 was bad enough to require a strong reaction for its basic violation of moral principles. Heisenberg, Planck, and the others, however, preferred to underrate the injustice and evil by rationalizing them as mere political epiphenomena, and to take a philosophical view that consented to a "few" injustices as inevitable—a very widespread rationalization in Germany at the time. One should contrast Heisenberg's relatively passive attitude to the dismissals of 1933 with the sharpening intensity of his reaction to what he saw as the threat to the sanctity of true theoretical physics posed by the rise of "German physics."

Even if Heisenberg and Planck had been able or willing to recognize the enormity of their mistaken optimism about Nazism in 1933–34, it is unlikely that they would have done other than they did in those years. Heisenberg's mentor Sommerfeld at one point did indeed change his mind about allowing German nationalist feelings to legitimate Hitler, and he wrote in August 1934 from Italy to Einstein:

> I write this letter from Italy. If I were to write it from Germany it would scarcely come into your hands. Regretfully I cannot pardon my countrymen all the injustice that has been done to you and many others, and that goes for my colleagues of the Berlin and Bavarian academies. The political immaturity of the German people has much guilt, and so too has the policy of our [former] military opponents. . . . Above all I may assure you that the national spirit that was so strongly stamped on me has been thoroughly broken by the misuse of the word "national" by our rulers. I would no longer object if Germany would now disappear as a power and merge into a pacified Europe.

However, this frank renunciation of German nationalism was too much for Sommerfeld, and he struck out the last two sentences (beginning with "Above all . . . ") before posting the letter to Einstein.[41]

Heisenberg pursued his mistaken policy with some passion, and at the cost of some unpleasantness to himself. When a group of prominent professors including Martin Heidegger rallied together at Leipzig University in November 1933 to declare public support of Hitler, Heisenberg absented himself. One reason for this was that the main organizer was the Nazi physicist Johannes Stark, whom Heisenberg intensely disliked as a rabble-rouser who had introduced extreme political antisemitism into the scientific world with his attacks on Einstein and was threatening to destroy the new physics. But Heisenberg was also appalled by the proletarianization of scholarship that this development promoted—students trying to tell teachers what and what not to teach, disruption of lectures by political slogan-

---

41. Sommerfeld to Einstein, 27 August 1934, in *Albert Einstein / Arnold Sommerfeld, Briefwechsel: Sechzig Briefe aus dem goldenen Zeitalter der modernen Physik*, ed. A. Hermann (Basel, 1968), pp. 113–116, which includes a facsimile showing the original crossed-out sentences.

izing, and deans eating ice creams in academic processions (particularly repellent to someone so brought up on academic propriety as Heisenberg). Despite difficulties with some of his Nazi students over this, Heisenberg managed to bring them round, and they even gave him a torchlight procession in his honor. The district leader of the Nazi Students' League was invited by Heisenberg to his home, and obliged by recommending to the minister of education that Heisenberg be exonerated from charges of opposition to the Führer and the state. Thus, what may have looked like an act of resistance at the start turns out in the end to be an act of collaboration. It was a typical Heisenberg compromise, in which the central moral issue was evaded and true moral principle sacrificed for a cleverly rationalized temporary success.[42]

The same lack of firm principle undermined what could have become a true act of resistance in 1935. The dismissal of previously exempted Jews such as war veterans from government office in May 1935 seemed to Heisenberg to betray the concordat reached between Planck and Hitler in 1933. Heisenberg courageously instigated a letter of protest to the Saxon ministry of education, arguing that the new dismissal policy violated "the intention of the law." Those who engineered the petition, some of them Nazi party members, were quickly slapped down, and this brought Heisenberg to his own moment of decision. Again, he failed to face up to the question. He began by approaching Planck for moral advice—yet he well knew that Planck could never advocate resignation or political resistance. Heisenberg was indeed relieved to have Planck tell him that resigning would do no good, since it would go unreported. Heisenberg had been at the critical point of finally defying authority by resigning and emigrating, but now lost his nerve and sought a fatal compromise. Once Heisenberg had shirked the test of resignation at this crucial juncture, there was no real chance of his resigning at a later stage; he had effectively decided to stay on in Germany come what may. The Nazi administrators were well aware of this kind of mentality, having encountered it in so many celebrated as well as less well known cases in their two years of office. They knew the horse had been broken, though he might still need careful handling on occasion.

Heisenberg, of course, had a ready rationalization for his failure to leave. Henceforth, he told his mother, his task was "to oversee in science the values that must become important for the future. That is in this general chaos the only clear thing that is left for me to do. The world out there is really ugly, but the work is beautiful."[43] The inner truth of physics was now the highest morality. For Heisenberg the need to ensure the existence of oases of scientific truth, around which new clusters of disciples (like those in his youth group) might "crystallize," constituted an overriding idea of "responsibility."[44] Heisenberg made much of this after

---

42. Cassidy, pp. 323 f., and 605 (for the ice cream).

43. Cassidy, pp. 327–329.

44. Cassidy, p. 317, however, prefers to see most of Heisenberg's responses to Nazism as "frustratingly weak, insensitive, even repugnant."

the war, arguing that he could not have withdrawn even into an "inner emigration" because that would have meant abandoning responsibility to science and to Germany. As he told Goudsmit, "I have never been able to have the least sympathy for those people who withdraw from all responsibility" (or as his good Leipzig physicist friend, Friedrich Hund, put it, "One doesn't leave a country just because one doesn't like its politics").[45] Heisenberg's shallow idea of responsibility was very German, and quite misconceived in Western terms. Responsibility consisted not just in staying on in Germany and protecting science, as Heisenberg believed. It lay rather in staying on and fighting openly against Nazism, as Laue had, or secretly, as did Rosbaud.[46] Heisenberg's notion of "responsibility" as the acquisition of influence in Nazi circles ("It is important to be clear that this was actually the only way really to achieve anything," in his words) was actually a rationalization of collaboration and of self-interest. It conceded the inevitability of Nazism, avoided opening one's eyes to other possible paths of resistance, and ended up achieving nothing except a few mentions of relativity in textbooks and lecture courses.

The main basis of Heisenberg's "resistance" to Nazism was his defense of the "Jewish" theoretical physics of Einstein's relativity theory. (For a time, his own quantum mechanics was targeted also because of its association with Jewish physicists like Max Born.) In 1934 the Nazi ideologue Alfred Rosenberg had reprimanded Heisenberg for defending relativity and mentioning Einstein's name. This set the stage for the serious attack of early 1936 in the Nazi official newspaper *Völkischer Beobachter* under the heading "German and Jewish Physics," labeling Heisenberg the "spirit of Einstein's spirit" and the proponent of a "Jewish physics" opposed to "German physics."[47] Heisenberg reacted with alacrity. Somewhat disreputably descending to the level of replying in the *Beobachter*, he implicitly identified the cause of physics with his own personal status, and so infused a highly emotional element into the issue. This was made all the more painful by the fact that the attacks were jeopardizing Heisenberg's imminent nomination to his

45. Cassidy, pp. 317 f., 603. In ordinary democratic politics this may be true, but the case in question was Nazi Germany; Hund was consistent in this apolitical stance, serving Stalin just as unconcernedly after the war.

46. The massive weight of German conformism affected even those foreigners who had embraced German high culture, as the Dutch physicist H. Casimir admits in his *Haphazard Reality* (New York, 1983), p. 192, when explaining why he had not joined the Resistance: "A good deal of German culture had gone into my idiosyncrasy. I had learned much from German books, German was the first foreign language I spoke fluently, my father had been strongly influenced by the German philosophers—he hated the Nazis perhaps most of all because they destroyed his image of Germany. That made it difficult for me to identify Germany—even Nazi Germany—with the Devil." (A colleague at Leiden had told Casimir: "With the Devil you cannot negotiate, with the Devil you cannot plead or argue; the Devil you can only fight.")

47. W. Menzel, "Deutsche und jüdische Physik," *Völkischer Beobachter*, 29 January 1936, translated (with Heisenberg's reply) in *HPNS*, pp. 119–124. See A. Beyerchen, *Scientists under Hitler* (New Haven, 1977), pp. 141 ff.; Cassidy, pp. 349–352.

long-coveted chair of physics at Munich.[48] More respectably, Heisenberg again resorted to a petition, but he had by now learned the lesson of the ill-fated petition
of 1935.[49] This time the petition was couched in terms of the utility of science—
even apparently "Jewish" science—to Germany: Failure to teach the new physics
including relativity would negatively affect the production of scientists and tech-
nologists required by the Four-Year Plan. The petition, signed by seventy-five
physicists, was well received by the national Education Ministry, and it seemed
that the cause of the new physics was won and Heisenberg's dignity affirmed—
together with the Munich chair. Unfortunately, Heisenberg's success had confirmed his belief that the future lay in clever compromise and collaboration with
various Nazi dignitaries—an unfortunate lesson learned.[50]

48. Heisenberg, "Zum Artikel 'Deutsche und jüdische Physik'" (28 February 1936), reprinted in
GWH, C V, 9–11, and in H. Rechenberg, ed., *Deutsche und jüdische Physik*, Munich, 1992, pp. 78–80.
Translated in *HPNS*, p. 137.

49. "An den Herrn Reichsminister für Erziehung . . . ," printed in Rechenberg, *Deutsche Physik*,
pp. 81–83, and GWH, C V, 12–13. Translated in *HPNS*, p. 137.

50. Cassidy, pp. 337, 349–363. Texts are in GWH, C V, and Rechenberg, *Deutsche Physik*. See Beyerchen, *Scientists under Hitler*, for a detailed account. For the general atmosphere of collusion that in-
fected German science see H. Mehrtens, "Mathematics in the Third Reich: Resistance, Adaptation,
and Collaboration of a Scientific Discipline," in *New Trends in the History of Science*, ed. R. P. W. Visser
(Amsterdam, 1989), pp. 141–166.

CHAPTER 18

The Himmler Connection

Heisenberg's "Honor," 1937–44

The apparent success of his new collusionist strategy soon led Heisenberg into the most contaminating of all his compromises.[1] On the verge of moving to Munich in July 1937, Heisenberg was shattered to find himself the object of a violent attack in the SS newspaper *Das Schwarze Korps,* intended to debar him from his university chair. Heisenberg was denounced as a "white Jew" and a virtual traitor—"the Ossietzky of physics. . . . They [Heisenberg, Planck, et al.] are all representatives of Judaism . . . who must be eliminated just as the Jews themselves."[2] Among Heisenberg's crimes were his defense of relativity in Nazi official journals, his refusal to sign a manifesto supporting Hitler, his obtaining his Leipzig chair through Jewish influence, his dismissal of German assistants in favor of Jewish ones, and his harboring of Jews and foreigners in his institute at Leipzig. Although these alleged acts might have commended Heisenberg as an anti-Nazi, he declined this identification and preferred to refute each of the "charges." Heisenberg now embarked on a morally disastrous campaign to have his lost "honor" restored that perverted his conduct for the next eight years.

Stung by an explosive combination of personal affront and insult to physics, Heisenberg asked the Ministry of Education that he be dismissed from his Leipzig chair unless the ministry showed its willingness to protect him from attack. Pride and anger, rather than any true spirit of resistance to Nazism, were now driving Heisenberg to offer his resignation. Heisenberg decided to go for broke by having

1. For a fascinating reconstruction of Heisenberg's relations with Himmler, see Cassidy, pp. 379–395.

2. Translated in *HPNS*, p. 152. Carl von Ossietzky, an outspoken pacifist opponent of the Nazi regime imprisoned in a concentration camp, won the Nobel Peace Prize in 1936, which resulted in Hitler's banning Germans from accepting Nobels.

his mother approach Himmler's mother, an old family acquaintance, to prepare the Reichsführer to receive a rather demanding letter.

> I must ask for a fundamental decision [Heisenberg stiffly notified Himmler on 21 July 1937]. . . . If Herr Stark's view of me agrees with that of the government I shall obviously be asking my release from post. But if this is not the case, as the Ministry of Education has expressly assured me, then I ask you as Reichsführer-SS to afford me active protection against such attacks in your official newspaper.

Heisenberg concluded by admitting his apolitical attitudes, but affirming his patriotism—that is, stating his loyalty to the Nazi regime.[3]

Himmler took his time replying to this importunate letter. When he did so in November, he asked Heisenberg for rebuttal of Stark's charges. Heisenberg rapidly answered, detailing how his conduct had always been justified: The 1936 petition had been authorized by an SS officer; the dismissal of a German assistant had been necessitated by his incompetence; Heisenberg had refused to sign Stark's 1934 manifesto because of his misgivings about its organizer; and so forth. Heisenberg emphasized again his loyalty to the regime, though he strongly believed, he said, that scientists should demonstrate their loyalty in scientific rather than political terms.[4]

Himmler now entrusted the preparation of the report on the case to the Security Service (SD) of the SS, headed by his intimidating associate Reinhard Heydrich. Over the next six months, officials of the scientific section of the SS's Cultural Division, including the physicist Johannes Juilfs (later known as Mathias Jules), interviewed Heisenberg in what seems to have been a sympathetic manner.[5] Nevertheless, some hints of nastier treatment were dropped to Heisenberg, who became quite frightened, especially when the presence of some morals-police officers suggested that there might be some question of homosexual involvements in the physicist's old youth group. So terrified was Heisenberg by his encounters with the SS that in later life (his wife relates) he had nightmares about the Gestapo marching up the stairs. He was especially troubled by the threat to his "inner autonomy"—his inner moral freedom—posed by his interlocutors at the Berlin Gestapo headquarters.[6]

3. Letter excerpted in A. Hermann, *Die Jahrhundertwissenschaft: Werner Heisenberg und die Physik seiner Zeit* (Stuttgart, 1977), p. 144. Paraphrased in A. Beyerchen, *Scientists under Hitler* (New Haven, 1977), pp. 160 f. The letter seems to have disappeared from the Heisenberg-Archiv. (Several items relating to Himmler and other sensitive materials have been reserved from public use by Mrs. Heisenberg.)

4. Beyerchen, *Scientists under Hitler*, p. 161; Cassidy, pp. 386 f.

5. Cassidy, pp. 387–391 (who calls the main interrogator, Johannes Juilfs, by the name "Mathias Jules"). After the war Heisenberg repaid the debt by writing "Persil-certificates" to aid such helpful SS acquaintances as Juilfs/Jules. For Heisenberg's denazification activities, see below, chap. 21.

6. Cassidy, pp. 389–391. Elisabeth Heisenberg, *Inner Exile: Recollections of a Life with Werner Heisenberg*, trans. (Boston, 1984), pp. 55 f. Unfortunately the SS's file on Heisenberg has not been found; but the report was certainly favorable (Cassidy, p. 618).

Finally in July 1938, Himmler received the report on Heisenberg, and informed Heydrich on 21 July that thenceforth the physicist was to be protected as a good German patriot who would be useful for the promotion of a new healthy German scientific life and who might also work well with the *Ahnenerbe*, the SS's research organization: "Heisenberg is a decent person, whom we cannot afford to lose or to silence." The same day Himmler wrote to Heisenberg telling him that there would be no further attacks in *Das Schwarze Korps* and expressing the hope that they would meet at the end of the year to "talk things over thoroughly man to man." A postscript added the crucial recommendation—already practiced by Heisenberg— that in the future the audience should be made aware of the "distinction between scientific results and the personal and political attitude of the scientists involved."[7] Himmler had adopted Heisenberg's apolitical principle of suppressing Einstein's name while speaking of his discoveries.

The report that Himmler received has not been found, but its contents may be surmised from a later affidavit prepared by the SS in May 1939 in connection with the Ministry of Education's consideration of Heisenberg's candidacy for the still-open chair at Munich. The author was doubtful about sending Heisenberg to Munich, since that would be a slap in the face to the Party organs that had opposed the nomination, but favored promoting the physicist to Vienna, where he would be usefully influenced by the Nazi staff of the university. Though his original ideas had been somewhat "Jewish" in their theoretical context, Heisenberg had now become more Aryan in his approach to physics. He was of good character, and though, as was typical of many of his class, he was an apolitical, Heisenberg was still ready to serve Germany unconditionally. He had, indeed, told the SS investigators that "one is either born a good German or one is not." This was reflected in his strong military record; Heisenberg had fought with the radical nationalist Lützow Freikorps against the leftists during the Munich revolution of 1918, and had actually volunteered for army reserves in 1935, and again during the Munich crisis of 1938. There were some question marks. His political attitude was certainly not as clear as it should have been; he had declined to take part in the 1933 Leipzig rally for fear his foreign colleagues might have misunderstood his action. But "over the course of several years, Heisenberg has allowed himself to be convinced more and more of the right of Nazism through its successes and is today positive toward it. He is, however, of the view that active political activity is not suitable for a university teacher, save for the occasional participation in indoctrination camps and

7. Facsimiles of the Himmler letters are in S. Goudsmit, *ALSOS* (New York, 1947), pp. 115–119. They are taken from documents in the Ahnenerbe Files, Berlin Document Center; and the Goudsmit Papers, AIP, box 11, folder 98. Translated also in *HPNS*, pp. 175 f., from copies in the Prandtl Papers, Göttingen. Goudsmit's memorandum on a missing copy of a Himmler letter to the SS Dozentenführer in Leipzig thanking him for a "very thorough and accurate report on Heisenberg" and repeating the substance of the Himmler letter to Heydrich is in NA, RG 77, MED Foreign Intelligence Unit, entry 22, box 167.

the like." Eventually, it was hoped, Heisenberg could also be brought to understand the rightfulness of Nazi antisemitic policy; already he was rejecting "the excessive infiltration of Jews into German living space."[8]

Heisenberg's honor was now satisfied enough to keep him in Germany. In 1938 he had told Sommerfeld that he had "turned to Himmler and requested from him the protection of my honor. . . . Now I actually see no other possibility than to ask for my dismissal if the defense of my honor is refused. . . . You know that it would be very painful for me to leave Germany. I do not want to do it unless it must be absolutely so. However, I also have no desire to live here as a second-class person." In other words, Heisenberg was willing to live in Nazi Germany as a first-class person, but not as a second-class one. Not moral resistance, but personal status, rationalized as being identical with the interests of Germany and German physics, was the benchmark of Heisenberg's "honor."[9]

From 1937 until late in the war Heisenberg regarded Himmler as the patron of his honor. After receiving Himmler's exonerating (and "somewhat friendly") letter of 21 July 1937, Heisenberg scribbled a delighted reply, profusely thanking Himmler for setting him free from great anxiety and assuring him that a proper clarification of the misunderstandings arising from the confusion of politics and science will show the Reichsführer just "how unjustified had been the attacks on my honor."[10] As the matter of Heisenberg's appointment to the Munich chair or another dragged out, and as Himmler deferred the "man-to-man" meeting that Heisenberg so desperately desired, the correspondence between the two continued with apolitical eagerness: "A man-to-man conversation would be the best way to settle completely the misunderstandings that have formerly led to the injury of my honor."[11] Heisenberg's recipe for the restoration of his honor was threefold: First, his new physics (including relativity) should be allowed to prevail over—and be defended from the attacks of—the "German physics" faction; second, his position in his current Leipzig chair should be reinforced, and at the same time a new prestigious chair found for him at Munich or elsewhere; third, he should be al-

---

8. The affidavit is in the Bundesarchiv Potsdam, REM 2943, 370–371, and is paraphrased in M. Walker, *Nazi Science: Myth, Truth, and the German Atomic Bomb* (New York, 1995), pp. 134–138, as well as in Cassidy, p. 391. It has now been translated in *HPNS*, p. 195. For Heisenberg's latent antisemitism see above, and also below, chap. 21, for a violent postwar encounter with Max Born.

9. Heisenberg to Sommerfeld, 14 April 1938, Sommerfeld Nachlass, Deutsches Museum, Munich, 1977–28/A, 136/18. See Cassidy, p. 384. As Cassidy (p. 394) observes, "the moral element was sacrificed to professional advantage."

10. Heisenberg to Himmler, 23 July 1938, copy in Goudsmit Papers, box 11, folder 98 (cf. Cassidy, pp. 393 f.).
Heisenberg to Sommerfeld, 23 July 1938, Sommerfeld Nachlass, 1977–28/A, 136/29, expresses delight at Himmler's friendly letter, which Heisenberg has asked the Reichsführer to circulate.

11. Heisenberg to Himmler, 14 June 1939, Goudsmit Papers, box 11, folder 98. See the frequent enthusiastic references to his contacts with Himmler and his staff in Heisenberg's letters to Sommerfeld of 1938–39, especially those of 21 October 1938; 15 and 25 February, 3 March, 13 May, 8 June, 17 December 1939; 27 October 1940 (Sommerfeld Nachlass).

lowed to publish an article promoting the new physics in an official Nazi science journal. Heisenberg pursued these three points with obsessive self-interest. By the time that war was imminent, Himmler had informed Heisenberg that he would be called to Vienna and allowed to publish an article in the Nazi science journal *Zeitschrift für die gesamte Naturwissenschaft* (*Journal for General Science*). As it turned out, it took until 1942 to translate Heisenberg into a new chair—at Berlin—and until 1943 to arrange finally the publication of his article.[12] But by 1939 Heisenberg had assured himself that staying on in Nazi Germany was the right and honorable thing to do.

True, for a time, especially under the personal pressure of the 1937 attack in *Das Schwarze Korps*, Heisenberg had been tempted to leave. He had contemplated a secret offer from Columbia University in 1937–38, but, as he later wrote to his mother: "When I thought about New York, it was less the thought of the intrigues of Herr St[ark] that was decisive, but more the prospect of living for many more years in an environment that makes work—for the sake of which I now exist—almost impossible."[13] There was no political or moral sense of opposition to Nazism in this decision, merely anxiety for his own physics. This would have been understandable enough in a normal context, but it was deplorable in the extraordinary circumstances of the 1930s. That anxiety was removed by Himmler's coming to the rescue of his honor in 1938–39. And, of course, "patriotism" reinforced Heisenberg's decision to stay on. While on holiday in April 1939 at Badenweiler, Heisenberg and his wife crossed to France. Gazing back across the Rhine hills, he whispered to Elisabeth, "How can I ever leave?"[14] This sentimental patriotism may seem harmless, but to accept it as true patriotism means doing an injustice to those Germans who liked the landscape and the cultural life just as much, but nevertheless left voluntarily out of conscience. To Heisenberg, remaining in Germany was worth almost any price— as long as he did not have to be a "second-class person." One has the strong impression that Heisenberg's "patriotism" stemmed ultimately from a refusal to face up to the facts because he was afraid of the uncomfortable consequences that would have to be drawn. His inability to place his own private contentment in perspective and the essential triviality of his understanding of the evil of the Third Reich are exposed in another justification he offered for not emigrating: His decision not to emigrate, he once admitted, was determined by his fear that he would not be able "to find anywhere else in the world the small private circles in which one could make music with another in the deepest mutual understanding."[15]

---

12. Himmler to Heisenberg, 7 June 1939, Goudsmit Papers, box 11, folder 98. Cf. Walker, *Nazi Science*, p. 138; Cassidy, pp. 394–398. For the article, "Die Bewertung der 'modernen theoretischen Physik'" (1943), see below.

13. Heisenberg to his mother, 27 September 1938, quoted in Cassidy, p. 387.

14. Cassidy, p. 402, quoting an interview with Mrs. Heisenberg.

15. According to A. Hermann, *Werner Heisenberg in Selbstzeugnissen und Bilddokumenten,* 3d ed. (Hamburg, 1979), p. 27.

Thus, by 1937 Heisenberg had shown himself to be a politically reliable person, serving in the army reserves, acquiescing in the purging of Jews from science, and proving his German patriotism to the new rulers of Germany, who were sufficiently sure of his loyalty to allow him to go abroad to Britain, America, and elsewhere on visits in 1938–39.[16] Writing to his mother in 1939, Heisenberg confessed, "I have the feeling that now everything is in place, as far as this depends on me. Of course, many difficulties could still come from the outside. But I will deal with them much more easily than with the inner difficulties."[17] The old German dichotomy between inner and outer freedom enabled Heisenberg to stay on and serve German science—and Himmler.

Among the "inner difficulties" that were troubling Heisenberg may be accounted the intensifying anti-Jewish measures of the regime. In 1938 Heisenberg found himself apologizing to his old friend Pauli for the fact that only "Aryans" were being allowed to celebrate Sommerfeld in a German publication (not seeming to realize how much worse an apology without rectification made matters; a true apology would require Heisenberg's own removal from the list of contributors, and indeed from Nazi Germany itself, instead of conforming to the regime's policies).[18] Heisenberg might claim that he excluded Jews from German science in order to save science, but the practical result of his actions was to isolate and discredit Jews, while exploiting Jewish contributions for the effective furtherance of Germany and of Nazism. The shamefulness of this opportunistic injustice never seems to have occurred to Heisenberg; after a few pro forma regrets and a little agonizing, Heisenberg was able to justify himself by getting back to normal very quickly and resuming his teaching of the new physics unhindered. The *Kristallnacht* pogrom of November 1938, which was particularly violent in Leipzig, did impinge on Heisenberg. In a letter to his mother Heisenberg, clearly shaken, told how he and Elisabeth were "still completely in shock from the last nights." A friend had told them how Jewish families had been dragged screaming to the train station and deported.[19] But Heisenberg's short-lived shock does not appear to have changed his mind about collaborating with the Nazi regime.

When he visited America in the summer of 1939, Heisenberg's friends found his attitudes incomprehensible. They were mystified as to how any rational, let alone decent, person should want to stay on in Germany, particularly when that person seemed to be having such a rough time in pursuing science. While staying with Goudsmit and other friends in Michigan, a famous discussion took place, of which various versions are extant. One eyewitness report describes how, when Fermi and Goudsmit began an aggressive questioning of Heisenberg, he seemed at first to waver; but then Mrs. Fermi said that anyone must be crazy to stay in

16. Cassidy, pp. 392, 403.
17. Heisenberg to his mother, 23 January 1939, quoted in Cassidy, pp. 413 f.
18. Cassidy, p. 408.
19. Heisenberg to his mother, 12 November 1938, quoted in Cassidy, p. 401 (cf. p. 394).

Germany, whereupon Heisenberg launched into a vehement objection.[20] Heisenberg's rationalized version has it that on being asked by Fermi why he did not emigrate, he replied that he could not abandon his young circle. Besides, Heisenberg lectured the group, "people must learn to prevent catastrophes, not to run away from them." Heisenberg insisted that he could not leave because "Germany needs me," and argued that the Hitlerite excesses would soon blow over; in any case, Germany could not win a war.[21] The last comment seems improbable, for by 1939 Heisenberg was aware that during his foreign trips he was constantly under surveillance by German spies who reported any unwise words uttered, and that to express defeatist sentiments would complicate his hard-won position at home. Other sources have claimed also that Heisenberg actually opined that a German victory in the forthcoming war was likely.[22]

On returning to Germany, Heisenberg regaled a family gathering at his Bavarian cottage with his vision of an explosive that could destroy New York, remarking in his usual objective way that whoever first possessed this explosive could blackmail the whole world. His sister-in-law spotted this amoralism masquerading as objectivity and commented ironically in a letter: "I am very glad to hear these lovely prospects of means of destruction."[23]

No wonder that when Heisenberg was called in September 1939 to participate in the Weapons Research Office's uranium project, he happily joined in, spurred on as he was by scientific and patriotic instincts alike, all scruples swept away by years of compromise and self-deception.

. . .

Work on military projects was a scientific imperative for scientists on all sides during the war, but the apolitical mentality of German scientists rendered them oblivious of the evil of their aggressive regime and conscienceless in their readiness to serve it. There was a precedent for this profoundly amoral behavior in the 1914 war when Fritz Haber introduced the use of poison gas. Tear gas had been used already, but Haber and his colleagues (including Otto Hahn, who served in a gas unit, but not Max Born, who refused to join in) racked up the barbarization of warfare without a thought for the violation of the Hague Conventions.[24] Given

20. Max Dresden's recollection, cited in Cassidy, pp. 411–413.
21. Heisenberg, *Physics and Beyond*, pp. 169–172.
22. Cf. Cassidy, pp. 411–413.
23. Edith Kuby-Schumacher to Erich Kuby, 30 August 1939, in Erich Kuby, *Mein Krieg* (Munich, 1975), p. 13.
24. See L. F. Haber, *The Poisonous Cloud: Gas Warfare in the First World War* (Oxford, 1986). This book by Haber's son occasionally slips into some rather German thinking—e.g., p. 28: "As long as the Germans were prepared to ignore the moral issue posed by the Hague Conventions, they would have done better [*sic*] to damn the consequences and rely for their initial surprise on the more powerful weapon [phosgene, rather than chlorine]."
Haber displayed a horrifying enthusiasm—in the name of patriotism—for the use of poison gas. His wife pleaded with him to abandon his work and committed suicide partly in disgust. In the 1920s

this German background of ruthlessness, it cannot really be doubted that had Heisenberg been able to produce an atomic bomb, he certainly would have done so. Whatever his private reservations might have been, they would assuredly not have deterred him from acting as a loyal son of Germany. Everything so far described in his mentality leads to this conclusion, and it is confirmed by his actual conduct and opinions during the war years.[25]

Throughout the war, Heisenberg continued his dialogue with Himmler and the SS in order to guarantee the integrity of theoretical physics and his own honor. With the invaluable help of Weizsäcker as a diplomat, a series of encounters, known jocularly as "religious colloquies" (*Religionsgespräche*), between Heisenberg and his rivals was arranged by the SS, at which arcane questions of physics and ideology were debated. These meetings convinced the Nazi University Lecturers' League's assessor of scholarship, Gustav Borger, that "Heisenberg's political position is in no way to be designated argumentative. He is undoubtedly the unpolitical academic type."[26] This helpful testimonial (in return for which Borger received his own "Persil-certificate" for denazification in 1947) opened the way to Heisenberg's victory over "German physics" at a final debate held at scenic Seefeld in the Tyrol in November 1942 and attended by thirty scientists and ideologists including Heisenberg and his old SS acquaintance Johannes Juilfs. As ever, the compromise was shameful: Relativity theory was to be taught, but divorced from Einstein's name. Indeed, Einstein was seen as a sort of Jewish profiteer of Aryan ideas. The report (formulated by Weizsäcker) found that "before Einstein, Aryan scientists like Lorentz, Hasenohrl, Poincaré, etc., had created the foundations of the theory of relativity, and Einstein merely followed up the already existing ideas consistently." The final paragraph of the Seefeld report denounced the forcing of relativity theory into a world philosophy of relativism "as has been attempted by the Jewish propaganda press of the previous era."[27] Heisenberg himself propagated this lie when he argued to a member of the Prussian Academy of Sciences that special relativity would have arisen even without Einstein.[28]

Haber acted as a consultant on the use of gas for the Spanish and other militaries. On this (and Born's refusal) see M. F. Perutz, "The Cabinet of Dr. Haber," *New York Review of Books*, 20 June 1996, 31–35.

25. Cassidy, p. 424, finds it "difficult to comprehend the motives and rationale that allowed Heisenberg and his colleagues to place their great abilities so easily at the service of the German army at war"; however, the extensive evidence of Heisenberg's peculiarly German attitudes amassed by Cassidy suggests an answer to this problem. The obituary by N. Mott and R. Peierls, "Werner Heisenberg," *Biographical Memoirs of Fellows of the Royal Society* 23 (1977): 213–251, at p. 232, sees Heisenberg's work on the uranium project as arising out of simple wartime patriotism, and neglects the German mentality and the context of Nazism. Heisenberg's war work cannot be equated with that of Allied scientists.

26. Borger to Party Chancery, 9 September 1942, Institut für Zeitgeschichte, Munich, "Amt Rosenberg/Hauptamt Wissenschaft: Heisenberg," MA 116/5. See Cassidy, p. 454.

27. Goudsmit, *ALSOS*, pp. 152 f. Beyerchen, *Scientists under Hitler*, p. 192. The minutes of the Seefeld meeting and Weizsäcker's report are in Goudsmit Papers, box 25, folder 12.

28. Cassidy, p. 454.

The public certification of Heisenberg's triumph took the form of the publication of an article (written in 1940) in the Nazi *Zeitschrift für die gesamte Naturwissenschaft*, the stronghold of "German physics." In 1942 Heisenberg had been immensely gratified by his dual appointment to the directorship of the Kaiser-Wilhelm-Institute for Physics and a chair at Berlin. But the publication of the article—the final element of the threefold restoration of his honor that Heisenberg had proposed to Himmler in 1938—had still been obstructed. Finally, in February 1943 Heisenberg wrote to Himmler, thanking the Reichsführer for "the public reestablishing of my honor" by the academic appointments, and requesting him to intervene with the journal.[29] Himmler's personal staff replied, stating that they would intervene positively, and the article duly appeared at the end of the year. It contained a revisionist account of the development of modern physics, rationalized with all of Heisenberg's expert glibness:

> America would have been discovered if Columbus had never lived, and so too the theory of electrical phenomena without Maxwell and of electrical waves without Maxwell, for the things themselves could not have been changed by the discoverers. So too undoubtedly relativity theory would have emerged without Einstein. Certainly it may be shown that in details other scholars had already bent their thought in the right direction; through the works of Voigt, Lorentz, and Poincaré one was standing right in front of the complete formulation of special relativity theory.[30]

(Heisenberg never seems to have applied this interesting theory of inevitable discovery to his own discoveries of matrix mechanics and the uncertainty principle.)

Not surprisingly, Heisenberg's public toadying led to his receiving high honors. Goering recommended him to Hitler for the War Service Cross in October 1943, and Goebbels's intellectual weekly made him the subject of a cover story in May 1944 as a "German national leader."[31] And, of course, when Himmler tried to develop his own atomic bomb project in 1944, his staff could always rely for assistance on their long-standing friendly relations with Heisenberg.[32] Heisenberg's relations with Himmler, which had begun in a spirit of self-protection, had all too seamlessly flowed into acquiescence and collusion.

29. Heisenberg to Himmler, 4 February 1943, Heisenberg-Archiv, Munich and Berlin (copy kindly supplied by H. Rechenberg).

30. Heisenberg, "Die Bewertung der 'modernen theoretischen Physik,'" *Zeitschrift für die gesamte Naturwissenschaft* 9 (1943): 201–212, reprinted in GWH, C V, 14–25, and also in H. Rechenberg, ed., *Deutsche und jüdische Physik* (Munich, 1992), pp. 90–106.

31. Cassidy, p. 464. See "Deutsche Volksführer: Werner Heisenberg," *Das Reich*, 14 May 1944, p. 1.

32. See above, chap. 13.

CHAPTER 19

Justifying Nazi Victory, 1941–45

Himmler's confidence in Heisenberg's loyal usefulness was certainly borne out by the series of propaganda trips Heisenberg made to occupied European countries during the war. These offensive and ignoble visits, later lightly dismissed by Heisenberg as of little significance, shamelessly manifested to the international scientific community his compromise with Nazism.[1]

The most notorious of Heisenberg's trips was the much-debated visit to Niels Bohr in Copenhagen in September 1941. Such "cultural propaganda" expeditions had been mounted in the 1914 war by Heisenberg's own mentor Sommerfeld, who had justified his lecturing to German troops in Belgium and to a Flemish section at the reorganized University of Ghent by invoking the need to assert "[international] German culture" on "ancient German soil."[2] Heisenberg's Copenhagen visit may have had a slight element of this cultural imperialism to it, but it seems to have been inspired by more complicated motives. Weizsäcker had given a lecture in Copenhagen in March 1941, and that visit seems to have passed off amicably.[3] This success may have suggested to Heisenberg that they might use the contacts of his colleague's father, Ernst von Weizsäcker, with the German ambassador in Denmark to help protect Bohr's position, while conveniently legitimizing the German occupation by implicating the Danish physicist in exercises in cultural collaboration.[4]

1. Cassidy, pp. 464–473; M. Walker, "Physics and Propaganda: Werner Heisenberg's Foreign Lectures under National Socialism," *Historical Studies in the Physical Sciences* 22 (1992): 339–389.

2. M. Eckert et al., eds., *Geheimrat Sommerfeld—Theoretischer Physiker: Eine Dokumentation aus seinem Nachlass (Deutsches Museum)* (Munich, 1984), p. 130.

3. Bohr to Weizsäcker, 13 March 1941, inviting the German to dinner, Bohr Scientific Correspondence, 26, Archive for History of Quantum Physics, Berkeley; copy in AIP.

4. Heisenberg felt he had done " a good job" in protecting Bohr through the good offices of the German ambassador in Copenhagen, who was under instructions from Ernst von Weizsäcker (see the interview in J. J. Ermenc, *Atomic Bomb Scientists: Memoirs, 1939–1945* [Westport, Conn., 1989], pp. 71 f.). The

(There may also have been an idea of making Weizsäcker director of Bohr's Institute as a means of protecting him.)[5] Weizsäcker's proposal to have Heisenberg accompany him on his next visit to Copenhagen, however, ran into bureaucratic obstruction, though it was eventually cleared thanks to the threat of intervention from Weizsäcker's father in the Foreign Ministry in early September 1941, and the visit took place later in the month.[6] The catalyst in this seems to have been Carl-Friedrich von Weizsäcker's alarm at press reports of American experiments for the development of a 5 kg atomic bomb; the mission thus assumed a crucial intelligence dimension, aiming at ascertaining whether Bohr knew of Allied progress, and also whether Bohr thought a bomb feasible.[7]

The behavior of Heisenberg and Weizsäcker during their days in Copenhagen did not augur well for the sensitive private conversation that Heisenberg planned on having with Bohr. Though Weizsäcker's preparatory correspondence had expressed a desire for Bohr and the Danes to participate in the German Cultural Institute's conference and had graciously stated that Bohr was not being "forced" to come, this sensitivity quickly evaporated after Heisenberg and Weizsäcker's arrival in Copenhagen.[8] Weizsäcker attempted to compromise Bohr and his colleagues by telling them that if they did not attend the conference, they would be faced with the imposition of an SS institute. Though this threat may have seemed impressive to Weizsäcker and Heisenberg—to judge from their own past conduct—it cut little ice with the Danes: "The Germans always excused the acceptance of something bad on the ground that if it was not, then something worse would have to be accepted." Weizsäcker then made matters worse by bringing the director of the German Cultural Institute to Bohr's offices and pushing him past the secretary into Bohr's own room unannounced.[9] Meanwhile, during several lunches at the Bohr Institute, Heisenberg antagonized his hosts by

story is embroidered in the Weizsäcker interview printed in D. Hoffmann, ed., *Operation Epsilon: Die Farm-Hall Protokoll . . .* (Berlin, 1994), pp. 351 f. Weizsäcker rejects Walker's contention that the whole visit was redolent with cultural propaganda, which he sees as merely a cover arrangement.

5. In a letter of 21 January 1977 to R. Peierls (copy supplied by Sir Rudolf Peierls), Goudsmit writes: "Early April 1945 when the armies entered Göttingen, I met Houtermans. He told me about that visit. He claims that Bohr's Institute had to be Aryanized and that von Weizsäcker was to be the new director. Von Weizsäcker could have effectively protected Bohr. Heisenberg came along to smooth over the transition. It failed because of the misunderstanding between Bohr and Heisenberg. Von Weizsäcker calls this a plausible story but denies that it was true."

6. See correspondence cited in Walker, "Physics and Propaganda," pp. 364 f.; and in general, M. Walker, *German National Socialism and the Quest for Nuclear Power, 1939–1949* (Cambridge, 1989), pp. 223–227.

7. See Weizsäcker's letters of 4 and 5 September to the HWA Wa F/1 and the Ministry of Education, citing the press reports, all transcribed in NA, RG 77, MED, microfilm A-1218, roll 5 (*Manhattan Project History*, vol. 14, *Foreign Intelligence*, supp. 1, app. A). See above, chap. 10.

8. Weizsäcker to Bohr, 15 August 1941, in Bohr Scientific Correspondence, 26.

9. J. G. Crowther, *Science in Liberated Europe* (London, 1949), pp. 106 f., drawing on Danish accounts. Cassidy, p. 440, however, dates the intrusion to Weizsäcker's first visit of March 1941.

speaking with great confidence about the progress of the German offensive in Russia. . . . He stressed how important it was that Germany should win the war. To Christian Møller, for instance, he said that the occupation of Denmark, Norway, Belgium, and Holland was a sad thing, but as regards the countries in East Europe, it was a good development because these countries were not able to govern themselves. Møller's answer was that so far we have only learned that it is Germany which cannot govern itself.[10]

A postwar British report on the Copenhagen visit concluded that though Heisenberg was not a Nazi, he was an "intense nationalist, with the characteristic German deference to the authorities in control of the nation. He is said to have expressed the opinion that war is a biological necessity."[11] Aware of such remarks, Bohr had difficulty in talking himself into agreeing to meet with Heisenberg, while Mrs. Bohr at first refused to have him to dinner during this visit, but finally relented under her husband's pleading.[12]

By the time the occasion for the momentous after-dinner conversation with Bohr himself arrived, things were thus well and truly prejudiced in every sense, and this is reflected in the various conflicting accounts we have of the tête-à-tête. Even the location of the talk is disputed: Heisenberg has it taking place in the Tivoli gardens or the Faelledpark; Bohr's friends place it in his study at home or at the Institute office.[13] As to its purpose and content, as usual Heisenberg is difficult to pin down and flits in his various recollections from theme to theme. A draft affidavit of 1948 in defense of Ernst von Weizsäcker for the Nuremberg Tribunal has Bohr asking Heisenberg if nuclear energy was likely to be exploited during the war and receiving the reply "Yes, I know that is so." Heisenberg claims that he meant here only a reactor, but implies that Bohr mistakenly took him to be referring to a bomb.[14] A private letter of the same year improves on this: Of course, says Heisenberg, he understood that a reactor would work and also that plutonium from reactors could be used to make bombs—but he thought both the uranium-235 and plutonium bombs to be fantastic propositions since he overestimated the technical effort involved. Still, he was deeply worried about the possibility of giving powerful leaders—"not only Hitler"—such weapons. Thus, when he saw Bohr, Heisenberg asked him whether

10. S. Rozental to M. Gowing, 6 September 1984, quoted in A. Pais, *Niels Bohr's Times in Physics, Philosophy, and Polity* (Oxford, 1991), pp. 483 ff. I am grateful to Professor Rozental for amplifying to me in letters of 21 May 1984 and 27 January 1985 the tenor of these conversations of 1941.

11. Crowther, *Science in Liberated Europe*, p. 108.

12. Details told by Bohr to Ruth Ananda Anshen, as reported in T. Powers, *Heisenberg's War: The Secret History of the German Bomb* (New York, 1993), pp. 122, 509.

13. See the useful information in Pais, *Niels Bohr's Times*, p. 484. Also N. Blaedel, *Harmony and Unity: The Life of Niels Bohr* (Madison, Wisc., 1988), p. 235.

14. Cassidy, p. 437, citing Weizsäcker Defense Exhibit, no. 303 (NA, RG 238, microfilm M-897, roll 119).

physicists had the moral right to work on atomic problems during wartime. Bohr asked back whether I believed a military application of atomic energy were possible, and I replied: Yes—I knew that to be so. I put my question again, and Bohr answered to my astonishment that the war work of physics in every country was unavoidable and therefore well-justified. . . . Bohr took my question as indirect information about the state of our [atomic energy] knowledge.[15]

Here Heisenberg blames Bohr for justifying the military work of atomic scientists of all nations, including Nazi Germany, and at the same time regrets that Bohr drew the erroneous conclusion that Heisenberg was successfully developing a German bomb. A moment's thought will show that both these ideas are ridiculous postwar rationalizations by the imaginative Heisenberg. Given all we know of Bohr's impeccable character and his view of Nazi Germany, he simply could not have given his approval to Heisenberg's working on an atomic bomb for Hitler. Moreover, if Bohr had done so, why did Heisenberg not then set Bohr's mind at rest by intimating that indeed he himself was not working on such a bomb?

Heisenberg here intimated another line of apology of which he was fond—the postulate that all politicians were men of amoral power and that supplying Hitler with a bomb was not essentially different from giving the bomb to others; Heisenberg thus placed himself in the same moral predicament as that of Bohr and the Allied scientists who also worked on the bomb. What Bohr would have made of this is not hard to imagine. Even Heisenberg himself later felt obliged to moderate his words somewhat, as in an interview of 1965 (though he introduced there other absurdities including the blatant falsehood that both he and Weizsäcker had always thought that America would be the first to make reactors and so, it is implied, develop a bomb):

We saw really from September 1941 an open road before us to the atomic bomb. We saw thus that atomic bombs could, in principle, be made. We found that now a terrible situation existed for all physicists, especially for us Germans, and certainly it was more horrible for the Germans than for all others, for the pictures conjured up by giving atomic bombs into Hitler's hand were dreadful.[16]

Heisenberg now made the German atomic scientists subject to the most exquisite pangs of conscience, and depicted his going to Copenhagen as a pilgrimage aimed at "getting Bohr's absolution." One would have thought that any genuine moral scruples would not have required going to an external figure for confirmation; and again, if the reactor was indeed the open road to the plutonium bomb, a person of such moral refinement would have surely refrained from the enthusiastic participation in the race to achieve a critical reactor to which Heisenberg devoted himself from 1941 to 1945.

Sometimes Heisenberg himself exposed the absurdity of his claim to have been asking Bohr for advice in matters of conscience, as in a BBC interview of 1965:

15. Heisenberg to B. L. van der Waerden, 28 April 1948, in Goudsmit Papers, AIP (IMF 29-1190).
16. Heisenberg, interview by D. Irving, 23 October 1965 (IMF 31-541/542).

We felt that in this situation the physicists had some influence on the further development of the project, because the physicists could argue in two ways. We could say, one can make atomic bombs, therefore one should try and make atomic bombs. We could also argue by saying, well, it requires such an enormous industrial effort that it will actually weaken our war effort during the next years and probably the bombs won't be ready before the end of the war, therefore it's no use to make bombs. Now, since in this way the physicists seem to have a strong influence on the further development, I felt that it was good to ask for [Bohr's] advice.[17]

Now this is very amusing as an example of Heisenberg's rationalizing skills and ability to make up plausible arguments on either side of a fence, but it does not show why Heisenberg had to ask Bohr's advice about what seemed to be a technical matter as to whether bombs could or could not be made without disrupting the German war effort. Moreover, if one had to ask which of the alternatives to adopt, then one's mind was still open to either of them and so Heisenberg was willing in principle to make a bomb for Hitler. In trying to refute one aspect of reproach, Heisenberg generally opens the way to another.[18]

Let us now turn to some of the other accounts of the Heisenberg meeting with Bohr. Bohr himself left no public description of what happened, although there are indications that he did write on it privately.[19] However, Niels's son Aage, who was in his father's confidence in these matters, has written a couple of terse sentences:

In a private conversation with my father, Heisenberg brought up the question of the military applications of atomic energy. My father was very reticent and expressed his scepticism because of the great technical difficulties that had to be overcome, but he had the impression that Heisenberg thought that the new possibilities could decide the outcome of the war if the war dragged on.[20]

In a footnote to this passage, Aage Bohr took special pains to deplore as entirely false Robert Jungk's claim that "the German physicists had submitted a secret plan to my father, aimed at preventing the development of atomic weapons through a mutual agreement with colleagues in the Allied countries."

17. Heisenberg, BBC interview, 2 March 1965, text in GWH, C V, 44.

18. In *Physics and Beyond: Encounters and Conversations,* trans. (New York, 1972), p. 182, Heisenberg puts forward the same issue, saying the conflicting technical views of the feasibility of the bomb could be argued "with equal conviction," and he blames Bohr for getting so frightened by his comments that he lost track of Heisenberg's essential point that the bomb required too great an effort to be feasible. Pais, *Niels Bohr's Times,* p. 484, is dubious about Bohr having been "frightened," though he may indeed have been "taken aback" by Heisenberg's démarches.

19. It seems that Bohr was so distressed by the fabrications in Jungk's book (which Jungk himself has largely disowned in recent years) that he wrote a letter to Heisenberg complaining, "Your version is wrong." But the letter was never posted and was later found by the family inside a copy of the Jungk book. (Information partly from Professor Gerald Holton.)

20. A. Bohr, "The War Years and the Prospects Raised by the Atomic Weapons," in S. Rozental, ed., *Niels Bohr: His Life and Work As Seen by His Friends and Colleagues* (Amsterdam and New York, 1967), pp. 191–214, at p. 193.

A close colleague of Bohr's, S. Rozental, has recalled the aftermath thus: "I can only remember how excited Bohr was after that conversation and that he quoted Heisenberg for having said something like: You must understand that if I am taking part in the project, then it is in the firm belief that it can be done."[21] This certainly has the ring of Heisenberg's voice. As for Mrs. Bohr, she retained very sharp memories of the episode, for which she never forgave Heisenberg and Weizsäcker. At a meeting in Copenhagen in 1963, she caught sight of the two German physicists and, without being asked, "suddenly blurted out" to Goudsmit, who was standing beside her: "That wartime visit of those two (pointing at Heisenberg and Weizsäcker) was a hostile visit, no matter what people say or write about it."[22] Bohr himself may have been slightly more forgiving, even if Heisenberg's and Weizsäcker's claims after the war to have been told by him that he understood and approved their conduct are too heavily colored by self-delusion to be accepted. They seem to have mistaken Bohr's fervent desire to avoid discussing the painful incident as somehow confirming their versions of it.[23] Most certainly Bohr's old friendship with Heisenberg was shattered by the visit of 1941, and though a certain formal friendliness was restored, it was never the same as before—thenceforth relations were civil, but strained.[24] Bohr must have felt completely betrayed, first by Heisenberg's collusion with the Nazi regime, and, as if that were not bad enough, by the heedless attempt to compromise the Danish physicist's own repu-

21. Rozental to Gowing, quoted in Pais, *Niels Bohr's Times,* p. 483.

22. Goudsmit to Peierls, 21 January 1977, copy supplied by Professor Peierls; file copy in Goudsmit Papers, box 10, folder 97; and also recalled by Erik Rudinger, according to Cassidy, p. 441. In a letter to Mrs. Bohr of 28 September 1964 (Goudsmit Papers, box 6, folder 26) Goudsmit asked her for details of her repudiation of Jungk's account, but I have not found any written information that may have been supplied. According to a letter to me from Professor John A. Wheeler, 18 April 1984, Mrs. Bohr retained a very sharp memory of the 1941 Heisenberg conversations.

23. For instance, Heisenberg, *Physics and Beyond,* pp. 201 f. Cf. Weizsäcker's interview in Hoffmann, *Operation Epsilon,* p. 353; his memoir in "Heisenberg im Urteil seiner Schüler," *Bild der Wissenschaft* 22 (1985): 138–147; and an interview of 1984 reprinted in his *Bewusstseinswandel* (Munich, 1988), p. 369, where he claims to have been told kindly by Bohr at Princeton in 1950, "You know, I had full understanding for the fact that in a war everyone has the immediate duty of loyalty toward his own country. On that account I certainly do not reproach Heisenberg. So why should we speak any more about it?" (Weizsäcker's plea to Bohr of 16 March 1950 to meet with him is in Bohr Scientific Correspondence, 33). In this misreading of Bohr's mind, Weizsäcker's powers of self-deception are quite remarkable (as also in his assertions that the purpose of Heisenberg's mission was to bring physicists together for the postwar period and ensure that physics helped the cause of peace, and that Heisenberg heroically "risked his neck" for this end).

Bohr showed enormous restraint and correctness in writing on scientific matters to Weizsäcker a month after the disastrous visit; Weizsäcker replied in equally professional terms, but Bohr can hardly have forgiven Weizsäcker at that point (letters of 18 October and 3 November 1941, in Bohr Scientific Correspondence, 26). Later correspondence (ibid.) of 1945 shows Bohr responding kindly to an appeal from Weizsäcker's mother to notify him at Farm Hall of the family's situation. Again, this does not prove that Bohr approved of Weizsäcker's moral conduct.

24. Cassidy, p. 515.

tation. During the 1930s Bohr had been impressed by Heisenberg's efforts to help Jewish scientists and by his apologies "for all that which is now happening in this country."[25] It must, therefore, have been a great sadness for Bohr in 1941 to have had to listen to the specious justifications of German conquest coming from someone he had taken to be a decent man.

When the element of atomic weapons was added to these already offensive propositions of Heisenberg's, the mixture must have become explosive. In late 1946 Bohr let slip some of this when he told Rudolf Ladenburg that Heisenberg and Weizsäcker had during their visit expressed their "hope and belief" that if the war lasted long enough, nuclear weapons would win the war for Germany.[26]

Some sense of Bohr's anger may be gleaned from another postwar German account, but by someone who had been asked by Heisenberg to try to appease Bohr shortly after the original fiasco. The German scientist Hans Jensen, reportedly a socialist or communist and friend of Heisenberg and Houtermans, informed Bohr in 1942 that the Germans were not intent on making a bomb. Bohr, who did not fully trust Jensen, nevertheless told him how much he had resented Heisenberg's lecture at the German Cultural Institute and the attempt to involve him in the proceedings. Bohr felt especially angered by Heisenberg's defense of the occupation of France as being less brutal than that of Poland. As to matters of conscience about nuclear weapons, Bohr said that "Heisenberg should deal with his conscience himself" and asked Jensen to deliver this message: "Tell Professor Heisenberg I am not the pope. I cannot give him absolution." Though Bohr and British Intelligence were suspicious of Jensen as a possible agent provocateur, he seems to have tried to send from Norway a message to Britain that Heisenberg was working on both a U235 bomb and a "power machine" and, although doubtful of the former project, was certain of the latter's succeeding. In the first edition of his autobiography Heisenberg seized on Jensen's visit to Bohr as a vindication of the truth of his own accounts of the meeting; but there is not the least evidence that he was aware of Jensen's possibly treasonous contacts, nor that Jensen ever fully informed Heisenberg of all of Bohr's comments. Significantly, Jensen himself asked Heisenberg to remove references to his visit from later editions of the autobiography for fear that he (Jensen) might be deemed a traitor.[27]

Word of the Heisenberg-Bohr meeting percolated slowly abroad both during and after the war. Christian Møller, whom Heisenberg had regaled with his theory of the benefits of Nazi conquest, visited Stockholm in March 1942 and told Lise Meitner of the episode. Meitner wrote ironically of it to Laue: "I had Dr. M with

25. Heisenberg to Bohr, 30 June 1933, cited in Cassidy, p. 321.

26. Ladenburg to Goudsmit, 23 October 1946, Goudsmit Papers, quoted in Walker, *German National Socialism*, p. 225.

27. See Powers, *Heisenberg's War*, pp. 158–161, for Jensen's late testimony. (Cf. A. Kramish, *The Griffin* [Boston, 1986], pp. 131 f.) Powers unwarrantedly concludes that Heisenberg was as much a resister as Jensen may actually have been. But even Jensen's status is problematic; he had joined the Nazi Party in 1937!

me one evening and that was very nice and pleasing. . . . Half-amusing and half-depressing was his report about a visit of Werner and Carl-Friedrich . . . I became very melancholy on hearing this; at one time I had held them to be decent human beings. They have gone astray."[28] Laue replied that he himself had "often wondered about the inner attitude of Werner and Carl-Friedrich. I think I understand their psychology. Many, especially the young, cannot come to terms with the great irrationality of existence, and therefore build castles of air in their thought. There is a powerful striving to find in something that one cannot get rid of at least some good sides. They aren't alone in this."[29]

The Bohr conversation was resurrected soon after the war by Heisenberg, who had by now convinced himself of the altruism of his Copenhagen mission. In 1947 Heisenberg traveled to Copenhagen with the aim of reestablishing friendly relations with Bohr and perhaps also bringing the Danish scientists round to the German version. However, when Heisenberg brought up the matter of the 1941 visit, Bohr flatly refused to discuss it with him and suggested he get in touch with Goudsmit directly.[30] Doubtless Heisenberg took this response as somehow confirming his own version, or so he made out in later interviews in which he falsely claimed he had enjoyed a long evening's talk with Bohr on the subject.[31] But the recollection of the British officer Ronald Fraser, who liaised with the German scientists at Göttingen and arranged the visit with Bohr himself, even accompanying Heisenberg to Copenhagen, is quite different. Heisenberg had represented to Fraser that he wished to go for two reasons: first, to expound his new theory of superconductivity to Bohr; and second, to obtain food for his family. But there was no thrashing out of the 1941 meeting.

> The whole story of "a kind of confrontation" [with Bohr in 1947] . . . is a typical Heisenberg fabrication—maybe a bit brighter than a thousand others, but like them all a product of his *Blut und Boden* guilt complex, which he rationalizes that quickly that the stories become for him the truth. . . . Pitiful, in a man of his mental stature.

As Fraser had said in an earlier letter in answer to a request to provide a clear picture of the German atomic project from his lengthy contacts with German scientists in 1946–48, "there was too much self-deception among them for that."[32]

---

28. Meitner to Laue, 20 April 1942, Meitner Papers, Churchill College Archives, Cambridge. Quoted also in Kramish, *The Griffin*, p. 120.

29. Laue to Meitner, 26 April 1942, Meitner Papers.

30. See the correspondence summarized in Cassidy, p. 515.

31. W. Heisenberg, interview, *Der Spiegel* 28 (3 July 1967): 79–83, reprinted in GWH, C V, 45–49. See also idem, *Physics and Beyond*, pp. 201 f., where Heisenberg fools himself into thinking that Bohr's refusal to enter into discussion is really just a case of difficulty in remembering the original episode. One is left with a typical Heisenberg impression of innocent geniality presiding over the 1947 encounter.

32. Fraser to Irving, 27 August 1966 and 19 January 1966, in IMF 32. Cf. Heisenberg, interview by Irving (IMF 31-564).

But what actually did happen in 1941? Two main thrusts to Heisenberg's presentation to Bohr can be deduced, one political, the other scientific. The days leading up to the talk saw Heisenberg making his case for the benefits of German conquest to all and sundry at the Copenhagen Institute, so Bohr would have been well prepared for this line. Some accounts suggest that indeed Bohr opened the talk by reproaching Heisenberg for defending the invasion of Poland; Heisenberg thereupon replied that though Poland was a tragedy, Germany had not destroyed France in similar fashion. This provoked Bohr, and matters were quickly made worse by Heisenberg's telling Bohr that Germany would soon defeat the Russians and that that would be a "good thing."[33] But even Heisenberg might have been daunted at making too crude a eulogy of German power in front of his old highly critical mentor, and so a more subtle apology would have been offered.

To reconstruct this apology, the political context of September 1941 must be remembered: France and the West had been defeated in the most amazing fashion in 1940, and now it seemed that the feat was about to be repeated even more spectacularly in the East against the Soviet Union. Britain seemed likely to lose North Africa and the Middle East and to be contained, if not forced out of the war—and the United States was not yet involved. A new European order under German patronage seemed inevitable, and Heisenberg would have already dreamed up his usual rationalizations of its "good sides." The most attractive line of presenting the necessity of collaboration in the New European Order would have been to appeal to Bohr's belief in the social responsibility of the scientist. The possibility of future advances in atomic energy would have seemed to Heisenberg a trump card; more than ever, scientists had to cooperate in order to mitigate the evil aspects of politics and promote social good and scientific progress, and the proper use of nuclear energy would be the key item in this program. This reconstruction may explain a central contradiction in Heisenberg's versions of the mission to Copenhagen: If he did indeed see an "open road" (via plutonium) to the atomic bomb from 1941 (as he claimed later) and if he also believed that the bomb could not be built before the end of the war, why did he feel he had to go to Copenhagen to see Bohr? There was no immediate danger of a breakthrough demanding Bohr's swift intervention, but it was certainly an opportune time to discuss with Bohr how to pursue that "open road" in the postwar period.

If the deceptive layers of Heisenberg's and Weizsäcker's postwar rationalizations of the meeting are stripped away, then traces of this reconstructed political argument begin to surface. Heisenberg later emphasized the need to plan for "in-

---

33. According to the reconstruction in Powers, *Heisenberg's War*, p. 123. Powers does not seem to notice how these glib apologies for German conquest invalidate his general argument that Heisenberg was so moved by conscience that he obstructed the development of a German bomb. Someone with as little capacity for moral insight—apart from the trivial—as Heisenberg repeatedly shows himself to have would never have had the moral stature to block actively the development of a bomb (unlike say, Laue).

ternational understanding among physicists" in a postwar era when atomic energy would be realized.[34] But by the time Heisenberg was writing and saying this, his understanding of the "postwar era" as the era of a defeated Nazi Germany was quite different in its shape from the "postwar era" of a Pax Nazica that appeared inevitable in September 1941. Heisenberg, of course, chose to forget this critical alteration. In talking to Bohr in 1941 about his "postwar" vision of scientific cooperation, Heisenberg had been offering him the opportunity to collaborate on exploiting atomic energy in a Nazified Europe, not the liberated Europe of the postwar period following a German defeat. Weizsäcker performed a similar sleight-of-mind in claiming that the purpose of the visit was to bring physicists together for the postwar period and ensure that physics helped the cause of peace. Such a happy scheme may have been desirable in the postwar Europe that did emerge, but what would it have been like in the postwar Europe that Heisenberg and Weizsäcker envisaged in September 1941?[35] A fundamental historical fallacy underlies all these self-deceiving accounts.

Having offered Bohr the opportunity of working in a Pax Nazica with cosmetic ameliorations, Heisenberg compounded his discreditation in his mentor's eyes by displaying how interested he was in the possibility of atomic bombs. Even Heisenberg admits that he told Bohr that "it was now possible in principle to build atom bombs." Of course, Heisenberg would have argued that a bomb was most unlikely to be developed in the near future or during the present war, but what did that mean? It meant that such bombs would eventually become feasible in the "postwar era" of the Pax Nazica. Heisenberg seems to have been carried away by his scientific arrogance into boasting that he understood how to build a bomb and to have intimated that he was involved in an active German project.[36] Indeed, Weizsäcker admits that Heisenberg, on returning to their hotel, reported: "I said . . . Well, you see a bomb can be made from that and we are working on it."[37]

There is no doubt, despite Heisenberg's later adamant denial,[38] that some technical discussion took place with Bohr on the subject of atomic weapons. When

34. For instance, in *Physics and Beyond*, p. 182.

35. Weizsäcker, "Heisenberg im Urteil," p. 147. Writing to Goudsmit on 7 November 1948, Paul Rosbaud found this kind of apology "silly and disgusting. I remember only too well that many people in Germany were prepared to forgive Hitler many of his evil deeds, because he began this 'crusade' against bolshevism. Hitler defending Western civilization!! . . . I used to tell these people right from the beginning of Hitler's war against Russia that he is the man who opens through his war the road for bolshevism" (NA, RG 200, Goudsmit Papers, box 1, folder 15).

36. See Aage Bohr's comment that Copenhagen's contacts with German physicists strengthened the "impression that the German authorities attributed great military importance to atomic energy" (A. Bohr, "War Years," p. 193). A source who knew the Bohrs and Heisenberg has told me that Heisenberg used these pompous words to Bohr: "We Germans, you know, we have the bomb" (meaning the key to the bomb).

37. Weizsäcker to Powers, quoted in Powers, *Heisenberg's War*, p. 126.

38. See Heisenberg, BBC interview (GWH, C V, 44):

Bohr came to Los Alamos in 1943 he raised for discussion ideas for a reactor-bomb (including a drawing by Heisenberg, or a copy thereof) that had previously arisen in the course of the 1941 conversation. Such a reactor-bomb, however, would have seemed somewhat chimerical in view of its huge size and also the difficulty of obtaining sufficient enriched uranium to fuel it for explosion. Even less probable was the possibility of obtaining the critical mass of U235 (thought by Heisenberg to be in the range of tons) needed for a pure-U235 bomb. Whether or not Heisenberg also talked to Bohr about the possibility of reactors producing plutonium for a bomb is a moot point, though Heisenberg would probably have regarded the idea as too much of a military secret to be divulged. In their 1941 talk, therefore, Bohr and Heisenberg would have concluded that there were no dangerous prospects for an atomic bomb in the near future. This is borne out by Bohr's not having taken any action to alert the Allies in 1941 that a German bomb was imminent. It was only in 1943, when approached by Chadwick, that he began to worry that he might have missed something.[39]

Seen in this dual political and scientific context, it seems clear that what upset Bohr at this meeting of September and turned him permanently against Heisenberg was not fear that a German atomic bomb was imminent, but rather disgust that Heisenberg was planning for atomic research in the imminent Pax Nazica. It seemed that Heisenberg had totally forgotten the humanity and decency that had earlier bound him to Bohr. As Bohr told the Russian scientist Eugene Feinberg in 1961 (and as Weizsäcker recounts without any trace of embarrassment or understanding), it was amazing how "a person whose opinions have slowly changed can completely forget his original opinion." According to what Bohr told Feinberg, Heisenberg was so convinced of Germany's impending victory over the Soviet Union that he thought it "a good thing," and then went on to try to get Bohr and the Danes to collaborate with the Germans in science.[40] In a word, Heisenberg had "Nazified" himself—a term we shall meet again later—without even realizing it.

One final piece of neglected evidence raises problems about Heisenberg's good faith in going to Copenhagen. After the war Heisenberg is reported to have written that he learned just after the September visit that Bohr was in contact with the

---

Dr. Black: "Professor Heisenberg, looking back, is it possible that you were seeking from Bohr advice as to whether your judgement that atomic bombs could be made was correct or not?"

Heisenberg: "No, that is absolutely impossible. I never asked him any questions about physics in that connection. I just wanted to have his human advice."

39. For the Heisenberg drawing of the reactor-bomb and the Bohr-Chadwick correspondence, see above, chap. 10.

40. Weizsäcker, *Bewusstseinswandel*, pp. 377–383, esp. p. 378 (attempting to gloss the Bohr encounter in a favorable light by new arguments that raise far more difficulties about Weizsäcker's attitudes than they resolve). For the original Russian account of Bohr's remarks, see E. Feinberg, "Werner Heisenberg: The Tragedy of a Scientist" (in Russian), *Znamja*, no. 3 (1989): 124–143.

Allied scientists. The Gestapo had intercepted a secret message from Bohr to British scientists and had delivered it to Heisenberg. Indeed, Heisenberg had suspected as much about Bohr's contacts even before his visit.[41] Now Heisenberg recalled that he heard from the Gestapo *after* going to Copenhagen; but considering Heisenberg's flexible memory, it would not be surprising, and would make a great deal of sense, if, in fact, he had been told of this *before* the visit. This would explain just why he would have had to talk to Bohr—namely, in order to pump him for information. In any case, the Gestapo's involvement in any aspect of the Heisenberg-Bohr relationship is a stunning admission. Once Heisenberg had been notified, he would have had to provide information on Bohr, and most certainly, if he had indeed visited Copenhagen after being briefed by the Gestapo, he would have had to write up an official report on Bohr. Yet we have no surviving SS files relating to this matter, suggesting that either Heisenberg was lying about the Gestapo involvement, or that the files have been lost. Whatever the case, intelligence factors—whether Weizsäcker's efforts to find out about the reported American bomb project, or Heisenberg's fishing for information from Bohr—seem to have played a serious role in Heisenberg's trip to Denmark.[42] In Copenhagen soon after the war, Bohr himself brought up the intelligence aspect when he discussed the Heisenberg visit with Victor Weisskopf. According to Weisskopf's account of what Bohr told him, Heisenberg seemed to want to know if Bohr knew anything about the atomic program of the Allies. Heisenberg wanted to propose a scientists' agreement not to work on the bomb and he also invited Bohr to come to Germany to establish better relations. But if Bohr may have been angered by all this, he was also puzzled as to whether Heisenberg was being honest, or rather was being used, and he was not at all sure of what Heisenberg really wanted.[43]

Heisenberg's conviction that Germany had to win the war had not waned two years later when he made another propaganda visit, this time to Holland, where he managed to give grave offense to several Dutch physicists just as he had done in Copenhagen. During a long walk with Hendrik Casimir, Heisenberg propounded his usual defense of Nazi conquest:

> Heisenberg began to lecture on history and world-politics. He explained that it had always been the historic mission of Germany to defend the West and its culture against the onslaught of the Eastern hordes. . . . Neither France nor England would have been sufficiently determined and sufficiently strong to play a leading role in

41. This account comes from Cassidy, p. 439, but no source is given. I am seeking further information. The matter is not mentioned in the various detailed treatments by Walker. It is possible that the Gestapo approached Heisenberg after intercepting Bohr's letter of 1943 to Chadwick, rather than in 1941.

42. An echo of intelligence objectives appears in E. Heisenberg, *Inner Exile*, trans. (Boston, 1984), p. 79, where she says it was her husband's hope that Bohr could convey to the Americans that the Germans did not expect to build a bomb.

43. V. Weisskopf, interview by Powers, cited in Powers, *Heisenberg's War,* p. 125.

such a defense, and his conclusion was—and now I repeat in German the exact words he used—"da wäre vielleicht doch ein Europa unter deutscher Führung das kleinere Übel" (and so perhaps a Europe under German leadership might be the lesser evil). Of course I objected that the many iniquities of the Nazi regime, and especially their cruel and mad anti-Semitism, made this unacceptable. Heisenberg did not attempt to deny, still less to defend, these things; but he said one should expect a change for the better once the war is over. And one had to recognize they were a consequence of the great power of the leader that was also part of the German tradition. . . . Perhaps [Heisenberg's] greatest shortcoming was that he was unable to grasp the full measure of depravity of what was then the ruling group in Germany.[44]

This accords with what Casimir told G. P. Kuiper of the U.S. Army in June 1945, though he was then more explicit in stating that Heisenberg had known of the concentration (death?) camps as well as the German plunder of occupied Europe. Still, Heisenberg believed that "Germany must rule. . . . Democracy cannot develop sufficient energy to rule Europe. There are therefore only two possibilities, Germany and Russia. And then a Europe under German leadership would perhaps be the lesser evil."[45] Heisenberg's apolitical morality here descends into a typically German amoral politics: the belief that ruthless might is always right. His complete incapacity to grasp the nature of Western liberal democracy was to be very much still in evidence in several of the distasteful conversations recorded in 1945 at Farm Hall, where his inability to distinguish between Nazi Germany, Soviet Russia, and the democratic West was all too apparent.

That this was not just a personal aberration of Heisenberg's but characteristic of many reasonable Germans may be seen from remarks made by other German visitors to Holland. When Casimir asked the atomic physicist F. Kirchner if he still believed in a German victory after Stalingrad, the visitor admitted sadly that this was unlikely—"unless," he said hopefully, "Germany and Russia could still come to terms, for that would be an unassailable bloc. And, after all, our ideologies are essentially the same." Loyalty to Germany was what mattered, not ideology. Richard Becker, who admitted to Casimir his detestation of the evils caused by Germany and was sure that "the bill will be presented, all right," nevertheless told his host:

Still, you must understand that I am a German. I do not want to see our troops annihilated at Stalingrad, and if I am called upon to assist the war effort of my country, I shall feel obliged to do so. Perhaps it is illogical, but that is my position.[46]

44. H. Casimir, *Haphazard Reality* (New York, 1983), pp. 208, 210. The visit was coordinated by H. A. Kramers, who still declined to collaborate on a scientific article with Heisenberg. Kramers, who felt strongly about German persecution of the Jews, may have on this occasion—and certainly in other contexts—asked Heisenberg to intercede on behalf of prisoners in concentration camps, but there is no indication this had any effect, according to M. Dresden, *H. A. Kramers: Between Tradition and Revolution* (New York and Berlin, 1987), pp. 454–458.

45. Kuiper's army report is cited in Cassidy, pp. 472 ff., and Walker, "Physics and Propaganda," pp. 379–382.

46. Casimir, *Haphazard Reality*, pp. 206 f.

If Heisenberg knew of atrocities against the Jews during his visit of October 1943 to Holland, he certainly would have known even more after going to Poland two months later, especially as he was staying with his old school friend Hans Frank, the Nazi General-Governor of occupied Poland, in Kraków. It was notorious that Heisenberg "never failed to mention that he was on very good terms with his '*Schul- und Dufreund* Frank,'" known in other circles as the "Butcher of Poland," though this evidently did not faze Heisenberg.[47] Heisenberg's wife has recalled his telling her father about a mass execution of the Jews in Poland that he had received written information about from a colleague, and so would have known what sort of things to expect in the "East."[48] In any case, there can be little doubt that the garrulous Frank would have boasted to his old chum about recent progress in solving the Jewish Question in his domain.[49] The whole Kraków atmosphere reeked of "the Jewish Question," and indeed the official sponsoring organization of Heisenberg's visit dealt directly with its solution. This was the notorious Institut für Ostarbeit (Institute for the Colonization of the East, in effect), which provided specialized advice to the German colonizers of Poland on how to liquidate the Jewish presence in Poland as well as on how to destroy the Polish intelligentsia and social elites.[50] Heisenberg had originally been invited in 1941, but on that occasion the Education Ministry had prevented him from traveling to Poland on the ground that he was too "politically controversial a figure."[51] That Heisenberg had no particular moral objection to going east to the slaughterhouse is clear from his earlier authorizing of the printing—in Frank's Nazi newspaper in Kraków, the *Krakauer Zeitung*, on 25 and 27 January 1942—of a lecture of November 1941 he had given in Leipzig.[52] This lecture, titled "The Unity of the Scientific Outlook on Nature," contained some phrases that would have struck any audience hearing it as a ringing endorsement of Hitler's New Order and its conquests: "We are witnessing a change in the external features of the world. The struggle [*Kampf*] for its reshaping is carried on with all our resources and absorbs all our powers. In

47. Rosbaud, report on Heisenberg, 12 August 1945, Goudsmit Papers, box 28, folder 41.

48. E. Heisenberg, *Inner Exile,* p. 49.

49. Frank's extensive official diary contains many references to gatherings at which he told an approving audience of anti-Jewish measures, including an announcement on 16 December 1941 that since disease and starvation had not proved completely effective, more drastic methods were about to be used (see H. Frank, *Das Diensttagebuch des deutschen Generalgouverneurs in Polen, 1939–1945,* ed. W. Präg and W. Jacobmeyer [Stuttgart, 1975], p. 459). For an amazing dismemberment of Frank's mentality and that of the German occupiers of Poland, see his son Niklas Frank's *In the Shadow of the Reich,* trans. (New York, 1991; originally published as *Der Vater*).

50. See M. Burleigh, *Germany Turns Eastward: A Study of Ostforschung in the Third Reich* (Cambridge, 1988).

51. See Walker, "Physics and Propaganda," pp. 360 f.

52. Listed in D. Cassidy and M. Baker, *Werner Heisenberg: A Bibliography of His Writings* (Berkeley, 1984), pp. 24 f.

such times, changes in the world of the mind, of which science is a part, automatically recede into the background."[53]

Frank was determined to have his old friend visit, and in May 1943 used the award of a "Copernicus Prize" (Copernicus having been Germanized) to invite Heisenberg to stay with him during the ceremony in the Wawel Castle in Kraków. Heisenberg abjectly replied, noting his special pleasure in receiving the prize as it could be interpreted as yet another case of the rehabilitation of theoretical physics. The visit was deferred for various reasons, but eventually the General-Governor's friend arrived in Kraków in December, where on 15 December 1943 he gave his lecture at the Institut für Ostarbeit, thereby further redeeming his honor.[54] (After the war, Heisenberg lightly explained the visit by saying that he found it difficult to turn down an invitation from his old school friend.)[55]

Given this general endorsement of Nazi conquest, how are we to interpret a recently published manuscript tract allegedly proving Heisenberg's "resistance" to Nazism in 1941–42? There are indeed some passages in his privately circulated text of those years, entitled *Ordering of Reality*, that to an innocent Western reader seem to indicate hostility to Hitler; but if they are read in the context of Heisenberg's German mentality—especially his apolitical acceptance of political power—these strange statements may easily be reconciled with support of a victorious Nazi Germany.[56] The tract is basically an attempt to rationalize to himself the providential purpose of the Nazi dictatorship while admitting the evil of war and power. Like Heidegger, Heisenberg sees war and power as aspects of a destructive modernity and seeks redemption in science and "human" values. If all modern war and power-seeking is evil, then Nazism loses any special status of evil and becomes much like any other power-state—regrettable but necessary—and justified and rationalized because it leads to a higher aim of human redemption.

Heisenberg sets his philosophical apology for Nazism in a pseudo-historical framework derived from Hegel, Burckhardt, and Nazi theories of history. The present war is a struggle between Anglo-Saxon ideas of law-based society and German (and Russian) metapolitical communities based on race, nation, and, in the case of Soviet Russia, universalism. Heisenberg, it must be emphasized, does

---

53. W. Heisenberg, "Die Einheit des naturwissenschaftlichen Weltbildes" (lecture delivered at Leipzig University, 26 November 1941), first published in 1942, reprinted in GWH, C I, 163, and translated without embarrassment in his *Philosophical Problems of Nuclear Science*, trans. (London, 1952), chap. 6, p. 77.

54. See Walker, "Physics and Propaganda," p. 383. (For the Copernicus Prize, see Burleigh, *Germany Turns Eastward*, p. 279.) The visit is recorded summarily in the published edition of Frank's diary (Frank, *Diensttagebuch*, p. 762), but the full nine-page entry for that day is missing from the complete microfilmed text in NA, microfilm T-992, roll 9, frame 1353.

55. See Heisenberg, interview by Irving, 23 October 1965, p.32 (IMF 31-557).

56. Heisenberg, "Ordnung der Wirklichkeit" (1942), in GWH, C I, 218–306. The quotations and paraphrases that follow come from pp. 292, 297, 299, 303–305. See Cassidy, pp. 447–451.

not see the war as a struggle between good and evil. In this crucible of world-history, great leaders are created by historical forces, and their work, like Caesar's, will be continued by others after their deaths. These historical revolutions are accompanied by shifts in human consciousness, such as the emergence of the new "this-worldly" religions of Nazism and Communism. For Heisenberg the present war is seen in relativistic terms as essentially another "war of religions" in which old "demons" in new disguises are being unleashed:

> The catastrophes of these decades . . . mean that the weight of human thought displaces and shifts the foundations. . . . The darkest demons immediately appear and play the chief role in this domain . . . the demons bind themselves continually with that splendid phantom that misleads man in all epochs—political power.

Heisenberg does not mean here to damn Hitler exclusively as *the* "demon," as his apologists would have it, but rather to see Hitler as one of the demons of political power in general, like Stalin, Roosevelt, and Churchill.[57] They are all repellent to a fastidiously apolitical Heisenberg, who dislikes the violence of "political power, which is always founded on crimes . . . even if it may also consequently produce good effects when it is stamped on a great human community as order." Here is in a nutshell Heisenberg's doctrine of the "good side" of Nazism: All political power is bad and war is evil, but at least Hitler and Germany are stamping an order—the New European Order—on humanity, which will survive the brutal means by which it is being imposed. But being squeamish, Heisenberg feels bound to remark in a typical platitude that it is more important "to treat others humanly than to fulfill professional, national, or political duties." It is a principle that Heisenberg himself failed to follow; though he was sometimes willing to intercede weakly to protect odd students or colleagues, he never allowed this "human" duty to infringe on his national duty to obey the rulers of Germany. As he lamely preaches:

> For us there remains nothing but to turn to the simple things; we should conscientiously fulfill the duties and tasks that life presents to us without asking much about the why or the wherefore. . . . And then we should wait for what happens.

This abdication of moral resistance is rooted in loyalty to Germany, regardless of its regime. Like Heidegger, Heisenberg has an almost infantile patriotic sensibility: "*The world of God* remains thus the greatest good fortune that we may ask of the world—the consciousness of the homeland [*das Bewusstsein der Heimat*]." Remaining in Germany, accepting Nazi policies, justifying Nazi conquest—all this is done out of the need to belong to the native soil of *Heimat*.

---

57. Heisenberg's term "demons" seems to have been influenced by the well-known book of Frank Thiess, *Das Reich der Dämonen* (Berlin, 1941), which described the barbarianization of the ancient Greek and Roman worlds. The book was banned soon after its publication on account of its allegorical implications, which figure also in Heisenberg's essay. But it was scarcely an "anti-Nazi" book.

To this naive emotionalism Heisenberg added a sophisticated worldly rationale of fatalism and the amorality of power, which he derived largely from a crude reading of the nineteenth-century Swiss historian Jacob Burckhardt. Burckhardt had argued pessimistically that in the modern industrial age, historical forces were producing national states that exemplified more than ever the essential amorality of the political and whose apparently evil deeds could be made tolerable only by their possible long-term benefits.

No good results [Burckhardt had written] can exculpate an evil past. But men must come to terms even with the greatest horrors once they have happened. . . . The state founded on sheer crime is compelled in the course of time to develop a kind of justice and morality, since those of its citizens who are just and moral gradually get the upper hand. . . . Without the foreknowledge of the evildoer, great historical purposes lying in the remote future are furthered by his deeds. . . .

Now evil on earth is assuredly a part of the great economy of world history. It is force, the right of the stronger over the weaker . . . carried on in the early stages of humanity by murder and robbery and later by the eviction, extermination, and enslavement of weaker races. . . .

Yet from the fact that good came of evil . . . we cannot in any way deduce that evil and misery were not, at the outset, what they were. Every successful act of violence is evil.[58]

Burckhardt's pretense of an amoral, fatalistic, and objective Archimedean point outside events from which he could complacently justify world history, all the while remaining self-righteously "moral" himself, thus gave Heisenberg an easy authority for his own Olympian rationalizations of German conquest. Indeed the notion that the power-state was amoral, inevitable, and irresistible was a dominant feature of German political and historical thinking that was evidenced in the German preoccupation with Machiavellianism and the astonishing degree to which moral indifferentism pervaded the professional mentality of the German administrative elite. It is all too apparent in the comment of Ernst von Weizsäcker to Ulrich von Hassell, who did indeed oppose Nazi crimes: "Great historical changes cannot be carried out without a certain amount of crime." As a Western historian has remarked, "If Hitler had won, the Weizsäcker class would have said just that. It would have felt guilty about the unfortunate crimes which had accompanied Nazism—but it would have welcomed Hitler's successes."[59] Heisenberg fell into this mold of thinking, reducing

58. J. Burckhardt, *Reflections on History*, trans. (London, 1943; originally published as *Weltgeschichtliche Betrachtungen*), pp. 39, 206, 213, 215. For Heisenberg's reading of Burckhardt, see E. Heisenberg, *Inner Exile*, p. 154, and J. C. O'Flaherty, "Werner Heisenberg on the Nazi Revolution: Three Hitherto Unpublished Letters," *Journal of the History of Ideas* 53 (1992): 490. Whether Burckhardt would actually have justified Hitler's regime in the light of its all too excessive evil is another matter, but Heisenberg clearly thought that he would have.

59. Hugh Trevor-Roper, "Aftermaths of Empire," *Encounter*, December 1989, 4. Cf. R. C. Baum, *The Holocaust and the German Elite: Genocide and National Suicide in Germany, 1871–1945* (Totowa, N.J., 1981). On Ernst von Weizsäcker's treatment of Hassell, see below. Weizsäcker Senior had been enthusiastic

Burckhardt's doctrines to a mere acceptance of might is right, in the face of which the individual was powerless to resist politically or externally: "The individual can contribute nothing to [the great transformations of history] other than to prepare himself internally [*innerlich*] for the changes that will occur without his action."

The only true refuge for the apolitical idealist lies in the inner freedom of the intellect, especially in science: "In this innermost realm science and art will no longer be divided; it is perhaps for modern man the only place where truth is wholly pure and no longer cloaked and violated by human ideologies and desires." The search for inner freedom and morality, rather than the corruption of ordinary politics, which is nothing more than power seeking, thus led Heisenberg into acceptance of Nazism and war.

Read in the context of Heisenberg's apolitical German patriotism, there is nothing, therefore, in *Ordering of Reality* to suggest that he wished to resist the Nazi regime, hoped for its defeat, or found it more evil than any other "power-state." Rather the reverse: Nazi Germany was in the long run of history, Heisenberg fervently believed, a providential force for good. This was the appalling attitude he took with him on his visits to Copenhagen, Holland, and Poland and freely expressed, to the distress of most of his hosts.

Even though Heisenberg believed in preserving decent behavior within his own small intimate circle, his patriotism and his general idea of conformism to political power made him cautious about intervening to protect colleagues in any way that might be construed as "resistance" or "betrayal" of Germany. Indeed, his response to certain life-or-death situations has been described as "pitifully weak." Sometimes, his scrupulous interventions could be effective, as in the case of a Polish student at Leipzig, Edwin Gora, on whose behalf Heisenberg approached the Gestapo. But Gora was of ethnic German descent, and so there were good bureaucratic grounds on which Heisenberg could appeal to the authorities—and in this case Mrs. Heisenberg was around to encourage her husband.[60] When it came to more difficult cases, Heisenberg really did not do much other than make weak and pointlessly safe gestures, not just out of fear, but because he was temperamentally incapable of any defiance of authority unless he felt it was forced upon him by the need to defend "physics" and his "honor." Thus, in the notorious case of Goudsmit's parents, whom Dutch colleagues had urged him to save from deportation to a death camp, Heisenberg could bring himself only to write a meek letter couched in very vague terms. Obviously he did not feel that their

---

about the destruction of Czechoslovakia and the war against Poland, and had also as early as January 1938 looked forward to a war with England as inevitable.

60. E. K. Gora, "Einer, den Heisenberg doch rettete," in *Werner Heisenberg in Leipzig, 1927–1942*, Abhandlungen der Sächsischen Akademie der Wissenschaften zu Leipzig, Mathematisch-naturwissenschaftliche Klasse, Band 58, Heft 2 (Berlin, 1993), pp. 91–93, which adds crucial information not in the English-language original, "One Heisenberg Did Save," *Science News* 109 (20 March 1976): 179. See Cassidy, p. 431.

fate—unlike his own scientific honor—was worth a direct approach to Himmler.[61]

Heisenberg's cautious conformism in anything political explains his peculiar connection with the anti-Hitler members of the Wednesday Club, the elite non-political circle of sixteen mandarins—German patriots all—that Heisenberg joined in December 1942. Some of the members figured in the 20 July 1944 plot to assassinate Hitler, but though Heisenberg was sounded out on this by nonmembers earlier, he evidently was too apolitical to become involved and was kept ignorant of the plot itself. At the meeting of 12 July, a week before the attack on Hitler, Heisenberg was the host at the Kaiser-Wilhelm-Gesellschaft guest house and gave a talk titled "The Nature of the Stars," handing in the minutes on 19 July before going off to his Bavarian cottage. In the aftermath of the plot's failure, several members, including Erwin Planck, were rounded up, but Heisenberg seems miraculously to have escaped the interest of the Gestapo. Perhaps he was protected by Himmler and Speer, or perhaps he was indeed helpful to the authorities in his usual frank way, or perhaps the Gestapo was less than thorough in its inquiries into the Wednesday Club, but the apparent failure even to question Heisenberg is strange.[62]

How Heisenberg viewed the July conspirators is not known, but his near silence on the matter is extremely disturbing.[63] It suggests that even long after the war Heisenberg believed the resisters guilty of betraying Germany by their attack on legitimate authority—even if that were Hitler. This suspicion is reinforced by a parallel reticence on the part of Weizsäcker—"a diplomat and opportunist"[64] —

---

61. Cassidy, pp. 484 f.; cf. Goudsmit, *ALSOS*, pp. 46–49. Walker, *German National Socialism*, p. 109, unconvincingly argues that Heisenberg was taking a dangerous risk in writing and could not have done more. In a letter published in *Nuclear News*, October 1970, Goudsmit observed that the desire to "'preserve German leadership in physics' was stronger than [the] desire to help persecuted physicists and other Nazi victims. The friendship with Himmler's family was not invoked for that purpose." Goudsmit later, perhaps too generously, conceded that he himself could not have done more, and "doubt[ed] that Heisenberg could have effectively saved people." But Heisenberg's mealy-mouthed phrasing still rankled: "Nevertheless, I do not understand why he [Heisenberg] wrote 'on grounds which are not known to me' in his 1943 letter which was in answer to Coster's request to save my parents" (Goudsmit to Gora, 2 April 1976, Goudsmit Papers, box 11, folder 98). Given, however, Heisenberg's direct channel of communication to Himmler, it cannot be denied that a direct appeal to Himmler was certainly available to the physicist and stood some chance of success despite Goudsmit's reservations.

That Heisenberg in his respect for obedience and conformity was not so much evil, but rather a prisoner of German mentality, may be illustrated from a trivial parallel example—his ineffectuality in obtaining housing for himself and his family at Hechingen, which he could easily have done by disregarding the usual rules (Cassidy, p. 489).

62. See K. Scholder, *Die Mittwochs-Gesellschaft: Protokolle aus dem geistigen Deutschland, 1932 bis 1944* (Berlin, 1982), pp. 15, 43 ff., 305, 368. Cassidy, pp. 459 ff.

63. The only instance I know of where Heisenberg comes remotely close to approving the "replacing" of Hitler by the opposition is in his letter of 5 January 1948 to Goudsmit, p. 5 (Goudsmit Papers, box 10, folders 95–96), but it is an extremely weak and vague statement of a self-serving nature that attempts to shift the blame to the Allies for not supporting the German opposition!

64. Rosbaud to Goudsmit, 18 July 1958, Goudsmit Papers, box 28, folder 45.

whose political and moral views were closely entwined with those of his mentor Heisenberg. According to one source, Weizsäcker viewed the plot in strongly disapproving terms. At a private social evening, a sympathizer with the plotters expressed regret at the failure of the coup. Weizsäcker reacted angrily, insisting that he would not stay in the same room with a person who held such opinions, and that one of them must leave.[65] Of course, it is possible that Weizsäcker was simply alarmed that the other man was acting as an agent provocateur, but the physicist's general behavior and opinions during the war, together with his apparent refusal after the war to endorse the actions of Ulrich von Hassell and the other July conspirators, strongly indicate that he was giving vent to his true German patriotic feelings of revulsion at such treason.[66] The episode is vividly reminiscent of an encounter that had taken place in 1942 between Weizsäcker's father and Hassell. On 29 April Weizsäcker Senior had called Hassell into his study to warn him of Gestapo surveillance and to tell him to curb his tongue and burn his papers, especially those containing names and references to conversations. Weizsäcker told Hassell harshly that he should "spare him the embarrassment" of his presence in future. When Hassell tried to defend himself, Weizsäcker sharply interrupted: "Get this straight! If you do not want to understand me, then I must break off!"[67]

Carl-Friedrich idolized his father as a moral exemplar and, we may assume, modeled his own reactions to the July plot on those of his father. Both Weizsäckers may have been willing to help their dissident friends, but only to a degree; they would have drawn the line at approving seditious grumbling and certainly abhorred an act of treason. When Paul Rosbaud compiled a list of about twenty-four names of those scientists who had fervently hoped that Germany would lose the war, he emphasized that Heisenberg and Weizsäcker "were *not* on my list."[68]

Weizsäcker's moral smoothness as well as his talent for always portraying himself as an innocent are aptly illustrated by another sorry tale of a visit abroad. According to the French physicist Frédéric Joliot, Weizsäcker had given a lecture in wartime Paris that had been boycotted by the French, as had also had a lunch

65. Private information.

66. See, for instance, Weizsäcker's curious omission of Stauffenberg from his discussion of German guilt in his article "Hitler und die Deutschen," in his *Bewusstseinswandel*, pp. 289–297. Neither Stauffenberg nor the July plot are discussed here—nor indeed in the whole book—despite the central relevance of these to the moral history of Germany under Hitler. For more on Weizsäcker's peculiar attitudes, see below, chaps. 20 and 21.

67. U. von Hassell, *Vom andern Deutschland* (Zurich, 1946), p. 264 (also in new ed., *Die Hassell-Tagebücher, 1938–1944* [Berlin, 1988], pp. 316 f.): "Verstehen Sie mich doch! Wenn Sie mich nicht verstehen wollen, dann muss ich abbrechen!" (English version in *The Von Hassell Diaries*, trans. [Garden City, N.Y., 1947], pp. 256 f.). See below, chap. 20, for Lewis Namier's devastating critique of Weizsäcker's pretensions to resistance.

68. Rosbaud to Goudsmit, 18 July 1958, Goudsmit Papers, box 28, folder 45. On the partial list were "Laue, Hahn, Strassmann, Rompe, Riehl, Regener, Paschen, Mattauch, etc." Rosbaud was perhaps a bit free in attributing a "fervent hope" of German defeat to some of these.

arranged in his honor. Joliot had actually spoken to Weizsäcker about the "bad taste" of his lecturing in occupied Paris, but Weizsäcker managed to persuade his French friend that he had been forced by the German authorities to give the lecture. Joliot had naively accepted this, believing Weizsäcker to be anti-Nazi and "trustworthy." To this shifty behavior of Weizsäcker's should be contrasted the response of Otto Hahn, who, when asked by the German officials to go similarly to Paris, had refused, "not wishing to confront Joliot as a victor." Knowing this, Joliot himself later wondered why Weizsäcker had not also refused.[69]

Nothing during the war forced Heisenberg to reconsider the validity of his theory that Nazism had its good side and that a Nazi victory was in Europe's interest. On hearing of the D-day invasion in June 1944, Heisenberg welcomed it not as a portent of Nazi defeat, but merely for hastening the end of the war, "one way or the other."[70] Did this mean he would have welcomed an Allied victory? Given Heisenberg's general attitude, it should not be thought that he was careless about which side actually won. Far more likely, the phrase signified a hope that the forces would fight themselves to a stalemate and so end the war, if not with a German victory, at least without a defeated Germany. By the end of the year, Heisenberg had given up hope of Germany's "winning" the war in the sense of its maintaining control of Europe. At a dinner in Zurich hosted by the Swiss physicist Paul Scherrer in December 1944, Heisenberg faced angry questioning about atrocities against the Jews and how he could have stayed on in a country led by Hitler. He replied, "I am not a Nazi, but a German." When Gregor Wentzel told Heisenberg, "Now you have to admit that the war is lost," Heisenberg sadly conceded, "Yes, but how fine it would have been if we had won this war."[71]

69. Goudsmit's report on a conversation with Joliot in Paris, 31 August 1944, NA, RG 77, MED, microfilm M-1108, roll 2, file 26, Harrison-Bundy Files.

70. Heisenberg to his mother, 15 June 1944, quoted in Cassidy, p. 490.

71. N. Dawidoff, *The Catcher Was a Spy: The Mysterious Life of Moe Berg* (New York, 1994), pp. 206, 401. Cassidy, p. 492; Goudsmit, *ALSOS*, p. 114; Powers, pp. 402, 565. According to Cassidy, p. 634, Heisenberg in a letter of 22 April 1948 to van der Waerden denied having said this; Goudsmit to van der Waerden, 26 April 1948 (Goudsmit Papers, box 11, folder 98), speculated rather kindly that "he probably made that statement, but perhaps did not give it at that time the same meaning it has now." Goudsmit seems to have backed off from actually calling Heisenberg a liar.

Wentzel's testimony was important for helping to persuade some German-Jewish scientists in America after the war that Heisenberg had wished for a German victory: "With the help of some of the documents which I obtained in Germany I have tried to convince my colleagues here about the deplorable attitude of most of the German scientists. I did not succeed, and the hardest disbelievers were the refugees. Not until Gregor Wentzel from Zurich visited here did a few of them finally admit I had been right" (Goudsmit to Rosbaud, 22 August 1946, Goudsmit Papers, box 28, folder 43).

Heisenberg's defeatist remarks caused him some trouble with the Gestapo, from whom Gerlach had to extricate him (see Gerlach's interview by Irving, in IMF 29-1230/1240).

CHAPTER 20

Decency and Indecency at Farm Hall, 1945

On reading through the Farm Hall transcripts, one is constantly struck by the absence of any serious moral reflection on the evil of Nazi Germany, on the physicists' relationship to the Third Reich, and on their participation in the uranium bomb project. Of course, there is the effort led by Weizsäcker, Wirtz, and Heisenberg to mount a moral manifesto, showing their horror of the atomic bomb and explaining that they had never intended to prepare such a weapon for Hitler; but that is more an evasion than an acceptance of moral responsibility.[1] The shallow moralizing of the assembled German physicists and their utter inability to come to terms with the fact that their Germany had produced such evil are all too evident in the silences and attempts at self-exculpation that punctuate the transcripts.

Typical, if amusing, is the slippery way in which they agree to redefine just who is a "Nazi." In one sequence of conversations sparked by fear that their Nazi pasts might cause them trouble, the scientists one after another attempt to wriggle out of their embarrassment. Convinced that Heisenberg and Gerlach kept on bringing up the question of Party membership for their own nefarious purposes, Bagge claims he was forced to join the SA (the *Sturmabteilung,* or Storm Troopers), but not the Party, though he was a member of the Nazi University Lecturers' League (*Dozentenbund*)—like Wirtz and Weizsäcker—but again because it was compulsory. Then Bagge seems to forget his own denial of having been a Party member, and recalls that his mother enrolled him in the Party without telling him! Meanwhile, Diebner explains to Hahn that he was actually a Freemason who suffered under

---

1. See above, chaps. 1–3. Cf. Cassidy, pp. 521 f.; J. Bernstein and D. Cassidy, "Bomb Apologetics: Farm Hall, August 1945," *Physics Today,* August 1995, 32–36. See also the detailed running commentary on the Farm Hall transcripts by J. Bernstein, *Hitler's Uranium Club* (Woodbury, N.Y., 1996).

the Nazis, never voted for them, but somehow became a member of the Party. "Everyone knows my views . . . I was never a National Socialist and never took any part in politics." He was merely an opportunist Party member who had promised Wirtz that he would look after him if things went well for the Nazis, and expected Wirtz's aid if things went badly.[2] Earlier Diebner had been carried away by the possibility of becoming a British citizen and repented fulsomely that "then [I would] have nothing more to do with the Party again. I would willingly take an oath never to have anything to do with the Party again!"[3] This stream of self-contradiction and rationalization verges on the comical, but it is symptomatic of a general refusal on the part of the scientists to face responsibility for their role in the German catastrophe. Occasionally, however, some of them shrewdly spotted one another's half-truths. After Gerlach had boasted of his defiance of the Nazis and left the room, Bagge observed acidly: "They could do nothing against him. He knew Goering personally. His brother was in the SS and that's how he managed to stay on. Gerlach gets a certain personal amusement out of annoying people. It wasn't just his [anti-Nazi] convictions."[4]

The only point at which an inkling of the horror in which they were implicated surfaces is when Wirtz, who had trouble keeping the truth to himself on other occasions, blurted out, in response to Heisenberg's musing upon how a Polish-Jewish colleague had been murdered, the following admission:

> We have done things which are unique in the world. We went to Poland and not only murdered the Jews in Poland, but, for instance, the SS drove up to a girls' school, fetched out the top class and shot them simply because the girls were High School girls and the intelligentsia were to be wiped out. . . . That's what we did.[5]

This sort of moral awareness was, however, quickly suppressed and occurred very rarely indeed in the transcripts made during the physicists' six-month internment.

More frequent are the ruminations on power politics laced with opportunism and cynicism. There are many conversations in which their amoral theory of *Realpolitik* is applied to the new postwar situation of Anglo-Saxon versus Russian

2. See *OE*, pp. 50–55.

3. Ibid., p. 39.

4. Ibid., p. 53. The scientists also make merry at the planting of that "wicked Nazi Bomke" as a spy in Hahn's institute (ibid., p. 75). Heisenberg—possibly for prudential reasons—had, however, provided Bomke with a warm testimonial to his scientific abilities ("a very versatile and good physicist"). See the file on Hans Bomke, who had worked on an ultracentrifuge at the KWIC from 1938 to 1941 and then with the German Post Office *Forschungsanstalt* from 1941 to 1943, in Goudsmit Papers, AIP, box 25, folder 13.

5. *OE*, p. 55. Wirtz's conscience had also bothered him during a wartime visit to Norway, when in a talk with Dr. Wergeland at Oslo, "he seemed to regret deeply all the behaviour and the brutality of Nazis in Norway and German efforts to extend and win the war" (according to Paul Rosbaud's account of the uranium project, 5 August 1945, p. 4, Goudsmit Papers, box 28, folder 42).

power blocs. In not one of these exchanges is any mention made of the moral superiority of Western democracy to Soviet totalitarianism; consequently, Heisenberg and Weizsäcker speak blandly at times of going over to the Russians if the West proves unamenable to them. In the new era of superpower blocs contending for Europe, Weizsäcker is (according to one of his colleagues) at one point "more or less resigned to the idea of becoming Russian one day."[6] Heisenberg varies in his prudential assessment of the German options. At one point he says:

> The sensible thing for us to do is to try and work in collaboration with the Anglo-Saxons. We can now do that with a better conscience because one sees that they will probably dominate Europe. . . . We have no possibility of switching over to the Russians even if we wanted to. . . . We can do it with a good conscience because we can see that in the immediate future Germany will be under Anglo-Saxon influence.[7]

This naked deference to power politics in which "good conscience" is reduced to German interests provoked even the flexible Wirtz to exclaim: "That is an opportunist attitude"—to which Heisenberg replied that it was difficult at times to do otherwise, while Weizsäcker contented himself with commenting that he would prefer to work for neither side.[8]

Heisenberg's facility for amoral rationalization is evident in the following noncommittal comment:

> The only choice for us is either to join this Western European bloc or join in with Russia. My own feelings are that the Western European bloc is better, but I can understand someone saying that we ought to join up with the Russians. This is a standpoint which could be discussed.[9]

So much for Heisenberg's commitment to the values of Western democracy. For him, all that matters is German interests—and perhaps, even more, the honor of German science and his own scientific activity. It is these same concerns that motivated his compromises with Nazism and his remaining in Germany. If now the Russians can further his ambitions, Heisenberg is insouciant about the Stalinist dictatorship:

> If we find we are only able to eke out a meagre existence under the Anglo-Saxons, whereas the Russians offer us a job for say 50,000 roubles, what then? Can they expect us to say: "No, we will refuse the 50,000 roubles as we are so pleased and grateful to be allowed to remain on the English side?"[10]

6. *OE*, p. 39.

7. Ibid., pp. 88–90.

8. Ibid., p. 90.

9. Ibid., pp. 144 f. In an interview of 1967 Heisenberg recalled having discussions with Weizsäcker on the future shape of politics, where only one or two superpowers would be able to have an "independent" politics, a process accelerated by the atomic bomb (J. J. Ermenc, *Atomic Bomb Scientists: Memoirs, 1939–1945* [Westport, Conn., 1989], pp. 48 f.).

10. *OE*, p. 172.

Heisenberg was so blinded by this opportunistic mentality that he rashly threatened his British captors with deserting to the Russian side. He reads a draft letter out to Hahn and

> says that the letter, in fact, implies that, unless he is generously treated by the Western Allies, he will seriously consider working for the Russians. . . . "I would consider if I shouldn't go to the Russians after all. . . . The Russians are much more generous than the English. . . . I don't know at all that the future of Europe does not lie with the Russians after all. . . . [If the Americans leave Europe], then we are bound to work with the Russians."[11]

The amorality of Heisenberg's scientific ambition is made all too plain:

> I don't want to do petty physics. . . . If the final decision is that I can't do any proper physics and I go back to Germany again, naturally they, too, will realize that I am then going to consider doing physics with the Russians after all.[12]

Pushed to the wall, Heisenberg would not allow even German patriotism to prevail over his "honor"—that is, the same need to be a first-class citizen able to do proper physics that had motivated his behavior under Hitler. And the same thirst drove Heisenberg's closest intimates:

> *Wirtz:* From what I have seen in England during these months, I should not like to settle down here . . . no matter what conditions in Germany may be. It might be different, of course, if they were to offer me some terrific position. . . .
>
> *Weizsäcker:* No, for that sort of thing, one could only consider America or Russia.[13]

We find here the same unreconstructed lack of commitment to democracy that had facilitated Heisenberg's constant compromises with the Nazi regime. In its place there is merely cynical opportunism masquerading as high moral principle and devotion to science. As Laue later recalled, "I did not hear the mention of any ethical point of view. Heisenberg was mostly silent."[14]

This is not to say that German patriotism—in its proper place—was no longer esteemed in the scientists' minds. Indeed, their patriotic mentality led the Germans into the following arrogant rationalizations, which were sardonically reported by their British guards.

> The general attitude seems to be that the German war was a misfortune forced on the Germans by the malignancy of the Western Powers, who should by now have forgotten that it had taken place (the guests seem to have done so). . . .
>
> Both Wirtz and Weizsäcker have argued that the Japanese war was engineered by President Roosevelt, who deliberately allowed the attack on Pearl Harbour. . . . In

11. Ibid., pp. 201–203.
12. Ibid., p. 203.
13. Ibid., p. 270.
14. Laue to Rosbaud, 1959, in A. Kramish, *The Griffin* (Boston, 1986), p. 247. See above, chaps. 1–3.

any case, Commodore Perry's first expedition to Japan was the prime cause of the war, which was, therefore, the responsibility of the Americans.[15]

German patriotism, giving birth to German paranoia about perpetual victimization by the West, usefully removed the need to face up to the real moral issues posed by the collaboration of the interned scientists with the Nazi regime. Instead Heisenberg preferred to regard the Allies as though they were simply a new and less intelligent brand of "Nazis" whose interfering was to be managed just as he had managed their Nazi predecessors.

> The American militarists who are already at loggerheads with scientific opinion . . . would not accept any argument of ours, but would merely say something like this: "There you are, the usual Nazi arrogance."[16]

Hearing this sort of thing, it was no wonder that the British were so unfavorably impressed with "the inborn conceit of these people, who still believe in the Herrenvolk. This applies to every one of the guests, with the possible exception of von Laue."[17] In his moral arrogance Heisenberg was totally unable to comprehend just what it was that the British officers held against him when he compared the "English" to Hitler, a heedless comparison he continued to draw in letters written many years after the war.[18]

The truth of this characterization is borne out by a wealth of vignettes in the transcripts. There is Heisenberg cunningly proposing that to protect their own reputation in Germany the scientists must pretend to accept Allied control "with fury and gnashing of teeth"; there is Heisenberg slyly congratulating Hahn after an angry session in which he "went for" a British officer. Or the businessman Heisenberg opining that "if the Americans [have] not got so far with the engine . . . then we are in luck. There is a possibility of making money." There is the crafty Heisenberg proposing: "We'll make the commander drunk and then he'll talk. . . . Yes, that is the right sequence of events. First, there will be an afternoon when we will go for him and break him down, and then an evening when we will make it up." And Weizsäcker offering to ensure that Laue doesn't mess things up in Germany, saying he would be willing to "undertake a little intrigue to see that Laue doesn't get back either until you [Heisenberg] get back." And, almost farcically, there is the picture of the guests all standing rigidly to attention while the British national anthem is played on VJ day—a happy exhibition of respect for authority and propriety, combined with a desire to be on the winning side as ever.[19] Manipulativeness, exploitation, opportunistic ambition, utter lack of moral principle—these are the overwhelming impressions left by even cursory readings of the Farm Hall tran-

15. *OE*, p. 230.
16. Ibid., p. 263.
17. Ibid., p. 169.
18. Heisenberg to Irving, 23 May 1966, in IMF 32.
19. *OE*, pp. 33, 92, 108, 171, 192, 262 (references not in sequence).

scripts. These conversations expose the mentality that permitted German scientists to collude in the Third Reich, whatever particular reservations they may have had. In sum, the transcripts reveal the elements of German life, sensibility, and behavior that made it possible for Hitler to be accepted by the German people as a society.

When it comes to moral thought, an interesting remark by Heisenberg shows vividly just how remote German mentality was from conventional Western attitudes: "We wouldn't have had the *moral courage* [emphasis added] to recommend to the Government in the spring of 1942 that they should employ 120,000 just for building the thing up."[20] In other words, it was not moral objections in a Western sense that precluded Heisenberg from committing himself to a full-scale bomb project in 1942, but rather his shortage of a peculiarly German sort of "moral courage" that had to do with the professional and fiscal responsibility of a patriotic scientist! And when Heisenberg does admit piously that he is "glad at the bottom of [his] heart" that Speer had decided on a reactor engine instead of a bomb project in June 1942, this does not mean that he would have refused to work on a bomb should that have been Speer's decision, even though Heisenberg himself may well have preferred the less dangerous path that was actually taken and doubted in any case whether a bomb could be made.[21] As Heisenberg commented in the same conversation, "we were not 100% anxious to do it"—which suggests that he may have been 50% or 75% anxious to make a bomb![22] Heisenberg's readiness, even if sometimes reluctant, to do whatever the political authorities commanded is reflected in the mealy-mouthed phrasing he uses here and elsewhere in the transcripts. This is the sad truth behind Heisenberg's cryptic postwar statements that the German scientists "were spared the moral decision whether they should make an atomic bomb."[23]

Attempts to camouflage the truth from themselves as well as others found their high point in Weizsäcker's concoction of an alibi of moral opposition to the German atomic bomb. But the fluctuations and self-contradictions in Weizsäcker's remarks at Farm Hall betray a sense that the retrospective claim of moral conscience was simply too difficult and absurd to maintain with any consistency. Weizsäcker's agility in rapid rationalization is evident in the following sequence of inventions (some of the more blatant contradictions are italicized):

> I believe the reason we didn't do it was because we the physicists didn't want to do it, on principle. *If we had all wanted Germany to win the war, we would have succeeded.*
>
> Even if we had got everything that we wanted, it is by no means certain whether we would have got as far as the Americans and the English have now. . . . It is a fact that *we were all convinced that the thing could not be completed during this war.*

20. Ibid., p. 76.
21. Ibid., p. 78.
22. Ibid., p. 77.
23. Heisenberg to Goudsmit, 3 October 1948, in Goudsmit Papers, and in different phrasing in his "Research in Germany on the Technical Application of Atomic Energy," *Nature*, 16 August 1947, 211–215, at p. 214 (GWH, ser. B, 417), and its MS draft. For this article and its draft, see above, chaps. 1–3.

If we had started this business soon enough, we could have got somewhere. . . . *We might have had the luck to complete it in the winter 1944–45.*

I don't think we ought to make excuses now because we did not succeed. . . . *It is quite certain that we would not have succeeded* as they would have smashed up the factories.

One can say it would have been a much greater tragedy for the world if Germany had had the uranium bomb. Just imagine, *if we had destroyed London with uranium bombs,* it would not have ended the war, and when the war did end, it is still doubtful whether it would have been a good thing.[24]

Quite remarkable in the last comment is Weizsäcker's statement that it was merely "doubtful" whether destroying London with an atomic bomb would have been a "good thing."

Heisenberg and Weizsäcker may not have hoped the war would end with a German victory, but they certainly wished that it might end without a German defeat. As Heisenberg remarked with his usual rationalizing facility after hearing the news of Potsdam, "at any rate, it would have been infinitely worse if we had won the war." This mood led him to impute to Gerlach what was his own characteristically patriotic mentality: "Heisenberg said [to Hahn] . . . Gerlach was the only one of them who had really wanted a German victory, because although he realised the crimes of the Nazis and disapproved of them, he could not get away from the fact that he was working for Germany."[25] By 1945 Heisenberg may have abandoned his preference for a great German victory, but his reading of Gerlach reflected faithfully his own ardent desire for German victory that had been expressed without embarrassment to colleagues in Denmark and Holland in 1941–43.

Equally difficult to sustain was the rationalization of their having worked at all on the uranium project when it still seemed in 1939–41 that it might produce a bomb in a reasonable time. The Farm Hall scientists sought to evade the real issue by two main lines of justification. The first was to justify their having worked on the uranium project by their lack of success. This failure they saw as inevitable since Allied bombing and other factors interdicted an industrial effort on the scale that was required. Second, there was the self-righteous tendency to excuse their own work by intoning a general condemnation of atomic weapons and blaming their Allied

---

24. *OE*, pp. 76–78. For Weizsäcker's role in compiling the Farm Hall Memorandum, see above, chaps. 1–3.

In an interview of 1984 with the magazine *Stern,* Weizsäcker made some telling admissions:

Weizsäcker: "I was rescued only by divine grace—that it did not succeed. For it would have turned out lethally wrongly. I undertook with youthful carelessness a project that I would not begin again were I in the same position today."

Interviewer: "The idea then was: We want to build the bomb, so we might have something in our hand?"

Weizsäcker: "Yes. Or at least we wanted to get as near to a bomb as we could."

Reprinted in Weizsäcker, *Bewusstseinswandel* (Munich, 1988), p. 365.

25. *OE*, p. 82.

counterparts for having succeeded in producing this horror. In this all too easy moralizing, what is missing is any confrontation of their moral guilt in having worked for Hitler on the bomb project in 1939–41, when it still seemed a very feasible operation. Weizsäcker in particular tried hard to evade this issue when he opined that "even the scientists said it couldn't be done," thus making out the whole uranium project to have been knowingly futile. But the blatant falsity of this line was apparent to his colleagues at Farm Hall. Bagge immediately interjected:

> That's not true. You were there yourself at that conference in Berlin. I think it was on 8 September that everyone was asked . . . —and everyone said that it must be done at once. Someone said, "Of course, it is an open question whether one ought to do a thing like that." Thereupon Bothe got up and said, "Gentlemen, it *must* be done." Then Geiger got up and said, "If there is the slightest chance that it is possible—it must be done."

Weizsäcker lamely responded, "I don't know how you can say that. 50% of the people were against it." But he was cleverly contradicted by Harteck to the effect that "of those who did understand it, one third spoke against it. . . . We knew that it could be done in principle, but on the other hand we realised that it was a frightfully dangerous thing."[26]

The interesting question arises of just how convincingly Heisenberg and his colleagues were deceiving *themselves*, since sometimes a recognition of the truth and the true moral question was able to break through, as with Wirtz's admission of German atrocities in Poland. One such occasion is afforded by the usually careful Weizsäcker during a discussion of what the "right position" should have been in Nazi Germany. When Heisenberg sagely recommends that "each of us must be very careful to see that he gets into a proper position" in the new Germany, Weizsäcker momentarily confesses that under the Nazis "the right position would really have been in a concentration camp, and there are people who chose that."[27] Obfuscate the issue as they might and deceive themselves and others as they did almost all of the time, the German scientists knew ultimately that they had failed the moral test.

To accept the shifty rationalizations of Heisenberg and his friends at Farm Hall at face value is to do a great disservice to the moral integrity of those German atomic scientists who did behave honorably, particularly Wolfgang Gentner and perhaps Hans Jensen, and, of course, the outspoken Max von Laue. Pointlessly interned at Farm Hall, Laue had something of a rough time there, principally at the hands of Weizsäcker, who acted quite viciously.[28] But even though browbeaten into a kind of

---

26. Ibid., pp. 85 f.

27. Ibid., p. 110.

28. Laue to Rosbaud, 1959–60, quoted in Kramish, *The Griffin*, p. 244; Weizsäcker applied his "influence, which he knows how to use with everybody who happens to be in power" to isolate Laue from his British guards as well as his fellow Germans at Farm Hall. See above, chaps. 1–3.

solidarity that he later regretted, Laue must have been aware of the unsavoriness of his colleagues' psychological maneuverings. In 1944 Einstein had written admiringly of Laue that "it was particularly interesting to see how in his case he tore himself loose step by step from the traditions of the herd under the working of a strong feeling of justice."[29] (A similar integrity was manifested in the non-Jewish mathematician Hermann Weyl's recollection of why he left Göttingen for America: "I could not bear to live under the rule of that demon who had dishonored the name of Germany, and although the wrench was hard and the mental agony so cruel that I suffered a severe breakdown, I shook the dust of the fatherland from my feet.")[30] Now, if Laue, for all his independence of mind, could still submit to the demands of German patriotic solidarity at Farm Hall (and for some time after, as his article of 1948 defending his colleagues from the charge of having been Himmler's armorers shows), that indicates just how difficult it was for scientists—including even Jews—educated in Germany to attain an objective (Western!) understanding of the situation. This may be seen in the case of Lise Meitner, with whom Laue corresponded provocatively throughout the war, though, of course, their letters were subject to censorship. As their 1942 discussion of Heisenberg's visit to Copenhagen showed, Meitner and Laue could be clear-eyed about the moral vacuity of their colleagues.[31] But in general Meitner, like Laue, was inhibited from condemning those colleagues who voluntarily remained in Germany and colluded with the regime. They were reluctant to make moral judgments on others, and accepted in good faith some of the moral justifications put forth. It was only in June 1945 that the details of the Belsen horror camp finally penetrated Meitner's shell of self-defense and opened her eyes to the fundamentally mistaken line to remain in Germany that had been taken by even the best-intentioned of German scientists—and indeed by herself until forced to flee in 1938. On 26 June she wrote a letter to Paul Scherrer in Zurich full of hostility toward Heisenberg and Weizsäcker. Criticizing Weizsäcker's recent book on physics for its pseudo-mystical "flight from reality," which she found "to some extent an intellectual dishonesty," Meitner accused Heisenberg of

> permitting himself intellectual dishonesty in a different form. I have heard remarkable things about him from young Danish colleagues concerning his 1941 visit with Carl-Friedrich to Copenhagen to stage a thoroughly unwelcome German physics congress. He was quite possessed by wishful thinking of a German victory and he developed a theory of the superior nations and of those inferior peoples over whom Germany should rule.[32]

29. Einstein to Born, 7 September 1944, in A. Einstein and M. Born, *The Born-Einstein Letters*, ed. and trans. M. Born (New York, 1971), p. 148. (I have amended the English to conform more accurately to the German.)

30. Quoted in R. Wistrich, *Who's Who in Nazi Germany* (London, 1982), p. 337.

31. See above, chap. 19.

32. Meitner to Scherrer, 26 June 1945, Meitner Papers, Churchill College Archives, Cambridge. (The words beginning with "superior . . . " and ending with " . . . inferior" are difficult to read and are

The following day Meitner wrote to her old friend and colleague Hahn in an unprecedented tone, angrily berating him, herself, and all their colleagues for having stayed on—and finding especial contempt for Heisenberg's "unforgivable" visit of 1941 to Niels Bohr in Copenhagen.

In my thoughts I have written very many letters in recent months to you, because it was clear to me that even people such as you and Laue did not understand the true situation. . . . Laue wrote to me that . . . Wettstein's death was a loss in a greater sense because Wettstein with his diplomatic skills could in the aftermath of the war have been of great use. How could a man who had never set himself against the crimes of the last years be of use for Germany? That indeed is the misfortune of Germany, that you all lost the measure of right and fairness. You yourself wrote to me in March 1938 that Hörlein [Professor Heinrich Hörlein, treasurer of the Kaiser-Wilhelm-Institute for Chemistry] had told you that horrendous actions would be taken against the Jews. He thus knew of all the planned and later executed crimes—yet still was a member of the Nazi Party. And you also despite this regarded him as a most upstanding human being, and allowed yourself to be guided by him in your behavior toward your best friend.

You all worked for Nazi Germany. And you tried to offer only a passive resistance. Certainly, to buy off your conscience you helped here and there a persecuted person, but millions of innocent human beings were allowed to be murdered without any kind of protest being uttered.

I must write this to you, because so much depends for both Germany and yourselves on your recognizing what you allowed to happen. . . . I and many others believe that a way for you would be to publish an open declaration that you are conscious that through your passivity you have incurred a joint responsibility for what happened. . . . But many believe that it is too late for that. They say that you first betrayed your friends, then your men and children in that you let them stake their lives on a criminal war—and finally that you betrayed Germany itself, because when the war was already quite hopeless, you did not once arm yourselves against the senseless destruction of Germany. This sounds irredeemable, yet believe me, I write all this to you out of the most honorable friendship.

You really cannot expect the rest of the world to mourn for Germany. What we have heard these days of the uncontained horrors in the concentration camps exceeds everything that one had feared. When I heard on the English radio a very factual report from the British and Americans on Belsen and Buchenwald, I took to howling out loud and could not sleep the whole night. If you could have seen for yourself those who came here from the camps. A man like Heisenberg and many millions with him should be forced to see these camps and the martyred people. His appearance in Denmark in 1941 is unforgivable.

You yourself may perhaps recall how when I was still in Germany (and today I know that it was not only stupid, but a great wrong that I had not immediately

---

here reconstructed.) See N. Dawidoff, *The Catcher Was a Spy: The Mysterious Life of Moe Berg* (New York, 1994), pp. 220 ff., 404.

left) I often said to you: "As long as only we and not you have sleepless nights, things will not be better in Germany." But you had no sleepless nights, you did not want to see, it was too uncomfortable. I could give you so many examples, great and small. I beg you to believe me that all I write here is an attempt to help you all.[33]

The letter was never delivered, and by the time contact was reestablished between herself and Hahn, Meitner had calmed down.[34] But her revulsion at the betrayal by her German colleagues may still be read between the lines of their subsequent, apparently warm, correspondence. Without changing the anti-German gravamen of the earlier letter, but now trying to soften the personal animus toward Hahn, Meitner told him in September 1945 that he should understand that "despite its harsh-sounding outspokenness about German matters, it [her letter of 27 June] was filled with the most honorable friendship for you."[35] Three years later, Meitner veiled her criticism of Hahn's own failure to leave Germany by referring to her own: "Today it is very clear to me that it was a grave moral fault not to leave Germany in 1933, since in effect by staying there I supported Hitlerism."[36] Other Germans have put it even more succinctly. General Roettiger observed caustically: "People spoke of loyalty, honor, etc., but what they really meant were

33. Meitner to Hahn, 27 June 1945, Meitner Papers. Printed in F. Krafft, *Im Schatten der Sensation* (Weinheim, 1981), pp. 181 ff. Berg promised Meitner to deliver the letter, but it never reached Hahn—more's the pity. See also above, chap. 2. For a critical view of Hahn's often whitewashed relations with Meitner in the matters of her flight from Germany in 1945 and her exclusion from the Nobel Prize of 1945, see R. L. Sime, "A Split Decision?" *Chemistry in Britain* (June 1994): 482–484; and Sime's biography of Meitner, *Lise Meitner: A Life in Physics* (Berkeley, 1996).

An angry letter from Bruno Walter to Wilhelm Furtwängler of 13 January 1949 echoes Meitner's strictures. "Throughout the [Nazi] years . . . you performed high service to this regime through your prominent image and great talent . . . [your] presence . . . abetted every horrible crime . . . you carried your title and positions during this time. In light of all that, of what significance is your assistance in the isolated cases of a few Jews?" (printed in S. H. Shirakawa, *The Devil's Music Master: The Controversial Life and Career of Wilhelm Furtwängler* [New York, 1992], p. 364). I hope to compare the behaviors of Heisenberg and the conductor in a future book.

34. Did Hahn later receive a copy of the letter? According to P. Rife, "Lise Meitner: The Life and Times of a Jewish Woman Physicist" (Ph.D. diss., Union for Experimenting Colleges and Universities, 1983), pp. 327, 497, an "original" or "carbon copy" was later "in the possession of Marie-Louise Rehder, Otto Hahn's personal secretary for many years," thus suggesting that Hahn did indeed see the contents of the letter at some point. His reaction is not known. Even after the war, some Austro-German scientists such as Meitner failed to understand British attitudes toward Germany. During an evening with James Chadwick in Washington in February 1946, where they agreed that Hahn was not a Nazi, Meitner was still taken aback by Chadwick's sharp opinion that even the most decent Germans shared responsibility for the crimes of the Third Reich, as she told Otto Frisch (Sime, *Lise Meitner,* p. 336).

35. Meitner to Hahn, 20 September 1945, Meitner Papers.

36. Meitner to Hahn, 6 June 1948, printed in F. Krafft, "Lise Meitner: Her Life and Times . . . ," *Angewandte Chemie* (international English ed.) 17 (1978): 826–842, at p. 829.

personal cowardice and a shirking of moral responsibility."[37] And Gerhart Hauptmann, when asked why he did not emigrate, retorted: "Because I'm a coward. Do you understand? I'm a coward"[38] —a refreshing change from Heisenberg's special pleadings and elaborate rationalizations and evasions.

37. Quoted in M. Messerschmidt, "The Wehrmacht and the Volksgemeinschaft," *Journal of Contemporary History* 18 (1983): 719–744, at p. 738.

38. Quoted in R. Hanser, *A Noble Treason* (New York, 1979), p. 86.

CHAPTER 21

Heisenberg's Peculiar Way, 1945–48

Heisenberg doesn't seem to be willing even now to condemn the Nazis openly. Instead, he tries to impress upon the world how excellent the quality of German scientific work was, even under the Nazis and how, after all, their intentions were only peaceful. The only mildly anti-Nazi article I have seen by Heisenberg is a speech to the students at Göttingen, in which he points out that science has nothing to do with race or religion. I think his speech would have been much stronger if he had given examples of the destructive influences of the Nazi doctrine.[1]

SAMUEL GOUDSMIT, 1948

I got yesterday from Lise Meitner a small book written in memory of Dietrich Bonhoeffer . . . I was deeply moved when I read the following sentences [in German]: " . . . I pray for the defeat of my country, for I believe that to be the sole possibility of paying for the whole suffering that my country has caused the world." You will understand when I tell you that exactly the same was my daily prayer from the first day of the war to the last. I don't make this confession to other people in this country [Britain]—they might not understand it.[2]

PAUL ROSBAUD, 1946

Heisenberg's selective memory and rationalizing faculties operated continuously after his release from Farm Hall. But his behavior and mentality always bore the imprint of years of German nationalist and cultural conditioning, as his disturbing attitude to the denazification of former SS officers exemplifies. Heisenberg is know to have been fairly free in providing "Persil-certificates" (*Persil-scheine*), whitewashing certificates, for former associates with embarrassing affiliations. One such was Johannes Juilfs (alias Mathias Jules), the SS scientific officer who had carried out the investigation into Heisenberg's political reliability for Himmler in 1937–38. A member of the SA before switching to the SS in 1933 and leader of the Nazi student organization, Juilfs joined the SS/SD in 1938, served under Helmut Fischer, and rose to the rank of *Obersturmführer*. He was scientifically trained, being at one time an assistant to Laue, and was later attached to Heisenberg at the Kaiser-Wilhelm-Institute for Physics and Berlin University.[3] Though the letter that Heisen-

---

1. Goudsmit to Michael Perrin, 27 August 1948, Goudsmit Papers, AIP, box 17, folder 180.

2. Rosbaud to Goudsmit, 9 August 1946, Goudsmit Papers, box 28, folder 43. See below for Rosbaud's despair at the tendency of some British scientists and officers to side with such "loyal" decent Germans as Heisenberg.

3. These details come from Juilfs's file in the Berlin Document Center. (Cassidy, pp. 390 f., 461, 618, refers to him under the name "Jules.") See also above, chap. 18. For Fischer, see above, chap. 13.

berg wrote on Juilfs's behalf to the denazification tribunal is not available, its tenor may be deduced from another letter in which he recalled Himmler's investigation about his sharp critique of "Aryan physics." Heisenberg recollected that he went several times to the SS headquarters in Berlin and spoke with "Dr. Juilfs, who placed himself openly and very energetically on my side." Subsequently Heisenberg received a letter from Himmler "that publicly restored my honor."[4] Heisenberg diplomatically omitted Juilfs's enforcement of the ban on mentioning Einstein's name (in 1942, Juilfs had influenced Heisenberg to write to Sommerfeld to persuade him to delete Einstein's name from his new book). One may contrast this with Laue's repeated naming of Einstein in lectures given at Stockholm in 1943, which led to his being reprimanded by Mentzel of the Reich Education Ministry. Laue, with tongue in cheek, sent a copy of the reprimand to Weizsäcker "since you have often striven for the official recognition of relativity theory." A concerned Weizsäcker wrote back to remind Laue of the conclusion of the Seefeld meeting that "a great part of the content of special relativity had already been discovered by Lorenz and above all Poincaré and the share of these two researchers compared to that of Einstein has not always been sufficiently valued. . . . Personally I would put the essence of the debate in these terms: Relativity theory would have been discovered without Einstein, but it was not discovered without him."[5] Weizsäcker's timid advice to Laue in this matter must have proved quite amusing to its recipient, but it emanated from an essentially collusionist mentality in dealing with Nazism that had been modeled on the conduct of his father, the State-Secretary Ernst von Weizsäcker, whom he idolized and sought to defend during the latter's trial for war crimes.[6] This collusionism also motivated Weizsäcker's attempt to rehabilitate the estimable Juilfs by coauthoring with him a physics textbook in 1952 so as to help the former SS officer obtain a teaching post in Hannover.[7] (Weizsäcker had himself also been rather more tarred than Heisenberg by actual membership in Nazi formations.)[8]

4. Testimonial for Werner Erler, 25 April 1947, in Heisenberg-Archiv, Munich and Berlin; copy supplied by Dr. H. Rechenberg. For Max Planck's similar willingness to issue whitewashing certificates, see H. Albrecht, "'Max Planck: Mein Besuch bei Adolf Hitler'—Anmerkungen zum Wert einer historischen Quelle," in *Naturwissenschaft und Technik in der Geschichte*, ed. H. Albrecht (Stuttgart, 1993), pp. 41–63, esp. pp. 60 f.

5. Exchange of 26 May and 2 June 1943 between Laue and Weizsäcker, in Goudsmit Papers, AIP, box 25, folders 12–13; NA, RG 200, Goudsmit Papers, box 6, folder 32 (inserted temporarily in box 8) (IMF 29-1065/1066).

6. For Ernst von Weizsäcker's devious attempts to exculpate himself, see L. Namier, *In the Nazi Era* (London, 1952), pp. 63–83.

Contrast Carl-Friedrich's character with the far more honest attitudes of his brother Richard, who, as President of West Germany in the 1980s, made unprecedentedly forthright admissions of German responsibility for the Holocaust.

7. C-.F. von Weizsäcker and J. Juilfs, *Physik der Gegenwart* (Göttingen, 1952); the preface thanks Juilfs for his "devoted cooperation." See Cassidy, pp. 390 f.

8. See the file on Weizsäcker in the Institut für Zeitgeschichte, Munich, Archiv, MA 116: "Beauftrage des Führers für die Überwachung der gesamten geistigen und weltanschaulichen Schulung der

Another useful friend of Weizsäcker's whom Heisenberg sought to exonerate after the war was Gustav Borger, head of the Scientific Section of the Nazi University Lecturers' League (*Dozentenbund*), who had recommended Weizsäcker for a chair at the Nazified University of Strassburg. Borger was active in arranging the Seefeld *Religionsgespräch* at which Heisenberg and Weizsäcker were able to have "theoretical physics" approved by divorcing it from its "Jewish" origins. In his denazification testimonial for Borger in 1947, Heisenberg reciprocated by saying that the former Nazi official "has to be thanked for ensuring a favorable decision at Seefeld for modern theoretical physics and an unfavorable one against the antisemitic physicists."[9] Here Heisenberg was dexterously resorting to his customary

---

NSDAP" (Amt Rosenberg), Hauptamt Wissenschaft. The reports in connection with his nomination for the Strassburg chair of physics remark on his "lack of any political activity," but say he "might be drawn to active political work in Strassburg through energetic work by the leaders of the Nazi teachers there" (letter of G. Borger, National Head of the Nazi University Lecturers' League [*Dozentenbund*], 12 November 1941). A later report naively remarked that "Weizsäcker has no understanding of political questions" (H. Roessner, 30 June 1942). Weizsäcker was a member of the Nazi University Lecturers' League, though he claimed that as a university lecturer (*Dozent*) he had been obliged to join.

Weizsäcker's attitude was so disreputable that after the war Goudsmit devoted some effort to trying (unsuccessfully) to keep him out of the United States, as correspondence in NA, RG 200, Goudsmit Papers, box 6, folder 32 (misplaced in box 8) shows. Following a meeting with Edward Teller and Weizsäcker in which Teller had argued on the latter's behalf, Goudsmit told Teller (22 November 1949) "that the general theme you followed, namely that the position of his father forced him to act as he did, is utterly ridiculous. . . . I was glad that you were present at our interview. . . . You can't be completely blind." Goudsmit had written—too late—at length to Robert Hutchins, chancellor of the University of Chicago, to try to have an invitation to Weizsäcker canceled. He made clear that his objection was not to "what Weizsäcker might do here," but because the invitation would enhance the reputation in postwar Germany of a scientist who "is not the proper person to educate German youth along the lines of democracy. . . . The objectionable characteristic of both father (Ernst) and son lies in their philosophy of compromise. This is a very common and usually forgivable weakness, but it should not occur in a man whom we single out to teach our way of life to German youth. . . . His illogical position of compromise shows most clearly in the way he tried to twist some of the basic ideas of physics into the Nazi philosophy . . . in November 1942 . . . at Seefeld. It seems natural that von Weizsäcker was given the task of writing the summary conclusion of this meeting. The first draft was written by a certain Dr. Sauter; von Weizsäcker edited it and toned down a couple of paragraphs. . . . The resulting document is a masterpiece of dishonest compromise." This position was repeated in letters to Edwin Kemble and James Conant at Harvard in 1950 and 1952, and in a letter of 6 February 1952 to Joseph Koepfli, the Science Adviser of the State Department, declaring Weizsäcker "unfit for entry in the United States." In an interesting response of 17 January 1950, James Franck agrees with Goudsmit's hostile opinion of Weizsäcker, but says he thinks it worth trying to educate the German physicist in Western standards of moral and political behavior. Weizsäcker had told Franck that "he had done as he had done because he thought it was right to take a realistic attitude toward the situation. . . . Of course, I did not agree with him. . . . I have neither forgiven him nor forgotten what he did. . . . [But] if I am right that he finally saw the situation and himself undistorted by his selfish excuses, he may try to influence the minds of young Germans toward the right attitude. You may regard me as a hopeless optimist."

9. Testimonial for G. Borger, 6 June 1947, Heisenberg-Archiv; copy from H. Rechenberg. Borger had earlier in 1943 congratulated Heisenberg on the award of the Copernicus Prize from Hans Frank.

half-truths; by referring to the rout of the "antisemitic physicists," he was suggesting to the denazification tribunal that somehow Borger was also against Nazi antisemitism or protective of Jewish physicists—neither of which was true. All that mattered to Heisenberg, of course, was that the truth of theoretical physics be preserved, even if its Jewish origins were to be rejected.

The tendency of Heisenberg's testimonials to erode the stigma of membership in the SS and the Nazi Party is evident in his letter on behalf of G. von Droste, who had written to him delicately noting that Heisenberg must be aware of his membership in the SA in 1933 and his subsequent automatic transfer to the Party in 1938; but "since you know well enough my position against the political events of the time, may I ask you to give me with good conscience an exculpatory testimonial. . . . I have to be 'legally prepared' for the denazification tribunal." In "good conscience," of course, Heisenberg supplied on 8 January 1947 the following certificate:

> I often discussed at that time (1939–43) political questions with Herr von Droste and found that he was as sharply critical of the crimes and failings of Nazism as I. I never had the impression that in his thought and behavior, he participated in the bad side of Nazism.[10]

This fallacious belief in the "bad side of Nazism" (*den schlechten Seiten des National Sozialismus*) was what enabled Heisenberg to write "in good conscience" that Droste was not a real Nazi, but rather a "good Nazi." (Lise Meitner, who also received a letter from Droste telling her how she must recall he had never really been a Nazi, dismissed it as "lies from beginning to end"; what she did recall was his customary attire being an SA brown shirt. Nevertheless, and this is the worrying part for what it says about the persistence of German habits of mental equivocation, Meitner did write on his behalf, saying that "I knew very little about the details of your [Party] membership so in that sense I can state . . . that you did not propagate Nazi ideas or express them by your manner.")[11]

So too with Pascual Jordan, the old colleague of Heisenberg's and Born's at Göttingen in the 1920s who later became a rabid Nazi publicist. In 1948 Jordan asked Max Born for a testimonial that would minimize his involvement in Nazi activities and emphasize rather his heroic decision to stay on in Germany to protect the Jewish contribution to theoretical physics in opposition to the "radical Nazi side" (i.e., the "bad side" of Nazism). Born politely declined, sending instead a list of relatives and friends who had died under the Nazis. However, such an appeal to the "good side" of Nazism and the preservation of physics impressed Heisenberg, and he supplied Jordan with at least two whitewashing documents stating

10. Droste to Heisenberg, 22 December 1946, and Heisenberg to Droste, 7–8 January 1947, Heisenberg Archive; copies from H. Rechenberg.

11. R. L. Sime, *Lise Meitner: A Life in Physics* (Berkeley, 1996), p. 350.

that he had "never reckoned with the possibility that Jordan could be a [bad] Nazi," and omitting mention of his propagandistic work for the Third Reich.[12]

One would have thought that commonsense morality, as well as self-interest, would have led Heisenberg at the least to distance himself from former SS scientific staff and Nazi Party members with whom he had come into contact during the Third Reich. But Heisenberg's misconceived German morality moved him rather to distinguish between "good" and "bad" Nazis, largely determined by which Nazis had proven useful to him and German science. Such a grotesquely narrow conception of morality might well have served to vindicate Himmler himself by reference to Himmler's invaluable protection of Heisenberg's "honor" in 1937–38 and after.

No doubt these gentlemen of the SS had purged themselves in Heisenberg's mind by their defense of "theoretical physics" during the Seefeld "religious discussions" and on other occasions, but that such—as Paul Rosbaud put it, "shocking and largely unintelligible"—discussions should have taken place at all was a disgrace. In Rosbaud's words, these "discussions should have been beneath the dignity of physicists of Heisenberg's and Weizsäcker's calibre."[13] Any gain from them was as empty and tainted as the denazification acquittals of their SS patrons. But by 1945 Heisenberg had habituated himself over a twelve-year period to such compromises in pursuit of his honor, and finding justifications for SS members hardly stretched his rationalizing powers. His attitude should be compared with that of Rosbaud, who was appalled at the reinstatement of so many Nazi types under a mask of democratic humbug. Where Rosbaud did try to excuse individual Nazis, it was out of a genuine humanity and recognition of their individual decency rather than the glib support given by Heisenberg to those who had helped to preserve both his honor and that of German science. Thus, Rosbaud always found a good word for Pascual Jordan, whom he personally liked and believed to have remained genuinely "decent" during the war, unlike Heisenberg and his testimonial-toting acolytes, whether nonmembers of the Party or members of the SS.

> I don't care much [said Rosbaud] whether somebody was a member of the Party or not, I ask only: How has he behaved and how will he probably behave now? . . . I

12. N. Wise, "Pascual Jordan: Quantum Mechanics, Psychology, National Socialism," in *Science, Technology, and National Socialism,* ed. M. Renneberg and M. Walker (Cambridge, 1994), pp. 224–254, at pp. 251 f., citing documents in the Staatsbibliothek Preussischer Kulturbesitz, Berlin, Handschriftenabteilung, Nachlass Born, 353 and 1003 (Jordan to Born, 23 July and 15 August 1948; Born to Jordan, 21 October 195[4?]7), and the Heisenberg Papers, Max-Planck-Institut für Physik, Munich.

It must be said, however, that Paul Rosbaud never regarded Jordan as a true Nazi and remained friendly with him after the war. In a note to Goudsmit of August 1945 Rosbaud asserted, "I had many frank discussions with Jordan, and I enjoyed arguing with him very much. There was never any feeling against his Jewish colleagues; for many of them, he had nothing but admiration" (Goudsmit Papers, AIP, box 28, folder 41).

13. P. Rosbaud, review of *Brighter Than A Thousand Suns,* by R. Jungk, *Discovery,* March 1959, 96–97. In a letter to *Nuclear News,* October 1970, Goudsmit referred to Weizsäcker's final summary of the Seefeld meeting as "a sickening concoction of compromise."

have no objection at all to people such as Brill or Drescher-Kaden, who were both members of the Party, [but] have done more to help Jews or people in danger than most of the nonmembers, especially Drescher.[14]

But the whole denazification process was in danger of becoming, thanks to the technicalities exploited by Heisenberg's "Persil-certificates," a distortion of justice and history.

The problem is quite simple, the denazification is left to the Germans, and many Nazis had their alibis ready, the testimonials of friends who testify that they were all antifascists, although they had joined the Party. Besides, there are many others who had never joined the Party, either because they were too clever and careful, or people who tried to join but were not accepted. . . . I come to the conclusion that real denazification is a problem of many years, it cannot be solved only by questionnaires. Drescher-Kaden, the mineralogist, certainly has a bad one . . . nevertheless he is one of the most decent personalities I have ever met, a man comparable in his decency only to Laue, who [Drescher?] has saved the lives of many persons, including my own. On the other hand, Schneiderhöhn, the mineralogist in Freiburg, has a fine questionnaire. He was rejected by the Nazis and was at that time very unhappy, but today he is writing letters to everybody, denouncing Drescher.[15]

As Rosbaud ironically remarked in 1948, "most of our old friends are either back in their old jobs or at least denazified or busy to get testimonials—and they get their testimonials. . . . They will show you some nice letters from people whose names I don't want to tell you and you will learn from these letters that they have been very nice fellows and sometimes have even said nasty things about Adolf."[16]

Heisenberg's behavior in the denazification arena exposes the shallowness of his moral response, his endorsement of traditional mentality in justifying service to the state as an unpolitical ideal, and his exaltation of the advancement of science as the prime moral criterion of scientists' behavior in the Third Reich.

Heisenberg never opened his eyes to the enormity of Nazi evil, though he had heard of it in Poland during his visit to Hans Frank in 1943, just as he never spoke of the use of slave labor to manufacture the metallic uranium plates for his various reactor experiments. But he must assuredly have known about this, since he was active in negotiating for accelerated production.[17] In any case, all of his extant statements show just how Heisenberg regarded the crimes of Nazi Germany and their punishment—as less significant than the preservation of Germany herself

14. Rosbaud to Goudsmit, 17 February 1947, Goudsmit Papers, box 28, folder 43.

15. Rosbaud to Goudsmit, 9 August 1946, Goudsmit Papers, box 28, folder 43. In general see D. Phillips, ed., *German Universities after the Surrender: British Occupation and the Control of Higher Education* (Oxford, 1983); I. D. Turner, ed., *Reconstruction in Post-War Germany: British Occupation Policy and the Western Zones, 1945–1955* (Oxford, 1989).

16. See Rosbaud to Goudsmit, 8 February 1948, 26 May 1949, Goudsmit Papers, box 28, folder 43.

17. Cf. M. Walker, *German National Socialism and the Quest for Nuclear Power, 1939–1949* (Cambridge, 1989), p. 133.

and above all of German science. This deformation of moral sense lies at the bottom of his inexplicable obtuseness of behavior both during and after the war.

Rosbaud had noted it during a rare talk with Heisenberg in 1940 or 1941, his recollections of which are worth quoting in extenso:

> I did not meet Heisenberg very frequently, and I don't know why. Of course, I saw and spoke with him at the meetings of the Physikalische Gesellschaft, but when I wanted some personal advice, I went to Laue, Sommerfeld, or Planck. It may be because I did not like this club of his at Leipzig University, young and highly intelligent people with some sort of arrogance which I dislike. . . . All my sympathies and my admiration for his scientific genius were naturally on his side. We were all fighting for him and against "Deutsche Physik." . . . [When he got the Nobel Prize] there was a demonstration of a few students against him when he entered the lecture room. He asked the few Nazi students: "Who do you think has done more for Germany, you or I?" The majority of the students applauded him. . . .
>
> In the meantime, the situation had changed. He was invited by Himmler to have a talk, and he never failed to mention that he was on very good terms with his good old school friend [*Schul-und Dufreund*] Frank, governor-general of Poland. Modern physics became "admissible at court." . . . The great advantage of modern physics was, of course, that it could be used in Germany's war effort. . . . This rehabilitation of modern physics, due nearly entirely to Heisenberg's efforts, was, of course, a great triumph. I wonder whether it was a triumph for his reputation, too!
>
> In 1940 [1942?] when he was Director of the [KWIP], I went to see Heisenberg. I remember all the points we discussed; I did not agree with him.

Rosbaud had argued that the Nazis had no true respect for science, but Heisenberg lightly remarked that they were still good for "giving you money if the plan . . . is large enough," for instance, for a large astronomical observatory. When Rosbaud objected that the Nazis would simply put a Nazi hack in charge of it, Heisenberg was not fazed: Our "good people" could still work there. At this flippancy, Rosbaud angrily objected that no decent astronomer would work under such conditions, but the point was lost on the opportunistic Heisenberg.

> After having discussed this point we spoke about war and I told him quite frankly my ideas. As he did not agree with me, I thought I had better go and I went away depressed. I never had any more personal talk with him except about professional questions. I heard later, when I was in Norway, that he expressed the same opinion in a conversation with Niels Bohr.
>
> As I knew he was completely in accord on every point with his friend von Weizsäcker, I avoided any further contact with him too.[18]

Obviously "the same opinion" about the war that Heisenberg expressed to both Rosbaud and Bohr was his usual line about the desirability of a German vic-

18. Rosbaud, deposition of 12 August 1945, Goudsmit Papers, box 28, folder 41.

tory. Writing in 1950, Rosbaud told Goudsmit a little more about Heisenberg's line.

> I am shocked and depressed about the childish and, I would almost say immoral, views of such a great scientist. He has not changed a bit and has not learned anything. There was never a revolution in Germany, neither in 1918, 1933, or 1945. He expressed the same views when I had my last long talk with him in 1940 or 41, and he thought that only when Germany has won the war, this "purification" will take place. It was from then on that I did not want to see him anymore, and that apart from occasionally saying "hello" I had no contact with him whatsoever.[19]

This was in reply to a letter from Goudsmit relating how his latest encounter with Heisenberg had found the latter as willfully blind as ever to the moral evil of Nazism:

> Heisenberg was here. I invited him to give a lecture and then saw him again later. His visit was quite friendly but I had occasion to discuss our differences of opinion with him. I still cannot understand his rationalization.
>
> The line he follows now is very similar to that which he expressed before the war. He believes that what happened in Germany was a "revolution." In a revolution, he says, low-grade people always have an opportunity to come to the top and do a great deal of damage. However, in the long run, normal selection will return—the low-grade people will be pushed out and reasonable people will again be in power. In the discussion, he was willing to admit the time to reach equilibrium might be fifty or one hundred years, rather than the few years he had in mind, and by that time there might not be any reasonable people left. But, he still goes on defending all the evil things in Germany as being the normal by-products of any social revolution.[20]

During the war Rosbaud had realized perfectly well how Heisenberg's self-serving moral sophistry was shared by his colleagues on the uranium project. A few days after the big Speer-Heisenberg meeting at Harnack-Haus in June 1942, the scientists learned of Speer's decision not to press ahead with the bomb project. One evening at Restaurant Orient, on Fasanenstrasse near the Kurfürstendamm, a group of twelve physicists were professing their moral relief at not having to develop a bomb. A rather intoxicated Rosbaud was finally provoked by the cant he was hearing to shout out: "If any one of you knew how to make the bomb, he would not hesitate a minute and tell your Führer how to destroy the rest of the world in order to get the highest order of the Iron Cross." Rosbaud admits that "they were decent enough not to denounce me after this, but my remark was followed by [icy silence]." The stunned scientists, evidently frightened that Rosbaud might be an agent provocateur who would report their reactions to the Gestapo,

---

19. Rosbaud to Goudsmit, 25 October 1950, copy supplied by Dr. A. Kramish from Goudsmit Papers, box 28, folder 45.

20. Goudsmit to Rosbaud, 20 October 1950, Goudsmit Papers, box 28, folder 45.

quickly split up and vanished.[21] But, of course, Rosbaud had hit both nails on the head—the first, that their advice to Speer stemmed from technical ignorance about how to build a bomb, and the second, that their moralizing was empty cant.

Neither Rosbaud during the war, nor Goudsmit after it, could open Heisenberg's eyes to the moral turpitude of hobnobbing with the SS in the alleged interest of theoretical physics or of working on a bomb project—however unfeasible—for the Nazi tyranny.[22] Heisenberg was all too ready with his repertoire of rationalizations, ranging from the moral superiority of German scientists over their Allied counterparts for not having produced a bomb to the essential harmlessness of the German project as pure disinterested science.[23] This rush to apology could easily boil over into outright offensiveness, as Heisenberg himself recognized on one occasion. Writing to his old Dutch friend B. L. van der Waerden, who had remained on in Germany during the war (to the distress of other Dutch scientists), Heisenberg ventured:

> In every case I had regarded it a crime to make atomic bombs for Hitler. But I find it also not good that they have also been given to other wielders of power who have used them. On the other hand from past years I have learned something that my Western friends do not yet completely wish to admit—that in such times almost no one can avoid committing crimes or supporting them through inaction, be he on the German, Russian, or Anglo-Saxon side.

After writing this somewhat barefaced claim to moral superiority to—or at least moral equality with—Allied scientists, Heisenberg drew back and thought he had better gloss it.

> On reading over this letter, I notice that the last sentence may be misunderstood in two respects. First, one could think that I wished to mark Oppenheimer or Fermi as criminals, or, second, it might be thought that I myself would have been ready under the circumstances to commit any sort of crime "for Hitler." I hope you know me well enough to know that neither of these views is intended. What I mean is that the breaking up of all the legal orders among the great peoples [*Völkermassen*] of this earth has forced each of them as he struggles [*kämpft*] for his preservation to be as brutal as his enemy—and this in turn then weirdly hastens the process of dissolution. But I shall not write too much on these matters.[24]

21. Rosbaud to Goudsmit, 30 April 1958, Goudsmit Papers, box 28, folder 44. Cf. A. Kramish, *The Griffin* (Boston, 1986), p. 129, which gives a slightly different version of Rosbaud's words: "Nonsense! If you knew how to build it, you'd present it to your Führer on a silver platter." See above, chaps. 3 and 12.

22. When Rosbaud sat at the same table with Heisenberg in Hamburg after the war, they "greeted each other very coolly, and did not say anything else" (Rosbaud to Goudsmit, 26 May 1949, Goudsmit Papers, box 28, folder 43).

23. For the irrelevance of the "harmlessness" argument, see Philip Morrison's review of Goudsmit's *ALSOS* in *BAS* 3 (1947): 354, 365; Morrison's reply to Laue's dissent, ibid. 4 (1948): 104; and Goudsmit's remarks, ibid. 3 (1947): 343. See also Cassidy, pp. 516 f.

24. Heisenberg to van der Waerden, 28 April 1948, in IMF 29-1191/1192. For van der Waerden's questionable moral status, see H. Casimir, *Haphazard Reality* (New York, 1983), p. 196: "A German re-

To escape the obvious corollary that Oppenheimer and Fermi had criminally provided the "wielders of power" with atomic bombs, Heisenberg again turned fatalistic world-historian and provided a vision of a descent to universal barbarism that magnanimously rendered the Americans no guiltier than the Germans. As usual, Heisenberg had blinded himself to the special guilt of Germany, which he obviously regarded as merely having been "struggling" for its own national "preservation," just as had Britain and America.

Heisenberg's embarrassing habit of justifying the Nazi regime's "good side" and insisting that it would have been "so fine" if Germany had won the war was particularly dismaying to Jewish scientists. In the course of their sharp-edged correspondence in the late 1940s Heisenberg told Goudsmit that though he had been aware of the "horrifying consequences" of a German victory, he had not wished to see Germany defeated out of fear of the Allied "hate that Nazism had sown"— an abjectly compromising admission that Germany should win because of the threat of Allied revenge on Nazi evil. Goudsmit was especially infuriated by Heisenberg's pitiful attempt to excuse himself and his colleagues by claiming that their contributions to Nazi success had been merely "small-scale." Goudsmit retorted that this was just a self-serving rationalization, fabricated for an absurd goal of preserving relativity and quantum theory under Hitler. "How could you ever think these were important issues?" he demanded of Heisenberg.[25]

When Heisenberg visited the United States in the late 1940s, he regaled Hans Bethe (a German-Jewish refugee) with his usual justifications. "Give us some years and we would have educated the Nazis. . . . Yes, I knew of atrocities, but was afraid of Allied revenge if the Germans lost." As to the atomic bomb, Heisenberg averred he had worked on it purely to save scientists from being enlisted. Hearing this, Bethe did not show any anger, but he was deeply appalled.[26] A certain incomprehensibil-

---

maining in Germany did not thereby condone the crimes of National Socialists; to a certain extent, a Dutchman staying on in Germany did."

25. Heisenberg to Goudsmit, 23 September 1947, and Goudsmit to Heisenberg, 1 December 1947, in Goudsmit Papers, box 10, folders 95–96. See Cassidy, pp. 515 f.

26. H. Bethe, conversation with author, 12 October 1995, confirming material previously reported in J. Bernstein, *Hans Bethe, Prophet of Energy* (New York, 1980), pp. 74 f.: "His [Heisenberg's] third reason was that in 1942 he had come to the conclusion that the Germans should win the war. That struck me as a terribly naive statement. He said that he knew the Germans had committed terrible atrocities against the populations on the Eastern Front—in Poland and Russia—and to some extent in the West as well. He concluded that the Allies would never forgive this and would destroy Germany as a nation— that they would treat Germany about the way the Romans had treated Carthage. This, he said to himself, should not happen, therefore, Germany should win the war, and then the good Germans would take care of the Nazis. It is unbelievable that a man who has made some of the greatest contributions to modern physics should have been that naive. But he seems to have said similar things to people during the war. He never mentioned anything to me about the morality of making a nuclear weapon."

In our conversation Professor Bethe agreed with my general view of the peculiarity of German mentality, remarking that the first time he thought he was among sane people was when he visited Cambridge in 1930. He thought he had been "born to be an Anglo-Saxon."

ity about Heisenberg's performance may have restrained Bethe, as it probably did others whom Heisenberg favored with his historical and moral interpretations. His otherwise well-inclined obituarists were rather mystified by what they heard:

> There were many instances of remarks which caused resentment, though nobody has collected them or checked them in great detail. One typical example is told by the people to whom the remark was addressed: visiting the house of a German refugee scientist [*Francis Simon*] during his stay in England in late 1947, Heisenberg commented "the Nazis should have been left in power for another fifty years, then they would have become quite decent." If this is correctly remembered, it was a strange remark to make to a man who had been dismissed in spite of his having served in World War I, and who had lost relatives and friends in extermination camps, in a conversation in which Heisenberg was anxious to re-establish cordial relations.[27]

This way of thinking and behaving provoked a violent scene when Heisenberg met his old friend Max Born again in Germany after the war. At Cambridge in 1934 Heisenberg had already distressed Born by his lack of feeling in inviting Born—but not his family—back to Germany.

> Heisenberg became rather embarrassed and answered, "No, I think your family is not included in the invitation." This made me very angry. I broke off the discussion and went into the house, where I told Hedi. We could not understand how Heisenberg, whom we knew as a decent, humane fellow, could have agreed to convey such a message to me. I have never talked to him about it. But later he, and others, described to me the situation in Germany at the time, the pressure under which they lived; thus I came to a kind of understanding, though not of forgiving this lack of feeling and tact—to use the mildest expressions.[28]

Following the war, Heisenberg visited Born at Edinburgh in December 1947 and evidently tried out the same gambits he used with Simon and others to justify a German victory. Born, who had long been somewhat skeptical and ironic about Heisenberg's mental agility, probably put up with this—in part, out of bewilderment and incredulity, no doubt. But the meeting left a deeply unpleasant impression on him, for a few months later Born wrote of it to Einstein as follows:

> By the way, Heisenberg visited us last December, as pleasant and intelligent as ever, but noticeably "Nazified" [*merklich "angenazit"*].[29]

27. N. Mott and R. Peierls, "Werner Heisenberg," in *Biographical Memoirs of Fellows of the Royal Society* 23 (1977): 213–251, p. 236. N. Kurti in a letter to the *Times Literary Supplement*, 18 June 1993, gives one of Heisenberg's remarks to Simon in 1947 in the German original: "*Man hätte die Nazis nur fünfzig Jahre dran lassen wollen; dann wären sie auch anständig geworden.*"

28. Max Born, *My Life* (London, 1978), pp. 269 f. For Born's ironic clarity of understanding of Heisenberg in the 1930s see his comments in W. Pauli, *Wissenschaftlicher Briefwechsel mit Bohr, Einstein, Heisenberg u.a.*, ed. K. von Meyenn (New York, Berlin, and Heidelberg, 1979–93), 2:168. See above, chap. 17.

29. Born to Einstein, 31 March 1948, in A. Einstein and M. Born, *The Born-Einstein Letters*, ed. and trans. M. Born (New York, 1971), p. 166; see also German original in idem, *Briefwechsel, 1916–1955*, with

Heisenberg, blandly insensitive as ever, noticed nothing much amiss. Though he had detected on his British trip "the undertone of a consciously anti-German feeling, especially among Jewish colleagues," Heisenberg had found "Born wholly charmingly hospitable—it was like old times."[30] But on a later occasion Born was to experience a shock. When an optimistic Born and his wife traveled to Göttingen in 1953 to receive the freedom of his old university city and also inquire about restitution, they found that Heisenberg's temper had soured, perhaps under the pressure of his public dispute with Samuel Goudsmit in 1948, which had fatally compromised his "honor" in Western eyes.[31] Heisenberg's stacked-up resentment over the Allied victimization of Germany, the attacks on his "honor" by Jewish-German scientists in the West, their harping on the Holocaust, their failure to understand the plight of Germany and German scientists, the effective "betrayal" of Germany by those same Jews now coming—like Max Born—to seek material compensation and psychological guilt from a humiliated Germany—and a humiliated Heisenberg—all this broke forth in a scandalous antisemitic outburst. The following is related by Born's Scottish secretary of long-standing who knew him for many years at Edinburgh University and was also close to Paul Rosbaud, who confirmed her hostile impression of Heisenberg.

> Paul spoke of the belief amongst Heisenberg's colleagues of his being a ruthlessly ambitious opportunist, greedy for power and advancement. He was apparently known to be prone to fits of frightening anger and black rage—when things did not work out according to his plans—and vented this on those around him, e.g. secretaries, technicians and junior colleagues. It was also believed that the main reason for sending his wife and children deep into the country was not so much because of the danger of bombing, but to get quit of her increasingly dangerous tendency to drop bricks by artlessly referring to confidences he had given her, in the most dangerous company where all ears were permanently alert for any careless or indiscreet talk. . . . I remember how Paul said with a twist of derision and scepticism that it was entirely characteristic of the man's arrogance that he was so furious when the Allies refused to allow him immediately to return to a position of power to rebuild physics in Germany immediately after his internment, during which he had persisted in alleging his very diluted Nazi allegiance. . . .
>
> I told Paul that although I was curious about Heisenberg from his portraits in

---

preface by Heisenberg (Munich, 1969), p. 226. As usual Born was rather too understanding; in his comments added in the 1969 English version, *The Born-Einstein Letters*, p. 167, he retreated, saying "my opinion of Heisenberg was probably not justified. Later on he explained to me what work had been during the Hitler period. . . . Irving ['s book] . . . justifies his behaviour." (Born died in 1970.)

30. Heisenberg to Sommerfeld, 5 January 1948, Sommerfeld Nachlass, Deutsches Museum, Munich, 1977–28/A, 136/49.

31. Max Born, *My Life and My Views* (New York, 1968), p. 43, but no date is given. It is difficult to fix the date of the Borns' visit to Göttingen, since it is omitted from the obituaries and other biographical sources I have seen, including H. Born and M. Born, *Luxus der Wissenschaft* (Munich, 1969). But Anita Kerkmann of the Born Nachlass in the Preussischer Kulturbesitz, Staatsbibliothek zu Berlin, kindly informs me that the visit took place in July 1953.

various textbooks, I had been repelled by the naked arrogance revealed in those pictures—and his behavior towards Max Born years after the war on the occasion of the Borns returning to Göttingen to arrange restitution of his pension rights at Göttingen, and reparation for the property confiscated by the Nazis when they fled over here in 1933. Heisenberg was by then Professor in Göttingen and when the Borns went to visit him at that time, they were met with anti-Jewish sneers and obscenities and in the end Heisenberg spat on the floor at Max Born's feet! Before they had set off Max spoke with naive anticipation of meeting Heisenberg again—they had never been able to believe that he could have been a dyed in the wool Nazi and Max expressed the somewhat naive belief that since they still remembered Heisenberg with friendship, surely Heisenberg must have retained some friendly feelings towards them. While I could hardly comment on this, I felt a little worried and uneasy about this simple trustfulness. When they returned and that first morning when I warmly enquired about their trip and how they had fared, very reluctantly Max Born confided in me about this great shock and painful encounter and I was both horrified and deeply angered to think of anyone treating my little Maxie [*a Scottishism!*] in such a loathsome way. Later Mrs. Born gave me her version and ended with a statement which I never forgot and said simply at the end, "And my poor Max, he wept." . . .

This was one of the stories Nick Kemmer wanted me to repeat to him before he wrote his review . . . and after I had repeated it, he then said what puzzled him was that years later at some international meeting or other, he had seen Max and Heisenberg apparently amicably talking to each other. I did not doubt that statement—I had already seen the Borns' quakerish ignoring of that first denazified Austrian—and learned what is actually meant by "turning the other cheek." Indeed, when Max Born first confided this story after his return, he begged me to keep it confidential since this Heisenberg had already gained so much hostility and suspicion that must irk him—and would be punished enough without either he or Hedi circulating that ugly experience amongst other colleagues and friends. . . . Max had patted my hand and said simply that he and Hedi had had so many more years of learning to forgive [*than had I*].[32]

True to his word, Born never told even his own son about this episode,[33] but the

32. Kramish, *The Griffin*, p. 44, first reported this incident, but editorial intervention led to its being placed in a context that suggested it occurred in the 1930s (in 1933, according to p. 118), rather than after the war. I am most grateful to Dr. Kramish for providing me with a copy of the original testimony.

The episode is alluded to in Nicholas Kemmer's review in *Nature* 313 (28 February 1985): 826, of Heisenberg's *Collected Works* and Elisabeth Heisenberg's *Inner Exile:* "I am reminded of the way a formerly close colleague of Heisenberg's returned from a postwar reunion in deep distress—a gulf remained unbridged." However, Born's official obituary by N. Kemmer and R. Schlapp, "Max Born," *Biographical Memoirs of Fellows of the Royal Society* 17 (1971): 17–52, discreetly omits mention of the matter.

Cassidy, p. 325, remarks that "anecdotal claims to the contrary, Heisenberg maintained a cordial relationship with both Born and Schrödinger to the end of their lives," but one should not confuse an outwardly correct relationship with a genuinely cordial one, nor do friendly relations disprove the fact of Heisenberg's onslaught on Born.

33. Information from Professor Gustav Born, London, who finds it hard to credit the story.

account nevertheless rings true in terms of what is known about Heisenberg's character from other sources, particularly his arrogance and temper. Heisenberg was always possessed of a deep pride that when wounded would give rise to child-like fury and resentment. He was so furious, for example, at being outdone by his brother in minor things that he refused to speak to him at times. And when a visiting Japanese physicist beat Heisenberg at table tennis, at which he had rigorously trained himself to become an expert, "Heisenberg was so unhappy and upset about this failure that he did not show up at his [Leipzig] institute for more than a week and never again played table tennis with the Japanese visitor. Heisenberg's ferocious ambition and his insistence on continued admiration made it necessary that at all times he be acknowledged as the best." These may sound like trivial matters, but it should be remembered that even when the magisterial presence of Niels Bohr should have acted as a psychological or prudential restraint on Heisenberg while he was arguing for uncertainty at Copenhagen in 1927, Heisenberg worked himself up into such a mental state that he jeopardized their whole relationship by his displays of temper and tantrums. Similarly too his antagonism to Schrödinger's wave mechanics overrode the boundaries of rationality. The Göttingen meeting with Max Born should be placed in the context of this behavioral syndrome, where Heisenberg's wildly emotional and ambitious—above all, proud —character was allowed to undermine his scientific achievement and raise serious questions about his personal morality.[34] This volatile personal makeup of pride, extreme ambition, anger, arrogance, and envy was ready to be ignited by anyone who cast doubt on his view of his moral conduct during the Hitler years and challenged his rationalizations of Nazism in the postwar years when Heisenberg's ego was still fragile and he felt his own integrity, both moral and scientific, to have been called into question.

Max Born's reference to Heisenberg's having appeared as "Nazified" as ever on his visit of December 1947 to Edinburgh shows just how far Heisenberg had internalized, perhaps without realizing it, the imprint of the years he spent under Nazism. No doubt the ironic term *Nazified* embraced Heisenberg's near-mindless German patriotism, his justification of his collusion and compromises with the Third Reich, his apologetic rationalizations of the Nazi war effort, his historical theories about the crisis of the modern world requiring the emergence of Nazism—and his latent antisemitism typical of the German intellectual class. Even in his autobiographical *Physics and Beyond* Heisenberg was unable to break out of the German antisemitic mentality and make straightforward statements about Jews and the evil of antisemitism. The most he could manage was to disapprove of the vulgar antisemitic protests against Einstein and to regret the emigra-

---

34. For the table-tennis affair, see M. Dresden, *H. A. Kramers: Between Tradition and Revolution* (New York, 1987), p. 264, and for his fraternal competitiveness, Cassidy, p. 15. For Heisenberg's violent behavior toward Bohr and Schrödinger in 1925–27 see Cassidy, pp. 213 ff., 241–246, and above, chap. 16.

tion of Jewish physicists from Germany.[35] By 1939, it will be recalled, the SS had hopes of activating Heisenberg's antisemitism, thanks to his rejection of "the excessive infiltration of Jews into German living space."[36] (Even so liberated an individual as Heisenberg's brother-in-law, Fritz Schumacher, who in the late 1930s moved to England out of disgust with the Nazi regime, had absorbed antisemitic elements and sympathized with the "good side" of Nazism during its first years in power.)[37]

Heisenberg's view of Einstein was a mixture of admiration, distrust, and a certain element of contempt. In a condescending obituary of 1955 Heisenberg the worldly-wise political and historical philosopher found Einstein flawed in his political attitudes by "an almost naive belief in the possibility of solving political problems through goodwill." Einstein, he claimed, had mistakenly believed that peace might be obtained through controlling national states (and especially Germany). These apparently reasonable comments on Einstein's pacifism and aversion to nationalism have about them a strong whiff of disapproval, implying a certain moral deficiency on the part of Einstein for his lack of German patriotism (one of Heisenberg's supreme values). But Heisenberg's moral strictures go further. It was, says Heisenberg, a "tragic aspect" of Einstein's life that the infamies of Nazism moved him to urge Roosevelt to develop an atomic bomb, which "killed as many thousands of women and children who were just as guiltless as those [*viz.*, *Jews*] for whom Einstein was anxious to intercede." The shockingly antisemitic implication here is that out of selfish Jewish concern Einstein had contributed to the making of an Allied atomic weapon that was used immorally to kill other innocents for whom he felt no compassion.[38]

35. See L. Poliakov, *The History of Anti-Semitism*, vol. 4 (Oxford, 1985), p. 334, which points out the lack of any true engagement with the problem of antisemitism by Heisenberg, and the tendency to portray Einstein as an "honorary Aryan." For the permeation of German culture by antisemitic presuppositions, see P. L. Rose, *German Question/Jewish Question: Revolutionary Antisemitism in Germany from Kant to Wagner*, 2d ed. (Princeton, 1992). (See above, chaps. 16 and 18, for Heisenberg's latent antisemitism; also Cassidy, pp. 71, 97, 135 f.)

36. Quoted in M. Walker, *Nazi Science: Myth, Truth, and the German Atomic Bomb* (New York, 1995), p. 138. See above, chap. 18.

37. See the frank statements in the biography by Schumacher's daughter Barbara Wood, *E. P. Schumacher: His Life and Thought* (New York, 1984), pp. 30, 58 f., 65 (though at p. 97 the author seems to think that Heisenberg's stance in Nazi Germany was "uncompromising"!). Immediately after his capture by the Americans, Heisenberg sought to make contact with Schumacher, loudly lamenting the destruction of Germany and looking forward to a rapid rebuilding of German science (Heisenberg to Schumacher, 6 May 1945, Goudsmit Papers, box 10, folder 93).

38. W. Heisenberg, "The Scientific Work of Albert Einstein" (1955), in his *Across the Frontiers* (New York, 1975), pp. 5–6. Heisenberg psychologically evaded the problem of Nazi antisemitism in his postwar writings, which, like Weizsäcker's, prefer to avoid mentioning Auschwitz. For instance, in his lecture "Science as a Means of International Understanding" (1946, Göttingen) (translated in his *Philosophical Problems of Nuclear Science* [London, 1952]) Heisenberg is silent about the relevance of Auschwitz to the problem of science and the state, though the scientific chemical methods of killing used at Auschwitz were in everyone's mind at the time.

Einstein had always had a jaundiced opinion of the German mentality that Heisenberg so ably represented. In 1933 Einstein had written to Max Born: "You know, I think, that I have never had a particularly high opinion of the Germans (morally and politically speaking). But I must confess that the degree of their brutality and cowardice came as something of a surprise to me."[39] Einstein never wavered in this view. On being invited to renew his ties with the Kaiser-Wilhelm-Society (now the Max-Planck-Gesellschaft) in 1949, Einstein refused, saying:

> The crime of the Germans is truly the most abominable ever to be recorded in the history of the so-called civilized nations. The conduct of the German intellectuals— seen as a group—was no better than that of the mob. And even now there is no real indication of any regret or any real desire to repair whatever little may be left to restore after the gigantic murders. In view of these circumstances, I feel an irrepressible aversion to participating in anything that represents any aspect of public life in Germany.[40]

Einstein understood perfectly well that there had been no true self-reckoning with conscience on the part of Heisenberg and those German scientists who shared his self-deceiving point of view that all should now be forgiven from both sides after the war as though it had been a simple misunderstanding and gentlemen should now shake hands. Einstein's view of Heisenberg must have been far more biting than Born's, but as usual this did not deter Heisenberg from doing his best to paper over a disastrous rift.[41] In describing the only occasion after the war when he and Einstein are known to have met (at Princeton in 1954), Heisenberg claimed:

> Einstein invited me to visit him at his home. . . . I had been warned beforehand that my visit should last only a short time, since Einstein was obliged to spare himself, on account of a heart condition. Einstein, however, would have none of this, and with coffee and cakes I was made to spend the whole afternoon with him. Of politics, we said nothing.[42]

Although some of this cozy picture may be true (for example, the fact that the conversation was confined to physics), it is impossible to believe that Einstein, well aware of Heisenberg's shameful compromises with Nazism, could have regarded his guest with equanimity. Another account seems more truthful.

> About Einstein on Heisenberg after '45, I heard the following from the late Helen Dukas, Einstein's secretary. One day, after the war, the bell at 112 Mercer St. rang. She opened the door. There stood Heisenberg, who had not announced his coming

39. Letter of 30 May 1933, in Einstein and Born, *Born-Einstein Letters*, p. 114.

40. Quoted in B. Hoffmann and H. Dukas, *Albert Einstein: Creator and Rebel* (New York, 1972), p. 237.

41. Little is known about Einstein's opinion of Heisenberg's behavior under the Third Reich, though I hope to obtain new information shortly.

42. W. Heisenberg, *Encounters with Einstein, and Other Essays* (Princeton, 1989), p. 121. GWH, C IV, 124. (The lecture of Heisenberg's from which the quote is taken was delivered in 1974.)

ahead of time. He asked to see Einstein. Helen went upstairs to tell Einstein what was up. Einstein was furious, he had no desire—to put it mildly—to see Heisenberg. Being a courteous man, he did receive him, however. I do not know anything more as to what happened during this visit.[43]

. . .

Unfortunately, several well-intentioned British scientists were taken in by Heisenberg's slick half-truths and impositions, leaving Rosbaud and the German-Jewish exiles to appear somewhat ranting and unreasonable in their objections and outrage. In 1948 Rosbaud wrote despairingly to Goudsmit:

> Heisenberg has been in this country and stayed several weeks. . . . He was a great success and had an enthusiastic reception in Cambridge. . . . Lord Pakenham was apparently deeply impressed by him. He also had talks with Simon and Peierls, who were not so much impressed. I have, of course, not seen him. Heisenberg's position is very strong and, I think, people over here look at him as at some German apostle. . . . Weizsäcker too is on his way to England invited by some Christian associations and, no doubt, he will also be very successful. . . . Don't think that Heisenberg will ever agree with you . . . he will never learn to be humble but he will always be arrogant. People will look at you or Simon or Peierls as being biased, at me as an illoyal [*sic*] and unreliable citizen and at Heisenberg as a truly patriotic and reliable German of the best type. And thousands of Germans who suffered under the Nazis . . . will soon be forgotten. It is a very pessimistic and depressing view I am taking.[44]

Though he believed there to be only one properly moral choice to be made in the end, Rosbaud was ready to admit that the Germans had indeed faced a difficult choice as to whether they should support or betray their country, and he did not blame all of those who, after agonizing, made the wrong moral decision to work for a German success. Of Walther Gerlach, Rosbaud remarked: "His desire was absolutely honest, he loved his country and wished the best to her and did not want her to perish. He suffered under this dilemma and many times I thought to have persuaded him that Hitler and the war were both inseparable and that he had to reduce war work to the least." To Rosbaud, Gerlach appeared "absolutely incorruptible" and at least retained his integrity in deciding to work for the war effort. But Heisenberg seemed opportunistic, ambitious, and dishonest in his various rationalizations of the need for a German victory, even if he were as sincere in his love of Germany as was Gerlach.[45]

---

43. A. Pais to author, 5 August 1991.

44. Rosbaud to Goudsmit, 25 April 1948, Goudsmit Papers, box 28, folder 43.

45. See Rosbaud's notes of 1945 on Gerlach, Goudsmit Papers, box 28, folder 42, and the comments on Heisenberg cited elsewhere in this chapter.

Rosbaud also implied that Siegfried Flügge had left the Heisenberg group for moral reasons; at any rate he regarded him as "very decent" and as hoping that the Nazis would lose their war (Rosbaud to Goudsmit, 24 February 1947, Goudsmit Papers, box 28, folder 43).

Rosbaud doubtless had both Heisenberg and Gerlach in mind when he wrote in his essay of 1945 on German attitudes in the Third Reich of "those [scientists] who wanted to win the war (be it for reasons of obviously false but honest patriotism)—they did not realize that it would never be this Germany which they had in their minds which would win the war but the Nazis for whom they often showed contempt, even hatred—be it for reasons of their own comfort."[46]

But the naive British inclination in some quarters to give Heisenberg and other patriotic Germans the benefit of the doubt—even respect them—disturbed Rosbaud in the years after 1945.

> The most terrible dilemma for every decent German was in his behaviour against his own country. I sometimes have the uneasy feeling that [the] BBC, of course, had to challenge the Germans to fight the Nazis . . . but that the average American or Englishman had contempt for every German following this advice. Maybe no one but a German can understand that "Right or wrong, my country" has completely lost its validity in Nazi Germany. . . .
>
> Have they [the resisters] betrayed Germany? No, they betrayed the Nazis and in so doing they worked . . . for right and freedom of their own country. I think they were really good Germans.[47]

In 1947 he told Goudsmit:

> I know that many people in this country don't understand me and don't agree with me. . . . It is a very great danger, if high officers . . . declare that they cannot blame German scientists, who have done such brilliant war work, for their loyalty to Hitler Germany and if they say that they like these scientists much better than the Germans who have been disloyal to their country.[48]

But what to Heisenberg and innocent foreigners seemed quite reasonable explanations of his conduct struck some more critical British observers of the time as belonging to a "madhouse mentality" that was quite alien to Western minds. A British report by E. W. B. Gill of 1945 characterizes the "general German scientific outlook" thus:

> When one has learned to disregard the impression, frequently arising when talking to these people [German scientists], that one is examining the occupants of a madhouse, it is possible to get a fair idea of their outlook. . . . The average German scientist was indifferent to politics, a phenomenon not unknown in more civilised coun-

46. P. Rosbaud, "The Attitude of Germans, Especially German Scientists, during the Nazi Regime" (1945), Goudsmit Papers, box 28, folder 42, p. 3.

47. Ibid., p. 4.

48. Rosbaud to Goudsmit, 22 June 1947, Goudsmit Papers, box 28, folder 43. In a later letter of 8 February 1948, Rosbaud told Goudsmit that "people like me are regarded as traitors—and not only by the Germans!" (Goudsmit Papers, box 28, folder 43). For Rosbaud's fear that the British could not understand Bonhoeffer's prayer—and his own—for the defeat of their own country, see his letter to Goudsmit of 9 August 1946 (Goudsmit Papers, box 28, folder 43), quoted in the epigraph of this chapter.

tries. What is, however, more difficult for us to understand is their almost fanatical zeal for pure research which put them in a world quite apart. . . . Regarding themselves as creatures of another world, the tendency was of course to disclaim all responsibility for the real world and to regard it merely as a somewhat reluctant supplier of funds for the prosecution of science. . . . [Summing up an American report]: "The better grade are not ill-disposed to the Allies and they seem to regard the initial stages of the occupation as a temporary and regrettable interruption of their work—at Göttingen some asked if they could not get grants from the Carnegie Institute for resuming their work." This last sentence reveals indeed the madhouse mentality we have to deal with.[49]

A key scientific officer of the British Control Commission confirms this picture. Ronald Fraser was the British officer at Göttingen in charge of reintegrating Heisenberg and his colleagues into the international scientific community and thus had ample opportunity to observe the peculiar way in which his protégés' minds worked, especially that of Heisenberg, whose historical account of the uranium project he had himself translated for *Nature* in 1947.[50] Fraser had long experience of German mentality, having studied in Munich in the 1920s, where he had been well acquainted with the latent antisemitism in German scientific circles.[51] He was therefore very equipped to understand the peculiar mentality of Heisenberg and his colleagues. When Fraser was approached by David Irving to confirm Heisenberg's story of going to Copenhagen in 1947 to have Niels Bohr corroborate his version of the earlier visit of 1941, he was able quickly to set matters straight.

I can indeed recall my visit [in 1947] to Bohr with Heisenberg. The object of that particular exercise was threefold.

49. Major E. W. B. Gill, "German Academic Scientists and the War," 20 August 1945, pp. 2–3 (IMF 31-1234/1235). Gill was chief of the Scientific and Technical Branch (British) of FIAT.

50. Otto Hahn, while remarking that Fraser was correct in his relations even though he could not conceal a certain anti-German attitude, acknowledged the British officer's helpfulness and tact in escorting him to Stockholm in 1946 to receive the Nobel Prize and also his facilitation of the founding of the Max-Planck-Gesellschaft (O. Hahn, *Mein Leben* [Munich, 1968], pp. 193 f., 205, 211 ff., 216). At p. 220 Hahn refers to Fraser on his departure from Göttingen as "our friend." (For Heisenberg's *Nature* article of 1947, see above, chap. 1.)

51. Ronald Fraser died in 1985 in New Zealand, where he had retired. His son Conan Fraser has communicated to me the following reminiscence: "Munich 1926 . . . German physics was at its most virulent, when all Jewish contributions to the learned journals were ignored. This meant that a handful of research students were doing experiments of which even I knew the answers. . . . Then came Stern's manifesto "On the Method of Molecular Rays" which I read one morning, breathlessly, in the library. In came Ruchardt, Wien's chief assistant. I burst out, "Do you know Stern? What sort of man is he?" Said Ruchardt, "He is a hideous Jew. I do not speak with him!" . . . So I went to work with Stern—a genial Jewish little man, completely human. And what a lab! Simply bursting with ideas, mostly divulged over the midday meal at which we all gathered. And it was there that I first met Rabi. I thought he was a "Galicianer" (a Jew from the East) and for two days we conversed in dog German until I discovered he was American!" Conan Fraser adds that "Rabi was a life-long friend."

a) Heisenberg had just completed a new theory of super-conductivity, which he was anxious to expound to Bohr. . . .
b) I used a) as a lever with Bohr to persuade him to receive his prodigal son . . . this was but one of my countless moves to open the windows of the German scientists' Nazi prison to the west.
c) Heisenberg's expressed wish to be given an opportunity of asking Niels Bohr verbally to arrange for a supply of Danish provender to supplement the calories to which his numerous offspring were officially entitled.

Your version . . . and even more your marginal source are way off the beam. The whole story of "a kind of confrontation" in the matter of his 1941 natter with Bohr in the Tivoli gardens is a typical Heisenberg fabrication—maybe a bit brighter than a thousand others, but like them all a product of his *Blut und Boden* guilt complex, which he rationalizes that quickly that the stories become for him the truth, the whole truth and nothing but the truth. Pitiful, in a man of his mental stature. . . .

Yours more in sorrow than in anger,
Ronald Fraser[52]

It is tempting to speculate how in this case the rationalization occurred: Heisenberg would have tried to open up the subject of the 1941 meeting, Bohr silenced him by saying he did not want to talk about the past and that it was over—and Heisenberg took this as confirmation that Bohr sympathized and agreed with his own version. After all, both Heisenberg and Weizsäcker recalled other postwar meetings with Bohr where they had allegedly been told that all that wartime stuff was behind them. But while Bohr had simply meant to spare their feelings (and his own too) by not bringing up the sore subject of Nazi collusion and their "hostile visit" (as Mrs. Bohr put it), Heisenberg and Weizsäcker interpreted this as agreement and forgiveness. From the same meeting, it was possible for Bohr and Heisenberg to take away quite opposing versions of what had transpired.

52. Fraser to Irving, 27 August 1966, in IMF 32. See also Cassidy, p. 515, for this visit. Also Heisenberg's interview of 23 October 1965 by Irving, p. 39 (IMF 31-564). The arrangements for the visit are in Bohr Scientific Correspondence, Archive for History of Quantum Physics, Berkeley, and AIP; see Fraser to Bohr, 18 July 1947, and Bohr to Fraser, 19 July 1947, BSC, 29; the latter says the visit will be "most welcomed." See also Heisenberg to Bohr, 15 September 1947, BSC, 29, in which he says he is most thankful for the visit.

Goudsmit raised the whole Heisenberg question with Bohr in a letter of 2 December 1947 (BSC, 29), but the reply—if one was indeed written—is not in the public Bohr Scientific Correspondence, nor is it in the Bohr Papers in Copenhagen (according to information from Finn Aaserud and Felicity Pors), nor in the Goudsmit Papers. Goudsmit enclosed with his note a copy of the Himmler letter of 21 July 1938 to Heydrich, so that Bohr was fully aware of the background. It would be most interesting to have Bohr's written reaction to this Himmler document.

Cassidy, p. 515, relates that when Heisenberg in correspondence tried to enlist Bohr's support against Goudsmit, he was brushed off, and that thereafter relations between Bohr and Heisenberg remained "civil but strained."

This German mentality of Heisenberg and his friends, fertilized by astounding powers of self-delusion and rationalization, spun the tissue of deception and self-deception that produced the Heisenberg version and the cocoon of fabrication and denial that has blurred the history of Heisenberg's work on the atomic bomb to the present day.

Select Bibliography

A NOTE ON SOURCES

The basic source for the history of the German uranium project is the set of nearly four hundred reports dating from 1939 to 1945 captured by the Allies and listed in Lore R. David and I. A. Warheit, *German Reports on Atomic Energy: A Bibliography of Unclassified Literature,* TID-3030 (Oak Ridge, Tenn.: U.S. Atomic Energy Commission, Technical Information Service, 1952). These are available in microfiche copies in the National Archives, College Park, Maryland, RG 242, Captured German Records, and also in the Niels Bohr Library of the American Physical Society, College Park, Maryland (formerly in New York). These need to be supplemented by records of the Kaiser-Wilhelm-Society and the Reich Research Council (Reichsforschungsrat); though incomplete, some of these papers survive respectively in the Archiv zur Geschichte der Max-Planck-Gesellschaft, Berlin, and in the Bundesarchiv, Koblenz. (A number of the Reichsforschungsrat files were formerly in the Library of Congress, Washington, which has retained microfilm copies.) A great deal of material bearing on German atomic research remains in the somewhat rambling files of the ALSOS Mission, now in the National Archives. Many crucial documents, as well as important correspondence, are to be found in the Samuel Goudsmit Papers, at the Niels Bohr Library. A portion of the Goudsmit Papers, held by the National Archives, is yet to be declassified.

Information gathered about the German project by British sources is in the Public Record Office, London, including the celebrated Farm Hall transcripts, which were declassified in 1992 (with copies in the National Archives, Washington). However, several important items relating to British Intelligence, including the reports of their agent Paul Rosbaud and the briefing and debriefing of Niels Bohr in October 1943, are not yet available.

Most German papers dating from the period after 1945 have to be handled with caution, since at the very least they tend to be informed by hindsight. Diaries by Otto Hahn, Erich Bagge, and Karl Wirtz have been published in heavily edited and incomplete forms. Letters by Max von Laue are available through the Lise Meitner Papers at Churchill College, Cambridge, and other sources, but the great bulk of correspondence by Hahn, Gerlach, and Heisenberg himself is now held in German repositories, which are governed by privacy laws that are likely to restrict access for many years to come. This applies also to Hahn's diary, which I have not been able to see.

Published German memoirs and interviews are subject to the same reader's caution already mentioned in dealing with the diaries.

A large variety of material mentioned above may be found in the four-roll microfilm edition of sources published by David Irving, *Records and Documents Relating to the Third Reich*, group 2, microfilms 29–32, *Records of German Atomic Research Programme, 1938–1945* (Wakefield, Yorkshire: EP Microform Ltd., 1973), though several items appear to have been withheld from the final compilation.

Heisenberg's own writings have been listed in D. C. Cassidy and M. Baker, *Werner Heisenberg: A Bibliography of His Writings* (Berkeley, 1984). (See also D. C. Cassidy, *Uncertainty: The Life and Science of Werner Heisenberg* [New York, 1991].) The available Heisenberg papers dealing with the uranium project have been collected in W. Heisenberg, *Gesammelte Werke/Collected Works*, ed. W. Blum, H.-P. Dürr, and H. Rechenberg, ser. A, pt. II (Berlin, 1989). The Heisenberg-Archiv itself, comprising papers and correspondence, has been housed in Munich, but is to be transferred to the Archiv der Max-Planck-Gesellschaft in Berlin. Access so far to the Heisenberg-Archiv has been restricted; moreover, some private papers have reportedly remained in the hands of the family.

Several key sources have either been destroyed or disappeared. The scientific papers in this category include the crucial text of Heisenberg's address to the June 1942 meeting with Speer attended by scientists and high officials of the military and munitions ministry; and a significant paper by C-F. von Weizsäcker, "Die Energiegewinnung aus den Uranspaltungsprozess durch schnelle Neutronen," 7 February 1940. Heisenberg is said to have burned relevant correspondence at the end of the war (see *OE*, p. 65), though he once claimed that after hearing about the Hiroshima bomb at Farm Hall in 1945, "I sat down and fetched up my old notes and sketches" (A. Hermann, *Werner Heisenberg in Selbstzeugnissen und Bilddokumenten*, 3d ed. [Hamburg, 1979], p. 86); it is not known exactly which papers Heisenberg may have brought with him to Farm Hall. Kurt Diebner, for much of the war the scientific administrator of the project, also destroyed all his papers. Diebner's own superior was the head of the Army Weapons Research Office, Erich Schumann, who, it was feared by the German scientists, had kept notes on everything (*OE*, pp. 93 f.). After the war, Schumann wrote a history of the project that seems to have run into publication difficulties with the British Control Commission. At any rate, the whereabouts of the manuscript is not known.

The archives of the Army Weapons Research Office, which until 1942 controlled the uranium project, have largely disappeared from view. Fragments of them exist in the Bundesmilitärarchiv in Freiburg. It is possible that they might have been captured by the Soviet Russian forces and so may yet reemerge, though inquiries to Russian sources have proved fruitless. As examples of what was contained in the Research Office's archives, one may cite, first, the secret patent for an atomic bomb of sorts taken out in 1941, and second, the lengthy analytical survey of the whole project (including discussion of reactor-bombs and plutonium) prepared for a decisive meeting in February 1942. Fortunately, a copy of the latter document (the HWA Report) has survived in private hands, and it is not unreasonable to expect that other copies of original Research Office papers may reappear. It is also likely that the German scientists taken to Russia to work on Stalin's bomb in 1945 brought important documentation with them, if one may judge from an extensive SS report on a bomb project of 1944 (now held at Yad Vashem Archives in Israel) that may well have been obtained from East German or Soviet sources.

PRIMARY SOURCES

Heisenberg

The collected edition of Heisenberg's works, *Gesammelte Werke/Collected Works* [= GWH], ed. W. Blum, H.-P. Dürr, and H. Rechenberg (Berlin, Munich, and New York, 1984), contains his writings on politics and philosophy as well as his scientific papers. Nearly all the material is taken from previously printed sources, though the uranium papers are largely published for the first time. The bulk of manuscript materials held by the Heisenberg-Archiv (in the process of transfer from Munich to the Max-Planck-Gesellschaft in Berlin) and the Heisenberg family remains unpublished, though often quoted in the secondary literature.

Scientific Papers on the Uranium Project

Heisenberg's wartime papers on the uranium project are assembled in his *Gesammelte Werke/Collected Works* [= GWH], ed. W. Blum, H.-P. Dürr, and H. Rechenberg, series A, part II (Berlin, 1989). Among the most noteworthy are:

"Die Möglichkeit der technischen Energiegewinnung aus der Uranspaltung," 6 December 1939 (G-39); GWH, A II, 378; IMF 29-374.

"Bericht über die Möglichkeit technischer Energiegewinnung aus der Uranspaltung (II)," 29 February 1940 (G-40); GWH, A II, 416; IMF 29-398.

"Die theoretischen Grundlagen für die Energiegewinnung aus der Uranspaltung," 26 February 1942 (no G number); GWH, A II, 517; IMF 29-1005.

"Die Energiegewinnung aus der Atomkernspaltung," 6 May 1943 (G-217); GWH, A II, 570; IMF 31-197.

Correspondence

Heisenberg and W. Bothe. Bothe Nachlass. Archiv zur Geschichte der Max-Planck-Gesellschaft, Berlin, III Abt., Rep. 6.

Heisenberg and G. von Droste. Heisenberg-Archiv, Munich and Berlin.

Heisenberg and S. Goudsmit. Goudsmit Papers. AIP, box 10, folders 93–97. (Partially in IMF 29-1185/1194.)

Heisenberg and H. Himmler. Goudsmit Papers. AIP, box 11, folder 98.

———. Heisenberg-Archiv, Munich and Berlin.

Heisenberg and D. Irving. IMF 31 and 32.

Heisenberg and A. Sommerfeld. Sommerfeld Nachlass. Deutsches Museum, Munich, 1977–28/A, 136/18, 136/29.

Heisenberg and B. L. van der Waerden. IMF 29-1130/1131.

Heisenberg's Historical Accounts

Memorandum of 7 August 1945. Printed in German in GWH, C V, 26–27. MS Draft in Bothe Nachlass, Archiv zur Geschichte der Max-Planck-Gesellschaft, Berlin, III Abt., Rep. 6.

"Über die Uranbombe (1945)." Ed. H. Rechenberg. *Physikalische Blätter* 48 (1992): 994–1001.

"Über die Arbeiten zur technischen Ausnutzung der Atomkernenergie in Deutschland." *Die Naturwissenschaften* 33 (1946): 325–329. Reprinted with a postscript in the Einstein commemorative volume *Helle Zeit—Dunkle Zeit*, ed. C. Seelig (Zurich, 1956), pp. 133–144, and in GWH, C V, 28–32, 143–157. The "slightly abridged" English version, "Research in Germany on the Technical Application of Atomic Energy," *Nature*, no. 4059 (16 August 1947): 211–215, is reprinted in GWH, ser. B, 414–418.

"Unveröffentliches Vorwort zu einer Aufsatzsammlung (1948)." In GWH, C V, 35–36.

Heisenberg's historical letter to the *New York Times*, 30 January 1949. Reprinted in GWH, C V, 42.

"The Third Reich and the Atomic Bomb." *BAS* 24 (1968): 34–35. The German text, "Das Dritte Reich versuchte nicht, die Atombombe zu bauen," was published in the *Frankfurter Allgemeine Zeitung*, 9 December 1967, and is reprinted in GWH, C V, 50–52.

Physics and Beyond: Encounters and Conversations. Trans. (New York, 1972.) Originally published as *Der Teil und das Ganze* (Munich, 1969; reprinted in GWH, C III).

Nazism and Politics

"Selbstbiographie" (1933). In GWH, C IV, 12.

"Questions of Principle in Modern Physics" (1936). In his *Philosophical Problems of Nuclear Science* (London, 1952). Reprinted in GWH, C I, 118.

"Zum Artikel 'Deutsche und jüdische Physik'" (28 February 1936). Reprinted in GWH, C V, 9–11, and in H. Rechenberg, ed., *Deutsche und jüdische Physik* (Munich, 1992), pp. 78–80.

"Die Einheit des naturwissenschaftlichen Weltbildes." Lecture of 26 November 1941 at Leipzig University. First published in 1942. Reprinted in GWH, C I, 163, and translated in his *Philosophical Problems of Nuclear Science* (London, 1952).

"Ordnung der Wirklichkeit" (1942). In GWH, C I, 218–306.

"Die Bewertung der 'modernen theoretischen Physik.'" *Zeitschrift für die gesamte Naturwissenschaft* 9 (1943): 201–212. Reprinted in GWH, C V, 14–25, and in H. Rechenberg, ed., *Deutsche und jüdische Physik* (Munich, 1992), pp. 90–106.

"Lebenslauf." MS of 1943. In GWH, C IV, 14.

"Science as a Means of International Understanding" (1946, Göttingen). Translated in his *Philosophical Problems of Nuclear Science* (London, 1952).

Testimonials for Werner Erler, G. Borger, and G. von Droste (1947). Heisenberg-Archiv, Munich and Berlin.

"The Scientific Work of Albert Einstein" (1955). In Heisenberg, *Across the Frontiers* (New York, 1975).

"An den Herrn Reichsminister für Erziehung. . . . " Printed in GWH, C V, 12–13, and in H. Rechenberg, ed., *Deutsche und jüdische Physik* (Munich, 1972), pp. 81–83.

Encounters with Einstein, and Other Essays. Princeton, 1989.

Interviews

"Das deutsche Atombomben-Geheimnis: Interview mit Professor Werner Heisenberg." *Die Welt,* no. 39 (12 August 1946): 3.

BBC interview. In GWH, C V, 44.

Interviews by D. Irving. IMF 31-526/567; IMF 31-616/620.

"'Gott sei Dank, wir konnten sie nicht bauen'—*Spiegel*-Gespräch mit . . . Werner Heisenberg." *Der Spiegel* 28 (3 July 1967): 79–83. Reprinted in GWH, C V, 45–49.

Interview by J. J. Ermenc. In *Atomic Bomb Scientists: Memoirs, 1939–1945* (Westport, Conn., 1989), pp. 43–45.

Other Original Sources
Public Record Office, London (= PRO)

AB 1/9.

AB 1/40.

AB 1/356.

AB 1/485.

AB 1/494.

AB 1/494, "MS 2."

AB 1/495.

AB 1/566.

AB 1/581.

AB 1/615.

AB 1/646.

CAB 21/1262.

CAB 104/186.

FO 935/55.

FO 1031/241.

WO 208/5019 (Farm Hall transcripts; copy in NA, RG 77, MED Foreign Intelligence Unit, entry 22, box 163).

Churchill College Archives, Cambridge

Chadwick Papers.
Meitner Papers. Meitner-Hahn correspondence.
———. Meitner-Laue correspondence.
———. Meitner-Scherrer correspondence.

National Archives, College Park, Md. (= NA)

RG 59. Decimal Files 740.0011, EW/29326; microfilm M-982, roll 158.
———. Decimal Files 740.0011, EW/30782; microfilm M-982, roll 168.
RG 77. MED Decimal Files 319.1, boxes 50 and 53 (Oppenheimer, "Explosion from Fast Neutron Reactions," 27 May 1944).
———. MED Decimal Files 337, box 63, "Conferences" (Bethe and Teller, "Explosion of an Inhomogenous Uranium-Heavy Water Pile").
———. MED Decimal Files 337, box 63 (Oppenheimer-Groves correspondence).
———. MED Decimal Files 371.2, box 64, exhibit A, "Goudsmit Mission" folder.
———. MED Foreign Intelligence Unit, entry 18, boxes 144–145 (London Office).
———. MED Foreign Intelligence Unit, entry 22, box 163 (Farm Hall transcripts).
———. MED Foreign Intelligence Unit, entry 22, box 164, folder "Germany."
———. MED Foreign Intelligence Unit, entry 22, box 165.
———. MED Foreign Intelligence Unit, entry 22, box 166, folder 32.23-24, "Patents."
———. MED Foreign Intelligence Unit, entry 22, box 166, folder 32.24-1, "German Research Institutes."
———. MED Foreign Intelligence Unit, entry 22, box 167, folders 202.3, 32.12-1 and -2, 32.60-1.
———. MED Foreign Intelligence Unit, entry 22, box 168, folder 202.3-1, "Appraisal of Enemy Bomb Production."
———. MED Foreign Intelligence Unit, entry 22, box 169, folder 32.21.
———. MED Foreign Intelligence Unit, entry 22, box 169, folder 32.7002-1.
———. MED Foreign Intelligence Unit, entry 22, box 170, folders 32.60-A-1.
———. MED, microfilm M-1108, roll 2, folders 19 (Bohr, "Memorandum," 3 July 1944) and 26.
———. MED, microfilm A-1218, roll 5 (*Manhattan Project History*, vol. 14, *Foreign Intelligence*, Supplement 1).
RG 84. Decimal Files 863.4, Bern Confidential File, box 14, "Uranium" folder.
———. Decimal Files 863.4, Bern Confidential File, box 14, no. 2958.
RG 165. G-2, Military Intelligence Division, Correspondence, 1917–1941, box 1573, 2655-B-392/393 (= MID Report no. 18,214).
RG 200. Goudsmit Papers, boxes 1,4,5,6,7,8.
RG 227. OSRD/S-1, box 5, Ladenburg folder.
———. OSRD/S-1, Bush-Conant files, microfilm M-1392, roll 1, folder 5.
———. OSRD/S-1, microfilm M-1392, roll 7, folder 75.
———. OSRD/S-1, microfilm M-1392, roll 11, folder 170 (Fisk-Shockley, "Study of Uranium," 1940).
RG 238. Microfilm M-897, roll 119.

RG 242. Captured German Records (also in AIP), German Atomic Research Reports, "G" series. Microfiches. Indexed and abstracted by L. R. David and I. A. Warheit in L. R. David and I. A. Warheit, eds., *German Reports on Atomic Energy: A Bibliography of Unclassified Literature*, USAEC-TID-3030 (Oak Ridge, Tenn., 1952). Originals (not seen) in USAEC Technical Information Service, Oak Ridge, Tennessee. Microfiche copies in Niels Bohr Library of the American Institute of Physics, College Park, Md.; and the Library of the Kernforschungszentrum, Karlsruhe. Individual "G" reports cited in text and footnotes have not been listed in this bibliography.
———. Microfilm T-580, roll 872.
RG 319. ALSOS/RFR files, boxes 12 and 16.

Library of Congress, Washington, D.C. (= LC)

MS Division. 18,806.2, container 230, reel 134: ALSOS 104 (microfilms PB 20489 and 20503).
———. ALSOS Microfilms, rolls 141 and 143.
———. Cordell Hull Papers, folder 184.
———. Oppenheimer Papers, box 20.
———. Photoduplication Service Room. U.S. Department of Commerce, Office of Technical Services (OTS), *Auszüge deutscher Patent-Anmeldungen* (index to microfilmed German patents).
———. *FIAT Microfilm Reel Index* (= microfilm PB-92000).

U.S. Official Collections

Defense Technical Information Center (DTIC), Cameron Station Army Base, Virginia. BIOS Reports 1949, vol. 1; BIOS Final Report no. 538, item no. 28 (Jones, "German Patent Records," March 1946). Accession no. ATI 70297 / JIOA. Some BIOS Final Reports are also held in the Library of Congress, as well as in the British Library Documentary Supply Centre, Wetherby, West Yorkshire, and the Imperial War Museum, London (Duxford Depot, Halstead Exploitation Centre Records [not seen]).
USAF Historical Research Agency, Maxwell Air Force Base, Alabama. U.S. 9th Air Force, P/W Interrogation Detachment, Military Intelligence Service, folder "Interrogations" 533.619, B-5 1945. no. 4, "Atomic Bomb—German, Investigations, Research, Developments and Practical Use," 19 August 1945 (= Microfilm B-5737 [Lieb, "Report on Speer Ministry's Nuclear Physics Project"]).

Niels Bohr Library, American Institute of Physics, College Park, Md. (= AIP)

Archive for the History of Quantum Physics. Bohr Scientific Correspondence (= BSC), microfilms 26, 29, 33.
Goudsmit Papers. Box 6, folder 26; box 10, folders 93–97; box 11, folder 98 (Himmler); box 14, folder 142; box 17, folder 180; box 25, folders 12–15; box 27, folder 35 (Houtermans, "Evaluation of Physicists in Sowjetrussland"); box 27, folder 38; box 28, folders 41, 42 (Rosbaud, 5 August 1945, on the history of the German uranium project; cf. IMF 29-1174; and "Attitude of Germans, especially Scientists"), 43, 44, 45, 52.

————. Goudsmit-Charlotte Houtermans correspondence, box 28, folder 52.
————. Goudsmit-Peierls correspondence, box 10, folder 97.
————. Goudsmit-Perrin correspondence, box 17, folder 180.
————. Goudsmit-Rosbaud correspondence, box 28, folders 42, 43, 45.
————. Houtermans-Blackett correspondence, box 10, folder 93 (IMF 31-1149).
Oral History Interviews (= OHI). Interviews with Bohr, Chadwick, Frank, Peierls, and Reiche.

Niels Bohr Archive, Copenhagen

Chadwick-Bohr correspondence.

Jewish National and University Library, Jerusalem

Einstein Archives. Einstein-Schuman correspondence.

Yad Vashem Archives, Jerusalem

Wiesenthal Archive. M-0/339 ("Rechenschaftsbericht," 1944).

Archiv zur Geschichte der Max-Planck-Gesellschaft, Berlin

Hahn Nachlass. "Die deutschen Arbeiten über Atomenergie," 2 February 1946 (MS not
    seen).
————. Diary (*Tagebuch*) (MS not seen).
Generalverwaltung. I. Abt. Rep. 1A, Nr. 1652 and 1653, "Aktennotiz aus Personalakten
    Peter Debye."
————. I Abt. Rep. 1A, Nr. 1935 ("Entstehung der 'Forschungsschutz GmBH,'"1956).
————. II Abt. Rep. 1A Gründung, Nr. 1/1–4 (Respondek, "Report on the History of the
    KWG," 12 November 1970).
————. III Abt. Rep. 6, Bothe Nachless (Heisenberg, "Draft Article," 1946).

Berlin Document Center

Ahnenerbe files.
Juilfs file.
Neitzel file.

Bundesarchiv, Koblenz (= BA)

NS 19/new 371.
R 3/1504.
R 3/1579, folder 1.
R 3/1583.
R 3/1593.

Bundesarchiv-Militärarchiv, Freiburg; and Bundesarchiv, Potsdam

Bundesarchiv-Militärarchiv, Freiburg. RH8 (Hwa WaF), 1362, 1714, and 1771; RH8, I, II, III.
Bundesarchiv, Potsdam. REM 2943, 370–71.

Deutsches Museum, Munich

Sommerfeld Nachlass, 1977–28/A, 136/15, 136/49.
Laue Nachlass. Max to his son Theodor (copy in Goudsmit Papers, AIP, box 14, folder 142).

Institut für Zeitgeschichte, Munich

Archiv. "Amt Rosenberg: Hauptamt Wissenschaft: Heisenberg," MA 116/5.
———. MA 116, Weizsäcker file.

Staatsbibliothek Preussischer Kulturbesitz, Berlin

Handschriftenabteilung. Born Nachlass, 353 and 1003.

Bagge Papers, Kiel

Bagge, E. Diaries. MS (not seen in toto; partially reproduced in E. Bagge, K. Diebner, and
    K. Jay., *Von der Uranspaltung bis Calder Hall* [Hamburg, 1957], and in IMF 29-106).
"Deutsche Geheimberichte zur Nutzbarmachung der Kernenergie aus den Jahren 1939–
    1942" (bibliography contained in the HWA Report).
"HWA (Heereswaffenamt) Report, 1941–42."

Irving Microfilmed Material

Numerous "G" reports and other materials are reproduced in the microfilms in
D. Irving, ed., *Records and Documents Relating to the Third Reich*, group 2, *German Atomic
Research* (Wakefield, Yorks., 1973), microfilms 29–32. Among relevant items are:

Ardenne, M. von. Original typescript (IMF 32).
Fraser-Irving correspondence (IMF 32).
Gill, E. W. B. "German Academic Scientists and the War," 20 August 1945 (IMF 31-
    1234/1235).
Perrin, M. Interview (IMF 31-1333).
Weizsäcker, C.-F. von. Interview (IMF 31-620).
Weizsäcker-Irving correspondence (IMF 31 and 32).

Irving Papers, London

Irving-Goudsmit correspondence.

Rose Papers, State College, Pennsylvania

Anshen, R. Correspondence and telephone discussion with author.
Ardenne, M. von. Correspondence with author.
Bagge, E. Correspondence with author.
Dilworth [Occhialini], C. Correspondence with author.
Fleischmann, R. Correspondence with author.
Frank, Sir Charles. Correspondence with author.
Höcker, K.-H. Correspondence with author.

Pais, A. Correspondence with author.
Peierls, R. Correspondence with author.
Rozental, S. Correspondence with author.
Weizsäcker, C.-F. von. Correspondence with author.
Wheeler, J. A. Correspondence with author.
Wirtz, K. Correspondence with author.

Interviews and Correspondence Not Listed Above

Groves, L. Interview by J. J. Ermenc. In *Atomic Bomb Scientists: Memoirs, 1939–1945* (Westport, Conn., 1989).
Weizsäcker, C.-F. von. Interview by D. Hoffmann, H. Rechenberg, and T. Spengler. In *Operation Epsilon . . . ,* ed. D. Hoffmann (Berlin, 1993).

PUBLISHED SOURCES AND SECONDARY LITERATURE

Adler, F., and H. von Halban. "Control of the Chain Reaction Involved in Fission of the Uranium Nucleus." *Nature* 143 (13 May 1939): 793.
Akten der Partei-Kanzlei der NSDAP: Rekonstruktion . . . . Munich: Institut für Zeitgeschichte, 1983–.
Albrecht, H. "'Max Planck: Mein Besuch bei Adolf Hitler'—Anmerkungen zum Wert einer historischen Quelle." In *Naturwissenschaft und Technik in der Geschichte,* ed. H. Albrecht, pp. 41–63. Stuttgart, 1993.
———, ed. *Naturwissenschaft und Technik in der Geschichte.* Stuttgart, 1993.
Albrecht, H., and A. Hermann. "Die Kaiser-Wilhelm-Gesellschaft im Dritten Reich (1933–1945). In *Forschung im Spannungsfeld von Politik und Gesellschaft: Geschichte und Struktur der Kaiser-Wilhelm-/Max-Planck-Gesellschaft,* ed. R. Vierhaus and B. vom Brocke. Stuttgart, 1990.
Alvarez, L. *Alvarez.* New York, 1987.
Amaldi, E., and E. Fermi. "On the Absorption and the Diffusion of Slow Neutrons." *Physical Review* 50 (1936): 899–928. Reprinted in E. Fermi, *Collected Papers* (Chicago, 1962–65), 1:892–942.
Anshen, R. N. *Biography of an Idea.* Mt. Kisco, N.Y., 1986.
Ardenne, M. von. *Ein glückliches Leben für Forschung und Technik.* Zurich, 1972. 2d ed., *Sechzig Jahre für Forschung und Fortschritt: Autobiographie* (Berlin, 1984); 3d ed., *Die Erinnerungen* (Munich, 1991).
———. Review of *Heisenbergs Krieg,* by T. Powers. *Die Welt,* 8 May 1993, book section.
Association for the Use and Diffusion of Documentation (UDD). *Subject Outline of the Unpublished Applications for Patents Filed at the German Patent Office during 1940 to 1945.* Paris, 1950.
Badash, L. "Otto Hahn, Science, and Social Responsibility." In *Otto Hahn and the Rise of Nuclear Physics,* ed. W. R. Shea, pp. 167–180. Dordrecht, 1983.
Badash, L., et al. "Nuclear Fission: Reaction to the Discovery in 1939." *Proceedings of the American Philosophical Society* 130, no. 2 (1986).
Bagge, E., and K. Diebner. "Zur Entwicklung der Kernenergieverwertung in Deutschland." In E. Bagge, K. Diebner, and K. Jay, *Von der Uranspaltung bis Calder Hall,* pp. 9–80. Hamburg, 1957.

Bagge, E., K. Diebner, and K. Jay. *Von der Uranspaltung bis Calder Hall.* Hamburg, 1957.

Barth, K. *Eine Schweizer Stimme, 1938–1945.* Zurich, 1948.

Baum, R. C. *The Holocaust and the German Elite: Genocide and National Suicide in Germany, 1871–1945.* Totowa, N.J., 1981.

Berg, H. C. *Random Walks in Biology.* Princeton, 1983.

Berninger, E. *Otto Hahn in Selbstzeugnissen und Bilddokumenten.* Reinbek, 1974.

Bernstein, J. "The Farm Hall Transcripts: The German Scientists and the Bomb." *New York Review of Books* 13, no. 14 (13 August 1992): 47–53.

———. *Hans Bethe, Prophet of Energy.* New York, 1980.

———. *Hitler's Uranium Club.* Woodbury, N.Y., 1996.

———. Review of *Heisenberg's War,* by T. Powers. *Science* 259 (26 March 1993): 1923–1926.

Bernstein, J., and D. C. Cassidy. "Bomb Apologetics: Farm Hall, August 1945." *Physics Today,* August 1995, 32–36.

Bethe, H. "Bethe on the German Bomb Program." *BAS,* January–February 1993, 53–54.

———. "Niels Bohr and His Institute." In *Niels Bohr: A Centenary Volume,* ed. A. P. French and P. J. Kennedy, pp. 232–234. Cambridge, Mass., 1985.

Beyerchen, A. *Scientists under Hitler.* New Haven, 1977.

Blaedel, N. *Harmony and Unity: The Life of Niels Bohr.* Madison, Wisc., 1988.

Boelcke, W. A., ed. *Deutschlands Rüstung im Zweiten Weltkrieg: Hitlers Konferenzen mit Albert Speer, 1942–1945.* Frankfurt, 1969.

Bohr, A. "The War Years and the Prospects Raised by the Atomic Weapons." In *Niels Bohr: His Life and Work As Seen by His Friends and Colleagues,* ed. S. Rozental, pp. 191–214. Amsterdam and New York, 1967.

Bohr, N. "Recent Investigations of the Transmutations of Atomic Nuclei" (1939). In *Collected Works,* by N. Bohr, ed. E. Rudinger, R. Peierls, et al., 9:443–466. Amsterdam, 1986. Originally published in 1941.

———. "Resonance in Uranium and Thorium Disintegrations and the Phenomenon of Nuclear Fission." *Physical Review* 55 (1939): 418–419.

Bohr, N., and J. A. Wheeler. "The Mechanism of Nuclear Fission." *Physical Review* 56 (1939): 426–450.

Bonhoeffer, D. *No Rusty Swords: Letters, Lectures, and Notes, 1928–1936.* Trans. New York, 1965.

Born, H., and M. Born. *Der Luxus des Gewissens.* Munich, 1969.

Born, M., ed. *The Born-Einstein Letters.* Trans. New York, 1971. Originally published as A. Einstein and M. Born, *Briefwechsel, 1916–1955* (Munich, 1969), with preface by Heisenberg.

Born, M. *My Life.* London, 1978.

———. *My Life and My Views.* New York, 1968.

Bower, T. *The Paperclip Conspiracy.* Boston, 1987.

Broad, W. J. "Saboteur or Savant of Nazi Drive for A-Bomb." *New York Times: Science Times,* 1 September 1992.

Brooks, G. *Hitler's Nuclear Weapons.* Barnsley, England, 1992.

Brown, A. *The Neutron and the Bomb: A Biography of Sir James Chadwick.* Oxford, 1997.

Burckhardt, J. *Reflections on History.* Trans. London, 1943. Originally published as *Weltgeschichtliche Betrachtungen.*

Burleigh, M. *Germany Turns Eastward: A Study of Ostforschung in the Third Reich.* Cambridge, 1988.

Calic, E. *Secret Conversations with Hitler: The Two Newly Discovered 1931 Interviews.* Trans. New York, 1971.

Casimir, H. *Haphazard Reality.* New York, 1983.

Cassidy, D. C. "Atomic Conspiracies." Review of *Heisenberg's War,* by T. Powers. *Nature* 363 (27 May 1993): 311–312.

———. *Uncertainty: The Life and Science of Werner Heisenberg.* New York, 1992.

———. "Werner Heisenberg." In *Dictionary of Scientific Biography,* supp., 17:394–403. New York, 1990.

Cassidy, D. C., and M. Baker. *Werner Heisenberg: A Bibliography of His Writings.* Berkeley, 1984.

Cassidy, D. C., and W. Sweet. "A Lecture on Bomb Physics: February 1942." *Physics Today,* August 1995, 27–30.

Churchill, W. *The Gathering Storm.* New York, 1948.

Clark, R. W. *The Birth of the Bomb.* London, 1961.

———. *The Greatest Power on Earth.* London, 1980.

———. *Tizard.* Cambridge, Mass., 1965.

Compton, A. H. *Atomic Quest: A Personal Narrative.* New York, 1956.

Craig, G. *The Germans.* New York, 1982.

Crowther, J. G. *Science in Liberated Europe.* London, 1949.

Dawidoff, N. *The Catcher Was a Spy: The Mysterious Life of Moe Berg.* New York, 1994.

"Deutsche Volksführer: Werner Heisenberg." *Das Reich,* 14 May 1944, p. 1.

Dewdney, A K. *The Magic Machine: A Handbook of Computer Sorcery.* New York, 1990.

Dewey, J. *German Philosophy and Politics.* New York, 1915. Reprint, New York, 1942, 1979.

Diebner, K. See Tautorus, W.

Diebner, K., and E. Grassmann. *Künstliche Radioaktivität: Experimentelle Ergebnisse.* Leipzig, 1939. Additions in *Physikalische Zeitschrift* 40 (1939): 297–314; 41 (1940): 157–194.

Dippel, J. V. H. *Two against Hitler.* New York, 1992.

Dresden, M. *H. A. Kramers: Between Tradition and Revolution.* New York and Berlin, 1987.

Droste, G. von. "Wirkungsquerschnitte von Uran." In *FIAT (Field Information Agency, Technical—OMGUS) Review of German Science, 1939–1946: Nuclear Physics and Cosmic Rays,* ed. W. Bothe and S. Flügge, pt. 2, pp. 197–208. Wiesbaden, 1948.

Dumont, L. *German Ideology.* Chicago, 1994.

Dundes, A. *Life Is like a Chicken Coop Ladder: A Portrait of German Culture through Folklore.* New York, 1984.

Eckert, M., et al., eds. *Geheimrat Sommerfeld—Theoretischer Physiker: Eine Dokumentation aus seinem Nachlass (Deutsches Museum).* Munich, 1984.

Einstein, A. *Investigations on the Theory of the Brownian Movement.* London, 1926.

———. *The World As I See It.* Trans. New York, 1949.

Einstein, A., and M. Born. *The Born-Einstein Letters.* Ed. and trans. M. Born. New York, 1971. Originally published as *Briefwechsel, 1916–1955* (Munich, 1969), with a preface by Heisenberg.

Einstein, A., and A. Sommerfeld. *Albert Einstein/Arnold Sommerfeld, Briefwechsel: Sechzig Briefe aus dem goldenen Zeitalter der modernen Physik.* Ed. A. Hermann. Basel, 1968.

Elon, A. *Journey through a Haunted Land: The New Germany.* London, 1967.

Encyclopaedia Britannica. 1971 ed. S.v. "Diffusion Theory."

Ermenc, J. J. *Atomic Bomb Scientists: Memoirs, 1939–1945.* Westport, Conn., 1989.

Evans, R. J. Review of *The Devil's Music Master,* by S. H. Shirakawa. *Times Literary Supplement,* 13 November 1992.

Farias, V. *Heidegger and Nazism*. Trans. Philadelphia, 1989.

Feinberg, E. "Werner Heisenberg: The Tragedy of a Scientist" (in Russian). *Znamja*, no. 3 (1989): 124–143.

Fermi, E. *Collected Papers*. Chicago, 1962–65.

———. *Nuclear Physics*. Rev. ed. Chicago, 1950.

———. "On the Motion of Neutrons in Hydrogenous Substances" (1936). In E. Fermi, *Collected Papers*, 1:980–1016. Chicago, 1962–65.

———. "The Temperature Effect on a Chain Reacting Unit" (1942). In E. Fermi, *Collected Papers*, 2:149–151. Chicago, 1962–65.

Feynman, R. *The Feynman Lectures on Physics*. Reading, Mass., 1963.

FIAT—Berlin Patent Office Activities. FIAT Technical Bulletin T-50. N.p.: Office of Military Government for Germany—U.S., 1947.

Fichte, J. G. *Addresses to the German Nation*. Trans. New York, 1968.

Fischer, H. J. *Erinnerungen*. 2 vols. Quellenstudien der Zeitgeschichtlichen Forschungsstelle Ingolstadt, vols. 3 and 6. Ingolstadt, 1984–85.

———. *Hitler und die Atombombe: Bericht eines Zeitzeugen*. Asendorf, 1987.

———. "Völkische Bedingtheit von Mathematik und Physik." *Zeitschrift für die gesamte Naturwissenschaft* 3 (1937–38): 422–426.

Fleischmann, R. "Warum Forschungsinstitut der Medizinischen Fakultät der Reichsuniversität Strassburg?" Lecture. 1988.

Flügge, S. "Die Ausnutzung der Atomenergie." *Deutsche Allgemeine Zeitung*, no. 385–386, "Beiblatt" (15 August 1939).

———. "Kann der Energieinhalt der Atomkerne technisch nutzbar gemacht werden?" *Die Naturwissenschaften* 27 (9 June 1939): 402–410.

Forman, P. Review of *Heisenberg's War*, by T. Powers. *American Historical Review* 99 (1994): 1715–1717.

Frank, F. C. *Operation Epsilon: The Farm Hall Transcripts*. Bristol, England, and Berkeley, 1993.

Frank, H. *Das Diensttagebuch des deutschen Generalgouverneurs in Polen, 1939–1945*. Ed. W. Präg and W. Jacobmeyer. Stuttgart, 1975.

———. *Diaries*. NA Microfilm Publication T-992.

Frank, N. *In the Shadow of the Reich*. Trans. New York, 1991. Originally published as *Der Vater*.

French, A. P., and P. J. Kennedy. *Niels Bohr: A Centenary Volume*. Cambridge, Mass., 1985.

Frisch, O. R. "Early Steps towards the Chain Reaction." In *Rudolf Peierls and Theoretical Physics*, Progress in Nuclear Physics, vol. 13, pp. 18–27. Oxford, 1977.

———. "Nuclear Fission." In *Annual Reports on the Progress of Chemistry for 1939*, pp. 7–24. London: The Chemical Society, 1940.

———. "Recollections." In *All in Our Time*, ed. J. Taylor. Chicago, 1975.

———. *What Little I Remember*. Cambridge, 1979.

Gamow, G. *One, Two, Three . . . Infinity*. 2d ed. New York, 1961.

Gimbel, J. *Science, Technology, and Reparations: Exploitation and Plunder in Postwar Germany*. Stanford, 1990.

Glasstone, S. *Sourcebook on Nuclear Energy*. 2d ed. Princeton, 1958. 3d ed., Princeton, 1967.

Glum, F. *Zwischen Wissenschaft, Wirtschaft, und Politik*. Bonn, 1964.

Goebbels, J. *The Goebbels Diaries*. Ed. and trans. L. P. Lochner. London, 1948.

———. *Tagebücher, 1942–1943*. Ed. L. P. Lochner. Zurich, 1948.

Goldberg, S., and Powers, T. "Declassified Files Reopen 'Nazi Bomb' Debate." *BAS* 48 (September 1992): 32–40.

Goldschmidt, B. *Atomic Rivals.* New Brunswick, N.J., 1990.

Gora, E. K. "Einer, den Heisenberg doch rettete." In *Werner Heisenberg in Leipzig, 1927–1942,* Abhandlungen der Sächsischen Akademie der Wissenschaften zu Leipzig, Mathematisch-naturwissenschaftliche Klasse, Band 58, Heft 2, 91–93. Berlin, 1993.

———. "One Heisenberg Did Save." *Science News* 109 (20 March 1976): 179.

Goudsmit, S. *ALSOS.* New York, 1947. Reprint, Los Angeles, 1983.

———. "Heisenberg on the German Uranium Project." *BAS* 3 (1947): 343.

———. Letter to *Chemical and Engineering News* (U.S.), 15 September 1947.

———. Letter to *New York Times.* 9 November 1947.

———. Letter to *Nuclear News.* October 1970.

———. "Nazis' Atomic Secrets." *Life,* 20 October 1947, pp. 124–134.

Gowing, M. *Britain and Atomic Energy, 1939–1945.* London, 1964.

———. "James Chadwick and the Atomic Bomb." *Notes and Records of the Royal Society of London* 47 (1993): 79–92.

———. "Niels Bohr and Nuclear Weapons." In *Niels Bohr: A Centenary Volume,* ed. A. P. French and J. P. Kennedy, pp. 266–277. Cambridge, Mass., 1985.

Graetzer, H. G., and D. L. Anderson. *The Discovery of Nuclear Fission.* New York, 1971.

Groves, L. R. *Now It Can Be Told: The Story of the Manhattan Project.* London, 1963.

Haber, L. F. *The Poisonous Cloud: Gas Warfare in the First World War.* Oxford, 1986.

Hahn, D. *Otto Hahn: Begründer des Atomzeitalters.* Munich, 1979.

———. *Otto Hahn: Erlebnisse und Erkenntnisse.* Düsseldorf, 1975.

Hahn, O. *Mein Leben.* Munich, 1968.

———. *My Life: The Autobiography of a Scientist.* Trans. New York, 1970.

———. *A Scientific Autobiography.* Trans. New York, 1966.

Hahn, O., and F. H. Rein. "Einladung nach USA." *Physikalische Blätter* 3 (1947): 33–35.

Halban, H. von., F. Joliot, and L. Kowarski. "Liberation of Neutrons in the Nuclear Explosion of Uranium." *Nature* 143 (1939): 470.

Hanle, W., and E. Bagge. "Peaceful Use of Nuclear Energy during 40 Years." *Atomkernenergie-Kerntechnik* 40 (1982): 1–10.

Hanser, R. *A Noble Treason.* New York, 1979.

Harteck, P. Interview by J. J. Ermenc. In *Atomic Bomb Scientists: Memoirs, 1939–1945.* Westport, Conn., 1989.

Hassell, U. von. *Vom andern Deutschland.* Zurich, 1946. New ed., *Die Hassell-Tagebücher, 1938–1944* (Berlin, 1988). Translated under the title *The Von Hassell Diaries* (Garden City, N.Y., 1947).

Haxel, O. "Der Beitrag der schnellen Neutronen zur Neutronenvermehrung im Uran." In *FIAT* [= Field Information Agency, Technical] *Review of German Science, 1939–1946: Nuclear Physics and Cosmic Rays,* ed. W. Bothe and S. Flügge, pt. II, pp. 165–173. Wiesbaden, 1948.

Heilbron, J. L. *The Dilemmas of an Upright Man: Max Planck as Spokesman for German Science.* Berkeley, 1986.

———. *Max Planck, ein Leben für die Wissenschaft, 1858–1947.* Stuttgart, 1985.

Heine, H. *History of Religion and Philosophy in Germany.* Ed. P. L. Rose. North Queensland, 1982.

Heisenberg, E. *Inner Exile: Recollections of a Life with Werner Heisenberg.* Trans. Boston, 1984.

Henning, E., and M. Kazemi. *Chronik der Kaiser-Wilhelm-Gesellschaft zur Förderung der Wissenschaften.* Veröffentlichungen aus dem Archiv der Max-Planck-Gesellschaft, vol. 1. Berlin, 1988.

Hentschel, K., and A. Hentschel, eds. *Physics and National Socialism: An Anthology of Primary Sources.* Basel, Boston, and Berlin, 1996.

Hermann, A. *Die Jahrhundertwissenschaft: Werner Heisenberg und die Physik seiner Zeit.* Stuttgart, 1977.

———. *Max Planck in Selbstzeugnissen und Bilddokumenten.* Reinbek, 1973.

———. *The New Physics.* Bonn, 1979.

———. *Werner Heisenberg in Selbstzeugnissen und Bilddokumenten.* 3d ed. Hamburg, 1979.

———. *Wie die Wissenschaft ihre Unschuld verlor: Macht und Missbrauch der Forscher.* Stuttgart, 1982.

Herneck, F. "Ein alarmierende Botschaft." In his *Wissenschaftsgeschichte.* Berlin, 1984.

Hershberg, J. G. *James B. Conant: Harvard to Hiroshima and the Making of the Nuclear Age.* New York, 1993.

Hewlett, R. G. and O. E. Anderson, Jr. *A History of the United States Atomic Energy Commission.* Vol. 1, *The New World: 1939–1946.* University Park, Pa., 1962.

Hinsley, F. H. *British Intelligence in the Second World War.* Cambridge, 1988.

Hoffmann, B., and H. Dukas. *Albert Einstein: Creator and Rebel.* New York, 1972.

Hoffmann, D. *Operation Epsilon: Die Farm-Hall-Protokolle oder die Angst der Alliierten vor der deutschen Atombombe.* Berlin, 1993.

Hoffmann, K. *Otto Hahn.* Berlin, 1979.

———. *Schuld und Verantwortung: Otto Hahn, Konflikte eines Wissenschaftlers.* Berlin, 1993.

Hutton, R. S. *Recollections of a Technologist.* London, 1964.

Irving, D. *The German Atomic Bomb: The History of Nuclear Research in Germany.* New York, 1967. 2d ed., New York, 1993. Published in the United Kingdom as *The Virus House* (London, 1967).

———. *Records and Documents Relating to the Third Reich.* Group 2, *German Atomic Research.* Microfilms 29–32. Wakefield, Yorks., 1973. Microfiche.

Joffé, A. *Promenades aléatoires et mouvement Brownien.* Montreal, 1969.

Johnson, J. A. *The Kaiser's Chemists: Science and Modernization in Imperial Germany.* Chapel Hill, N.C., 1990.

Joliot-Curie, F., and I. Joliot-Curie. *Oeuvres scientifiques complètes.* Paris, 1961.

Jones, R. V. "Meetings in Wartime and After." In *Niels Bohr: A Centenary Volume,* ed. A. P. French, and P. J. Kennedy, pp. 278–287. Cambridge, Mass., 1985.

———. *Most Secret War: British Scientific Intelligence, 1939–1945.* London, 1979. Published in the United States as *The Wizard War* (New York, 1978).

Jungk, R. *Brighter Than a Thousand Suns: A Personal History of the Atomic Scientists.* Trans. Harmondsworth, 1960. Reprint, 1982.

———. *Trotzdem: Mein Leben für die Zukunft.* Munich, 1993.

Kaempffert, W. Letter to *New York Times.* 9 November 1947.

———. "Nazis Spurned Idea of an Atomic Bomb: Dr. Heisenberg Says German's Research Was Far Advanced but Lacked Hitler Support." *New York Times,* 28 December 1948. Reprinted in GWH, C V, 37–40.

———. "Why the Germans Failed to Develop an Atomic Bomb Is Now Revealed in Two Reports." *New York Times,* 26 October 1947.

Kant, I. *Metaphysics of Morals.* Trans. Cambridge, 1991.

Kater, M. *Das "Ahnenerbe" der SS, 1935–1945.* Stuttgart, 1974.

———. *Doctors under Hitler.* Chapel Hill, N.C., 1989.

Kemmer, N. Review of *Collected Works,* by Werner Heisenberg, and *Inner Exile,* by Elisabeth Heisenberg. *Nature* 313 (28 February 1985): 826.

Kemmer, N., and R. Schlapp. "Max Born." *Biographical Memoirs of Fellows of the Royal Society* 17 (1971): 17–52.

Kirsten, C., and H.-J. Treder. *Albert Einstein in Berlin, 1913–1933.* East Berlin, 1979.

Klotz, I. "Captives of Their Fantasies: The German Atomic Bomb Scientists." *Journal of Chemical Education* 74 (February 1997): 204–209.

———. "Germans at Farm Hall Knew Little of Atomic Bombs." *Physics Today,* October 1993, 11–15, 135.

Koehler, W. "Gespräche in Deutschland." *Deutsche Allgemeine Zeitung,* 28 April 1933.

Krafft, F. *Im Schatten der Sensation: Leben und Wirken von Fritz Strassmann.* Weinheim, 1981.

———. "Lise Meitner: Her Life and Times . . . ." *Angewandte Chemie* (international English ed.) 17 (1978): 826–842.

Kramish, A. *The Griffin.* Boston, 1986.

Krieger, W. *The Germans and the Nuclear Question.* Fifth Alois Mertes Memorial Lecture 1995, German Historical Institute, Washington, D.C., Occasional Paper no. 14.

Kuby, E. *Mein Krieg.* Munich, 1975.

Kurti, N. Letter to the *Times Literary Supplement,* 18 June 1993.

Ladenburg, R. "Study of Uranium and Thorium Fission Produced by Fast Neutrons of Nearly Homogeneous Energy." *Physical Review* 56 (1939): 168–170.

Lanouette, W. *Genius in the Shadows: A Biography of Leo Szilard.* New York, 1993.

Laqueur, W. *Young Germany: The History of the German Youth Movement.* New York, 1962.

Laue, M. von. "Die Kriegstätigkeit der deutschen Physiker." *Physikalische Blätter* 4 (1948): 424–425. Reprinted, from the manuscript, in E. Henning, "Der Nachlass Max von Laues," *Physikalische Blätter* 48 (1992): 938–940. Translated under the title "The Wartime Activities of German Scientists," *BAS* 4 (1948): 103.

Laurence, W. L. *Men and Atoms.* New York, 1959.

Leeb, E. *Aus der Rüstung des Dritten Reiches (Das Heereswaffenamt, 1938–1945): Ein authentischer Bericht des letzten Chefs des Heereswaffenamtes* (= *Wehrtechnische Monatshefte,* supp. 4). Berlin and Frankfurt, 1958.

Leggin, A. "Potomac Postscripts." *Chemical and Engineering News* 26, no. 11 (15 March 1948): 733.

Lemmerich, J. *Die Geschichte der Entdeckung der Kernspaltung.* Berlin, 1988.

Lifton, R. J. *The Nazi Doctors.* New York, 1986.

Löwith, K. *My Life in Germany before and after 1933.* Trans. Urbana and Chicago, 1994.

Logan, J. L. "The Critical Mass." *American Scientist* 84 (May–June 1996): 263–277.

Logan, J. L., and R. Serber. "Heisenberg and the Bomb." *Nature* 362 (11 March 1993): 117.

Ludwig, K.-H. *Technik und Ingenieure im Dritten Reich.* Düsseldorf, 1974.

MacPherson, M. C. *Time Bomb: Fermi, Heisenberg, and the Race for the Atomic Bomb.* New York, 1986.

Macrakis, K. *Surviving the Swastika: Scientific Research in Nazi Germany.* New York, 1993.

Mahoney, L. J. "A History of the War Department Scientific Intelligence Mission (ALSOS), 1943–1945." Ph. D. diss., Kent State University, 1981.

Manchester Guardian, 7–14 August 1945.

Mann, T. "What Is German?" *Atlantic Monthly,* May 1944, pp. 78–85.

Mattauch, J., and S. Flügge. *Kernphysikalische Tabellen.* Berlin, 1942. Translated under the title *Nuclear Physics Tables* (New York, 1946).

McMillan, E., and P. Abelson. "Radioactive Element 93." *Physical Review* 57 (1940): 1185–1186.

Mehrtens, H. "Mathematics in the Third Reich: Resistance, Adaptation, and Collaboration of a Scientific Discipline." In *New Trends in the History of Science*, ed. R. P. W. Visser, pp. 141–166. Amsterdam, 1989.

Menzel, W. "Deutsche und jüdische Physik." *Völkische Beobachter*, 29 January 1936.

Messerschmidt, M. "The Wehrmacht and the Volksgemeinschaft." In *Journal of Contemporary History* 18 (1983): 719–744.

Moore, W. *Schrödinger: Life and Thought*. Cambridge, 1989.

Morrison, P. *Nothing Is Too Wonderful to Be True*. Woodbury, N.Y., 1995.

———. "Reply to Dr. Von Laue." *BAS* 4 (1948): 104.

———. Review of *ALSOS*, by S. Goudsmit. *BAS* 3 (1947): 354, 365.

Mott, N., and R. Peierls. "Werner Heisenberg." *Biographical Memoirs of Fellows of the Royal Society* 23 (1977): 213–251.

Muller, R. *The Wonderful, Horrible Life of Leni Riefenstahl*. 1993. Documentary film. Also discussion in the *New York Times*, 26 September 1993, 14 October 1993, 13 and 16 March 1994.

Namier, L. B. *In the Nazi Era*. London, 1952.

O'Flaherty, J. C. "Werner Heisenberg on the Nazi Revolution: Three Hitherto Unpublished Letters." *Journal of the History of Ideas* 53 (1992): 487–494.

Office of Technical Services, U.S. Department of Commerce. *Bibliography of Scientific and Industrial Reports, Prepared by the Office of Technical Services*. 6 vols. and supps. Washington, D.C., 1947–48.

———. *An Informal Introduction to German Patent Applications (1940–1945) in the Library of Congress*. Library of Congress, Washington, D.C., n.d. Mimeographed.

———. *Numerical Index to the Bibliography of Scientific and Industrial Reports, Volumes 1–10, 1946–1948*. Washington, D.C., 1948.

Oliphant, M. "The Beginning: Chadwick and the Neutron." *BAS* 38 (1982): 14–18.

Osenberg, W. "Allgemeine verständliche Grundlagen zur Kernphysik." 8 May 1943. IMF 29-1062/1063.

Ott, H. *Martin Heidegger: A Political Life*. Trans. New York, 1993.

Pais, A. *Niels Bohr's Times in Physics, Philosophy, and Polity*. Oxford, 1991.

Pauli, W. *Wissenschaftlicher Briefwechsel mit Bohr, Einstein, Heisenberg, u.a.* Ed. K. von Meyenn et al. New York, Berlin, and Heidelberg, 1979–93.

Peierls, R. "Atomic Germans." *New York Review of Books*, 1 July 1971, pp. 23–24.

———. *Bird of Passage*. Princeton, 1985.

———. "Critical Conditions in Neutron Multiplication." *Proceedings of the Cambridge Philosophical Society* 35 (1939): 610–615.

———. "Reflections on the Discovery of Fission." *Nature* 342 (21–28 December 1989): 852–854.

Perrin, F. "Calcul relatif aux conditions éventuelles de transmutation en chaîne de l'uranium." Parts 1 and 2. *Comptes Rendus de l'Académie des Sciences* 208 (1 May 1939): 1394–1396; (15 May 1939): 1573–1575.

Perrin, J. *Les atomes*. 2d ed. Paris, 1936.

Perutz, M. F. "The Cabinet of Dr. Haber." *New York Review of Books*, 20 June 1996, 31–35.

Pfau, R. *No Sacrifice Too Great: The Life of Lewis L. Strauss*. Charlottesville, Va., 1984.

Phillips, D., ed. *German Universities after the Surrender: British Occupation and the Control of Higher Education*. Oxford, 1983.

Pippard, B. Review of *Heisenberg's War*, by T. Powers. *Times Literary Supplement*, 28 May 1993, 3.

Planck, M. "Mein Besuch bei Adolf Hitler." *Physikalische Blätter* 3 (1947): 143. Reprinted with other texts in J. L. Heilbron, *Max Planck: Ein Leben für die Wissenschaft, 1858–1947* (Stuttgart, 1988).

Poliakov, L. *The History of Anti-Semitism.* Vol. 4. Trans. Oxford, 1985.

Powell, C. F., and G. P. S. Occhialini. *Nuclear Physics in Photographs.* Oxford, 1947.

Powers, T. *Heisenberg's War: The Secret History of the German Bomb.* New York, 1993.

Rabi, I. I. *Science: The Center of Culture.* New York, 1970.

Rechenberg, H. *Deutsche und jüdische Physik.* Munich, 1992.

————. *Farm-Hall-Berichte: Die abgehörten Gespräche der 1945–46 in England internierten deutschen Atomwissenschaftler: Ein Kommentar.* Stuttgart, 1994.

————. *Die langerwarteten Farm-Hall-Berichte—Sensation oder "Alter Schnee"?* Munich, 1993.

————, ed. "Über die Uranbombe (1945)," by W. Heisenberg. *Physikalische Blätter* 48 (1992): 994–1001.

Rhodes, R. *The Making of the Atomic Bomb.* New York, 1986.

Riefenstahl, L. *Leni Riefenstahl: A Memoir.* New York, 1993.

Rife, P. "Lise Meitner: The Life and Times of a Jewish Woman Physicist." Ph.D. diss., Union for Experimenting Colleges and Universities, 1983.

Ring, B. *Origines du Centre de Recherches Nucléaires.* Vol. 1, *Implantation d'un générateur de neutrons aux Hospices Civils de Strasbourg, 1941–1944.* Strasbourg, [1988?].

Rosbaud, P. Review of *Brighter Than a Thousand Suns,* by R. Jungk. *Discovery* 20 (March 1959): 96–97.

————. "Secret Mission." *Times Literary Supplement,* 5 June 1948, 320.

Rose, P. L. "Did Heisenberg Misconceive the Atomic Bomb?" *Physics Today,* February 1992, 126.

————. *German Question / Jewish Question: Revolutionary Antisemitism in Germany from Kant to Wagner.* Princeton, 1994.

Rosenfeld, L. *Selected Papers.* Boston, 1979.

Rozental, S., ed. *Niels Bohr: His Life and Work As Seen by His Friends and Colleagues.* Amsterdam and New York, 1967.

Rudolf Peierls and Theoretical Physics. Progress in Nuclear Physics, vol. 13. Oxford, 1977.

Runge, G., ed. *Correlation Index: Document Series and PB Reports.* New York, 1953.

Scheel, W. Address to the Einstein-Laue-Hahn-Meitner Centenary Symposium of the Max-Planck-Gesellschaft. In *Reden zum 100. Geburtstag von Einstein, Hahn, Meitner, von Laue,* Dokumentationsreihe der Freien Universität Berlin. Berlin, 1979.

Scholder, K. *Die Mittwochs-Gesellschaft: Protokolle aus dem geistigen Deutschland, 1932 bis 1944.* Berlin, 1982.

Seaborg, G., et al. *The Transuranium Elements.* New York, 1949.

Seelig, C., ed. *Helle Zeit—Dunkle Zeit.* Zurich, 1956.

Serber, R. *The Los Alamos Primer.* Berkeley, 1992.

Sereny, G. *Albert Speer: His Battle with Truth.* New York, 1995.

Shirakawa, S. H. *The Devil's Music Master: The Controversial Life and Career of Wilhelm Furtwängler.* New York, 1992.

Silber, J. R. "Kant at Auschwitz." *Proceedings of the Sixth International Kant Congress.* Washington, D.C., 1996, I, 177–211.

Siegmund-Schultze, R. "The Problem of Anti-Fascist Resistance of 'Apolitical' German Scholars." In *Science, Technology, and National Socialism,* ed. M. Renneberg and M. Walker, pp. 312–323. Cambridge, 1994.

Sime, R. L. *Lise Meitner: A Life in Physics*. Berkeley, 1996.

————. "Lise Meitner's Escape from Germany." *American Journal of Physics* 58 (1990): 262–267.

————. "A Split Decision?" *Chemistry in Britain*, June 1994, 482–484.

Simon, L. E. *German Research in World War II*. New York, 1947.

Smoluchowski, M. *Abhandlungen über die Brownsche Bewegung und verwandte Erscheinungen*. Leipzig, 1923.

Smyth, H. DeW. *Atomic Energy for Military Purposes: The Official Report on the Development of the Atomic Bomb*. Princeton, 1945.

Sontheimer, K. *Antidemokratisches Denken in der Weimarer Republik: Die politischen Ideen des deutschen Nationalismus zwischen 1918 und 1933*. 2d ed. Munich, 1968.

Speer, A. *Infiltration*. New York, 1981.

————. *Inside the Third Reich*. New York, 1970.

Stern, F. *The Failure of Illiberalism: Essays on the Political Culture of Modern Germany*. Rev. ed. Chicago, 1975.

Strauss, L. *Men and Decisions*. New York, 1962.

Stuewer, R. H. "Niels Bohr and Nuclear Physics." In *Niels Bohr: A Centenary Volume*, ed. A. P. French and P. J. Kennedy, pp. 197–220. Cambridge, Mass., 1985.

————, ed. *Nuclear Physics in Retrospect*. Minneapolis, 1979.

Szilard, L. *The Collected Works of Leo Szilard*. Ed. B. T. Feld and G. W. Szilard. Cambridge, Mass., 1972.

————. *Leo Szilard: His Version of the Facts*. Ed. S. R. Weart and G. W. Szilard. Cambridge, Mass., 1978.

————. "Reminiscences." In *The Intellectual Migration: Europe and America, 1930–1960*, ed. D. Fleming and B. Bailyn, pp. 94–151. Cambridge, Mass., 1969.

Talmon, J. L. *Political Messianism: The Romantic Phase*. London, 1960.

Tautorus, W. [K. Diebner]. "Die deutschen Geheimarbeiten zur Kernenergieverwertung während des zweiten Weltkrieges, 1939–1945." *Atomkernenergie* 1 (1956): 368–370, 423–425.

Theweleit, K. *Male Fantasies*. Trans. Minneapolis, 1987.

Thiess, F. *Das Reich der Dämonen*. Berlin, 1941.

Thomson, G. P. "Anglo-U.S. Cooperation on Atomic Energy." *BAS* 9 (1953): 46–48.

Times (London), 7–14 August 1945.

Toronto Star, 8 April 1933.

Tracy, J. D., ed. *Luther and the Modern State*. Sixteenth Century Essays and Studies, vol. 7. Kirksville, Mo., 1986.

Trevor-Roper, H. R. "Aftermaths of Empire." *Encounter*, December 1989, pp. 3–16.

Turnbull, P. "The 'Supposed Infidelity' of Edward Gibbon." In *The Historical Journal* 25 (1982): 23–41.

Turner, I. D., ed. *Reconstruction in Post-War Germany: British Occupation Policy and the Western Zones, 1945–1955*. Oxford, 1989.

Turner, L. "The Nonexistence of Transuranic Elements." *Physical Review* 57 (1940): 157.

————. "Nuclear Fission." *Reviews of Modern Physics* 12 (1940): 1–29.

U.S. Department of Commerce, Office of Technical Services. *Bibliography of Scientific and Industrial Reports, Prepared by the Office of Technical Services*. 6 vols. and supps. Washington, D.C., 1947–48.

————. *An Informal Introduction to German Patent Applications (1940–1945) in the Library of Congress*. Library of Congress, Washington, D.C., n.d. Mimeographed.

————. *Numerical Index to the Bibliography of Scientific and Industrial Reports, Volumes 1–10, 1946–1948.* Washington, D.C., 1948.

Walker, M. *German National Socialism and the Quest for Nuclear Power, 1939–1949.* Cambridge, 1989.

————. "Heisenberg, Goudsmit, and the German Atomic Bomb." *Physics Today,* January 1990, 52–60. Also ensuing correspondence: ibid., May 1991, 13–15, 90–96; ibid., February 1992, 126.

————. "Legends Surrounding the German Atomic Bomb." In *Science, Medicine, and Cultural Imperialism,* ed. T. Meade and M. Walker, pp. 178–204. London, 1991.

————. "Myths of the German Atomic Bomb." *Nature* 359 (8 October 1992): 473–474.

————. *Nazi Science: Myth, Truth, and the German Atomic Bomb.* New York, 1995.

————. "Physics and Propaganda: Werner Heisenberg's Foreign Lectures under National Socialism." *Historical Studies in the Physical Sciences* 22 (1992): 339–389.

————. Reply to P. L. Rose, *Physics Today,* February 1992, 126.

————. Review of *Heisenberg's War,* by T. Powers. *Times Higher Education Supplement,* 4 March 1994, 22.

————. "Selbstreflexionen deutscher Atomphysiker: Die Farm-Hall-Protokolle und die 'deutsche Atombombe.'" *Vierteljahrshefte für Zeitgeschichte* 41 (1993): 519–542.

————. *Die Uranmaschine: Mythos und Wirklichkeit der deutschen Atombombe.* Berlin, 1990. "Vorwort" by R. Jungk.

Weart, S. *Nuclear Fear.* Cambridge, Mass., 1988.

————. "The Road to Los Alamos." *Journal de Physique* 43, no. 12 (December 1982), supp. (*International Colloquium on the History of Particle Physics, 21–23 July*) (= *Colloque C8, Supplément au no. 12, Journal de Physique, tome 43, decembre 1982*), pp. 301–321.

————. *Scientists in Power.* Cambridge, Mass., 1979.

————. "Secrecy, Simultaneous Discovery, and the Theory of Nuclear Reactors." *American Journal of Physics* 45 (1977): 1049–1060.

Weinberg, A. Letter to *Physics Today,* December 1994, 84.

Weizsäcker, C.-F. von. *Bewusstseinswandel.* Munich, 1988.

————. "Heisenberg im Urteil seiner Schüler." *Bild der Wissenschaft* 22 (1985): 138–147.

————. "Ideas on the Philosophy of Science"; "The Meaning of Quantum Mechanics"; "The Political and Moral Consequences of Science." Lectures given at CERN, Geneva, January 1988. Transcription.

————. "Die Illusion deutscher Atombomben: Aus einem Brief an den Herausgeber, Göttingen, 14 October 1955." In *Helle Zeit—Dunkle Zeit,* ed. C. Seelig, pp. 130–132. Zurich, 1956.

————. "Wir waren heilfroh . . . ." Interview. *Stern,* August 1984, 55–56. Reprinted in his *Bewusstseinswandel* (Munich, 1988).

Weizsäcker, C.-F. von, and J. Juilfs. *Physik der Gegenwart.* Göttingen, 1952.

Weizsäcker, C.-F. von, and B. L. van der Waerden. *Werner Heisenberg.* Munich, 1977.

Wheeler, J. A. "The Discovery of Fission." *Physics Today,* November 1967, 49–52.

————. "Niels Bohr and Nuclear Physics." *Physics Today,* October 1963, 36–45.

————. "Some Men and Moments in Nuclear Physics." In *Nuclear Physics in Retrospect,* ed. R. H. Stuewer, pp. 217–322. Minneapolis, 1979.

Wigner, E. F. *The Recollections of Eugene P. Wigner.* New York, 1992.

Wilson, R. R. "Niels Bohr and the Young Scientists." *BAS* 41 (August 1985): 23–26.

Winnacker, K., and K. Wirtz. *Nuclear Energy in Germany.* Trans. La Grange Park, Ill., 1979.

Wirtz, K. "Historisches zu den Uranarbeiten in Deutschland in den Jahren 1940–1945." *Physikalische Blätter* 3 (1947): 371–379.

———. *Im Umkreis der Physik.* Karlsruhe, 1988.

Wise, N. "Pascual Jordan: Quantum Mechanics, Psychology, National Socialism." In *Science, Technology, and National Socialism,* ed. M. Renneberg and M. Walker, pp. 224–254. Cambridge, 1994.

Wistrich, R. *Who's Who in Nazi Germany.* London, 1982.

Wolin, R., ed. *The Heidegger Controversy: A Critical Reader.* New York, 1991.

Wood, B. *E. P. Schumacher: His Life and Thought.* New York, 1984.

Zierold, K. *Forschungsförderung in drei Epochen: Deutsche Forschungsgemeinschaft.* Wiesbaden, 1968.

Index

Aaserud, F., 39
Abelson, P., 132–33
Academy of Aeronautical Research, 184
Adler, F., 123
AEG Electrical Company, 185
ALSOS, 23–27, 52, 58, 60, 63, 188, 325
Alvarez, Luis, 62
Amaldi, Edoardo, 145n44
American Physical Society, 23, 84
Anderson, Sir John, 159
Anshen, Ruth Nanda, 60
Antisemitism: academy and, 250, 256; Einstein and, 200n3, 317–20; Germany and, 4, 44–46; Hahn and, 250; Heisenberg and, 241–42, 267, 284, 317; Kant and, 230–31; Luther and, 228; Mann and, 233; science and, 200, 306; Wagner and, 232
Appleton, E. V., 105
Ardenne, Manfred von, 47, 48, 136–40, 202
Army Weapons Department, 167, 327
Atomic bomb, 97, 109, 190; Bagge and, 64; Bohr and, 29–30, 83–84; Britain and, 91–95; Chadwick and, 92–94; conceptualization of, 9; construction of, 204; France and, 90–91; Germany and, 95–98; Hahn and, 76; United States and, 88–90. *See also* Plutonium bomb; Reactor-bomb
Atomic energy, 168, 179
"Attitude of Germans, Especially German Scientists during the Nazi Regime" (Rosbaud), 250
Autocatalytic bomb, 165

"Back of an envelope" calculation, 115, 123, 207, 211
Bagge, Erich: atomic bomb and, 64; diary of, 41, 116n2, 326; Farm Hall and, 206, 212, 214; HWA Report, 146; Nazi University Lecturers League, 292; papers of, 168, 333; plutonium bomb and, 214; SS and, 293; Uranium Club and, 106
Baker, M., 326
Barth, Karl, 229
Becker, Karl, 97n54, 173
Becker, Richard, 283
Bell Telephone Laboratories, 87
Beller, Maria, 199n44
Bernstein, Jeremy, 72, 161n48, 212
Bethe, Hans, 160–62, 313–14
Bethe-Teller Report (1944), 161–63
Bibliography of Scientific and Industrial Research Reports, 149
Bohr, Aage, 161n48, 275
Bohr, Niels, 2, 26; atomic bomb and, 29–30, 83–84; autocatalytic bomb and, 165; Bohr Library, 325; Chadwick and, 157, 159; "Chain Reactions in Nuclear Fission," 86; critical mass and, 86; fast-neutron fission and, 87, 107; Frisch and, 82; Heisenberg and, 51, 62, 74, 154–66, 271–82, 301, 322–23; Rosbaud and, 159, 310–11; U235 and, 83; uncertainty and, 221, 317; Weizsäcker and, 155
Bomb temperature, 110
Bomke, H., 148

Compositor:	Impressions Book and Journal Services, Inc.
Text:	Baskerville
Display:	Baskerville
Printer and Binder:	Edwards Brothers